Alfred Marshall in his garden shelter at Balliol Croft, 1920.

The Correspondence of

Alfred Marshall, Economist

THE CORRESPONDENCE OF
ALFRED MARSHALL, ECONOMIST

Volume 3. Towards the Close, 1903–1924

A Royal Economic Society Publication

Edited by

JOHN K. WHITAKER
University of Virginia

CAMBRIDGE UNIVERSITY PRESS
Cambridge, New York, Melbourne, Madrid, Cape Town, Singapore, São Paulo

Cambridge University Press
The Edinburgh Building, Cambridge CB2 2RU, UK

Published in the United States of America by Cambridge University Press, New York

www.cambridge.org
Information on this title: www.cambridge.org/9780521558860

First published 1996
This digitally printed first paperback version 2005

A catalogue record for this publication is available from the British Library

Library of Congress Cataloguing in Publication data
(Revised for v. 2- v. 3)

Marshall, Alfred, 1842–1924.
The correspondence of Alfred Marshall, economist.

Includes bibliographical references.
Contents: vol. 1. Climbing, 1868–1890—vol. 2. At the summit, 1891–1902—vol. 3. Towards the close, 1903–1924.
1. Marshall, Alfred, 1842–1924—Correspondence. 2. Economists—Great Britain—Correspondence. 3. Neoclassical school of economics. I. Whitaker, John K. (John King). II. Title.
HB103.M3A4 1996 330.15′7 95-8022
ISBN 0-521-55888-3 (v. 1)
ISBN 0-521-55887-5 (v. 2)
ISBN 0-521-55886-7 (v. 3)

ISBN-13 978-0-521-55886-0 hardback
ISBN-10 0-521-55886-7 hardback

ISBN-13 978-0-521-02354-2 paperback
ISBN-10 0-521-02354-8 paperback

CONTENTS

INTRODUCTION

The present volume continues Marshall's correspondence up to the year of his death, 1924, and thus completes the entire edition. The reader should turn to the introductory matters of Volume 1 for general information on Marshall's biographical background and on the editorial principles and procedures followed throughout the edition. It suffices to note here that when individuals mentioned in this volume are not explicitly identified or cross-referenced they will normally be listed in the Biographical Register, below. Cross-references take the form [740] for reference to letter number 740, [740.1] for reference to footnote 1 of letter number 740, and so on. Cross-reference to the other volumes is explicitly indicated as such.

The volume opens in the year 1903, a doubly significant one in Marshall's life. It saw the successful conclusion of his campaign to establish a new Tripos in economics and related subjects. And it saw his literary aims diverted from completion of his *Principles* to composition of a book bearing on the fiscal controversy provoked by Joseph Chamberlain's campaign for protection and imperial preference.

The campaign for the new Tripos, and the burdens of organizing and managing it, placed Marshall under heavy strain, especially as extra resources were not provided to staff the new courses. Even by 1908, only one new lectureship in economics had been established. Despite this, and in part because of his willingness to support two young lecturers from his own pocket, Marshall soon became convinced that a brilliant creative group of young scholars was in the making, and this did much to compensate the burdens of his Professorship and the cramping of his own literary efforts. Marshall's faith was to be largely justified by the rapid rise of the new 'Cambridge School' to world eminence after his retirement in 1908.

The memorandum on the fiscal issue that he was induced to write in the summer of 1903 for the then Chancellor of the Exchequer, C. T. Ritchie, turned Marshall's mind to the composition of a semi-popular work dealing with the economic and historical conditions underlying the controversy of the day. This book was to prove an incubus against which he struggled for the next fifteen years. The eventual appearance of *Industry and Trade* in 1919, and the last-gasp publication of *Money Credit and Commerce* in 1923, far from exhausted the matters he blithely planned in 1903 to dispose of within the year. Even more did they fall short of the long-envisaged rounding out of the *Principles* into a comprehensive general treatise.

Release from professorial cares upon retirement in 1908 seems to have brought

Marshall a sense of liberation and to have induced a new expansiveness in correspondence and controversy. (See, for example, the 1909 letters to Lord Reay, or the 1910 controversy with Karl Pearson.) But declining health, ebbing vitality, and above all the frustrating difficulty of completing his literary plans, all conspired after 1910 to limit his interests and activities and increase his isolation—Maynard Keynes remaining, however, an attentive link to the world of affairs. After 1914, the anxieties of horrifying war, and the rapid economic changes that the war induced or augured, all increased Marshall's perplexities. The story of the last decade of his life is largely the story of his sad but brave struggle, despite failing strength, to capture for posterity the economic wisdom he had garnered so patiently over so many decades.

ABBREVIATIONS

BLPES	British Library of Political and Economic Science.
Collected Writings	*The Collected Writings of John Maynard Keynes.* Managing editors Sir Austin Robinson and Donald E. Moggridge (Macmillan, London, 1971–89, for the Royal Economic Society: 30 vols.).
Diaries	Diaries of John Neville Keynes (Cambridge University Library, Additional Manuscripts 7853–8, covering 1903–8).
Early Economic Writings	*The Early Economic Writings of Alfred Marshall, 1867–1890*, ed. John K. Whitaker (Macmillan, London, 1975, for the Royal Economic Society: 2 vols.).
Elements	Alfred Marshall, *Elements of the Economics of Industry, being the First Volume of Elements of Economics* (Macmillan, London, 1892, revised 1896, 1899, 1907).
Guillebaud	*Alfred Marshall's Principles of Economics: Ninth (Variorum) Edition*, vol. 2, ed. Claude W. Guillebaud (Macmillan, London, 1961, for the Royal Economic Society). (Vol. 1 is simply a reprint of the eighth edition of the *Principles.*)
Industry and Trade	Alfred Marshall, *Industry and Trade: A Study of Business Technique and Business Organization; and of their Influences on the Conditions of Various Classes and Nations* (Macmillan, London, 1919, with additional 'editions' in 1919, 1920, 1923—only the first involving significant alteration).
Memorials	*Memorials of Alfred Marshall*, ed. Arthur Cecil Pigou (Macmillan, London, 1925, for the Royal Economic Society).
Mill's *Principles*	John Stuart Mill, *Principles of Political Economy with some of their Applications to Social Philosophy* (Parker, London, 1848: several further editions). The standard edition is that appearing as *Collected*

Works of John Stuart Mill, Volumes Two and Three (University of Toronto Press, Toronto, 1965).

Money Credit and Commerce — Alfred Marshall, *Money Credit and Commerce* (Macmillan, London, 1923).

Official Papers — *Official Papers of Alfred Marshall*, ed. John Maynard Keynes (Macmillan, London, 1926, for the Royal Economic Society).

Principles (3) — The third edition of Alfred Marshall, *Principles of Economics, Volume I* (Macmillan, London, 1895).

Principles (4) — The fourth edition of the *Principles* (Macmillan, London, 1898).

Principles (5) — The fifth edition of the *Principles* (Macmillan, London, 1907).

Principles (6) — The sixth edition of the *Principles*, introducing the new title *Principles of Economics: An Introductory Volume* (Macmillan, London, 1910).

Principles (7) — The seventh edition of the *Principles* (Macmillan, London, 1916).

Principles (8) — The eighth and final edition of the *Principles* (Macmillan, London, 1920).

Ricardo's *Principles* — David Ricardo, *On the Principles of Political Economy and Taxation* (Murray, London, 1817, revised 1819, 1821). The standard edition is that appearing as *The Works and Correspondence of David Ricardo, Volume One*, ed. Piero Sraffa (Cambridge University Press, London, 1951, for the Royal Economic Society).

Wealth of Nations — Adam Smith, *An Inquiry into the Nature and Causes of the the Wealth of Nations* (Strahan and Cadell, London, 1776, with three further editions). The standard edition is that appearing as *The Glasgow Edition of the Works and Correspondence of Adam Smith, Volumes One and Two* (Clarendon Press, Oxford, 1976).

LIST OF MANUSCRIPT COLLECTIONS[1]

Bishopsgate Institute, London, G. Howell Papers
BLPES, Beveridge Papers
BLPES, E. Cannan Papers
BLPES, Courtney Papers
BLPES, Miscellaneous Letter Collection
British Library, Macmillan Archive
Bundesarchiv, Koblenz, L. J. Brentano Papers
Cambridge University Library, Diaries of J. N. Keynes
Cambridge University Library, F. W. Maitland Papers
Cambridge University Library, University Archives
Columbia University Library, J. B. Clark Papers
Columbia University Library, H. L. Moore Papers
Columbia University Library, E. R. A. Seligman Papers
Foxwell Papers [privately owned]
Harvard University Archives, C. W. Eliot Papers
Harvard University Archives, F. W. Taussig Papers
Harvard University Archives, A. A. Young Papers
Harvard University, Houghton Library, W. Rothenstein Papers
King's College, Cambridge, O. Browning Papers
King's College, Cambridge, J. M. Keynes Papers
King's College, Cambridge, J. T. Sheppard Papers
Levasseur Papers [privately owned]
Lund University Library, K. Wicksell Papers
Manchester Central Library, T. C. Horsfall Papers
Marshall Library, Cambridge, J. N. Keynes Papers
Marshall Library, Cambridge, Marshall Papers
Nuffield College, Oxford, H. D. Henderson Papers
Robertson Papers [privately owned: now deposited at Trinity College, Cambridge]
Royal Library, Stockholm, G. Cassel Papers
Royal Library, Stockholm, E. F. Heckscher Papers
St John's College, Cambridge (Archives), College Records
St John's College, Cambridge (Archives), J. R. Tanner Papers
St John's College, Cambridge (Library), E. A. Benians Papers
St John's College, Cambridge (Library), Letter Collection
Seeley Library, Cambridge, History Board Minutes
Sheffield University Library, W. A. S. Hewins Papers

Staatsbibliothek, Berlin, L. Darmstädter Collection
Trinity College, Cambridge, W. T. Layton Papers
Trinity College, Cambridge, H. Sidgwick Papers
University College, London, W. Ramsay Papers
University of Amsterdam, N. G. Pierson Papers
University of Illinois, J. H. Hollander Collection
University of London Library, C. Booth Papers
University of Newcastle-upon-Tyne, H. Bosanquet Papers
University of Toronto, Thomas Fisher Rare Book Library, J. Mavor Papers
Yale University, Sterling Library, A. T. Hadley Papers

[1] For details of these collections and precise archival identifications for them see Appendix II.

BIOGRAPHICAL REGISTER

As explained in the description of editorial practices in Volume 1, this register describes all individuals mentioned but not specifically identified in the body of the present volume, with the exception of a small number of names deemed to be so well known that identification would be otiose. Unless otherwise indicated, reference is to Cambridge on academic matters and Britain on general matters. The symbols (*) or (**) following a name or abbreviated identification indicate that a fuller description is provided in the Biographical Register of Volumes 1 or 2, respectively.

Acton, Lord (1834–1902). Eminent historian (**).

Alston, Leonard (1875–1953). Born in Australia and educated at Cambridge, Alston, a rather enigmatic figure, served as Deputy Professor of History and Political Economy at Elphinstone College, Bombay 1904–5, and eventually as University Lecturer in Economics at Cambridge 1926–40—probably after some years of private 'coaching' in Cambridge. He published mainly on politics, but his books include *Elements of Indian Taxation* (1910) and *Functions of Money* (1932).

Archbold, William Arthur Jobson (1865–1947). Lecturer on economic history for the Economics Tripos in its early years. A member of Peterhouse, Archbold obtained a first in the Law Tripos of 1887, followed by a Whewell Scholarship in international law. He remained in Cambridge as Secretary to the Board of Indian Civil Service Studies, Secretary to the Appointments Association, and finally Assistant Secretary to the Local Examination and Lectures Syndicate, meanwhile lecturing on historical subjects and publishing variously. He eventually left Cambridge for a career as educational administrator in India.

Armitage-Smith, George (1844?–1923). Economist and educational administrator. Principal of Birkbeck College, London, 1896–1918, where he was also Lecturer on Economics and Mental Science. Dean of the recently instituted Faculty of Economics of London University 1904–6. Author of *The Free Trade Movement* (1898), *Principles and Methods of Taxation* (1906), and other works.

Ashley, William James (1860–1927). Economic historian (*).

Asquith, Herbert Henry (1852–1928). Liberal statesman. Home Secretary 1892–5, Chancellor of the Exchequer 1905–8, Prime Minister 1908–16. Created Earl of Oxford and Asquith, 1925.

Auspitz, Rudolf (1837–1906). Austrian businessman and economist (*).

Babson, Roger Ward (1875–1967). American business forecaster and writer, founder of the Babson Statistical Association and Babson College.

Bagehot, Walter (1826–77). Journalist and writer on literature, politics, and economics (*).

Balfour, Arthur James (1848–1930). Conservative statesman and writer on philosophical and theological subjects. Prime Minister 1902–5 (*).

Bastable, Charles Francis (1855–1945). Irish economist (*).

Bauer, Stephan (1865–1934). Swiss economist, Professor at the University of Basel from 1899. An expert on labour questions and closely associated with the International Labour Office, Basel.

Beaulieu, Pierre-Paul Leroy. *See* Leroy Beaulieu, Pierre-Paul.

Benians, Ernest Alfred (1880–1952). Benians had a lifelong association with St John's, where he was a Fellow 1906–33 and Master 1933–52. As undergraduate and research student there he had obtained firsts in both parts of the Historical Tripos, 1901–2, and won the Adam Smith prize of 1906. A specialist in colonial history, he served as College Lecturer in History from 1910 and University Lecturer in History 1926–34. After 1913, service as Local Adviser to Indian Students, then as Tutor and Senior Tutor at St John's, absorbed his energies and he published very little. His most significant scholarly contributions were in connection with the *Cambridge Modern History* and the *Cambridge History of the British Empire*, of which he was joint editor. In his early academic career Benians was a protégé of Marshall, who groomed him to lecture on modern imperial and American history for the new Economics Tripos.

Bentham, Jeremy (1748–1832). Eminent social philosopher and propounder of utilitarianism.

Beveridge, William Henry (1879–1963). Empirical economist and social and administrative reformer. After a first in 'Greats' at Oxford (Balliol) in 1901, Beveridge's early career was varied. Throwing over a projected legal career, he became Sub-warden of Toynbee Hall in 1903, and—influenced by the Webbs—involved himself extensively in educational, social, and journalistic endeavours, publishing in 1908 his inductive study *Unemployment: A Problem of Industry*. Entering government service in 1908, he worked mainly in the Board of Trade (initially as Winston Churchill's personal assistant). Beveridge left government service in 1919 to become Director of the London School of Economics, continuing until 1937. From 1937 to 1944 he was Master of University College, Oxford. His advisory work and writings during the Second World War, especially the so-called 'Beveridge Plan', paved the way for the post-1945 'welfare state'. He was created first Baron Beveridge in 1946.

Bismarck, Prince Otto Edward Leopold (1815–98). Germany's 'Iron Chancellor', Prussian architect of German unification and social reform.

Böhm-Bawerk, Eugen von (1851–1914). Austrian economist (*).

Bonar, James (1852–1941). Civil servant and economist (*).

Bonar Law, Andrew. *See* Law, Andrew Bonar.

Booth, Charles (1840–1916). Shipowner and social investigator (*).

Bosanquet, Helen Dendy (1860–1925). Social economist and poor-law expert (**).

Bowley, Arthur Lyon (1869–1957). Economist and statistician (**).

Brentano, Ludwig Joseph (1844–1931). German economist (*).

Browne, George Forrest (1833–1930). Ecclesiastical historian, antiquary, academic administrator, and churchman. Bishop of Bristol 1897–1914 (**).

Browning, Oscar (1837–1923). Cambridge historian and character (*).

Bryce, James (1838–1922). Historian, jurist, and statesman (**).

Bücher, Karl Wilhelm (1847–1930). German economic historian, Professor at Leipzig. His *Industrial Evolution* (1901; 1893 in German) is his best-known work.

Bullock, Charles Jesse (1869–1941). American economist, an expert on public finance. After a Wisconsin Ph.D. (1895), Bullock settled at Harvard where he taught economics 1903–34 and authored successful textbooks.

Campbell-Bannerman, Henry (1836–1908). Liberal statesman. A Member of Parliament 1868–1908, he held various Cabinet posts in Liberal administrations, becoming leader of the Liberals in the House in 1899 and serving as Prime Minister 1905–8.

Cannan, Edwin (1861–1935). Economist (**).

Carey, Henry Charles (1793–1879). American protectionist economist and social philosopher (*).

Carver, Thomas Nixon (1865–1961). American economist and sociologist of conservative tendency. A student of R. T. Ely (*) and J. B. Clark, with a Ph.D. (1894) from Cornell, Carver served as Professor of Political economy at Harvard, 1900–32.

Cassel, Karl Gustav (1866–1945). Swedish economist (**).

Chamberlain, Joseph (1836–1914). Conservative statesman whose various campaigns, especially that initiated in 1903 for tariff reform and imperial preference, galvanized British political life (**).

Chapman, Sydney John (1871–1951). Economist and economic adviser (**).

Churchill, Winston Leonard Spencer (1874–1965). Statesman. Prime Minister 1940–5 and holder of many Cabinet posts from 1908 onwards. In particular, President of the Board of Trade 1908–10, Home Secretary 1910–11, First Lord of the Admiralty 1911–15, Minister of Munitions 1917–18, Secretary for War 1918–21. Knighted 1953.

Clapham, John Harold (1873–1946). Economic historian. A protégé of Marshall (**).

Clark, John Bates (1847–1938). American economist (*).

Clay, Henry (1883–1954). Economist and economic adviser of conservative inclination. A student at University College, Oxford, Clay lectured for the Workers' Educational Association, 1909–17. After a brief spell in the Ministry of Labour he became a Fellow of New College, Oxford, 1919–21, then moved to Manchester, first as Jevons Professor of Political Economy 1922–27, and afterwards as Professor of Social Economics 1927–30. Joining the Bank of England, he served as economic adviser to the Governor 1933–44. His career closed as Warden of Nuffield College, Oxford, 1944–9.

Cognetti di Martiis, Salvatore (1844–1901). Italian economist and sociologist, Professor at Turin. His translation of Marshall's *Principles* into Italian was only partly completed at his death.

Cohn, Gustav (1840–1919). German economist (*).

Colson, Léon Clément (1853–1939). French engineer, statistician, and economist. Trained as an engineer at the École Polytechnique and the École des Ponts et Chaussées, Colson combined a career at the French Ministry of Public Works with teaching economics and statistics at various *grandes écoles*. His *Cours* is his best-known economic work.

Conrad, Johannes (1839–1915). German economist and statistician (**).

Cournot, Antoine Augustine (1801–77). French mathematician, philosopher and economist (*).

Courtney, Leonard Henry (1832–1918). Politician, lawyer, journalist, and economist (*).

Cunningham, William (1849–1919). Economic historian and churchman (*).

Cunynghame, Henry Hardinge (1848–1935). Civil servant, polymath, and amateur economist (*).

Darwin, Charles Robert (1809–82). Naturalist (*).

Darwin, Erasmus (1881–1915). Only son of Horace Darwin (1858–1928), the youngest son of Charles Darwin. A member of Trinity, Erasmus obtained a second in Part I of the Mechanical Sciences Tripos, 1905. He was killed at the battle of Ypres, 1915.

Darwin, George Howard (1845–1912). Mathematician and astronomer. Second son of Charles Darwin (*).

Davies, Theodore Llewellyn (1870–1905). Civil servant and one-time student of Marshall (**).

Dawson, William Harbutt (1860–1948). Author and editor. Educated at the University of Berlin, Dawson devoted much of his life to educating the British public about things German. His copious writings ranged widely over literary, historical, and social topics. The organizer and editor of *After-War Problems* (1917), to which Marshall contributed an essay.

Derby, Lord (1865–1948). Statesman. George Edward Villiers Stanley succeeded his father as seventeenth earl in 1908. He held various minor posts under Conservative administrations 1895–1905. During the 1914–18 war he was Director of Recruiting 1915–16, taking the first tentative steps towards conscription. Subsequently he was Secretary of State for War 1916–18.

Dicey, Albert Venn (1835–1922). Jurist and legal scholar (**).

Dickinson, Goldsworthy Lowes (1862–1932). Political philosopher and essayist who played a prominent role in the foundation and early operation of the Economics Tripos (**).

Dietzel, Heinrich (1857–1935). German economist. Professor at Bonn from 1890 and author of *Theoretische Sozialökonomie* (1895), Dietzel was a liberal of the old school, avoiding the historicist extremes of many of his contemporaries.

Dixon, Frank Haigh (1869–1944). American economist. Recipient of an 1895 Ph.D. in economics from the University of Michigan where he taught until 1898, Dixon was an expert on railway and transport economics. He served as chief statistician at the Bureau of Labor Economics 1910–18, and was a faculty member at Dartmouth 1903–19 and Princeton 1919–38.

Dunbar, Charles Franklin (1830–1900). American economist (*).

Dupuit, Arsène-Jules-Émile Juvenal (1804–66). French civil engineer and economist (**).

Ede, William Moore (1849–1935). Churchman, sometime student of Marshall (*).

Edgeworth, Francis Ysidro (1845–1926). Economist (*).

Eliot, Charles William (1834–1926). American educational administrator and reformer. President of Harvard, 1869–1909 (**).

Elliott, Thomas Henry (1854–1926). Civil servant and officer of the Royal Economic Society (*).

Engels, Friedrich (1820–95). Anglo-German socialist writer and organizer, Karl Marx's chief collaborator and literary executor.

Fauquier, Francis (1704?–1768). Lieutenant Governor of Virginia, 1758–68, and author of the economic tract, *An Essay on Ways and Means of Raising Money* (1756).

Fawcett, Henry (1833–84). Economist and politician (*).

Fawcett, Millicent Garrett (1847–1929). Suffragist and writer on economics, wife of the above (*).

Fay, Charles Ryle (1884–1961). Economic historian and protégé of Marshall, Fay became in later life a chief repository of Marshallian lore, gleefully but affectionately recalling the quirks and eccentricities of his old teacher. An undergraduate contemporary of Maynard Keynes at King's, Fay obtained firsts in both parts of the Historical Tripos, 1904–5, coming under Marshall's influence. He commenced to lecture for the Economics Tripos in 1907 while still a research student at the London School of Economics, and was elected a Fellow of Christ's in 1908, the year his *Cooperation at Home and Abroad* appeared. He remained active in Cambridge teaching and life, with an interruption for military service, until 1921, when he moved to Toronto as Professor of Economic History. In 1931 he returned to Cambridge as Reader in Economic History, occupying this position until retirement. The author of *Life and Labour in the Nineteenth Century* (1920), *Great Britain from Adam Smith to the Present Day* (1928), and other works.

Fisher, Irving (1867–1947). American economist (**).

Flux, Alfred William (1867–1942). Economist and statistician (*).

Foxwell, Edward Ernest (1851–1922). Younger brother of Herbert Somerton Foxwell (*).

Foxwell, Herbert Somerton (1849–1936). Economist and bibliophile (*).

Galton, Francis (1822–1921). Eugenicist (**).

Gide, Charles (1847–1932). French economist who taught in Paris from 1898 onwards. A critic of untrammelled individualism, co-author with Charles Rist (1874–1955) of the classic *A History of Economic Doctrines* (1915 in French).

Giffen, Robert (1837–1910). Economist and statistician (*).

Goschen, George Joachim (1831–1907). Statesman, financier, and economist (*).

Gossen, Hermann Heinrich (1810–58). German pioneer of marginal utility economics (*).

Grant, Ulysses Simpson (1822–85). US civil-war general. Eighteenth President of the USA, 1869–77.

Green, George Edward (1863–1931). Historian and early lecturer on elementary economics for the Economics Tripos. As a member of St John's, Green obtained a first in the History Tripos of 1885 and held a Whewell Scholarship in 1886. Subsequently admitted to Caius as assistant lecturer in history, he became established as a private 'coach'. Ultimately he turned to schoolmastering.

Guillebaud, Claude William (1890–1971). Economist, Fellow of St John's, and Marshall's nephew (**).

Guyot, Yves (1843–1928). French economist and publicist (**).

Gwatkin, Henry Melville (1844–1916). Dixie Professor of Ecclesiastical History 1891–1916 (**).

Hadley, Arthur Twining (1856–1930). American economist and college president (*).

Hasbach, Wilhelm (1849–1920). German economist (**).

Head, Frederick Waldegrave (1874–1941). Historian and churchman, an early lecturer on history for the Economics Tripos. A first in the Historical Tripos of 1896, and a Whewell Scholarship in 1897, led to a Fellowship at Emmanuel, where Head served variously as History Lecturer, Dean, Chaplain, Tutor, and Senior Tutor. After 1922 he devoted himself to clerical activities and served as Archbishop of Melbourne 1929–41.

Headlam, James Wycliffe (1863–1929). Historian. After a first in the Classical Tripos, Headlam became a Fellow of King's in 1890 and also served as Professor of Greek and Ancient History at Queen's College, London, 1894–1900. During 1903–4 he lectured on history for the new Economics Tripos. Abandoning Cambridge he then served as a school inspector 1904–20 and finally as historical adviser to the Foreign Office, 1920–8.

Heckscher, Eli Filip (1879–1952). Swedish economist and economic historian. Trained at Uppsala, Heckscher was associated with Stockholm University College of Commerce, serving as Professor of Economics and Statistics 1909–29, and Director of the Institute of Economic History 1929–45. A prolific author, whose interests turned increasingly to economic history, he is best known for his pioneering 1919 contribution to international trade theory and his comprehensive study *Mercantilism* (1935; 1931 in Swedish).

Henderson, Hubert Douglas (1890–1952). Economist. With a first in Part II of the Economics Tripos of 1912, Henderson returned to Cambridge after wartime government service to take up a Fellowship at Clare and lecture on economics. Combining this with editorship of the *Nation and Athenaeum* 1923–30, he collaborated closely and successfully with Maynard Keynes. From 1930 to 1944 Henderson served in various advisory capacities and in 1945 he was elected Drummond Professor at Oxford, where he was also a Fellow of All Souls. His introductory *Supply and Demand* (1922), which had considerable success, was influenced significantly by Marshall's *Principles*, but Henderson's scholarly output remained sparse.

Hewins, William Albert Samuel (1865–1931). Economist, historian, and politician (**).

Higgs, Henry (1864–1940). Civil servant and economist (**).

Hilton, John (1880–1943). Civil servant, statistician, journalist, and expert on industrial relations. Apprenticed at age 16 as a mill mechanic in his native Lancashire, Hilton soon rose to managerial status in the cotton-spinning industry. After a year of convalescence in Russia, 1907–8, he turned to lecturing and technical journalism and was acting secretary 1912–18 of the Garton Foundation, which was inspired by Norman Angell (1872–1967). Hilton served at the Ministry of Labour as Assistant Secretary and then Director of Statistics 1919–31, having been Secretary of the Committee on Trusts in 1919. As the rather surprising choice for Professor of Industrial Relations at Cambridge from 1931, his mark was made rather as a journalist and broadcaster than as a scientist and scholar.

Hobson, John Atkinson (1858–1940). Economic writer and self-confessed economic heretic (**).

Hollander, Jacob Harry (1871–1940). American economist. Hollander was trained, and subsequently spent his entire career, at the Johns Hopkins University, Baltimore. He is remembered mainly for his studies in the history of economic thought, but was also active and influential as a government adviser on questions of finance and taxation.

Horsfall, Thomas Coglan (1841–1932). Social reformer (**).

Howell, George (1833–1910). Labour leader, politician, and author (*).

Jannet, Claudio (1844–94). French economist and economic historian (**).

Jenkin, Henry Charles Fleeming (1833–85). Engineer and occasional writer on economics (**).

Jenks, Jeremiah Whipple (1856–1929). American economist and government adviser. Trained at Michigan and Halle, Jenks was Professor of Political Economy at Cornell 1891–1912, and subsequently Professor of Government at New York University. He was adviser on trusts to the US Industrial Commission of 1899 and a member of the Immigration Commission of 1907. After 1899 his involvement in multifarious government advising and inquiries absorbed much of his time, nevertheless he wrote widely on practical issues of the day.

Jevons, Herbert Stanley (1875–1955). Son of William Stanley Jevons, Herbert was educated at University College, London, and Cambridge—where, as a member of Trinity, he obtained a first in Part I of the Natural Sciences Tripos 1896. After study in Heidelberg, he served as demonstrator in Petrology at Cambridge 1900–1, and as Lecturer in Mineralogy and Geology at the University of Sydney 1902–4. Turning, as his father had done, from natural to social science, he next taught economics and political science at the University College of South Wales and Monmouthshire, Cardiff, 1905–11. This was not a success, and after involvement in housing reform in the South Wales coalfield he went into exile, teaching economics in Allahabad 1914–23, and Rangoon 1923–30. He published among other works *Essays on Economics* (1905) and—again emulating his father—*The British Coal Trade* (1915).

Jevons, William Stanley (1835–1882). Economist and logician (*).

Johnson, William Ernest (1856–1931). Logician, mathematician, psychologist, and economic theorist (**).

Kenny, Courtney Stanhope (1847–1930). Legal scholar. A member of Downing, of which he was a Fellow 1885–1907, Kenny headed the Law and History Tripos of 1874. He lectured in law at Trinity 1881–6, and served as University Reader in English Law 1888–1907, then Downing Professor of the Laws of England 1907–18.

Keynes, Florence Ada (1861–1958). Wife of John Neville Keynes and mother of John Maynard Keynes (*).

Keynes, John Maynard (1883–1946). The precocious senior of the three children of Florence and John Neville Keynes, Maynard soon showed unusual intellectual powers. Educated at Eton and King's College, Cambridge, he emerged disappointingly as only Twelfth Wrangler in the Mathematical Tripos of 1905. But he had made his mark on Cambridge as President of the Union (1905) and as a prominent member of the influential coterie of Apostles. In conjunction with preparation for the Civil Service Examination, he came in 1906 under the influence of Marshall, who encouraged him to contemplate a future as economist. Entering the India Office in 1906 (he would have preferred the Treasury) Maynard soon established himself as a rising star, but Cambridge still called. Continued work at a thesis on probability theory for the Fellowship competition at King's succeeded in late 1908 after an earlier rebuff. Meanwhile, in June 1908, Maynard left the civil service to become a lecturer for the Economics Board in Cambridge, a private arrangement financed by Pigou, the new professor, and apparently brokered by Marshall.

Maynard threw himself into economics teaching. He was appointed as Girdlers' Lecturer in December 1910 and succeeded Edgeworth as editor of the *Economic Journal* in 1911, continuing until 1944. Keynes's first major work *Indian Currency and Finance* appeared in 1913 and he served as a youthful member of the Royal Commission on Indian Finance and Currency, 1913–14. During the war of 1914–18 Keynes became a prominent and influential figure in the Treasury, which he represented at the Paris Peace Conference of 1919. Dismayed at the tenor of the proceedings he withdrew from official life and returned to Cambridge, rapidly producing his powerful polemic *The Economic Consequences of the Peace* (1919), eventually followed by *A Revision of the Treaty* (1922). The long-promised revision of his Fellowship thesis eventually appeared as *A Treatise on Probability* (1921) and was followed by the orthodox *Tract on Monetary Reform* (1923).

Keynes had kept steady contact with Marshall in the years after 1908 and his remarkable memorial essay appeared in the *Economic Journal* for September 1924, shortly after the latter's death. It is hardly necessary to enter into the multifarious activities, academic, advisory, literary, and journalistic, into which Keynes entered in the years that followed, or into the nature and impact of the major works, *A Treatise on Money* (1930) and *The General Theory of Employment, Interest and Money* (1936), through which Keynes established himself as a dominant figure in the twentieth-century economic landscape.

Keynes, John Neville (1852–1949). Logician, economist, and educational administrator. Marshall's longtime colleague and one-time protégé (*).

Làl, Manohar (1879–1949). Indian economist, lawyer, and public servant. A member of St John's, Làl obtained firsts in both parts of the Moral Sciences Tripos, 1902–3, and was a Whewell Scholar 1904. He came under Marshall's influence, winning the Cobden Prize for 1904 and being called to the Bar in the same year. Returning to India, he served as Principal of Randhir College, Kapurthala 1906–9, then Minto Professor of Economics at Calcutta University 1909–12. His subsequent career was devoted to law and public service. He held high public office, particularly as finance minister for Punjab 1937–46. Knighted in 1941.

Lassalle, Ferdinand (1825–64). German socialist writer and proponent of cooperative production.

Laughlin, James Laurence (1850–1933). American economist, professor at the University of Chicago from 1892 (*).

Lavington, Frederick (1881–1927). Lavington entered Cambridge as a mature student, having worked in banking for eleven years. He obtained firsts in both parts of the Economics Tripos 1910–11. After service with the Board of Trade, he returned in 1918 to Cambridge as an economics lecturer, concentrating on monetary economics. Lavington worked very much on lines set out by Marshall, and his originality came to be recognized only after his untimely death. His main contributions were his *English Capital Market* (1921) and his *Trade Cycle* (1922).

Law, Andrew Bonar (1858–1923). Conservative statesman. Born in Canada, but educated mainly in Glasgow where he rose to prominence in business, Law was a Member of Parliament 1900–10 and 1911–23. Soon singled out for office as Parliamentary Secretary to the Board of Trade 1902–5, he emerged as a supporter of Joseph Chamberlain's tariff-reform proposals. Law succeeded Balfour in 1911 as Conservative leader in the Commons. From 1916 to 1919 he served successfully as Chancellor of the Exchequer in Lloyd George's coalition government. When the latter fell in 1922, Law briefly led the ensuing Conservative administration as Prime Minister.

Layton, Walter Thomas (1884–1966). Layton came up to Trinity in 1904, planning to take the new Economics Tripos. He had already obtained a degree in history and economics while studying at University College, London, and had acquired experience in applied economic research as a protégé of Sanger. He achieved firsts in both parts of the Tripos in 1906–7 and was awarded a research studentship in economics at Caius. He received the Cobden Prize in 1907 for an essay on relative wages, and in 1908—together with Maynard Keynes—was made a lecturer for the Economics Tripos at an annual stipend of £100 provided by Pigou. He also began to contribute regularly to *The Economist.* A Fellow of Caius in 1909, and a University Lecturer in 1911, his reputation as an applied economist was cemented by his *An Introduction to the Study of Prices* (1912). He served in the Board of Trade and the Ministry of Munitions during the war, working closely with Lloyd George and Winston Churchill and playing a key role in the organization of the war effort. In 1919 he became Director of the Iron and Steel Federation, but left in 1921 to assume the editorship of *The Economist,* meanwhile having been seconded for a year to the League of Nations. He continued as editor until 1938 and served also as Chairman of the *News Chronicle* 1930–50. He was a leading figure in the newspaper world, and—a lifelong Liberal—took an active part in public affairs and in the war effort of 1939–45. He was knighted in 1930 and created Baron Layton in 1947.

Leathes, Stanley Mordaunt (1861–1938). Historian and civil servant, one-time student of Marshall (**).

Lees-Smith, Hastings Bertrand (1878–1941). Born in India and destined for a military career, Lees-Smith resigned a cadetship at Woolwich to study at Oxford, where he was a member of Queen's College. He became closely associated with Oxford's Ruskin College after the foundation of this working-man's college in 1899, and also served as Lecturer and subsequently Reader in Public Administration at the London School of Economics from 1906 to

1941. A Liberal Member of Parliament, 1910–18, and a prominent Labour Member 1922–3, 1924–31, and 1935–41, he served as Postmaster General in the Labour administration of 1929–31.

Le Play, Pierre Guillaume Frédéric (1806–82). French mining engineer and social engineer, author of *Ouvriers Européens* (1855), a pioneering study of the budgets and activities of individual working-class families.

Leroy Beaulieu, Pierre-Paul (1843–1916). French economist and journalist, Professor of Political Economy at the Collège de France from 1880. Now mainly remembered for his contributions to public finance, he was hostile to post-1870 trends in both economic policy and economic method.

Levasseur, Pierre Émile (1828–1911). French historian and economist (*).

Lexis, Wilhelm (1837–1914). German economist and statistician (**).

Lieben, Richard (1842–1919). Viennese banker and economist (**).

Liefmann, Robert (1874–1941). German economist, professor at Freiburg and author of *Die Unternehmerverbände* (1897), *Kartelle, Konzerne und Trusts* (1919), *Grundsätze der Volkswirtschaftslehre* (1920), and other works.

List, Friedrich (1789–1846). German writer on economics and promulgator of protectionist ideas. Author of *The National System of Political Economy* (1856: 1841 in German).

Lloyd George, David (1863–1945). Statesman. Of humble origin, and initially a solicitor, the 'Welsh Wizard' represented the same Welsh constituency in Parliament from 1890 to 1945. A Liberal, he served as President of the Board of Trade 1905–8, Chancellor of the Exchequer 1908–15, Minister of Munitions 1915–16, Secretary of State for War 1916, and Prime Minister of the coalition government 1916–22. His pre-war Chancellorship and his Premiership were among the most striking episodes of British political history during the first half of the twentieth century.

Loch, Charles Stewart (1849–1923). Poor-law expert. Born in India, and educated at Balliol in its heyday, Loch served as Secretary to the Council of the Charity Organisation Society 1875–1914. He soon became a leading proponent of the COS position on social reform and played an influential role on various Royal Commissions, especially the Poor Law Commission of 1906–9. Loch published considerably on the aims and methods of charity and related socio-economic subjects. He held the Tooke Professorship of Economic Science and Statistics at King's College, London, 1904–8, and was knighted in 1915.

Lotz, Walther (1865–1941). German economist (**).

Lowe, Joseph (fl. 1807–23). Economic writer, author of *The Present State of England* (1822) which proposed a form of price index or 'tabular standard'.

Lowe, Robert (1811–92). Liberal politician. An Oxford-educated barrister, who entered Parliament in 1852 after several years in Australia, Lowe served as Chancellor of the Exchequer 1868–73 and Home Secretary 1873–4. He was created first Viscount Sherbrooke in 1880.

McCulloch, John Ramsay (1789–1864). Scottish economist (*).

Macgregor, David Hutchison (1877–1953). Economist. A protégé of Marshall and early Lecturer for the Economics Tripos (**).

Mackenzie, John Stuart (1860–1935). Philosopher (**).

Macmillan, Alexander (1818–96). Publisher (*).

Macmillan, Frederick Orridge (1851–1936). Publisher, knighted 1909 (*).

McTaggart, John McTaggart Ellis (1866–1925). Hegelian philosopher (*).

Mahaim, Ernest (1865–1938). Belgian economist (**).

Maitland, Frederic William (1850–1906). Eminent legal scholar: Downing Professor of the Laws of England, 1888–1906 (**).

Malthus, Thomas Robert (1766–1834). Economist and student of population (*).

Marshall, Mary Paley (1850–1944). Economist and Marshall's wife (*).

Marx, Karl Heinrich (1818–83). German socialist writer and agitator (*).

Mavor, James (1854–1925). Canadian economist and economic historian, Professor at Toronto (**).

Menger, Carl (1840–1921). Austrian economist (*).

Meredith, Hugh Owen (1878–1964). A member of King's, and a Fellow 1903–8, Meredith obtained firsts in Part I of the Classics Tripos, 1899, and Part II of the History Tripos 1901. Turning to economics, he lectured for the Economics Tripos 1904–5, was Lecturer in Economic History and Commerce at Manchester 1905–8, Girdlers' Lecturer in Economics at Cambridge 1908–11, and Professor of Economics at Belfast 1911–46. The author of *Protection in France* (1904) and *Outlines of English Economic History* (1908). Evidently one of Marshall's students, but not a favourite or a close disciple.

Mill, James (1773–1836). Historian, economist, and leading light among the philosophical radicals. Father of John Stuart (**).

Mill, John Stuart (1806–73). Philosopher—especially social philosopher—of eminence and an influential economist (*).

Moore, Henry Ludwell (1869–1958). American economist and statistician, a pioneering figure in the development of econometrics. The author of *The Laws of Wages* (1911), *Generating Economic Cycles* (1923), and other works. Trained under Carl Menger at Vienna and John Bates Clark at Johns Hopkins in Baltimore, Moore's career was spent mainly at Columbia, where he taught from 1902 to 1929. He visited London in 1909 and 1913, studying mathematical statistics with Karl Pearson.

Morley, John (1838–1923). Politician and man of letters. A prolific author and biographer, editor of the *Fortnightly Review* 1867–82, Morley was a Liberal Member of Parliament 1883–95 and 1896–1908. He served as Chief Secretary for Ireland, 1886 and 1892–5, and Secretary of State for India 1905–10. Created Viscount Morley in 1908.

Moulton, John Fletcher (1844–1921). Lawyer and judge (**).

Newton, Sir Isaac (1642–1727). Inventor of Newtonian mechanics and author of *Philosophiae Naturalis Principia Mathematica* (1687).

Nicholson, Joseph Shield (1850–1927). Scottish economist (*).

Nourse, Edwin Griswold (1883–1974). American agricultural economist. Nourse, a 1915 Ph.D. from Chicago, taught at the University of Arkansas 1915–18 and Iowa State College 1918–23. He then assumed various leadership roles in the Brookings Institution in Washington DC and served as first chairman of the President's Council of Economic Advisers 1946–9.

Oldham, Henry Yule (1862–1951). Geographer and early lecturer for the Economics Tripos. An Oxford graduate of 1886 (Jesus), Oldham was admitted to King's in 1893 upon being appointed University Lecturer in Geography. He was subsequently Reader in Geography, 1898–1908 and University Lecturer in Historical and Economic Geography 1908–21.

Palgrave, Robert Harry Inglis (1827–1919). Banker and economist (*).

Pantaleoni, Maffeo (1857–1924). Italian economist (*).

Papi, Giuseppe Ugo (1893–?). Italian economist. A law graduate who turned to economics, which he taught from 1927 onwards at various Italian universities but especially at the University of Rome. General secretary of the International Institute of Agriculture 1938–48, and subsequently associated with the Food and Agriculture Organisation of the United Nations. Author of *Escape from Stagnation* (1933) and many other works.

Pareto, Vilfredo (1848–1923). Italian engineer, economist, and sociologist. Although born in France, and spending his last thirty years in Switzerland, Pareto was quintessentially Italian. A brilliant engineering student at Turin, he had an extended business career during which he developed, as a confirmed liberal, a strong interest in the political and economic questions of the day. But it was not until 1890, prodded by Pantaleoni, that his attention turned to economic theory. He soon made his mark, and was appointed Walras's successor at Lausanne in 1892. Here he made fundamental contributions to economic theory and published his *Cours* (1896–7) and *Manuale* (1906), but his interest in economics had waned by the latter date as he turned increasingly to larger sociological questions.

Patten, Simon Nelson (1852–1922). American economist (**).

Payne, Sarah (*c.* 1862–1920). The Marshalls' faithful and indispensable servant. She entered into service with them in Bristol as a young woman and remained intimately involved in their lives until her death.

Peace, James Bennet (1864–1923). University Printer 1916–23, Fellow and Bursar of Emmanuel 1893–1920, University Lecturer in Mechanical Engineering, 1903–8.

Pearson, Karl (1857–1936). Biometrician (*).

Pethick-Lawrence, Frederick William (1871–1961). Politician and social reformer. One-time student of Marshall (**).

Phelps, Lancelot Ridley (1853–1936). Economist and poor-law authority (*).

Pierson, Nicolaas Gerard (1839–1909). Dutch economist and statesman (**).

Pigou, Arthur Cecil (1877–1959). Economist. Marshall's student and chosen successor (**).

Pitt, William 'the younger' (1759–1806). Statesman (**).

Plunkett, Horace Craven (1854–1932). Irish pioneer of agricultural cooperation and a prominent figure in Irish affairs. A Member of Parliament 1892–1900, and Vice President of the Department of Agriculture and Technical Instruction for Ireland 1899–1907. Author of *Ireland in the New Century* (1904) and other works. Knighted in 1903.

Price, Langford Lovell Frederick Rice (1862–1950). Economist and economic historian (*).

Pryme, George (1781–1863). Cambridge's first Professor of Political Economy (*).

Ramsay, William (1852–1916). Chemist, Knighted 1902 (*).

Rau, Karl Heinrich (1792–1870). German economist (*).

Rayleigh, Lord (1842–1919). John William Strutt, third Baron Rayleigh, succeeded his father in 1873. Senior Wrangler in the year, 1865, when Marshall was Second Wrangler, Strutt soon established himself as one of the leading physicists of his era. A Fellow of Trinity, 1866–71 and Cavendish Professor of Experimental Physics 1879–84, he thereafter conducted his researches independently at a laboratory on the family estate. He received, jointly with William Ramsay, a Nobel Prize in 1904 for the discovery of argon. His wife, née Evelyn Balfour, was the sister of both A. J. Balfour and Mrs. Eleanor Sidgwick.

Reay, Lord (1839–1921). Donald James Mackay, eleventh Baron Reay, the scion of an expatriate Scottish family, spent his earlier years in Holland, migrating to Britain only in 1875. He served effectively as Governor of Bombay 1885–90 and was Under Secretary of State for India 1894–5. He remained active thereafter in public—especially educational—affairs, serving as the first President of the British Academy 1901–7.

Ricardo, David (1772–1823). Economist and financier (*).

Ritchie, Charles Thomson (1836–1906). Conservative politician. A Member of Parliament 1874–92 and 1895–1905. He held office as President of the Local Government Board 1886–92, President of the Board of Trade 1895–1900, Home Secretary 1900–2, and Chancellor of the Exchequer 1902–3. Created first Baron Ritchie in 1905.

Robertson, Dennis Holme (1890–1963). Robertson had a distinguished undergraduate career at Trinity, obtaining firsts in Part I of the Classical Tripos and Part II of the Economics Tripos, 1910–12, and winning the Cobden Prize. He became a Fellow of Trinity in 1914, publishing his Fellowship dissertation, *A Study of Industrial Fluctuation*, in 1915. Military service, distinguished by award of the Military Cross, drew him from

Cambridge, but the return of peace saw him back in Trinity primed to play a prominent role in the small but distinguished group of teachers for the Economics Tripos. He became a University Lecturer in Economics in 1924 and a Reader in 1930. His most significant work, *Banking Policy and the Price Level*, appeared in 1926. Intellectual exchange with Maynard Keynes, initially fruitful, eventually led to a frustrating impasse and distracted Robertson from the development of his own ideas. He left Cambridge in 1938 for the Cassel Professorship in Economics at the London School of Economics, but returned in 1944 (having been extensively involved in govermental work) in order to succeed Pigou, and indirectly Marshall, as Professor of Political Economy. He retired in 1957, but retained until his death the Trinity Fellowship to which he had been re-elected in 1944. He was knighted in 1953.

Rogers, James Edwin Thorold (1823–90). Economist and economic historian (*).

Roosevelt, Theodore (1858–1919). Twenty-fifth President of the United States, 1901–8.

Rothenstein, William (1872–1945). Painter, noted for portraiture. Principal of the Royal College of Art 1920–35. Knighted 1931.

Sanger, Charles Percy (1871–1930). Lawyer and economist (*).

Sauerbeck, Augustus (?). Pioneering Anglo-Swiss compiler of price indices. This shadowy figure, employed by a wool broker, provided price index data regularly to the *Journal of the Royal Statistical Society* from 1886 until his retirement in 1913, when the *Statist* took over the task of continuing the 'Sauerbeck index'.

Schloss, David Frederick (1850–1912). Civil servant and expert on industrial relations. Educated at Oxford (Corpus Christi) Schloss was called to the Bar in 1875. After considerable involvement in social and industrial reform in London, where he aided Charles Booth's enquiries and assisted the organization of women workers, Schloss became associated with the Labour Department of the Board of Trade in 1893, taking up a permanent position in 1899. Best known for his *Methods of Industrial Remuneration* (1892).

Schmoller, Gustav von (1838–1917). German economist (*).

Schönberg, Gustav Friedrich von (1839–1908). German economist (*).

Scrope, George Julius Poulett (1797–1876). Geologist and frequent writer on economics. A Liberal Member of Parliament 1833–67, he was actively involved in the economic debates of the period. A reformist, but a critic of the ideas of Ricardo and Malthus.

Seager, Henry Rogers (1870–1930). American economist (**).

Seligman, Edward Robert Anderson (1861–1939). American economist (*).

Shirras, George Findlay (1885–1955). Educated at the University of Aberdeen, and an expert on public finance, Shirras spent most of his career in India, partly in teaching and academic administration and partly in government service, especially as Director of Statistics 1914–21. He returned to

Britain to serve as Professor of Economics at University College, Exeter, 1940–5. The author of *The Science of Public Finance* (1924) and other works.

Shove, Gerald Frank (1887–1947). Shove, a member of King's and an Apostle, obtained only a second class in Part I of the Classical Tripos, but switching to economics found his metier with a first in Part II of the Economics Tripos of 1911. Although encouraged by Maynard Keynes, Shove—a pacifist—was initially unsuccessful in establishing an academic career, and it was not until 1923, after some years as a private 'coach' in Cambridge, that he was appointed University Lecturer (subsequently Reader) in Economics, and not until 1926 that he became a Fellow of King's. Shove published little but was an influential teacher and critic in the Cambridge School that was rising to world dominance in the 1920s and 30s. His wife, Fredegond, was daughter to F. W. Maitland. Shove's Apostolic connections and his links with Maynard Keynes tied him to 'Bloomsbury'.

Sidgwick, Eleanor Mildred (1845–1936). Wife of Henry Sidgwick and Principal of Newnham 1892–1910 (**).

Sidgwick, Henry (1838–1900). Philosopher and occasional writer on economics (*).

Smart, William (1853–1915). Educated at the University of Glasgow, Smart devoted some years to business before turning to an academic career in 1886. He served as Adam Smith Professor of Political Economy at Glasgow from 1896, and is chiefly remembered for his enterprise in translating and communicating the ideas of the Austrian School to English-speaking readers, especially his *Introduction to the Theory of Value on the Lines of Menger, Wieser and Böhm-Bawerk* (1891).

Smith, Adam (1723–90). Scottish economist and philosopher (*).

Smith, Hubert Llewellyn (1864–1945). Civil servant, economist, and social investigator. Educated at Oxford (Corpus Christi), Smith obtained a first in Mathematics, 1886, and won Oxford's Cobden Prize in the same year. After lecturing on political economy for Oxford Extension and the Toynbee Trust, and serving as Secretary to the National Association for the Promotion of Technical Education, 1888–92, he commenced his long and fruitful association with the Board of Trade, first as a Commissioner for Labour and subsequently as the Board's Permanent Secretary 1907–19. From 1919 to 1927 he acted as chief economic adviser to the government. In retirement he directed the *New London Survey of Life and Labour* (1928–35). Knighted 1908.

Sorley, William Ritchie (1855–1935). Philosopher (*).

Spencer, Herbert (1820–1903). Evolutionary philosopher (**).

Stephen, Leslie (1832–1904). Man of letters (*).

Tanner, Joseph Robson (1860–1931). Historian and colleague of Marshall at St John's (**).

Taussig, Frank William (1859–1940). American economist (**).

Taylor, William George Langworthy (1859–1941). American economist. Trained at Harvard, Taylor subsequently studied in Paris and Leipzig. He was Professor of Economics at the University of Nebraska 1893–1911 and author of *The Credit System* (1913). His interests extended to spiritualism, horsemanship, and immortality—on all of which he published works in his years of retirement.

Thornely, Thomas (1855–1949). Historian and lawyer, University Lecturer in History, 1883–1907, and an early lecturer for the Economics Tripos (**).

Thünen, Johann Heinrich von (1783–1850). German economist and agriculturalist (*).

Todhunter, Isaac (1820–84). Cambridge mathematician (*).

Tooke, Thomas (1774–1858). Merchant and economist (*).

Turgot, Anne Robert Jacques (1727–81). French philosopher, economist, and administrator (*).

Wagner, Adolf Heinrich Gotthelf (1835–1917). German economist (**).

Walker, Francis Amasa (1840–97). American economist (*).

Walras, Léon (1834–1910). French economist (*).

Ward, Adolphus William (1837–1924). Historian, literary scholar, and academic administrator (**).

Ward, James (1843–1925). Philosopher and psychologist (*).

Webb, Beatrice (1858–1943). Student and reformist critic of economic, political, and administrative institutions (*).

Webb, Sydney James (1859–1947). Husband and inseparable co-worker and co-organizer with the above (*).

Westcott, Brooke Foss (1825–1901). Theologian and churchman (**).

Westlake, John (1828–1913). Legal scholar, Whewell Professor of International Law 1888–1908 (**).

Whewell, William (1799–1866). Philosopher, mathematician, and scientist (*).

Wicksell, Johan Gustav Knut (1851–1926). Swedish economist. Educated at Uppsala, and initially intending to become a mathematician, Wicksell turned to economics relatively late in life, his attention and energies meanwhile having turned to social issues. His serious study of economics commenced only in 1885 but by 1893 the first of his seminal works, *Value Capital and Rent* (in German, translated 1934) had appeared. He was to make important contributions to the theories of capital, factor pricing, public finance, and macroeconomics. However, his radical social views and propagandist activities, together with the need to qualify in law, hampered his appointment to a university post, and it was not until 1900 that he was appointed to teach economics and law at Lund University, where he remained until retirement in 1916. Retirement years in Stockholm brought him into contact with an able younger group of Swedish economists and involved him in official work for government and central bank. Recognition of Wicksell's stature as one of the most significant economic thinkers of his era was delayed, but his posthumous reputation greatly exceeds that of his initially more prominent contemporary, Gustav Cassel.

Wieser, Friedrich von (1851–1926). Austrian economist (**).

Young, Allyn Abbott (1876–1929). American economist. Young received a Ph.D. from the University of Wisconsin in 1902 and taught, among other places, at Stanford 1906–11, Cornell 1913–20, Harvard 1920–7, and the London School of Economics, 1927–9. His high reputation stemmed more from his abilities as teacher and critic than from the extent of his publications, although two of his articles achieved classic status.

Yule, George Udny (1871–1951). Statistician. Yule was a protégé of Karl Pearson at University College, London, and taught in London from 1894 to 1912. In the latter year he moved to Cambridge as University Lecturer (subsequently Reader) in Statistics, continuing until 1931 and becoming a Fellow of St John's in 1922. Yule was by no means an uncritical follower of Pearson and played a significant role in the development of statistical theory in Britain.

CHRONOLOGY FOR ALFRED MARSHALL, 1903–1924

1903 The Syndicate established by the University to 'enquire into the best means of enlarging the opportunities for the study in Cambridge of Economics and associated branches of Political Science' reported in favour of the establishment of a new Tripos in Economics etc., Marshall having taken a prominent part in its proceedings. The Report was approved by Senate (June), thus establishing the new Tripos as of October 1903 and establishing a new Special Board to administer it. The first examinations were scheduled in 1905 for Part I and 1906 for Part II.
Prepared during the summer a memorandum on the fiscal controversy for the then Chancellor of the Exchequer (C. T. Ritchie).

1904 Setting the uncompleted second volume of *Principles* aside, commenced work on a proposed short volume on international trade and the fiscal issues of the day. This work, which Macmillan's had agreed to publish, was the seed from which *Industry and Trade* eventually emerged in 1919.
The British Association met in Cambridge (August) involving the Marshalls in extensive entertaining of foreign guests for Section F.

1906 Published a pamphlet *Introduction to the Tripos* in order to publicize the new Tripos.

1907 Published 'The Social Possibilities of Economic Chivalry', *Economic Journal*, 17 (March), pp. 7–29, based on an after-dinner speech to the first Congress of the Royal Economic Society in January. See *Memorials*, pp. 323–46.
The fifth edition of *Principles* published.
The Marshall portrait appeal launched by Marshall's admirers.

1908 The portrait of Marshall by W. Rothenstein completed.
Resigned as Professor of Political Economy and succeeded by A. C. Pigou. Marshall's manœuvrings in favour of Pigou led to an irreparable breach with Foxwell.
Awarded an honorary Sc.D. by Cambridge University.
The 1903 Memorandum on the Fiscal Policy of International Trade published as a House of Commons Paper, having been referred to in debate.

1910 The sixth edition of *Principles* published, 'Volume I' being eliminated from the title and the promise of a second volume formally withdrawn.
Embroiled (in alliance with J. M. Keynes) in controversy with Karl Pearson over the latter's studies of the effects of parental alcoholism.

1916 The seventh edition of *Principles* published.

1917 Published 'National Taxation After the War', pp. 313–45 of *After-War Problems*, ed. W. H. Dawson (Allen and Unwin, London).
1919 *Industry and Trade* published by Macmillan.
1920 The eighth and final edition of *Principles* published.
1922 Members of the Royal Economic Society present an Address to Marshall on his eightieth birthday.
1923 *Money Credit and Commerce* published by Macmillan.
1924 Marshall's death (13 July).

In addition to the publications listed above, the *Journal of the Institute of Bankers*, 25 (February 1904) includes a report of Marshall's comments on E. J. Schuster, 'Foreign Trade and the Money Market'. (See [791.2] for further details.)

LIST OF LETTERS REPRODUCED IN VOLUME 3

LETTERS 733–1148

733. To Frederick Macmillan, 7 January 1903[1]

7. 1. 03

Dear Mr MacMillan,

Much of my life is spent in answering correspondents. If I answered all fully, the whole of it would go. Consequently I have made a rule never to do any paid work in the way of reviewing or advising. But I shall always be glad to tell you what I think of the quality of anybody's work, so far as I can do so without making a special study.

I know something of D^{r}.. Cassel. I think he has a fine, powerful mind, that he is a genuine student in the highest sense of the world;[2] & that anything written by him can be used with perfect safety for the higher education. There is a marked gap in economic literature on the subject of the underlying causes which govern the movements of interest & discount recorded in the City articles. Anything wh Dr Cassel said on the subject would be sure to be suggestive original & true as far as it went. But it might be a little wanting in inside knowledge of the money market, & the relative proportions of the forces that are in effective work in it.[3]

I have no doubt that the book would be bought by all professional students; & that the better class of young students would be recommended to read it.

D^{r}.. Cassel stayed with me for a couple of days;[4] & [I][5] have quite a feeling of affection for him, & *for his mind.*

I think there has been some little misunderstanding about my Corrigenda.[6] I sent the Revise to the press by my wife, & she brought home a rather troubled story. I had regarded Corrigenda—at all events *post mortem Corrigenda*—as things for wh the Author was solely responsible. And I wished to pay for them entirely myself, as in the case of one of my previous editions—the third, I think. I had 50 proofs printed, & sent some to friends in America. That caused a long delay before I was ready with the revise. Perhaps I should have mentioned this when writing to you about them.

Yours very truly | Alfred Marshall

[1] British Library, Macmillan Archive. From Balliol Croft.

[2] Possibly 'word' was intended.

[3] Gustav Cassel, *The Nature and Necessity of Interest*, which was published by Macmillan (London and New York, 1903), is presumably the work in question here.

[4] See Vol. 2 [659].

[5] Word apparently omitted.

[6] See Vol. 2 [731].

734. To Nicolaas Gerard Pierson, 20 January 1903[1]

20. 1. 03

Dear D^{r}.. Pierson,

Thankyou very much for your book.[2] I have been very busy, & have not, as I had hoped to have done ere this, mastered its substance. But I have read the chapter on Index numbers, a subject wh. happened to be in my mind: & I have pondered over the contents.[3] The contents puzzle me, as you would expect. But the notion of putting off production to the second volume seems less strange to me now than it would have some years ago: for indeed I find I am going to talk, a good deal more than I had expected to do, about it in my second volume; & it will be most instructive to me to see how you treat it. Of course I miss a centralized discussion of 'Distribution & Exchange': but by dipping in here & there, I have seen how you manage, with consummate skill & strength, to bind together its *disjecta membra*:[4] & I am quite sure that if you can succeed in making people see the underlying unity of your thought, you will have done an excellent service to economic study. For as the boy 'hates knowledge' so the man hates being forced to read an argument too long to be taken at one sitting: & if your plan of splitting it up into compartments will induce him to read, & enable [him][5] to see the fundamental unity, as you see it; your book will I am sure be the model on which the treatment of economics will be based hereafter. That will be rather bad for me: but it will be a good thing for the world, & I can rejoice at it.

As to index numbers, I agree very much with you, & think Edgeworths answer was valid only against the extremer pessimism of your articles, wh seem to go beyond the chapter in your book.[6] That is, I hold with you that the mechanical interpretation of index numbers is useless. I think that in fact they do not lie very badly; but in order to know how badly they lie we must analyse. The index number is rather the binding of an important book, than the book itself. Each leaf needs study: & the index number, in my view, is useful in helping us to settle down to the study of the book. Also, as a thing in itself, it is useful to quote against sweeping doctrines about price movements, wh partisan currency enthusiasts of all denominations shout at us. Such are my views, wh I had thought of submitting to your judgement long ago, when your articles appeared.

Just now I am largely taken up with the work of a Committee, 'Syndicate' we call it, appointed to inquire into a proposal, the general nature of which is indicated in the *Plea* wh I send separately.[7]

My wife & I are looking forward much to seeing you & Mrs Pierson in May or June, when I hope to know more of & to have learnt more from the noble book wh you have sent me.

Again many thanks | Yours very sincerely | Alfred Marshall

[1] University of Amsterdam, Pierson Papers. From Balliol Croft. Reproduced as letter 1191 in J. G. S. G. van Maarseveen (ed.), *Briefwisseling van Nicolaas Gerard Pierson 1839–1909* (De Nederlandsche Bank, Amsterdam, 1990–3: 4 vols.).
[2] N. G. Pierson, *Principles of Economics, Volume I* (Macmillan, London, 1902). The second and final volume was published only in 1912.
[3] That is, the Table of Contents.
[4] Separate parts.
[5] Word apparently omitted.
[6] See N. G. Pierson, 'Index Numbers and Appreciation of Gold', *Economic Journal*, 5 (September 1895), pp. 329–35; 'Further Considerations of Index Numbers', *Economic Journal*, 6 (March 1896), pp. 127–31. F. Y. Edgeworth, 'A Defence of Index Numbers', *Economic Journal*, 6 (March 1896), pp. 132–42.
[7] Marshall's pamphlet, *A Plea for the Creation of a Curriculum in Economics and Associated Branches of Political Science* is reproduced in *Guillebaud*, pp. 161–78. It had been widely disseminated in 1902 as a preliminary for Marshall's campaign for a new Tripos. The University Syndicate established to consider and report on the question was still sitting. For details see Vol. 2 [687.3, 722.1, 726.1, 731.3].

735. To Percy Alden, 28 January 1903 (incomplete)[1]

28. i. 03

Dear Mr Alden,
. . . I think that unemployment is a symptom of several distinct social maladies, which require different treatment.

For instance, the occasional unemployment of capable energetic workers of all grades is, I think, a wholly different disease from systematic unemployment. It seems due to the inability of beings of finite intelligence to forecast coming economic needs and opportunities with perfect precision: I believe that this form of unemployment is not increasing, but rather diminishing: and that it can be further diminished by a better understanding of the causes of trade fluctuations and changes; and by the widening of world markets: while something may be gained through the diffusion of the notion, that to spend the whole of one's income in prosperous times and to be without resource when the tide turns, is inconsistent with the respect that every one owes to himself.

On the other hand, systematic unemployment is, I believe, caused by the existence of large numbers of people, who will not or can not work steadily or strongly enough to make it possible that they should be employed regularly. They are hunters for odd jobs, which are generally 'soft' jobs. A large part of the present unemployment seems to me to be this kind: that is, it is a symptom of disease rather than a cause. And remedies addressed to the symptoms of it are likely, I fear, to increase the disease.

No doubt we ourselves, society at large, are responsible for the existence of this disease, more than the victims of it are. And we ought not to be afraid of very large expenditure of public and private funds in removing or lessening the causes of the disease; on methods of which you and our common friend Lawrence are high authorities. I refer especially to methods for de-urbanizing life, in the

sense in which urbanized life is enfeebled life. This should, I think, be supplemented by kindly but severe discipline of those who are bringing up children under physical and moral conditions which will make them recruits to the great army of the habitually unemployed....
Yours very truly, | Alfred Marshall

[1] Printed in *Memorials*, pp. 446–7. Original not traced. From Balliol Croft. The precise enquiry about unemployment to which Marshall is responding remains unclear.

Percy Alden (1865–1944) was associated with Pethick-Lawrence, editing *The Echo* during 1901–2. He had been Warden of Mansfield House University Settlement, 1891–1901, and served as a Radical Member of Parliament, 1906–18. See his *The Unemployed: A National Question* (King, London, 1905); also *The Unemployable and the Unemployed* (Headley, London, 1908), by Alden and Edward E. Hayward.

736. From John Bates Clark, 3 February 1903[1]

616 W. 113th St.,
New York, Feb. 3, 1903.

Dear Professor Marshall:—

When I received your very welcome letter[2] and filed it for a careful reply I did not think that almost the whole of January and a day or two over would pass before the reply could be written. The letter has, in the interim, been much in my mind and I have only waited for a quiet afternoon in which I might reread it and make reply in a way that would express my interest in the subject. I have unwisely let myself be loaded by a multitude of extra appointments which have crowded together at this particular time, and today is the first day for a very long time in which I have had the hours at my disposal. I do not mean again to be under such a pressure.

As for the sequence of the sentences at the bottom of my p. 370 and the top of 371,[3] I imagine you may be looking for a connection which does not exist. The connection which I see, as I now read the passage, is that Professor[4] has made one concession concerning the connection of rent with price and that Professor Marshall has made one, while my argument claims more and maintains that the connection extends to all rents.

I wonder whether we do differ as to the static state. I do not now see that we differ much, if at all. I do not myself think that such a state is, in itself and for itself, worth talking about. A static ocean is an unreal thing and so unlike the real sea that it is not in itself worth studying; and yet a study of it gives some important facts about the actual sea. I never for a moment, in studying the static economic state, think of the study otherwise than as a mode of investigating certain facts and laws of the real and dynamic world. The creation of such a state is a bit of heroic imagining and it has not appeared to me to be necessary to supply the causes of the stationary conditions of the economic world; and yet when I do this, I imagine certain forces that produce change paralyzed, leaving others unimpaired. That is one way of creating an imaginary equilibrium. It never seems to me that the equilibrium is possible in any part of the real world.

In so far as there remains a real difference of thought between us I think the citation from the lower paragraph on your page 608[5] does, as you suggest, indicate it. I should always think of the social capital as steadily increasing and as not the same amount for any two days, but in considering what changes will occur in consequence of the manufacturer's decision to add a floor to his mill rather than to buy bonds, I should think of the other additions to the productive plant of society which would have been made if he had bought the bonds and consider that the ultimate effect of his decision will be the prevention of certain marginal investments of capital, or what is the same thing, the making of certain marginal additions to the total stock of capital goods. I should not think of this man as accelerating his accumulation for the specific purpose of adding to his mill, but should think of him as going on the even tenor of his way, in so far as spending and saving are concerned, and as deciding whether to use his own capital or to lend it, just as he would decide whether he would borrow money from a bank or refrain from borrowing it and so let others have it,—by comparing the earning power of the capital in the use that will be made of it in his mill with the earning power that it would have in some other use. I should rely on this general proposition:—the amount of capital at one instant in existence is fixed and the fact that part of it is at this instant in the form of a floor of A's mill prevents that part of it from being at this time embodied in a floor of B's mill or in other marginal investments. The static state helps me by furnishing the standard toward which the apportionment of capital in the dynamic world is always tending. I should think of the comparative quantities of goods and of their relative values as connected with the apportionment, and should regard the portioning out of land among different uses as akin, in this respect, to the parceling out of the capital.

I have made a long letter, proportionate to my interest in the subject and the pleasure that the correspondence has given me, notwithstanding the delay I have allowed to occur in writing. I have just now one advantage which I may lose some day:—I can say 'It will all be explained in my volume on Dynamic'. I really do hope that the value of the static studies may be put in a clearer light when the results of them are at hand in the shape of a beginning of a comprehensive dynamic study. If only I could bring the study out easily and soon![6] We shall see what we shall see, and in the meanwhile I hope to do more work in that line than I have been doing. In the hope that you are well and that your eagerly awaited second volume has made more rapid progress than mine has made, I am

Yours very truly, | John B. Clark.

[1] Columbia University Library, J. B. Clark Papers. Possibly a fair copy.

[2] See Vol. 2 [732].

[3] See Vol. 2 [727.5, 732.2] for the details of the cited passage from J. B. Clark, *The Distribution of Wealth* (Macmillan, New York, 1899).

[4] The intended reference was probably to Wieser, who is mentioned immediately before the cited sentences on pp. 370–1 as insisting that only 'the part of rent that is not differential, but general, is an element in price making'.

[5] Of *Principles* (*4*). See Vol. 2 [732.3] for details.

[6] Clark's *Essentials of Economic Theory* (Macmillan, New York, 1907) fell short of meeting this ambitious aim.

737. From Nicolaas Gerard Pierson, 15 February 1903[1]

Feb. 15 [1]903
8 Groothertoginnelaan | 's Gravenhage

Dear Professor Marshall

Many thanks for your kind letter.[2] Of course by sending you a copy of my book I never meant that you should be expected to read it, or even the largest part of it. Only, I should like to know your opinion, at some future time, on a few subjects

p. 217–225 Wages and interest
" 228–232 Money and interest
" 288–300 Providing employment
" 454–461 My conception of the dispute regarding Currency theory and Banking princ.
" 536–542 'On the balance of payments' explanation of gold drains.
" 587–590 My conception of the desideratum: fixity of value of money.

In all this, I fancy, there is something that goes out of the beaten track. It may be wrong for all that.

I also should be desirous to know whether I fully grasped your idea on pp. 527 and sq.[3]

Your remark that on the subject of Index Numbers I spoke more reservedly in my book than in The Economic Journal is quite true.[4] Not being a mathematician I felt rather reluctant to repeat assertions which among mathematicians had met with some opposition.

I would ask you not to overrate the bearing of my observations regarding the distribution of the subject matter. Of course, what I said on the desirability of putting Production at the close fully expresses my opinion. But this question is not so *very* important.

Thanks for your 'Curriculum',[5] but I am sorry to say that I am not sufficiently well acquainted with the English System of higher education to follow you *entirely*. I hope you will explain to me all this when I come to see you on the month of May.

There will be much to talk over.

With our best regards to Mrs. Marshall,
Yours truly | Pierson

[1] The original is pasted inside the cover of a copy of vol. 1 of Pierson's *Principles* [734.2], now in the Marshall Library. Reproduced as letter 1195 in J. G. S. G. van Maarseveen, *Briefwisseling* [734.1].
[2] See [734].
[3] Here Pierson deals with bills of exchange and foreign exchanges. The point at issue is obscure.
[4] See [734.6].
[5] See [734.7].

738. To Arthur Cecil Pigou, 19 March 1903 (incomplete)[1]

19. iii. 1903

My dear Pigou,

I have just been reading your article in E. J.[2] ... Well! Am I right in supposing that your main argument is this—

Though we may pass from the utility curve of an individual to the demand curve of a nation (or other group) as regards bread or milk or any other commodity which is valued only for its direct benefit to us, yet we cannot do that for commodities which we value partly because they impart social distinction. For a large change in the supply all round of such a commodity alters the conditions which we have assumed to be practically constant when making out the curve for an individual.

So far as I can see, I concur in this: and think something of the sort ought to have been said by me. But of course I have always insisted that the demand price of a group is not any approximate measure of satisfaction, save on the assumption that people of different incomes and also of different sensibilities are evenly distributed throughout the group. And next it may be said that the continued references to the effect of changes in fashion include in their purview such changes as alter the distinction-giving power of a thing....

Next, is your second chief point that, since some moving forces are not associated with great pleasure, possibly not even with great satisfaction, therefore the consumers' surplus shown by the curve may diverge far (even in a society where all are about equally well-off) from being a measure of aggregate pleasure or even aggregate satisfaction? If so I again quite agree. I must some time consider whether I have sufficiently emphasized the fact that the schedule deals with satisfaction only in so far as that arises out of the number and excellence of the things which a man has, and not out of the quality of the man himself....

Alfred Marshall

[1] Printed in *Memorials*, p. 433. Original not traced. From Balliol Croft.
[2] A. C. Pigou, 'Some Remarks on Utility', *Economic Journal*, 13 (March 1903), pp. 58–68.

739. To Charles Booth, 31 March 1903[1]

31. 3. 03

My dear Booth,

Thank you much for your angelic book: holy & beautiful outside and in. I cannot profess to be a connoisseur of the pictures with which it abounds. But I find myself drawn on to read a good deal, wherever I look in. But most of all do I yearn for the focussing in the last volume.[2] To that you will of course give the very best of yourself. And I look to it as among the most valuable of economico-ethico-spiritual goods that have ever been vouchsafed to the world. I heard some one whose words are very weighty & who takes great interest in your work, a very eminent man & one older than either of us, say 'Booth gives materials, but he does not build with them enough'. I was interrupted in my reply by a man with a much bigger voice than mine; & the party almost at once broke up. But, thinking over it afterwards, I felt that a person who merely read you & did not vibrate in echo to you—a la Marconi[3]—might not see how much construction there is latent in all you do. There seems to me quite as much when you do not point directly to action as when you do; sometimes even more: that seems a paradox, but I mean it in all soberness & reverence. But now in your last volume you must for the sake of all, for knowledge, for progress, for ideals—and I will throw in, though somewhat irrelevantly, for Booth—for the sake of all you must make that volume the best thing you possibly can. The best of the kind that has been done, I know it will be anyhow. But I want it to be even better [than][4] that—ever so much.

Our best love to you & Mrs Booth.

Yours eagerly | Alfred Marshall

[1] University of London Library, Booth Papers. From Balliol Croft.

[2] A third and expanded edition of Booth's *Life and Labour of the People of London* was published in 17 vols. (Macmillan, London) in 1902–3. It comprised: first series: *Poverty* (4 vols., 1902); second series: *Industry* (5 vols., 1903); third series: *Religious Influences* (7 vols., 1902–3); final volume: *Notes on Social Influences and Conclusion* (1903). The volume Marshall had received was most probably from the third series.

[3] Guglielmo Marconi (1874–1937), Italian pioneer of wireless telegraphy who had recently established transatlantic transmission.

[4] Word apparently omitted.

740. To Ludwig Joseph Brentano, 4 April 1903[1]

9: 4: 1903.

Dear Professor Brentano,

It would be difficult to conceive a more pleasant letter than yours: and I thank you heartily for it.[2] But unfortunately I am not perfectly free. Two years ago I gave permission to a young man—Hugo Ephraim, Leipzig, Scharnstorn-strasse, 511—to translate my book.[3] Last July he wrote that he had translated three quarters of it but would have to suspend work at it for about a year, as he wanted to take his Doctor's Degree sooner than he intended. He hoped however to finish within the stipulated time, i.e. by July 1904. Of course I would infinitely rather that the translation were brought out under your high auspices, and by such a man as Dr Kestner.[4] Herr Ephraim was unknown to me when he asked for leave to publish,[5] and I do not think he has made any definite arrangement with a publisher. I did not stipulate for any payment, but merely that the translation should be a good one. I am now writing to him, referring to you as an economist of the very highest rank, but not giving your name. In any case it would be a pity that so much of the translation should be done twice over: and what I should like best under the circumstances is that[6] the translation of this volume should be completed by Dr Kestner, the first part of it revised by him, and the whole published by your Publisher under your auspices, in the names of Dr Kestner and Herr Ephraim.

Yours most truly, | Alfred Marshall

[1] Bundesarchiv Koblenz, Brentano Papers. Typewritten with handwritten corrections. From Balliol Croft.

[2] Brentano had apparently offered to arrange and supervise a German translation of *Principles* (*4*).

[3] Hugo Ephraim (1869–?) published a Liepzig dissertation on the history of weaving in 1904.

[4] Friedrich Julius Felix [Fritz] Kestner (1879–1914?) had published a Liepzig dissertation on the German iron tariff in 1902.

[5] Mistyped as 'pulish' in the original.

[6] Followed in the original by an undeleted 'tha'.

741. From Hugo Ephraim, 13 April 1903[1]

Leipzig d. 13. 4. 03

Dear Sir;

In reply to your [letter][2] of 8 iv, which I received this morning, I beg to inform you, that I feel *most agreeably* surprised by it.

Though not 2/3 of the agreed time have passed yet, I felt always troubled by the thought, that I would not be ready in time, and that I would not find a worthy publisher.

I feared, that *a great amount of work and time* would be spent in vain.

Certainly I would have spared no pains, to carry through the printing of the translation, when finished!

A friend of mine, pupil of Prof. Brentano in Munich told me some time ago, that this gentleman has a special interest for a translation of your work. I have not the honour, to know Professor B. personally, but I had the intention to appeal to his intervention later on, your permission supposed.

Possibly he is the economist of the very high rank, you refer to !?!

I welcome your proposal and hope, that an arrangement in your way will be possible.

I have translated: Book I. II. III. IV, and Book V Chapt. 1/5 (without remarks). I beg to propose, that my cooperator begins with Book VI, while I finish Book I/V. But I wish, (you will enter my situation) that my cooperation will not be 'thrown into the shade'.

Awaiting your further informations with pleasure, I remain, Sir,

Yours very truly | Hugo Ephraim

[1] Bundesarchiv Koblenz, Brentano Papers. Sent to Brentano with [742]. For Ephraim see [740.3].
[2] Illegible abbreviation.

742. To Ludwig Joseph Brentano, 19 April 1903[1]

19 4 03

Dear Professor Brentano,

I inclose a very satisfactory letter from Mr Ephraim.[2] His desire that his co-operation should not 'be thrown into the shade' seems reasonable. Possibly he has guessed that you are the eminent economist to whom I referred in writing to him: and possibly Dr Kestner[3] is the friend of whom he now speaks.

In any case it would perhaps simplify matters if Dr Kestner would enter into negociations with him direct. Both their names might appear on the title page, and a note—possibly included in an Introduction by you—might specify the shares of each in the work.[4]

As regards any payment that can be extracted from the publisher, I have only to say, with Messrs Macmillan's concurrence, that I wish for none of it. I shall be more than satisfied by the mere fact that the book is well translated and well published. If you would arrange the rest, and especially give the book as much of your blessing as you honestly can in writing to a publisher and in an Introduction, you would confer on me a very deep obligation; & render me

Yours very gratefully | Alfred Marshall

[1] Bundesarchiv Koblenz, Brentano Papers. Typewritten with handwritten corrections. From Balliol Croft. The typist's rendering 'Macmillan' was left unaltered despite Marshall's penchant for 'MacMillan'.
[2] See [741, 740.3].
[3] See [740.4].
[4] When the translation appeared in 1905, it was attributed to Hugo Ephraim and Arthur Salz with a preface by Brentano. See [827.2], below.

743. To Oscar Browning, 15 May 1903[1]

15. 5. 03

My dear Browning

I should be ungrateful indeed if I forgot the splendid services which King's has rendered & is rendering to History in general & especially to History looked at from that point of view which is most interesting to the Economist. I know also that many Kings men have given to economics a larger share of their time than they would have done if their sole object had been to lay out their work so as to reap the largest possible harvest of marks.

I meant only that the purely historical systematic work set for the Tripos consisted of English economic and English constitutional history: that the history of England is traced over (say) 8 centuries on these two sides, & that there is no systematic study of international movements of the kind which we want for the XIX century for the proposed Tripos.

Economics as well as economic history is practically an English subject for the Historical Tripos as it is for Part I of the Moral Sciences Tripos. A few of us are gradually wedging in international books: but the time for studying them is really at a later stage than 'Historical' economists generally reach.

I am very grateful to the Historical Faculty, & most especially to the Kings Branch of it for what it has done for economics. But it remains true that I have never known any one who, while reading for the Historical Tripos, obtained a high class knowledge of economics. Clapham & Pigou learnt almost all that they know about economics after they had taken their degrees. You must of course take the first two paragraphs of my speech together & not a *bit* of *one* sentence by itself. I have repeated in my speech the main tribute wh I made in speaking with you to the training of the Historical School (especially à la Kings) in the middle of the second column of p 773.[2]

Yours sincerely | Alfred Marshall

[1] King's College, Cambridge, Browning Papers. From Balliol Croft. The Economics and Political Science Syndicate [734.7] had reported on 4 March, recommending the establishment of a new Tripos (see *Reporter*, 10 March 1903, pp. 528–38, for the text). This Report was debated by Senate on 7 May and a full account appeared in the *Reporter*, 14 May 1903, pp. 763–74. The report of Marshall's speech is reproduced in Appendix I, below. It seems likely that Browning had objected to the statement in Marshall's first paragraph that recent international history was not represented in the Historical Tripos.

[2] This refers to Marshall's statement: 'The instinct of proportion seemed to be developed by the students for this Historical Tripos; but very few of them got beyond the merest elements of economic science'. See Appendix I, p. 400.

744. To Ludwig Joseph Brentano, 18 May 1903[1]

18. 5. 03

Dear Brentano,

I wonder whether I may encourage Herr Ephraim[2] to put himself into direct communication with you. If you adhere to your most noble promise to write a Preface to the translation, he would need to come into contact with you ultimately: and, unless I hear from you to the contrary within a week or so, I shall be bold enough to encourage him to write to you, as he wishes to do.

Our proposal for a new curriculum meets with almost unanimous support from British economists. But unfortunately one influential Cambridge man, Cunningham, is strongly, even bitterly opposed to it; as you will see by the inclosed cutting from the *Times*.[3] There is also a large body of conservatives who believe only in the old fashioned studies; & we shall have a hard fight for victory. I hope we shall win, but am not sure. The decisive vote of the Senate will be taken soon.[4]

I am bringing out a 'Fly', as we call it, containing some extracts from some letters I had received about it.[5] I will send you a copy tomorrow.

With renewed thanks, I am | Yours sincerely | Alfred Marshall

P.S. I have forgotten to say that Ephraim thinks he can finish the translation by the middle of next year. But he might go to press with the first half at once: so not much time need be wasted.

[1] Bundesarchiv Koblenz, Brentano Papers. From Balliol Croft. Partly reproduced in H. W. McCready, 'Alfred Marshall: Some Unpublished Letters', *Culture*, 15 (September 1954), pp. 300–8 at pp. 307–8. See [742].

[2] See [740.3].

[3] Cunningham, although a member of the Economics Syndicate, had stood aloof from its proceedings. In alliance with MacTaggart he had announced implacable resistance to the establishment of a new Tripos, and the two refused to sign the Syndicate's Report. Cunningham introduced his specific alternative proposals only in a printed memorandum for the Syndicate of 9 March 1903 (Marshall Papers), when the Report (dated 4 March) had already been submitted. This manœuvre was evidently designed to provide ammunition for the coming public debate into which Cunningham entered vigorously. The cutting from *The Times* sent to Brentano was presumably a report of the Senate debate of 7 May [743.1]. (See *The Times*, 11 May 1903 (11d): condensed without attribution in the *Cambridge Review*, 14 May 1903, pp. 290–1).

[4] The Senate vote on the Syndicate's recommendations was to take place on Saturday 6 June, 1903.

[5] See [747] below.

745. To Oscar Browning, 18 May 1903[1]

18. 5. 03

My dear Browning

It passes my comprehension to guess by what malignant accident the absurd story has got about that we are asking the University to admit people to a degree on Part I of the Economic Tripos + Part II of the Historical.[2] That we do not do this any one can discover who will take the trouble to read our regulations: that we could not possibly have done it is obvious *a priori*, because we were not invited to overhaul the regulations for the Historical Tripos. Of course the Historical Board will have to consider on what terms, if any, persons coming from the new Tripos (if created) are to be admitted to either part of the Historical. When they do that, they will presumably arrange that the terms are of fitting difficulty. But for our Syndicate to have done that would have been an unparalleled & even an impossible impertinence.

Of course it was our duty to consider on what terms Historical (& other) men might be admitted to our Tripos. And we did spend a *long time* in discussing the question whether any one who had taken Part I of the Historical (or Moral Science) where economics is represented might be admitted to our Part I. I myself voted against it. But the majority were against me, heavily: & I am now convinced they were right.

As to those who have taken Part II of the Historical Tripos: they have necessarily qualified for a degree already. So we of course did not waste our time on discussing their case.

As to Clapham, I think he is a much better economist than he would have been if he had wasted the time which he spent on the XI–XVIII centuries. But I think he would have become by now an immeasurably better economist if he had given his best years of study to the course now proposed for the Economic Tripos, in wh there is a vast deal of just that history wh gives sense of proportion in dealing with *quite modern* economic problems; & had read his earlier centuries in recreative hours either before or after his degree.

Yours very sincerely | Alfred Marshall

[1] King's College, Cambridge, Browning Papers. From Balliol Croft.

[2] An unnamed correspondent of the *Cambridge Review* (May 14 1903, p. 291) had remarked:

> The first part of the proposed Economic Tripos seems to coincide so closely with the course already taken by many students preparing for the second part of the History Tripos, that they may be said to be almost identical. Is it intended that men who have passed the first part of the Economic Tripos should be able to find an easy avenue to a degree by presenting the same work over again to History examiners?

The allusion is to the option for an economics concentration in Part II of the existing History Tripos. Success in Part I Economics was not proposed to be sufficient for award of a degree.

746. To Joseph Robson Tanner, 20 May 1903[1]

20. 5. 03

My dear Tanner

Macgregor (who helped me with correcting papers last year) will give my general course for me next year. I am moving him to write to you.

Pigou—if our scheme gets through—will probably offer lectures on my behalf in the Lent & Easter Terms on the history of labour, chiefly XIX century English; no formal application can well be made until after the vote on the 6th..[2] If that is in the negative, Pigou will probably give for me a set of lectures like that wh he is giving this term. I am wording my own course-titles vaguely, so that he may be free to pick out any part that he likes.[3]

I am much obliged indeed for your vigour about the Review.[4] You are *the* man. I have had some correspondence & conversation with Reddaway.[5] He had discovered a lot of mares-nests. One was that Part I of the new Tripos was to be absurdly easy. The economics wh in the History Tripos occupy but two papers were to be spread out over three. I said we intended a higher standard, & have implied that in our preamble: also we shall show it in our list of books. He is still not quite satisfied, as the list of books will have no permanent authority. I think he is unreasonable about this. But perhaps it may be well to put it about that there is a firm intention on the part of all concerned to keep the standard high.

Yours sincerely | Alfred Marshall

[1] St John's College, Cambridge, Tanner Papers. From Balliol Croft.

[2] See [744.4].

[3] Pigou did in fact offer in 1903–4 the lectures envisaged: see *Reporter*, 10 October 1903.

[4] Tanner had written to the *Cambridge Review* on 15 May to answer a complaint from an anonymous correspondent who signed himself 'Y'. The point at issue was whether the growth of the history staff had been a natural evolution, which might justify similar expectations for the eventual growth of the number of economics teachers, as Sorley had suggested in the debate on the Report of the Economics Syndicate (*Reporter*, 14 May 1903, p. 770), or whether it had been an unrepeatable consequence of recommendations of the Parliamentary Commissioners. Tanner disproved emphatically Y's contention that the latter was the case and that Sorley's evidence depended upon his particular choice of dates. See *Cambridge Review* 14 May 1903, pp. 295–6; 21 May 1903, p. 314. The letters were published under the respective headings 'Economy in Observation' and 'Economy in Investigation'.

[5] William Fiddian Reddaway (1872–1949), historian of King's and Fitzwilliam Hall. Presumably 'Y' was he. His correspondence with Marshall has not been traced.

747. To Members of the Cambridge University Senate, 20 May 1903[1]

In the discussion of the proposed Tripos for Economics and associated branches of Political Science, which was held in the Senate House on May 7th,[2] several speakers expressed a wish that some letters which I had submitted to the Syndicate[3] should be circulated to the Senate. In compliance with that wish, the following selection is submitted. The original selection was made to answer a question, raised at a meeting of the Syndicate, whether there was good reason for believing that a curriculum of the kind under discussion would be of much service to any but professional students; and, in short, whether there was a real demand in the country for it. The present selection is on the same lines; but with some variations in detail. I should perhaps explain that I made no canvass for expressions of opinion. I merely sent my *Plea for the creation of a curriculum in economics and associated branches of political science*[4] to a few men of affairs with whom I had happened to come into contact, or who had taken part in recent public discussions on the education of business men. I seldom asked for an answer. But nearly all to whom I sent the Plea wrote expressing in definite terms their agreement with Sections (2) and (3) of it, which deal with matters of general interest, to the exclusion of academic detail.[5]

Mr Gibb, General Manager of the North Eastern Railway, writes:—

Two distinct tendencies amongst business men are, I think, observable at the present time. There is a growing desire on the one hand, that young men who enter business with the hope of reaching the higher posts of management, shall come with faculties trained by thorough education and by studies of University rank. But this desire is balanced and seriously checked by a conviction, which seems to me to become more intense and more definite, that the courses of study at the Universities need considerable revision to render them suitable for students who intend to enter public life. If the right kind of training is provided there will be an ample rush of students to take advantage of it, and employers will quickly apply their business instincts to the matter and detect in the finished University product an item of value for business purposes.

I have no hesitation in saying that if I were choosing between two candidates for railway employment, of equal capacity, one of whom had gone through the ordinary curriculum, and the other had taken his degree through some such curriculum as is suggested in the Plea, I would give the preference to the latter. I should consider that he had obtained a mental training practically as good as the other for the needs of a business career, and, besides that, something more of special value for his individual work.

Sir Thomas Sutherland, G.C.M.G., Chairman of the Peninsular and Oriental Company, after saying that many business men must go to work at eighteen years of age, continues:—

In the case of that smaller class, who are destined to a business career, but who are also privileged to spend three or four years at one of our Universities, ... your 'plea' would appear to me, to be in every sense a wise and valid one. Most men whose sons were intended to follow this life, would, I think, be only too happy to enter them for a curriculum such as that indicated in your paper. I should certainly embrace the opportunity myself.

From a letter by Sir John Glover, Shipowner, to Mr N. L. Cohen, submitted to the Senate by permission:[6]

I have read Mr Marshall's *Plea for the Creation of a Curriculum in Economics*.... It is the absence of such a Curriculum that explains the far-offness of men who come from the Universities to business life.... As an increasing portion of the students have to be concerned in affairs somehow, as lawyers, as writers, as politicians, and as men of business in the higher direction of manufactures, and commerce—it seems to me that to turn men out without such studies means waste of very precious human time and faculties.

Sir Clinton E. Dawkins, K.C.B., formerly Financial Member of Council of Governor General of India, Member of the Firm of J. S. Morgan & Co., writes:—

I am glad to find myself in general and hearty agreement with you in your main contention. This I can say with the more pleasure because certain schemes for business training that I have seen put forward went far in the direction of technical preparation, and ignored the advantages of that general education of mind and character afforded at the old Universities.

I do not believe that you will get men with a broad outlook or what I may call a free play of mind who have started early on technical preparation for business. But I equally believe that those who have passed into a University, and are subjected to its influences, should have the opportunity of a training in economics of the same character as the training given to intending lawyers or physicists.

Mr R. H. I. Palgrave, F.R.S., Banker, after receiving the Report of the Syndicate, writes:—

The scheme has been carefully thought out and should become the accepted course for the classes of men whom you aim at receiving. There are a great many men—besides those intended for the professional Study of Economics, and highest branches of business—to whom such a Tripos as you intend to establish, should be attractive.... There are difficulties in the way of men destined for business going to Universities at all—the time consumed, the habits acquired—besides the expense. I can quite think however that there are parents to whom your existing courses of study do not appeal and who might quite take to the Economic Tripos.

Mr Le Marchant, Member of Council of India, Banker, First Class in *Litt. Hum.*, writes:—

A systematic course of study such as you propose would provide men with an intellectual equipment of great value and prepare them for constructive work in many lines of practical life.

Sir David Dale, D.C.L., Bart., Ironmaster, Chairman of Section A of Royal Commission of Labour, one of the four representatives of England, at the Berlin Labour Conference, 1890, writes:—

Section 3 of your Plea and that which precedes it on page 7 specifically commend themselves to my judgment and to my rather long and varied experience of what is needed for the due equipment of a young man who is destined for higher administrative duties either in business (commercial or manufacturing) or in public life, and that this training should be provided at the older Universities seems to me of great importance. Many young men to whom it would be invaluable would miss it if it were obtainable only at Modern Colleges.

Your allusions to the beneficial influence of such a course of study as you advocate on the large employer commend themselves to me.

The late Mr Albert Fry, Master-Engineer, Master of Merchant Venturers, Bristol, Chairman of Council of University College, Bristol, wrote:—

I wish you may succeed. Such a curriculum would be a great boon to young men intended for a business career.

A man now coming from a university and entering a business office has no key to the wider interests of what is going on and is only wearied with unmeaning detail: after a while if he is the right sort he sees what it is all about and is interested, but he has a bad time first. A proper education would save him most of this, I think.

Mr Charles Booth, Hon. LL.D., Camb., F.R.S., Merchant, Author of *Life and Labour of the People in London*, writes:—

I am in cordial agreement with the 'Plea' you make for the creation of a curriculum in Economics and associated branches of Political Science at Cambridge.

It is already generally recognised that a University training is desirable for any whose lot it is to inherit commercial positions of even moderate importance (my three junior partners are all University men), and this although no pains has been taken to make the higher training offered applicable to their future.

That a curriculum such as you suggest would be an attraction to young men of this class is certain, and in my view it is no less sure that it would be of great and solid value both in business and for any form of work involving public responsibility.

I hope too that the widening of training in these subjects might lead men of other antecedents to appreciate the depth of the interests that really underlie the life of a business man.

Mr Walter Leaf, Litt.D., Merchant, Vice-President of London Chamber of Commerce, writes:—

I have great pleasure in signing the memorial. I have been recently engaged in an enquiry into the education of young men who are destined to take leading positions in commerce and industry, and have been specially impressed with the scant opportunities afforded them by our present system for gaining the breadth of view which, as you rightly say, is becoming more and more necessary for the leaders and managers.[7]

The Right Hon. A. J. Balfour, M.P., writes:—

I am hardly in a position to form any judgment on the modifications you propose in the existing Tripos System at Cambridge for the purpose of giving opportunities for further study of Economics. But I am entirely at one with you in thinking that there is a pressing need for promoting economic research. The conditions of industry, national and international, are now widely different from those which prevailed when our classic works on political economy were written. There is much to be done in the direction of submitting these new phenomena to scientific treatment; and I most earnestly hope that if any change in our curriculum is required to enable Cambridge to take its full share in these investigations, that change will be adopted.

The Right Hon. John Morley, M.P., writes:—

Thank you for sending me the short piece on an Economic Curriculum. I have read it with the very liveliest interest and sympathy. It fits in remarkably with the view of society and history which Mill used to press upon me. You draw attention to one of the very first of our educational necessities.

The Right Hon. James Bryce, M.P., writes:[8]—

I have read your paper with great interest and concur generally.... The connection of legislative and administrative problems with economic science grows closer as Government is more and more asked to interfere, and as *laissez faire* is less and less regarded.... I should certainly try for Post Graduate as well as Tripos courses. To get even a few men to stay for them would be a great gain. And we might hope for students from U.S. and Colonial Universities.

Sir T. H. Elliott, K.C.B., Secretary to the Board of Agriculture, formerly Private Secretary to the President of the Local Government Board, writes:—

I have no hesitation in expressing my agreement with the general propositions you make in your address to the members of the Senate.

My own point of view is of course mainly that of the Civil Service, in which I have lived and worked for more than thirty years, and of Local Authorities of all grades with the Members and Officers of which I have been continuously brought in contact. In both cases the advantages of training in Economics and the associated branches of Political Science can scarcely be overestimated, in the interests alike of the individuals themselves and of those they serve. It is not too much to say that from the very outset, the prospects of a man who has received such training are superior to those of others who have not. There is a constant demand for the services of men who have been taught and have accustomed themselves to grapple with intricate social and financial problems, and such men obtain early opportunities of commending themselves to the approval of those upon whose esteem and goodwill advancement necessarily depends. The reason is of course clear. A well-trained Economist has been taught to be accurate and comprehensive in the collection of facts, to distinguish between the real and the apparent, to 'seek for the Many in the One, and the One in the Many'—as you yourself put it—and to follow a chain of abstract reasoning without being entangled in its links. At the same time he has acquired knowledge of direct service to him in his work. I am sure that an intending Civil Servant could not be better equipped for his work by means of any other scheme of study than one on the lines you propose.

The Bishop of Winchester[9] writes:—

A curriculum such as you propose would, I believe, obtain many eager students; and it has the great advantage of lifting what are called 'merely material' questions into their proper relation with the higher thought of the age and the advance of political science.

Master John Macdonell, C.B., of the Supreme Court, Editor of Smith's *Mercantile Law*, writes:—

I am much struck by your scheme. It is excellent; it is needful; and it must sooner or later be realised, I should think.

I have in my mind three or four young men, probably examples of large classes, to whom your scheme offers just what they want. The first is likely to be a country gentleman—to live the life of a squire under modern conditions. The second aspires to be a Member of Parliament. The third will probably rule a large business; the fourth is likely to be concerned in the administration of charities. All these men, if intelligent, must study economics, and the question is whether they will do so perfunctorily and superficially or not, in fragmentary fashion or with a knowledge of the whole region.

All of them will 'pick up' their notions; all of them will be disposed to exaggerate the value of their own experience, to be intolerant or 'faddists', unless you give them a comprehensive economical training.

Canon W. Moore Ede, who used to assist Bishop Westcott in arranging conferences between employers and employed, writes:—

For clergy, men of business, and all who have to work among their fellow men, a knowledge of economics is of more service than anything else.

Letters generally with the same tendency as the above, and in every case expressing strong sympathy with the movement were received from the following,[10] among others:—

Lord Avebury.
Lord Brassey.
Lord Windsor.
The Bishop of Bristol.
Sir Joseph Dimsdale, M.P., Banker, late Lord Mayor of London.
Sir Thomas Wrightson, M.P., Bart., Ironmaster.
Sir John Evans, Paper Manufacturer; President of the British Association, 1897–8.
Sir David Salomons, Electric Engineer.
Sir George Livesey, South Metropolitan Gas Company.
Mr T. E. Young, Ex-President of the Institute of Actuaries.
The Right Hon. L. H. Courtney.
Sir R. Giffen, K.C.B.
Mr C. S. Loch, Secretary of the London Charity Organization Society.

20 May, 1903. Alfred Marshall.[11]

[1] A printed 'fly' circulated in anticipation of the vote on the Report of the Economics Syndicate to be taken on 6 June. From a copy in the Marshall Papers.

[2] See [743.1].

[3] A typewritten copy, dated 1 October 1902, of this submission of letter extracts to the Syndicate is preserved in the Marshall Papers. The covering note read as follows.

> In accordance with the request of the Syndicate I send you copies of the salient passages of a few of the letters which I read at the meeting on May 29th. I will lay these letters on the table, with marks indicating the passages which I have selected for reproduction. They bear almost exclusively on the probable demand for systematic education in economics by students

> preparing for the higher ranks of business, and for public life. But one or two of them touch the more vital question how Cambridge may do her part in training professional economists who will be able to apply high scientific faculty and sound knowledge of affairs to the great problems of the coming generation. I am prepared, if desired, to circulate a second series of extracts from letters bearing on both these questions.

Quotations from Sutherland, Palgrave, Le Marchant, and Ede were not included in the earlier version, while the quotations from Leaf and Bryce were rather different, as noted below.

4 See [734.7].

5 The full letters from which these extracts were taken were reproduced in Vol. 2 in the following cases: Gibb [702], Sutherland [701], Dawkins [698], Le Marchant [695], Dale [706], Fry [707], Booth [697], Leaf [696], Elliott [699], Macdonell [692]. Biographical and other information given there is not reproduced here. Marshall's editorial annotations are evident on the originals, and a comparison of the extracts with the full letters will reveal minor variations. The originals of the letters from Palgrave, Balfour, Morley, Bryce, the Bishop of Winchester, and Moore Ede have not been traced.

6 The original letter of 14 June 1902 is preserved in the Marshall Papers. Sir John Glover (1829–1920), shipowner, was associated with Glover Brothers and the Mercantile Steamship Company: knighted 1900. Nathaniel Louis Cohen (1847–1913), businessman and member of the London County Council, was associated with the London Chamber of Commerce.

7 The earlier typed version had added the remainder of the body of Leaf's letter.

8 The earlier typed version had quoted a quite different passage, possibly from a different letter:

> (a) England is behind in economic science now-a-days if one looks to the quantity of good work produced. Much more—perhaps not of first rate, yet of high, quality, appears in the U.S.A. (b) Geography ought to have a place not only on its physical side but on its politico-legislative side; because it is calculated to set men thinking. The whole world must now be under the eye of the business man and the economic thinker. (c) The connection of legislative and administrative problems with economic science grows closer as Government is more and more asked to interfere, and as laissez faire is less and less regarded.

9 Herbert Edward Ryle (1856–1925), Hulsean Professor of Divinity at Cambridge 1887–1901, Bishop of Exeter 1901–3, Bishop of Winchester 1903–11, Dean of Westminster 1911–25.

10 For the letters from Avebury, the Bishop of Bristol (George Forrest Browne), and Giffen, see [694, 688, 678] in Vol. 2. The other letters mentioned have not been traced. Thomas Brassey (1836–1918), first Earl Brassey, was the son of Thomas Brassey (1805–70) the railway contractor. A Member of Parliament (1868–86), the younger Brassey was deeply interested in labour questions and naval affairs, Governor of Victoria 1895–1900. Robert George Windsor-Clive (1857–1923), fourteenth Baron Windsor, was made first Earl of Plymouth in 1905. He was a distinguished public servant, serving as Commissioner of Works, 1902–5. The other individuals listed may be identified more briefly. Joseph Cockfield Dimsdale (1849–1902), knighted 1894; Thomas Wrightson (1839–1921), knighted 1900; John Evans (1823–1908), knighted 1892; David Lion Goldsmid-Stern-Salomons (1851–1925) (Sir David Salomons) succeeded to a baronetcy in 1873; George Thomas Livesey (1834–1908), knighted 1902; Thomas Emley Young (1843–?), writer on insurance and finance.

11 The printed pamphlet has marginal notes as follows: '*Railway experience* [Gibb]. | Demand for University training | with a preference for that of an economic curriculum | *Ship-owning experience* [Sutherland, Glover]. | The curriculum attractive to business men; | it would lessen the far-offness of University men in business. | *Financial experience* [Dawkins, Palgrave, Le Marchant]. | The curriculum would give broad outlook, appropriate to businessmen, | also to others. | *Manufacturing experience* [Dale, Fry]. | Such training should be accessible without loss of the social training of the old Universities; | it would promote class sympathy | and increase mental activity of young business man. | *Mercantile experience* [Booth, Leaf]. | Business wants University men especially if

trained in economics; | which would give much needed breadth of view. | *Legislative experience* [Balfour, Morley, Bryce]. | Modern problems need modern studies. | The scheme would have been approved by Mill. | Economics and public affairs. | Need for post graduate work also. | *Administrative experience* [Elliot]. | The curriculum approved in the interests of Local Government, | where there is a constant demand for men trained in social and financial science. | It is especially suited for intending civil servants. | *Other points of view* [Winchester, etc]. | Need for looking at higher side of material questions. | The citizen is ever deciding economic issues: he ought to be trained for his decisions'.

748. To Members of the Cambridge University Senate, 5 June 1903[1]

The Proposed New Tripos.

I must apologize humbly for bringing out a fly-sheet so late. I consulted some friends yesterday as to whether any point in the Syndicate's scheme remained to be defended: and the answer was in the negative. But during the night it occurred to me that if so able and kind a critic as Professor Gwatkin could think his proposals would go any considerable way towards affording adequate scope for economic study, it might be well to restate even at the last hour the main grounds of our appeal.

Cambridge curricula are arranged for students who can as a rule spend only three years in the portal that leads from boyhood to the responsibilities of life. A few can give a fourth or a fifth year: but their numbers are small; and by the age of twenty-two examinations have done a man nearly all the good they can do him, but not nearly all the harm.

Of course study should be broad as well as thorough: but three years are too short for a thorough study over a very wide area. I think it is well that some Universities give precedence to breadth, and insist on only so much thoroughness as can be combined with great breadth. I am certain it is well that one University urges all those students who are capable of thorough work to attain thoroughness at all costs, and to combine it with as much breadth as they can. For if a man has not learnt to be thorough before he is twenty-two, he will never learn it. If the legacy of his youth to his manhood is thoroughness in thought, combined with some width of knowledge and much breadth of interest; his manhood will put this capital stock out to usury and acquire large intellectual riches. An ideal curriculum from this point of view is therefore one which fills three years with studies which all bear on some centre of intense intellectual activity. For then a considerable breadth may be obtained in the very process of developing thoroughness.

A historical curriculum for instance may be concentrated about great and fertile ideas. It may call forth some of the highest faculties of the mind in weighing evidence; in reading the character of witnesses who have left but slight indications behind them; and, above all, in tracing some one or more broad and complexly interwoven strains of that evolution of human life and action, which is always one and yet never repeats itself at all. In such work a great part may be played by economic history provided it is treated very seriously. But, so far as I am capable of forming an opinion, I agree with Dr Maitland both in thinking that the apparent simplicity of early economic history is delusive; and in thinking that the present Historical curriculum might be made to afford a higher intellectual training for some classes of historians if it contained rather more history and rather less of other things.[2]

On the other hand I think that one Part of the Historical Tripos combined with one Part of the Economics Tripos, might be made to offer an ideal course for those who aim at the supremely important work of the economic study of history and the historical study of economics; due provision being of course made, as is done now by the Historical Tripos Regulations, for preventing the same subject from being offered twice by any candidate. And here I may observe that a small place is allowed to history before 1800 in the proposed Tripos, solely in order to avoid needless duplication. Had there been no Historical Tripos, I am certain that no member of the Syndicate would have been content without making provision for an optional study of economic history so thorough as to occupy at least half of the student's three years.

Judged by the above test, the new curriculum may I think claim to be ideal in its way, and that way the best for two important classes of students. Anyone who sets himself to prove that it makes little or no provision for many things which ought to be known by the economist, by the business man and the citizen, has an easy task. I am prepared to make out a list of the kind, which should supply material for many years' study. Perhaps I may here raise the edge of the veil on the secrets of the Council Chamber. On my return to Cambridge last September I was told by a friendly member of the Syndicate who had been in residence during the vacation, and who had exceptional means of forming a judgment, that not more than one or two votes besides my own would be given for a new Tripos. But, when we came to details, the difficulty was not to find three years' work almost essential to the economists, and to business men and citizens in responsible positions. The difficulty was how to find room for this thing and that thing, which were almost essential; and which if not attacked before the age of twenty-two, were not likely to be mastered in later years. Thus we could not find room for a technical study of the methods of science (we make room only for a non-technical study); mathematics up to the elements of the differential calculus, a somewhat detailed history of the eighteenth century, and a systematic study of the development of economic doctrine. Gradually opinions changed on the Syndicate. And at last the division was very much as had been expected—twelve against two: but the twelve were Ayes instead of Noes.[3]

The scheme thus recommended has unity and variety. It requires that more than the equivalent of one year should be given to the study of history chiefly during the nineteenth century. It is understood that no detailed questions will be set on earlier centuries, but that comparisons between recent and earlier conditions will be required. The central idea of the two papers on history in Part I[4] is to trace the action of modern influences, and especially of those which enable anything important said anywhere to be heard within twenty-four hours over the whole civilized world: to see how they have at once enlarged the area over which national sentiment is keen and strong, because it is based on thorough knowledge; and at the same time have woven the whole western world into a single nation for many purposes. This historical study leads up to Part II, and through Part II to the work of life. In Part II economics proper is to be carried to its higher analytic and realistic developments. It is supposed that the knowledge of economics required in Part I will be about half as much again as that now required in Part I of the Moral Sciences Tripos, and about twice as much as that required if the economic option is taken in either part of the Historical Tripos. Starting with that knowledge the student is supposed in Part II to carry back the history of selected portions of economics as far as may be needed—for instance, the study of foreign trade would run back over many centuries, while that of some labour problems would scarcely get behind the nineteenth. He would combine this historical survey with exacter analysis, and more realistic study of present international conditions than would be possible for Part I. Thus he would be prepared for dealing in mature age with problems for which few Englishmen are properly equipped now.

I will give one illustration. The growing distance between the owners of a business and its operatives, due to the development of joint stock companies and other causes, has quickened the attempts, in which England led the way, to give the operatives a direct interest in their work; the impulse coming partly from humanity and partly from business calculations. Latterly this movement has made rapid progress in other countries: it has proved itself capable of greater elasticity and strength than could have been predicted ten years ago; and many of the ablest English business men are now studying it. But England would have been further advanced if the foreign movement had been studied earlier, and with special reference to the extent to which it needs modification for English use. For instance, methods which are suitable where the unskilled workers come mainly from Eastern or Southern Europe are not directly applicable where nearly all are of Teutonic extraction: and *vice versa*. In all such matters other countries eagerly seek guidance from her and from one another: England alone learns little save from her own experience.

All students will be required to make some study of the modern complex State, in its Imperial, Provincial, and more narrowly local aspects. They will resign to those, who elect the Historical curriculum, a detailed study of those constitutional questions which have their origin in far off centuries: but some of them at least will get a real hold of those equally vital questions which have been created in recent times—a task for which no adequate room is found in the Historical curriculum. And if they should set their faces towards law or diplomacy they will have the option of combining studies which are already close neighbours in almost all the Universities except the English.

Thus around the central group there are arranged other subjects, for which, excepting in the case of Law, no full provision is made in any existing curriculum: which are so diverse from economics, in the narrow sense of the term, as to call forth a great variety of mental activities, and yet are so closely bound up with the central group, that all work at them will stimulate and be stimulated by work at that group. Together they will exercise the higher and scientific imagination as thorough and concentrated work alone can do.

Surely the University will not refuse our petition for a Tripos which opens a free path to true work. By a very little effort it can have two ideal Triposes, one historical, the other mainly economic, each helping the other. Surely it will not yield to the suggestion of Professor Gwatkin that it would grievously injure the Historical Tripos without to any great extent enlarging the scope for economic studies.

5 June 1903. Alfred Marshall.

I have abstained from quoting the opinions of external economists, though those who have written to me are almost as unanimous in approving the new movement as are the Cambridge economists resident and non-resident to whom I referred in the Senate House.[5] But I will quote one, because his name has been introduced into the controversy as apparently supporting the notion that a study of business problems here is likely to have little realistic value.[6] Professor Jenks, who is perhaps the highest authority upon Trusts, after a strong eulogy of the proposal of the Syndicate, writes thus under date 2 June 1903:[7]

> If I may judge by my own experience in the United States, the association of students who are preparing for a professional career and those who propose to enter business life will be a benefit to both. Unless economic theory is really founded upon actual facts of business life, I fear it is poor theory; but I am glad to believe that most of the more prominent economists of the present day,—and it is certainly true of those of Cambridge,—are basing their theories upon facts, so that their teaching of economics does bring students into actual touch with the business life of to-day. On the other hand, too, business men in their talk with me at home often express regret that they do not have the wide outlook in business matters which can come only from a study of business principles and of the history of business.

[1] A printed flysheet issued on the eve of the Senate vote on the proposed Economic Tripos. From a copy in the Marshall Papers. The usual flurry of flysheets accompanying a controversial vote had been called forth. The Marshall Papers contain copies of flysheets from the following: Cunningham (26 May), G. E. Green with W. F. Reddaway [746.5] (2 June), H. M. Gwatkin (2 June), J. W. Headlam (1 June), J. M. E. MacTaggart (1 June), all in opposition to the new Tripos; and from

G. Lowes Dickinson (4 June), H. S. Foxwell (30 May), F. W. Maitland (2 June), and J. R. Tanner with S. M. Leathes (28 May), all in support. The more reasonable opponents (including Gwatkin) argued that the existing channel of Part I History, Part II Moral Sciences, could be widened to accommodate Marshall's goals. However, Maitland's firm opposition to further dilution of the History Tripos, when combined with the division of opinion among the historians, carried decisive weight. The vote on the Syndicate's recommendations was affirmative: 103–76 on the crucial issue of establishing the new Tripos, and 75–10 on the proposal for a new Board of Studies. All subsidiary proposals were unopposed. See *Reporter*, 9 June 1903, pp. 933–4.

2 Marshall appended here the following footnote:

> 'Agrarian history becomes catastrophic as we trace it backwards' (*Domesday Book*, p. 365). And Karl Bucher goes to the root of the matter, in my opinion, when he says (*Industrial Evolution*, p. 153):—'The complex nature of all social phenomena renders it just as difficult for the investigator of to-day to reconstruct the economic conditions of life of the nations of antiquity and of the Middle Ages as to forecast even with the most lively and powerful imagination the ultimate consequences of the 'socialistic State of the future'. We shall not arrive at an understanding of whole epochs of early economic history until we study the economic side of life of primitive and uncivilised peoples of the present with the care we to-day devote to Englishmen and Americans.

See F. W. Maitland, *Domesday Book and Beyond: Three Essays in the Early History of England* (Cambridge University Press, Cambridge, 1897); Karl Bücher, *Industrial Evolution* (Holt, New York, 1901: translated from the German by S. Morley Wickett).

3 The 'Noes' being Cunningham and MacTaggart. See [744.3].

4 Described in the Syndicate's Report [743.1] as 'Recent Economic and General History'.

5 See Appendix I.

6 An 'Economical Interview' with Cunningham, reported in the *Cambridge Review* (7 May 1903, pp. 277–8) had invoked Jeremiah Jenks as arguing the practical irrelevance of the economic theory of competition.

7 Jenks's letter has not been traced.

749. To Henry Hardinge Cunynghame, 14 June 1903 (incomplete)[1]

14. vi. 03

My dear Cunynghame,

I am no authority on either agricultural or military questions; and I am very far from wishing to offer myself as a witness before the Commission on Food Supply in Time of War: indeed I could not do it. But the matter has been much in my mind during many years; and I think I should like to be sure that certain questions which have occurred to me have been considered, if only to be put aside as unpractical. Will you kindly look through the following?

A. *The Question of Storing*

1. Is it not worth while to induce the growers of wheat which is ultimately to be consumed here to store it here rather than at a distance, if that can be done cheaply?

2. Can it not be done cheaply by enacting that (say) 1s. per ton shall be paid to everyone who on (say) the first Monday night in every month posts a sworn

statement that he has on that night a certain number of tons of wheat in store at a certain place? (His statement need not be checked save by occasional surprise visits, with penalties for fraudulent declarations. I reckon this amount would not only make it amply worth while to store grain here rather than abroad, but might even make it worth while to carry over grain from one year to another.)

3. Would not the English farmer obtain by this route some reward for the service which he renders in keeping a stock of wheat on hand? Is not such a reward just?

4. Might the plan possibly be extended at a lower scale to other grains, which on emergency could be used as bread-stuffs?

B. *Military Questions*

5. Could we not in time of war with continental nations obtain grain from U.S. more easily than from Canada? Even if grain for us were made contraband of war, would it not suffice to convoy ships containing U.S. grain from the nearest friendly or neutral European port, to which they could run safely; while Canadian grain would be prize of war in all its course across the Atlantic?

6. If we were at war with U.S., would Canadian wheat reach us? If they kept their own grain at home, would they not certainly cross the border and seize or destroy Canadian grain which they thought was coming to us?

7. If U.S. government forbad the exportation of grain to any part of Europe, would not it speedily cause such ruin among their own farmers as to cause the evasion or abrogation of the rule? And if they allowed its exportation to, say, France or Germany, should we not be able to buy most of what we wanted from markets to which that wheat came, directly or indirectly?

[1] Printed in *Memorials*, pp. 447–8, under the heading 'Food Supply in Time of War'. Original not traced. From Balliol Croft. Cunynghame was a member of the Royal Commission on Supply of Food and Raw Materials in Time of War, a response to fears raised by Germany's growing naval power. Marshall did not give evidence, but Cunynghame and others presented storage schemes of the sort suggested by Marshall. The Commission's Report appeared in 1905 (Cd 2643–5). For further details see John K. Whitaker, 'The Economics of Defense in British Political Economy, 1848–1914', in Craufurd D. Goodwin (ed.) *Economics and National Security: A History of their Interaction* (Duke University Press, Durham, NC, 1991), especially pp. 51–2.

750. To John Neville Keynes, 15 June 1903[1]

15. 6. 03

My dear Keynes

The growing heat of the Preferential Tariff discussion makes me rather afraid of my half-promise to give a non technical course on International Trade. So I have drafted a notice on the subject to see how it looks. If published at all it will appear in the Reporter just before next Full Term.[2] I rely *very much* on your discretion in such matters; &, as we may not have time to talk it out this afternoon, I should be much obliged if you would scribble remarks on this copy. I have other copies. I should of course take a balanced position as far as possible on the political issues, & generally adhere to the lines of my address to B Ass^{n} Section F in 1890.[3]

I am thinking of rewriting my *Plea* as a description of the Tripos: partly as an advertisement, & partly to save myself from writing long letters.[4]

Yours ever | A.M.

I will come to Syndicate Buildings at 4 25.

[1] Marshall Library, J. N. Keynes Papers. From Balliol Croft.

[2] Marshall did not offer such a course, although Pigou, MacTaggart, and Meredith offered in the Lent Term 1904 an unofficial series of lectures in support of free trade, perhaps provoked by Cunningham's offering in the Michaelmas Term of 1903 a series of lectures on 'The Rise and Decline of the Free Trade Movement': see *Reporter*, 13 October 1903; *Cambridge Review*, 26 November 1903, p. 98.

[3] 'Some Aspects of Competition', *Memorials*, pp. 256–91.

[4] See [751].

751. To Frederick Macmillan, 18 June 1903[1]

18. 6. 03

Dear Mr MacMillan

I have been asked to put my *Plea*[2] into a permanent form. I am rearranging it, together with parts of other occasional papers, cutting out whatever seems dead now. I propose to use it—with the concurrence of the new Board of Economic Studies—largely as a means of making the new Tripos known to head masters of schools and others.[3] So I shall give away about half the edition; and of the remainder I expect most to be sold either in Cambridge or—to a small extent—in America. I propose that the price should be perhaps 1s in paper; 1/6 or 2s in cloth. The whole affair is so small & so local that I was inclined to ask the University Press to manage the whole thing. But if you think it better that this Tract should go with my graver work, I should of course be very glad to put it in your hands.[4]

I propose to insert the effective—not the technical—part of the new Regulations: & also the inclosed extracts from letters,[5] the type of wh is standing at the University Press.

Yours very truly | Alfred Marshall

[1] British Library, Macmillan Archive. From Balliol Croft.

[2] See [734.7].

[3] In a follow-up letter of 20 June (not reproduced here) Marshall indicated that he proposed to send the pamphlet to 'about 100 headmasters, and about 130 other persons (including about fifty College Tutors)'.

[4] The 34–page pamphlet was to appear as: A. Marshall, *The New Cambridge Curriculum in Economics and Associated Branches of Political Science: Its Purpose and Plan* (Macmillan, London, 1903).

[5] See [747]. Only the extracts from letters by Gibb, Dawkins, Booth and Elliott were included in the new pamphlet.

752. To Herbert Somerton Foxwell, 29 June 1903[1]

29. 6. 03

My dear Foxwell

The list of books wh you have was framed to be produced in case Cunningham should reproduce in the Senate House,[2] or in a Fly, his assertion that the Economic & General History chiefly of the nineteenth century is an impossible subject, as 'there are no good books on it'.[3]

My own view of that subject is that it is designed to be the history of man in the broad: with enough political & other 'general' history to make the economic view of man full & human, & enough of economics to insure that political & social growth are throughout considered in relation to their economic affinities.

Consequently I suggested a good many books on 'labour': because 'labour' is so large a part of mankind, & its history is so full of 'human' as distinguished from material concepts. But I tried to avoid technical economic books. Webbs *History of Trade Unions* & Bowley's *Wages*, are perhaps most in that direction.[4] Everyone says the list is too long & I should concur in striking out those two & perhaps some more. On the other hand I know of no book on the history of trade, money, or taxation; unless it be Deweys new book (wh is less technical than Taussigs) which seems to me eminently suitable,[5] & I certainly think there should not be a detailed book on cooperation, partly because the subject is narrow, but more because the books are bad. This is my explanation.

But my paper is only to start not to solve the question. It is open to you & Tanner to add what you will, & eject what you will. I may be converted. But at present I incline to think that books on the history of trade, crises, &c ought to find their place among the *ten* papers allotted to economics and not in the *one* (ie 1/2 × 2) allotted to broad economic history.[6] That is my view: but it is for you & Tanner to improve on it.

The Wealth of Nations is in Part I of the Mo Sc Tripos, & also in the Historical Tripos. It never occurred to me that anyone would dream of omitting it from Part I of our Tripos. I have some fear of putting the whole of it above the line.[7] I had thought of proposing Book IV above: the whole thing below. Ricardo & Malthus seem on a different footing. But I should incline to putting the whole or a part of them below the line: I have no strong opinion: (Keynes views are, *on this one point*, rather extreme I think) & Ashleys selections from the Classics never pleased me.[8]

The chief good I have got from US Census is the study & comparison of the maps; & from Vol VIII, or rather the introduction to it. I have got several people besides myself to work at that. By accident I have two copies, & one of them is with Oldham; who will I hope use it next Term a good deal.[9]

I have recently written a long statement in the University Library Recommendation Book explaining why—though contrary to the usual course—the XIX Volumes of the Industrial Commission should be bought.[10] I have lent the chief volumes—those on Trusts & Transportation, more than almost any other books. I always say it is better to know those four fat volumes than all else that has been written on their several subjects put together. Macgregor & Làl (but this is confidential) are thinking of writing on the first of the Cobden Essays—on Trusts.[11] I have talked with them; & the books suitable for them are to be placed on the window side of my dining room. (Another set for Pigou is on the opposite side, & the two must not be mixed.)[12] Macgregor & Làl are to borrow the books as they want them. (For reasons not worth detailing, I have decided to let people have the run of my study only when I am in Cambridge myself). They will not specially care probably about the Industrial Commission for a few days; & you might borrow one or two volumes if you like. If you do be sure to return them as soon as you have done with them.

I dont think any book on US industries stands out. I am always reading, & trying to get each writers personal equation, & set off one against another. E.g. the series in the *Century* on Trusts,[13] which was almost certainly in the interests of the Trusts, seemed to me very instructive. The pick of such articles I cut out & bind. But as they bear on International Trade Competition, they are on their way to the Tyrol by goods train.

Yours wearily
but very sincerely } Alfred Marshall

P.S.[14] Thank you for your suggestions.[15] I have acted on all of them. I am not sure that my words always bear the construction you put on them. But anyhow it is an improvement to get them definitely in your direction as far as possible.

As to the XIX history list, perhaps you wd show my letter to Tanner i.e. its first pages.

[1] Foxwell Papers. From Balliol Croft. Foxwell wrote on the envelope 'Marshall on Books'. The new Tripos was first to be examined for Part I in 1905 and for Part II in 1906, so that the selection of books recommended for Part I was a matter of some urgency. Supplementary regulations for both parts had been approved by the new Board on 15 June (*Reporter*, 25 June 1903) and a full list of lectures offered under the Board's aegis appeared in the *Reporter*, 10 October 1903. The approved list of books for Part I finally appeared in the *Reporter*, 10 November 1903.

[2] That is, in the 7 May debate: see [743.1].

[3] This probably alludes to remarks or submissions made by Cunningham during the Syndicate's deliberations. The two history papers in Part I of the new Tripos were to cover 'Recent Economic and General History'. Marshall's preliminary book list is untraced.

[4] Beatrice and Sidney Webb, *The History of Trade Unionism* (Longmans Green, London, 1894); Arthur Lyon Bowley, *Wages in the United Kingdom in the Nineteenth Century* (Cambridge University Press, Cambridge, 1900). Neither work was included in the final list.

[5] Davis Rich Dewey, *Financial History of the United States* (Longmans Green, New York, 1903); Frank William Taussig, *The Tariff History of the United States* (Putnam, New York, 1888: fifth edition 1900). Dewey's book was included in the final list.

[6] Since economic and general history shared two papers, economic history could be credited with one.

[7] Books above the line were required: those below only recommended.

[8] The views of J. N. Keynes on this matter are not ascertainable. Ashley was the editor of a series of 'Economic Classics' published by Macmillan in New York in the 1890s, the first three volumes comprising selections from the *Wealth of Nations*, Ricardo's *Principles*, and Malthus's *Essay on the Principle of Population* (1798, 1803).

[9] Oldham was to lecture on Economic Geography for the new Tripos. Marshall's reference is probably to: US Census Office, *Census Reports of the Twelfth Census of the United States Taken in the Year 1900* (Washington, DC, 1901–2: 10 vols.). Vols. 7–10 deal with manufactures.

[10] United States Industrial Commission, Reports (Government Printing Office, Washington, DC, vols. 1–5, 1900, vols. 6–18, 1901, vol. 19, 1902). Vols. 1, 2, 13, 18 dealt with Trusts and Combinations while vols. 4, 9 dealt with Transportation. The 'four fat volumes' were presumably vols. 2, 4, 9, 13. Vol. 2, prepared by Jenks, was included in the final list.

[11] The first of the six topics available to candidates for the 1904 Cobden Prize was 'The causes and effects of Commercial and Industrial Trusts, and the extent to which it is possible and desirable to introduce legislative restrictions on their operations'. Làl was to be awarded the prize, Macgregor receiving 'special commendation'. (*Reporter*, 28 April 1903; 13 December 1904.)

[12] Closing parenthesis omitted in the original.

[13] *The Century Magazine*, 65 (43 NS), covering November 1902 to April 1903, had published a series of five articles on 'The Great Business Combinations of Today', dealing with the following 'so-called' Trusts: Beef, Steel, Sugar, Tobacco, and Steamship. The editor, in introducing the series, observed that the aim was 'not to present a partizan view of these organizations ... but to supply in an interesting manner authoritative information as to the facts and claims which bear upon the subject' (p. 148). Macmillan and Company were the British distributors for this American monthly, which would therefore have been quite accessible to Marshall.

[14] Written on the last side, which bears the superscription 'Should have been p 1'.

[15] Probably on the draft of Marshall's pamphlet [751.4].

753. To Herbert Somerton Foxwell, 30 June 1903[1]

I shd have said that for the general history of economic changes in England during XIX century I rely chiefly on Walpole aided by Social England.[2] Walpole e.g. discusses admirably I think the non technical side of crises for wh people are then ready, though not for the technical.

[1] Foxwell Papers. Postcard, postmarked 'JU 30 03'. From Balliol Croft.

[2] Spencer Walpole, *A History of England from the Conclusion of the Great War in 1815* (Longmans Green, London, 1878–86: 5 vols.—revised 1890 in 6 vols.); Henry Duff Traill (ed.), *Social England* (Cassell, London, 1893–7: 6 vols.). Both works were included in the final list (see [752.1]), Traill (vols. 5 and 6) being 'below the line'. Traill and Marshall had been schoolfriends.

754. From Theodore Llewelyn Davies, 2 July 1903[1]

Treasury Chambers,
Whitehall, S.W.
2 July, 1903.

Private.

Dear Professor Marshall

I know very well how entirely your time is occupied with important work which has been too long delayed, and I hear from Higgs that you are just about to leave England. Still I am sure you must be very much concerned with what the newspapers call the 'fiscal problem'. I don't suppose you would be able to find time to take part in newspaper or magazine controversies and I would not venture to bother you on my own account. But in talking matters over the Chancellor of the Exchequer[2] expressed a strong wish that he might have the advantage of any unofficial expression of your opinions, or any suggestions as to the right method of handling the questions, which you might be able to offer: and it is at his desire that I now write.

Mr. Ritchie does not wish to impose any fetters on your discretion or convenience as to the method or scope of any observations with which you can favour him. You will no doubt have seen in the newspapers the questions raised. Of course they fall mainly under two heads:—

(1) Imperial Preferential Tariffs—involving import duties in this country on Food and perhaps other more or less Raw Materials

(2) Retaliatory Duties—adopted primarily perhaps for the purpose of Tariff negotiations, but involving almost certainly permanent and systematic protection of Manufactures.

Of course endless issues arise out of these two main points: e.g. whether, and if so how far and in what directions, the circumstances which formerly made Free Trade the best policy for this country have altered: whether the development of business organisation in the direction of Trusts and the like makes Free Trade more, or less, expedient: whether the advance of Germany and the U.S.A. under Protection weakens the old Free Trade arguments—whether the 'dumping' of goods here by tariff-protected Cartels is a formidable evil, and especially whether a determined attempt to destroy an important industry in this country by such means could under any conditions be successful: and, if so, how it ought to be combated.[3]

We can hardly ask you for a full statement of your views as to the incidence of Import Duties, but perhaps you might be able to state summarily your views as to the Incidence of Duties on Corn, Meat and Dairy Produce in this country, (a) with and (b) without preference for Colonial products.

Any answer you may be able to give to the Chancellor shall of course, *if* you should so desire, be treated as private—or if you prefer to send me any part of your remarks in as rough a form as you please, I shall be grateful for them. Indeed, I should very much like a talk, in addition to anything you can send in writing, if there is any time and place that would be convenient to you before you go away. Of course you have expressed opinions in print already on some of these subjects: it may save you trouble to refer to them.

Yours sincerely | T. Ll. Davies

I was very much pleased the Tripos went so well, I hope to hear more about it from Dickinson on Sunday.

TLlD

[1] Marshall Papers. Typewritten with postscript added by pen. Reproduced in John C. Wood, 'Alfred Marshall and the Origins of his "Memorandum on the Fiscal Policy of International Trade" (1903): Some Unpublished Correspondence', *Australian Economic Papers*, 21 (December 1982), pp. 261–9, at pp. 263–4. For further background on the fiscal controversy and Marshall's part in it see A. W. Coats, 'Political Economy and the Tariff Reform Campaign of 1903', *Journal of Law and Economics*, 11 (1968), pp. 181–229; John C. Wood, 'Alfred Marshall and the Tariff-Reform Campaign of 1903', *Journal of Law and Economics*, 23 (October 1980), pp. 481–95.

[2] C. T. Ritchie.

[3] Marshall subsequently added in red ink the marginal notes 'Part II F-M' and 'N', the latter against the passage dealing with cartels. The first sentence of the next paragraph has 'Part I' as a marginal note and also '§ 29'. These notes appear to connect the questions raised to the sections where answers were provided in the Memorandum Marshall was to produce (in its final form this is reproduced in *Official Papers*, pp. 367–420: see especially p. 369 for a description of the organization of the Memorandum).

755. To Theodore Llewelyn Davies, 14 July 1903[1]

Stern
Enneberg 14. 7. 03
South Tyrol

Dear Llewellyn Davies

On reaching my summer quarters here I found your letter awaiting me.[2] I am sorry for the delay.

I will send you a Memorandum in a few days. It will necessarily be brief. But I will endeavour to develop any points on w^h.. the Chancellor may desire to know my opinions more fully, in a later letter.

Unfortunately the rather long time w^h.. I have given to International Trade has not resulted in much print as yet. The problems now in the air occupy a large space in that part of my Vol II w^h.. is nearly ready for press: but I get very little time for my own work except in the summer.

In the *Economic Journal* pp 265–7 of Vol XI, you will find a compressed statement of my views as to the incidence of Customs duties, in the course of a letter (reprinted from the *Times*) on the Tax on Coal.[3]

I am telling my servant to send you a paper on 'Some Aspects of Competition' 1890.[4] The views there expressed as to the relative suitability of a discriminating

'Protection' for a country whose industries are still immature, & its absolute unsuitability for England, have been confirmed by the history of the last few years. (So called Retaliation & Preferential duties are on a somewhat different footing). But on the other hand the chief interest now in the latter half of the paper lies in the fact that all discussion of American 'Trusts' of even a dozen years of age are nearly obsolete now. The paper suggests that the fiduciary element from w^{h}.. they derived their name might disappear, & consolidation be substituted for federation. That has come about even more quickly than I expected. But are the consolidations themselves stable? I incline to think that any change in our fiscal system w^{h}.. assumes that the present position of 'Trusts' is likely to be maintained without considerable modification w^{d}.. be premature; even if nothing else could be urged against it.

Yours sincerely | Alfred Marshall

1 Marshall Papers, from a copy in Mrs Marshall's hand. Reproduced with some inaccuracies in J. C. Wood, 'Origins' [754.1], pp. 264–5. The spelling 'Llewellyn' is Marshall's.

2 [754]: presumably forwarded from Balliol Croft.

3 For the text see Vol. 2 [639, 642] and for bibliographic detail see [639.1].

4 See *Memorials*, pp. 256–91, for the text of Marshall's Presidential Address to Section F of the British Association.

756. To William Albert Samuel Hewins, 14 July 1903[1]

14. 7. 03

My dear Hewins

Many thanks for your letter of the 6th.. wh I have just received.[2] But I must not let you remain under the impression that there is 'not any substantial difference of opinion between us on the economic question'. I have no time for controversy, & least of all for controversy by post. So I indicated, or tried to indicate, my differences as mildly as possible.[3] But misconceptions in such a case are to be avoided. And so I trust you will forgive me if I state bluntly and categorically that I dissent from your economic arguments, & even from your statements as to fact, to an extent wh I had not anticipated in the very least.

If I really thought there was any danger that the scheme wh you advocate would be put into practice, I should feel bound to break through my rule against taking active part in the discussions of the market place. I do not care much about a preferential duty on wheat *by itself*.[4] For though I differ from almost every one of your conclusions as to its effects, I think it would be stopped abruptly before it had done much harm. But I object to your position as it is being developed because, whatever your original intentions, you seem to me to have been entangled in the meshes of a very astute body of Protectionists. Your positions—in the same way though not to the same extent as those of Chamberlain himself—seem to me incapable of being maintained permanently, & worked out to their logical consequences, without resulting in Protection of the most malignant kind, to wh I understand that you, if not he, are truly opposed.

As to Germany, your references to Hasbach & other statements seem to me to indicate that you do not really know German opinion. Protectionists by profession, there as elsewhere, are of course wild with delight at the notion that we may abandon free trade. But most of the intelligent Germans whom I meet agree that free trade is the only policy wh really suits England. And the same is true of the Americans & others.

Further I believe that the adoption of Chamberlains scheme would lead to friction with the Colonies wh would inevitably disrupt the empire: for everyone would expect to gain from measures the aggregate economic effect of which must be loss: & everyone would be sure that others had had a selfish interest in & an unjust gain from the move.

Also in spite of what you say, I am certain it would estrange the U.S. I value the affection of the, say, 30,000,000 of our cousins who live there for its own sake: I do not know that I do not value it almost as much as that of the 11,000,000 who live in our dependencies. And further, our Empire must collapse ere long if the dominant power in the Pacific is not on our side: & that power must be the U.S.

Please forgive my frankness, & do not trouble to reply.

Yours very sincerely | Alfred Marshall

P.S. I was very sorry to miss the Pol Econ Club dinner.[5] But I have been on the strain for an unusually long while; & though in splendid health generally, I have got my brain into a morbid weak feverish state; & found a break compulsory. I am much interested in all you say & follow it eagerly. But it is only frank to say I am not convinced. The problems which are spoken of as 'new' have occupied my attention during the last ten years very closely. Indeed the relation between big capital combinations & protection was one of the chief problems wh sent me to visit the American protectionists in 1875. But my general conclusion is that, though the new forces necessitate modification in all doctrines relating to international trade these modifications turn out to be less than might have been expected *a priori*. And without being at all Cobden-Club-ite, I regard the new movement inaugurated by Chamberlain with great distrust.

For one detail I have paid close attention to the causes of the movements of the price of wheat in England since 1800: & I believe that rightly interpreted, they tend to support the doctrine that taxes on wheat raise its prices *generally* by about their full amount. I say that while of course aware that the rough & ready proof that they must have this effect is generally lax in logical form: & that the whole position is very complex.

I agree—as a politician—with the last paragraph of the resolution of the Manchester Chamber of Commerce.[6] But I do not attach any value to my own opinions on political issues.

[1] Sheffield University Library, Hewins Papers. From Stern, Austria, but on Balliol Croft notepaper.

[2] Letter not traced. At this time Hewins was intensively involved in promoting the tariff campaign, serving as economic adviser to Joseph Chamberlain. Most prominent among his polemical writings of the period were the sixteen articles he published in *The Times* from June to December 1903 under the pseudonym 'An Economist'—see the report published in the *Economic Journal*, 13 (September 1903), p. 445, for a summary of his arguments. It is probably to the earlier articles in this series, but perhaps also to other recent pamphlets sent by Hewins, that Marshall is reacting. For background see A. W. Coats, 'Political Economy and the Tariff Reform Campaign' [754.1]; W. A. S. Hewins, *The Apologia of an Imperialist* (Constable, London, 1929: 2 vols.), vol. 1, pp. 62–81. In December 1903 Hewins was to resign his Directorship of the London School of Economics to head Chamberlain's non-official Tariff Commission, which aimed to develop 'scientific' tariff proposals.

[3] This suggests a previous letter from Marshall, not traced.

[4] The duty on wheat, imposed in 1902 by his predecessor, had been repealed in Ritchie's April budget, precipitating the 1903 controversy by undermining hopes of modifying the duty to incorporate imperial preference.

[5] At the Political Economy Club dinner of 3 July Hewins had opened a discussion on the question 'Should closer commercial relations between the United Kingdom and the Colonies be encouraged, and, if so, by what means?'

[6] Hewin's latest article as 'An Economist' (*The Times*, 11 July 1903, 6a,b) had observed: 'as long ago as 1888, the Manchester Chamber of Commerce showed, by a resolution passed in that year, that they had gone a long way from the position of 40 years earlier'. For a report of the resolution see *The Times*, 20 December 1888 (12c), but since the resolution consisted of a single paragraph, Marshall may have had some other resolution in mind. See Vol. 1 [256], for his initial reaction to the 1888 resolution.

757. To Frederick Macmillan, 17 July 1903[1]

Stern, im Enneberg | South Tyrol
17. 7. 03

Dear Mr MacMillan

I write to continue my reports as to translations of my Vol I.[2] Part I of the Italian translation was brought out some time ago.[3] The French translation seems to hang fire; though I understand it is being proceded with.[4] The German translation was undertaken by a young man, whose work was interrupted after he had got through about half.[5] Meanwhile Prof Brentano wrote urging that a translation should be made.[6] As a result one of his pupils is to finish the translation; Brentano is to write a preface; & Cotta[7] is to publish it on terms arranged by Brentano subject to my approval. These are:

> Nothing to be paid to me for the first edition. If there is a second edition Cotta is to pay me & to the translators lump sums, & thereby acquire the copyright.

He asks me, through Brentano, whether I consent in principle; & if so how much I demand.

I trust that the original translator will not be left out in the cold, even if the book does not reach a second edition. Subject to this I am inclined to agree. But I do not know how much to ask for, and I do not know whether some part of whatever I get would not properly belong to you. I should myself be inclined not to ask for very much. May I trouble you to be so very kind as to tell me frankly your opinion on the whole subject?

I do not hear that copies of my new pamphlet[8] have arrived at Balliol Croft. I trust that the binder is not negligent.

Yours very truly | Alfred Marshall

Frederick MacMillan Esq
Another German[9] applied recently for leave to translate & seemed to be acting in connection with Mess[rs] Duncker and Humblot.

[1] British Library, Macmillan Archive.
[2] Previous reports not traced.
[3] The Italian edition had been undertaken by Salvatore Cognetti de Martiis. It was completed in 1905 after the latter's death. See Riccardo Faucci (ed.), 'Una Fonte per la Storia della Cultura Economica Italiana nell'età del Positivismo: Le Carte di Salvatore Cognetti de Martiis', *Annali della Fondazione Luigi Einaudi*, 13 (1979), p. 429 where a brief letter of enquiry of 4 June 1899 from Marshall is reproduced.
[4] A French translation of *Principles (4)* with some additions from *Principles (5)* was to appear as *Principes d'Économie Politique* (Giard and Brière, Paris, 1906–9: 2 vols.). Translated by F. Sauvaire-Jourdan and F. Sauvinien-Bouyssy. No information as to the genesis of this translation has been discovered.
[5] See [741].
[6] See [740].
[7] The publishing house of J. G. Cotta, Stuttgart, the eventual publishers of the German translation: see [826.2] below.
[8] See [751.4].
[9] Not identified.

758. To Ludwig Joseph Brentano, 17 July 1903[1]

Stern, im Enneberg
17. 7. 03

My dear Brentano,

I am filled with confusion at my carelessness in telling you that it was on the *Wednesday*, & not the *Thursday*, morning that I expected to pass through Munich. I was really worn out by the work connected with the construction of our new economic curriculum; & had to leave home before I had finished some urgent business. I had got into quite an unhealthy state of nervous strain. Even when I got to the mountains, and vigorously shut my mind to all economic matters while awake, I kept on dreaming economics at night! I am now settling down to work rather too soon. But some letters of a more or less public character relating to the 'Tariff Issue,' wh have been forwarded to me here, leave me no choice.[2]

So my stupidity may perhaps be pardoned, though I deeply regret that it has added so much trouble unnecessarily to the great & good work which you are so very kindly undertaking on my behalf.[3]

I have no hesitation in accepting with great gratitude the general principles of your proposal. I believe I have full power of action, independently of the consent of my English publisher, MacMillan. But it is just possible that he may have the right to object to any formal assignment of the copyright. He has behaved very generously in all matters; & I think it is unlikely he would press his rights obstructively, even if he has any. But I have thought it proper to write to him before giving a formal reply.[4] I consulted him before accepting Mr Ephraims original proposal.[5]

One little difficulty occurs to me. Nothing is said about Volume II (In fact there will probably be two more volumes, if I live to finish my task). But if Mr Cotta obtains the exclusive right of publishing a translation of my Vol I, I should have no choice but to accept any terms he might offer for my Vols II & III. I think this point should be cleared up.

It might perhaps be well that he should say how large he proposes that the first Edition should be. But of course it would not be to his interest to lock up too much capital in a very large edition which might sell slowly, or not at all. So I do not press this point.

With these reservations I endorse provisionally all that you have done for me, and give you my most earnest and hearty thanks for it. I will write again definitely as soon as I have heard from MacMillan.

No. Ashley is not 'An Economist.'[6] There are so few people in England who would have written as rapidly & interestingly as he has done, that I am sure I should have found out ere now, by a process of exhaustion, who he is *not*, & therefore who he *is*. But unfortunately he told me about writing, in strict confidence, before he began. And as I *know*, I must not say.

I have ventured to write him some remonstrance: but I have declined invitations to answer him.[7] I am, however, engaged at this moment in formulating my own opinions on some of the chief matters wh are now before the country: & I must of course incidentally traverse many of his statements and arguments. The paper which I am writing will probably be published, in some form or other, before the crisis is reached.

Chapman of Manchester is writing a series of articles in the Daily Mail wh practically answer many of 'An Economist's' arguments: & I think he is doing it very well.[8] Of course he is very young.

Bastable also is, I believe, preparing something & no doubt many others will write more or less directly on the issues raised by 'An Economist,' as soon as it is clearly known what they are.

But there are two difficulties. One is that 'An Economist' has not committed himself to supporting Chamberlain: he keeps his own scheme up his sleeve. He keeps on assuring us that he is not a protectionist, but a most divinely enlightened free-trader. He writes quickly & apparently without consistency.

The second difficulty is that, though writing as 'an economist,' he is even more dogmatic and omniscient in his capacity of statesman than in that of economist. And his later letters, even while professedly talking sheer economics, assume premises which he considers himself to have established as a politician. So if one answers him, one must mix up politics and economics.

For that work the better class of newspapers & members of Parliament are better fitted than economists of the chair; who make it a duty to bring out arguments which tell against their ultimate conclusion, as faithfully as those which tell for it.

But in fact the situation seems to me to be changing with astonishing quickness. Chamberlain is a man of resource and rapidity; & may save the situation with some complete change of front: & he may go over to the side of the 'Protection-against-Trusts' people, & leave the agrarians in the lurch.[9] If he does he may save himself; but I do not really fear that he will succeed in bringing about an effective dear-food-treaty with our colonies.

Much of the change in public opinion seems to have occurred since I left England. But I lay great stress on the action of the Daily Mail. That has, you know, a circulation of one and a quarter million or more. (It now telegraphs its recent news and articles to Manchester, & is set up in duplicate in Manchester. Thus it reaches the industrial districts before any other London paper.) It has always been regarded as devoted to Chamberlainism. It started the discussion of his new move with some strong pronouncements in favour of it as a whole. Then it remained silent for about ten days. When it spoke again, it was very cold to the 'dear food' position. And the copy, which has just come in contains a leader, that is I believe representative of the 'way the cat is jumping.' I send it & another.[10]

Retaliation—especially against indirect bounties, & against 'dumping' down sugar & other things at less than cost price—seems to me more insidious, & more likely to lead to real Protection than 'Imperial federation.' And the fight may last many years, even many generations.

Yours most sincerely & gratefully, | Alfred Marshall

[1] Bundesarchiv, Koblenz, Brentano Papers. Partly reproduced in H. W. McCready, 'Alfred Marshall and Tariff Reform, 1903: Some Unpublished Letters', *Journal of Political Economy*, 63 June 1955), pp. 259–67 at pp. 260–2.

[2] See [754, 756].

[3] See [740].

[4] See [757].

[5] See [741] for the earliest extant letter about Ephraim's proposal.

[6] 'An Economist' was actually Hewins: see [756.2].

[7] See [756] for the remonstrance. According to Hewins (*Apologia* [756.2], vol. 1, p. 67) Marshall had declined an invitation from *The Times* to respond to Hewins's articles, and had also refused a request that he contribute a piece on the tariff question to one of the monthlies.

[8] Chapman published four articles on the free-trade side of the tariff issue in the *Daily Mail* between 30 June and 11 July 1903.

[9] That is, opt for retaliatory tariffs aimed against unfair competition rather than agricultural protection aimed to safeguard Britain's food supply and imperial ties.

[10] See 'The Free Food League', *Daily Mail*, 14 July 1903 (4b).

759. To Ludwig Joseph Brentano, 20 July 1903[1]

20. 7. 03 Stern im Enneberg

My dear Brentano

'An Economists' seventh article in The Times of last Thursday is monstrous,[2] I am sure you will think. By accident I have with me a copy of Conrads table, a part of which he quotes as to relative prices in England France & Prussia. But I have no access here to Prussian prices for individual years: I cannot check his statements as to the number of years in wh prices were high. And I do not even know what were the real causes of all the broad movements. In particular I do not know whether currency depreciation had anything to do with the high prices in 1816–20; but I have a notion it had. Of course the duty did not materially affect prices in Province-Prussia at the earlier times. Altogether the argument seems to me most objectionable & if I had access to my books I should I think write to the Times about it. But you could do it much better than I; for you can read between the lines of the Statistics. I can do that for England, of course, but not for Prussia. As regards England I have told 'An Economist' that, though I cannot 'controvert' I may feel forced to publish prematurely an explanation of wheat prices in England in the XIX century, wh I have already written for my second volume. But in no case could I tackle thoroughly the Prussian prices. Will not you? Do!

Yours sincerely, | Alfred Marshall

The return post between here & England takes six days: so of course I have not heard from MacMillan.

P.S. *Confidential*[3] | I hate mystery. So I am going to take the other horn of the dilemma & tell you *in strict confidence* that what I have been, and still am, engaged on here is a Memorandum on the whole of the Chamberlain proposal, written privately for the use of a leading member of the English Cabinet at his request.[4] I had at first intended to make it short. But the course of the discussion in England & especially the Tracts, which are being issued by the million under Chamberlains auspices from Birmingham—have induced me to make it long and to publish its substance ere long. The first Part wh I sent off a few days ago relates to the incidence of import duties, on which the 'Tracts' contain some misleading extracts from Sidgwick's Political Economy.[5] Here also I have taken occasion to propose an alternative to the history of English wheat prices published by 'An Economist.' The second half is an answer—in brief—to the question—'How have the changes of the last sixty years modified the basis of our present fiscal system?' My answer is:—'In many ways. But on the balance they have rendered it more urgently necessary for England (not for all other countries) than ever.' In particular I am urging that 'Trusts,' 'Kartelle' &c are much more injurious to the country in which they are than to the countries in which they sell at low prices; & that their growth is a strong argument for Free Trade. If, as seems not unlikely, England reintroduces Protection in order to fight foreign Trusts, she will in my opinion give herself over to the dominion of Trusts at home. I have ordered the Fortnightly Review: but it has not come yet. I thought you would wish me to speak with special frankness on this point.[6] 'An Economists' letters to the Times are increasingly hard to reconcile with his private letters to me.[7] I give him up.

A.M.

[1] Bundesarchiv Koblenz, Brentano Papers. Reproduced in McCready, 'Alfred Marshall and Tariff Reform' [758.1], pp. 262–3.

[2] *The Times*, 16 July 1903. Hewins argued, by reference to the effects of German duties on corn, that no simple prediction of the effects of tariffs could be given. The statistics in question were drawn from J. Conrad and others, *Handwörterbuch der Staatswissenschaften* (Fischer, Jena, 1892–5). See McCready, p. 262 n. 19.

[3] This postscript, on a separate sheet, was most probably appended to the next letter, but McCready's attribution to the present one is followed to avoid confusion.

[4] See [754].

[5] H. Sidgwick, *Principles of Political Economy* (Macmillan, London, 1883). The precise passage being utilized has not been ascertained.

[6] Brentano's article 'The Proposed Reversal of English Commercial Policy' was to appear in the *Fortnightly Review*, 80 (74 NS), August 1903, pp. 212–21. Brentano's view was that wider use of retaliatory tariffs would sap the basis for protectionist policies and thus promote free trade in the longer run. See McCready, p. 263 n. 24.

[7] Not traced. See [756] for Marshall's only surviving 1903 letter to 'An Economist' (Hewins).

760. To Ludwig Joseph Brentano, 24 July 1903[1]

Stern 24. 7. 03

My dear Brentano

Many thanks for your letters and papers. I have not had time to look at them properly yet. In no case shall I answer 'An Economist'—(He is not Bonar, for Bonar is very dilettanti, he does not know enough to write these letters.)[2] One of my grievances against him is that he does not know his Jacob. My history of English wheat is to a considerable extent based on facts which Jacob was directly or indirectly instrumental in bringing to light.[3] Some time I shall publish a different view of that history. But I shall not meddle with German prices. I wish you would.

But my chief object in writing now is to warn you that you are doing the worst thing for the cause of free trade you possibly can by advocating special duties on goods which have export bounties.[4] It is all right theoretically. But it *can not* be done, without also levying countervailing duties on people who slaughter[5] goods in foreign markets. All our protectionists know this: & are insisting that the German &c taxes on our imports give in effect 'a bounty'—that is their regular phrase—to the German &c producers of rival goods, which they use in underselling us at home. This is *the chief danger* in the present movement. Chamberlain will not get any considerable tax on corn. But he may get countervailing duties on goods which interested people declare have received an indirect bounty. E.G. there is a considerable danger of the revival of part of our navigation laws: for while German shippers declare ours get more indirect bounties than they do, ours say the contrary. Who is to decide? Answer: The Statesman whose election agents have a distinct notion as to which kind of half-lie will be most effective at the voting booths.

If he[6] is to [be][7] prevented from bringing England's fiscal policy back to protection to manufactures, it must be by insisting that what Government might do, if it could follow out every secret bargain, is quite different from what it can do in practice: that in *fact* foreign bounties have never done any considerable harm to any British industry, with the exception of the sugar industry (& the harm done there was much exaggerated): & that the remedy wh the Protectionists are proposing would put us under the heel of English combinations: it would make some of the rich a little richer & the people a great deal poorer. 'An Economist' wrote me a warning letter that that is the chief danger:[8] but I knew it before. So please don't help to destroy Englands free-trade, in your anxiety to stop a system which I admit to be most injurious to the country which adopts it; but *not* to the country to which it sells.

Excuse haste, | Yours most truly & gratefully, | Alfred Marshall

I believe 'An Economist' to [be][9] genuinely opposed to vulgar protectionism. But he has been carried off his legs by ambitious notions about colonial federation: & he seems to me unable to perceive obvious inconsistencies in his own position. He seems to argue as a special pleader rather than as an economist.

Please don't send me a *third* guess. If you do, you *must* be right! There are not many left for you to guess from.

[1] Bundesarchiv Koblenz, Brentano Papers. Reproduced in H. W. McCready, 'Alfred Marshall and Tariff Reform' [758.1], pp. 263–4.

[2] See [756.2].

[3] William Jacob (1762–1851), Comptroller of the Corn Returns, 1822–42. Author of *Report on the Trade in Foreign Corn, and on the Agriculture of the North of Europe* (London, 1826). See *Official Papers*, pp. 380–1; *Industry and Trade*, p. 755 n.

[4] See [759.6].

[5] That is, dump at a price below cost.

[6] That is, Chamberlain. The preceding example, written on the reverse of the previous sheet, was inserted as an afterthought.

[7] Word apparently omitted.

[8] This letter from Hewins not traced.

[9] Word apparently omitted.

761. To Herbert Somerton Foxwell, 2 August 1903[1]

Confidential for you and Keynes Stern, im Enneberg, South Tyrol: 2. 8. 03

My dear Foxwell,

I am not yet free of my Fiscal Problem correspondence. But I have come to a halting stage: & so I feel I ought not to keep you waiting longer for my rough suggestions.[2]

As to the official descriptions of the books which are to be above or below the line,[3] no solution seems to me quite satisfactory. The Moral Science Regulations seem to exclude books wh are not suitable for being read through. On the whole the Historical phrases seem to me best; & I have copied them.[4] But please consider carefully, & try for something still better. I can't think of anything.

The order in which I have arranged the books is purely fortuitous: I have put them down just as they came. Ultimately I assume the order will be alphabetical.

I have a strong desire to see Pierson & Hadley above the line.[5] The former book is a paragon of usefulness: and Hadleys realistic chapters are I think the best & most stimulating that I know. I incline to think that Nicholson[6] must go above the line. For though I personally am irritated by the intellectual slovenliness, as it seems to me, of every single passage of his which deals with difficult questions & is not a direct repetition[7] of old work; & while I feel bound to let students know that I do not regard him as a man of high calibre; & while even I think a man is more likely to get intellectual mischief than intellectual benefit from reading it; yet, as his book is to a certain extent a competitor with mine on the booksellers shelves, I don't think I dare appear to take advantage of my position to keep him out of the list. And it has occurred to me that you also are perhaps not as free to vote according to your intellectual conscience about him, as you are about (say) Bastable or Dunbar.

You will notice that I have failed in the attempt to get good books in French.[8] I expect *Pareto* is the ablest:[9] but he is very un-real & cranky, I think. *Beaulieu*[10] is level headed, but prodigiously dull. *Gide* is, I think, quite empty: & he is translated into English. *Jannet* is amateur, but he is interesting. *Roussiers* has an astonishing faculty for describing in detail things wh he has but a bowing acquaintance with: & I have not read his *last* book on 'Syndicats industriels', wh is more concerned with France than most that he writes; & may be based on sounder knowledge.[11] If Tanner or others can suggest good French books for the historical subject (No 3), we might take over Levasseurs *Population Française Comparée* &c Vol III, into our subject (No 4). Or it might go in both.[12] It seems to me better *of its kind* than any other book wh has occurred to me is of its kind, with the doubtful exception of *Pareto*. Please work at this. If called on, I am prepared to recommend many more German books. But there is nothing which I wish to run against Schönbergs Vol I (really two large volumes), which is compressed, though long; & which contains a great deal that is representative of the best German work in several directions.[13] Parker[14] is afraid that an excess of German books on the list may be deterrent. He does not object to French.

Bonar's little book[15] reached me shortly before I left England. It seemed to me rather *dilettanti*, though excellent in its way. On the whole I did not think it would prove exactly the right book for us. But I have not read it. I hope you will have an opinion on it.

And I hope you will generally make this list a very much better thing than it is now, before we come before the Board with it. I understand the position as to Committees to be this.

I For Political Science Ward[16] + Dickinson

II For History, you + Tanner / Keynes + (myself as consulting physician)

III For Economics you + myself + (Keynes as consulting physician)

I wonder whether my memory is right?

I expect that Committees I & II should have an informal understanding with one another as to books on the border line between their special provinces & of course Committees II & III. Perhaps it might be a good plan for you Keynes & me to have a meeting somewhere about Sep 26 to make up the list for Economics. There would be an advantage perhaps in holding it at Balliol Croft; because all the books wh I have proposed, & some others about which I am in doubt, are there. And those, wh you or Keynes suggest to be added, I shall certainly wish to buy; if I have not them already.

I had intended to talk about Fiscal Issue. But this has run to such length, that I must stop. You are sure to know all the little gossip I know, and ever so much beyond. I am rather greedy, the smallest contributions thankfully accepted.

This will probably be our address till near the near of August. After that we hope to carry out a long projected plan, often nearly acted on, to come home by the fringe of debateable land between Western and Eastern civilization: ie part of Hungary, Bohemia, Silesia & the Tiltau district of Saxony, wh I understand to be very interesting because it is so far removed in character from the rest of Saxony: though so near in distance. All which is not to the point except thus. Any letter posted to me before August 22nd is almost sure to reach me. After that my address may be uncertain till I get home about September 20th.

Postal arrangements here are exceptionally bad. Our newspapers (even a Frankfurter Zeitung with a printed direction) often go astray. So I will say for security, that I have written you a letter & two postcards[17] none requiring any answer: & that I have got none. Please tell me how Nicholson is.

Best love to you & Keynes | Yours ever | Alfred Marshall

[1] Foxwell Papers. Presumably accompanied by a list of books, not traced.
[2] About the list of economics books to be recommended for Part I of the new Tripos. [752] had focused on the question of history books. For the final version of the economics list see [777], below.
[3] See [752.7].
[4] The precise difference between the practices of the two Boards remains obscure. For Marshall's own wording see the enclosure to [777].
[5] N. G. Pierson, *Principles of Economics, Volume I* [734.2]; A. T. Hadley, *Economics: An Account of the Relation between Private Property and Public Welfare* (Putnam, New York, 1896). Both works were above the line in the final list.
[6] J. S. Nicholson, *Principles of Political Economy* (Black, London, 1893–1901: 3 vols.). This work was included above the line in the final version, but only as an option.
[7] Written as 'repetion' in the original.
[8] The regulations required that the Part I examination questions in economics and history 'shall include quotations from French and German writers' (*Reporter*, 25 June 1903, p. 1133). None of the authors Marshall proceeds to mention appeared in the final list.
[9] The allusion is presumably to Pareto's *Cours d'Économie Politique* (Librairie de l'Université, Lausanne, 1896–7), his only major work published initially in French.
[10] That is, Paul Leroy Beaulieu.
[11] Paul de Rousiers (not Roussiers), *Les Syndicats Industriels de Producteurs en France et à L'étranger* (Colin, Paris, 1901). For Rousiers (1857–1934) see vol. 2, [709.9]. This work was not included in the final list.
[12] Pierre Émile Levasseur, *La Population Française. Histoire de la Population avant 1789 et démographie de la France comparée à celle des autres nations aux XIXe Siècle* (Rousseau, Paris, 1889–92): vol. 3, part 1 was included above the line in the economics listing only. See *Reporter*, 10 November 1903, and [777].
[13] Gustav Schönberg, *Handbuch der Politschen Ökonomie* (Laupp, Tübingen, third edition 1890), included below the line in the final list.
[14] Probably Edmund Henry Parker (1858–1928), banker and Borough Treasurer of Cambridge, a member of the Economics Syndicate proposing the new Tripos (see vol. 2 [722.1]).
[15] James Bonar, *Elements of Political Economy* (Murray, London, 1903), not included in the final list.
[16] Adolphus Ward, chairman of the newly established Special Board for Economics and Politics—more briefly the Economics Board—that was to manage the new Tripos.
[17] Marshall sent *three* picture postcards to Foxwell from Stern (10, 24, 31 July; Foxwell Papers). Each bore a short procastinatory message.

762. To Herbert Somerton Foxwell, 5 August 1903[1]

5. 8. 03
Stern im Enneberg | South Tyrol

My dear Foxwell

The still peace of mountain woods has taken out my evil spirit; & I no more dream economics at night. But luckily I awaked last night & saw a picture of the list of books I had sent you.[2] It looked too short. I thought there must be something wrong. So I looked when daylight came, & found I had omitted bodily the books on one of the slips wh I had made out for the purpose some time back. I now inclose them, amended.

Post takes 3 days each way between here & Cambridge, if it comes at all; wh is not always. So I reckon that tomorrow you will be maledicting my list if in

Cambridge. I am contrite & conscious of guilt (the last smudge[3] meant that I had to kill a gnat, & his death-throes shook my hand). So I shall bend my back to the Smiter.

I think we should add to the list a notice that a knowledge of the books relating to economic history & geography, especially English, in the list for Subject 3 will be assumed in Subject 4.[4]

If we have Malthus Population, wh I gather you wish, & to which I do not object, I think Levasseur's *Population Française* Vol III must be in the list for *Economics;*[5] & on the whole I am drifting to think it would be more appropriate there than in the historical list. For it contains a good deal of high class realistic training in Statistical Method. And Levasseur's Classes Ouvrières depuis 1789[6] is pretty solid in the old edition, & will be very heavy & also just what we want when the second edition is out.

One idea has just occurred to me. Perhaps we ought not to ignore the French Classics even in Part I. So I am suggesting *doubtfully* Turgots *Reflexions:* though unfortunately I believe it is translated into English.[7] But of course questions could be set containing quotations in the original.

My apologies to Keynes, as well as to you, for my egregious carelessness.

Again I say take care of yourself. The last time I saw you you looked overstrained: & so my wife thought when she cycled over to you just before we came away. We hereby authorize & empower your better half to take strong measures with you if needful.

Yours ever | Alfred Marshall

[Enclosure][8]

Addenda to draft list of books on Economics for Ec Tr Part I

Above the line

Mayo Smith *Economics & Statistics*
Jevons *State in Relation to Labour*
Smart *Distribution*
Gilman *Dividend to Labour*
Webb *Industrial Democracy*

Below the line

Ingram *History of Pol Econ?*
Turgot *Réflexions?*
Higgs *Physiocrats?*
Boehm Bawerk *Theory of Capital?*
J B Clark *Distribution?*
Schloss *Methods of Industrial Remuneration*
Ellis *Market Fluctuations*
Bowley *Englands Foreign Trade*

Darwin *Bimetallism*
Giffen *Stock Exchange Securities*
Walker *Money*

[1] Foxwell Papers.
[2] See [761.1, 2].
[3] The word 'guilt' was written only at the second attempt.
[4] Subject 4 in Part I of the new Tripos was Economics while Subject 3 was economic and general history, as is implied in [761].
[5] See [752.8, 761.12]. Both works were included above the line in the list finally adopted.
[6] Pierre Émile Levasseur, *Histoire des Classes Ouvrières en France Depuis 1789 Jusqu'à nos Jours* (Hachette, Paris, 1867). The second edition bears the title *Histoire . . . Ouvrières et de L'industrie en France de 1789 à 1870* (Rousseau, Paris, 1903–4: 2 vols.). This was included below the line in the eventual list of history books for Part I of the new Tripos: see *Reporter*, 10 November 1903.
[7] A. R. J. Turgot, *Réflexions sur la Formation et la Distribution des Richesses* (1766: English translation, Macmillan, New York, 1898). See [761.8] on the reason for regretting the existence of a translation.
[8] See [777] for Marshall's subsequent full list and for details of the list eventually approved. The question marks may have been added by Foxwell.

763. To Ludwig Joseph Brentano, 5 August 1903[1]

Stern
5. 8. 03

My dear Brentano

I have heard from Mr MacMillan.[2] He leaves the matter entirely to me. But he suggests that I should ask Messrs Cotta to pay me £20 for each thousand copies of Vol I after the first thousand: no payment whatever being made for the first thousand. If the copy-right is not to pass to Messrs Cotta, I should not need to obtain any security from them as to Vol II (& the possible Vol III). But if they ask for the copyright of Vol I, I should want an understanding as to the later Volume or Volumes. I am inclined to think that the simplest plan would be to make the agreement that Messrs Cotta should publish Vol II (& possibly Vol III) on the same terms as Vol I, *if they wish to do so*; & that if & when they do that the copyright of the whole work, in German, remains with them. But in case they should not wish to translate & publish Vol II (& the possible Vol III) on these terms, then that I should have the liberty of arranging with another publisher for a translation of the whole work. That is to say the present contract would be not for the transfer of the copyright to them, but for giving to them an 'Option' to take the copyright of the whole work at any time within six months after the publication of my second volume in English. That would I think give them all that they want; & secure me against a possible, though improbable, contingency of being helpless as to a German translation of my Vol II.[3]

Perhaps you will be so very kind as to communicate this suggestion to Messrs Cotta, & thus add to my great obligations to you,

Yours sincerely | Alfred Marshall

[1] Bundesarchiv Koblenz, Brentano Papers.

[2] Macmillan's response to Marshall's letter [757] has not been traced.

[3] It is curious that Marshall makes no provision for revision of vol. 1 of his Principles, the translation being of *Principles* (*4*). Perhaps, still hoping to complete the second volume, he did not forsee the substantial changes to be made in *Principles* (*5,6*).

764. To Ludwig Joseph Brentano, 12 August 1903[1]

Stern
12. 8. 03

My dear Brentano

I have just finished & despatched the second half of my Memorandum.[2] It is alas! very long.

Rumours are current in England that Hewins is 'An Economist' of the *Times*: I pass that rumour on to you for what it is worth.

Many thanks for your letter from Cotta.[3] I quite agree to there[4] being 1500 copies in the first edition for which no payment is made. If you should think £20 is at all a high price to ask for my royalty on each subsequent 1000 copies, please kindly tell me so. I care very little about money.

Your & Mrs Brentano's very kind invitation to my wife & me to stay a couple of days at Amberg[5] on our way home is most attractive. I have not stayed with any friend for many years. I abstain on the same ground that I decline all invitations to dinner. But I should have doubted whether I could bring myself (and my wife) to obey my rule in this case, if we had been going North from here. But our plans are to go Eastwards early in September to Pesth, which we have never seen; & then to make a circuit through either Breslau or Prag. We have schemed long for this: & in fact we chose a place near the Pusterthal Bahn[6] with that object in view.

If I were a German or a Frenchman I should want to put out the Protectionist fire around me. But I am not sure that if you & Yves Guyot[7] had your way, you would not in the name of free trade burn down the poor English free trade house as fuel for the fire engine with which to pump water on your home conflagration. I am not angry: but am not glad.

I admit however, that if [it][8] should be possible to identify a parcel of goods which are sold below cost price in England, no *great* harm would be done by putting a special tax on that *special parcel*. I am suggesting this in my Memorandum: though I do not believe the thing can be done practically.

Yours very sincerely, | Alfred Marshall

No I probably shall not go to the meeting of the International Statistical Institute.[9] I never attend public meetings.

If you can save trouble by acting on my behalf with Mess[rs] Cotta, please kindly do so. It is practically certain that I shall approve whatever you do.

A.M.

[1] Bundesarchiv Koblenz, Brentano Papers. Substantially reproduced in H. W. McCready, 'Alfred Marshall and Tariff Reform' [758.1], pp. 264–5.
[2] See [754].
[3] See [757.7]. Letter not traced.
[4] Mis-spelt 'their' in the original.
[5] Perhaps Ambach, Brentano's usual summer address, was intended?
[6] A railway.
[7] See Yves Guyot, 'Mr Chamberlain's Programme in the Light of French Experience', *Fortnightly Review*, 80 (74 NS), August 1903, pp. 1–18. See also [759.6].
[8] Word apparently omitted.
[9] The International Statistical Institute was to meet in Berlin, 20–5 September 1903. Foxwell attended: see *The Times*, 22 September (4a).

765. From Theodore Llewelyn Davies, 13 August 1903[1]

Treasury Chambers, | Whitehall, S.W.
13 August, 1903.

Dear Professor Marshall,

I ought to have acknowledged before the receipt of Part I of your Memorandum. I have had it printed at once and I now enclose 3 proofs together with your original MS. so that you may correct it.[2]

The Chancellor has read your Paper, and I know he was very much pleased with it; but he has not had time at present to do more than to ask me to thank you very heartily for it, and especially for the trouble which you have taken under circumstances so particularly trying. Myself I have felt quite guilty, when I think how we have spoilt the holiday which you so badly need. I only hope you will be able to get a really good rest before the Term begins.

I need not say how very valuable the Memorandum appears to me, nor how very useful it will be just at the present moment.

Just one point occurs to me, which I venture, with much diffidence, to suggest for your consideration. Is not paragraph 29 expressed in a way which might be capable of being misunderstood, and certainly might be unfairly quoted?[3] I mean, especially, the statement that the price here would probably not rise by the full amount of the Tax? In view of the fact that the increase in our Colonial Wheat supply would be gradual, and that the World's demand for Wheat is continually growing, it would appear that Foreign producers could have no difficulty in disposing of the produce of their existing plant and land, and would merely be deterred from increasing the output by bringing new and less advantageous land under cultivation, or by cultivating more extensively. Consequently, it would be only the element of rent, would it not, that would not be borne by the consumer, namely, the element representing the differential advantage of the worst land cultivated in Foreign countries after the imposition of the Duty, as compared with the worst that would have been cultivated had there been no Duty, and would not this be an almost negligible amount?

Again, I think your whole argument implies that the price in this country, though it need not be higher by the full amount of the tax than it would have been in the absence of the tax, is certainly higher by the full amount of the tax than the price in the free markets of the world. Consequently, in so far as we make the Foreign producer pay the tax we give a bounty to all other consumers who are our competitors? If this point is true, I think it would weigh so much with practical men that it might be worth stating.

I hesitate to trouble you any further; but I will venture to send you a short Paper which I drew up myself.[4] If, without much trouble, you could indicate with a blue pencil any points you think wrong, I should of course be very much obliged.

I shall await Part II with much interest.

Will you please return 1 proof corrected ?

I will let you have plenty of copies when struck off.

Please excuse this letter wh. is written of course under great pressure.

Yours sincerely | T. Ll. Davies

[1] Marshall Papers. Typewritten with the last three sentences added by hand. Reproduced in John C. Wood, 'Alfred Marshall and the Origins' [754.1], at pp. 265–6. See [754] for the background.

[2] Wood reports finding in the Public Record Office an anonymous printed memorandum on the fiscal question that he deems to be Parts I and II of Marshall's first version. See his 'Alfred Marshall and the Tariff Campaign' [754.1], p. 481 n. 3. It is suggested below that his attribution is dubious: see [962.6].

[3] The point at issue seems to be the effect on price in the home market of an English tax on imports of wheat from non-colonial sources.

[4] Not traced.

766. To Abdullatif Camrudin Amirudin Abdul Latif, 15 August 1903[1]

The Tyrol
15. 8. 03

My dear Latif,

I am sorry that, through my absence from home, your letter of the 19th of July[2] has only just reached me.

I do not recollect exactly what I wrote to you last Autumn. But so far as I can recall its substance, I said that I thought you should consult your College Tutor as to the advisability of your becoming a candidate for a Fellowship at St John's.

I think I wrote just after having heard the report of the Whewell Scholarship Electors. That was a strong Report; and no doubt its substance could be obtained in an official form—from Prof Maitland, the Secretary to the International Law

Scholarship Board, or in some other way. Meanwhile if you write to your Tutor, you are at liberty to state that I told you that that Report gave unusually strong approval of your work.

If you should stand and be elected, you might then consider whether you would like an academic career in Cambridge. If so you would have to take your chance with others for lectureships &c. In economics there is large room for teachers, but little money to buy them with. At present in fact there is practically no money.

If you chose that course, & made a reputation as a competent scholar & effective teacher, it is conceivable that in some way or other you might obtain a post as teacher of Indian Law & Economics in relation to one another. I have heard it said that it would probably be as easy to obtain a special endowment for a lectureship on Indian Economics, as for almost any other: but I have no direct knowledge on the subject.

I do not recollect that I specially suggested for you an English rather than an Indian career. I did not fully understand what your expectations in India are; nor do I even now.

But, unless you are specially drawn to an English academic career with all its pecuniary risks, I should I think feel inclined to suggest for your consideration the following plan:—

(i) To ask your Tutor whether he thinks there would be a considerable chance of your obtaining a Fellowship; taking account not only of your claims, but of others who might be candidates—a point on which I know nothing. If his answer is encouraging, then to apply for leave to come over next October year (1904), & stand. I presume you would not be of too old a standing[3] then: but your Tutor will know, if you do not.

(ii) Whether you are elected or not, to resolve to make yourself known in India as a man who studies the economic problems of India in a scientific spirit; i.e. seeking to find out things that are *a* true, *b* practically important *c* not so obvious as to be picked up easily by the hasty thinker. There is an urgent demand for work of this kind; and especially for natives of India who will do it. You must be aware, and you will not mind my speaking plainly, that a considerable proportion of those natives who have written on Indian economics, have written rather as politicians than as students. I mean they have convinced themselves rather easily what is the right practical aim for which it is best to work in their country's interest; & then they have studied with a view to get such facts and arguments as will promote that aim. The scientific student on the other hand, however strongly he may have become convinced that a certain aim is right, seeks to find & to make known, arguments & facts that bear on it, without any bias towards those which tell on the side of the aim which he believes to be right. He is just as pleased to discover & to publish an argument against his aim, as an argument for it.

I suggest therefore that, assuming you to stay in India, you should resolve to make yourself master of some large and difficult subject in which all your faculties & advantages will be turned to account. It should be one which

(a) cannot be studied by an Englishman as easily as by a native
(b) requires a knowledge of economics and, perhaps, of law
(c) goes to the root of some of India's chief difficulties & can help to show how to develop some of her chief latent faculties.

Work for the work's sake. Never stop to think whether what you say will be popular or not. Be true; & in time it will be known that you are true.

You may have to live among Philistines at present. But the best & truest minds English & Native will soon recognize you as a comrade. And after a few years, you are quite certain, I feel sure, to be called on for your opinion on high matters. For there is no one whom the English Government—at all events when in the hands of a high minded man, as it generally is—so much wants, as a Native who will be trusted by English & Natives alike, to think carefully & to speak what he believes to be true fearlessly & without desire for favour.

Great as might be your influence in Cambridge, if you could obtain[4] the trust of the Natives who go there to study, & guide them aright, I think you might in India, do even more towards making the world better than it would have been if you had not been born into it. And that is the one thing that is worth living for.

Yours very sincerely | Alfred Marshall

I will ask my servant to send you a little book about the new Curriculum. You will note that we hope often to have a 'Special Subject' relating to India, when the Tripos is in full swing.[5]

[1] From a photographic copy in the Marshall Papers. The original, not traced, was presumably sent to India. Latif (subsequently Alma Latifi) of St John's had obtained firsts in the Law Tripos (Part I 1900, Part II 1902), and had been elected to a Whewell Scholarship for International Law in 1902. He did not return to Cambridge but had a distinguished career as an administrator in India.

[2] Not traced.

[3] That is, too long a time would not have elapsed since graduation.

[4] Preceded by an undeleted 'get' in the original.

[5] Among possible special subjects listed in Marshall's *New Cambridge Curriculum* [751.4] was 'the existing political and administrative organisation, of some foreign country, or of India, or of some other dependency or colony of the United Kingdom' (p. 34).

767. To Ludwig Joseph Brentano, 15 August 1903[1]

Stern
15. 8. 03

My dear Brentano,

Thank you much for Messrs Cotta's letter[2] which I return with thanks. In my last letter I said that I was perfectly willing that the first edition, for which no honorarium should be paid for me, should consist 1500 copies.[3] I understand that, that being concluded, Messrs Cotta are willing to pay me at the rate of £20 per 1000 copies for all subsequent editions, whatever be the size of those: and that the same arrangements should hold for the several editions of Vol II (& a possible Vol III) as hold for Vol I. These terms I have great pleasure in definitely accepting. I am much obliged to you and to them, & hope that progress will be able to be made quickly.

I do not know whether Messrs Cotta will wish me to sign a formal agreement. If so, I should be glad if [it] could be written in Latin and not German characters. I am very much puzzled by German characters, & I notice that their letters contain some Latin characters.[4]

Yours very sincerely | Alfred Marshall

P.S. I have just been reading your article in the Fortnightly:[5] I have had no time during the last month to read anything very carefully. I hope it will do good: though I believe that if the sale of German slaughter goods[6] in England leaves 'thousands of workmen without bread' in England, it leaves tens of thousands without bread in Germany. I mean it makes German industry much more unstable than it does English. With this exception, I cordially & heartily concur in & admire the article; & I am very grateful to you for it.

One little suggestion I will venture on. The English statistics of exports & imports of *silver* are fairly trustworthy, but not those of *gold.* For English tourists, especially those who frequent the semi-anglicized hotels, take large numbers of sovereigns in their pockets; & these escape the notice of the customs officers. All of these that are not quite full weight are sent back to England; & in most cases by bullion dealers, who of course report them to the customs officers.

No doubt a few come back in the pockets of German visitors to England; but not very many. Our net import of gold, though considerable, is therefore rather less than is indicated by the statistics.

I have mislaid Messrs Cottas letter. I will send it when I find it.

[1] Bundesarchiv Koblenz, Brentano Papers. Postscript reproduced in H. W. McCready, 'Alfred Marshall and Tariff Reform' [758.1], p. 265.

[2] Not traced. Presumably the letter referred to in [764].

[3] See [764], also [763].

[4] The contract with Cotta (signed on the publisher's behalf by W. Koebner on 3 September) was signed on 5 September by Marshall, who retained a copy now in the Marshall Papers. It covered all three possible volumes in the way he had suggested.

[5] See [759.6]. Marshall's quotation is from p. 221.

[6] See [760.5].

768. To Ludwig Joseph Brentano, 18 August 1903[1]

Stern
18. 8. 03

My dear Brentano

I think you had misread Mess[rs] Cottas letter. The proposal that the payment should be at the rate of £20 per 1000 copies after the first edition was theirs, as you will see. My last letter to you was intended to indicate this.[2]

You have probably seen the full text of the manifesto[3] ere now. I think, but I am not sure, that I shall be able to send you a spare copy if you have not one.

It was mainly drafted by Edgeworth in consultation with Bastable & Nicholson: I having declined to draft it, because when I was asked to do so I thought there was nothing sufficiently definite to kick against. Afterwards, when Chamberlain & his League[4] committed themselves to the most glaring economic falsities, I changed my mind, & suggested that one should be drafted in England. The first draft was sent to me about three weeks ago, but miscarried in the post. When I got the first draft there were several things wh I disliked & three or four which I could not sign. So I expected to have to be left out. But Edgeworth was very good, & obtained the consent of the others to those changes about wh I felt strongly. Finally Cannan—who has much literary skill—helped in verbal changes, and now I think that on the whole we may be proud of it.

I declined to join the English Sociological Association, partly because I thought the people who were getting it up were not quite the right men for doing it if it had to be done; & partly because I have never ceased to be ashamed of being a member of the so-called 'Institut International de Sociologie.'[5] Its publications seem to me to have no adequate *raison d'être*. Sociology is a magnificent aspiration: but the greater part of sociologists seem to me to divide their time impartially between prehistoric institutions, without much knowledge of early history; & the last new fashion in philanthropy without a knowledge of economics. Perhaps the gas may be squeezed out of it in the coming time, but I am too old to meddle with it.

Yours most truly | Alfred Marshall

Thanks for useful hints about Buda-Pest. Also for those about the Statistical elections.[6] But unfortunately I could not profit by those, as I should have wished to. For I had sent off my voting paper some time ago.

[1] Bundesarchiv Koblenz, Brentano Papers. Substantially reproduced in H. W. McCready, 'Alfred Marshall and Tariff Reform' [758.1], pp. 265–6.

[2] See [767]. In the absence of letters from Cotta it is difficult to judge who initiated the proposal, but [763] certainly suggests that it was proposed by Marshall.

[3] A free-trade 'manifesto' signed by fourteen academic or ex-academic economists including Marshall had been published in *The Times*, 15 August 1903, partly to counter Hewins's articles written as 'An Economist' [756.2]. The signatories were to be severely criticized for claiming scientific authority for positions widely deemed politically debatable. For details see A. W. Coats, 'The Role of Authority in the Development or British Economics', *Journal of Law and Economics*,

7 (October 1964), pp. 85–106, especially pp. 99–103. For Marshall's own retrospective assessment of the episode see the report (from *The Standard*) of his comments on L. L. F. R. Price, 'Economic Theory and Fiscal Policy', *Economic Journal*, 14 (September 1904), pp. 372–87, that is reproduced on pp. 483–4 of the same issue. See also *The Times*, 20 August 1904 (8e) for a full report of the session of the British Association at which Marshall's remarks were made and for a variant version of them.

[4] The Tariff Reform League, centred in Birmingham.

[5] The Institut was the creation of René Worms (1869–1926), French sociologist. Marshall had told J. N. Keynes in a letter of 5 November 1900 (Marshall Library, J. N. Keynes Papers) that 'I am an original member, & was a V.P in 1899 (or 8, I forget which). He seduced me with sweet phrases: & he has never done me any harm. But he has not yet made it clear to me why the Institut exists. There is no subscription; &, I confess it in confidence & with a shamed face, I have only once bought the Annals.'

[6] Presumably for the International Statistical Institute [764.9].

769. From Theodore Llewelyn Davies, 25 August 1903[1]

Treasury Chambers, | Whitehall, S.W.
25th August, 1903.

I have to acknowledge several things, with many thanks. First, Part II of your Memorandum,[2] which only reached me on the 22nd and which I sent to the printer. I have only read it hastily and won't try to criticise at this stage, beyond saying that I am myself too hide-bound not to feel some abhorrence from even your statement of the Infant Industry argument: but that I am delighted and re-assured to find you backing so powerfully the line on which my ideas have been going as regards most-favoured-nation system, commercial treaties and retaliation. I will send any comments I can with the proof.

Next, I am very glad indeed you approve generally of my Paper, and very much obliged for your comments.[3] I think you are right about (a) at the beginning.—I put it in, thinking of cases like Greek currants, to which you refer in Paragraph 15, and which Lowe mentioned in discussing Incidence in his 1869 Budget speech.[4] Is there not something in this, even apart from definite monopolist organisation in Greece?

And, now, as to your Memorandum generally.—When I first wrote, I had no idea that you would be able to reply so fully, and no definite arrangement was in my mind as to how your answer should be treated. But I had no hesitation about printing it at once when it came in. It is now clear that the Government does not mean to consult Economists generally in a systematic way—in fact, I do not know that any others have been consulted (unless it be the 'Times' pet!), and under all the circumstances there would be no question (even if we had your permission) of issuing your Memorandum by itself officially.[5] So, I hope it will be satisfactory to you—as I gather from your letters it would be—that the position should stand thus: that the Chancellor of the Exchequer asked you for your views: that you communicated to him a Memorandum which was and remains altogether your property: that he printed it for his own convenience, and for his private use: that he, incidentally, for your convenience, I hope, supplied you with some of the prints: but that the question of publication remains entirely in your own hands, except that he would prefer that, in case of publication, any reference to his intervention in the matter should be omitted. I needn't say that I hope you may manage to publish it soon.[6]

Yours sincerely | T. Llewelyn Davies

[1] Marshall Papers. Typewritten, without salutation. Reproduced in J. C. Wood, 'Alfred Marshall and the Origins' [754.1], at pp. 267–8. See [754, 765] for background.

[2] See [765.2].

[3] Not traced. Imports of Greek currants were regarded as having a price-elasticity of supply that remained low for a considerable time.

[4] See *Official Papers*, p. 377. Robert Lowe (1811–92), Chancellor of the Exchequer, 1868–73, under Gladstone, and subsequently first Viscount Sherbrooke. See *Hansard*, third series, 195, for his famous Budget speech of 8 April 1869, reported in *The Times*, 9 April (4a–f, 5a, b).

[5] *The Times* had taken Chamberlain's side in the tariff debate, and its 'pet' was Hewins (see [756.2]).

[6] Marshall's 'Memorandum on the Fiscal Policy of International Trade' was to be published by the House of Commons only in 1908: see [912–15] below. For the text see *Official Papers*, pp. 367–420.

770. To Ludwig Joseph Brentano, 26 August 1903[1]

August 31 to Sep 4
Hotel Ronacher
Bruneck

Till August 31
Stern

26. 8. 03

My dear Brentano

I return Mess[rs] Cottas agreement signed.[2] It seems clear & satisfactory in every way; & I am very much obliged to you for all the trouble you have so kindly taken about it.

Our Manifesto[3] has been furiously attacked by the Times, by Foxwell & by one or two other persons. Hewins has written in his own name a 'superior' answer to it.[4]

There is no doubt that one or two phrases in it were not the best possible. But the chief grounds of attack seem to me quite invalid: they are (1) that it is premature to judge Chamberlain's scheme, because it is not yet known (the fact that the Birmingham League[5] of wh he is officially known to be the chief director, though he may not be consulted on minor details, issues its hundreds of thousands or millions of leaflets weekly, is left out of sight) and (2) that economists ought not to assume to speak with authority on matters in which there is a large political element. The blemishes in the drafting to which I have referred give perhaps more countenance to this charge than I should have wished but substantially I think that the points on wh we do speak are such as economists have always been expected to speak decidedly about.

Many of our opponents attack us because we deny Protectionist axioms; & they may be neglected.

People who agree with us are very polite: but that does not count for much.

On the whole my first feeling that a Manifesto is more vulnerable than a letter by an individual remains. The Manifesto must be short, & yet must cover a large ground. And as no one feels that its wording is exactly what he would have chosen himself, no one is very eager or even well qualified to defend it. Edgeworth is in some sense under special obligation to do so. But there are few men as able as he is, who would be so likely to get the worse of a controversy, even when they have the right on their side. So we just lie low, & bend our backs to the smiters.

I will certainly send you my Memorandum, when it is available. I do not yet know whether it will be published, or merely circulated privately among the Cabinet.[6] In the latter case I shall probably bring out its substance remodelled & enlarged, as a small book.
Yours very sincerely | Alfred Marshall

[1] Bundesarchiv Koblenz, Brentano Papers. Substantially reproduced in H. W. McCready, 'Alfred Marshall and Tariff Reform' [758.1], p. 266.
[2] Presumably this was a preliminary version of the contract: see [767.4].
[3] See [768.3].
[4] *The Times*, 20 August 1903. This was only the beginning of a spate of letters and commentary in that newspaper. See A. W. Coats, 'Political Economy and the Tariff Reform Campaign' [754.1], for details.
[5] See [768.4].
[6] He could hardly have yet received [769].

771. To Helen Dendy Bosanquet, 18 September 1903[1]

18. 9. 03

Dear Mrs Bosanquet

I am glad your 'Strength of the People' has reached a second edition.[2] I have a constitutional objection to the publication of private letters. I think few people can do it safely, & I less than others. For I am one of the most reckless & rapid of letter writers, & am very slow in writing for publication. I find I have your letter of 30 Sep. 1902.[3] If you will send me my letters, I will see if I can agree to a part of them being published; should you desire it. But my recollection of them—jogged by rereading yours—is that they were wordy & personal; & if anything is said on the subject at all I expect it should be put in fewer words & more objectively.

I have only just returned from the Continent & am pressed with correspondence.
Yours very sincerely | Alfred Marshall

[1] University of Newcastle-upon-Tyne Library, Bosanquet Papers. From Balliol Croft.
[2] Helen Bosanquet, *The Strength of the People* (Macmillan, London, 1902; second edition 1903). Mrs Bosanquet had requested permission to reproduce their previous correspondence (Vol. 2 [717–9]) in the forthcoming second edition of her book. Her letter of request has not been traced.
[3] See Vol. 2 [718].

772. From Charles Thomson Ritchie, 19 September 1903[1]

Welders, | Gerrard's Cross, | R.S.O. | Bucks.
September 19th

My dear Sir,
I should like to express my thanks for the great trouble you have taken in drawing up the admirable paper you sent me on the proposed fiscal changes.[2] I am only sorry that the corrections of the proof which I know you sent off were lost in the post.[3] But without these corrections the paper is a most valuable one and was so described to me by the Prime Minister[4] to whom I sent a copy.
Believe me, | Yours faithfully | C. T. Ritchie

Professor Marshall

[1] Marshall Papers. Reproduced in J. C. Wood, 'Alfred Marshall and the Origins' [754.1], at p. 269. Ritchie had been forced to resign as Chancellor of the Exchequer, Chamberlain's activities having divided the Cabinet irreconcilably. The public announcement occurred on 17 September, when Chamberlain's resignation as Colonial Secretary was also announced.
[2] Marshall's 'Memorandum': see [769.6].
[3] See [776].
[4] A. J. Balfour.

773. To Charles Thomson Ritchie, 21 September 1903 (incomplete)[1]

I make bold to express my gratitude for the stand which you have made.[2] Mr. Balfours *Notes*[3] attract me in many ways. But I do not think he realizes how slippery & steep is the slope on wh. he proposes to take a few little steps. I think he overrates the injury done to us by foreign tarifs & our power of obtaining by special negotiations better terms than we now get under the most favoured nation clause.
I have the honour to remain | Yours faithfully | Alfred Marshall

[1] Marshall Papers. From a transcript in Mrs Marshall's hand headed 'Copy of part of Letter to the Right Hon C. T. Ritchie. 21. 9. 03'. Reproduced in J. C. Wood, 'Alfred Marshall and the Origins' [754.1], at p. 269.

[2] In resigning to uphold free-trade principles, although in truth Balfour's manoeuvrings had left little option.

[3] A. J. Balfour, *Economic Notes on Insular Free Trade*, a semi-official pamphlet, issued 16 September 1903, which supported retaliatory tariffs.

774. To Edwin Cannan, 21 September 1903[1]

21. 9. 03

My dear Cannan,

Working through a large accumulation of print wh I found on my recent return from the Continent, I have at last reached the Times report of your paper at the British Ass^n a week ago.[2] Its language is more vigorous than any for wh I have courage: but its substance seems to me excellent. I venture to offer you my humble tribute of hearty thanks & admiration for it.

At the same time let me thank you for the 2nd Ed^n of your *Theories of Prod^n* &c,[3] wh I was very glad to see. I trust to make a closer acquaintance with it later on.

Yours sincerely | Alfred Marshall

[1] BLPES, Cannan Papers. From Balliol Croft.

[2] *The Times*, 16 September 1903 (9c–e). Cannan's paper 'What is Success in Foreign Trade?' was summarized as part of the report on a well-attended session of Section F of the British Association that had been held on the previous day and was devoted to the tariff controversy. Cunningham and Bowley had also read papers. Cannan gave a trenchant defence of free-trade principles, buttressed by scepticism as to the superior wisdom of government.

[3] E. Cannan, *A History of Theories of Production and Distribution in English Classical Political Economy* (King, London, 1893: second edition 1903).

775. To Helen Dendy Bosanquet, 21 September 1903[1]

21. 9. 03

Dear Mrs Bosanquet

I have crossed out from my letters one or two references to individuals, which are not essential, & which would require to be recast in order to fit them for publication.[2]

I have also drawn a line in pencil through all about the explorer & the pilgrims.[3] For I think that the letters are too long for publication; & should be curtailed. And these passages seem to raise side issues, as to which we did not, perhaps, quite understand one another; & as to which the public might easily misunderstand both of us, & feel bored to boot. On these grounds I should rather prefer the omission of these passages & the consequential ommission of the passage in your letter through wh I have also drawn a pencil line.[4] I do not however positively require the omission of these passages: I merely think it would be advisable.

I have made a small alteration on p 3 of my second letter, partly because as it stood it was in apparent (though not real) discord with a passage p 786 (Ed IV. Book VI ch XII § 19) of my Principles.[5] I had forgotten it: but Mary has reminded me of it.

I have also cut out the end of my second letter,[6] as not of public interest.

I do not know whether there is any part of your own letter wh you are inclined to omit. If so, please, do so; provided of course no part of my second letter hangs on it. With these reservations & suggestions, I am happy to comply with your request & to consent to the publication of our correspondence.[7]

Yours very sincerely | Alfred Marshall

[1] University of Newcastle-upon-Tyne Library, Bosanquet Papers. From Balliol Croft. See [771].

[2] Probably the references to Giffen and Rothschild in Marshall's letters of 28 September and 2 October 1902 (Vol. 2 [717, 719]).

[3] Passages bearing on this example occurred in each of Marshall's 1902 letters.

[4] Only the printed version of Mrs Bosanquet's letter of 30 September 1902 (Vol. 2 [718]) is available, so that the suggested deletion cannot be ascertained.

[5] The phrase 'think it is may be nearly *two*' in [719] was altered to 'think it is very much larger', the amount in question being the unnecessary expenditure of the well-to-do. The cited page in *Principles* (*4*) had stated 'Perhaps £100,000,000 annually are spent even by the working classes, and £400,000,000 by the rest of the population of England in ways that do little or nothing towards making life nobler or truly happier'.

[6] The last two sentences in the body of Vol. 2 [719].

[7] The three 1902 letters were reproduced in the preface to the second edition of Mrs Bosanquet's book [771.2], pp. vii–xii. A comparison of the versions of Marshall's two letters published by Mrs Bosanquet and the texts reproduced in Vol. 2 will reveal various further minor changes in wording which do not, however, involve substantive alterations. Interestingly, the versions of Marshall's letters published in *Memorials* (pp. 443–5) restore some of these changes, and must therefore have been based on the manuscripts, although accepting the main deletions.

776. To Ludwig Joseph Brentano, 29 September 1903[1]

29. 9. 03

My dear Brentano

You have no doubt followed the whirligig of English affairs: & I can tell you nothing much. But my own opinion, partly fortified by some little conversation with a man who has been much on the inside of politics,[2] is that Balfour will succeed in getting the majority of the conservative party to adhere to Retaliation, with special reference to 'dumping' by 'export prices'; that at the next general election the Liberals & Conservatives will be nearly equal, probably the Liberals in a majority; but that the Irish will be able to enable the Opposition, whether it be Liberal or Conservative, to pass a vote of censure: & that they will do this when it suits their purpose. Finally *the* great fight will probably be before the election resulting from that vote: unless of course a war or some other catastrophic event puts all ordinary politics into the shade. Sooner or later I fear that the 'dumping' question will be the ruin of our free trade. But I am quite sure we shall never have any considerable taxes on food: even a 5s per quarter duty on wheat is I think *most* improbable. These guesses are however very wild.

I spent my last fortnight at Stern in rewriting that Memorandum[3] of wh I told you. It was horribly confused & out of proportion: & I got it into fairly good order. But I had no rough copy of my second draft: and my letter containing it was *lost in the post*! Practically my Summer's work has been almost wasted. I shall however *perhaps* rewrite it again by aid of the original draft, expand it a little & publish it about Christmas. I am not sure at all. If I do, I will of course send you a copy.[4]

I send you back under a separate cover *Ucke*;[5] & at the same time several copies of errata in my Principles.[6] Perhaps you would kindly send two to Dr. Kestner. I do not know his address; or I would send them direct. Herr Ephraim has a copy already.[7]

I am very sad. I feel that Chamberlain (who organizes the cleverest appeals to selfish ignorance *all round*) needs to be combated by rougher &—to speak frankly—more crude and unscientific arguments & methods than I have either the taste or the faculty for.[8]

Yours very sincerely | Alfred Marshall

[1] Bundesarchiv Koblenz, Brentano Papers. From Balliol Croft. Substantially reproduced in H. W. McCready, 'Alfred Marshall and Tariff Reform' [758.1], pp. 266–7.

[2] T. Llewelyn Davies?

[3] See [754, 769.6].

[4] See [787] below for the further evolution of this project.

[5] Probably a borrowed copy of Arnold Ucke, *Die Agrarkrisis in Preussen während der zwanziger jahre dieses jahrhunderts* (Niemeyer, Halle, 1888), a Halle dissertation.

[6] Marshall had prepared an errata slip to *Principles* (*4*) in 1902. See Vol. 2 [731].

[7] Kestner [740.4] and Ephraim [740.3] were translating *Principles* (*4*) into German.

[8] On the day this letter was written Marshall also drafted a preface with an eye on publication of his Memorandum. The manuscript, preserved in the Marshall Papers, reads as follows. (The transcription published in J. C. Wood, 'Alfred Marshall and the Tariff-Reform Campaign' [754.1], pp. 493–4, is somewhat garbled.)

> I have made it a rule to avoid taking part in the discussion of a burning political question, even if it contains a large economic element. For however clearly a professional economist may distinguish in his own mind those aspects of the question on which his studies directly bear from those on wh he has no special knowledge, the distinction is apt to be ignored by partisans on either side. And if he allows himself to be drawn into the heat of the fight he may himself lose sight of the distinction. He may at last swerve a little from that straight path, in wh the student rejoices to discover & to promulgate a new truth or a new argument that tells against his own conclusion as much as one that tells on his side. He desires to influence the public. The public will not [discern] subtle distinctions, or complex reasoning. A full discussion of the economic bases of the problem will repel them; & be ineffective. He must lighten the discussion: he must ignore many difficulties. Brought into association with experienced controversialists, he is tempted to work them for their ends & to some extent by their methods. If he yields to the temptation, he may ere long begin to adjust his light & shade so as to bring to undue prominence those facts & arguments which tell for his conclusions. His

advocacy may thus become effective; but at some cost of that impartial sincerity which belongs to the student.

But every rule has its exceptions. And the political issues which are now chiefly before the public differ from all others of equal importance that have arisen in this country at all events during the last two generations in the extent to which the leaders on either side have formally accepted certain distinctly economic statements and arguments as a part—not the whole—of the basis of their positions.

The *Economic Notes* issued by the Prime Minister [Balfour] are a new precedent: I think a good precedent. No one, & least of all the academic economist, can fail to be attracted by its charm, or to concur in the greater part of its arguments. But some of them seem open to objection. Taken all together [they] do not, I think, cover the whole ground; they ignore some vital considerations. The immediate step suggested is small; & might involve no great national risk if it were certainly to be the last step. But it is on a slope which experience & reason alike seem to show is steeper & more slippery than almost any other in the whole region of economic practice. The hazard is therefore great: & the student seems therefore bound to present his own opinions on those academic points raised by the Prime Minister.

The economic utterances of the late Colonial Secretary [Chamberlain, whose resignation had been announced publicly on 17 September] and of the Reform League of wh he is President are of a different kind. The policy which he would have the country pursue may for what I know be wise. But I do not think it is. And I know that some of the economic propositions which he has laid down as a basis of his policy are invalid. Many million copies of the propositions have been circulated among people who have had no scientific training. Economists seem therefore bound to contradict these statements; & that was, so as I know anything of the matter, the real motive of a public letter which was issued by most [of] the professional economists in the country in August; but which was much misunderstood.

And there is one further point. An economist is after all a human being, & has his affections & enthusiasms like others. I have a passion for Anglo Saxon ideals. They are chiefly developed in this country & in the United States. If I had to choose either part, I would frankly prefer the former. But I believe that Englishmen have more to learn from . . .'

The manuscript breaks off at this point. This preface was replaced by a quite different one (*Official Papers*, pp. 367–8) when the Memorandum was eventually published in revised form in 1908.

777. To Herbert Somerton Foxwell, 6 October 1903[1]

6 Oct. 1903.

Dear Foxwell

I submit, after consultation with you, a draft list of books on Economics for discussion to-morrow. I have arranged those above the line on one shelf in my study, those below on a second shelf; and I have put on a third shelf those which are not in the list, but which seem to have some claim on our attention. This will I hope facilitate our work to-morrow. My own notion is that those above the line in a *science* should be such as nearly every student may be expected both to read and to buy; & that they should therefore be few[2] in number. Again, if the books above the line are numerous, those below it are apt to be regarded as added for ornament only: whereas if those above the line are less than enough for a first class man, he is likely to exercise his spontaneity in making selections from those below the [line].[3] I propose to work at the books on history to-morrow morning in a similar way: but I shall not be able to get very far with them.

Yours sincerely | Alfred Marshall

[Enclosure][4]
Draft list of books for the three papers on Economics in Part I of the new Tripos. Suggestions, which appear specially doubtful, are inclosed in brackets.

Students are expected to read (at least four of) the general treatises on Economics by Hadley, J. S. Mill, Nicholson, Pierson, Sidgwick: also Bowley, Elements of Statistics Part I; Keynes, Scope and Method of Political Economy; (Seignobos, La Méthode Historique appliquée aux Sciences Sociales): also Bagehot, Lombard Street; Bastable, International Trade; Clare, Money Market; (Conant, Banks of Issue); Dunbar, History and Theory of Banking; Goschen, Foreign Exchanges; Jevons, On Money, and Investigations in Finance: also (Emery, Stock and Produce Markets); (Hadley, Railway Transportation *or* Colson, Transports et Tarifs); Jenks, Trusts; (Greene, Corporation Finance): also Booth, Life and Labour in London Second Series—'Industry' Vol. 5; Bowley, Wages in United Kingdom; Gilman, Dividend to Labour; Jevons, State in relation to Labour; Levasseur, La Population Francaise Comparé a celle des autres Nations Vol. III: also Bastable, Public Finance.

The attention of students is further directed to the following books which may be read with advantage if time suffices; they will require to be studied, with others, for some one or more of the compulsory or alternative papers in Part II.

Turgot, Reflexions sur la nature des richesses; Adam Smith, Wealth of Nations; Ricardo, Principles; Jevons, Theory of Political Economy: also (Boehm-Bawerk, Positive Theory of Capital); (J. B. Clark, Distribution of Wealth); Mayo Smith, Economics and Statistics, Schoenberg, Handbuch der Politischen Oekonomie, Vol. I: also Attfield, English and Foreign Banks; Bastable, Commerce of Nations; Board of Trade 1903, Report on British and Foreign Trade & Industry; Bowley, Englands Foreign Trade; Clare, Foreign Exchanges; J.B. Clark, The Control of Trusts; Ellis, Market Fluctuations; Giffen, Essays in Finance, Second Series, and Stock Exchange Securities; Wells, Recent Economic Changes: also (Ashley, The adjustment of Wages;) Booth, Life & Labour in London Second Series, 'Industry', Vols 1–4; Labour Commission, Final Report; Rae, Contemporary Socialism; Smart, The Distribution of Income; Webb, Industrial Democracy: also (Adams, Public Finance).

[1] Foxwell Papers. From Balliol Croft. A typed carbon copy, with 'you' replacing the typed 'Foxwell' as the sixth word of the text. A similar letter was probably sent to Keynes. The letter pertains to the choice of economics books to be listed for Part I of the Economics Tripos. See [761, 762].
[2] Mistyped 'efw' in the original.
[3] The original reads 'list'.

[4] Typed carbon. A fuller identification of the many works mentioned is not attempted.

When the list was finally approved by the Economics Board the following changes had been made (*Reporter*, 10 November 1903.) Students were advised 'to read the general treatises by Hadley, Marshall and Pierson together with at least one of those by J. S. Mill, Nicholson and Sidgwick'. J. B. Clark, *Control of Trusts*, and A. Smith, *Wealth of Nations*, were elevated 'above the line', while Conant, Banks of Issue, was relegated below. Hadley, *Railway Transportation*, was retained above the line and Colson, *Transports et Tarifs*, was listed below. The following works disappeared: Boehm-Bawerk, Positive Theory of Capital; J. B. Clark, *Distribution of Wealth*; Bowley, *England's Foreign Trade*; Clare, *Foreign Exchanges*; Giffen, *Stock Exchange Securities*; Ashley, *The Adjustment of Wages*. The following works were added below the line: 'Howell, Labour movements; Menger, The right to the whole produce of labour (edited by Foxwell); Jevons, Coal question; Malthus, Principles of population; Conrad, Handwörterbuch der Staatswissenschaften; Palgrave, Dictionary of Political Economy; Tooke and Newmarch, History of prices'. The official reports below the line were amplified as follows: 'The Reports of the Royal Commissions on the depression of trade and industry, 1885–6, Gold and silver, 1887–8, Labour, 1892–4, Agricultural depression, 1894–7, Local taxation, 1898–1901; The current Statistical Abstracts published by the Board of Trade, and its Report on british and foreign trade and industry 1903 (Cd. 1761)'.

778. To John Neville Keynes, 10 October 1903[1]

10. 10. 03

My dear Keynes,

I think it is essential that Foxwell should have an opportunity of being present when M^c^Taggarts motion is discussed. And he lectures on Tu Th in London. Friday is barred by M^c^Taggart's lectures. I think the meeting shd be on a Monday or a Wednesday. I think also that a month's notice is not too short for so important a motion; for amendments may need careful consideration. So far as students are concerned, it practically makes no different when the matter is settled, provided notice be given to them some time in this Academic Year.

I am clear that my wishes go against M^c^Taggart's resolution, & with the spirit of your Amendment. But I am not quite sure that I understand its wording. Do you mean 'optional' as an *additional* or as an alternative subject. The two plans seem to me to work in different ways: & I prefer the latter. I have said that I should not think it right to urge the retention of P.E. in the Mo Sc Tripos against the wishes of the Mental Science element. For instance, if a resolution for omitting it were passed by the Board, I should certainly not ask the Senate to disapprove their Report. But I have also said that, *if* I vote on the Board at all about it, my vote will be for not ejecting P.E altogether.

It is not at all unlikely we may have an adjourned meeting of the Economics Board on Wednesday 21 or 28. I suggest therefore that the meeting might perhaps be called for Wednesday Nov 4; & that you should draw up a careful Amendment, perhaps in consultation with Foxwell or Sorley or both. I think you three agree on some points on wh I do not go the whole way with you; & so I w^d^.. rather be left out. But as at present advised, I expect to vote for any resolution on wh you three are agreed.

Yours very sincerely | Alfred Marshall

So many of what I regard as Chamberlains fallacies have been recently exposed, to the apparent conviction of even simple-minded men, that my anxiety is less than it was when I last spoke to you about it. So I feel free to lie low, at all events for the present.[2]

Sarah[3] thinks it was you who telephoned to this house yesterday. So I infer that the VC has told you confidentially about the Girdlers.[4]

[1] Marshall Library, J. N. Keynes Papers. From Balliol Croft. With the establishment of the Economics Tripos, the role of economics in the Moral Science and History Triposes, and their relation to the new Tripos, needed to be considered. The consideration was not long delayed. MacTaggart gave notice at a meeting of the Moral Science Board on 9 October that he would move to expel economics (hitherto a compulsory subject) from Part I. This motion, seconded by James Ward, was considered and passed 4-2 with 2 abstentions at the next meeting on 26 October. An amendment by Keynes, seconded by Foxwell, that economics remain as an alternative was defeated 4-3 with 1 abstention. After considerations of various further changes in the Tripos (including the non-controversial deletion of an economics specialization in Part II), a Report to Senate was agreed by the Board on 3 February 1904. The Senate discussion of this report occurred two weeks later. For Marshall's remarks in this discussion see Appendix I below. (Moral Science Board Minutes; *Reporter*, 9, 23 February 1904)

[2] A letter to Keynes of October 17, otherwise of little interest, added the postscript:

> We have not been able to continue our talk about Chamberlainism. As to his statements about purely economic matters we should probably agree. I am not sure whether we do as to ideals. So I venture to call your attention to the first leader of the current *Economist*: it says just what I would say, except only that it does not travel on to discuss the Anglosaxon, as distinguished from the British Empire, ideal.

Marshall Library, J. N. Keynes Papers: see 'Mr Chamberlain's Scheme', *The Economist*, 61 (10 October 1903), pp. 1710–11.

[3] Sarah Payne, the Marshalls' servant.

[4] This is the first intimation of the possibility of the new Tripos being supported by the Girdlers' Company, a London Livery Company. The current Vice Chancellor was Frederic Henry Chase (1853–1925) of Queens'. The minutes of the Cambridge University Association for 6 December 1902 had recorded in connection with 'the proposed School of Economics' that the Girdlers' Company had been approached and had agreed to receive a deputation. The Economics Board reported on 21 October 1903 receipt via the General Board of an offer from the Girdlers' Company of £100 a year for three years for 'a Readership in Economics'. Pigou was appointed to the ensuing Girdlers' Lectureship in June 1904 and the lectureship was to be extended well beyond the proposed three-year term. (See Minutes of the Economics Board and of the Cambridge Association, Cambridge University Archives.)

779. To Joseph Robson Tanner, 23 October 1903[1]

23. 10. 03

My dear Tanner

If you have heard, or should hear before our meeting on Wednesday, any proposals likely to be made as to the conditions on wh those who have taken Economics Tripos Part I may be admitted to Historical Tripos Part II, w[d].. you kindly let me know, so that I may think over them a little in advance.[2]

If I had to make a proposal myself, it would be, I think, that they should be required to take (in addition to the Essay) not less than six & not more than *eight* (instead of not less than *four* & not more than *six*) of the papers indicated in Regulation VII; subject to the condition that he may not take Political Economy. I think he nearly always would take Economic History; & I should not see any objection to compelling him to do so.

Yours ever | A.M.

[1] St John's College, Cambridge, Tanner Papers. From Balliol Croft.

[2] The recent establishment of the Economics Tripos raised the question of the relation of that subject to the Historical Tripos, just as it had in the case of the Moral Sciences Tripos (see [778.1]). At the History Board meeting on 27 October, Tanner and A. W. Ward were constituted a committee to consider the matter. Their report was approved, with amendments, at the next meeting on 24 November. Regulation VII for the History Tripos was modified to impose additional restrictions on candidates for History Part II who had completed Economics Part I. They were to take the maximum number of papers (six plus the essay), and were not to take political economy. Economic history was not excluded. (History Board Minutes, Seeley Library. See *Reporter*, 12 January 1904, for the formal report.)

780. To Joseph Robson Tanner, 25 October 1903[1]

25. 10. 03

My dear Tanner,

I think I prefer my form for the modification of VII: but I do not care very much.

On the other hand I should regard it as a great evil to turn Economics out of Part I, unless Economic History after 1485 goes with it.

You will recollect that a Resolution was carried at the Historical Board, when its present main Regulations were being drafted,[2] to the effect (I forget the words) that students should be encouraged to study economic analysis in connection with Economic History. Cunningham then said:— 'Under those circumstances, it will be impossible for me to continue to teach economic history'. I then moved that the Resolution just passed be rescinded: & it was. (Had he said that he was tired of teaching economic history, I do not think I should [have][3] moved. But that is a side issue.)

If Economics appears only in Part II: then in Part I the only part of history subsequent to 1485 wh will remain, will be just that part for the understanding of which, even in Cunninghams opinion economics is needed. That seems to me wholly illogical.[4]

My own solution wd be this. I do not pretend that modern analytical methods can be applied to medioeval phenomena by a young student without much aid from his teacher. But I object to his being taught dogmatically a tissue of statements wh are called history, but which really, in my opinion, are its antithesis, & without any opportunity of forming a judgement for himself.

Domesday Book[5] has no dogmas; it is a continued application of the analytical method: it is a noble training for the mind, & it will, I believe, gradually supersede the antagonistic view of medioeval times given by Cunningham. Even if his conclusions were as generally true, as I believe them to be generally false, the method by wh they are reached would I believe exercise a deadening effect on the mind. The whole difference is this: I believe early economic history especially on the agricultural side to be 'catastrophic' in Maitlands phrase,[6] & like the ice on the lower reaches of a glacier, not that on a pond. It is only because we are not near that the crevasses & pinnacles of wh the glacier is made seem to be smooth. Cunningham seems to me like a man who applies a crude form of spurious physical science to explain why the lower part of a glacier is stationary; & is so smooth that, if [it][7] were only level, one could skate on it nicely. His pupils look at it from a distance & say 'Oh, how smooth! What a pity it is not level!'

Consequently I suggest that there should be in Part I a single paper on economic history with Domesday Book as its backbone supplemented by Cunningham Vol I[8] & Ashley[9] (who is of course in many ways nearer to Maitland than to Cunningham): later economic history to go to Part II.

Pardon Prolixity | Yours very sincerely | Alfred Marshall

[1] St John's College, Cambridge, Tanner Papers. From Balliol Croft. See [779.2].

[2] Probably at the Board's meeting of 16 May 1896, but the episode is not distinguished in the Board's minutes. The same story was recounted to Foxwell in March 1899: see Vol. 2 [589].

[3] Word apparently omitted.

[4] Although Tanner seems to have proposed it (see [783]), there does not seem to have been a serious move to remove political economy from History Part I, despite the fact that its inclusion had been fortuitous in the first place (see Vol. 2 [518.2]).

[5] The allusion is to F. W. Maitland, *Domesday Book and Beyond* [748.2].

[6] See [748.2].

[7] Word apparently omitted.

[8] W. Cunningham, *The Growth of English Industry and Commerce* (third edition: Cambridge University Press, Cambridge, 1896–1903: 3 vols.). The first edition of 1882 had one volume and the second edition of 1890–2 had two. Vol. 1 of the third edition (essentially the same as the first edition or as Vol. 1 of the second edition) dealt with the early and middle ages.

[9] W. J. Ashley, *An Introduction to English Economic History and Theory* (Longmans, London, 1888–93: 2 vols.).

781. To Helen Dendy Bosanquet, 28 October 1903[1]

28. 10. 03

Dear Mrs Bosanquet,

Many thanks for letting me see this proof. I have found two obscure passages in my first letter. I ought to have found them before. Do not trouble to incorporate my suggestions for their amendment, if you cannot do so conveniently.

A Query on p vi is perhaps rather more important.[2] If by 'well-being' is meant *true* wellbeing & not the pleasures derived from display & sumptuous feeding, then my contention is the opposite of what the passage on p vi seems to suggest. I contend that it would be possible to provide opportunities of healthy play for all children, & to bring fresh air & light more generously into all urban homes, & in other ways to lessen the *real* evils of the poorer classes, without trenching on that expenditure of the rich which is necessary for their *true* well-being. I think this is *possible*. But I think also that the attempt to do it in a hurry would be dangerous; for, carelessly done, it might sap the springs of freedom & energy. And in that danger I see the most urgent of all the calls on the efforts of students such as you and me.

Yours very sincerely | Alfred Marshall

[1] University of Newcastle-upon-Tyne Library, Bosanquet Papers. From Balliol Croft. The portion beginning 'I contend' was reproduced in *Memorials*, pp. 445–6. See [771.2].

[2] On p. vi of the preface to the second edition of her *Strength of the People*, in introducing the reprinted letters, Mrs Bosanquet wrote 'the most important criticism is one received privately, for which I am indebted to Professor Marshall ... the question in my mind ... was whether the hardship in the life of the poor could rightly be represented as necessary to the well-being of the rich. I still think that this is not the case, but the view should not be stated in such a way as to obscure the very real economic relations which bind together the mass of the industrial community'. The passage may, of course, have been modified before publication in the light of Marshall's comment on the proof.

782. To Oscar Browning, 28 October 1903[1]

28. 10. 03

My dear Browning

When you upset my applecart for the time by an interruption, the use of wh I cannot even now guess, I was in an awkward position; I could not give the correct reply. I was arguing that the Trinity[2] as contrasted with the King's route to economics had not proved itself successful. You burst in with but Pigou studied economic history before economics. My answer was necessarily repressed: it was, 'he never came under Dr Cunninghams influence at all: he tried to listen to his lectures; but, like other able men, found them designed merely to enable the weakest of students to understand his own book, a waste of time for men who already knew how to read for themselves'. But I could not say that.

Of course Pigou owed his position as Captain of Harrow mainly to his knowledge of English history. I find that he did not come to my lectures in his first year: but before coming to them in his second year he had read my Principles through, & he adds that he had read my Economics of Industry as well as Mrs Fawcett 'some time ago'.[3]

Finally he is not a mere Historical Tripos man. For he took up economics in Mo: Sc: Tripos Part II.

From first to last the whole working of his mind has *not* been on Cunninghams lines, but on the opposite. Why then should you have insisted on interrupting me & prevented me from explaining what I had to say, wh was the outcome of much thought during the last three years (as well as before); which all told on your side, & for wh I wanted all the patience I could get from a Board several members of which have more interest in medioeval chronicles than in modern analysis?

Yours very sincerely | Alfred Marshall

Pigou has just come in. He tells me that the entry 'some time ago' on his paper means 'at school'.

[1] King's College, Cambridge, Browning Papers. From Balliol Croft. The events referred to had occurred at the History Board meeting on the previous day. See [779.2].

[2] That is, the Cunningham approach.

[3] Based on the record slip Marshall had each of his students complete. The 'Economics of Industry' would be the *Elements*. Presumably the allusion is to Millicent G. Fawcett, *Political Economy for Beginners* (Macmillan, London, 1870: eighth edition 1896).

783. To Oscar Browning, 30 October 1903[1]

30. 10. 03

My dear Browning

I think you misunderstood me. I was not traversing your remarks,[2] nor trespassing on your ground in any way. I was answering that one of Tanners suggestions which alone concerned me: viz that economics should be extruded from Part I. I was arguing that that kind of study of modern economic history which alone was possible *prior* to a study of economics was not likely to educate a race of students who would be eminent among (historical) economists; & that in fact it had not done so. Any reference I made, directly or indirectly to the Kings School was complimentary; but I was concerned only with one point viz how to arrange economic studies so as best to educate (historical) economists.

Yours sincerely | Alfred Marshall

[1] King's College, Cambridge, Browning Papers. From Balliol Croft. See [782.1].

[2] The drift of Browning's remarks has not been ascertained.

784. To Oscar Browning, 30 October 1903[1]

No 2 30. 10: 03

My dear Browning

Since posting my letter to you, I have recollected that I did make some remarks on the general position: though I believe that they were after the interruption by you wh bothered me so.

I said in effect: if you like to turn economics bodily out of the Tripos, you are of course within your rights; there is something to be said pro as well as (more) to be said contra. But the plan of keeping it in the Tripos, & forcing people to read it at a time at wh it is too late to make their study of modern economic history intelligent is *not* reasonable.[2]

Yours ever | AM.

[1] King's College, Cambridge, Browning Papers. From Balliol Croft. A postscript to [783].

[2] The History Board made no changes at this time in the roles of economics and economic history in either part of the Historical Tripos.

785. To Francis Henry Astley Manners-Sutton, 19 November 1903[1]

Dear Sir,

I deeply regret that I am unable to co-operate in the great work which the Unionist Free Food League is doing, for I have ever acted on the principle that academic economists should avoid joining leagues and should belong to no political party, unless indeed, they give themselves largely to politics, as Professor Fawcett did. I have much sympathy with those who argue that the changes of the last half-century in the economic condition of the Western world have been immense and not wholly to the advantage of this country, and that, therefore, it is right to examine the foundations of our tariff policy thoroughly and with an open mind. About 30 years ago I became convinced that a protective system, if it could be worked honestly as well as wisely, might on the whole benefit countries in a certain stage of industrial development, and that set me on the inquiry whether a free-trade policy was wholly right for England. I have pursued that inquiry ever since, and have gradually settled down to the conclusion that the changes of the last two generations have much increased the harm which would be done to England by even a moderate protective policy, and that free trade is of more vital necessity to England now than when it was first adopted.

Yours very faithfully, | Alfred Marshall

[1] Published in *The Times*, 23 November 1903, in a short article 'Fiscal Policy' announcing a public meeting to be addressed by various luminaries of free-trade bent, presumably organized by the Unionist Free Food League, of which Manners-Sutton (1869-1916) was secretary. Also reproduced in the *Economic Journal*, 13 (December 1903), p. 659. From Balliol Croft.

786. From Albert Venn Dicey, 25 November 1903[1]

All Souls College, | Oxford.
25 November 1903

My dear Marshall,

Very many thanks for your most kind letter[2] which I have just received. I can hardly say what a pleasure it was delivering the Address at Newnham & seeing so many of my friends there.[3] I am a little anxious by the way that no one should suppose that, though I spoke from a mere scheme, I had the folly or rashness to speak extempore. The address was an expansion of part of a series of Lectures, all of which I have written in the rough (& hope soon to publish) on the Relation between Law & Opinion in England during the XIXth Century,[4] & my main difficulty during the address was to drop out enough points to bring it within a reasonable compass.

I received your letter just before starting for a lecture & will consider it most carefully. I have no doubt whatever you are right in the belief that Adam Smith had, no less than Bentham, much to do with the legislation about trade combinations, but on looking at the Life of Place,[5] where the whole matter is gone into in detail, it seems to me clear that the Combination Act, 1824, was the direct work of Benthamites. The policy of it was advocated by M^c^Cullock in 1823,[6] the Act was brought forward by Joseph Hume, & it was 'dodged'—if I may use the expression—through Parliament by Place.[7] I do not suppose however that on this point you & I essentially differ. I have always assumed, perhaps hastily, that in 1825–1830. the Benthamites & the political economists might be broadly identified, at any rate in so far as accepting in the main the teaching of Adam Smith.

I am very much obliged for the reference to Mill's Political Economy.[8] Can you refer me to any other passages where Bentham, or the Benthamites, or Mill have dealt at all thoroughly with the effect of 'combined' action, or the right of association? I cannot find anything material on the matter in Herbert Spencer, but my knowledge is probably at fault. I found some year or two ago that Leslie Stephen fully agreed with me in the belief that the Utilitarians as a body had not taken much account of combined action.

I much regretted not having time to point out the curious likeness between the development of the Combination law in England & the development of the Combination law in France. This particular address will probably never be published—the substance will in some shape or other, come into my book. I am looking forward much to seeing you & Mrs Marshall on Sunday week, but my arrangements are uncertain because George Trevelyan[9] has invited me to meet members & friends of the Working Men's College,[10] & everything I do must be governed by the effort to promote the cause of the College.

Please tell Mrs Marshall that I was infinitely vexed with myself for having to ask her name. The truth is my eyes deceive me so much both positively & negatively that even when, as in this case, I feel morally sure who was the friend speaking to me, I am compelled to make certain that I am under no error and I was dazed, as well as pleased by finding so many friends about me.

Yours sincerely | A V Dicey

[1] Marshall Papers. In the hand of an amanuensis, but signed by Dicey.
[2] Not traced.

[3] Dicey had given the annual Sidgwick Memorial Lecture at Newnham College on Saturday 21 November. See *Cambridge Review*, 26 November 1903, p. 98.
[4] Dicey's classic work, *Lectures on the Relation Between Law and Public Opinion in England during the Nineteenth Century* (Macmillan, London) was to appear in 1905.
[5] Graham Wallas, *The Life of Francis Place, 1771–1854* (Longmans Green, London, 1898).
[6] See the copious bibliography of McCulloch's writings in D. P. O'Brien, *J. R. McCulloch: A Study in Classical Economics* (Allen and Unwin, London, 1970). The Combination Act 1824 repealed previous restrictions on workers' combinations.
[7] Joseph Hume (1777–1855), Scottish radical politician; Francis Place (1771– 1854), reformer and agitator.
[8] Presumably Mill's *Principles* rather than the similarly titled work by his father, James Mill.
[9] Probably George Macaulay Trevelyan (1876–1962), historian, of Trinity College, but possibly his father Sir George Otto Trevelyan (1838–1928), statesman and author.
[10] Dicey was the (part-time) Principal of the College, located in Great Ormond Street, London.

787. To Frederick Macmillan, 12 December 1903[1]

12. 12. 03

Dear M[r] MacMillan

I am thinking of bringing out a book of 200–300 pp on *National industries & international trade*. It is to be an economic monograph adapted for the general reader, supplemented by some detailed statements & some rather difficult reasonings for the serious student. These are to be in a sense *pièces justicatives*[2] for the main text, but to be printed as appendices. They will for the greater part be taken out of the M.SS. of Vol II of my *Principles*.

It is almost certain that I shall be coming to London on Wednesday afternoon. May I call on you at about 11.30 on Thursday morning? In fact any time after eleven would suit me well. In case I do not come to London, I will telegraph not later than Tuesday morning; & will write more at length on my plan. I incline to begin to print after Christmas.

Yours very truly | Alfred Marshall

Frederick MacMillan Esq

[1] British Library, Macmillan Archive. From Balliol Croft.
[2] 'justificatives' was probably intended: that is, justifying or documenting pieces.

788. From James Mavor, 16 December 1903[1]

Toronto, Dec. 16th, 1903.

Dear Professor Marshall,

I am extremely glad to know that you have come out squarely against Mr. Chamberlain.[2] I own that when I saw the pronouncement of the economists in the Times in August[3] I thought it was premature. It seemed to me that it would have been better to wait until Mr. Chamberlain had promulgated his scheme.

He has now done so and nothing remains but to fight it hard. It is really difficult to believe that any person of his experience in political affairs should have had the audacity to advance a scheme so utterly immature to say the least of it. Even from the protectionist point of view it is evidently only half considered and from an imperialist point of view his suggestion that the Colonies should practically devote themselves to the production of raw materials is too absurd for serious discussion. He seems to be playing for the support of the Colonies but he is doing it so clumsily that he can only provoke irritation.

The present position of the United States is profoundly instructive. The association of the trusts and the tariff is absolutely undoubted. It is useless for Mr. Chamberlain to instance the Thread and the Alkali trusts.[4] The first was devised by Coats' German manager to cope with the tariff-produced conditions in the United States, and the second is not so much a trust as a combination of firms to deal with a situation brought about by the introduction of new processes and the need of tiding over the period of transition. The U.S. trusts are much more formidable and are undoubtedly the offspring of the tariff. Moreover the system of U.S. finance which has developed under the shadow of the tariff and the trust is fundamentally unsound and unless it had been buttressed by heavy borrowings from Europe during the past few years it could not have endured. As it is, industry has been paralyzed by a demoralized money market. The 'bull' movement has come to an end and fortunes even quite great have during the past twelve months been simply wiped out. The result is general stagnation in industry. Workmen are being dismissed by the tens of thousands and the steamers to Europe from New York are full of returning immigrants. To some extent those who are returning are foreign workmen who have been induced to come to the United States by the prospect of high wages, and who have earned these wages during the period of brisk production of the few past years. Now with their savings in their pockets they are returning to Europe where they realize that notwithstanding the lower scale of earnings, industry is not subject to quite so wild fluctuations as it is in America, and where on their savings they may live more comfortably than they could possibly[5] do on this side of the Atlantic.

The concentration of industry in the U.S. in the hands of the great trusts has not been accompanied by the concentration of immediately available capital. The banking system of the U.S. is partly to blame for this, but the principal causes are the want of a sufficient number of men of financial ability of the order necessary to deal with suddenly inflated values, and of adequate available cash reserves. These suddenly inflated values require steady ability and vast reserves to support them, and neither the ability nor the reserves exist in a sufficiently available form. In order to remedy this to some extent it is understood that Morgan, Rockefeller and other important groups[6] have made up their minds to accumulate these reserves in cash. To accomplish this accumulation they must sacrifice their existing stocks and obtain ready money. This process has been carried on to a certain extent and it has intensified the strain in the money market and has caused the banks interested to impose a check upon the withdrawal of funds for industrial purposes. The labour difficulties which have ensued as a result of this and other movements have frightened employers, who refrain from embarking in new enterprises, and the consequence is a general condition of extreme peril. All this is of course not due exclusively to the tariff, but the plain fact is that these huge combinations live on the tariff and by means of it are able to control the market to a certain extent, to corrupt the State legislatures and municipalities and even to influence the federal legislature and executive.

It is impossible to foresee what is going to happen in the U.S. but many intelligent persons there look forward to intensified labour troubles this winter, to a great outcry against the trusts and to the most strenuous efforts to attack them through the tariff by demanding a modification of it. If Bryan[7] were not such a fantastic person, he might be able to build up a fusion party of dissatisfied Republicans and Democrats and sweep the country. Roosevelt is understood to be honestly opposed to the trust system, but nevertheless he owes his election to it, and he is moreover a protectionist. It is nevertheless possible that he may kick over the party traces and avow himself an advocate of a greatly modified protection.

Yours very sincerely | (Signed) James Mavor.

[1] University of Toronto, Thomas Fisher Library, Mavor Papers. A typed copy (not carbon) of a letter whose original has not been traced.
[2] See [785].
[3] See [768.3].
[4] These British 'trusts' were dominated by J. P. Coats and Company, and the United Alkali Company, respectively. See Francis W. Hirst, *Monopolies, Trusts and Kartels* (Dutton, New York, 1906), pp. 152–73.
[5] 'Possible' in the original
[6] The financiers John Pierpoint Morgan (1837–1913), John Davison Rockefeller (1839–1937), and their associates.
[7] William Jennings Bryan (1860–1925) of 'cross of gold' fame, unsuccessful presidential candidate 1896, 1900, 1908.

789. To Frederick William Pethick-Lawrence, 12 January 1904[1]

12. i. 04

My dear Lawrence,

I thought your article[2] extremely interesting: and in every way an improvement on Chamberlain's scheme. But I could not follow all your arguments completely.

New elements are introduced by the Colonial exemption. I think the result would be vast arbitrage operations by which nearly all British dependency securities in the hands of foreigners (especially French and Dutch) would be transferred to England in exchange for Argentine, U.S.A. and others. In so far as this was done we should not get much of the tax: the commercial interests of the empire would be knit together: but it might weaken our position in time of political friction. For at such a time it is specially convenient to us to be able to bring capital home by selling international securities. Colonials do not serve well. And further the chauvinism of certain factions of foreign nations, especially the French, is sometimes mitigated by the commercial interests of other factions; who in consequence speak out when they might otherwise have kept silent. The effect of French holdings of Kaffirs was, I believe, very important in this respect.[3] Of course if the Colonies would really bear their share of imperial military burdens, that would not matter. But in fact they only make believe.

The difference between the yield on good U.S.A. and U.K. securities is nearly £1 per £100: I do not feel sure that changing the £1 into 19s. 6d. would have a very great effect on the course of investment. I think that is governed mainly by (a) rate of average yield, and (b) confidence that the investor knows what he is about. The average Englishman is much more sure of his ground when comparing two English railways than two U.S.A. or two Canadian railways. I do not deny that sentiment influences a large number of small investors: but I do not think it influences much the great bulk of large investments.

For these reasons I should put items 3, 5 and 6 at the end of your article lower than you do. (I quite go with 4.)[4]

Coming to your letter. I do not object to taxing foreigners if we do it by a simple plan, i.e. one that is really simple, not one that merely looks so, like Charles Booth's.[5] But who are foreigners? In this whole controversy, nothing has angered me more than the action of Chamberlainites, and especially his Canadian bodyguard, in reviling the U.S.A. as 'foreigners'. The last page of the inclosed typed speech of mine indicates my views on that.[6] I am not sure that the tax would *immediately* increase employment at home, except in so far as the price of English securities is kept high by sentiment. Nothing seems to cause a sharper *temporary* bout of unemployment than the buying back by foreigners of their own securities held in England. It causes dumping, or at least semi-forced sales of foreign goods; and so temporarily disturbs the English employment market.

And I do not see how the investor in foreign securities evades English taxes: other than those which have been imposed since the goods were made, by the exportation of which he—or his predecessors in title—obtained control of the means of purchasing foreign securities. Also I fear that a firm, which sold largely in U.S.A. and was thinking of starting a branch there, might be decided by the tax to send one of the partners over there to start an independent factory. What I mean is that, if Smith and Brown decide that this foreign branch shall stand wholly in Brown's name, he obtaining a foreign domicile, the plan is defeated.

I have said all I can against your scheme: for I think you put its merits too high. And I am not prepared, as at present advised, to look with favour on *any* scheme which differentiates against our greatest colony.

I admit however that U.S.A. are no longer in great need of external capital: and that your scheme would be much less offensive and friction-making from their point of view than Chamberlain's.

Yours very sincerely, | Alfred Marshall

[1] Printed in *Memorials*, pp. 453–5. Original not traced. Presumably from Balliol Croft. Neither the original nor the preceding letter from Pethick-Lawrence has been traced.

[2] F. W. Pethick-Lawrence, 'The Taxation of Foreign Investments', *Contemporary Review*, 85 (January 1904), pp. 58–64. See *Economic Journal*, 14 (January 1904), p. 157, for a notice which reports 'An addition of 6d in the £ tax on incomes derived from foreign investments would give an impartial preference to the Colonies and encourage British industry'.

[3] Presumably in modifying French views on the Boer War.

[4] At the end of his article Pethick-Lawrence had listed six points of contrast between the implications of his own and Chamberlain's proposals. Point 3 claimed 'By my proposal the revenue would benefit by about 1 million a year' as opposed to a 2 million loss. Point 5 claimed that farmers and farm workers would be benefitted, rather than large gains going to landlords. Point 6 claimed that 'British securities would be "appreciated", British enterprise, industry and labour encouraged in all directions', whereas Chamberlain's scheme would help only a few industries at the expense of others and of consumers. Point 4 claimed that the assistance to colonies and dependencies would be uniform rather than highly selective.

[5] C. Booth, 'Fiscal Reform', *National Review*, 42 (January 1904), pp. 686–701. For a brief description of Booth's arguments for a uniform tariff, lowered for imports from Imperial sources, see *Economic Journal*, 14 (March 1904), p. 158. Booth was a prominent member of Chamberlain's Tariff Commission [756.2].

[6] See [791.2].

790. To the Committee, the Cambridge University Association, (January?) 1904[1]

Ten students in their first year, of whom two are women, have declared the intention of presenting themselves for the Tripos in Economics and associated branches of Political Science next year (1905).[2] Several others propose to take that Tripos after Part I. of some other Tripos to which they are already committed. And now, as heretofore, several students, whose main studies lie in another direction, are reading Economics systematically. Some are graduates; some come from other countries, chiefly in Central Europe and Asia; and among them there are a few of exceptional ability. There seems every reason for hoping that the Tripos will soon take a prominent place in the University, and need a large teaching staff.

My own chair is well endowed. But there is no other post in the University which is definitely associated with Economics and recent economic history, though provision for the purely historical, as distinguished from the analytical, study of the economic conditions of earlier times is made in connection with another Tripos.[3] One lecturer on Economics has a small and not necessarily permanent college stipend; and one college lecturer is giving himself mainly to

Politics in connection with the department of Economics and Politics.[4] But all the other teachers for the department are either without any public salary at all, or being connected with some other department are doing extra work for this almost gratuitously.[5] There is therefore an urgent need for about £2000 a year, of which half might be used as salaries for four Readers or Lecturers attached to the department, while the other half might be distributed among those who are working partly for this and partly for other departments. A further £1500 a year will perhaps be needed later on to make the staff fairly complete for teaching purposes.

Economics is however a subject in which the chief occupation of an academic teacher ought to be the study of those new problems, and new versions of old problems, which are ever making their appearance, at home and abroad, and especially in the outlying parts of the Empire. For instance, in a central British University there ought to be a trained economist whose whole energies are devoted to the great and various economic problems of the Continent of India. An ideal equipment for Economics and associated branches of Political Science in a great national University would therefore demand a staff of from fifteen to twenty teachers. Each of them should occasionally lecture over a rather wide range of subjects: for extreme specialization is much to be deprecated in Economics. But his thoughts as a teacher should be mainly given to matters which occupy him as a student. This ideal equipment should be kept in view; though at present nothing more can be expected than that Cambridge should in this department contribute a small quota to the sum total of the new work that is being done in the world.

No lecture room is assigned to the department at present. It needs two at least at once. Perhaps they would cost a capital sum of £500.

The department needs a small handy library for ordinary students. But the requirements of an advanced student would be met by bringing together into one room in the University Library those books which specially belong to the economic department. He would need to consult frequently books belonging to other departments; and an adequate special provision for his needs would require a duplication of a considerable part of the Library. It is however deeply to be regretted that the University could not afford to buy Professor Foxwell's unique collection of rare economic books with which the liberality of the Goldsmiths' Company has endowed the University of London.[6]

[1] From pp. 8–9 of a printed pamphlet issued by the Cambridge University Association. This pamphlet of 24 pages revised and updated the Association's earlier *Statement of Needs* (on which see Vol. 2 [587]). A copy, bound with other Association pamphlets, is in the Rare Book Room, Cambridge University Library (Cam b 899.17). The Association's minutes for 3 February 1904 (Cambridge University Archives) record that the revised statement of needs was nearly complete: hence the tentative dating of Marshall's contribution, which seems to have been sent in his own capacity rather than on behalf of the Economics Board. However, the lack of reference to the support promised by the Girdlers' Company [778.4] may suggest an earlier composition date.

[2] The numbers actually completing Part I successfully in the years 1905–8 were: 1905 (5 men, 5 women); 1906 (4 men, 1 woman), 1907 (6 men, 2 women); 1908 (7 men, 1 woman). For Part II, first offered in 1906, the numbers were 1906 (2 men, 1 woman); 1907 (4 men, 1 woman); 1908 (5 men, 4 women).

[3] Cunningham?

[4] Foxwell and Dickinson?

[5] The following lectured under the auspices of the Economic Board for 1903–4. Marshall, Foxwell, Dickinson, Pigou, Macgregor, Oldham (economic geography), Thornely (politics), Johnson (mathematical economics), Green (elementary economics), Headlam (general history), Archbold (later economic history), and Head (general history). For 1904–5, Benians and Meredith joined the list, while Headlam dropped off. See *Reporter*, 10 October 1903, 8 October 1904. (All individuals mentioned are listed in the Biographic Register.)

[6] See Vol. 2 [625.2].

791. From Arthur Twining Hadley, 7 March 1904[1]

March 7th, 1904

My dear Mr. Marshall:—

I was delighted to get the typewritten copy of your remarks before the Institute of Bankers.[2] There is no question at all that you are right. How to get at the matter is a more difficult problem. The whole system of representative government has taken such a shape that it causes the real or supposed interests of the several parts to be preferred to the collective interests of the whole. When parliaments or congresses were deliberative bodies for the formation of public opinion this evil was not very seriously felt. But since this function has been taken out of their hands by newspaper conventions and other agencies, they have become mere means for registering local demands. In Great Britain itself you are protected from the worst abuses of this practice by a code of Parliamentary ethics which, though indefinite, is in certain ways very powerful, and makes a member follow his own judgement as to what is to the interest of the country in preference to the judgement of those who elected him for what is to their own interest. (This is an awkward sentence, but I suspect the meaning is clear enough.) In the United States we are worse off in this respect than in England, and most of the colonies are worse off than in the United States. I really think that most of the evil in tariff laws results from this political difficulty, rather than from divergence of economic ideals. I only wish that I saw how we were to get at the root of it.

Pray remember me most kindly to Mrs. Marshall, and believe me

Faithfully yours | [A. T. Hadley]

[1] Yale University, Sterling Library, Hadley Papers. From an unsigned carbon copy.

[2] The typescript, with an unsigned compliments slip from Marshall, is preserved in the Hadley Papers. The text was printed in the discussion of E. J. Schuster, 'Foreign Trade and the Money Market', *Journal of the Institute of Bankers*, 25 (February 1904), pp. 58–83, followed by discussion pp. 83–122: see pp. 94–8 where Marshall expands 'On the theme that the maintenance of Free Trade is essential to the position of Great Britain' (*Memorials*, p. 506). A summary of Marshall's

speech is given in the *Economic Journal*, 14 (March 1904), p. 109, ending in his plea 'our true ideal is to be found not in little Anglo-Saxondom but in great Anglo-Saxondom'.

792. To Alfred William Flux, 19 March 1904 (incomplete)[1]

19. iii. 04

My dear Flux,

I was just settling down to a belated letter of thanks to you for your generous and strong aid on pp. 281–3 of the current *Quarterly Journal of Economics*;[2] and for your article in the *Canadian Bankers' Magazine*,[3] when your letter of the 8th arrived.

I am very glad that you are coming to England and that you will be here at the British Association meeting.[4] We have asked Dr and Mrs Pierson to stay with us for that. I hope you will get put up somewhere in our neighbourhood so that we may see you during the meeting, and that you will be able to look in on us in June. We have taken lodgings in Norfolk for July and the first half of August.

Thank you *very much* for your most kind offer to read the proof of my new book.[5] . . . The first half, which is only half written, is on the causes and nature of Industrial Leadership treated historically as well as analytically. The second is on International Trade; while at the end is to come an application of the basis thus provided to current issues. The second part is to be as scientific as is compatible with an attempt to catch the general reader; but free use is to be made of appendices throughout. I am going to be a little venturesome in it: and shall be most grateful for your kindly help.

In the last part I am going to give a little freedom to my *sentiment*, as distinguished from my reason; and to speak as a citizen rather than specially as an economist. There also I shall be grateful for help. But sentiment is like a butterfly; no amount of friendly discipline will make him go by a rational bee-line.

Our best regards to Mrs Flux.

Yours very sincerely, | Alfred Marshall

[1] Printed in *Memorials*, pp. 407–8. Original not traced. From Balliol Croft.

[2] A. W. Flux, 'The Variation of Productive Forces: Further Comment', *Quarterly Journal of Economics*, 18 (February 1904), pp. 280–6. Here Flux defends Marshall on diminishing returns from criticisms levelled in that journal by Charles J. Bullock, 'The Variation of Productive Forces', vol. 16 (August 1902), pp. 473–513.

[3] 'The Journal of the Canadian Banker's Association (Vol XI., No. 2) has an article on the condition of British industry by Professor Flux. The writer contends that no case exists for a preferential tariff policy on the ground that British trade and commerce must otherwise decline': *Economic Journal*, 14 (June 1904), p. 337.

[4] The British Association was to meet in Cambridge 17–24 August. Flux was scheduled to deliver a paper on 'the relation between improvements in agriculture and economic rent'. See *Economic*

Journal, 14 (June 1904), p. 331, where the presence of 'a galaxy of foreign experts including Professor Bauer, Professor Hasbach, Dr. Körösi, Professor Mahaim, Dr. Pierson, M. Yves Guyot' was forecast. The reports of the meeting in *The Times* (17 August (6a), 20 (8a, 12a), 23 (4a), 24 (8a), 25 (4a), 27 (2e)) indicate that Lotz, Dietzel, Mavor, and Mandello were also among attendees from abroad, but that Hasbach may have withdrawn: also that Dietzel's paper was read 'in his absence' by Professor Arndt of Frankfurt (20 August (8e)). The President of Section F was William Smart. József Körösi (1844–1906) and Gyula Mandello (1868–1919) were Hungarian statisticians: Paul Arndt (1870–1942) was a German economist specializing in monetary questions.

[5] See [787].

793. To Henry Hardinge Cunynghame, 7 April 1904 (incomplete)[1]

7. iv. 04

My dear Cunynghame,

I am glad indeed that you are writing a book on curves. . . . I do not know on what lines you are writing, nor whether the history of those MSS.[2] would be in any way relevant. But I would like you to have its outline in your hand, in case you should wish to use any part thereof.

In 1874–7 I nearly completed the MSS. of a book on Foreign Trade.[3] What I then regarded—though I do not do so now—as a fairly realistic treatment of the problem, adapted for the use of business men and other non-academics, was the text. Then followed appendices, consisting of the foreign trade curves; and also the other class of curves in order to get at consumers' surplus (a) in open market, (b) in monopoly sales: where I wanted to get in some hyperbolas drawn by a certain machine you know of.[4] I wanted these, because I found all methods of representing the 'total benefit' of foreign trade by their special curves very troublesome. Also I wanted to get out in print those hyperbolas, etc. And lastly, in the appendices, I developed or tried to develop the abstract notion of international trade between employers' associations and trade unions.[5]

Consequently the Appendix had no realism about it: all that seemed in any way real was put into the first part, which was to be in bigger print.

The first chapter was 'philosophical', on the abstract idea of an economic nation. Then came the chapters on foreign trade which Sidgwick printed (you know I was very ill and consented to his printing some chapters for private circulation, but left the selection to him); then came a chapter applying those curves to the incidence of import and export duties and bounties. He did not print that: I wish he had. It was quite finished. Some of the others were not.

But my case II, that of increasing returns, never seemed to me of much practical use; and in later years I warned people off it, on the ground that, if time was allowed for the development of economies of production on a large scale, time ought also to be allowed for the general increase of demand.

And now, in recent years, I have gradually gone away from the fundamental hypothesis on which the curves are based. They lead to the result that a great part of an import duty will probably fall on the export nation: and I have become convinced that, though the reasons which the old free-traders gave for the opinion that import duties are paid almost entirely by the consumer are wrong, yet their result is pretty well true. And on inquiry I found I had fallen into a trap. I had followed Mill in taking a yard of cloth as *representative* of England's exports and Germany's imports: which I still think is right. But then I had glided, as he had done, unconsciously into regarding the demand for imports in general as having a similar character to that for a single commodity. And I now think that is illegitimate, and vitiates a great part of my curves. My old chapter on the incidence of import duties is at least as slashing as Edgeworth's articles. But I do not believe his conclusions, nor those of Seligman, whom the Birmingham League and Ashley quote with such reverence.[6] I have never said anything about the subject of this page in print as yet. But I hope soon to explain what are, in my opinion, the conditions which govern the incidence of import duties. My Volume II could not be got ready in tolerable time. So I have decided to bring out an intermediate book. . . .

This is long. But I do not apologise. For it takes us back to those queer rooms with the litle windows close to the floor, from which I used to look out on noble elms, and in which I used to see some faces that I still love very much: and to one of these this is sent by a worn-out old pedagogue

Alfred Marshall

[1] Published in *Memorials*, pp. 448–50. Original not traced. From Balliol Croft.

[2] Marshall's privately printed 'Pure Theory of Foreign Trade: Pure Theory of Domestic Values' of 1879. See *Early Economic Writings*, vol. 2, pp. 129–66, 186–236.

[3] See *Early Economic Writings*, vol. 1, pp. 57–66.

[4] The machine invented by Cunynghame for Marshall in the early 1870s. See *Guillebaud*, pp. 7–8.

[5] The surviving portions of the text and appendices, together with the appendices printed by Sidgwick (see note 2), are reproduced in *Early Economic Writings*, vol. 2, pp. 3–236.

[6] Edgeworth's main articles on international trade are collected in his *Papers Relating to Political Economy* (Macmillan, London, 1925: 3 vols.). The allusion to Seligman is presumably to his *On the Shifting and Incidence of Taxation* (revised edition, Macmillan, New York, 1899: for the first edition see Vol. 2 [443.2]).

794. To Ludwig Joseph Brentano, 6 May 1904[1]

6. 5. 04

Dear Brentano,

You will receive by this or the next post an official invitation to attend the meeting of the British Association which will be held this year in Cambridge August 17–23.[2] I do hope very much you will come. And for once I do wish our little house were not quite so small. For we have just asked D[r] and Mrs Pierson to stay with us; & they will occupy our only double room. We have only a bachelors room free. But should you be able to come, & should you come en garçon, it would give my wife and me the *very greatest* pleasure to receive you. I do not know whether you have met Pierson: he is, I think a most charming man, & very much after your heart. Mrs Pierson[3] also is pleasant.

I hear that Professor Hasbach has been asked, but no other German. I have selected Lexis, whom I do not know, but who seems to me a very strong man. I was rather drawn to Dietzel whom I have found exceptionally instructive on the fiscal question. But I did not like to go so far at present.[4]

Yours very sincerely | Alfred Marshall

[1] Bundesarchiv Koblenz, Brentano Papers. From Balliol Croft.

[2] See [792.4].

[3] Pierson had married Catharina Rutgera Waller in 1862.

[4] See [801], below.

795. To Thomas Coglan Horsfall, 13 May 1904[1]

13. 5. 04

Dear Mr Horsfall,

I am unable to turn away from my belated book to read anything else. So I can only send you my thanks & good wishes. You seem to me to be doing noble work: & both the books wh you send me[2] must I am sure be productive of great good.

I rejoice in p 155 of '*The example*':[3] for that shows that you are not as uncompromising an advocate of broad streets where the workmen live under the dominating influence of the rich, as I once feared, and as I might have gathered from something I noticed in turning over the pages of this book—I can't put my hand on the page just now. I am increasingly convinced that in this respect the German plan has evils so great as to go far to outweigh all its other excellencies. In fact I am not sure that I would not rather have the English plan as a whole than the unmixed broad streets cutting up the ground into quadrangles some 100 or 150 yards square; beautiful without, but whited sepulchres, where the joy that should belong to the young is stifled in odious propriety. I cannot tell you how much I deplore the great influence which you are exerting in this most mischievous direction, as I regard it. On every other subject, I think, I agree with what you say, & am most grateful for the excellent services you are rendering to the nation.

Yours sincerely | Alfred Marshall

[1] Manchester Central Library, Horsfall Papers. From Balliol Croft. Horsfall was to read a paper on the development of towns to Section F at the British Association meeting in Cambridge in August. See also Vol. 2 [606, 635].

[2] T. C. Horsfall, *The Improvement of the Dwellings and Surroundings of the People: The Example of Germany* (Manchester University Press, Manchester, 1904: A Supplement to the Report of the Manchester and Salford Citizens' Association for the Improvement of the Unwholesome Dwellings and Surroundings of the People). There is no obvious candidate for the other book sent by Horsfall.

[3] p. 155 of *The Example* was part of a compilation of quotes from a German pamphlet on town planning: Herman Josef Stuebben, *Die Bedeutung der Bauordnungen und Bebauungsplaene fuer das Wohnungswesen* (Vanderhoeck und Ruprecht, Göttingen, 1902). 'While a well-considered net of broad streets for traffic must be provided for ... care must also be taken to provide narrower trafficless streets, and thus to promote the building of the more desirable small dwelling house ... [also] an adequate supply of light and air in the interior of the blocks of building....'

796. To Ludwig Joseph Brentano, 16 May 1904[1]

16. 5. 04

My dear Brentano

I am very grieved indeed that you cannot come.[2] But I cannot blame you. I should not be present myself, if I were free to be away. For I think that when people have things to write which they cannot get out the tongue should yield precedence to the pen. But all the more because I know how very busy you are, am I most grateful to you for sparing time to care for the translation of my poor book. I am most heartily grateful to you.

And yet I am ashamed to look you in the face, even by post. For I feel certain you sent me some copies of a German newspaper with articles by yourself; &, if so, I have certainly put them away carefully somewhere. But where? I have three times, since your last letter came in, gone over every place in my study where they could possibly be. But I cannot find them. I can only find *Die Zeit* for 11 June & 9 July and Deutschland with the article on *Getreide Zölle als Mittel gegen Not der Landwirthe*.[3] Of these the last seems to me much the most suitable for English readers at *this* stage. They have heard about their own Corn Laws so much from their own writers that I expect Editors might think they w^{d}.. not care to hear more. But the broad outlook of the Deutschland article, with its skilful blending of English and German problems, is just what I should like, if I were an Editor. Perhaps you were thinking of selecting the most appropriate parts of this, and working them up with others from other articles. If so I think the result might be even better.

I am certain that the Editors of the Independent Review would be very proud to receive an article from you. But I have no connection with the Review. I am merely on rather intimate terms with Dickinson, who is a member of the Editorial Committee. I expect that in this matter it is best for you to write direct. But if you think there would be any advantage in showing this *Deutschland* article, with perhaps some others to Dickinson, & suggesting that—if the Editors approve the notion— they should approach you on it, I should be *most* happy to do so.

Yours very sincerely | Alfred Marshall

I am very glad that Prof Lotz is coming. I am trying to get him & his wife put up near me. He will be a great bulwark & will I suppose be able to present your views together with his own.[4]

[1] Bundesarchiv Koblenz, Brentano Papers. From Balliol Croft.
[2] To the meeting of the British Association: see [792.4, 794]. Brentano's letter has not been traced.
[3] This was also published as a pamphlet (Schwetschke, Berlin, 1903). The other items have not been traced. Brentano does not appear to have published an article in the British monthlies or quarterlies, but did eventually produce, under the Cobden Club's aegis, his *Political Economy and Fiscal Policy* (Cassell, London, 1910), a discussion of tariff issues.
[4] Lotz was a colleague, previously a student, of Brentano.

797. To Frederick Macmillan, 25 May 1904[1]

25. 5. 04

Dear Mr. MacMillan,

I am afraid it was rather under false pretences that I induced you to arrange with the printers for keeping my type up till the whole of my MSS was in their hands. I then estimated its length at about 300 pp., & hoped I might possibly get it out in June, though I felt there was truth in your remark, as you looked over the proposed contents, that it was a large undertaking for so short a time.

Since then the situation has changed a good deal. Several books have appeared setting out the principles of international trade with reference to current issues. Also it is now clear that Mr. Chamberlain has not captured any considerable section of the working classes, & that the critical fight over his programme, if ever there is one at all, will not take place during 1904.

Two or three of the books which have been written seem to me admirable *pieces d'occasion*; &, between them, they perhaps rather glut the market for that kind of book. But on the other hand, there is I think a growing demand for a careful study on rather broader lines than theirs. And as time does not press, I propose to try to write one.

I have been drifting to this conclusion gradually, being indeed partly pushed to it by the increasing difficulty of writing quickly what I want to say. About 150 pages are already in type or with the printer: & the remainder of Part I (which is on the characteristics of the leading industries of different countries) will occupy at least 50 more pages. I now think the book may run to 400, or possibly 450 pages. I am resolutely giving to it every moment of time which is in my own command. But the British Association, alas! is coming to Cambridge this summer, & so I shall have less time than usual for undisturbed writing. And, though I will try to get the book ready by October, I do not feel at all sure of doing so. If I miss October I shall probably have to run on till January.

What then must be done about the type? I told you that I should want to refer forwards in the text to supplementary passages in the appendices. It would have been rather convenient to name the specific pages. But I find that references in more general terms will suffice. And anyhow this matter is of small importance to me in comparison with freedom to go at my own pace.

So perhaps it would be best to fix a certain number of pages, as large as you consider reasonable, which I may have in type simultaneously. And then as soon as I approach that number, I will print off the early chapters so as to liberate type. On this plan I should be inclined to print rather slowly during the early summer.

I shall be grateful for any suggestion you may have to make.

Yours very truly | Alfred Marshall

[1] British Library, Macmillan Archive. From Balliol Croft. Typewritten with corrections by hand. See [787].

798. To Alfred William Flux, 26 May 1904 (incomplete)[1]

26. v. 04

My dear Flux,

... I have been drawn in for an unusual amount of festivities much against my will. I have not attended a big dinner for ten years, and hoped I might never have to do so again. But I have to be responsible for Leroy Beaulieu, who arrives tomorrow;[2] and so must go to three! straight on end. ... Towards the end of June, I have to go to Oxford.[3] Then from 17 to 23 August this house is to be a sort of Hotel with at least one Dependance, for British Association foreign guests— Pierson, Lotz and Dietzel, and probably some others.[4] So I shall not have the repose of the blessed, which the would-be cautious writer so craves.

Consequently I don't know what is to happen to my book. I have got about 150 pp. in type; and I have made special arrangements for having it all set up before I read it. Now, however, it is certain that the book will not be out till the autumn and probably not till later. For the course of events has lessened the demand for short books—there are already several good ones out; and the Tariff Issue will probably not get to a head within the next six or twelve months. Also I find that the further I go the slower I go. Just at present I am getting out of the industrial problems of Germany into those of U.S.A. That will bring my Part I to 200 pp. or more. Only after that shall I begin International Trade, and severe analysis. ...

Yours very sincerely, | Alfred Marshall.

[1] Printed in *Memorials*, pp. 408–9. Original not traced. From Balliol Croft.

[2] Paul Leroy Beaulieu, together with several other distinguished participants in the triennial meeting of the International Association of Academies, was to be awarded the honorary degree of Doctor of Letters by Cambridge University at a ceremony on Saturday 28 May. The meeting, held in London, 25–30 May, had divided itself between Oxford and Cambridge for the weekend. See *The Times*, 24 May (6a), 27 (8c), 28 (8d), 30 (10d), especially the last.

[3] Marshall was awarded an Honorary D.Sc. at the Oxford Encaenia, 22 June 1904.

[4] See [792.4].

799. To Henry Hardinge Cunynghame, 28 June 1904 (incomplete)[1]

28. vi. 04

My dear Cunynghame,

Your kind and generous letter[2] makes me all the more regret that I have not been able as yet to read your article in the September number of the *Econ. Journal.*[3] Just now I am inquiring how much of the progress of U.S. industries, which is popularly attributed to the Law of Increasing Returns, is really due to it. I can't answer the question: but I am sure there is a large error in the common estimate....

I believe that we differ a little as to the function of curves. I like to keep them as simple as possible, and to fill in qualifications and limitations *in the text.* I recollect that this was the reason of my not following you in the use of successive cost curves.[4] Human nature varies: and I know some people find your method simpler than mine. (I may be wrong, but I think the majority do not.) And it is a very great gain that things should be treated from two points of view.

If there could be imagined an improvement in your discussion, it would perhaps be that you should indicate that such qualifications as you put into your diagrams are only samples of a great many others which might be introduced. If they were all introduced, the diagrams would be a mass of curves; and I prefer to keep all that I can out of the diagrams. I have hinted this in my note on them in my *Principles*, p. 524.[5]...

As to International Trade curves:—Mine were set to a definite tune, that called by Mill. It is improbable that I shall ever publish them: but I am not certain.[6] I am rather tired of them.

I find that it takes a long time to get men to understand the theory: though, when they do, they are proud of it, and are rather contemptuous of any one who undertakes to teach them without understanding it. There is no subject on which I lecture so many times to the same men from different points of view. One of these is that which I understand you are following. I set a question as to the immediate and ultimate effects of an import duty on some thing (named in the question); and, in answering it myself, I often follow what I call 'the practical man's route.' I talk of prices throughout, and work up to generalities; and thus get a good *part* of the science of International Trade as a side issue to a special problem. I say 'a *part*': for much that is most interesting from my point of view cannot, I think, be conveniently reached by this route.

But I always find that the best men are relieved when I go over the ground again, starting with aggregates and subordinating details. My experiences on this matter are so numerous that I think it is impossible I can ever be convinced that your method is *the* method.

But I am sure it is *a* method: and I am *most heartily* glad that a man of your very high constructive force is tackling it: it will be a great boon to all students, here and elsewhere. For indeed there is no subject, I think, on which English thought has led the way so consistently as this.

I have promised Macmillan to keep the text of the book I am writing (not the *appendices*) in a form as attractive as I can to the practical man: and I shall probably go *much* more nearly on the price-of-particular-commodities line than in lecturing to an advanced class: but I do not yet know *how* much more.

Of course I shall not touch a curve of any kind in the text....

I doubt whether I should be able to add usefully to the long letter I have now inflicted on you, if I saw your MSS.[7] For I *do* want my time. But I will try if you wish it.

Yours affectionately, | Alfred Marshall

[1] Printed in *Memorials*, pp. 450–2. Original not traced. From Balliol Croft.
[2] Not traced.
[3] H. H. Cunynghame, 'The Effect of Export and Import Duties on Price and Production Examined by the Graphic Method', *Economic Journal*, 13 (September 1903), pp. 313–23. This article popularized the now-familiar back-to-back diagram for the partial equilibrium analysis of the market for an internationally traded commodity.
[4] SeeVol. 2 [406, 8], for Marshall's early and much less temperate reaction to Cunynghame's successive cost curves.
[5] The cited footnote on p. 524 of *Principles* (*4*) appears on p. 463 of *Principles* (*8*).
[6] They were eventually to appear in 1923 in appendix J of *Money Credit and Commerce*.
[7] Presumably of Cunynghame's forthcoming book, *Geometrical Political Economy* (Clarendon, Oxford, 1904).

800. To Johan Gustav Knut Wicksell, 26 July 1904[1]

26. 7. 04

Dear Professor Wicksell,

I have not been reading anything about interest lately. I have not read Prof Cassels book, nor Prof Bohm Bawerk's recent criticisms on myself,[2] nor indeed some of your own work wh I have noted as likely to be specially instructive.

I think it is probable I am in considerable agreement with Prof Cassel. For a student, who had come to Cambridge with the opinion that the founders of Economics of all nations were inferior in common sense to most children of ten, & very much inferior to his worthy self, gave Prof Bohm Bawerk as his authority. I replied, 'I do not think Prof Bohm Bawerk has caught their real meaning. I regard personal controversies as great waste of time; but if you will select any one of the great writers as a test case, I will give a lecture on his doctrines of interest'. It happened that several other members of the class were present at the conversation, & the notion was approved & they selected Turgot. I therefore did—what I had not done before—compared Turgots words with Prof Bohm Bawerks account of them; I made full notes for the lecture. I read out alternately passages from Turgot & from Prof Bohm Bawerks account of Turgot.[3] I then gave Turgot & Prof Bohm Bawerks book to the class & asked them to pass the books from hand to hand, adding 'a fortnight hence, I will ask the question in lecture—have I done justice to Prof Bohm Bawerks treatment of Turgot'. The answer was yes! I forget details: but I think I found not only that the opinions which Prof Bohm Bawerk had read into some of Turgots passages, were not really there; but also that in other sections to which discussions on these matters more properly belonged, Turgot had expressed categorically the exact opposite of the opinions attributed to him. I have lent the notes of this lecture to several persons, and I may have lent them to Prof Cassel; though I do not recollect whether I did or not. No one who has read the notes has questioned the conclusion to which they point.

I am very busy. But my profound respect for you has made me write fully on a subject of which I am very weary.

Yours sincerely | Alfred Marshall

[1] Lund University Library, Wicksell Papers. From Balliol Croft. Reproduced in Torsten Gårdlund, *The Life of Knut Wicksell* (Almqvist and Wicksell, Stockholm, 1958), pp. 339–40. Wicksell's previous letter has not been traced. For background see P. D. Groenewegen, 'Turgot's Place in the History of Economic Thought: A Bicentenary Estimate', *History of Political Economy*, 15 (Winter 1983), pp. 585–616, especially pp. 610–15. Also see [733].

[2] In attacking Böhm-Bawerk's treatment of Turgot, Cassel had acknowledged 'suggestive remarks' on the matter from Marshall. (*Nature and Necessity*, [733.3], p. 22 n.) This probably accounts for Wicksell's approaching Marshall. The criticisms of Marshall had been levied in the second edition of E. von Böhm-Bawerk, *Geschichte und Kritik der Kapitalzins-Theorien* (Wagner, Innsbruck, 1901). In the substantially unchanged fourth edition (Fischer, Jena, 1921) see especially pp. x–xx (the introduction to the second edition) and pp. 482–96. The fourth edition is translated as *Capital and Interest Volume I: History and Critique of Interest Theories* (Libertarian Press, South Holland, Illinois, 1951): see especially pp. 378–93 and 436–43. A much earlier translation of the appendix on recent literature, added by Böhm Bawerk to the second edition of his *Geschichte* appeared as *Recent Literature on Interest* (Macmillan, London, 1903): see especially pp. 21–48.

[3] A. R. J. Turgot, *Réflexions* [762.7]. Böhm-Bawerk's criticisms of Turgot date from the first edition of his *Geschichte* (Wagner, Innsbruck, 1884), translated as *Capital and Interest* (Macmillan, London, 1890).

801. To John Neville Keynes, 8 August 1904[1]

Church Farm | Upper Sheringham
8. 8. 04

My dear Keynes

Thank you very much for your letter,[2] & all that you have done.

I should be very glad that an honorary degree should be conferred on Giffen, or on Edgeworth. Giffens later work seems to me less careful than his earlier. But he has done good service & has earned national gratitude. I should regard it as an excellent thing to do to honour him. And to honour Edgeworth would I think be as good a thing to do, perhaps even a little better. Booth being already provided for, there is I think no English economist whose claims are equal to theirs.

I know Bauer a little; I like him in a way. He is industrious & careful: but I do not think he holds any very high position among German economists.

Schmoller was to have given an address at St Louis:[3] but he had to withdraw, family causes, I think, prevented him from travelling. Wagner would I believe not come; & his ferocity against England w[d] make an invitation not very appropriate just now. Putting them aside I think Lexis is distinctly the ablest & strongest German Economist: indeed as an all round man, I think he stands first in the world. After consulting the Com[ee] of Section F, I moved Seward[4] to invite him to the Association. But he did not answer. If he had accepted, I had intended to write to you to ask you to move for a degree for him. He is a decided protectionist, I believe. But he writes on all matters gravely & carefully: he is not a politician, as Wagner & even Schmoller are now to some extent. I do not know him personally.

Next to him, I think come, in the opinion of Germans generally, Conrad, & perhaps after him the two Anglophils Brentano & Cohn. Both have been asked to come. Cohn has not answered. Brentano cannot come.

All these have long lives behind them. Lotz & Dietzel seem to me as able as any of them, & to have more interesting minds than almost any of them. The prominant position which Lotz takes at the meetings of the Social Verein, shows I think that he is thought by Germans worthy of a place in the first rank.

Yours very sincerely | Alfred Marshall

We stay here till Tuesday week. I am writing away from my stock of paper & am short of supplies.[5]

[1] Marshall Library, J. N. Keynes Papers. Concerning nominations for honorary degrees. The occasion and outcome are unclear. No degree ceremony seems to have accompanied the British Association meeting in Cambridge of 17–23 August, on which see [792.4, 794].

[2] Not traced.

[3] At the Congress of Arts and Sciences Universal Exposition, 1904. Wagner had also declined, but Conrad attended the Congress.

[4] Albert Charles Seward (1863–1941), botanist, a Fellow of Emmanuel, formerly of St John's, was one of the Local Secretaries for the Cambridge meeting.

[5] One sheet of the letter had been torn in half.

802. From Johan Gustav Knut Wicksell, 10 August 1904[1]

Linero, Lund, 10. VIII. 04

Dear Professor Marshall

I thank you very much for your kind letter.[2]—I have read over and over again the passages in Turgot quoted by Böhm-Bawerk as well as all those who seem to have any bearing whatever on the subject, but I cannot possibly convince myself that B.B. has misstated Turgots meaning, though as usual he may have failed in making as it were a little too much of it.

It cannot be denied, I think, that for Turgot the buying of a piece of land is a real investment of capital of the same kind as if capital is really sunk in some (agricultural, industrial or commercial) enterprise and that the possibility of making the firstnamed 'investment' regulates the rate of interest in the others (which all of course is radically false). And he *seems* to believe that the saleprice of a piece of land is determined in an *independent* way by the play of supply and demand so as to give by comparison with the rent of the land in question a real determination or explanation of the height of interest. It is true that Turgot in a later paragraph shows that he knows very well that the saleprice of land is determined itself by the rate of interest but this gives not, as far as I can see any clue to his true meaning; if he had stated this at once he would never have been able to reason as he does in the paragraphs quoted by Böhm.—In his later treatise: *Mémoire sur les prêts d'argent*[3] Turgot speaks with somewhat more caution, but even there he occasionally falls back on the possibility of investing capital in buying land as regulating the rate of interest.

As you are busy I by no means pretend to have any answer on this but if you possibly could let me have your notes on the subject it would interest me very much and I should return them as soon as possible.

Yours respectfully | K. Wicksell

[1] Lund University Library, Wicksell Papers. From a handwritten copy presumably retained by Wicksell. Reproduced in T. Gårdlund, *The Life* [800.1], pp. 340–1.

[2] See [800].

[3] A. R. J. Turgot, 'Mémoire sur les Prêts d'Argent', in G. Schelle (ed.), *Œuvres de Turgot* (Alcan, Paris, 1913–23), vol. 3, pp. 154–202; partly translated as 'Extracts from "Paper on Lending at Interest" (1770)' in P. D. Groenewegen (ed.), *The Economics of A. R. J. Turgot* (Nijhoff, The Hague, 1977), pp. 149–63.

803. To Johan Gustav Knut Wicksell, 26 August 1904[1]

26. 8. 04

Dear Professor Wicksell,

The British Association has just finished its meeting at Cambridge.[2] We had an unprecedented—for England—concourse of economists; & the week was most pleasant, though most fatiguing.

I seize the first free moment to answer your very considerate letter. I will be frank. I have decided not to answer, probably not even to read Prof Bohm-Bawerk's criticisms on myself. I am therefore debarred from any indirect attack upon him. If I had time for personalities I should respond to his frontal attack by a frontal movement of defence. As it is I prefer to lie low, & to take without reply any chastisement he may inflict on me. But while lying low, I do not wish to shoot at him *en enfilade*. It is possible I may be *compelled* to break silence: but hope not.

Now I fear that if I send you my notes I may be drawn on gradually to waste—from my point of view—much time in arguing a point which has little or no interest to me; &, at the same time, to seem to be attacking Prof Bohm Bawerk indirectly. If you strongly desire to see my notes, & will promise me that you will not in *any way* bring me into the controversy, I will send them.

I have just looked at them again, but without comparing them with the originals; & I have not read Prof Cassel. But the general effect left on my mind is to confirm my previous opinion that Turgot's doctrine, rightly interpreted, is a monument of genius & falls very little short of the best that is known today about interest.

Yours sincerely | Alfred Marshall

[1] Lund University Library, Wicksell Papers. From Balliol Croft. Reproduced in T. Gårdlund, *The Life* [800.1], pp. 341–2. See [800, 802].
[2] See [792.4].

804. To Claude William Guillebaud, 28 September 1904 (incomplete)[1]

28. 9. 04

My dear Claude

People who don't know how to select a wedding present, commonly go to a silversmith and ask his advice: and he generally recommends an inkstand. So some friends of ours who had many well-to-do friends, but not much money for their own house received as wedding presents, among other things, twenty four silver inkstands!

Now I am sure you have received *condolences* enough to enable you to dispose of them retail two or three a piece to each of your schoolfellows, who may happen to have fallen into a ditch, or the masters ill favour or any other misfortune, & would like to be soothed by a little soft-cream-lotion. So I shall try another plan.

I beg leave to *congratulate* you heartily on not having blown your head off, & on not having lost both your eyes. They say no one really wants two eyes for most purposes, & that a second one is given to him in order that he may run some risks, & yet be able to have one eye left to take care of him, & of which he may take care.

And I congratulate you very heartily on the courage and patience & level-headedness which you have shown throughout. These qualities are worth much more than one eye, perhaps than two.

In all this I am very serious: but I will congratulate you on yet another matter not perhaps quite seriously. You are now able, if you can only find the proper comrades to take part in playing again the following practical joke:—

Three friends went for a walking tour. It happened that. . . .

[1] Marshall Papers. From Balliol Croft. Only one folded sheet survives. Marshall's 14-year-old nephew (see Vol. 1, App. I) had recently lost an eye, thumb, and finger, from an explosion while attempting to make gunpowder.

805. To Harold Ernest Guillebaud, 3 October 1904[1]

3. x. 04

My dear Harold,

I am glad you are in the Sixth. Just for the present you must I suppose be content to live as a parasite of Greeks and Romans. But do not overdo it.

Do not overstrain your health; and do not shut your mind to broader and harder matters of thought than Classics suggest.

Recollect that two boys out of three, who show exceptional ability at public schools in England, are pushed into classical studies on narrower lines than prevail in Germany, or indeed anywhere save in England. And recollect that in after life the large majority of these boys are passed by numbers of others, who probably had less natural ability and certainly had less careful education. Recollect that, even in literature, the best strength is generally shown by people who at school did not narrow their thoughts mainly to classics.

I speak with deep feeling. From six to seventeen years of age I studied practically nothing but classics. I then obtained a place in the school which entitled me to a 'close' probationary classical fellowship at Oxford. (These things are abolished now.)[2] I spent the next five years mainly on mathematics and the next three mainly on philosophy. I have forgotten my mathematics and philosophy as well as my classics: but I am intensely grateful to them. And I am not very grateful to my classics.

For of course the *Knowledge* gained by them is of no great use to anybody. They are the most invigorating studies of which boys are capable up to the age of (say) fourteen: and there are some, though not many *ideas and ideals*, which older boys and men more easily assimilate, perhaps, if presented in Greek surroundings than if associated with modern problems. But, on the whole, the mental vigour of the chief adult men of the world has been trained chiefly in work that uses bigger muscles of the mind than those which are chiefly exercised by classics.

Do then your classics, but recollect that by a mere study of them your faculties—be they great or small—are much less likely to be made as strong, and as serviceable to your generation, as they would be if you passed on from them to work in which you would be standing on your own feet, and not merely carried by men who were great, *because they studied the problems of* THEIR OWN AGE. The Alexandrines were classical scholars: the great Greek genius was educated in direct work at real difficulties.

Your very affectionate | Alfred Marshall

Give my love to Claude[3] when you see him.

[1] Printed in *Memorials*, pp. 494–5. Original not traced. From Balliol Croft. Marshall's 16-year-old nephew was at this time a schoolboy at Marlborough. His uncle's advice did not prevent him from taking the Classical Tripos at Cambridge. See Vol. 1, App. I.

[2] See *Memorials*, pp. 2–12, for a more balanced account of Marshall's schooling.

[3] Harold's younger brother. See [804.1].

806. To the Council, St John's College, Cambridge, October 19 1904[1]

[1. Does this paper shew originality?][2]
My knowledge of the literature relating to the subject of this essay is not sufficient to enable me to judge the originality of Mr Benians in matters of detail. But the treatment as a whole bears strong marks of individuality; and its main ideas are thought out coherently on lines not resembling those of any history of Canada which I happen to have seen. My impression thus is that the essay shows a very considerable originality of that kind, which alone can be expected in work which is mainly occupied with the narration and coordination of facts.

[2. Does it give promise of higher work to follow? 3. What is your opinion as to its merits in general?]
In answering these questions I think the Council would wish me to take account of the conditions under which it was written, for indeed its weak points are of a kind to render any judgement as to the promise shown by it of little value, unless something is known of the time at the disposal of the writer, and of his freedom of action. The scope of the essay is sufficient to occupy a large part of the life of an able man; and is far too broad for a hurried essay. The essay shows frequent marks of haste. The style is very uneven, in some cases it is careful and strong; in some it is very loose. In some parts the facts have been digested; their essence has been collected, and superfluous details weeded out. In others the accessible facts relating to a subject have been brought together, and set out in clear order; but for the greater part they are allowed to remain mere facts (sometimes they are not even very important facts) little time having apparently been given to reconsidering them in relation to one another and re-writing the account of them so as to convert it into a living history. These faults however lose most of their significance when it is known that M^r.. Benians had less than a year to give to the work from first to last; and that indeed it is rather the first draft of a part of a large study, which he has been asked to undertake, than a self-contained piece of literature. For the Board of Economics and Politics in making out the list of books which it recommended to students, found that there were no satisfactory books relating to English colonies, and that therefore the students would be very dependent on lectures. The subject was generally recognized as important; and there was no one available for lecturing on it, who had made a special study of it. So M^r.. Benians was asked to prepare lectures on this subject (as well as on the history of India, for which there are good books).[3] Thus he had no choice as to his lines of work; he was compelled to make them too broad for the time at his disposal: and the haste and inequality of his treatment are not to be taken as signs of weakness or want of resolution.

Under these circumstances the essay seems to me to give very high promise of better work to follow. I think that if he turns several years to as good account as he has the last year in the study of colonial history, he will probably produce a book which will give him a high reputation and confer some lustre on the University. And the vast amount of work which he has put into his essay, seems to me, considering all the circumstances, to indicate that he has the zeal of a true student.

[4. Are there any points in connexion with the subject on which it is desirable to examine the candidate further?]
No.

19/10/04 (signed) Alfred Marshall.

[1] St John's College, Cambridge, College Archives. From a copy in another hand, probably a College clerk's. The report, on a printed form, gives Marshall's assessment of an essay by Ernest Alfred Benians on 'Economic Development of Canada to 1841'. Benians, an intending Fellowship candidate, who had obtained firsts in both parts of the Historical Triposes, 1901–2, held a Lightfoot Scholarship, 1903–6, and an Allen Scholarship (worth £250) in 1905. In 1906 he won the Adam Smith Prize and was elected a Fellow of St John's. For Marshall's subsequent reports on the progress of Benians's work in 1905 and 1906, see [829, 859] below.

[2] This and other interpolated questions stood at the head of the College's printed form and were referred to by number in Marshall's answers.

[3] Benians was down to lecture in the Lent and Easter Terms of 1905 on 'Economic and General History of the English Colonies and Dependencies' under the auspices of the Special Board for Economics and Politics. The course was due to be repeated in 1907. In Michaelmas Term 1906 Benians also lectured on 'Economic and General History of the United States'. See *Reporter*, 8 October 1904, 10 October 1906.

807. To Sydney John Chapman, 29 October 1904[1]

29. x. 04

My dear Chapman,

I am proud of your two books.[2] So far as I can see, your *Cotton Industry* is the best monograph of the kind that has ever been published. It is both a realistic-impressionist study of human life, and an economic treatise.

Work and Wages I have not yet seen much of. But I shall use it a great deal during the next few months. It fits in with my own work. I think the combination of Lord Brassey's knowledge of the inside of big affairs—a knowledge the lack of which at first hand has hampered me always and hampers me still—and his strong solid judgment combined with the faculties and mental elasticity which you have developed make a splendid team.

I have bought duplicates of them and taken them to the bookcase in L.L.R. 5: and at the same time Cunynghame's *Geometrical Political Economy*.[3]

I am awfully proud of the three Cambridge products.

I bragged indeed and said I thought that there were few Universities which could show as good a series as our Adam Smith Prize lot. First Bowley's which got him the Silver Medal of the Statistical Society at (I believe) an unprecedently early age, next Lawrence's *Local Variations of Wages*, next yours; and there is one good one still to come, that of Pigou on Arbitration and Conciliation, nearly ready for the Press.[4]

So I *am* proud of the 'Cambridge Stables'; and I think the quantity and quality of the work you have got through is wonderful. Our best regards to you and Mrs Chapman.[5]

Yours affectionately, | Alfred Marshall

You may be amused by this photograph of our house party (Edgeworth had gone), Sarah working the bulb.[6]

[1] Published in *Memorials*, pp. 455–6. Original not traced. From Balliol Croft.

[2] S. J. Chapman, *The Lancashire Cotton Industry: A Study in Economic Development* (Manchester University Press, Manchester, 1904); *Work and Wages in Continuation of Lord Brassey's 'Work and Wages' and 'Foreign Work and English Wages' with an Introduction by Lord Brassey* (Longmans, London, 1904–14: 3 vols.). Only Part I (1904) on Foreign Competition was available at this time, Parts II and III appearing in 1908 and 1914. For Brassey see [747.10].

[3] See [799.7]. L[iterary] L[ecture] R[ooms] 5, Marshall's usual lecture room, held a collection of economics books for use by students.

[4] The four had won the triennial Adam Smith Prize for the following essays: Bowley, 'Wages in the United Kingdom' (1894); [Pethick-]Lawrence, 'Local Variations in Wages in the United Kingdom' (1897); Chapman, 'Forms of Production and Distribution in the Cotton Industry' (1900); Pigou, 'A Study in the Principles and Methods of Industrial Peace' (1903). Bowley's prize essay was the basis for his 'great' paper to the Royal Statistical Society (see Vol. 2 [595.2]), which earned him the Guy Silver Medal in 1895, and was expanded in his *Wages in the United Kingdom* [752.4] of 1900. The essays by Lawrence and Pigou appeared in monograph form as: F. W. [Pethick-]Lawrence, *Local Variations of Wages* (Longmans Green, London, 1899); A. C. Pigou, *Industrial Peace* (Macmillan, London, 1905).

[5] Chapman had married Mabel Gwendoline Mordey in 1903.

[6] At the August meeting of the British Association in Cambridge: see [792.4]. Sarah is Sarah Payne.

808. From Frederic William Maitland, 6 November 1904[1]

Downing
6 Novr. 1904.

My dear Marshall,

As regards law in the Economics Tripos,[2] I do not want to revive overruled objections and I wish to suggest what will satisfy you. I should like to know therefore what you think of some such formula as the following to which Westlake and I tended yesterday afternoon.

'Candidates are required to study the principles of English, French and German law relating to contract in general and also to study more particularly the English, French and German law relating to (1) the sale of goods, (2) partnership, (3) bills of exchange'.

Our (1) (2) (3) are chosen *partly* because at these three points English law has been recently codified.

As you know, I forsee great difficulties. I think that the inclusion of foreign law to be read in foreign books, though highly desirable, will deter almost all candidates, and that if now and again one wishes to take up this subject, it will be worth no one's while to learn enough to teach him or even to examine him.

I believe that you would have done better to accept at least *pro tem.* what some of our law lectures could have provided: viz English contract and English tort. But I am not going to raise that point again, and I now only want to know whether the formula stated above would in a general way meet your wishes—for Westlake and I are proposing to make some inquiry in France and elsewhere about the best books.

Believe me | Yours very truly | F. W. Maitland.

[1] Cambridge University Library, Maitland Papers. Possibly a copy retained by Maitland. Reproduced in C. H. S. Fifoot (ed.), *The Letters of Frederic William Maitland* (Harvard University Press, Cambridge, 1965), pp. 318–9.

[2] Part II of the new Economics Tripos provided for four optional papers on law: International Law with reference to existing political conditions; International Law with reference to existing economic conditions; Principles of Law as applied to economic questions (two papers). No details had been proposed by the Syndicate. See *Reporter*, 10 March 1903; also Vol. 2 [726.1].

809. To Frederic William Maitland, 8 November 1904[1]

8. xi. 04

My dear Maitland,

Probably 'Company Law' is technically more serious than I know.[2] But I thought I had avoided the term. I want phrases to be as broad as possible. The Law relating to Joint Stock Cos., which I am most interested in just now, is proposed by J. B. Clark of Columbia.[3] Its main purpose is to *defeat* practices such as those from which the Mogul Co. suffered, and one of its main means is to *allow* railway poolings, federations and similar 'Northern Securities' practices.[4] I am not sure that I agree with this. I rather think I do not. But I am sure that economists of the next generation will have to consider questions of this sort very carefully: and that, if they do not know more law than I do, though I have read a good many law books and a great many appeal cases, they will be in a weak position. That is why, as I have so often said, I want them, while still plastic, to be taught how to read law books; though I do not want them to become lawyers in any sense of the term.

I knew of course that the Mogul case had nothing to do with Company Law. But I think that the XXth century will need much Company legislation which pivots around the same fiduciary relations of directors of Joint Stock Cos. (and especially of such of them as would be called Trusts in America, on the ground that they exercise a predominating—not necessarily monopolistic—influence in certain branches of trade) towards the public. The economists' complaint against the law generally is that it cares too exclusively for the shareholders, customers and creditors of the Joint Stock Cos.; and neglects the quasi-fiduciary obligations of the company and its directors to other classes.

I don't want you to pay attention to any detail, right or wrong, in this suggestion; but simply to go for as broad phrases as you can. In particular it would be a good thing if monopolies could be included—partly because the question of national, and even more of international, patent rights is growing rapidly in urgency. But even now I should like, if it were possible, though I fear it may not be, to include the general question of the basis and limitations of the right of a private business to the privilege of secrecy, when its dimensions become so large as to give it a semi-public character. That is the kernel of most of the legal questions which interest myself—and I believe other economists—to-day. What will be the kernel twenty years hence, I have not the smallest notion.

Yours very sincerely, | Alfred Marshall

1 Published in *Memorials*, pp. 452–3. Original not traced. From Balliol Croft.

2 Marshall had replied immediately to [808], in an untraced letter suggesting more coverage of corporate law. Maitland's 7 November reply (reproduced in Fifoot [808.1], p. 408) had expressed doubts about such a proposal in terms of the complexity and unsettled state of the subject, observing 'I doubt whether many of the questions about companies which you would like young economists to study really fall within the range of what we call "company law"—e.g. (this is only an example) the Mogul case had no company law in it'.

3 J. B. Clark, *The Control of Trusts* (Macmillan, New York, 1901), ch. 4.

4 For brief descriptions of the cases of Mogul Steamship Co. v. McGregor Gow and Co. (1892) and United States v. Northern Securities Co. et al. (1903–4) see F. W. Hirst, *Monopolies, Trusts and Kartels* [788.4], pp. 99–100, 60–3, respectively. The Northern Securities case was an important test of the Sherman Act of 1890.

810. To Frederick Macmillan, 16 November 1904[1]

16. 11. 04

Dear Mr MacMillan,

I send herewith the M.S.S. of a book by Mr A. C. Pigou on Industrial Conciliation & Arbitration. It obtained the Adam Smith Essay Prize here in 1903, and has since then been in a great measure rewritten.[2] On inquiry, I found that he was thinking of offering it to a publishing house which has not a very large connection among economists, & suggested that he should offer it to you. As he seemed bashful, I undertook to introduce him.

Mr Pigou is, I think, the ablest economist of his age (about 27) in England, & perhaps anywhere. I have no doubt that he will be among the leading economists of the coming generation; and I should like him to be connected from the first with the chief Publishers of economic books.[3]

I of course read the essay carefully in 1903; but such criticisms as I made on it were from the point of view of the economic student rather than the general public. If you should see your way to accept it, he would I am sure receive with gratitude any suggestions that your consummate judgement may offer for improving it from the publishers' point of view. The full table of contents will enable you to see its drift at once.

Mr. Pigou has written several articles in Quarterly and Monthly Magazines & elsewhere; and a pamphlet—*The Riddle of the Tariff* (Brimley Johnson)[4]—which has had considerable vogue.

Yours very truly | Alfred Marshall

[1] British Library, Macmillan Archive. From Balliol Croft. The postscript attached to [814] below may have been attached to the present letter as it consists of a separate sheet and there are no stylistic differences.

[2] See [807.4].

[3] Pigou's book was accepted and appeared in 1905 as *Principles and Methods of Industrial Peace.* Thus began an extensive and long-continued, but not exclusive, connection between author and publisher.

[4] Published in 1903 in London.

811. To the Editor, *The Daily Chronicle*, 23 November 1904[1]

I have no hesitation in giving an appreciative answer to your question whether a national memorial should be raised to Herbert Spencer. His attempt to lay down the outlines of a unified sociology was, in my opinion, premature by at least 100 years. He spread his strength over too wide an area; and his fame has suffered from many attacks, not always based on a generous interpretation of his words, by specialists, each of whom was more at home in his chosen ground than Spencer could be. And, again, his fame has suffered because his general remarks as to the principles of evolution dealt with conceptions which were themselves in process of rapid evolution; and the younger students of today are often inclined to find little that is both new and true in a saying of him which had sent the blood rushing through the veins of those who a generation ago looked eagerly for each volume of his as it issued from the press. There is probably no one who gave as strong a stimulus to the thoughts of the younger Cambridge graduates thirty years or forty years ago as he. He opened out a new world of promise; he set men on high enterprise in many diverse directions; and though he may have regulated English intellectual work less than Mill did, I believe he did much more towards increasing its vitality. He has, perhaps, been more largely read and exercised a greater influence on the Continent than any other recent English thinker except Darwin.[2]

I think he would have wished that any memorial raised to him should not be a statue, but some addition to the beauty or the extent of a public recreation ground. Of course, it might include a medallion portrait of him.

[1] Published with other responses in the *Daily Chronicle*, 23 November 1904, without address or date. The Dean of Westminster having refused to allow in the Abbey a memorial tablet to Herbert Spencer, the newspaper had solicited 'opinions of eminent scientists and others' on the possibility of an alternative memorial.

[2] The allusions are to John Stuart Mill and Charles Darwin.

812. To Joseph Robson Tanner, 7 December 1904[1]

7. 12. 04

My dear Tanner,

Làl tells me that he has not spoken to you about his chance of a Fellowship at St.. Johns; & that he is shy about it. He wants me to lead up to his conversation. I stopped him yesterday to tell him—as I might not see him between the publication of the Cobden Essay award[2] & his departure from Cambridge—I would break etiquette so far as to tell him that his essay was an excellent one, & would certainly have got the prize if it had been alone.

I will tell you further that the other two examiners, Nicholson and D. A. Thomas (MP for Welsh coal)[3] think Làls distinctly superior to Macgregor's. I do not: for though Macgregor has thrown out several immature suggestions, & his Essay was so hurriedly put together as to be very faulty in arrangement, its 420! typed pages contain an extraordinary amount of original thought. So I should give him the prize & Specially Commend Làl. As it is the Prize will be given to Làl, with commendation to Macgregor; or else divided.[4]

Làls essay is not remarkable for originality. But as a well studied compact (132 typed pages) account of the present position of the Trust question, it is a masterpiece of composition. Nicholson, who is a first rate judge of literary form, is enthusiastic about its English.

I thought very highly of Làl when I tried to get a Fellowship for him at another college:[5] but I now think much more highly. I should like him to lecture in England a little before he goes to India, if he does go there, to settle down. But I do not feel I have got inside him completely, in spite of his very great intellectual force and openness of mind.

I think *every* lecturer to honour men ought to be a doctor: ie that no one should be put on to lecture at all who had not written a doctor's thesis. But as the University in its haste has ordered men to be examined by their chums at the age of 40 or thereabouts I think the old lady may be congratulated on her latest achievement.[6]

Yours ever | Alfred Marshall

[1] St John's College, Cambridge, Tanner Papers. From Balliol Croft.

[2] See [752.11] for the topic chosen by the candidates and the final outcome.

[3] David Alfred Thomas (1858–1918), Member of Parliament for Merthyr Boroughs 1888–1910 and for Cardiff 1910–16, subsequently created Viscount Rhondda. A colliery manager and director, BA 1880 (Caius), he had been nominated as examiner by the Cobden Club.

[4] This paragraph was overwritten in red ink 'Strictly confidential'. Unusually large numerals were used in writing '420'.

[5] No record of this approach has been traced.

[6] Cambridge doctorates (other than honorary ones) recognized established scholarly reputation rather than the completion of scholarly training. Tanner was to be awarded the degree of D.Litt. in 1905.

813. To Johan Gustav Knut Wicksell, 19 December 1904[1]

19. 12. 04

Dear Professor Wicksell

I did not mean that I was quite ignorant of what Prof Boehm Bawerk has said about me.[2] My pupils occasionally bring me passages of his, & we have our little laugh at the way in which, after having misinterpreted my great masters, he misunderstands my humble self. This does not make me angry: for indeed he has always been very courteous to me, & has treated me far more generously than my masters. My only feeling of anger rises out of this:—While he was still at school, I learnt from the men whom he reviles everything which he has vaunted as a great discovery: and especially in America, he has been taken at his own valuation by people *who have never studied the great men* on whose burial places he dances his war dance. If then he accuses me of discounting backwards & reckoning interest forwards *over the same period of time* on the same economic goods (or sacrifices), why should I concern myself. A boy in a village school who made such a blunder in his arithmetic would be punished:[3] and he knows I am a trained mathematician. If he were really earnest in his desire to know what I mean, he would turn to my mathematical notes. He would find in my Note XIII a complete solution of his mystery; which simply arises out of his neglecting the 'starting point', shown by the limits to the integral.[4] He simply runs together and confuses a discussion in which the limits to the integral have reference to a starting point *prior* to the events in question, with another in which the starting point is *posterior*. England is going to the bad, because we English economists have not time and strength enough to deal with the real problems of our age. How could I be right in wasting my time by controversy about such paltry personalities. One of my pupils, now a lecturer, proposed to write an answer to him. But I said 'No,—you have more important things to do at present'. But perhaps he may later on.[5]

I send you my notes *for your own use exclusively*. I have not read them through since I wrote them six years ago. My edition of Turgot is that by Daire. A D 1844.[6]

I *never* go to the British Association. But in 1904 it came to Cambridge: and of course I acted as one of the hosts. In 1905 it is to meet in South Africa. If in any later year you should wish to take part in it, & will let me know some time before hand, I shall be proud to move the Committee of the Economic Section to send you an invitation. They are always pleased to welcome a distinguished foreigner, particularly if he speaks English well as you do.

Yours sincerely | but wearily | Alfred Marshall

[1] Lund University Library, Wicksell Papers. From Balliol Croft. Reproduced in T. Gårdlund, *The Life* [800.1], pp. 342–3. Presumably a reply to an untraced letter from Wicksell subsequent to [802].

[2] See [800.2].

[3] This echoes an annotation Marshall had made on pp. 36–9 of his copy of Böhm-Bawerk's *Recent Literature* [800.2] (copy in the Marshall Library):

> He seems not to catch the point that when a man pays a premium of £100 a year from 1860 to 1880 in order to get an annuity of say £300 from 1880 till the probable end of his life in 1895, the equation may be worked out from a basis in 1860, in wh case both premia and annuity will be discounted; or from a basis in 1880, in wh case the premia will be accumulated & the annuities discounted. He ought to know that a mathematician and the experts of the first rank who read his notes in proof cannot have made a mistake for which a schoolboy of 12 would be punished.

[4] Note XIII of *Principles* (*4*) corresponds to the same Note in *Principles* (*8*), apart from the alteration noted in [817.2] below. For Böhm-Bawerk's criticisms on this point see pp. 490–1 of the fourth edition of his *Geschichte* or pp. 386–8 of the 1951 translation [800.2].

[5] One can only guess at the identity of the pupil (Pigou?) as the issue does not seem to have been pursued in print.

[6] Eugène Daire and Hyppolite Dussard (eds.), *Œuvres de Turgot* (Guillaumin, Paris, 1844). Marshall's notes have not been traced.

814. To Frederick Macmillan, 20 December 1904[1]

20. 12. 04

Dear Mr MacMillan

Another of my pupils, Mr Manohar Làl, wants to bring out a book. He is one of a group of natives of India who have competed with Englishmen under great disadvantages, and have achieved success. He was alone in the first class of Part II of the Moral Sciences Tripos in 1903: he was bracketed first with another for the International Law Scholarship (Whewell Studentship) a week or two ago; and the essay on Trusts which he is now sending to St Martin's Street[2] has just been awarded the Cobden Prize against strong competition.[3]

I do not think he is of the same intellectual rank with Pigou: and if he had adhered to his intention of offering his essay to the Publishers of one of the current series of economic books, I should not have tried to turn him. Indeed I have just written him a letter[4] to be used for that purpose. But he now says he would prefer to offer the book to you, if you would accept it; and he is sending that letter to you. It is not a testimonial, but states frankly what I think to be the weak as well as the strong points of the essay.

It is not the work of a great constructive thinker: but it has almost every other virtue. It will I think be for the time, the most useful book on its subject; and will certainly do no discredit to the high fame of the chief publishers of English economic books.[5]

Manohar Làl has developed recently very fast. He will, I hope, settle down to a study of the economic possibilities of India; and as this great subject has never yet been handled by a trained economist, I have hopes that he will do good work for the empire, and leave his mark on history. He is to leave for India in a few weeks. Trusting that his case will receive your kind consideration

I am yours sincerely | Alfred Marshall

P.S. | My own book makes slow progress. Events move fast. The more obvious things are being repeated in periodical literature so frequently that much, which would have seemed fresh a year ago, would be stale now. Thus delay causes delay; for it makes me inclined to lay more and more stress on industrial conditions which underlie the fiscal issue of the day.

Thus I am giving a couple of months or so more than I had intended to do to the question, 'How far is it true that large industrial aggregations (Trusts, Cartels &c) in a country are a source of strength to her and of menace to her neighbours?'

I wish I could write faster: but my limited strength is heavily drained for the work of others, especially in connection with the new Tripos; & the nature of the task, wh I have set myself, demands much care & deliberation.

[1] British Library, Macmillan Archive. From Balliol Croft. See [810.1] concerning the date of the postscript.

[2] The location of Macmillan's office.

[3] See [752.11]. Làl was actually bracketed equal with two other candidates in the award of Whewell Scholarships for International Law.

[4] Not traced.

[5] Làl's book does not appear to have found a publisher.

815. From Johan Gustav Knut Wicksell, 6 January 1905[1]

Lund 6. 1. 05

Dear Professor Marshall

I beg to thank you very much for your kind letter and also for the notes which I have read with keen interest.[2]—I also have read once more the passages concerning you in B.-B.'s 1st volume (2d ed.)[3] and have been confirmed in my opinion that there really is nothing in them. He seems to be labouring under a sort of quaternio terminorum. He regards 'undervaluation of future commodities' and 'sacrifice of waiting' as something which could be *added together*, whereas indeed they are only different expressions for the very same thing.

On the other hand I think you are wrong in questioning (Principles 4th ed. p. 667n.)[4] the generality of his doctrine that 'every lengthening of a roundabout process is accompanied by a further increase of the technical result' by which of course he only means, that it always will be possible by *some* lengthening of the process to increase the result etc. Unless the process in question is of a quite discontinuous character this must be regarded as an obvious truth,[5] and it no doubt covers the whole field of the interest question from the productive or demand side, as admirably shown by B.B. himself in the last part of his 'positive theory'[6] which I for my part always have regarded as his main contribution to the theory of capital.

And I cannot help thinking that you somewhat overrate the earlier writers on interest, especially Turgot. Of course there are many *glimpses* of truth in Turgot but hardly a worked up theory. It cannot be denied, I think, that he regards the capital or money used in buying land as so much capital sunk or destroyed, and he totally oversees the fact that this capital in the hand of the seller of land is as much available for the purposes of production, as it was in the hand of the buyer. See f.i. his § 87 'Je suppose que tout à coup un très grand nombre de propriétaires de terres veuillent les vendre' &c. In the following § (88) he no doubt states the true relation between interest and the price of land,[7] and this remark would have been most valuable if standing in the beginning in stead of in the very end of his investigation, but if so the whole of it would at once have been seen to move in a circle. I take it, that in the rent of land he thought to have the fix archimedical point for determining the rate of interest, which he somewhat missed in the 'other uses' of capital, but in this opinion he of course was mistaken. This at any rate is my present view of the subject, I would not defend B.B. here, if I did not think that he is substantially in the right.—

Moreover the theory of capital and interest cannot be regarded as complete yet. As I have tried to show several times and of late in a review of Clark's and Hobson's books in Conrad's Jahrbücher (III F. Bd 26)[8] so long as capital is defined as a *sum of commodities* (or of value) the doctrine of the marginal productivity of capital as determining the rate of interest is never quite true and often not true at all—it is true individually but not in respect of the whole capital of society.

I think it would be a very great benefit if the main features of economic theory could be as it were agreed on and settled by the scientific world. I am convinced that thereby even the solution of the practical questions would be forwarded in the very best way.

Great many thanks for your kind promise to introduce me sometime to the British Association—I fear I shall not be able to go to Boulewayo next year. The notes are hereby returned with thanks.

Yours respectfully and thankfully | Knut Wicksell

[1] Lund University Library, Wicksell Papers. From a copy retained by Wicksell. Reproduced in T. Gårdlund, *The Life* [800.1], pp. 343–5. The original appears to have had an unrecorded postscript: see [817].

[2] See [813].

[3] See [800.2]. B.B. is Böhm-Bawerk, of course.

[4] This footnote in *Principles* (*4*) is substantially the same as one in *Principles* (*8*), pp. 583–4n. But several rewordings go unrecorded in *Guillebaud*.

[5] Apparently written as 'thruth' by Wicksell, who also seems to have written 'technical' as 'thecnical', 'thought' as 'thougt', and 'British' as 'Britic'.

[6] Eugen von Böhm-Bawerk, *Positive Theorie des Kapitales* (Wagner, Innsbruck, 1889: second edition 1902). Translated as *The Positive Theory of Capital* (Macmillan, London, 1891).

[7] These references correspond to ss. 88, 89 of the 1898 translation of Turgot's *Réflexions* [762.7], as also of the new translation included in P. D. Groenewegen, *The Economics* [802.3].

[8] K. Wicksell, 'Neue Beitrage zur Theorie der Verteilung', *Jahrbücher für Nationalökonomie*, third series, 26 (December 1903), pp. 817–24. A review of J. B. Clark, *The Distribution of Wealth* [736.3] and J. A. Hobson, *The Economics of Distribution* (Macmillan, New York, 1900).

816. To Joseph Robson Tanner, 27 January 1905[1]

27. 1. 05

My dear Tanner

My position was only half-hatched when we separated. And the half that was out of the shell was not quite representative. I hold that people who avoid Cambridge, because others are not compelled to study Greek, are like the man that migrated from a Slave State on the ground that a new law had deprived people of the freedom to wallop their own niggers.[2] I think he would not benefit by any education. But I think also that the notorious fact that many people know little more when they take high honours in the Classical Tripos than they did when they left school shows that that Tripos is not an element of strength to Cambridge. Oxford Greats[3] have their faults: but anyhow they are not a mere school-boy examination.

If we show that we recognize the modern age has higher responsibilities to meet than those for which medioeval education was arranged, I believe that we shall soon so far out run Oxford in the esteem of all broad minded & capable men that Oxford will, as is her wont, follow quickly in our wake.

Yours ever | A M

[1] St John's College, Cambridge, Tanner Papers. From Balliol Croft.

[2] A proposal to make Greek optional in the Previous Examination (or 'Little Go') became a source of intense national debate in 1904–5. For the Syndicate's proposal see *Reporter*, 17 December 1904. The final vote, taken in November 1905, resoundingly defeated the proposal mainly because of non-resident opposition, the resident MAs being evenly divided. For background see Sheldon Rothblatt, *The Revolution of the Dons* (Basic, New York, 1968), pp. 252–4. Marshall appears to be countering a suggestion that making Greek optional would repel some who might otherwise attend Cambridge.

[3] The Honour School of Literae Humaniores, Oxford's most prestigious course of study.

817. To Johan Gustav Knut Wicksell, 30 January 1905[1]

30. 1. 05

Very many thanks for your letter, & for the P.S. about my page 797.[2] I think the least confusing way of putting it is

$$V = \int_0^{T'} \tilde{\omega} R^t \frac{dv}{dt}\, dt.$$

In all probability I wrote it in this way at first & then inverted the limits, & forgot to complete the change by altering the sign of t. I am constantly coming to grief through only half carrying out the inversion of a mode of statement. Again many thanks.

I have been giving a great deal of time during recent years to a detailed study of American improvements in manufacturing technique. Many of the best of them consist of the substitution of 'direct' for roundabout processes. I regard round-about-ness as itself an obstacle to efficiency, and not as a cause of it.[3]

Yours ever | A.M.

[1] Lund University Library, Wicksell Papers. From Balliol Croft.

[2] See [815]. The postscript appears to have been omitted from Wicksell's copy of that letter. The reference is to the analysis of an investment project in Note XIII of the Appendix of Mathematical Notes in *Principles* (*4*), at the point where Marshall switches from discounting efforts backwards to the beginning of construction to the alternative of compounding them forward to the end of construction (which now becomes the time origin). The integral had been written with upper and lower limits 0 and $-T'$ (T' being the length of the construction period) so that R^{-t} should have replaced R^t. The change Marshall proposes was made in all subsequent editions of *Principles* (it is not recorded in *Guillebaud*). It implicitly changes the variable of integration from t to $-t$.

[3] Whatever its merits, this argument hardly bears on Böhm-Bawerk's position as it confounds shifts in technology with adaptations to capital accumulation given existing technology.

818. To the Editor, *The Times*, 7 February 1905[1]

Sir—You have justly observed that the discussion on compulsory Greek is stretching out towards broader issues than those in which it had its origin. May I speak to one of these?

The Headmaster of Uppingham recently said in your columns that the instruction in Latin and Greek gives 'education', but that instruction in 'science' is a 'mere imparting of knowledge'.[2] I wish to inquire whether studies can be arranged in any order of merit absolutely and without reference to the age and other conditions of the individual. I submit that those studies are best for a student in any phase which call into fullest play the faculties that belong to that phase and prepare the ground for those that belong to the next.

For instance, it may be that Kindergarten play in assorting flowers, whether it is called elementary botany or not, is more educative to a very young child than formal lessons in language. But the child soon outgrows this phase; and for several years to come his most educative study is that of words, for he is still too young to make a scientific study of things. His mind is ripe for a little, but only a little, of the strong discipline of mathematics; and some training in music and drawing seems to be enjoined by nature as well as by Greek precept. But experience shows that he has more to gain from handling words than from any other exercise, perhaps more than from all others put together. The materials for his work come to him gratis and in abundance; and, in building with them, he is called on to exert the highest spontaneity of which he is capable. Demands are made on his general intelligence, his judgment, his sense of proportion, his logical acumen, his perceptive sensibility, and his taste; and in a greater or less degree he can rise to these demands. He is architect, engineer, and skilled artisan all at once.

There seems also no doubt that Latin is the best language for some parts of this work. But we are all prone to seek the path of least resistance; and perhaps classical masters give more attention to teaching the boy to write Latin not much worse than he writes English than to the more difficult and important task of teaching him to write moderately good English.

The boy passes gradually out of this phase and becomes fit for the next. In that he may begin to make a scientific study of things, whether they be material, or the ideas which are the truest realities. This work cannot be taken prematurely and in considerable quantities without peril. If he attempts it for more than a few hours a week, his overstrained mind is likely to take refuge in vagueness and docile receptiveness. He needs to seek relative rest in literary pursuits.

But the very causes which make the study of things unfit to be the foundation of education require that some at all events of those who are responsible for the training of boys after the age of 16 should themselves have attained mastery in that study. No doubt work in Greek history and philosophy, if sufficiently thorough, does provide a route, pleasant if circuitous, by which some insight into one of the two great groups of things can be attained; and Oxford men love to use Greek thought and experience as stalking horses, from behind which they shoot at mental and political problems of our own age.

A merely classical training gives little grasp of the methods by which man is now increasing his knowledge of the processes of nature, and his power of compelling her to work in his service. The same reasons that render the scientific study of nature impossible for the young boy make it call upon the man for the fullest exertion of his powers; and even that will not suffice, unless he has fed his mind in advance by an alert study of the subject for several years. For the highest spontaneity can seldom be developed after the first bloom of early manhood has passed; and therefore as much of the material as can be grasped in the later years of school life should be acquired then. In any case that needful implement, a knowledge of French and German, can be brought with him to the University. But will he be guided to do this?

It is universally recognized that the classical headmasters of England's great schools are eminent in fine character, in ability, in energy, and in breadth of sympathy. But is it not true that their devotion to the glorious field of study which they have made their own, combined with their lack of any first-hand experience of the nature and scope of the higher scientific spontaneity, makes them unconscious partisans, however much against their will?

I speak with diffidence. But I believe that in our leading schools a boy is often led to believe that the classical part of his work is of a nobler sort than the rest. For instance, if he has not strength or inclination to do the work set him by all his masters, his choice is often influenced by the notion, whether well or ill founded, that the headmaster will treat a complaint by his classical master more seriously than if made by another. And the 'bread-and-butter' influence tends in the same direction. For scholarships, at the richest schools as well as at the Universities, are given on a more generous scale to classical studies than to others.

Under such conditions there must be a great chance that many of those boys who are good classical scholars, but have germs of yet greater proficiency in science, will not be advised in the best interests of themselves and of the country by classical headmasters, however conscientious. Indications of undeveloped scientific power, which are not easily read by a scientific student, are certainly in danger of being overlooked by a classical headmaster whose mind has more than enough occupation in other directions.

We are told truly that the country owes much to men who have taken honours in classics. But may it not be questioned whether she would not have owed even more to those same men if one half of her chief schools had been under masters who had the same insight into the potentialities of a scientific education as they have into those of a classical education? It is to be remembered that the large majority of the abler lads who come to Cambridge from our richest schools present themselves for the Classical Tripos. Most have been exceptionally favoured at home as well as at school; they have been accustomed from childhood to hear high questions discussed with knowledge, a sense of proportion, and dignified reserve. They have been taught by well-paid masters who are themselves among the best products of Oxford and Cambridge, and in classes not too large for thorough teaching. Further, they are boys whom a severe process of competition has proved to be brighter and more earnest students than the average even of those whose upbringing has been equally noble and costly with theirs. Many of them belong to powerful families, and have good introductions to learned professions, to the legislature, and to public administration. Some of their achievements are of very high quality; but is the aggregate as great as it might have been if their attention had not been directed almost exclusively to studies that are the highest of which young boys are capable, but have no just claim to that pre-eminence in later years?

Many Germans have told me that they hold it to be an urgent duty of the age to develop schools to which the keynote is given by modern instead of classical studies, a solid foundation of Latin being taken for granted, but which have the same social and educational rank as the best classical schools. Germany has recently strengthened her Real Gymnasia, and is bent on further reform; England lags far behind Germany, and is in doubt whether the time has come to wake up. The inequality which allows classical students to pass the Previous Examination without giving evidence of any considerable amount of work outside of their own special studies, while all other students are required to offer a great deal that will not help them directly in their future work, seems to me objectionable for many reasons. But just at present I am concerned to urge that its redress might encourage the governors of a few of our great schools to select headmasters from among those students of science who have a marked literary faculty and a high appreciation of the value of literary training.

I do not suggest that any attempt should be made to select a headmaster free from bias. A master is nothing unless he is an eager student; and an eager student who has no bias towards his favourite studies is not easy to find. If the utterances of any classical headmaster on this question had indicated an absence of all bias, I should have been tempted to question his character as a student. But I have not been tempted.

What I hope for, then, is that there may be a few schools of the first rank, richly endowed with scholarships, in which a boy who has about equal aptitudes for classics and for science will most probably be guided towards science. I believe that such schools would be found to turn out nearly as many able classical scholars as the schools which still followed the old model; and that others of their scholars would in after life enrich the world with great discoveries, and with large thoughts, which an old Greek, if he could come to life, would respect more highly than learned dissertations on the words and thoughts of even the greatest of the dead.

The social and economic sciences, that now specially interest me, have no considerable place in such a reform. But the international studies of life and work, to which my thoughts have been increasingly turned during recent years, have impressed on me the urgent need of some steps in the direction I have ventured to suggest, if England is not to fall from her high rank in reputation and in power.

I am, Sir, yours obediently,

Cambridge, February 7. Alfred Marshall.

[1] Printed in *The Times*, 3 March 1905 (15a-b). The delay in publication is probably due to the plethora of letters on the Greek question [816.2]. Marshall subsequently drew upon this letter in composing appendix K of *Industry and Trade.*

[2] See the letter from E. C. Selwyn published under the heading 'Compulsory Greek', *The Times*, 28 January 1905 (11b, c). What Selwyn actually wrote was that the terms of his appointment obliged him to promote 'practical and liberal' education, adding that 'Practical education includes "science", liberal education includes Greek. As [the headmaster] is pledged to education, and not to the mere imparting of knowledge, he is bound to do his best to preserve Greek from extinction in his school' (Edward Carus Selwyn (1853–1918) was headmaster of Uppingham 1887–1907 and a one-time Fellow of King's.)

819. To Charles William Eliot, 6 March 1905[1]

6. 3. 05

Dear President Elliott,

I often think of your illuminating conversation about education, when you kindly took me into the heart of Harvard life in 1875.[2] Since then, ten years of ill health followed by a vain attempt to make up for lost time, has prevented me from taking part in movements for educational reform, except in my own special department. Recently however there has been a movement for broadening the basis of our entrance examination. The details of the new scheme were perhaps not well chosen in all respects; and anyhow it has just been rejected by a large majority in the biggest vote ever given here.[3] Probably the majority would have vanished if those clergymen to whom the University has granted a degree on too easy terms, as she does indeed to all Poll men, and some Honour men, had been eliminated. Well, this movement seemed to me likely to fail of great results, even if approved by the University, if the direction of the studies of our ablest boys were left exclusively in the hands of head-masters who speak *de haut en bas* of all studies save classics. So I wrote the inclosed letter.[4] It has had no practical result. But as it is the only thing, relating to general education, in wh my stay at Harvard thirty years ago has borne any fruit, I venture to send it to you.

I ever think of Harvard with something of affection. If I see the record of a boat race or a football match, in wh Harvard has been engaged, I am always glad to find that 'Harvard won'.

Yours sincerely | Alfred Marshall

[1] Harvard University Archives, Eliot Papers. From Balliol Croft. The misspelling of Eliot is Marshall's.
[2] See Vol. 1 [23].
[3] See [816.2].
[4] See [818].

820. From Oscar Browning, 13 March 1905[1]

King's College, | Cambridge.
March 13. 1905

My dear Marshall

M^r^. Thoday a tenant farmer is anxious to address the Society for the discussion of social questions on the depopulation of the land.[2] Can you help him in the matter?

Believe me | yrs ever | Oscar Browning

[1] Trinity College, Cambridge, Layton Papers.
[2] See [821, 822.2].

821. From George Adams Thoday, 14 March 1905[1]

Christs College Farm | Fen Drayton | Cambridge
March 14th 1905

Professor Marshall
Madingley Road
My dear Sir,

I beg to say in explanation to the accompanying letter[2] of Oscar Browning Esq M.A. that the subject I should like to speak upon, would be English Landlordism, & the depopulation of Rural Districts. My views are that although Free Trade has caused a considerable depreciation in the selling value of land, other causes are responsible for equal depreciation.

As regards the letting value of land; the percentage in proportion to its selling value, for land not out of cultivation, is higher for Farms from 50 to 100 acres than at any other period; if there are Homesteads available.

In consequence of this growing demand for land in a fair state of cultivation, thousands of farmers have adopted what I term the 'Tenant Farmers Retaliation Remedy'; that consists of letting their Farms get out of cultivation, until a low rent can be secured; & then again reclaiming the whole or a portion, according to the temperament of the owner or the owners agent.

I should also propose to show how the Agricultural Holdings Acts,[3] have been manoeuvred, to aid in the removal of small & medium sized holdings.

The latest innovation likely to harass small holdings and further the depopulation of the twenty four parishes in this locality; or those where there are convenience for other than large holdings; is quite a new interpretation of the Union Assessment Committee Act 1862.[4]

It is quite clear to me that the new interpretation of the said Act, is to secure most of the advantages of the Agricultural Rates Act 1896,[5] to large occupiers, and those who have adopted the 'Tenant Farmers Retaliation Remedy'; while medium & smaller occupiers & good cultivators of the land, will be in a worse position than if the Agricultural Rates Act had not been passed.

I am, my Dear Sir | Your Obedient Servant | George Adams Thoday

[1] Trinity College, Cambridge, Layton Papers. Further information on Thoday has not been discovered.
[2] See [820].
[3] Presumably 46 and 47 Victoria, c. 61 (1883); 63 and 64 Victoria, c. 50 (1900).
[4] 25 and 26 Victoria, c. 103.
[5] 59 and 60 Victoria, c. 16.

822. To Oscar Browning, 15 March, 1905[1]

15. 3. 05

My dear Browning

I am not taking an active part in the management of the Social Discussion

Society. So I am writing to Mr Thoday to say that I have sent his letter and yours to Erasmus Darwin, the Secretary.[2] The subject seems a lively one: but I doubt a little whether the Committee will feel quite ready to tackle it.

The meeting at wh Crooks spoke[3] was lively: but even there political fervour was made to serve in lieu of evenly balanced & careful judgement, I fear.

Yours very truly | Alfred Marshall

[1] King's College, Cambridge, Browning Papers. From Balliol Croft. See [820, 821].

[2] Marshall's letter to Thoday, sent by Darwin (see [823.3]), has not been traced.

[3] The recently revived Social Discussion Society, with Erasmus Darwin as Secretary and Walter Layton as Treasurer, had held its first public meeting on Monday 6 March 1905. The speakers were Will Crooks and Canon Barnett, with Marshall in the chair. 'The text upon which Canon Barnett and Mr Crooks hung their discourses on "Unemployment" was the need of an alliance between the Universities and the industrial centres ... Even those who disagreed as to the practicability of the actual scheme for dealing with "unemployment" propounded by Mr Crooks, ought to have been, and evidently were, roused to enthusiasm by the earnestness which inspired his speech as well as by the dramatic force and the wit with which it was delivered'. *Cambridge Review*, 26 (9 March 1905), p. 244; see also 2 March, p. 228. (William Crooks (1852–1921), labour leader and radical politician, active in promoting unemployment-insurance schemes; Samuel Augustus Barnett (1844–1913), clergyman, long associated with Toynbee Hall and an old acquaintance of Marshall.)

The *Cambridge Daily News* of 7 March 1905 carried an extended account of the meeting from which it appears that Crooks had proposed the readying of public-works projects to be undertaken in slumps, and the provision of training schemes preparing workers for jobs in the colonies. The report of Marshall's introductory remarks is of considerable interest:

> The meeting ... was presided over by Professor Marshall who explained that it was the first meeting of the Society, which was the descendant of other and similar societies which had become defunct. The aims of the Society were to stimulate interest in social settlements and the discussion of social problems. The society which preceded it described its aims in similar terms: 'to hear statements from experienced persons as to the working of contemporary social movements, the knowledge of which cannot easily be obtained from books', and 'to enable members of the University to enter into the spirit of the work of those who are actively endeavouring to improve the conditions of social life'. Such a method had its limitations. It did not aim at subtle reasonings; it did not laboriously analyse in order to discover the causes that lay under the surface and were often more important than those which were easily seen. It did not even reach very far towards a discovery of the ultimate results of proposed remedies for social ills, which like drugs applied to the human body, often acted in the long run in the opposite direction to that in which they acted at first. That required long and patient study of the kind that their Medical School offered to those who would prescribe remedies for bodily ills. But medical students must be brought into direct contact with bodily life and sickness and death in the hospitals. And academic students of the working of economic causes needed in like manner to be supplemented by direct contact with social life and its ills. Every member of the University, and especially all who professed to care for and study social problems ought, if possible, to spend some time in a social settlement, or to attain the same result by other methods. But not all could do that, especially during their undergraduate career; and therefore it was all the more helpful to them to hear those who were immersed in the great whirling stream of modern social and industrial life tell how men and women and children worked and suffered, rejoiced and hoped, away from the still quiet of academic shades. (Applause)

823. To Erasmus Darwin, 15 March 1905[1]

15. 3. 05

My dear Darwin,

The inclosed letters[2] explain themselves. If I have done right, please post my letter to Thoday with or without a note from yourself. If I have done wrong, please kindly suppress my letter, & write to him direct.[3]

Yours very truly | [Alfred Marshall]

I send you a cheque for £1.1s as my contribution towards the travelling expenses of invited speakers &c. I think you should offer Crooks his expenses; probably you have done so.

I am a passionate admirer of Crooks: though I do not think that the considerations affecting 'unemployment' of which he took account are nearly as important as those wh he ignored.

[1] Trinity College, Cambridge, Layton Papers. From Balliol Croft. The signature has been cut out of the letter, presumably to add to an autograph collection. See [822.3] for background.

[2] See [820, 821]: see also [822.2].

[3] Someone, presumably Darwin, wrote on the original of [821] 'Answered by Prof. Marshall March [15?] saying [Thoday's] letter will be laid before the Committee. Note enclosed saying it will be laid before Committee next term'. Thoday does not appear to have addressed the Society at any time in 1905.

824. From George Adams Thoday, 23 March 1905[1]

Christ's College Farm | Fen Drayton, Cambridge

March 23rd 1905

My Dear Sir,

I beg to thank you, for your kindness in forwarding my letter[2] to Mr Erasmus Darwin, the Hon Sec of the Social Discussion Society.[3] I did not retain a copy of my letter of application to you, and was not aware that the brief facts I stated were of a very political nature; I have never addressed a meeting on political subjects. If politicians would bring forward, sound & effective measures, that would tend to encourage labourers to stay upon the land; landlords might obtain more rent for their land.

You will probably be surprised to learn that land upon which the rent, has been kept up to high figures, is such as was not good enough for the practice of the tenant farmers retaliation system, and some that by far the greater part was considered by the owners as almost worthless, when wheat was nearly 50/- per qr; & was 25 years ago practically unlettable except to strangers who did not know the nature of the land; has since yielded its owners an average net rental of 24/—per acre, besides what the owners have allowed for serious losses from floods on Arable Land, repairs to buildings &c, & taxes paid for the owners; while land good enough for the retaliation system that large premiums could be obtained in the former period, has in some cases yielded about half an average net rental.

In some other parishes, where the arable and also the pasture land, is sound & free from floods, that formerly let at 20 per cent higher than the average of this parish, in times of great agricultural prosperity; the rents have fallen to 9/- per acre.

I am, my Dear Sir | Truly Yours | George A. Thoday

Professor Marshall
Madingley Road | Cambridge

[1] Trinity College, Cambridge, Layton Papers. See [821.1].
[2] See [821].
[3] See [822, 823].

825. To Erasmus Darwin, 24 March 1905[1]

24. 3. 05

My dear Darwin,

I do not think I will reply to this letter.[2] My own opinion is that if he would be content—as he now intimates—to describe the difficulties, aspirations, and general experiences of the tenant farmer in his part of the world, he would be an excellent guest for the Society. But the particular remedies, which he proposes, seem to me[3] unsuited for discussion except by a committee of experts, or else by counsel for the prosecution of the alleged culprit—the existing law—followed by expert counsel for the defence. In that case a Jury of non-experts might perhaps bring in a fairly good verdict: but I am not sure that their time would be well spent in doing so, even if the counsel for the defence should be forthcoming.

Some years ago I read a good deal of Blue-book evidence[4] for and against various schemes of Tenant compensation. I felt that I could form something of an opinion after hearing both sides, but none at all after hearing only one.

This is of course partly repetition of what I have already said as to the good & evil of eloquence such as Mr Crook's.[5] Untrained thinkers can present the most vivid and instructive of pictures. But when they endeavour to establish doctrine or to prescribe remedy, the mischief which they do varies as the product of their intellectual limitations and their oratorical efficiency.

Yours very truly | Alfred Marshall

[1] Trinity College, Cambridge, Layton Papers. From Balliol Croft.
[2] See [824].
[3] Followed in the original by 'to'.
[4] That is, evidence resulting from governmental enquiries.
[5] See [822, 823].

826. To Edwin Robert Anderson Seligman, 18 May 1905[1]

18. 5. 05

My dear Seligman,

I am living a very retired life, & see little of the official world. Probably there are some old pupils of mine in official posts in India and China. But I do not keep in touch with men generally after they leave Cambridge, unless they are working at economics, or happen to be personal friends.

As regards India the two men whom I know best are—perhaps not quite as an accident—brother-correspondents with yourself of the British Economic Association. I inclose a note to one of them F. C. Harrison.[2] He is in the Public Service, and may perhaps eventually become Secretary for Finance to the Central Government. The other—O. V. Muller—is Professor at Elphinstone College, Bombay;[3] and is just now in England. I am to see him again in a fortnights time, & will then tell him about you. I fear that there is nothing else that I can do to help you.

I have sometimes thought of asking our Foreign office for a letter, wh I might show when making miscellaneous inquiries in Germany and elsewhere. I have never done so. But it might be a good plan. If your Ambassador applied to the English Foreign office, that office w^{d}.. of course act through the Indian & Colonial offices.

Wishing you all good speed; & hoping to see you in 1906, I am

Yours sincerely | Alfred Marshall

Muller will return to Bombay in September or October. Harrison you know has worked a good deal at currency; and in particular has made the only existing statistical estimate of the number of rupees in circulation in India. See *Economic Journal*.[4]

Harrison has changed his address several times, being moved from one post to another: and it is likely that Allahabad is obsolete. No doubt a letter sent to that address wd be forwarded. But as distances are great in India, it might be well to make sure where he is, before arranging your tour in detail.

[1] Columbia University Library, Seligman Papers. From Balliol Croft. Seligman's request for advice and introductions in connection with his trip to the Orient has not been traced.

[2] Francis Capel Harrison (1863–1938) had been one of Marshall's Oxford students, 1883–4, and was an authority on Indian monetary and financial questions. Marshall's note of introduction to him not traced. See also Vol. 2 [581].

[3] Oswald Valdemar Muller (1868–1916), born in Denmark, had been 20th Wrangler in 1890 (Jesus). He was Professor of History and Political Economy in Bombay, 1892–1916.

[4] See F. C. Harrison, 'The Composition and Amount of the Rupee Circulation', *Economic Journal*, 6 (March 1896), pp. 122–7.

827. To Ludwig Joseph Brentano, 13 June 1905[1]

13. 6. 05

My dear Brentano

I have just received six copies of my *Grundlagen* from Cotta;[2] & I write to express my hearty thanks for the very kind and flattering remarks you have made in your introduction; which, otherwise than in its over-praise of my poor efforts, seems to me admirable in every way. Again most hearty thanks. I think the publishers have done their part very well: and the translation seems to me remarkably good, especially towards the end. I am not sure that Ephraim[3] alone would have managed it quite well: and in this matter again my best gratitude is due to you.

My wife and I propose to pass through Munich in our usual way very late in June or early in July. That is we expect to arrive at about 7 a.m. Then after breakfast she goes to the Secession[4] and, if there is no special reason to the contrary, I go with her. Then at eleven we join our train again, and sleep amid the mountains. For I am always dead beat when I close my books in England, and yearn for the high air. I should like just to look in on you about 9.30 a.m.; and shake hands & thank you personally. But I know you are very busy just at that time of the year: and so I shall not venture to do so unless you tell me that you would be at leisure.

Again very gratefully yours | Alfred Marshall

[1] Bundesarchiv Koblenz, Brentano Papers. From Balliol Croft.

[2] The German translation of *Principles* (*4*) had just been published: A. Marshall, *Handbuch der Volkswirtschaftslehre, Bd. 1. Nach der 4.Aufl. des Englischen Originals.* (Übers. von Hugo Ephraim und Arthur Salz. Mit Einem Geleitwort von Lujo Brentano: Cotta, Stuttgart, 1905). Arthur Salz (1881–?), a student of Brentano, published a Munich dissertation in 1905 and went on to publish prolifically on economic topics.

[3] The original translator: see [740.3, 741].

[4] An exhibition of avant-garde painting.

828. To the Secretary, George Howell Appeal Committee, 20 August 1905[1]

Stern im Abtei | Pustertal, Tyrol

20. 8. 05

Dear Sir

I presume that M[r] Howell's collection is of that exceptional character which fits it to be preserved in its entirety. On that understanding, I shall be glad to join the Committee to wh you kindly invite me. But I wish your circular had made the point more clear. For I regard the acquisition of private collections en bloc by public institutions as generally a very great mistake, and one which may need to be remedied ere long by special legislation. As a rule I think private collections should be either dispersed, or weeded down to a third of their original size; & that even then public institutions to whose care they are intrusted should be instructed to continue the process of weeding in after years.

Yours very truly | Alfred Marshall

[1] Bishopsgate Institute, London. The appeal being launched was to purchase and find a home for George Howell's extensive library (eventually housed in the Bishopsgate Institute) and endow him with a small pension. See F. M. Leventhal, *Respectable Radical: George Howell and Victorian Working Class Politics* (Harvard University Press, Cambridge, 1971), p. 213.

829. To the Council, St. John's College, Cambridge, (October?) 1905[1]

I beg leave to submit to the Council of St John's College my report on Mr. Benians' Essay on the Settlement of Canada.

In reporting a year ago on an earlier draft of the Essay, I spoke more about its promise than about its performance.[2] I am glad to say that the present essay more than justifies my estimate of the promise shewn by the earlier one; and that it is a very considerable achievement.

The subject is one of those on which no one can claim to have said the final word, even after many years study and I have little doubt that the results of Mr. Benians' work during the coming year as Allen's Student[3] will carry a good deal further some of the suggestions which he now puts forward. But if it were published just as it stands, it would, I think be generally accepted as the standard authority for the present on the issues raised by it.

These issues are in substance:

(1) What are the causes which made the British dominions in North America relatively stagnant during a great part of the nineteenth Century?

(2) In what directions has her recent progress been aided by (a) the opening up of her richest lands, accompanied by the running short of the supply of attractive free homesteads in the United States; (b) the rise of a high national spirit among her people; and (c) the development of new methods of production adapted to the conditions of new countries.

These issues owe their main interest, of course, to the differences of opinion which are found among competent judges, on the question whether Canada's present rate of progress is likely to be continued without any great check for many years.

The facts bearing on these issues, more or less, are so numerous that much care was needed in selecting from them: and it may be true that a few of those recorded in the essay might with advantage have been relegated to footnotes. But, as a rule, the edifice is well built: each stone does work; it bears its share of the weight of the ultimate conclusion, and not more than its share. For though the style of the essay is not altogether even and sometimes errs through excess of emphasis, it will I think generally be found that the fault is in the style and not in the substance: the over strong statement is generally corrected or qualified later on.

Thus on the whole the essay seems to me to show the higher faculties of the historian developed in a degree that is not very often found even in writers of mature experience. I think it reaches and goes beyond the standard which may generally be expected of successful Fellowship theses; and gives reason to hope that he may become a distinguished member of the staff of the University.

If often happens that only the first twenty pages of a young man's essay are worth reading. Mr. Benians however is not seen at his best in his Introduction. His essay of last year had no marked style and was indeed a little diffuse. He has set himself to put strength into his style; and he has in a great measure succeeded. But he has not yet acquired the power of moving with a broad and easy sweep over large territories and his broader propositions lack restraint. But this fault belongs to the transitional stage in which he is. The improvement in his style during the last year has been so marked, that I expect him to succeed ere long in combining ease and strength.[4]

(Signed) Alfred Marshall.

[1] St John's College, Cambridge, College Archives. From a copy in the same hand as [806]. The copy is headed, 'Opinion of Professor A Marshall on the paper on The Progress of Settlement in Canada during the Nineteenth Century sent in by E. A. Benians'. A cover sheet indicates that it is the 1905 report. The four questions listed on the printed form (as in [806]) are not separately addressed.

[2] See [806].

[3] See [806.1].

[4] Benians did not obtain a Fellowship in the 1905 election but was successful one year later. For Marshall's final evaluation see [859].

830. To Ernest Alfred Benians, 6 November 1905[1]

6. 11. 05

My dear Benians,

I am very sorry that neither you nor Làl is elected.[2] I hear that Atkins' claims turned out to be stronger than had been supposed.[3]

My tongue is now free. I think the second edition of your essay is a vast improvement on the first from every point of view. It gives good hope that you may do excellent work. But there is no doubt that you have developed rather late, and that you must be patient.

The style of the earlier draft was without character. You are acquiring a much stronger style: but you are rather like a chorister, when changing his voice. When you take special pains over it, as in some of the introductory pages, it 'breaks'. But when writing easily, you do not write badly. That does not mean you should cease to take pains: but that you should read people who have good styles.

Yours very sincerely | Alfred Marshall

[1] St. John's College, Cambridge, Benians Papers. From Balliol Croft.
[2] To a Fellowship at St John's: see [829.4].
[3] John William Hey Atkins (1874–1951) held a Fellowship at St John's 1905–11. Lecturer in English at the University of Manchester 1903–6; Professor of English Language and Literature at University College, Aberystwyth, 1906–40.

831. To Frederick Macmillan, 20 November 1905[1]

20. 11. 05

Dear Mr MacMillan,

Thank you for your note. I am making the correction as you suggest. Originally I had taken interest on security of the first order as a little *over* 3%. Then Consols went up to 112, & so I took it in a later edition as rather under 3%: and either I or the compositor omitted to raise the remainder out of 4% to rather more than 1%.[2]

I am giving every fraction of free time & strength to *National Industries & International Trade.*[3] But I do not work fast; & the work direct & indirect demanded by the new Tripos is very heavy.

Also the book is changing its form a little. Its general notion is that the courses of trade are controlled by the contours of industry, as watercourses are controlled by those of the hills. And therefore I had always intended to treat the issues of International Trade as subordinate to those of National industries. But as I go on I incline to carry this subordination even further than I originally proposed; and so far as I can see the book will consist of about five or six hundred pages of text together with rather more than a hundred of Appendices. I fear it will not be ready for the public till some time in 1907. More than half the whole will be on National Industries.

I feel I must apologise to you for the delay: but really I cannot help myself. I regret it on account of its cost, and because it keeps me away from Vol II of my Principles. But I incline to agree with those who think that the Tariff controversy will not come to a head for two or three years: & I hope that any bearing my book may have on it will not altogether miss its aim.

It was found last year that some College Tutors were not well inclined to the new Economics Tripos, partly because they did not really understand it. So I printed off 2000 copies of the inclosed explanatory pamphlet[4] for gratuitous distribution chiefly through the Tutors: and the expedient seems to have answered. For this years entries for the Curriculum are good.[5] This pamphlet is less formal, but perhaps more to the present purpose than the booklet wh you kindly published for me.[6] Will you please decide whether the small remainder of that should now be thrown away.

Yours very truly | Alfred Marshall

[1] British Library, Macmillan Archive. From Balliol Croft.

[2] The passage in question appears to be that on pp. 588–9 of *Principles* (*8*). The change indicated was made between *Principles* (*2*), p. 623, and *Principles* (*3*), p. 670, but without error. However the same passage is used in *Elements* (pp. 284–5 of the final 1907 version) which was reprinted in 1905, and it is probably here that the error was found.

[3] See [787, 797, 814].

[4] Alfred Marshall, *Introduction to the Tripos in Economics and Associated Branches of Political Science* (Cambridge University Press, Cambridge, 1905). There are at least two different versions. The fuller one, which contains 16 pages of text and does not bear Marshall's name, is probably that sent to tutors.

[5] See [790.2] for the number successfully completing Part I in various years. Matriculants of 1905 would be most likely to take Part I in 1907.

[6] See [751.4].

832. To the Editor, *The Times*, 20 November 1905[1]

Sir,—In your Education Notes of last Saturday you refer to the increase of 1,490 in a single year in the number of students at American Universities and colleges who are receiving a 'commercial education'. While suggesting that the instruction given in some of these Institutions is of a more technical character than would be appropriate to the older English Universities, you seem to imply that they are neglecting even that part of the work which lies within their sphere.[2] But, not to dwell on the special 'certificate' for economic studies now offered by Oxford,[3] may I point out that Cambridge is making a great effort to perform her duty thoroughly in this direction?

Your own weighty leading article of April 17, 1902, contributed not a little to induce the Senate to establish a Tripos in economics and associated branches of political science.[4] The syndicate appointed to consider the subject reported that 'What is desired is not technical instruction, but an education of a high type which shall have the additional advantage of preparing the student to take, without unreasonable delay, a responsible place in business or in public life, and which shall have as high an educational value as that of any other school'.[5] During their first two years, academic and business students work together at economics combined with recent international history, both general and economic, and politics. But in their third year those who are looking forward to a career in the higher branches of business or in public life are invited to give much of their time to preparing for two realistic papers on the facts of business life and the application of economic principles to them.[6]

The task thus undertaken by our staff is difficult: and, as no examination for third-year students has yet been held, I will venture to illustrate the way in which it may be met, by quoting one or two realistic questions that were set to second-year students last June. They are:—

Give a brief discussion of the advantages and disadvantages of the system of piecework, and by reference to specific industries show how their relative importance varies in different circumstances.

Describe the function of the speculator in the organization of industry. Distinguish the speculative element in the work of the manufacturer and the wholesale merchant, and indicate the new kinds of speculation which have been made possible by modern business methods.

How is the output of a monopolistic industry likely to be affected if, having hitherto been allowed to discriminate between its customers, it is prevented by law from doing this? What light does your answer throw on the problem of Governmental interference with the rates chargeable by railway companies?

Our new curriculum is gradually becoming known. More students, and especially more sons of leading business men who are preparing to follow in their fathers' business, have entered this year than in either of its first two years. And, though we are hampered by a great want of funds for the payment of the younger lecturers, there are reasons for hoping that we may be helped. The 'Girdlers' lectureship in Economics' bears testimony to the liberality of a City Company[7] and the interest it takes in our work. Sir Henry Buckley has founded a scholarship for lads proceeding from Merchant Taylors' School to study economies at Cambridge.[8] And the beginning of an economics endowment fund has been made by a donation from Mr. N. L. Cohen.[9]

I may add that the secretary of the Cambridge University appointments board tells me that the applications to him from leading business firms for men who have received a Cambridge training of one sort or another is large and increasing fast, and that the reports which he receives of their work are as a rule very satisfactory.

Yours faithfully, | Alfred Marshall.

Cambridge, Nov. 20.

1 Printed in *The Times*, 23 November 1905 (4c), under the heading 'Education for Business Men'. Original not traced.

2 *The Times*, 18 November 1905 (16a) had commented in its Educational Notes on issues of business education raised in a paper read by S. J. Chapman at Cardiff on 7 November. The following comment is probably what provoked Marshall: 'Whether the older Universities will make any attempt to provide special training for students intending to enter business careers may be doubted; but, as indicating the needs for such training, it may be mentioned that one of the speakers in the discussion which followed the reading of Professor Chapman's paper expressed the opinion that Oxford and Cambridge graduates were useless as business men'.

3 Oxford had instituted in 1903 a post-graduate 'Diploma in Economics' without any notable emphasis on preparation for business. See Alon Kadish, *Historians, Economists and Economic History* (Routledge, London,1989), pp. 98–101. Also see the report summarized in the *Economic Journal*, 14 (September 1904), pp. 486–9.

4 See *The Times*, 18 April 1902 (7f)—not 17 April. The leader was invoked by the Memorial requesting a new Tripos (see Vol. 2 [687.3]) and was sympathetic to Marshall's *Plea* [734.7].

5 *Reporter*, 10 March 1903, p. 529 (pp. 528–38 for the full report). Marshall inserted the 'and' after 'public life' after eliding 'For such students the Syndicate believe, it is both possible and desirable to provide by constructing a curriculum in Economics and associated branches of Political Science'.

[6] Part II of the Tripos allowed candidates to take two papers on 'Advanced Economics, mainly realistic'.
[7] See [778.4].
[8] Sir Henry Burton Buckley (1845–1935), lawyer and judge, subsequently (1915) Baron Wrenbury, who had probably overlapped with Marshall at Merchant Taylors' School and had been a Fellow of Christ's 1868–82. The Buckley Scholarship was subsequently transferred to the control of the University as the Wrenbury Scholarship and the restriction to candidates from Merchant Taylors' dropped.
[9] See [747.6]. Details of the gift have not been discovered.

833. To the Editor, *The Times*, 14 December 1905[1]

Sir,—Your Educational Notes of November 18 implied that Cambridge made no provision for the education of business men.[2] You kindly allowed me to point out, on November 23, that Cambridge had created a full three years' curriculum, designed to enable those who are 'looking forward to a career in the higher branches of business or in public life' to obtain an appropriate education of full University rank.[3] They work side by side with others who hope to spend the rest of their lives in study: but from the first they can give a large share of their attention to the practical applications of the questions brought before them, and in their third year they are encouraged to specialize on those applications. Your Educational Notes of December 11, however, question whether this curriculum can serve its purpose: since it makes no direct mention of such subjects as 'balance-sheets, sinking funds, and depreciation, goodwill and the finance of machinery.'[4]

May I now be allowed to state that these subjects are not ignored? It is true that economics, like every other new study at Cambridge, must put up with a small staff; and that no place has been found in our staff for an accountant. But it must be remembered that we are not at present endeavouring to teach the principles of business to passmen, but only to Honour men, and that Honour students in their third year are able to read books of some severity without the detailed supervision which is needed for an ordinary commercial education. Accordingly, they are set to read the more important parts of standard treatises on factory accounts, depreciation, &c., and some points of special difficulty, such as those connected with the distribution of costs between different departments of the same business, the capitalization of goodwill, &c., are discussed in lectures.[5]

If the University should ever decide to adapt its pass examinations in economics[6] to the wants of those business men who do not aim at an education of the same high order as is given in our Honour courses, it will probably be necessary to have lectures on the common routine of accounting. And, if they are given by a professional accountant, he may be asked to give a short course adapted to the needs of abler students. It is, however, not probable that the

University will allow much time to be given even by passmen to absorbing prematurely technical information about those 'forms and accounts adapted to different classes of undertakings', on which your Educational Notes lay stress. For Honour men, at all events, such work is inappropriate. The three sacred years of their University life are already fully occupied with studies which claim to help the able business man to be a leader in the world.

Yours faithfully, | Alfred Marshall.

Cambridge, Dec. 14.

[1] Printed in *The Times*, 18 December 1905 (13c) under the heading 'Economics for Business Men'. Original not traced.
[2] See [832.2].
[3] See [832].
[4] *The Times*, 11 December 1905 (6f): 'the scheme of Part II. of the Economics Tripos is chiefly remarkable in connexion with the training of businessmen not so much for the subjects included as for those omitted. If there is one subject a knowledge of which is indispensable to a business man, it is surely the theory and practice of accountancy'. See also A. Kadish, *Historians* [832.3], p. 233.
[5] No accounting books were included in the list of economics books recommended for Part I (see [777]), while no formal recommendations for Part II economics books were made in Marshall's day, his individual guidance of advanced students sufficing.
[6] The optional Special Examination in Economics for the Ordinary B.A., responsibility for which now rested with the Economics Board.

834. To the Editor, *The Times*, 27 December 1905[1]

Sir,—I fear that any one who sees Mr. Vinter's letter in your columns of yesterday,[2] without referring to mine in your columns of the 18th,[3] may suppose that the subject of accounting is ignored in the curriculum which Cambridge has recently instituted for those preparing for the higher branches of business. For he states that I regard 'accountancy, &c.,' as inappropriate to Honour men. But I explained how the principles of accountancy are dealt with by us to the best of our limited means, though I am not sure that its detailed forms 'adapted to different classes of undertakings'[4] ought to be a part of academic education for any class of students. For they fill the mind, without enlarging it and strengthening it. And the ablest business men tell us that it is faculty rather than knowledge which the business man of to-day needs. It is a powerful and capacious mind, rather than one already crammed with dead matter, that a University should send out to the work of the world.

Professor Cayley's masterly pamphlet (1894) on the principles of bookkeeping by double entry[5] ends with the warning that bookkeeping routine, however perfect, is no guarantee of truth, but only of consistency between the several parts. For truth we need judgment; without it routine may lead to 'the fool's paradise of a fictitious amount to the credit of profit and loss.'

I am informed that on the technical side of this judgment, that which deals with the special conditions of different classes of undertakings, the only education which is of much value is that of experience; and that an expert in the valuation of shipping concerns, or of textile fabrics, would not willingly be responsible for the depreciation items in the accounts of an hotel or a mine. And I have the highest authority for saying that, in so far as the principles on which this judgment is based are general, they rest on the same foundations as economic science.[6]

No doubt in an ideally complete University these matters ought to be handled by a man who is both an expert accountant and an economist; and, if Mr. Vinter's business friends will endow the University for the purpose, I doubt not that the gift will be thankfully accepted. The economics department, to say nothing of others, could do well with many such gifts.

Yours faithfully, | Alfred Marshall.

Cambridge, Dec. 27.

[1] Printed in *The Times*, 29 December 1905 (5d) under the heading 'University Education for Business Men'. Original not traced.

[2] See the letter from James Odell Vinter, a businessman writing from Cambridge, published under the heading 'University Education for Businessmen', *The Times*, 26 December 1905 (8d). Suggesting an appeal to support the teaching of accountancy at Cambridge, Vinter had written 'Professor Marshall states that in the study of economics "no place has been found in our staff for an accountant." This is a sorry admission to be obliged to make; and until this defect has been remedied he must not claim that much is being done in the way of commercial education'.

[3] That is, [833].

[4] Vinter had echoed the phrase quoted by Marshall in [833] from *The Times* of 11 December.

[5] Arthur Cayley, *The Principles of Book-keeping by Double Entry* (Cambridge University Press, Cambridge, 1894).

[6] It is difficult even to conjecture the name of the 'high authority' invoked here.

835. To Johan Gustav Knut Wicksell (with postscript by Arthur Lyon Bowley), 22 January 1906[1]

22. 1. 06

Dear Prof. Wicksell,

The officers of the British association for 1906 are I think not yet appointed. Certainly they have had no formal meeting. But anyone can become a member of the Association for a single year by merely paying £1.1s. Therefore you will be safe even technically in telling your Government that you intend to go to the meeting. I am however sending round this letter to M[r] Bowley, who was the 'Recorder', i.e. the organizing Secretary of the Economic Section for last year in South Africa; and asking him to add a Postscript saying when and where this years meeting is to be held. If he says nothing to the contrary, you may assume that you would be justified in saying further that though no formal invitation has been issued yet, you have been privately informed that an informal invitation will be in all probability issued to you. I am quite sure that the Committee will be proud to welcome you.[2] I dare not go to such meetings myself; and in fact I shall probably be buried in the recesses of South Tyrol as usual.

Yours sincerely, | Alfred Marshall

Dear Sir,

I cordially endorse Prof Marshall's letter. I am writing to Prof. S. Chapman at Manchester who succeeds me in my office this year, & after some considerable interval you will receive definite information and an invitation. The meeting is at York, & begins (I believe) on Aug 1st.

Yours faithfully, | A.L. Bowley

Professor Wicksell

[1] Lund University Library, Wicksell Papers. From Balliol Croft. Presumably in response to an untraced letter from Wicksell. See [813, 815]. Bowley's postscript is written on Marshall's letter.

[2] Wicksell did present a paper in York on 'The Influence of the Rate of Interest on Prices'. See British Association, *Annual Report*, 75 (1906), p. 643. The paper was published in the *Economic Journal*, 17 (June 1907), pp. 213–20.

836. To Herbert Somerton Foxwell, 8 February 1906[1]

8. 2. 06

My dear Foxwell

I wonder if you have seen a good way out of our difficulty as to lectures for the first-year. I think we have the same aim; viz to make all lectures tell, and not to waste our small strength on duplication.

Another evil is the division of one course between two men. Thus in the present year you and Macgregor divide English economic history.[2] And if we provided a set of lectures to continue your course on economics,[3] there would be another danger of overlapping in some matters, and omission as to others.

Then again the time which men spend on history is too long. At first we had to get lectures as we could: and in more than one case the scope of a set of lectures was limited by the lecturer's inability to 'get up' an amount of history proportionate to the time which his lectures covered. As a result men often went to more than twice as many lectures on history (including geography) as on economics, though there are three papers on Economics and only two on history.[4]

Lastly there is another evil, I think. My notion is—I may be wrong—that the lectures which you affect are too much of the 'London School' type to suit our better third year men. And I constantly find really able and zealous students especially graduates of Fellowship level, who are interested in your subjects, and yet say they cannot find the time to attend your lectures. If you could get rid of some of your history of banking in another course, & lecture to third year men mainly on those matters on w^{h}.. even able men cannot see their way clearly without help, I think you might get a good class so far as quality goes.[5] (Last year I lectured a little on the causes wh govern the amount of deposits, and the influence of bank money on prices: and the men were much interested, but gave no sign that they had considerd the questions before. I have no time to lecture on this point now. Nicholson's *Banking Money*[6] does not touch such matters.)

I was struck by the keen interest wh you showed at the last Board Meeting in your lectures on history.[7] It set me on thinking that a way out of three or four of our difficulties might be found in your undertaking English Economic History in the nineteenth century, & giving two terms to it.[8] That is as much time as men ought to give to lectures on the subject: really rather more I think (Incidentally you might perhaps take the opportunity of admitting Newnham and Girton students to your lectures.[9] If they are to be examined—& I confess I think that too many of them *do* enter for our Triposes—we ought not to handicap them by excluding them from lectures that are almost necessary.)

Then Macgregor might give a full three terms course on economics, and cover a good many matters which Green leaves out as unsuited to the weaker men.[10]

I find and my wife finds that the easier half of theory of value is just that part of economics on which first year students need the most help. The refinements—e.g. as to rent in relation to value, and the interpretation of 'fair' or 'normal' cost in relation to things that conform to tendency towards Increasing Return, should not I think come into the first year. But all the rest seems to me to belong to it, for those men and women who are giving a fair ability and the prescribed full half of their time to economics. I know that Macgregor is inclined to seek out difficulties overmuch; though he is trying to smooth his mind out. But men who found him too hard would get what they want from Green.

What do you think of all this? Perhaps it would be better to talk than to write: since life is short. If you think some discussion would be good, may I cycle to you at Harvey Street[11] or in College on Wednesday? I think that is the only day that quite suits us both. I always prefer 10 am or 4 pm to other hours for appointments: later hours take the heart out of either the morning or the afternoon. I could come conveniently at 4 p.m. on Tuesday, or Friday.

I assented unguardedly to the suggestion that I thought there should be a general course in the third year as well as in the other two. It was not to the point at issue. But I do *not* think there should be a general course in the third year. I originally set myself down for Special courses for Part II: but found that on that plan large gaps would be left. So I chose the title 'General Course' as a makeshift for this year merely because it is absolutely elastic.[12] But each Special course must I think cover a considerable part of the whole. Macgregors course on Trusts &c takes very little burden off my shoulders. I think I am expected to cover more than my share of the whole area. I am willing to be responsible for a half of the third year teaching; or even a little more if need be. But I would prefer giving lectures for wh the term 'General Course' would not be appropriate. On the other hand when I lectured to freshmen, & covered most of the ground covered by Mill[13], merely avoiding high difficulties, I would not have liked any other title.

Yours sincerely | Alfred Marshall

[1] Marshall Papers. From Balliol Croft.

[2] For 1905–6 Foxwell offered 'Introduction to 19th century Economic History' in the Michaelmas Term and Macgregor offered 'The economic development of England since 1800' in the Lent and Easter Terms. (*Reporter*, 13 January 1906).

[3] Foxwell offered in 1905–6 an introductory course 'The Economics of Industry' in the Michaelmas Term. In the Lent Term his elementary lectures were on 'Currency and Banking'.

[4] In Part I of the Economics Tripos.

[5] Foxwell taught an advanced course, 'History of Currency and Banking', in the Lent Term of 1906.

[6] Presumably, J. S. Nicholson, *Banker's Money: A Supplement to a Treatise on Money* (Black, London, 1902).

[7] This was at the meeting of the Economics Board on 8 November 1905, where it had been agreed that Macgregor's economic history course meet twice a week and that he also offer an advanced course on Industrial Combination in the Lent and Easter Terms of 1906. (Economics Board Minutes, Cambridge University Archives.)

[8] No such change was to occur, Foxwell adhering to the set pattern of 1905–6.

[9] Admission of women was at the lecturer's discretion and Foxwell had always staunchly refused it.

[10] In 1905–6, first-year teaching of economics was provided for only by Foxwell's 'Economics of Industry' and by G. E. Green's 'Elementary Political Economy' which continued through all three terms. The basic second- and third-year courses were given by Pigou and Marshall, respectively. Cunningham also offerd his wayward 'Political Economy', but this was hardly directed to the Tripos. For the changes involving Macgregor that were made for 1906–7 see [839.4].

[11] Foxwell resided at 1 Harvey *Road*.

[12] For 1905–6 Marshall's course was entitled 'Advanced Economics'. He also offered an extra class on 'Some analytical difficulties'. Subsequently the title became 'Applied Economics' except in Michaelmas Term 1906 when it was 'National Industries and Trade'.

[13] Presumably Mill's *Principles*.

837. To Herbert Somerton Foxwell, 12 February 1906[1]

12. 2. 06

My dear Foxwell

I thank you much for full and clear letter. I am very sorry that I have occupied so much of your time. I had hoped to save it by suggesting a verbal discussion on points raised in my long letter. But though I regret the trouble imposed on you, I am very glad to have a full statement of your views. I do not think we could have come to the best conclusion in a conversation based on my letter alone: but with yours as well as mine, I think perhaps we may.

I have always known you to be a most excellent expositor. I have heard you speak many times; and have thought your method, your style, your lucidity and your geniality most attractive to your hearers, and most effective on behalf of the cause which you were advocating. And everything I have heard from others, whether young or old about you has been in the same direction. Ashley was staying with me when he attended your lecture a few years ago.[2]

Of course our ideals in economics are different. I have noticed that when a book or a pamphlet pleases you greatly you describe it as 'Scholarly': whereas I am never roused to great enthusiasm about anything wh does not seem to me thoroughly 'Scientific'.

I have two or three times referred to this difference, when discussing our curriculum, and described it as an advantage. I think it is very important that there should be considerable diversities of temperament among the teachers of any subject, and especially of one of which the past and the present are so meagre, and the future is so uncertain as economics.

I make it a rule not to ask students to discuss their teachers either directly or indirectly. But to say nothing of their papers, I see by mens faces when I am breaking new ground for them, and when not. It seems to me that our difference in temper causes you to lay greater stress upon accuracy as regards facts, & me to insist more on their wrestling with difficult analysis and reasoning. That of course means that I am now compelled to turn out of my lecture room nearly half—this year it was more than half—of the students whom ill advised College Tutors send to me. I do it by saying at once that I shall assume the text books, and going almost at once to some intricate reasoning which no one can possibly understand unless he knows his books fairly well.

But when I have proposed that my lectures were suitable for freshmen I have always referred them to books, and above all to Statistical Abstracts, for their facts; and have worked over the main reasoning with wh text books concern themselves. I do this unwillingly, and even perfunctorily, in regard to ground covered by my Principles Vol I; and avoid repeating what I have said in print as far as possible. I work by illustration as far as possible: scarcely ever giving facts for the sake of information, but being rather glad to get them in, when they can be used as a means of forcing people to think. When I get clear of my *Principles*, I am more at ease; I work more consecutively, but stop only on those points which I believe a man w^{d}.. ask his coach, if he had one, to explain.

That you lay what seems to me insufficient stress on what, from my own particular point of view, is at once the most arduous, the least attractive and the most essential duty of the lecturer, is the *only* objection wh, so far as I am aware, I have ever raised to your lectures. I regard your lectures as a most important part of our scheme; and I should regard your being displaced by young men as a great calamity.

I agree with you that the young men ought to do some drudgery; and I had that in mind when I suggested that Macgregor should give a full first years course, pitched rather higher than Green's.[3]

When we have got satisfactory courses for the compulsory papers, and for the central parts of the four 'advanced' papers in Part II, I think it will be a very great gain to have a special course on Socialism.[4] (But, to be frank, I think no one can lecture safely on German Socialism without having studied recent writings, including Marx's Capital Vols II & III, & other posthumous works.[5] I have not read them. But whenever I talk to Germans about Socialism, they come to the front. I have looked at them sufficiently to think they do not save Marx's position. But I should not be willing to lecture on the subject till I had read two or three thousand pages of recent German literature. Even Lassalle, whom I once read nearly through, seems to me quite incapable of being treated in lecture by aid of English sources only.) Another subject of the same kind is the history of English Economic theory. But I seldom find people want to borrow books about that. Not one in a hundred of those wh I lend relates to it, unless for men reading for the Civil Service Examination; though I *always* offer such books to third year students.

As things are, you being unwilling to lecture on English Economic history, the only thing to be done seems to me to follow the course to wh you agreed at the last Board Meeting, and to add on someone else's lectures on Economics at the end of yours. I think that the present plan under wh freshmen have their choice only between a set of lectures addressed mainly to historical students, and one which consists only of two lectures during each of two terms; while they are inundated with lectures on history, is unendurable. I should like the additional lectures to begin with the Wednesdays in the second Term, if you had no objection; since even for Freshmen the third Term is very short.[6]

I am very sorry indeed to hear that your heart gives you trouble. This makes me even more glad than I otherwise should have been that you have written so frankly. I do not wish to urge you to undertake anything for wh you are not inclined. And I trust that we may agree finally on some plan that provides fuller instruction in economics for Freshmen, and enables you to do only what you wish, and that in your own way, wh I quite recognize as being excellent of its kind.

Yours very sincerely | Alfred Marshall

Unless I hear to the contrary I will come to you at 4.30 on Wednesday (*after* tea) in College.

1 Marshall Papers. From Balliol Croft. Foxwell's doubtless expostulatory reply to [836] has not been traced.

2 Possibly Foxwell had instanced Ashley's praise.

3 See [836.10].

4 Probably proposed by Foxwell, an expert on the literature.

5 Vols. 2 and 3 of Karl Marx, *Das Kapital* (vol. 1 1867), had been published posthumously—edited by Friedrich Engels—in 1885 and 1896: English translations, appearing only in 1907 and 1909, were not available at this time.

6 See [836.10, 839.4].

838. To Edwin Cannan, 15 February 1906[1]

15. 2. 06

My dear Cannan

I am very glad that you are able to examine for the Cobden and Adam Smith Prizes. There have been some breakdowns among Adam Smith Prize writers; and I am not sure whether we shall have a very good crop. For that prize you and I are the only examiners; and the Essays are due to arrive in the last week of April. It makes no difference to me whether I read them before you do or after. Have you any preference as to time?

For the Adam Smith Prize each man selects his own subject.[2] For the Cobden Prize 'two or more' subjects are set by the Examiners and each candidate chooses one. Four, five or six seem to be good allowances for choice. Will you kindly send me two subjects any time between now and the end of March. I will ask M[r] Leadam of the Temple,[3] whom the Cobden Club have nominated as third examiner to send two more. I will add two myself & send the six on their round. We might then send to the V.C.[4] those of the six which all three regard as suitable.

Yours very truly | Alfred Marshall

[1] BLPES, Cannan Papers. From Balliol Croft.

[2] For the regulations of the Adam Smith Prize see Vol. 2 [337].

[3] Isaac Saunders Leadam (1848–1913), lawyer, author of several works on history, land laws, and agricultural policy.

[4] The Vice Chancellor of Cambridge University, at this time Edward Anthony Beck (1848–1916) of Trinity Hall.

839. To Herbert Somerton Foxwell, 24 February 1906[1]

24. 2. 06

My dear Foxwell,

I have seen Macgregor just now. There seems to have been some misunderstanding. I thought the arrangement was that your elementary course would be of three lectures a week for one Term, instead of two lectures a week for two Terms: that you would in addition give such third year (or rather '3,2') lectures[2] as you felt drawn to on Currency and Banking, Socialism, History of Economic Doctrine &c; varying perhaps a little from year to year.

The extra material wh you proposed for your first Terms elementary course, I understood you to describe as 'Distribution and Exchange'. But Macgregor, when asked whether he would carry on your course with three lectures a week for the remaining two Terms, said he did not know where the dividing line between your work & his would be as regards this subject. Broadly taken it would want much time. I told him that if he could agree with you on such points, everyone w[d].. be fully contented. He said something incidentally about the advantage of putting the elements of money very early in the course: & I said that you had spoken in the same direction. 'Perhaps you & Foxwell may agree that the best plan wd be for him to take the elements of money in the first Term, & for you to begin with Distribution & Exchange in the second'. I understood him to assent: but I seem not to have made my own meaning clear to him.

I now gather, though Macgregor does not seem clear on the point, that you feel disinclined to give up your Wednesday holiday.[3] If you do, I cannot complain. I had great scruples about suggesting it; and afterwards, I was not sure whether I ought to have suggested it.

But Macgregor & I think that if he lectures for three days in the second and third Terms, the men will get enough altogether without asking you to make any change in your first Terms lectures on the Economics of Industry.

We agreed further in a hurried talk—for he had to catch a train—that the title of his lectures might be

Lent Term	Easter Term
Distribution, Money Trade &c MWF	same course continued

Do you concur? It will be very pleasant if you do. Macgregor seems quite comfortable with this plan: he was not at ease with the other.[4]

I agree with you that there ought to be detailed lectures on small pieces of the whole subject. But I do not see how it is possible for a student preparing for the papers on 'General' or on 'Advanced Economics' to give full time to these pieces. On the other hand the Regulation which limits our choice of Special Subjects to *non* English pieces of history,[5] is 'Supplementary' and can be changed by Resolution of the Board. It was, I think, Maitland's notion: I never quite liked it. If you like to propose that its scope be enlarged, I will support you. I think, for instance, that 'English & Continental Socialism with special reference to the first half of the nineteenth[6] Century' wd make an excellent subject. So would 'Adam Smith & his relations to contemporary & later thought' or something of the kind. I am not picking my words: but merely indicating my drift.

Yours very sincerely | Alfred Marshall

[1] Marshall Papers. From Balliol Croft. See [836, 837]. Negotiations were under way for Foxwell and Macgregor to provide jointly a full elementary course in economics.

[2] '3,2' means that the course was primarily intended for third year students but might be suitable for some second-year ones. The notation was standard in the lists of lectures published in the *Reporter*.

[3] Foxwell's Cambridge lectures had long been given on Mondays and Fridays, and were to continue so. Presumably Tuesdays and Thursdays were devoted to his duties in London. His lectures in Cambridge had also long been restricted to the Michaelmas and Lent Terms.

[4] The solution eventually recorded in the lecture list for 1906–7 was that Foxwell offered 'Economics' (rather than 'Economics of Industry') in the Michaelmas Term (two hours per week)

and Macgregor continued the course in the Lent and Easter Terms (three hours per week, dropping to two hours per week for 1907–8). Foxwell's 'Currency and Banking' course in the Michaelmas Term was elevated from '1,2' to '2,3' (and to '3,2' in 1907–8). He continued to offer a '3,2' 'History of Currency and Banking' in the Lent Term. (*Reporter*, 10 October 1906, 9 October 1907).

[5] The Economics Board, in Supplementary Regulations adopted 15 June 1903, had specified that Special Subjects for Part II should deal with 'either the recent economic or general history, or with the existing political and administrative organisation, of some foreign country, or of India, or of some other dependency or colony of the United Kingdom'. (*Reporter*, 25 June 1903).

[6] Corrected from 'eighteenth'!

840. To Arthur Lyon Bowley, 27 February 1906 (incomplete)[1]

27. ii. 06

My dear Bowley,

I have not been able to lay my hands on any notes as to Mathematico-economics that would be of any use to you: and I have very indistinct memories of what I used to think on the subject. I never read mathematics now: in fact I have forgotten even how to integrate a good many things.

But I know I had a growing feeling in the later years of my work at the subject that a good mathematical theorem dealing with economic hypotheses was very unlikely to be good economics: and I went more and more on the rules—(1) Use mathematics as a shorthand language, rather than as an engine of inquiry. (2) Keep to them till you have done. (3) Translate into Engish. (4) Then illustrate by examples that are important in real life. (5) Burn the mathematics. (6) If you can't succeed in 4, burn 3. This last I did often.

I believe in Newton's Principia Methods, because they carry so much of the ordinary mind with them.[2] Mathematics used in a Fellowship thesis by a man who is not a mathematician by nature—and I have come across a good deal of that—seems to me an unmixed evil. And I think you should do all you can to prevent people from using Mathematics in cases in which the English Language is as short as the Mathematical....

I find mathematicians almost invariably follow what I regard as Jevons' one great analytical mistake, his eulogy of the Geometric mean in general: and do not see that, according to his use, erroneous weighting may do far more mischief with the Geometric Mean than with the Arithmetic Mean.[3] I always have to spend some time in convincing them of the danger.

Yours emptyhandedly, | Alfred Marshall

Another trouble is that mathematicians insist on assuming that, if p be the price which may vary to pr or to $\frac{p}{r}$, then the two variations are *prima facie* to be assumed to be equally probable. Whereas of course, if r is a considerable quantity, that is not true: Jevons has overlooked this also, I think, as a result of not thinking in English. But of course you know far more about these things than I do: and again I say I am an unprofitable Servant.

[1] Printed in *Memorials*, pp. 427–8. Original not traced. From Balliol Croft. The reason for Bowley's enquiry is not obvious. His *Mathematical Groundwork of Economics* (Clarendon, Oxford) was not to be published until 1924.
[2] The aspect of Newton's methods that Marshall had in mind remains obscure.
[3] W. S. Jevons, *Investigations in Currency and Finance* (ed. H. S. Foxwell: Macmillan, London, 1884), especially pp. 23–4.

841. To Edwin Cannan, 30 March 1906[1]

30. 3. 06

My dear Cannan,

I think both your questions are good in substance; but perhaps each might be improved in form.[2] I have to supply books &c for the Essay writers year after year: and I am beaten with many stripes if a subject is chosen on which the needful data are elusive.

I had intended to propose 'The immediate and ultimate effects on wages and profits in dangerous trades of the compulsory insurance by employers of their employees against accidents'.

On the whole I think I like that as well as your second question; but I am quite willing to withdraw it in favour of yours. I only fear that young men will not know at what level to put the 'coefficient of self sacrifice' which determines how much of the aid given to old people or school-children by the State goes to save the pockets & increase the self-indulgence of the able bodied members of families. But if you do not think that a grave objection, might I suggest that 'State assistance to parents' conveyed no clear meaning to me at first; and I do not know whether you have in view French proposals for remission of taxation proportionate to the number of the children in a family, or such things as free meals to all children (or only the poorest) in public elementary schools. I think it would be well to make it clear how far people are to treat it as a question on Malthusianism & how far as one on the ultimate incidence of bounties.

One of the questions set three years ago for the Cobden Prize was:—'The measurement & causes of the changes in the rate of interest in U.K. during XIX century, as indicated by the yields to the different classes of securities'. Mr D.A. Thomas proposed it. I liked it; but no one wrote on it.[3]

My feeling with regard to your question as it stands is that I could not direct people how to find out what the history was. At one time I tried to insert in my *Principles* a short broad statement as to the history of interest. But my search for facts left me a perfect agnostic. I thought that the historians on whom I should have to rely did not make sufficient allowance for the difference between loans that involved little trouble to the lender and such as go on today in cattle markets of 5% for 24 hours (i.e. over a million % per annum) on good security to an active lender.

So I fear that if people have to go back further than say 1700 they will lose much time on slippery chronicles; & I would therefore myself prefer to narrow the question to England in the last *two* centuries.

And now I want to ask you in return to give some searching criticism to the first draft of three subjects two of which I am thinking of proposing. They are:—

The changes in the relative wages of agricultural labourers, miners, textile workers, iron and steel workers and domestic servants in England during the last fifty years. Consider how far these changes are due to the quality of the work, and the faculties required in these several groups; and illustrate by reference to parallel changes in other countries.

The ethical and economic limits to the freedom of the officials of joint stock companies and of Government, central and local, to award to the employees high wages or other privileges, such as might be granted by a generous employer, but which, from a strictly business point of view, will not be remunerative even in the long run.

The chief changes in the character of commercial fluctuations during the last eighty years. Compare in particular those which culminated in 1826, 1873, and 1900.

Of course I should in any case propose only two of these.
Please kindly aid me as much as you can afford time to do.
Yours sincerely | Alfred Marshall

I return your letter for fear you have no copy of your questions.

[1] BLPES, Cannan Papers. From Balliol Croft. See [838].

[2] A letter from Cannan of 29 March (Cannan Papers) had proposed the following questions for the Cobden Prize: (1) The causes of variation in the general rate of interest, illustrated from the history of the last four centuries. (2) The influence which may be exerted on the earnings of labour by State-assistance to (i) parents, old people, or others, irrespective of their means, and (ii) the poor.

[3] See [813.4] and *Reporter*, 28 April 1903.

842. To Edwin Cannan, 2 April 1906[1]

2. 4. 06

My dear Cannan,

I shall withdraw the insurance question. But I think it is more definite than yours, and one of great theoretical difficulty. Labour Commission experience[2] has taught me a good deal about it. I don't think the statistical difficulties are very great as regards most of the dangerous trades. But the question whether Insurance or Factory &c Inspection is the better method of lessening danger & attracting a high quality of labour, so that net wages rise without cost to employer is very interesting to me. I believe the answer varies from one trade to another, one phase of civilization to another, & one country to another. It is one of those few questions on wh a highly trained economist could, in my opinion, render special service to the world by a study which went to the roots of the matter. I should not have proposed it, if I believed the primâ facie answer to be the right answer.

I will not trouble you any more till I have heard from Mr Leadam[3] again & am ready to send round a formal voting paper: but I think we must vote on the questions as they stand without allowing for the chance that they can be improved before publication. In fact what the author regards as an improvement may lead one of the others to wish to withdraw his vote in favour of the subject. The experience of 8 Cobden prizes weighs heavily upon me.

There is no hurry.

I inclose a paper giving an abstract of the evidence I wanted to give before the Aged Poor Commission. The paragraph marked was aimed at the Loch-Harold Cox position. But Loch objected to it as raising matter external to their inquiry. So the Chairman made me go to my *practical* suggestions, though I told him that they were merely to illustrate my creed.[4]

Yours sincerely | Alfred Marshall

[1] BLPES, Cannan Papers. From Balliol Croft. See [838, 841].

[2] This alludes to Marshall's experience as a member of the Royal Commission on Labour 1891–4.

[3] See [838.3].

[4] The paper was presumably the 'Preliminary Memorandum' Marshall had submitted to the Royal Commission on the Aged Poor of 1893. See *Official Papers*, pp. 199–204, especially pp. 201–2. Harold Cox (1859–1936), economist and journalist, was Secretary of the Cobden Club 1899–1904. Loch, a leader of the Charity Organisation Society, had been a member of the Commission.

843. To Edwin Cannan, 6 April 1906[1]

6. 4. 06

Dear Dr Cannan and Mr Leadam,

Will you kindly put your votes in the columns under your respective initials for or against each of the subjects, for which a key-word is given in the table below; while text and key-word are given on the adjoining papers.[2] It is proposed that the votes be interpreted thus:—

A. to denote strong liking,
B. " " approval
C. " " disapproval
D. " " strong disapproval, practically a veto

It is understood that each one will put A against his own subjects, whenever he would have done so if they had been proposed by another. Probably it will be best to propose four or five choices[3] to the candidates.

On receiving the voting paper, I will complete it; make out a draft report based on it, and circulate all the papers again. If the report is approved, it may be signed at once, and the matter finished. If not, I will base a new report on the suggestions made and circulate it.

Yours very truly, | Alfred Marshall

Dear Cannan,

Please kindly vote on the annexed paper & send to M^r I S Leadam, 1 The Cloisters, The Temple, E.C.

Yours AM

[Enclosure]

Subjects proposed by:—

E. CANNAN

I. INTEREST. The causes of variation in the general rate of interest, illustrated from the history of the last three centuries.

II. ASSISTANCE. The influence which may be exerted on the earnings of labour by State-assistance to (1) parents, old people, or others, irrespective of their means, and (2) the poor.

I.S. LEADAM

III. CURRENCY. The relations of currency to the general range of prices.

IV. MUNICIPAL. Municipal v. Private Enterprise.

V. PHYSIOCRATS. The relation of the doctrines of the Physiocrats to English Economic Theory.

A. MARSHALL

VI. WAGES. Changes in the relative wages of agricultural labourers, miners, textile workers, iron and steel workers, and domestic servants during the last 50 years; and the extent to which these changes are due to changes in the quality of the work & the faculties required in these several groups.

VII. CRISES. The chief changes in the character of commercial fluctuations in the last eighty years; with special reference to those which culminated in 1825, 1873, and 1900.

[1] BLPES, Cannan Papers. Typed carbon with corrections signature and postscript added by hand. From Balliol Croft. See [838, 841, 842]. For Leadam see [838.3].

[2] The enclosure, also a typed carbon, which was presumably accompanied by a voting paper, not traced.

[3] 'Choises' in the original.

844. To Edwin Cannan, 15 April 1906[1]

15. 4. 06

My dear Cannan

I agree that the Municipal Enterprise question[2] was too tersely worded. I think short questions are always to be avoided. But none of the better men w[d] have taken it as a 'burning question': though they might probably have shunned it on account of its intense difficulty. The historical element curiously predominates in the 4 survivors.[3]

Yours ever | Alfred Marshall

[1] BLPES, Cannan Papers. From Balliol Croft.

[2] See the enclosure to [843].

[3] The questions selected in their final form were:

(1) The causes of variation in the general rate of interest, illustrated from the history of the last three centuries.

(2) The chief changes in the character of commercial fluctuations in the last *eighty* years; with special reference to those which culminated in 1825, 1873, and 1900.

(3) Changes in relative wages of miners, textile workers, iron and steel workers, agricultural labourers, and domestic servants during the last fifty years; and the extent to which these changes are due to variations in the quality of the work and the faculties required in these several groups.

(4) The relation of the doctrines of the Physiocrats to British economic theory.

(*Reporter*, 1 May 1906. An earlier notice had misstated 'eighty' as 'thirty' in question 2.)

845. To Edwin Cannan, 23 April 1906[1]

23. 4. 06

My dear Cannan

Only one of the three Essays wh I had hoped for has turned up.[2] But [I][3] always had fear that the pressure of their official work w[d].. prevent two of those who proposed to write from completing their task. Of course we have only to declare whether this is worthy of a prize.

Yours sincerely | Alfred Marshall

[1] BLPES, Cannan Papers. From Balliol Croft. See [838]. The date is ambiguous and could perhaps be the 25th.

[2] For the Adam Smith Prize. The Prize for 1906 was awarded to Benians. See [859] below for Marshall's report on Benians's Fellowship essay.

[3] Word apparently omitted.

846. To John Maynard Keynes, 2 May 1906[1]

2. 5. 06

My dear Keynes,

I was very sorry to get your letter[2] this morning. But I must not urge you further. I think that if you went in for the Tripos, merely re-reading Economics in the ten days before it, you would *probably* get a first class: & that if you did not, you wd not injure your position, since it w^{d}.. be known that you had had very little time free for economics. But I must say no more.

The list of Cobden Prize subjects is reprinted ('eighty' being substituted for 'thirty' in the second subject) in the current Reporter.[3]

After you have taken your well earned holiday in August & September, I hope you may see your way to working at one of these, for your own good, for the glory of Cambridge and to the great satisfaction of

Yours very sincerely | Alfred Marshall

[1] King's College, Cambridge, J. M. Keynes Papers. Reproduced in *Collected Works*, vol. 15, p. 2. Maynard Keynes had been attending Marshall's lectures. The latter had written to Neville Keynes in December 1905 that 'Your son is doing excellent work in Economics. I have told him that I should be greatly delighted if he should decide on the career of a professional economist. But of course I must not press him'. (Transcribed into *Diaries*, entry for 3 December 1905, original not traced.) For background see D. E. Moggridge, *Maynard Keynes: An Economist's Biography* (Routledge, London, 1992), pp. 95–7; Robert Skidelsky, *John Maynard Keynes: Hopes Betrayed, 1883–1920* (Macmillan, London, 1983), pp. 165–6.

[2] Not traced.

[3] See [844.3].

847. From Sir Thomas Elliott, 24 May 1906[1]

Board of Agriculture and | Fisheries
4, Whitehall Place, S.W.
24th May, 1906.

My dear Marshall,

At a meeting of the Council of the Royal Economic Society held yesterday, I was asked, as its Chairman, to ascertain whether you would be disposed to allow yourself to be nominated as the President of the Society in succession to Lord Goschen, who has decided to relinquish the position owing to his advancing years and his desire to be relieved of public responsibilities.[2]

No one knows better than yourself the nature of the work which the Society is doing and its aspirations and the possibilities for the future. And there was a very general feeling amongst the members of the Council present yesterday that if you felt yourself able to undertake the general guidance and supervision of the proceedings and policy of the Society, as its President, we might look forward with confidence to doing even more useful public service in the future than in the past.

Of your eminent fitness for the position as an economist distinguished not only in your own country but all the world over it scarcely becomes me to speak. I should like you to feel however that your work as a thinker and a writer on the subjects with which the Society is concerned was very much present in our minds yesterday in arriving at the decision which it is now my privilege to communicate to you.

Believe me, | Yours very sincerely, | T. H. Elliott

Professor Alfred Marshall, M.A.

[1] Marshall Papers. Typewritten.

[2] Goschen had served as President since the 1890 inauguration of the Society, formerly the British Economic Association. Marshall was to decline the invitation (see [848]). Goschen's successor as President proved to be Richard Burdon Haldane (1856–1928), subsequently Viscount Haldane. Lawyer, politician, and philosopher, Haldane served as Secretary of State for War 1905–12, and was active in the promotion of university education.

848. To Sir Thomas Elliott, 25 May 1906 (incomplete)[1]

25. 5. 06

My dear Elliott

I shall always be proud of the invitation which you have transmitted to me on behalf of the Council of the Economic Association, & of the letter in which it was conveyed. I am wholly unworthy to be the successor of a man like Goschen; & I cannot but think that the Council might have made a dozen better choices. But when there is really critical work to be done, I think anyone who declines because he supposes others wd. do it better, is scarcely better than a soldier who makes an excuse for a strategic movement to the rear. And the task of presiding over the first annual Congress of the Association[2] is so high & important that my ambition calls me to do it as much as my fears warn me off it, & even more.

It is therefore with something more than regret that I am compelled to decline. I have just heard from Schloss,[3] who happens to be in Cambridge, that it is proposed to hold the Congress in October. That will mean that the arrangements for it must be made in the summer. Now the Summer is the only part of the year in which I can work to any good purpose. When I write at other times, I never know what I have already written on allied subjects, or even the same, in earlier parts of the book: in the summer only could I pass a tolerably good examination as to what there is in the book already, & what more I want to put into it. In Cambridge I am ever interrupted: I always bury myself in some inaccessible part of Tyrol. And in fact my wife has already taken a huge old fashioned room for us in a country inn for July & August; we had proposed to start about June 20 & make a détour to it.

I am too impractical & too little experienced to be able to flatter myself that in any case I could have contributed very much to the good guidance of the Society. But during the summer I could not even make an attempt to be of service in however humble a way at Committee meetings. & this special difficulty combined with my general inability to bear the strain of visits to London, & of discussion of all sorts, leaves me no choice but to decline etc...[4]

[1] Marshall Papers. From an incomplete transcript in Mrs Marshall's hand. See [847]. Elliot's brief, regretful, letter of acknowledgement of 26 May is in the Marshall Papers.
[2] Originally planned for 2 and 3 October 1906, the Congress was eventually held in London on 9 and 10 January 1907, Marshall giving an after-dinner speech on the 9th: see [863.2] below. For details of the Congress see *Economic Journal*, 16 (1906) pp. 325, 477, 638; 17 (1907), p. 1.
[3] Schloss was at this time on the Council of the Royal Economic Society.
[4] The transcript ends here.

849. To Frederick Macmillan, 9 June 1906[1]

9. 6. 06

Dear Mr MacMillan,

My book[2] proceeds slowly, though I give it all the time I can. I have made a good many changes on the proofs of the slips already in print; and have for some time been thinking that in this way, as well as by locking up the type, I am running up an unreasonable printers bill against the book. At last I have decided to have the remainder of the book, excepting perhaps the last few sheets, type written on paper of about the same size as the printers slips, and with two carbon duplicates.[3] In that way I shall have practically all the advantages of my present plan of having three copies of the back chapters in slips, and shall stop most of the charges against the book till the end is in sight. I think it is possible that the book may be ready in the autumn of 1907. I am working for that; but I have so often underestimated the time needed for it, that I do not speak with confidence.

I think that including contents &c it is likely to have about 800 pp. At a later stage I shall ask your advice as to whether it should appear in one or two volumes.

Do not trouble to acknowledge this.

Yours very truly | Alfred Marshall

Frederick MacMillan Esq

[1] British Library, Macmillan Archive. From Balliol Croft.
[2] The projected *National Industries and International Trade*: see [787, 831].
[3] Many such sheets are preserved in the Marshall Papers. Marshall's work appears to have been typed mainly by Miss M. Pate: see [916] below.

850. From Richard Lieben, 17 June 1906[1]

1 Appolzergasse, 6 | Vienna
June 17. 06

Dear Sir!

Mr H. Cuninghame in the introduction to his geometrical political economy expressed the confidence, that we—R. Auspitz and R. Lieben—would redress our having omitted your name in a future edition.[2] My friend Mr Auspitz deceased in March 1906 and I have little hope to see a new edition wanted in a near future and to profit of this occasion to give you your due place amongst our predecessors.

Therefore I take the liberty to aprise you, that we knew nothing about your privately printed papers, when our researches on the theory of price appeared and that I was not able to get a copy to this hour. Mr C. seems to underrate the extent of Austria and even of our town of Vienna in presuming, that some copies sent there—and not in trade—must necessarily reach all those, for whom they might be of interest. We would have been glad to cite your authority to corroborrate our views, as we did with all predecessors, to whom we are indebted. Mr C. reproaches us, that the foundation of our theory is the form of curves proposed by you in 1879. When I heard of this some months ago, I again requested my book seller to procure me a copy, but his researches were in vain. His agent addressed you personally and you have been kind enough to detail in your answer 25/4 06 where the contents of your paper are to be found: in Ch V Bk V, VII, VIII of your Principles and in Prof. Pantaleoni's Pure Economics.[3]

I have meanwhile consulted all the passages mentioned. I have found many interesting and original thoughts, but I could not find there such a coincidence, especially in the form of curves, as the critical remarks of Mr C. had made me expect. I found greater resemblance in fig. 52–58 of Mr C., the curves of foreign trade, taken from your paper. These curves are like ours, but they are not identical. Your coordinates are quantities of two articles of barter, while our ordinates are throughout not prices but quantities of money. There are other differences of perhaps more importance besides.

I beg you to believe, that we would not have failed to acknowledge, that you have been in the field before us, if we only had seen your privately printed writings before.

Respectfully yours | Richard Lieben

[1] Marshall Papers. The spelling of Cuninghame, aprise, and corroborrate, is Lieben's.

[2] H. H. Cunynghame, *A Geometrical Political Economy* (Clarendon, Oxford, 1904), p. 9.

> It is to be presumed that these gentlemen [Auspitz and Lieben] did not know of Marshall's previous work, in spite of the fact that copies of his [1879] memoranda had been sent to Austria. Whether, however, they did or did not know of it, we may trust that in any future edition they will give that just recognition to their predecessor that has been rendered to him by other writers in England, Italy, and America.

The allusions are to Rudolf Auspitz and Richard Lieben, *Untersuchungen über die Theorie des Preises* (Duncker and Humblot, Leipzig, 1889) and to Marshall's privately printed 'Pure Theory of Foreign Trade: Pure Theory of Domestic Values' [793.2].

[3] Correspondence not traced. The appropriate reference to *Principles* (*4*) would be to book v, ch. 12 (plus possibly chs. 3, 5, 11) and book iii, ch. 6, but these only deal with 'domestic values'. Marshall's offer-curve treatment of 'international values', which had a much closer affinity to the approach of Auspitz and Lieben, had been reproduced quite extensively in M. Pantaleoni, *Principii di Economia Pura* (Barbèra Florence, 1889), translated as *Pure Economics* (Macmillan, London, 1898): see pp. 226–50 (pp. 188–209 of the translation) where the demand–supply curves of 'domestic values' are also reproduced.

851. To Richard Lieben, 19 June 1906[1]

19. 6. 06

Dear Sir,

I have to thank you for your letter. I sent a copy of my privately printed MSS to either you or M^r^. Auspitz, I think the former, as soon as I had seen your book in 1889.[2] I addressed it to the University of Vienna. I received no answer. I had hoped to be told whether you had seen my paper before. I knew it was possible my missive never reached its goal; & that it was probable you had never seen my paper: though even to this day it seems to me not impossible that you have been unconsciously influenced by people who had obtained from my papers the fundamental idea developed by you & Dr Auspitz with so much ability.

My memory is very bad. But I have a notion that subsequent to the appearance of my dominant curve, that on p. 243 of Pantaleoni's Economia Pura 1889,[3] you wrote an article in an English journal,[4] & did not avail yourself of the opportunity to call attention to that curve.

Pupils are always more jealous for their preceptor than he is himself: & I think that perhaps you may under the circumstances bring yourself to excuse Mr. Cunynghames[5] zeal.

For myself I unhesitatingly accept without any reserve whatever your statement that you were not aware of the existence of my work when you & Dr. Auspitz wrote.[6]

I remain, with sincere respect | Yours very truly | Alfred Marshall

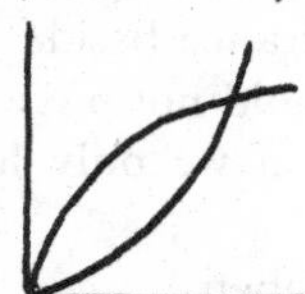

My curves of the [foreign trade] class [see fig.][7] were first used by me in lectures in 1872 or 3 when Mr Cunynghame was a student here. I practically never use any diagrams at all in lectures now, & have forgotten much that is in my own Principles.

[1] Marshall Papers. From a transcript in Mrs Marshall's hand. A reply to [850].

[2] See [850.2].

[3] [850.3]: see p. 203 of the translation.

[4] R. Lieben, 'On Consumer's Rent', *Economic Journal*, 4 (December 1894), pp. 716–9.

[5] Written as 'Cunnynghame', probably a copying error.

[6] Marshall subsequently added the following statement in a footnote (pp. 331–2) to *Money Credit and Commerce*, appendix J, where his foreign trade diagrams at last appeared.

> Some of the diagrams contained in this Appendix were reproduced, with my permission, by Prof. Pantaleoni in his *Principii di Economia Pura*, 1889, subsequently translated into English. In 1889 also appeared Auspitz and Lieben's powerful *Theorie des Preises*, in which use is made of diagrams similar to mine, which they had constructed independently. See a generous note by Dr Lieben in the *Zeitschrift fuer Volkswirtschaft*, Vol. VII.

[7] In the original the figure replaced '[foreign trade]'.

852. From Richard Lieben, 29 June 1906[1]

1 Appolzergasse, 6

Dear Sir

I thank you for your letter 19/6 06 and for your cordial acceptance of my statements and keep no ill feeling against Mr Cunynghame for his zeal.[2] I have shortly seen again your letter accusing receipt of our book, we had sent you, when published.[3] The most interesting printed M.S.S. you have kindly sent us then, as your last letter tells me, has never reached us, to my greatest regret. Mr Auspitz was M.P. of Austria and owner of a sugar manufactory, I am partner of a banking concern, both of us were in no relation with the university—we have not even a D^r's title—so the university may be excused, but not the post office in making no effort to find us. I would readily admit an indirect influence of your ideas, but in fact we worked under the direct impulsion of Walras and more so of Jevons for ten years, without the benefits of sympathy or interest for our pursuits of anybody we knew. Our university economists, most eminent men in their number, are perfectly innocent of mathematical treatment.

This our isolation has continued after our Researches had appeared and we never met in Austria or Germany such a reception as by Pf. Edgeworth and Irving Fisher.

This want of encouragement and a great want of rest caused me not to follow up newer publications as I ought have done. So I had Pantaleoni's book[4] for years on my shelf without looking at it.

So it seems we have followed your traces, quite independently, without knowing of it. As it happened to Walras, Jevons & Menger to meet at the discovery of marginal utility.

I see by your letter to the book seller,[5] that you have lost confidence in 'diagramatical fantasies', but I hesitate to ask a nearer explication, which you will no doubt give to the public.

Most respectfully yours | Richard Lieben

Bad Gastein 29/6 06 | (for a short stay—without any books)

[1] Marshall Papers.
[2] See [850.2].
[3] Doubtless 'acknowledging' was intended. The letter, not traced, was presumably written in 1889.
[4] See [850.3].
[5] Not traced. Presumably the letter of 25 April 1906 mentioned in [850].

853. To Charles Ryle Fay, 16 July 1906[1]

Stern in Abtei | Pustertal | South Tyrol
16. 7. 06

My dear Fay

I have just been looking at R. J. Thompson's paper on *Agriculture in Denmark* in the current (June) number of the Statistical Journal.[2]

He suggests that the success of Cooperation there is largely due to the homogeneity of the Danish farmers. The suggestion is new to me, & seems luminous. It might be worth while to investigate the following question:—

How far is it true that the success of any kind of coop^{n} in any country, (I omit Profit Sharing), tends to vary with the homogeneity of the class of the population to wh it is applicable?

Danish, Irish, Italian, German, and even French facts in agriculture seem to me on first blush favourable. But I may be wrong. You may think it worth while to find out.

Yours ever | A M

How far is it true that in Germany & France agricultural coopn is most successful in districts in wh there is greatest equality in
(*a*) the size of properties
(*b*) the size of farms?

[1] Marshall Papers. Fay was embarking upon a study of agricultural cooperation.
[2] Robert John Thompson, 'The Development of Agriculture in Denmark', *Journal of the Royal Statistical Society*, 69 (June 1906), pp. 374–411.

854. To Charles Ryle Fay, 7 August 1906[1]

Address for next three weeks

Stern in Abtei
Pustertal
South Tyrol
7. 8. 06

My dear Fay

Thank you for your full, kind & considerate letter about the Shaw Studentship.[2] The matter is entirely within your own competency; and I am no judge as to the wisdom of your course. It is very likely you are right. But your letter makes me think that you may not have considered all the difficulties of the case.

The Worts studentship has never yet been granted for an economic subject[3]: and you do not say that you consulted the Chairman or any other of the Trustees. The grant was intended to help you on your way. I don't think it was expected that it would support your extra expense to the end of your work: but the work was expected, I think, to be Cambridge work, & not London work. Consequently if when it is finished, you bring it out under the auspices of the London School, some people may think that Cambridge has been rather hardly treated. I doubt whether anything of the kind has yet occurred with regard to a Worts Grant; partly because I think there is no School in any other branch of science whose methods of Administration are like those of the London School of Economics in this particular relation. Perhaps you know what makes me say this. If not, I need only say here that there are, in my opinion, reasons for acting cautiously in the matter.[4]

If the London School are content that your work should be published ultimately as Worts work, there is no question on this head. If they would be content that it should be published as Worts + Shaw work (and therefore of course not in the special London series[5]) there is perhaps no question. But if they desire to bring it out in their series, then I think you should consult some person of grave & large experience as to whether you can quite fairly serve two[6] masters.

Another matter troubles me a little. When the Economics Board passed the Resolutions (1) that the Historical Subjects for Part I of the Tripos should be divided into three compartments, two of which should be taken in the first year, & the third (with Politics) in the second; and that they should be taught in a three yearly cycle

A, B
B, C
C A

and (2) that A, B, & C should be the histories respy (in XIX Century) of A England, B the Continent, C USA + British Dependencies:—when these two Resolutions were passed, I suggested that perhaps in 1907–8, when the C, A pair came on you might be ready and willing for A.[7] I think I have told you that already; & added that some opinion favourable to the suggestion was expressed and none that was unfavourable. But no official action of any kind was of course taken. I was therefore a little sorry when you told me that Fellowship exigencies required you to specialize on some subject;[8] I would rather that had waited. But I recognized *thoroughly* that you were right. I hoped however that during Term time in 1907–8[9] you would be able to give the greater part of your attention to your lectures. The class may be large; & the experience of last years large freshmans class shows that a large class goes to the bad if not looked after carefully. Do you think you will be able to do the work with credit to yourself, if you are under obligations to work during the Michaelmas and Lent Terms in London, and under the supervision of the London staff—(I am not quite sure what this means)? If you say no; then perhaps it may be possible to get Macgregor to repeat the lectures on A which he has recently given,[10] so that you may take A in 1908–9 when A, B are to be on the list. But I do not think that arrangement would be nearly as satisfactory as your taking both years: for indeed, A, B, & C have yet to be made. There are no decent books for those students who are unable to read very widely: and I had hoped that you would acquire a mastery of A. The Newnham & Girton students—if there are many of them—together with the men may be rather a heavy burden to be carried, if you have no rooms in College, & make London your home.

If on the other hand your home will be half in Cambridge, and you will be free to give a large part of your time during Term to Lecture subjects and

Lecture people, you may be able to do all that is needed to satisfy yourself and to rejoice Cambridge.

It has been greatly against the grain that I have brought myself to write this letter which may in some measure damp the joy which you naturally feel in your twofold fortune. But it seemed to me I ought to do so.

If London is complacent, then all is well. But I think your duty to Cambridge requires you to make sure that London will not be exigeant; or otherwise to consider whether you should in some measure change your position as to Cambridge.

Yours sincerely | Alfred Marshall

Macgregor is not likely to take history as his main work. The economics staff is too small for its work and we can't well expect him to lecture on economics & on history at the same time. Possibly Head might make a shift at A.[11]

In looking over my letter I fancy I may have laid more stress on your having a home in Cambridge *and* London during your Cambridge lectures, if you give them, than I had intended. I think it is a desideratum. But I think your having time to saturate yourself with the subject on wh you[12] lecture is much more important, especially in regard to your own credit.

[1] Marshall Papers.

[2] Fay had been elected to the Shaw Studentship, a research scholarship at the London School of Economics provided by Mrs George Bernard Shaw (formerly Charlotte Payne Townsend). The Studentship was of £100 a year for two years.

[3] Fay had been granted £60 from the Worts Fund of Cambridge University 'towards defraying the expense of a journey which he proposes to make on the Continent of Europe with the objective of investigating the comparative conditions of the Cooperative Movement in Germany, France, and other adjacent countries' (*Reporter*, 12 June 1906).

[4] Marshall's reasons remain obscure.

[5] That is, the series 'Publications of the London School of Economics'.

[6] 'too' in the original.

[7] The resolutions were passed at the meeting of 28 February 1906 (Economics Board Minutes, Cambridge University Archives). Fay did indeed lecture in the Lent and Easter Terms of 1908 on 'English Economic History during the 19th Century' (*Reporter*, 9 October 1907).

[8] In order to prepare a Fellowship dissertation. Fay, who had been an undergraduate at King's, was to become a Fellow of Christ's in 1908.

[9] Written '1807–8' in the original.

[10] Macgregor taught a course on British economic history only in 1905–6. See [836.2].

[11] Head lectured for the new Tripos on 'General and Economic History of Europe in the 19th Century' during 1905–6 and 1906–7. For 1903–5 he had lectured on 'General History of Europe to 1815'.

[12] Written 'your' in the original.

855. To Charles Ryle Fay, 22 August 1906[1]

Many thanks for your most pleasant & satisfactory letter.[2] As to the main point, by writing to the V. C.[3] (I thought he was Chairman, but was not sure) you put yourself in a perfectly safe position. I was alarmed lest you shd have omitted to do so. As to lectures I trust all will go right. May the prosperity, wh seems so[4] far to have fallen bountifully on you, continue throughout your travels. I shall want to hear all. Yours A M

[1] Marshall Papers. Postcard addressed to 'Herr Fay, Post Restant, Kopenhagen, Dänemark'. Postmarked 'Stern im Abtei, 22. 8. 1906'.

[2] Not traced. Presumably a reply to [854].

[3] The Vice Chancellor, Chairman of the Worts Fund trustees: see [838.4].

[4] Written 'to' in the original.

856. To Arthur Lyon Bowley, 7 October 1906 (incomplete)[1]

7. x. 06

My dear Bowley,

I ought to have thanked you before for your excellent and interesting Section F address.[2] I rejoiced to know that the whole meeting of the Section was eminently successful, at all events from the scientific, if not from the newspaper, point of view....

It is however true that the longer I live the more convinced am I that—except in purely abstract problems—the statistical side must never be separated even for an instant from the non-statistical: on the ground that, if economics is to be a guide in life—individual and more especially social—people must be warned off by every possible means from considering the action of any one cause—beyond the most simple generalities—without taking account of the others whose effects are commingled with it. And, since many of the chief of these causes have either no statistical side at all, or no statistical side that is accessible practically for common use, therefore the statistical element must be kept subordinate to general considerations and included among them....

And so you, who, in spite of your humility, are an economist by nature, should, I think, in the non-mathematical part of your work treat economic problems as a whole clearly and emphatically.

The vast services which you are rendering to economics would, I think, be doubled if you would do that: well that's too much, there's not room for it: say increased 'in a considerable ratio'.

Yours very sincerely, | Alfred Marshall

In the last two years I have given about a sixth of my lectures to almost purely statistical discussions of a general (non-mathematical) character. Each year I worked over rather carefully some hundred pages selected from the statistical parts of the two 'Fiscal Blue Books'.[3] And now that Pigou is taking 'Analytical Difficulties' I shall probably be able to do a little more in this direction.[4] But my main aim is to help people to read *through* figures, and reach the real values, the true relative proportions represented by them.

[1] Printed in *Memorials*, pp. 428–9. Original not traced. From Balliol Croft.
[2] Bowley had recently given his Presidential Address, 'On the use of Statistics and Statistical Methods' to Section F of the British Association, meeting at York. See British Association, *Annual Report*, 75, pp. 629–42. The address was reprinted in the *Journal of the Royal Statistical Society*, 69 (September 1906), pp. 540–58.
[3] Probably Board of Trade, 'British and Foreign Trade and Industrial Conditions—Memoranda, Statistical Tables and Charts' (first series, Cd 1761, 1903; second series, Cd 2337, 1905).
[4] An additional advanced class with this title had been offered by Marshall in 1905–6. It was taken over by Pigou for 1906–7 and continued by him in 1907–8.

857. To John Maynard Keynes, 14 October 1906[1]

14. 10. 06

My dear Keynes,

I am very sorry I missed you. I had been thinking of writing to ask whether you saw your way to entering for the Cobden Prize. Some of the subjects require hard thinking rather than laborious research,[2] & perhaps you might find time for one.

Yours sincerely | Alfred Marshall

[1] King's College, Cambridge, J. M. Keynes Papers. From Balliol Croft. See [846].
[2] See [844.3] for the list of subjects.

858. To Arthur Lyon Bowley, 15 October 1906 (incomplete)[1]

15. x. 06

My dear Bowley,

... In what I am writing I am bound to say something on the matter:[2] but it can only be in one or two paragraphs; and it cannot be based on thorough study. For general purposes indeed I rely more on my 'field work' in the workingmen's quarters of many German towns, and on my conversations with Germans in the Tyrol, than I do on Statistics. For the Statistics seems to me specially full of traps. 'Arbeitslosigkeit' for instance means something very widely removed from 'Unemployment,' and it is hard to find out how widely.[3] ...

A novelist has been quoted in support of the statement that German children never wear untidy shoes: they would rather go shoeless. I showed that to Dietzel and Lotz:[4] they burst into a roar of laughter. She had obviously only observed in summer: and then most children of the working classes go barefoot; those who would have tidy shoes in winter start in the morning with clean legs: those who would wear untidy shoes start with legs covered eight inches high with indurated street muck!...

This is not Statistical. But if you could take the statistical side up, and do a little field work in Germany, you might render a great service.

Yours sincerely, | Alfred Marshall

[1] Printed in *Memorials*, pp. 429–30. Original not traced. From Balliol Croft.
[2] The real wages of German and English workers (according to an interpolation in the *Memorials* version).
[3] Marshall had received a letter of 12 February 1906 from Richard Calwer (1868–1927), a German editor of business yearbooks and copious writer on economic topics, offering some account of such matters (Marshall Papers).
[4] Probably during the meetings of the British Association at Cambridge in August 1904. See [792.4].

859. To the Council, St John's College, Cambridge, (October?) 1906[1]

[1. Does this paper shew originality?]
The originality for which the subject of this paper gives scope is that of independent thought in collecting and assorting facts relevant to one issue after another and reasoning about them in such a manner as to force the conviction on the reader that the true solution or, at all events, a great part of it is before him. Though I can pretend to no acquaintance with Canada comparable to that of one who has resided there, special circumstances have induced me to make a collection of recent books relating to Canada; and I am able to say with some confidence that the more difficult part of the work in the paper has not been done by anyone else. Some of the broader causes which have till recently retarded the progress of Canada, & led many of the more enterprising of her sons as well as of her immigrants to seek their fortunes in the United States, have indeed been long common property. But from internal evidence, as well as from my reading of other writers, I am convinced that a great number of the most interesting and suggestive points made in the paper are new: and there is certainly no other account of Canadian developments which explain its retardation in a manner to be compared with that of the present paper: it is more solid, coherent, & convincing than anything else on the subject which I know.

[2. Does it give promise of higher work to follow?]
Its solidity indicates an ability & resolution of purpose giving much promise of higher work to follow. The progress made by Mr Benians since I last reported on his work to the Council has been very great. Especially has his style improved. It is not brilliant, & it is weighted by the necessity of stating the specific facts which are the foundations of his structure. Some of these are not very interesting: but he could not dispense with them; & he has apparently not felt free to stow them away in footnotes or appendices where they might be sought by anyone who was inclined to question the conclusions wh he based on them. But he has obviously endeavoured to avoid unnecessary details. And in spite of this difficulty, the style is easy, clear and not unattractive.

[3. What is your opinion as to its merits in general?]
I conclude that Mr Benians has established his position as a historical investigator of solid parts and scientific method: and that he would be a very valuable

addition to the teaching staff of the College & the University. He shows a mastery not only of historical, but also of economic method. Especially admirable is his treatment of economic geography a subject capable of high educational work, but hitherto not developed on scientific lines.

Alfred Marshall

[1] St John's College, Cambridge, College Archives. The printed form on which the report is written in Marshall's hand is headed 'Opinion of Professor Marshall on the paper on "The Progress of Settlement in Canada during the Nineteenth Century" sent in by Mr E.A. Benians'. The heading of the report (undated but clearly the third in the series) had been completed by the copyist of Marshall's previous reports [806, 829]. The questions enclosed in square brackets were printed at the head of the form and answered by number. The answer 'No' to the final listed question (see [806]) was deleted to provide space to extend the answer to the third. Benians was soon elected to a Fellowship at St John's where he was eventually to become Master.

860. To John Maynard Keynes, 20 November 1906[1]

20. 11. 06

My dear Keynes,

After you went it occurred to me that I do not know of anyone who is both able & free to devote a great deal of time to writing a Cobden Essay. For a long while every winning essay for Cobden & Adam Smith prizes has been a strong & fairly terse book of from 150 to 250 octavo pages: & I felt that with the time at your disposal you could not write an answer of that sort to any of the questions proposed.

But I think that if you wrote a comparatively short essay on Interest, without attempting original research as to its early history, but merely making what you could of the ordinarily received results, you would be very likely to find no one whose claims on the prize were stronger than yours. So I am rather reverting to your notion that you should write about that subject, & from the analytical & primâ facie point of view simply. It would not make a book; but it might make a very good Economic Journal article.[2]

I expect to be in Cambridge during nearly the whole of the Christmas Vacation. If you come home for the Public Office holidays[3] we might have a talk about it on say the 24th or the 26th at about 4—that is if you are drawn that way. I have looked out the bibliography of the history of interest & find it rather meagre. But I have one or two things to show you.

Yours sincerely | Alfred Marshall

[1] King's College, Cambridge, J. M. Keynes Papers. From Balliol Croft.

[2] See [844.3] for the list of possible topics. Keynes did not enter for the Cobden Prize which was won in 1907 by Walter Layton who chose the third topic, dealing with relative wages. Keynes was to win the Adam Smith Prize in 1909.

[3] Keynes, at this time a civil servant, was engaged at the Indian Office in London.

861. To Eleanor Mildred Sidgwick, 6 December 1906[1]

6. 12. 06

Dear Mrs Sidgwick

You may like to see the inclosed extract from the November number of the Harvard *Quarterly Journal of Economics*.[2] A few words in a list designed to guide the reading of specialists, if strong, count for more than most reviews. Personally, I am guided very much by these notes in buying books.

I cut up my magazines, & bind assorted articles; so I do no harm by tearing this out. Do not trouble to acknowledge it.

Yours sincerely | Alfred Marshall

[1] Trinity College, Cambridge, Sidgwick Papers. From Balliol Croft.

[2] Enclosed with the letter was the sheet comprising pp. 167–8 of the *Quarterly Journal of Economics*, 21 (November 1906), part of a listing of recent publications. The recently published *Henry Sidgwick: A Memoir* (Macmillan, London, 1906), prepared by Mrs Sidgwick and Henry's brother, Arthur, was described as 'An admirable memoir: valuable to economists as well as students of philosophy'. For Arthur Sidgwick see Vol. 2 [494.3].

862. To the Editor, *Tribune*, 12 December 1906[1]

I have no scheme for constituting a Second Chamber which appears free from grave objections. But if I started out to invent one my first draft would probably contain some such suggestions as these:—

1. The First Chamber to be elected for a period not exceeding four years.
2. The Second Chamber to consist of, say, eighty members, half of whom are to be elected by the First Chamber in each fourth year to serve for eight years.
3. The election to be on the (modified Hare's) proportionate representation plan.[2]
4. Either all peers to be eligible for the First Chamber, or at least half of the members elected into the Second Chamber at each election to be selected from the peers.

I think that every candidate for the First Chamber should be brought face to face with the electors, and therefore that the disadvantages of proportionate representation exceed its advantages in the case of such an election as that to the First Chamber; but I believe the plan would work well in the hands of a small and highly-expert body of electors. Though I am no politician, I have a notion that Parliament has much leeway to make up, and that any agitation for constitutional reform which hindered constructive work would be inopportune, and a great error under present circumstances.

[1] Printed in *Tribune*, 12 December 1906. Original not traced. The Liberals under Henry Campbell-Bannerman (1836–1908) had been returned by a landslide in January 1906, and there was growing friction between the Commons and the heavily conservative Lords, culminating in a major constitutional crisis 1909–11. The *Tribune* had instituted an inquiry 'as to the constitution and powers of the House of Lords', soliciting opinions from various individuals on 'the best way of securing the full recognition of the democratic will with the least disturbance to society', Marshall's was one of the responses reproduced. The short-lived newspaper *Tribune* was published only from 1906 to 1908 and had Liberal leanings.

[2] The allusion is to Thomas Hare (1806–91), pioneering proponent of proportional representation.

863. To the Editor, *Tribune*, 11 January 1907[1]

Sir,—Mr. Gwynne Davies, referring to my speech at the dinner of the Royal Economic Society on Wednesday,[2] objects to my remark that if the £1,700,000,000 which constitutes the total income of the country were divided out equally it would yield £40 a head, and that some hundred thousand or more artisan families have more than that, on the ground that a family has a claim to more than one person's share. My statement is correctly represented by you as being to the effect that many prosperous artisan families earn more than £40 a head, not more than a total of £40. For, indeed, 21s. a week all the year round, or £54 12s., is the family income at the upper limit of those eleven or twelve million persons who, by a careless misinterpretation of Mr. Charles Booth's statistics, are commonly spoken of as being on the 'verge of hunger'.

No provision had been made for a report of my speech, and I am under an obligation to you, Sir, for the excellent notice which you published.

The length of the speech, that informality which seemed appropriate to a festive meeting, and faults in exposition combined to hide the unity which underlay the whole. It was designed throughout as a statement of my views as to the special opportunities which this age has for developing economic chivalry, without which, in my opinion, a collectivist world would be a miserable failure, and by aid of which it might be possible to attain sound social conditions, with all the energy of free enterprise, and without the waste of large expenditure on hollow ostentation and even on costly real pleasures that, though solid as far as they go, are of little real worth.—I am, Sir, yours faithfully,

Alfred Marshall.

Cambridge, Jan. 11th.

[1] Printed in *Tribune*, 14 January 1907. Original not traced.

[2] Marshall's speech, 'The Social Possibilities of Economic Chivalry', had been given on 9 January at the Hotel Cecil after a formal dinner at the Congress of the Royal Economic Society [848.2]. An article based upon the notes for the speech was to appear under the same title in the *Economic Journal*, 17 (March 1907), pp. 7–29, and is substantially reproduced in *Memorials*, pp. 323–46. A short account of Marshall's 'discursive and diverting' speech appearing in *Tribune* of 10 January had elicited a short letter from Gwynne Davis of The Woodlands, Hither Green, making the criticism indicated. His letter had appeared in *Tribune* on 11 January.

864. To Macmillan and Company, 29 January 1907[1]

29. 1. 07

I do not want to make changes in my *Economics of Industry*[2] except as consequential on changes in my *Principles*. But I am contemplating rather considerable changes in that, & I fear the stock of it is not very large. Will you kindly let me know about how soon you think it will be necessary to go to press on each of the books.[3]

Alfred Marshall

[1] British Library, Macmillan Archive. A postcard addressed to 'Messrs. Macmillan & Co. Ltd.', and postmarked from Cambridge.

[2] That is, *Elements*.

[3] A note filed with Marshall's missive records that 269 copies of *Principles* (*4*) and 657 copies of *Elements* were in stock.

865. To Frederick Macmillan, 31 January 1907[1]

31. 1. 07

Dear Mr MacMillan,

I am much obliged for your kind & considerate proposal.[2] But on the whole I think it will be best to hasten the new edition of Principles Vol I; I think I can get that through the press rather quickly. I noted in October that the stock was not very large, so I worked at the new edition a little during the Michaelmas Term. I can utilize scraps of time between lecture work for such things, though not for my main writing.

The chief changes wh I propose are:—

(1) To transfer to an Appendix all those parts of Book I, wh I advise (p 9) students to postpone till they have read the rest of the volume.[3]

(2) To make several minor changes, chiefly in Book II.

(3) To write in nearly a chapter quite at the end of the volume.[4]

(1) is practically done; (3) is more than half done; & (2) will not occupy much time.

I shall not need more than one proof & that in pages except for Book I (where there is a good deal of new matter), and for perhaps about 40 pages extra.

I shall send the new matter to be put in slips in advance, & then return it to be printed with the surrounding old matter in pages. I can send Book I the only very troublesome one to press early next week if you think that advisable.

I propose to take full authors share of responsibility for correcting proofs & revises so far as new matter is concerned. But I shall be very glad if it can be understood that the Press is wholly responsible for setting up correctly all those paragraphs which are to be reproduced without change. I do not want to have to re-read for errors of the press any passages except those at which my pen has worked.

I think I can get my share done nearly as quickly as the Press could work. If I put it off at all, I should need to put it off till *National Industries* &c is off my hands. I could not pass two books through the press at the same time. I am, you know, having *National Industries* type written.[5] I think I shall see the end by next January; but it will not be ready for publication till about September.

When that is over I shall have to consider what part of my original project can be accomplished in my life time, supposing that to be fairly long. After a year's consideration, I shall probably recast Vol I as an independent treatise, keeping *National Industries & Trade* as another & aiming at perhaps two more before I cease. Meanwhile I may perhaps try to finish my *Elements* as a complete text book. I fear it is impossible to complete my *Principles* on the scale—so vastly enlarged during the present generation—required for it. Consequently I should like the new edition of my *Principles* to be calculated to last about four years.

As to the *Elements* I expect it is best to have 1000 copies printed at once from the plates; & to recast the plates so far as necessary—that will not be much—during the next Autumn.

Again thanking you, I am, | Yours very truly | Alfred Marshall

My intention is to resign my Professorship as soon as two generations of men have passed through the new Tripos; ie in June 1809:[6] & thenceforward to give myself wholly to writing.

[1] British Library, Macmillan Archive. From Balliol Croft.
[2] Presumably to reprint *Principles* (*4*) and postpone any revision.
[3] These were to become appendices A and B of *Principles* (*5*) and subsequent editions.
[4] This became book vi, Chapter 13, 'Progress in Relation to Standards of Life', of *Principles* (*5–8*). See *Guillebaud*, p. 703: also pp. 21–2 for a general description of the changes made in *Principles* (*5*).
[5] See [849].
[6] Presumably 1908 was intended. Parts I and II had first been sat in 1905 and 1906, respectively.

866. From Francis Ysidro Edgeworth, 9 February 1907[1]

All Soul's College, | Oxford.
Feb 9 1907

My dear Marshall

It has occurred to many of your economic friends that the time has come for having a picture of you painted, to be handed down to posterity. The idea was first voiced I believe by Price and myself almost simultaneously. The plan proposed is first to form a committee of representative men and then to appeal to a wider public. I have consulted several occupants of chairs and members of the Council of the Economic Society and find a unanimous wish to cooperate in this scheme. If some names are absent from a list which I enclose[2] it is simply because for the want of asking. I have thought it best not to proceed further in the matter without having obtained your consent which I hope will not be refused to so many friends and admirers.

Yours ever | F. Y. Edgeworth

[1] Marshall Papers.
[2] Not traced.

867. To Francis Ysidro Edgeworth, 11 February 1907[1]

11. 2. 07

My dear Edgeworth

Your kind letter telling me that you & Price & some others of my friends wish to have my portrait painted covers me with confusion. For why should you? I am filled with gratitude.

But when I look at the list of the names which you enclose, affection rises till it overshadows gratitude. My face is not worthy to be painted. But as you will it, I may not say nay. So I fall in with your most kind & flattering suggestion & tender hearty thanks for it.[2]

Yours very sincerely | Alfred Marshall

[1] Marshall Papers. From a copy in Mrs Marshall's hand.
[2] Subsequently a printed appeal was circulated, endorsed by a committee of 117 of Marshall's colleagues, friends, ex-students, and admirers. (There is a copy in the Library of St. John's College, Cambridge.)

868. To Frederick Macmillan, 23 February 1907[1]

23. 2. 07

Dear Mr MacMillan,

I have been working a good deal at *Principles* Vol I, to get it out of the way: I can now supply the printers with three sheets a week till it is done. But I do not think I shall be ready to recast it in about four years as I suggested in my last letter to you: and, on the whole, I think I should prefer that this edition should, like the last, be of 5000 copies if you have no objection.

Yours very truly | Alfred Marshall

Frederick MacMillan Esq

[1] British Library, Macmillan Archive. From Balliol Croft. See [865].

869. To Frederick Macmillan, 9 April 1907[1]

9. 4. 07

Dear Mr MacMillan,

I will do what I can.[2] I have just marked Sheet 18 'For Press'; and there are about 100 pp more with the Printers.

I saw them this morning: & if ever I should run short of copy for parts where I am making great changes, they will get into galley other parts, with which I will supply them, where no great changes are needed.

In the last ten years there has been a great deal of controversial writing, chiefly in U.S.A. as to the fundamentals of economics: & not a little of this has been specially concerned with my *Principles*. Much of it is not very solid, & some of it apparently written rather for the love of striking effects. But I have thought it necessary to read a good deal of it lately; &, without changing the substance in any way, I am modifying the form of about a hundred pages. Also I am writing a little new matter. I am giving myself wholly to it just now. But soon I must do other things for a few weeks.

Yours very truly | Alfred Marshall

[1] British Library, Macmillan Archive. From Balliol Croft.

[2] Presumably to expedite preparation of *Principles* (*5*).

870. From Charles Booth, 21 April 1907[1]

24, Great Cumberland Place, W.
21 April 1907

My dear Marshall,

I have been reading with delight your article on Economic Chivalry.[2] I had had the Economic Journal lying by me but had never taken it up, & all I knew of what you had said was gleaned from the newspaper reports of your speech which had interested me very much but were very incomplete. I think what you say is profoundly true & it seems to me that the facts only need recognition to become the moving force you desire to see. But it is difficult to get them recognised.

A full national life must help, & for me it is very full just now. I know you do not hold just the opinions I do—on Free Trade Modification on Imperialism & Preference[3]—on Poor Law & Old-age Pensions—on Town Development (perhaps) & Site values—but it is so wretchedly long since we have met & talked that I hardly know. We must meet.

Ever yours sincerely | Charles Booth

Kindest regards to Mrs Marshall

You would be pleased to hear of Aves' appointment—or rather engagement for the Home Office job in Australia.[4] I miss him much as he was helping me over the Poor Law Commission,[5] but I hope he will get further Gov^{t}. work, following on—& make a name.

[1] University of London Library, Booth Papers.
[2] See [863.2].
[3] Booth had become an adherent of Chamberlain's views and a member of his Tariff Commission.
[4] Ernest Harry Aves (1857–1917) had been appointed temporarily by the Home Office to report on the labour situation in the Antipodes. After a first in the Moral Science Tripos of 1884, he had been associated with the University Settlement movement, especially with Toynbee Hall, and had been a long-time assistant in Booth's enquiries into the London poor. He did indeed continue in government service.
[5] Booth was a member of the Royal Commission on the Poor Laws 1905–9.

871. To Courtney Stanhope Kenny, 29 April 1907[1]

Cambridge,
29th April, 1907.

Whewell Scholarships

Dear Kenny,

As Professor Westlake's letter of 16th December, 1906, may lead the Electors to reconsider the whole policy of the Examination for the Whewell Scholarships, I think it may be well that I should circulate two papers, bearing on the subject, which I wrote about fifteen years ago.[2] The first, written, I think in 1891, was shown to Professor Westlake, and to one or two of the Electors: but so far as I can recollect it was not circulated generally. The second, written about two years later, was shown to examiners for the Tripos[3] who came to consult me as to the scope of the examination.

I think there is much to be said for confining the Whewell Scholarship examination to various aspects of law. But I am as strongly convinced as ever that Dr Whewell did not intend law to dominate the examination.

I do not indeed doubt that his main purpose was to contribute to the formation of a strong body of experts on International Law, distributed among the chief countries of the world. I believe he looked forward to a time at which every nation would be willing, if not to accept the general verdict of such experts, yet at least to hesitate to impute malignity to another nation whose conduct was declared by the common opinion of experts in neutral countries to be technically correct.

But I believe him to have held that the *causae causantes* of international discords have their roots not in the technical interpretations of international treaties, conventions and 'laws', but in ethical sentiments and in economic interests, real or supposed: and that therefore a thorough grounding in ethical and economic principles should be required of all candidates for his scholarships.

I am far from urging that the 'dead hand' should constrain the action of distant generations who have new problems of their own, and new resources for handling them. I should therefore listen with an open mind to the argument that if Dr Whewell were alive, he would say that 'International Law' had become much larger, deeper and more coherent than in his time; and that on the whole the examination for his Scholarships should henceforth be exclusively legal. Should that opinion be adopted by the University, I think it would be right to apply for a new Statute setting aside such part of Dr Whewell's will as may be necessary for giving effect to the new view. But I think that we should conform to the spirit of the will, unless we are prepared openly to set it aside; and accordingly I submit respectfully that at least one full paper should be allocated to economics in the examination.

The study of international Treaties is so intimately connected with general history, that if Dr Whewell had not regarded economics and ethico-political philosophy as vital to the enlightened and wise treatment of international difficulties he would surely have found room among his Electors for the Regius Professor of History; and he might very properly have omitted the Knightbridge Professor and the Professor of Political Economy. In answer to this argument it has been urged that he had no great admiration for the then incumbent of the chair of history.[4] I am not aware how much authority there is for that statement: but I think Dr Whewell was looking forward to a longer time than the probable tenure of that chair by a man who was then not very young. And further, though he took a foremost part in the movement for founding a chair of Political Economy (Professor Pryme had no chair), he was the leading and most energetic supporter of a candidate for that chair other than the one who was elected.[5]

With this introduction I submit a copy of the papers already mentioned, with only one or two verbal changes.

Yours very truly | Alfred Marshall A.M.

[Enclosures.]

I.

Public International Law in Relation to Economics.

The following are instances of economic questions which have from time to time given rise to angry feelings between different nations; and have tended to bring about that tension which under the strain of some evil accident may cause a rupture, and which supervening on a state of tension may itself be the occasion of a rupture. It will be seen that almost every part of the second half of Mills' Political Economy[6] bears on one or more of these questions: and that even the analysis of Production and Distribution has some bearing, direct or indirect, on several of them.

The Conception of Rent in Relation to Profits.

What part of the gross produce from mineral and other properties owned by the State but worked by foreigners is the property of the State? E.g., what are the rights of Chili after conquering Peru with regard to Peruvian guano deposits on public land worked by Europeans?

International Trade.

What are generally the international effects of customs duties? How should international commercial treaties be interpreted? And, especially—with a view to England's interests—how are we to settle the constantly recurring disputes as to the meaning of the most Favoured Nation clauses; and of Reciprocity clauses in general? When is a duty differential against another nation? E.g., were Spain and Portugal right in denying our claim that we treated their wines and French on equal terms?

International Taxes.

What is the incidence of taxes levied by a State on persons resident within their boundaries, but possessing property outside of them? E.g., how far is a graduated legacy duty an infringement of international rights, if it is assessed directly or indirectly on property outside the boundaries of the State? When is a tax on the interest of government securities held by foreigners a partial repudiation?

Traffic.

What charge for lighthouse and other accommodation for foreign shipping is a legitimate charge for service rendered, and what are indirect ways of taxing foreigners, justifying reprisals? What taxation, direct or indirect, levied by Holland or Turkey on goods and passengers passing between the ocean and the upper Rhine or the Black Sea is an infringement of international comity? How are similar questions to be dealt with in the[7] case of railway traffic, especially when the railways or some of them are State railways? Does Canada act fairly by the United States as regards summer traffic through the Welland Canal? And how are we to judge the United States' proposals to put specially heavy charges on Canadian traffic to the sea board, when Canada's own ports are ice-bound?

International Currency.

What are the limits and the difficulties of international treaties as to currency? Has the treatment by France of the other members of the Latin Union as regards worn and token coins been overbearing?

International Migration.

Assuming it to be a rule of international comity that any nation should admit freely a subject of other nations in the absence of any special cause to the contrary; and that one such cause may be that the individual in question is likely to become a burden to the state:— on what principle should it be decided whether the rule is being used for different purposes so as to unfairly exclude those who are not really likely to become so liable.

Lastly the recent Berlin Labour Conference (1890)[8] may perhaps be the first of many international discussions, carried on by diplomatists and economists, as to the effects and the limits of agreements for parallel movements in different countries of the position which the State takes with regard to the claims of the working classes. And should any such agreement be reached, complex questions of international law may arise when it is alleged that any of the parties to it are breaking it or evading it; and if so whether the plea of necessity, (which is sure to be urged in such a case), is a valid one.

II.

Specimen Questions Illustrating the Bearing of Economics on International Law, and Suitable for an Examination Paper.

What are the advantages and disadvantages of specific and *ad valorem* duties respectively. In case the duties on goods which a country A. largely imported from country B. were changed from an *ad valorem* to a specific basis, how would you decide on the merits of a friendly remonstrance from the Government of B. to the effect that the change had really increased the burden on B's goods, while professing to leave the burden unchanged?

Under what circumstances is a tax on the income paid to the foreign holders of national bonds to be regarded as a partial repudiation?

What are the causes which govern the amount of currency per head required in different countries. In case of the agreement proposed at the Brussels conference of 1892 that £5,000,000 worth of silver should be bought and appropriated to currency purposes annually by the European states represented,[9] what inquiries should be made in order to assign to each state its fair share of this obligatory purchase?

What is the justification for charging light and harbour dues on the ships entering a port? Do they stand on the same footing as regards international comity as customs duties; and by whom are they ultimately borne?

If a state A. receives from another B. a tribute of a fixed sum in the currency of A., has B. any grievance (1) if A's currency being in a worn state it calls in that currency and replaces it by a full weight currency, (2) if A. retaining the weight of its currency unchanged levies a seignorage on it?

Give some account of the nature extent and causes of the recent changes of the value of silver in India. How would you estimate a change in the value of silver, with a view to the inquiry whether the English government was morally justified in raising the silver value of the dues paid by the Bengal Zemindars,[10] by measures that are not technically at variance with their contracts.

[1] Cambridge University Archives, Records of the Whewell Benefaction. From a typed carbon copy, with the recipient's name and Marshall's initials added by hand.

[2] The Whewell Scholarships for International Law, established in 1867, were supported by a trust established at the 1866 death of William Whewell by the terms of his 1863 will. Foxwell had been awarded one in 1872. Marshall took the occasion of a proposal from John Westlake, Whewell Professor of International Law, that changes be made in the conditions of award, to press for a greater role for economics. Westlake's 16 December letter was considered at the meeting of Whewell electors on 13 May 1907 (Westlake, although not an elector, was invited to attend). Marshall moved that 'in view of the new opportunities for the study of International Law in the curriculum of Economics and Politics, it is advisable that a part of the Whewell endowment should be devoted to the reward of proficiency in the papers on International Law, General Economics and Political Ideas, in Part II of the Economics Tripos'. A printed memorandum of 24 May 1907 from Marshall and Westlake—proposing with the support of the Economics Board that there be three scholarships, one opened up on Marshall's lines, instead of the usual two—was considered by the electors on 7 June 1907, but the matter lapsed thereafter. Westlake, like Marshall, was to retire in 1908.

[3] Presumably the Law Tripos.

[4] Charles Kingsley (1819–75). The Whewell electors comprised the Vice Chancellor; the Master of Trinity (Whewell's College), the Regius Professor of Civil Law (E. C. Clark), the Downing Professor of the Laws of England (Kenny), the Knightbridge Professor of Moral Philosophy (Sorley), and the Professor of Political Economy. Edwin Charles Clark (1835–1917) held the Regius Professorship 1873–1913.

[5] Whewell had supported J. B. Mayor: see Leslie Stephen, *Life of Henry Fawcett* (Smith Elder, London, 1885), pp. 117–22, for an account of the boisterous 1863 election won by Fawcett. George Pryme had held only the title of Professor of Political Economy before the establishing of a permanent chair in the subject.

[6] That is, Mill's *Principles*.

[7] 'This' in the original.

[8] The International Labour Conference, convened rather peremptorily by the German government, met in Berlin, 16–29 March 1890, but its proceedings were overshadowed by Bismarck's departure from office. For a description of its resolutions see *The Times*, 31 March 1890 (5a–c).

[9] An International Monetary Conference, instigated by the USA in the hope of increasing monetization of silver, met with little success in Brussels from 22 November to 19 December, when it adjourned until March 1893. The proposal Marshall describes was made but not adopted: see *The Times*, 26 November 1892 (5b-c).

[10] Landholders.

872. To William Albert Samuel Hewins, 21 May 1907[1]

21. 5. 07

My dear Hewins

Thanks for your letter.[2] I did not mean to advocate a sort of death-bed repentance. I think a man s^{hd}. be chivalrous all through his life; & that while engaged in business he should deal fairly with customers & generously with employees. But generosity to employees needs, I think, to be directed by considerations into wh I had no time to enter in what was, after all curtailments, a moderately prolonged dinner speech.

Yours sincerely | Alfred Marshall

[1] Sheffield University Library, Hewins Papers. From Balliol Croft.
[2] Not traced. Presumably containing comments on Marshall's 'Economic Chivalry' paper [863.2].

873. To an unknown correspondent, 6 June 1907[1]

6. 6. 07

Dear Sir

I am so busy, that I must ask you to put up with a short answer to the far reaching question wh you send me.

Prof. W. J. Ashley of Birmingham is unquestionably that one of the English advocates of Tariff Reform whose arguments are regarded with most respect by trained economists generally. His book on the Tariff Problem is published by King.[2]

I am not a member of the Cobden Club. When urged to join many years ago, I refused on the ground that some of their utterances grossly exaggerated the benefits of free trade, & underrated the compensatory benefits wh Protection might render—not indeed to England—but to New Countries & even Germany. The most reckless user of those clap trap arguments for free trade wh I loathed was Mr Chamberlain.

Tariff Reform advocacy generally is stained by just the same faults as those wh I disliked in Mr Chamberlains advocacy of free trade. Protection in a new country may increase the employment for her people after a time: But setting aside some intricate questions of 'Retaliation' & 'Dumping', as to which there is no general agreement among students, I believe I may assert with some confidence that no really trained economist, whether free trader or protectionist, thinks that protection would increase employment on the balance, except when used as List urged with consummate ability for educational purposes. I should say that Lists *National System of Political Economy* can be had in English.[3] I may add that I know of no treatise on Economics in general written from the protectionist point of view in English, wh has general vogue, except Prof R. Ellis Thompson's *Social Science*.[4] In 1875 I went to the United States chiefly to learn what I could from the Protectionists there; & I found that they regarded that book—though written by a young man—as to a large extent superseding Carey:[5] & that they adopted it as putting their case.[6] I do not know what changes it may have undergone since then. But my edition is a very able book; & I have not heard of any to supersede it; though I read as much of American & German economic literature as I do of English, if not more.

Sir Vincent Caillard's *Imperial Fiscal Reform*[7] stands next in rank to Ashleys book. He is not a trained economist; & occasionally makes rather wild remarks. But he has a very strong, original mind; and is always worth reading.

On the Free Trade Side nothing systematic has been written: those who know most are least willing to mix in the turmoil—a stronger word than this is really needed—of political conflict on the methods adopted by the Tariff Reform League.

But you will find good answers to some of their assertions in Prof Smarts *Return to Protection*,[8] in Mr Pigou's *Protective duties* & *The Riddle of the Tariff*[9] & elsewhere: but, for the greater part, time may be trusted to clear away much of the dust with wh the air is now filled: and no one who puts a high value on his own time, is likely to write controversially at length on the subject.

Yours truly | Alfred Marshall

1 BLPES, Miscellaneous Letter Collection. From Balliol Croft. Presumably in response to a request for advice on the tariff issue.

2 William James Ashley, *The Tariff Problem* (King, London, 1903).

3 Friedrich List, *The National System of Political Economy* (Longmans, London, 1885; original German publication 1841).

4 Robert Ellis Thompson, *Social Science and National Economy* (Porter and Coates, Philadelphia, 1875), no subsequent edition. Thompson (1844–1924) served for many years as Professor of Social Science in the University of Pennsylvania.

5 Henry Carey, leader of the Pennsylvania protectionists and copious writer on economic and social matters.

6 See *Early Economic Writings*, vol. 2, pp. 101–2. For details of Marshall's American visit see Vol. 1, [21–32], especially [31].

7 Sir Vincent Caillard, *Imperial Fiscal Reform* (Arnold, London, 1903). Vincent Henry Penalver Caillard (1856–1930), soldier and man of affairs, had become Chairman of Chamberlain's Tariff Commission in 1904.

8 William Smart, *The Return to Protection* (Macmillan, London, 1904).

9 Arthur Cecil Pigou, *Protective and Preferential Import Duties* (Macmillan, London, 1906); *The Riddle of the Tariff* (Johnson, London, 1903): see [810].

874. From Frank William Taussig, 2 August 1907[1]

Cotuit, Mass.
Aug. 2, 1907.

My dear Professor Marshall:

I have gladly availed myself of the opportunity afforded me of joining in the movement testifying the appreciation of your work, & have sent a modest (very modest) subscription to the Portrait Fund.[2] There is no living economist from whom I have learned more, & none to whom I should so gladly testify my esteem & admiration. Not least, I remember the true hospitality of Mrs. Marshall and yourself when we were in Cambridge,—a hospitality not the less cordial for your being taxed so much for foreign admirers & visitors. Mrs. Taussig joins me in cordial good wishes to both of you.

Believe me to be, with true regard | Very sincerely yours | F. W. Taussig.

1 Marshall Papers.

2 See [867.2].

875. To Herbert Somerton Foxwell, 8 August 1907[1]

8. 8. 07

My dear Foxwell

Many thanks. Though my own preference is for discussing the ground ideas on wh Socialists base their schemes, with but slight reference to their personal idiosyncracies, & with as little allusion as possible to burning issues of the day, I think I can do no harm by adding the words 'Some discussion of socialism being included under this head' after the statement that the General Papers in Part II 'are to lay stress on Public Finance, the Economic functions of Government, & the ethical aspects of economics generally'.[2]

And I am very glad to do so.

Yours ever | A. M.

[1] Marshall Papers. From Balliol Croft.

[2] This phrase comes from the pamphlet 'Introduction to the Tripos' [831.4] (p. 11 of the fuller version) which was doubtless being revised.

876. To Frederick Macmillan, 2 September 1907[1]

2. 9. 07

Dear Mr MacMillan,

I think the Pitt Press sent you my new Preface a few days ago, & that you now have the whole of the book[2] ready for binding.

It seems to me to be in the interest of the book that a copy shd be sent to every leading teacher of economics in English speaking countries. For people are often slow about buying a new edition of a big book of which they already have a copy: & yet, if the teacher has a different edition from that in the hands of the younger men, there is some confusion. So I have ventured to make out a rather long list of persons to whom I think the new edition might be sent. Nearly all of them are addicted to rather severe thinking: I have avoided those whose bias is towards easy & popular work, and also specialists in administration &c, unless they are specially influential.

I am not sure that I have included all the most important American teachers: perhaps your American House may think additions advisable. I have added two or three names on private grounds.

I have indicated names by my initials on the inclosed list,[3] with some MSS additions on p 27. There are about 50 in all.

I do not think it will be necessary to make great alterations in the little book: but I have not gone into the matter in detail. There are many small improvements in phraseology in the *Principles* wh I should introduce into the *Elements* if that were being set up afresh. But they would be troublesome and expensive, unless the time had come for throwing away the old plates: & I gather that that time has not yet come. But perhaps you will kindly consider the question and let me know at your leisure.[4]

If you decide that new plates are not needed, I should disturb very few pages. For the new matter in the *Principles* chiefly relates to subtle questions wh were wholly ignored in the Elements. I shd however insert a little of the new matter on Unemployment &c from the last chapter of the Principles.[5]

Yours very truly | Alfred Marshall

[1] British Library, Macmillan Archive. From Balliol Croft.

[2] *Principles* (*5*), printed at the Pitt Press in Cambridge.

[3] Not traced. Apparently based on a printed list.

[4] It was decided to reprint another 5,000 copies of *Elements* and delay major revision (letter of 5 September 1907 to Frederick Macmillan, Macmillan Archive).

[5] See [865.4].

877. From Hastings Bertrand Lees-Smith, 17 September 1907[1]

16 Park Terrace | Oxford
September 17th, 1907

Dear Professor Marshall

I am delighted to receive the new edition of your great work,[2] & thank you for paying me the compliment of having it sent to me. I began the study of economics with your Principles, & however widely I read on the subjects covered in your first volume, I never return to it without finding that all that is wisest has been there the whole time. I sincerely hope that you will have strength to carry out the work you project in the new preface,[3] & that those of your pupils who are not in Cambridge will be given the chance of learning still further from our greatest master

Yours sincerely | H. B. Lees Smith

[1] Marshall Papers.

[2] *Principles* (*5*). Lees-Smith was a lecturer at University College, Bristol (chartered as a University only in 1909) and also associated with Ruskin College, Oxford.

[3] See *Guillebaud*, pp. 45–6, for the relevant passage. Marshall projected, instead of the long-promised second volume of *Principles*, 'an almost independent volume, part of which is already in print, on *National Industry and Trade* . . . [which] may be followed at no very long interval by a companion volume on *Money, Credit, and Employment*'. He hoped eventually 'to compress these two volumes, together with some discussion of the functions of Government, into a single volume' that might complement *Principles*. Perhaps because of this hope, *Principles* (*5*) continued to be described as 'Volume One'.

878. From George Armitage-Smith, 19 September 1907[1]

3, Albert Terrace, | Regent's Park, N.W.
19. Sept 1907

Dear Prof. Marshall,

Allow me to thank you warmly for the copy of the 5th. Edition of your

'*Principles*' which you have kindly sent me. I shall value it greatly both for its own worth & as your gift.

From its first issue 'The Principles' has been the Text Book for advanced students in that Division of Economics, while the smaller Book has been the text Book for beginners, & I have had from *100* to *160* students per session for many years.[2]

I earnestly trust that your health & strength will be maintained to publish the complete work as set forth in your new preface.[3] Some of us who have been engaged in teaching Economics have been looking forward to the other Vols with a longing interest. It is a vast undertaking & will be a monument of exhaustive investigation & an invaluable heritage to the business man, as well as a permanent record of Economics' attainment at this stage of civilization. With much esteem & renewed hopes of vigour for its completion.

Believe me | Yours sincerely | G. Armitage Smith

[1] Marshall Papers.

[2] At Birkbeck College, which was affiliated to London University. Armitage-Smith was at this time Dean of the University's Faculty of Economics.

[3] See [877.3].

879. From Joseph Shield Nicholson, 21 September 1907[1]

Tummelbridge | Perthshire
21st. Sept. 1907

My dear Marshall

I thank you for the copy of the new edition of your Vol I. which I shall read in the course of the winter in connection with my Honours' class.

In the meantime I have looked through the new Preface and I learn with satisfaction that more of your systematic work may be expected soon.[2] It is highly desirable that students should have a wider view of the range of Pol. Econ., and should realise that three more thick volumes would be required to complete your work on the same scale as Vol I.

When I read Prof. Ashley's address I wondered what you would think of his account of Ricardo and other economists.[3] The address reminded me of the letters I used to get from Cliffe Leslie about thirty years ago.

I see you call it 'important'.

I trust your health is satisfactory. I have been taking a holiday this summer. In three more sessions I shall have earned my maximum pension for thirty years service and for many reasons should be glad to get rid of the strain of 150 class meetings every winter. Does the personal reference in your preface mean that you contemplate giving up your Profship.[4] It is no doubt an exacting position and personally I prefer Edingh. to Cambridge in spite of the longer hours of official duty.

Give my kind regards & remembrances to M^{rs}. Marshall. My elder daughter is coming up to Girton in Oct. 1908 to read math.[5]

Yours very sincerely | J. S. Nicholson

[1] Marshall Papers.

[2] See [877.3].

[3] A footnote to the Preface of *Principles* (*5*), dealing with Marshall's differences from J. B. Clark, was induced 'by Prof. Ashley's important address at the British Association, which was delivered when the text of this volume was in type'. Marshall charged that Ashley overrated differences among economists, yet failed to observe differences between Marshall and Clark as to the use of the 'statical method', the one point on which the two differed significantly. See *Guillebaud*, pp. 51–2; W. J. Ashley, 'Presidential Address' [to Section F], *Annual Report*, 76 (1907), pp. 579–92; reprinted as 'The Present Position of Political Economy', *Economic Journal*, 17 (December 1907), pp. 467–89. Marshall's footnote dealt briefly with the issues discussed in his 1902–3 correspondence with Clark (see [736] above and Vol. 2 [727, 730, 732]).

[4] 'I hope ere long to have more command of my time and my limited strength' (*Guillebaud*, p. 46).

[5] Marjorie Nicholson (1888–1936), subsequently Mrs Lee, obtained a third in Part I of the Mathematical Tripos of 1910 and a lower second in Part II of the Economics Tripos of 1912. She was an assistant in the Labour Exchange Service, 1913–15. (*Girton Register 1869–1946*, Cambridge, 1946.)

880. From Lancelot Ridley Phelps, 25 September 1907[1]

Oriel
25 Sep^{t}.. 1907.

My dear Marshall,

I am just back & have found your kind gift. It is most acceptable. The next generation will probably come to form its opinion of me by the books on my shelves with the inscription 'from the author'. My one chance of shining will be with borrowed light! & I rejoice to think that it will at least come from worthy fires, your own amongst the worthiest! But to drop badinage, it is very good of you. I have read through the new preface, & am a little out of heart at the postponement of much that we have been hoping to see.[2] But perhaps after all it will come sooner than we think.

I was sorry not to find M^{rs}. Marshall & yourself at home when I was in Cambridge in July. There is so much just now that I sh^{d}.. wish to have your opinions on, & our generation still values talk!

With very kind regards | I remain, my dear Marshall | Very heartily y^{rs}.. | L. R. Phelps.

[1] Marshall Papers.

[2] See [877.3].

881. From Jacob Harry Hollander, 1 October 1907[1]

The Johns Hopkins University | Baltimore, Md.
October 1, 1907

Dear Professor Marshall:

It was a great pleasure to receive a copy of the new edition of the 'Principles', and I congratulate you heartily on its appearance. The changes and additions, in so far as I have been able to study them carefully, seem admirable and insure the position of the treatise. For a number of years we have been using the book for our advanced undergraduate courses, and with undiminished success.

I was very greatly interested in the new plans for the succeeding volume, or volumes,[2] as I must now say, and in common with that body of friends and students whom you have stimulated and helped, I pray earnestly that your strength may endure for the full completion of the *magnum opus*.

I am very sensible of the kind spirit in which you have referred to my *Quarterly* paper on 'Ricardo's Theory of Value'.[3] I am trying my best to push forward a fuller exposition and criticism of the man and his work, but distractions, state and personal, intervene with maddening regularity to delay its progress.

With kind regards to Mrs. Marshall and yourself, believe me,

Faithfully yours, | Jacob H. Hollander.

[1] Marshall Papers. Typewritten.

[2] See [877.3].

[3] J. H. Hollander, 'The Development of Ricardo's Theory of Value', *Quarterly Journal of Economics*, 18 (August 1904), pp. 455–91. See *Principles* (*5* and *8*), p. 821, for Marshall's reference to Hollander's 'illuminating' paper.

882. From Herbert Somerton Foxwell, 2 October 1907[1]

1 Harvey Road, | Cambridge.
Oct. 2. 1907.

My dear Marshall

I have just received from Macmillans' at your instance the 5th. Edn. of your Principles. I am extremely obliged to you for again remembering me in this way. I have only had time so far to read the Preface, & to glance at the arrangement: but I propose at the first opportunity to read the book right through.

I am delighted with the Preface, which I think I like more than anything else you have written, & find myself in complete agreement with it.

The new arrangement too seems to me immeasurably better than the original one, especially from the point of view of the teacher, who has to consider the wants of the tyro.[2]

I believe that this altered arrangement alone will lead to a greatly increased use of the book for beginners of average ability.

But besides this the unity of the book & the sequence of the argument is greatly strengthened, more perhaps than you will feel yourself, because you had already grasped the whole before you began to write, & can hardly put yourself into the position of a reader who nibbles his way into the book from the first page.

These men will of course find the Preface extremely difficult, & cannot be expected to follow it: but it is I suppose inevitable that a preface of the critical type should imply at least a knowledge of the work it introduces.

I was surprised to find that in spite of small type for the Appendices the new ed^{n}. has 50 pp. more than the last. It does not look quite so large: perhaps the paper is thinner.

A William A Cecil of the Grenadier Guards, whom I take to be the son of Lord W^{m}. Cecil, & heir through his mother to a peerage,[3] wrote me an interesting & boyish letter saying that he was going into politics & wanted to study economics. I dont know if he has written to you. He can only attend lectures in the evenings, as he is on guard at Windsor in the morning: so on the whole I recommended him to go to the School of Economics but I may be able to look after him a bit. He, like the rest of his family, is much exercised in his mind about the Tariff Question: about which, I suspect, we shall hear less as time goes on, for Balfour sits very tight, & seems at present to have the control.

I recommended him alternatively (not knowing his bent) to read your book or Nicholsons. I hope he did not get yours, so that he may begin with the 5th. Edition.

We have had a good holiday in Barmouth—only one half day's rain—but the last week was a bit too hot—80° in the shade—not to speak of the scorching sun—& rather put a stop to our walks.

I hope you & M^{rs}. Marshall are as fit as when I saw you last.

I was delighted to hear of the Master's engagement.[4] He has long wanted to be married. It will be an excellent thing for the College, & I hope for himself too.

I was sorely tempted to take a little cottage on the Barmouth Estuary in which Ruskin & Charles Darwin are said to have lived: but my brother,[5] who kindly came to inspect it for me, condemned it as hopelessly damp.

I hear the general entry[6] is a record one.

Ever yours | H. S. Foxwell.

[1] Marshall Papers.

[2] The main rearrangement was the transfer of the extended historical accounts from book i to new appendices A and B: see [865]. Foxwell had favoured in 1898 making such a change in *Principles* (*4*): see Vol. 2 [541].

[3] William Amherst Cecil (1886–1914) eldest son of Baroness Amherst of Hackney (Lady William Cecil). A lieutenant in the Grenadier Guards he did not matriculate in Cambridge.

[4] Charles Taylor (1840–1908), Master of St. John's since 1881 and hitherto a bachelor, was to marry Sophia Dillon on 19 October 1907.

[5] Probably his medical brother William Arthur Foxwell (1853–1909). Ruskin is, of course, John Ruskin (1819–1900), author, artist, and critic.

[6] Presumably the entry to St John's.

883. To the Vice Chancellor, University of Cambridge, 4 October 1907[1]

4 October 1907

Dear Mr Vice Chancellor,

I have long resolved to retire from official work at the close of the current academic year; and, partly in order that I may be free to speak on the subject to others, I desire to communicate my intention formally to you without further delay. I should like my successor to be able to take part in the arrangement of the lecture list that will be published next June.

I therefore hereby resign the Professorship of Political Economy in this University as from the day following the Division of the Easter Term 1908.

For some reasons I am more sorry to leave my lecture room than I thought I ever could be. The main cause of this is the growth in recent years of a small but vigorous staff, which goes some considerable way towards the attainment of that division of labour which is necessary for the modern developments of economics. The unfailing kindness and generosity of my colleagues has lightened my labour in every possible way, & I shall ever be grateful to them.

But, not to lay stress on the fact that I have already passed the age at which it is generally expedient to make room for younger men, I must be able to give the remainder of my energies to attempting to finish however inadequately the task which I undertook long ago. The ill health, from which I long suffered, has indeed passed away. But, in spite of rigorous economy of my strength, I find that the number of hours in each year, during which my mind is of any considerable use, steadily diminishes: & I can now do very little effective writing during Term time. Therefore my course is clear.

I remain | dear Mr Vice Chancellor | Yours sincerely | Alfred Marshall

[1] Cambridge University Archives, Guard Book on Professorship of Political Economy. From Balliol Croft. The current Vice Chancellor was the classicist Ernest Stewart Roberts (1847–1912) of Caius. He served for two years from 1 October 1906.

884. To Frederick Macmillan, 4 October 1907[1]

4. 10. 09

Dear Mr. MacMillan

I had reckoned to finish a chapter of my new book before lectures begin, but I will stop in the middle & give the next week to the *Elements*.[2] I will start the Press at work on Monday, & hope I may be able to get my share done quickly.

Thank you for the twelve copies of my *Principles*.

I shall be glad when the publishers have come to some arrangement with the *Times*.[3] I dislike the methods & the tone of the *Times* manager. But, as you know, I think that the booksellers get too large a share of the price of those books which appeal to relatively small audiences. The net system as at present worked seems to me to put too great difficulties in the way of a man who must earn his living & yet wishes to think before he writes. Authors work: publishers exercise judgment & take risks. But I cannot discover what booksellers do for the extension of knowledge.

Yours sincerely | Alfred Marshall

[1] British Library, Macmillan Archive. From Balliol Croft. Reproduced in C. W. Guillebaud, 'The Marshall–Macmillan Correspondence over the Net Book System', *Economic Journal*, 75 (September 1965), pp. 518–38, at p. 535. Although the letter is clearly dated as 1909, this appears to be a slip of the pen as Guillebaud notes (p. 535 n.).

[2] See [876, 876.4].

[3] This refers to an extended dispute over the net-book system between the Times Book Club and The Publishers' Association, to be settled only in September 1908. For details see [885] and pp. 535–6 of Guillebaud's article. A blow-by-blow account of this 'Book War' is given in Charles Morgan, *The House of Macmillan (1843–1943)* (Macmillan, London, 1944), pp. 193–207.

885. From Frederick Macmillan, 5 October 1907[1]

Macmillan & Co. Ltd.
St. Martin's Street. | London. W.C.
October 5 1907

Dear Professor Marshall,

I am obliged to you for kindly promising to let the Pitt Press people have the corrections for your *Elements* next week. We are most anxious that the reprint should be ready by the time our stock of the present Edition is exhausted.

What you say about the Net Book System interests me very much & I should like to have an opportunity of discussing it with you at length.

The *Times* and its methods are only accidentally connected with net books. The Times Book Club was avowedly started because the proprietors found the circulation of their paper falling off in consequence, as they supposed, of the competition of the cheaper news-papers. They did not wish to reduce the price of their journal, but thought that if they offered their subscribers some inducement such as the free use of a circulating library, it would enable them to keep the price of their paper at three pence & at the same time increase its circulation.

The managers of the Book Club soon found that furnishing a Circulating Library for nothing was an expensive undertaking & came to the conclusion that the only way in which they could lessen the cost to themselves was to establish a monopoly of the Circulating Library business by underselling their rivals & driving them out of business: they thought that if they could accomplish this they would be in a position to dictate the prices at which they bought books from publishers. They began by offering to take large numbers of certain popular novels at absurdly low prices at the same time making it a condition of purchase that the publisher should spend a certain sum of money in advertising the book in the columns of *The Times*. For instance they offered to buy 1000 copies of a certain six shilling novel which we published if we would supply it to them at 3/- *and* spend £100 in advertising it in their paper. As the author of this book received a royalty of $1^s/6^d$ per copy & the book cost at least another $1^s/6^d$ to produce it is obvious that it would not have been worth our while to sell it to the Book Club for 3/- and to spend a sum equal to 2/- on each copy they bought in advertisements.

Considering the sort of people who are engaged in managing the Book Club one could imagine how they would proceed if they had succeeded in establishing a monopoly of the Circulating Library business, & the publishers with the assent of the authors whose books were likely to be affected declined to walk into the trap set by the astute Americans[2] & baited with extravagantly large orders. Finding themselves foiled the managers of the Book Club lost their tempers & proceeded to fling against the publishers as a body the most outrageous charges of every sort which their ingenuity could invent. They thought that they would be able to bully us but failed, & now they are sulking. I don't think we shall hear much more about them. I cannot find that they have in any way injured or affected our business.

The net book system is another matter. We began it, as you know, seventeen years ago because we found that booksellers had by insane competition & underselling each other, reduced the profits of their business to such an extent that in order to avoid bankruptcy they were giving their whole attention to 'fancy goods' & toys etc & devoting less & less space in their shops to the display of books. We are decidedly of opinion that the sale of books, particularly of solid books, is increased by having them kept in stock by a number of dealers in all parts of the country, and as it is of importance to us that our customers, who are the booksellers, should be solvent we tried to devise a plan which would enable them to buy good stocks of books and to pay us for them.

It was obvious that this could never be done so long as the booksellers were allowed to undersell one another because one persistent underseller in any town could always upset any agreement his rivals might make among themselves; so the publishers determined that in the case of certain classes of books they would only give trade terms to dealers on condition that the books were sold at the prices fixed on them by the publisher & not below. In fixing the trade terms we tried to hit upon a rate of discount which would be enough to give a bookseller a fair profit after paying his working expenses & yet not be large enough to tempt him to break the price. I think the terms arranged are reasonable—whether they are or not is a matter for discussion—but the *principle* is the same in any case, viz that the publisher should fix the price at which the books he publishes are to be sold.

The *net system* has been generally confined to books which retailers may be expected to speculate in to some extent & the sale of which is affected by a bookseller's exertions.

School books are not published at net prices because the bookseller does little more than act as a carrier or delivery agent. If we bring out a new Arithmetic or a Latin Grammar we have to do the pushing of it ourselves. We are in communication with nearly all the teachers of various sorts in the Kingdom to whom we send presentation copies & prospectuses & catalogues of any new book we think likely to suit them. We have a number of travellers who visit both Elementary & Secondary Schools not to sell books but to shew them and explain their merits. In fact we, the publishers, do all the *selling* of an Educational book and the bookseller only delivers it. This being so, we have not made school books *net* and they are therefore sold at discount prices. Indeed the prices at which Elementary School books (Readers, Geographies etc) are supplied to School Board or Educational Authorities are so closely cut that there is very little profit in them to the bookseller and the sale of them is nearly all in the hands of a few contractors who also supply stationery, School Appliances & things of that kind.

I have gone into these details for the purpose of letting you see that the net book system has not been adopted without consideration. Books which retailers ought to keep in stock & the sale of which they can push have been made net, with excellent results as any retail bookseller can tell you. Books which are unaffected by a bookseller's exertions are still sold at a large discount, and on such sales the retail bookseller gets only a carrier's profit.

I am | Yours sincerely | Frederick Macmillan.

[1] Marshall Papers. A reply to [884].

[2] Horace E. Hooper, an American speculator who had bought up the plates of the ninth edition of the *Encyclopaedia Britannica*, was prominently involved in the foundation and operation of the Times Book Club. However, the manager of *The Times*, Charles Frederic Moberley Bell (1847–1911) was English. See C. Morgan, *The House of Macmillan* [884.3], pp. 193–207.

886. To Frederick Macmillan, 7 October 1907[1]

7.10.07.

Dear Mr MacMillan

Thank you for your long & interesting letter. As you say, the matter is too large for discussion in writing. About eight or ten years ago I heard a great deal about the injury done to Privat-dozents & others—poor fellows who were not endowed by a Fellowship as I was—by the new rules of the booksellers combinations.[2] But I found that after all those rules had some elements of liberality which the later British rules lack. As a rule 10% is deducted for cash over the counter: and the bookseller sends out small bundles of books to each of his studious customers; who can read enough of them to see whether he wishes to buy them, even more easily & much more cheaply than he can by subscribing to the Times.

I hold that when a young writer is not subsidized by a Fellowship, every shilling taken out of his purse—assuming him to have high aims—is a greater national evil than the loss of five shillings by the well to do artisan or the loss of several pounds by a rich man. And the present system enriches the (relatively) rich shopkeepers largely at the expense of poor students.

I do not think that the bookseller should speculate, or at all events that the author should be charged for his doing so. I do not think that English booksellers—no, not even Germans—do stock largely those books which contain new constructive work. I believe I told you some time ago that in my opinion a score of booksellers shops in say Leeds would be of less service than, one central store to which all Publishers would send books on view (perhaps not selling any), and an organized carrying trade like that of news vendors.[3] I think that the author should receive a *share* (not necessarily a *half*) of the excess of the net cash price (not the three months credit price) over actual expenses of printing and binding: And that all the expenses of handling the books, whether wholesale or retail, should come out of the publishers share. If he liked to take the bookseller into partnership, that might be well: but I hope it would not come about. My reasons for this hope cannot be put shortly: and indeed I have already talked too long.

I have already sent all necessary corrections for the first half of my *Elements* to the Press. They consist chiefly of verbal changes—e.g. *last* century for *this* century—and additions in the blank spaces at the end of chapters. I have not displaced any page. But I find I am getting in a good deal more than I thought possible of the *Elements* into harmony with the new edition of the *Principles*: & I think it is possible that I may not wish to recast the book when the present edition has run out. Perhaps I may even write in a weeks time suggesting that this edition should be made larger than 5000 copies; or that, if the types hold out, the plates should be preserved for another edition. The new matter in Book V is unsuitable for the *Elements*; and having a free hand at the end of Book VI, I think I may get along fairly well.

I am much disquieted by the recent tendency to expect a dissolution of Parliament a year hence. I had wanted to get out my new book[4] before Tariff Reform again becomes a burning question.

Yours sincerely, | Alfred Marshall

[1] British Library, Macmillan Archive. From Balliol Croft. Reproduced in C. W. Guillebaud, 'The Marshall–Macmillan Correspondence' [884.1] at pp. 536–7. A reply to [885] which Guillebaud was unable to trace: see p. 536 of his article. Also see pp. 537–8 for his general evaluation of the long-running Marshall–Macmillan correspondence over the net book agreement, a correspondence that terminates with the present letter.

[2] Presumably in Germany.

[3] This was probably in verbal discussion, but a similar proposal is made in Marshall's unpublished 1897 letter to *The Times* (Vol. 2 [545]; see also [548, 571, 576] for pertinent 1897–8 letters to Macmillan).

[4] The long-projected *National Industry and Trade* (its most recent title: see [877.3]).

887. From Henry Rogers Seager, 10 October 1907[1]

Columbia University in the City of New York
School of Political Science
October 10, 1907.

Dear Professor Marshall:—

Please accept my warmest thanks for the copy of the new edition of your Principles of Economics which you were so good as to send me. I have long used it as representing the best statement of Economic theory for advanced students; and from a hasty examination am glad to see that the changes made in this last edition are all in the direction of adapting it better to the use of our American students.

With sincere respect, I am, | Very truly yours, | Henry R. Seager

[1] Marshall Papers. Typewritten. See [876].

888. From Frank Haigh Dixon, 10 October 1907[1]

1307 Fairmont St.
October 10th 1907

My dear Sir

I wish to acknowledge my very great indebtedness to you in the receipt of the fifth edition of your masterly treatise on Economics. We have long realized in the United States the indispensable character of this work in our study and teaching and a new edition comes as a most welcome addition to our working material. During the evenings of my Sabbatical year, I am greatly enjoying a leisurely reading of this volume with the added pleasure that comes from a familiarity with your earlier productions.

With my great respect | I am | Most sincerely yours | Frank Haigh Dixon | Professor of Economics | Dartmouth College.

Professor Alfred Marshall.

[1] Marshall Papers. On the printed letter stock of the Interstate Commerce Commission, Washington, DC, see [876].

889. To Ernest Alfred Benians, 12 October 1907[1]

12. 10. 07

My dear Benians,

Bowden of Pembroke has just been sent to me for advice.[2] I have called his attention to the fact that, in consequence of Oldham's absence from England, the pressure on his time will be very heavy in the Second Term.[3] He has read a good deal of Economics, but no history. So in this Term he might I think with advantage consider books on Colonial History a little: or if not in the Term, yet at all events in the Xmas Vacation. Others may be somewhat in the same case. Perhaps you could put them in the way of doing this either by remarks in lecture,[4] or in private conversation, when the time comes on.

Bowden has been in the Upper Sixth at Sedbergh[5] for two years, & seems to be solid. So he may be worth taking some trouble.

Yours very truly | Alfred Marshall

Miss Olivier (daughter of the Fabian, & Colonial office magnate—I almost think he is now Governor of Something) will be at your lectures.[6] She has read Karl Marx & no other economics! But my wife says she is a very good sort. She may not go to Foxwells Introduction to English History.[7] So my wife is urging her to read a good deal for you this term.

[1] St John's College, Cambridge, Benians Papers. From Balliol Croft.

[2] E. R. Bowden obtained a second class, first division, in each part of the Economics Tripos (1909–10).

[3] Oldham's lectures on Economic Geography, given in the Michaelmas Term of the 1906–7 academic year, were transferred to the Lent Term of 1907–8 (*Reporter*, 9 October 1907).

[4] Benians was down to lecture on 'Economic and General History of the United States' in the Michaelmas Term of the 1907–8 academic year and on 'Economic and General History of the English Colonies and Dependencies' during the two remaining Terms.

[5] The public school in north Yorkshire.

[6] Margery Olivier (1887–1974), daughter of Sydney Haldane Olivier (1859–1943), subsequently Baron Olivier, entered Newnham in 1907. She obtained a second class, first division, in Part I of the Economics Tripos in 1909 and a third in Part II in 1911. Sydney Olivier had been secretary of the Fabian Society, 1886–90, and was in the Colonial Service, serving as Governor of Jamaica, 1907–13.

[7] Foxwell refused to admit women to his lectures.

890. To Frederick Macmillan, 14 October 1907[1]

14. 10. 07

Dear Mr MacMillan,

I have been taking stock of the next few years; & considering the new edition of my little book[2] which is now complete in the hands of the Press: & I think I shall not be inclined to give any more time to that book for many years to come. It is now sufficiently in accord with the fifth edition of my *Principles*. And if the plates will hold out, I should like them to be used till after the sixth edition of my *Principles*, if that is ever called for.[3]

Yours sincerely | Alfred Marshall

None the less I am very much obliged to you for offering to have new plates made soon, if I desired it.

[1] British Library, Macmillan Archive. From Balliol Croft.

[2] *Elements.*

[3] *Principles* (6) was to appear in 1910. No substantial further changes were to be made in *Elements.*

891. From Frank William Taussig, 14 October 1907[1]

October 14, 1907.

My dear Professor Marshall:

Thank you very much for the fifth edition of the Principles. The changes in arrangement seem to me improvements, especially the grouping of the appendices at the end.[2] I have not noted with any detail the changes in the text, but shall do so in the course of the winter. For some years past I have read substantially the whole of it with the students in my advanced course on economic theory, and I can still say that nothing is so helpful and invigorating for them.

I note with interest and just a shade of amusement what you say in the introduction of my friend Clark and of the relation of his work to yours. You are over-modest about yourself and over-generous in what you say of Clark.[3] I rate him intellectually vastly! lower than I do you. He has ingenuity and a perverse sort of originality, but he has no power of sustained reasoning and no sober sense of the realities of life. Most of Böhm-Bawerk's criticism of him in our Journal seems to me just.[4]

By the way, there is no possibility that you would care to take a hand in this discussion? Needless to say, we should be very glad to have a statement of your conclusions on the controverted points.[5] I see that you are busy on the forthcoming (and surely welcome) books on the subjects that will make up volume two, and I should not make a suggestion for a digression if I thought it would make much drain on your time and energy.

Mrs. Taussig joins me in very cordial regards to Mrs. Marshall and yourself and I am as ever, with much respect and regard,

Very truly yours, | F. W. Taussig

[1] Marshall Papers. Typewritten on printed letter stock of the *Quarterly Journal of Economics*, Harvard University. The exclamation 'vastly!' was inserted by hand.

[2] This reverses his opinion of December 1897 when revision of *Principles* (4) was under way. See Vol. 2 [554].

[3] See [879.3]. Marshall wrote of Clark's 'profound and suggestive *Distribution of Wealth*' (*Guillebaud*, p. 51 n.: for Clark's book see [736.3]).

[4] Eugen von Böhm-Bawerk, 'Capital and Interest once More: I Capital vs. Capital Goods: II A Relapse to the Productivity Theory', *Quarterly Journal of Economics*, 21 (November 1906, February 1907), pp. 1–21, 247–82. There was a reply by Clark in May 1907 (pp. 351–70) and a rejoinder by Böhm-Bawerk (vol. 22, November 1907, pp. 28–47).

[5] Marshall did not subsequently contribute to the *Quarterly Journal of Economics* on this or any other topic.

892. From William George Langworthy Taylor, 20 October 1907[1]

Department of Political Economy and Commerce

The University of Nebraska
Lincoln
October 20, 1907

Professor Alfred Marshall,
Cambridge, England.

Dear Mr. Marshall:

I want to thank you most warmly for the recognition accorded me by the receipt of a copy of the fifth edition of the 'Principles' with the author's compliments. Ever since I have been acquainted with this great work I have regarded it as the standard in the Science which we serve, although with such unequal efficiency. There was that in it which appealed to my own conception, or rather capacity for conception—of economic life as nothing else that I had or have seen in print. Our mental life is partly a struggle to reconcile the ideal with the actual. Man is an animal that from the start had an adumbration of finality. He has since spent his time in bridging the gap in act and in thought. Most of his mistakes and 'bad reasoning' occur somewhere along this line of 'filling up the gap'.

I am deeply impressed with the services that you have rendered in 'Principles' Vol. I right along this line; and from unconscious mental digestion, perhaps, have acquired a taste for dynamic economics, including even the temporary inquiry as to whether 'Principles' itself was really dynamic. But I soon assured myself that it was; and perceived the futility of an absolutely separate *statics* and *dynamics*. Your preface to the fifth edition[2] states my own views on this subject.

Again, your statement of the biological nature of the dynamic problem exactly suits me. On this point I owe something to Professor Patten also I have been greatly impressed with the importance of the *crisis* as a dramatic point for a starting point in dynamic studies; and accordingly tried to formulate some suggestion of a bio-economic system a few years ago. The result was very crude, but was at least an expression of personality.[3] I take the liberty of sending a copy of this crude study, as well as some statistical studies of my pupil, Dr. Minnie T. England, designed to confirm or modify some of those generalizations.[4]

My talented pupil, Dr. Edith Abbott[5] writes me that she had the pleasure of a few words with you; and I was much gratified to learn that you recalled my name. With sincerest hopes for your health, I remain

Yours faithfully, | W. G. Langworthy Taylor

P.S. For many years your photograph has hung in my study. We obtained it through Miss Rogers of Oxford[6] whom my wife knew when she was a student at Lady Margaret Hall, Oxford.

[1] Marshall Papers. See [876].
[2] *Guillebaud*, pp. 45–55.
[3] Probably W. G. Langworthy Taylor, 'The Kinetic Theory of Economic Crises', *Nebraska University Studies*, 4/1 (1904).
[4] Minnie Throop England, 'On Speculation in Relation to the World's Prosperity 1897–1902', *Nebrasks University Studies*, 6/1 (1906); 'Statistical Inquiry into the Influence of Credit upon the Level of Prices', *Nebraska University Studies*, 7/1 (1907).
[5] Edith Abbott (1876–1957) became a prominent applied economist, concentrating on the economic position of women. Earning a Ph.D. from Chicago in 1905, she spent 1906–7 at the London School of Economics on a Carnegie Fellowship.
[6] Annie Mary Anne Henley Rogers (1856–1937), Secretary of the Association for the Education of Women in Oxford and a tireless promoter of women's education there. Daughter of J. E. Thorold Rogers.

893. From Charles Jesse Bullock, 21 October 1907[1]

Commonwealth of Massachusetts | Commission on Taxation
State House, Room 429 | Boston, Oct. 21, 1907

My dear Professor Marshall:

I received a short time ago a copy of the latest edition of your 'Principles of Economics' which you were good enough to instruct your publishers to send me with your compliments. I am greatly indebted to you for your courtesy.

In its present form you can well afford to leave your volume as an authoritative statement of the theory of production and distribution, which is not likely to be superseded speedily. I trust that you will have time and strength to bring the second volume to completion.

I chance to be engaged at present in an attempt to improve our system of local taxation in Massachusetts, but the work is temporary, and does not require me to give up my work at Harvard University.

With assurances of deepest respect, I remain,
Very truly yours, | Charles J. Bullock

[1] Marshall Papers. Typewritten. See [876].

894. From Jeremiah Whipple Jenks, 29 October 1907[1]

Cornell University | Political Economy and Politics
Ithaca, N.Y., Oct. 29, 1907

My dear Professor Marshall:

I wish to thank you for copy of the new edition of your Economics received a few days ago. I have been very much interested in noticing your new preface and the change in plan. I trust that I shall see before very long the two volumes which you mention on National Industry and Trade and Money, Credit and Employment.[2] On both of those subjects, as you know, I am very much interested, and I shall prize very highly indeed your mature judgment on those questions.

I trust that you and Mrs. Marshall are both of you in as good health as usual, and that you had your usual pleasant summer on the Continent.

I was appointed by the President last April a member of the new Immigration Commission, several of the members of which were in Europe this summer. I had thought some of going myself, but eventually it seemed better for me to devote my time this year to the study of the immigration situation here, the administration of our laws, etc., with our relations to Canada and Mexico in that connection. It is entirely possible that next summer there may be certain points left which may require my coming to Europe to look up. In that event I shall hope to have the pleasure of another visit with you.[3]

During this last summer in connection with the work of the Commission I had a long trip,—practically all round the borders of the United States from Quebec to Vancouver, then to the borders of Mexico and then back by the way of New Orleans. My wife and daughter went with me, and the trip was extremely interesting as well as valuable from the point of view of the Commission's work. The difference in the problem on the Canadian border and the Mexican border was very noticeable and most suggestive.

The National Civic Federation held last week an important conference on the subject of Trusts and Corporations which I had the pleasure of attending.[4] The resolutions, of which I have not with me a copy as I had to leave before the meeting ended, were to the effect that the Sherman Act should be amended so as to permit reasonable agreements in restraint of trade. They suggested also the appointment of a Commission to make a thoro study of the question and to recommend to the Federal Government and to the separate states conservative legislation which, while permitting reasonable agreements in restraint of trade, should yet ensure much greater publicity regarding the affairs of these corporations and a considerable restraint upon their methods of doing business. I will secure for you as soon as possible a copy of these resolutions and forward them. I am sure that you will be interested in seeing them. At this meeting were represented a great many different states by delegates appointed by the Governors, also large commercial bodies, Boards of Trade, etc., as well as a good many of the leading business men and students of the question thruout the United States. I think that the work of this Commission, followed up as it will be by a Committee to present the matter to Congress, is likely to have considerable effect.

With best wishes, I remain, | Very sincerely yours | J. W. Jenks.

[1] Marshall Papers. Typewritten. See [876].

[2] See [877.3].

[3] The Immigration Commission, 1907–10, established by Congress, undertook extensive enquiries and published voluminous reports. Jenks was one of three Commissioners selected by the President—Theodore Roosevelt—to cooperate with the six Congressional members. There is no indication that Jenks did meet Marshall in 1908.

[4] See National Civic Federation, *National Conference on Trusts and Combinations* (Proceedings of the National Conference, Chicago, 22–5 October 1907; National Civic Foundation, New York, 1908).

895. To Herbert Somerton Foxwell, 24 January 1908[1]

24. 1. 08

My dear Foxwell

Roberts[2] decided that it wd be best to say straight out that we want four lecturers at £200 a year each; & to whisper to ourselves that we hope we may get them. So that is what he will report.[3]

I entirely agree about Fay. I know a good deal about his essay, though I have not read it. I think it is a splendid piece of work. And the energy with wh he is throwing himself into his lectures is a glory & a delight to behold. He is a most splendid man, probably the best for attracting men to the Tripos that could be had anywhere.

Yours very sincerely | Alfred Marshall

[1] Marshall Papers. From Balliol Croft.

[2] E. S. Roberts, the current Vice Chancellor [883.1].

[3] The Economics Board had been asked to report on its needs in connection with a projected appeal of the Cambridge Association on behalf of the University.

896. To Macmillan and Company, 13 February 1908[1]

13. 2. 03[2]

Dear Sirs,

I do not feel at all strongly as to the possible pecuniary effect, good or ill, on my *Principles* of the publication of a Digest of it. But Economics is passing out of the phase in which it can profitably be studied in brief. I went to the University Library today to see what Waters could have made of a digest of Fawcett.[3] But it is not catalogued; (I surmise that there is scarcely any other book except some novels published by Mess[rs] MacMillan which the Library has not cared to put on its shelves.) So I am still at a loss to guess how even Prof Fawcett's sweeping & trenchant dicta can have been focussed into a few pages. The new spirit in economics is averse to sweeping dicta. It analyses; & indicates tendencies, with considerable detail of concrete fact in regard to wh the broad tendencies are shewn at work. Thus it tries to educate the student to see that the same principles may lead to widely different results, according as the matter to which they are applied differs in this or that detail. I cannot see how any part of this spirit can be retained in a short abstract.

It was the fear of such abstracts which led me to compress my larger book on lines thus set out:—

> The necessary abridgement has been effected not by systematic compression so much as by the omission of many discussions on points of minor importance and of some difficult theoretical investigations. For it seemed that the difficulty of an argument would be increased rather than diminished by curtailing it and leaving out some of its steps. The argumentative parts of the *Principles* are therefore as a rule either reproduced in full or omitted altogether.[4]

These lines have been approved generally by those experts who have published, or told me privately, their opinions on the subject. And as years have gone on, I have become strengthened in the opinion that a short book on large economic questions cannot be helpful. In particular an abridgement of those difficult parts of Books V and VI of the larger volume[5] which are ignored in the smaller,[6] would I think lead only to so confused a jargon of technical terms misapplied, that no credit could be given for work based on it. I doubt the possibility of finding a tolerably good market for such work.

I am unwilling to suggest that the copyright of anything I have written should be used to repress any efforts for the advancement of knowledge. But I do not wish it to be supposed that I think that an abstract of intricate reasonings on difficult questions can advance knowledge.[7]

Thanking you for the trouble you have taken in the matter.

I am | Yours faithfully | Alfred Marshall

Mess[rs] MacMillan & Co

[1] British Library, Macmillan Archive. From Balliol Croft.
[2] Stamped '14 Feb 1908' by Macmillan and Company, apparently upon receipt as was the usual practice, but conceivably written in 1903 as dated by Marshall.
[3] Cyril Aubrey Waters, *An Explanatory Digest of Professor Fawcett's 'Manual of Political Economy'* (Macmillan, London, 1887).
[4] Marshall incorporated this passage from the preface to *Elements* by pasting in a clipping from a printed copy.
[5] *Principles*.
[6] *Elements*.
[7] No digest was published and the proposer remains anonymous.

897. To Charles Ryle Fay, 21 February 1908[1]

21. 2. 08

Dear Fay

You *are* good! But I fear you may find the proposed task much heavier than it seems from afar: that at least is my experience in such cases.

And there is another difficulty. Head is an awfully good fellow, & most unlikely to be inclined to regard himself as slighted, and yet the course which you propose is so far constructive, that I think it is possible that he might think he would have liked to be asked whether he would cooperate.[2] He would supplement you in two ways. He knows the books; & could talk a short guide book to them—wh is after all the thing most useful for the men—better than you could without taking a good deal of trouble: and he would approach the whole subject with *political* interest rather than economic.

The weak point in the course you propose seems to me to be its discontinuity: it might perhaps even happen that no single question is set in wh the course could be turned to much account.[3] Why not call on Head; tell him about these men; say what you had thought of doing; ask him his views; & give him an opportunity of offering to take a hand? I shall feel quite certain that anything that you & he agree on will be a great & unmixed good.

If however you are disinclined to do this, & prefer to paddle your own canoe, that also will be good I think; if not quite so good. In that case I would venture to suggest that a part of each lecture should be given to helping the people to read the books sufficiently to get something of a continuous view of the whole. And it might be well to propose a rather shorter course: you could extend it later, if you thought well.

Anyhow you *are* good: & we shall all be most grateful to you.

Yours sincerely | Alfred Marshall

Many thanks for suggestions about wrong references. Mary is responsible for that department; & she thinks that if you would at some time give her a list of the pages where the errors are, that wd be most helpful.[4]

[1] Marshall Papers. From Balliol Croft.

[2] Fay was to begin soon to lecture on 'English Economic History during the 19th Century' while Head, who had hitherto lectured on the 'General and Economic History of Europe in the 19th Century', had stood down. See [854.7, 11].

[3] Tripos questions were set by the appointed examiners independently of the lectures.

[4] Presumably the errors were in *Principles* (*5*). Fay subsequently recalled 'a treasured postcard [not traced] acknowledging some verbal errors in the *Principles*, collected by Edwin Cannan and myself—"Thanks for the *errata*. I have handed them to Mary. The mistakes are her department. Yours A.M."' See C. R. Fay, 'Reminiscences of a Deputy Librarian' (1960), reproduced in John C. Wood (ed.), *Alfred Marshall: Critical Assessments* (Croom Helm, London, 1982), vol. 1, pp. 87–90 at p. 87.

898. To William Henry Beveridge, 1 March 1908[1]

1. 3. 08

Dear Mr Beveridge,

When I said the Fabian leaders seemed to me to 'pose too much' you surprised me by a rather strong dissent; though you had partly assented to the grounds on which I base this opinion. On thinking it over, I conclude you supposed me to mean that they were insincere in their professions of zeal for humanity. I am certain that all of them whom I know personally, ie the Webbs and Bernard Shaw are perfectly sincere in this matter; & I believe *the* same to be true of the others.[2] But I hold that they are ever 'posing' as *the* friends of the working classes; & that in so doing they are betrayed into words & deeds that are unworthy of their high & sincere professions. I refer to (1) the negative side of M[rs] Webbs work on Cooperation;[3] to (2) their successful intervention to prevent the main Report of the Labour Commission from being unanimous,[4] (those who brought out the Labour-Minority Report had intended to sign the Main Report also, many amendments to which were adopted on their recommendation; but, as they told some of the Majority-Labour members, who told the Commission, the Webbs intervened & told them not to): to (3) their persistent references to the attitude of the early economists towards the Factory Acts: and to (4) the design on the cover of their new book.[5]

I forgot to mention that Tooke, the leading economist of his age, the founder of the Political Economy Club, and the draftsman of the great 1830 Manchester 'Petition of Merchants' in favour of free trade, was the chief of the Assistant Commissioners by whom the abuses of child labour in the mines (wh were *incomparably* worse than those in the factories) were brought to light, & to their death.

Yours very truly | Alfred Marshall

[1] BLPES, Beveridge Papers. From Balliol Croft. According to a letter of 4 March 1908 to Annette Susan Beveridge (his mother), Beveridge had recently visited Cambridge to address a meeting chaired by Marshall who had also been the host at a Sunday lunch where 'he held forth to me (very nicely) on the wickedness of the Fabians & Sidney Webb in jeering at orthodox economists & he asked me for my views on his own book which I rashly gave—so I am now to read it through again & justify my statements or withdraw them'. (Beveridge Papers).

[2] Altered to 'ie' from '& especially'. George Bernard Shaw (1856–1950), Fabian, playwright, and social critic.

[3] Beatrice Potter, *The Cooperative Movement in Great Britain* (Swan Sonnenschein, London, 1891).

[4] The Labour Commission of 1891–4 on which Marshall, but not the Webbs, had served.

[5] The nature of this objection remains a puzzle.

899. To John Bates Clark, 24 March 1908 (incomplete)[1]

24. iii. 08

My dear Clark,

I thank you very heartily for your most kind and friendly letter.[2] I had thought you selected the Austrians for mention, partly in order to show that you bore them, and especially Böhm Bawerk, no ill-will on account of his rather rough method of thumping.[3]

I have in earlier years eaten my heart out with doubt and anxiety as to what acknowledgements I should make to others. I fear I am an awful sinner: but I have grown callous. My rule has been to refer in a footnote to anyone whom I know to have said a thing before I have said it in print, even though I may have said it in lectures for many years before I knew that it had ever occurred to him: I just refer, but say nothing about obligations either way; being quite aware that people will suppose me to imply obligations. Instances are Francis Walker and Fleeming Jenkin.

But perhaps in return for your good-natured confidence I may state the reason which has prevented me from making general acknowledgments in any Preface except the first. It is that my main position as to the theory of value and distribution was practically completed in the years 1867 to 1870; when I translated Mill's version of Ricardo's or Smith's doctrines into mathematics; and that, when Jevons' book[4] appeared, I knew at once how far I agreed with him and how far I did not. In the next four years I worked a good deal at the mathematical theory of monopolies, and at the diagrammatic treatment of Mill's problem of international values (parts of this were printed by Pantaleoni in a kindly way in his *Principii di Economia Pura*).[5]

By this time I had practically completed the whole of the substance of my Mathematical Appendix, the only important exception being the treatment of elasticity (Note III) and Edgeworth's contract curve Note XII bis.

Substantially my theory of capital as it exists to-day is completely outlined in Notes V and XIII–XIV; and my general theory of distribution (except in so far as relates to the element of time) is in like manner contained in Note XXI; to which the preceding notes and especially XIV–XX lead up.[6] I worked that out for the greater part while still teaching mathematics; and while still regarding myself as a mere pupil in the hands of great masters, especially Cournot, von Thünen and Ricardo; and while still extremely ignorant of economic realities. Between 1870 and 1874 I developed the details of my theoretical position; and I am not conscious of any perceptible change since the time when Böhm Bawerk and Wieser were still lads at school or College. . . .

I think there is an immense deal to be done still in

(1) elaborating the influence of time;
(2) studying complex interactions with special reference to the quantities concerned;
(3) allowing for the decadence of some economic influences and the rise of others;
(4) taking account of non-economic influences, and especially such as evade quantitative measurement;
(5) applications to practical problems as to which I look for much help from 'Essentials'.[7]

I see before me ten times as much work to do in these five directions as I can hope to do: and I am sure that after I am dead people will gradually discover ten times and more as much work as I see.

So I scarcely ever read controversies or criticisms. I have not read even a quarter of those which have been written about myself. The books, for instance, which I take to the Alps nearly every summer are almost exclusively concerned with matters of fact; though I try to read or skim any piece of analysis in which a man works to produce knowledge and not to controvert others. Thus I could not make acknowledgments to others properly: and I fall back on the plan already mentioned of referring in silence to any anticipation, of which I am aware, of a suggestion made by myself.

My whole life has been and will be given to presenting in realistic form as much as I can of my Note XXI. If I live to complete my scheme fairly well, people will, I think, realise that it has unity and individuality. And a man who has lost ten of the best years of his life—from 37 to 47—through illness, would, I think, be doubly foolish if he troubled himself to weigh and measure any claims to originality that he has.

One thing alone in American criticism irritates me, though it be not unkindly meant. It is the suggestion that I try to 'compromise between' or 'reconcile' divergent schools of thought. Such work seems to me trumpery. Truth is the only thing worth having: not peace. I have never compromised on any doctrine of any kind. As to the use of terms, that is a matter of mere opportunism and everyone should, I think, not merely compromise but positively yield against his own judgment, if he thinks that by so doing he can facilitate mutual understandings. For that reason I have shifted my use of the word capital, but I have not changed my doctrines as to capital by a hair's breadth: Irving Fisher seems to have misread me in this matter.[8] I hope you will forgive this scrawl.

Yours very sincerely, | Alfred Marshall

[1] Printed in *Memorials*, pp. 416–8. Original not traced. From Balliol Croft.
[2] Not traced.
[3] See [891.4].
[4] W. S. Jevons, *Theory of Political Economy* (Macmillan, London, 1871).
[5] See [850.3].
[6] The references are presumably to *Principles* (*5*), but its Mathematical Appendix is substantially the same as that of *Principles* (*8*).
[7] J. B. Clark, *Essentials of Economic Theory* [736.6], which had been published in October 1907. Marshall appears to have received a copy only recently or to be still expecting one. Surprisingly, the book never mentioned Marshall, but the preface drew attention to the work of Böhm-Bawerk and Wieser as 'Worthy of special attention, if citations had been given' (p. x). Few were.
[8] Probably an allusion to I. Fisher, 'Precedents for Defining Capital', *Quarterly Journal of Economics*, 18 (May 1904), pp. 386–408.

900. To Edwin Robert Anderson Seligman, 24 March 1908[1]

24. 3. 08

Dear Prof Seligman,

I ought to have written before to thank you for the new edition of your Principles.[2] It seems to me to have many excellent qualities, & to be likely to be read a good deal by students here as a secondary book: though the 'Special reference to American conditions', may prove unfavourable to its use as a main implement here.

Yours sincerely | Alfred Marshall

Thanks also for the pamphlet on the Crisis of 1907;[3] wh I expect to read with much interest.

[1] Columbia University Library, Seligman Papers. From Balliol Croft.

[2] E. R. A. Seligman, *The Principles of Economics, With Special Reference to American Conditions* (Longmans Green, New York, 1905: third edition, 1907).

[3] E. R. A. Seligman, 'The Crisis of 1907 in the Light of History': written as an introduction to *The Currency Problem and the Present Financial Situation* (Columbia University Press, New York, 1908).

901. To Sir George Darwin, 24 March 1908[1]

24. 3. 08

Dear Darwin

The only tolerably good small book dealing with Banking & the Exchanges is Clare's *Money Market* (MacMillan). Its treatment of the Exchanges is very slight. The same author has written *The A.B.C. of the Foreign Exchanges*, a book of about the same size (160 pp) dealing much more thoroughly with the Exchanges but still only from 'the practical' point of view: ie that of the banker & the City Editor.[2] It is really developed out of lectures given before members of the Institute of Bankers. It is admirably clear, & of the highest authority on technical matters: but it does not profess to deal with fundamental questions, such as—How far if at all are variations in the Exchanges causes (not mere indications) of permanent (or sub-permanent) variations in the general levels of prices. It is fairly international.

On the other hand *The Money Market* is narrowly British-technical. I don't think it is what Erasmus wants. What he does want is a part of a big book.

Volume I Part II of 'Dutch' Pierson's *Principles of Economics* is on *Money, Banking & the Exchanges*; & it has gradually established itself as *the* book for our Tripos students. It is masterly in technique & principle; and it is thoroughly international, though it gives special prominence to British questions. Its Chapter II on 'Banking in the principal countries' pp 449–515, and Chapter III on 'Bills of Exchange & Foreign Exchanges' pp 516–67; ie 127 pp in all is exactly what he wants; & though the whole volume is 604 pp long, I recommend you to send it. It is published by MacMillan.

Yours sincerely | Alfred Marshall

If you think he wants details of Exchange technique you might add Clares A.B.C.

[1] Original in the possession of Peter D. Groenewegen. From Balliol Croft. Pasted inside a copy of vol 1 of N. G. Pierson, *Principles of Economics* [734.2] previously owned by Darwin's nephew Erasmus, an organizer in 1905 of the Social Discussion Society in Cambridge: see [822.3, 823, 825]. According to a note in what appears to be Erasmus Darwin's hand the letter was the response received 'On a request whilst in USA for a book on foreign Exchange'; a request probably transmitted through his uncle who was well acquainted with Marshall, but perhaps through his father, Horace Darwin (1851–1928), fifth and youngest son of Charles Darwin and founder of the Cambridge Scientific Instrument Company. Previously reproduced in Groenewegen's 'An Unpublished Letter of Alfred Marshall', *Australian Newsletter on the History of Economic Thought*, 5 (1984).

[2] George Clare, *A Money Market Primer* (Effingham and Wilson (not Macmillan), London, 1892); *The A.B.C. of the Foreign Exchanges* (Macmillan, London, 1892: third edition 1907).

902. To John Maynard Keynes, 3 April 1908[1]

3. 4. 08

My dear Keynes,

Quite recently, since your father left England,[2] I have heard, in a round-about way, that it is just possible you might be willing to return to Cambridge, if you had work to do here. I have also heard that your chance of election to a fellowship at Kings next year is good.

Under these circumstances, & taking account of the fact that Macgregor is going to Leeds,[3] my course would have been clear if I had not been about to vacate the Professorship. I should then have asked you to allow me to propose you to the Economics Board as a lecturer on General Economics probably for the first year, but possibly for the second; and I should have said I would gladly pay you the £100 wh I have paid in similar cases.

But I shall cease to be a member of the Economics Board on April 21st: & at its last meeting I said that I should do nothing to hamper the freedom of the reconstituted Board which will meet (probably on June 3rd) to make up its lecture list.

It has however been suggested to me by the same person, to whom the notion of your coming to Cambridge to teach economics is due,[4] that there may be an advantage in calling your attention to the situation. I am in a position to state two things. First, (subject to some reserve in the case of one possible election to the Professorship in May[5]) if you approve, a suggestion will be made by a member of the Board on (probably) June 3, that you be asked to lecture. Secondly, if the Board concur—and I have no doubt that (subject to the above mentioned reserve) they will concur gladly—the sum of £100 will be forthcoming for you, just to make you feel that you really are a lecturer. I do not think that the £100 will be paid by me: but I can guarantee that it will be paid either from some other source or by me.

There is a certain air of mystery in this letter; and I dislike mystery. But later on you will understand that it was inevitable.

Answer at your convenience. There is no hurry.
Yours very sincerely | Alfred Marshall

[1] King's College, Cambridge, J. M. Keynes Papers. From Balliol Croft. Previously reproduced in *Collected Works*, vol. 15, p. 13.
[2] Scribbled as 'Eland' in the original.
[3] Macgregor had been appointed as Professor of Economics at Leeds in succession to Clapham, who was returning to Cambridge.
[4] Apparently Pigou, who was to succeed Marshall as Professor, and who was to provide the £100 per year paid to Keynes when he accepted this proposal. See [910].
[5] That is, the election of Foxwell.

903. From William Rothenstein, 21 April 1908[1]

11, Oak Hill Park, Frognal. | P.O. Hampstead
April 21 '08

Dear Prof. Marshall.

You have little idea believe me of how much pleasure you have given me in presenting me with your noble volume:[2] I take it as a very great compliment that you think me capable of appreciating it. I have already begun to read it, & I am greatly impressed with the extraordinary perception of human motives shown in it on every page. What pleases me above all is that your own standard of conduct & nobility is applied to other people, & that you refuse to believe that others have a much lower standard. I am always distressed when made aware of a man of high gifts & distinction looking on the rest of mankind with suspicion or contempt, & the generous spirit underlying your own views of men & women does not take away from their force. It always seems to me that the pursuit of science & art is useless to any one, unless it be expressed in the form of hope; men want support for their best motives, & if we can't encourage every thing which is fair & good, we have a very small place in the hierarchy of mankind. All I know is that I am reading your work with much inward stirring, & it is a very real delight to me to be made acquainted with your thoughts & views on so many matters of interest. I thank you de coeur for your charming kindness, & I would not have you think that I do not fully appreciate it. With many regards to M[rs] Marshall believe me

Sincerely yours | W. Rothenstein

[1] Marshall Papers. Rothenstein had been chosen to paint Marshall's portrait: see [866, 867].
[2] Presumably *Principles* (*5*).

904. To William Rothenstein, 2 May 1908[1]

2. 5. 08

Dear M[r] Rothenstein

I have been so awestruck by the pendulous left hand in my photographs, that

I have looked over a number of loose portraits (chiefly torn out of the *Worlds Work*):[2] & I cannot find a single one in which both hands are shown, either loose or one enfolding the other; which I like at all.

So I want to urge you to be good enough either to cut out my hands, or to let them be occupied. My own notion is to have my hat in my right hand on my knee, & my stick in my left rather like Gotz at the tag in the *Secession Catalogue*.[3] Will you kindly think over this before tomorrow?

Yours sincerely | Alfred Marshall

[1] Harvard University, Houghton Library, Rothenstein Papers. From Balliol Croft.

[2] *The World's Work ... A History of Our Times*, a profusely illustrated magazine published in New York between 1900 and 1932, when merged with *Review of Reviews*. An English edition was distributed by Macmillan and Company. Marshall had a long-standing interest in the collection and study of portraits.

[3] The Marshalls had hoped to visit the Secession exhibition at Munich in 1905: see [827]. The precise allusion remains obscure, but is probably to a paper tag marking the place in a copy of the Catalogue where a portrait of Gotz (not further identified) was reproduced.

905. From Lord Rayleigh, 20 May 1908[1]

Terling Place, | Witham, Essex,
May 2/08

Dear Prof Marshall

The Council has invited me to suggest some distinguished men for Hon. Degrees on the occasion of my installation on June 17.[2]

I should like to include yours if I should learn that you would accept this compliment if sanctioned by the Senate. I imagine the degree would be Sc. D.[3]

I am | Yours very truly | Rayleigh

[1] Marshall Papers.

[2] As Chancellor of the University of Cambridge.

[3] This honorary degree was awarded.

906. To Pierre Émile Levasseur, 24 May 1908[1]

24. 5. 08

Monsieur le Professeur et illustre Collègue

Je me trouve accablé par le grand honneur que la Section d'economie politique, statistique et finances me fait en voulant présenter mon nom à l'Académie des sciences morales et politiques, pour remplacer Lord Goschen comme Correspondent.[2] J'accepte avec reconnaissance la plus sincère la haute bienveillance que la Section daigne m'accorder; et je desire ajouter mes remerciments les plus cordiales pour la lettre lucide et plein de bonté, dans laquelle vous m'avez communiqué l'offre si agréable et flatteuse.

Je vous prie, Monsieur et illustre Collegue d'agreer l'expression de ma haute consideration et de mes sentiments de cordiale confraternité.

Alfred Marshall

Monsieur E Levasseur, Professeur de l'economie politique au Collège de France

[1] Levasseur Papers. In the possession of Arnold Heertje. From Balliol Croft. The spelling and accenting are Marshall's.
Précis: Thanks Levasseur for his proposal to nominate Marshall to succeed Goschen as a Correspondent of the Section of Political Economy, Statistics, and Finance, of the Academy of Moral and Political Sciences. He accepts the flattering invitation.

[2] Levasseur's letter (undated) is preserved in the Marshall Papers. The Section had twelve correspondents and its nominations were normally ratified by the Academy without debate.

907. To Adolphus William Ward, 30 May 1908[1]

30. 5. 08

Dear Master,

I have to express my deepest & most heartfelt gratitude for the most kind and generous resolution of the Special Board for Economics & Politics which you have just sent me.[2] What little I have been able to do for the progress of economics in Cambridge would have been impossible had not others cooperated genially & unselfishly. I have always been abundantly paid. Others have worked for the love of the truth & for the well being of the University, with little or no material reward: & this has always seemed to me to be one of the highest forms of chivalry.

And may I add a word of thanks to you. Your influential pleading of our cause before the Senate; and the invaluable counsel and guidance which you have given to the Board in general and to me in particular, have played a chief part in enabling the Tripos to see the light of day & to grow—as I hope & believe—towards a great future.[3]

As long as I live I shall cherish a happy and grateful remembrance of the kindness I have received from the whole Board, and from none more than from yourself.

Believe me to remain, | Dear Master | Yours very sincerely | Alfred Marshall

[1] Cambridge University Archives, Minutes of the Special Board for Economics and Politics, vol. 1.

[2] Ward, Master of Peterhouse, had forwarded on behalf of the Economics Board a copy of a resolution passed at the meeting of 20 May and 'since signed by all members of the Board'. (Ward's 30 May letter is preserved in the Marshall Papers.) The resolution read as follows:

> We desire to express to Professor Marshall on behalf of this Board our deep regret on learning that he has resigned the Chair which he has filled with so much lustre and with so much advantage to the University, and to offer him our thanks both for his services as Chairman of this Board and for the generosity with which he has for so many years supported the School of Economics destined to be long identified with his great name.

[3] Ward had been an influential member of the Economics Syndicate that had recommended the new Tripos, and was first Chairman of the new Economics Board, being succeeded by Marshall in 1906 and temporarily replacing the latter upon his retirement.

908. To Herbert Somerton Foxwell, 31 May 1908[1]

31. 5. 08

My dear Foxwell

Pigou is in my opinion likely [to][2] be recognized ere long as a man of quite extraordinary genius: and I hoped that he wd be elected to the Professorship. But I have just written a letter to the Master of Peterhouse expressing my gratitude to the Economics Board in general, & to him in particular, for their kindly treatment of me, & for their recent most generous resolution.[3] And I should like to add a word of special gratitude to you, the oldest of my colleagues. We differ in opinion a good deal, and in temperament perhaps even more: so that some things, for which I cared much, seemed of little importance to you. But so far as these differences permitted, you have cordially, heartily, and[4] generously supported and furthered my poor endeavours: Sometimes even your genial friendship has perhaps induced you to go a little further in the direction in which I was working, than your own unbiassed judgment would have prompted. For all this I shall ever feel myself your debtor: I shall ever look back on our association with pleasant & grateful memories.

I am sure that the University as a whole cherishes feelings of high regard for your wholehearted & very poorly remunerated services to it. I have not heard very much about it: the proceedings of the electors between 12 and 2 yesterday have been kept absolutely secret; but I have heard no one, not even among the most enthusiastic supporters of Pigou's claims, who is not deeply pained by the thought that it has not been possible to crown your long and trusty work by a[5] high reward.

Please do not answer this just now: for you must be feeling sore. But I wish you to know that though I think the Electors, acting as trustees, did their duty, I share with all of them to whom I have spoken a deep sorrow on your account and an affectionate gratitude towards you.

Yours in sympathy | Alfred Marshall

[1] Marshall Papers. From Balliol Croft. Pigou had been elected on the preceding day to the Cambridge Professorship of Political Economy vacated by Marshall's retirement, Foxwell having been an unsuccessful candidate. For details of the election, and of Marshall's blatant manoeuvring in Pigou's favour, see R.H. Coase, 'The Appointment of Pigou as Marshall's Successor', *Journal of Law and Economics*, 15 (October 1972), pp. 473–85; the present letter is reproduced at p. 480. See also the 'Reply' by A. W. Coats, (ibid., pp. 487–95) and also Trevor W. Jones, 'The Appointment of Pigou as Marshall's Successor: The Other Side of the Coin', *Journal of Law and Economics*, 21 (April 1978), pp. 235–43.

[2] Word apparently omitted.
[3] See [907, 907.2].
[4] Followed by a further 'and' in the original.
[5] Followed by a further 'a' in the original.

909. From Herbert Somerton Foxwell, 1 June 1908[1]

June 1st. 1908.

Dear Marshall

I am much obliged to you for the kind things you say in your letter. It is nothing less than the truth that I have tried, as you say, to give you loyal support during the time we have worked together, though not always in complete agreement as to points of policy.

But I must frankly say (I prefer not to mince matters) that at critical times in one's life one looks to one's friends for deeds rather than words.

The unexpected blow dealt me by a majority of my friends the Electors is the heaviest I have received in my life, or could receive, short of the loss of my wife & children. The chance of leading the school here is one that has never been out of my thoughts for the last twenty years, & has always been my supreme ambition. I had supposed that the candi[da]ture[2] of Pigou on this occasion was rather, as is so often the case with young men, a formal appearance, with a view to a more real contest some ten years later, when, in the natural course of things I should have given up active work. I was encouraged by the talk of the place, which has always been very generous to me, to believe that I should be elected, & had already begun to write my lectures & to prepare for the new duties, with many cordial promises of support from tutors. Perhaps I should have taken a more modest view of my deserts: but I thought experience & long service might count for something in an election to such a responsible post, the difficulties of which I certainly do not under-rate: & people are so polite now-a-days that it is only on illuminating occasions like this that one is able to realise what a poor figure one cuts in their real judgement. Of all my varied & heavy work the Cambridge lectures have always been the most enjoyable part. It is a further misfortune to me that an end is now put to my Cambridge work, for I never could have the assurance to address a Cambridge audience again, with the stamp of incompetency so publicly branded upon me by a body of experts, of whom I am bound to believe that they decided on a strict view of the merits of the case.[3]

In a less degree, the same stigma will make my work in London very difficult, & I would gladly give it up, but for pecuniary considerations.

If I had had the slightest idea that I should have been rejected in favour of an untried man young enough to be my son (I remember your dictum about economists under fifty[4]) I would never have put up. I could have well understood the preferance of Ashley or Cannon.[5]

I wish to say however that the new professor has my very best wishes: & that not the slightest shade of personal feeling exists, or has ever existed between myself & him. I will find some opportunity of letting him know this, but the situation is difficult & I have avoided unecessary writing.[6]

I gather from your letter, & from many other circumstances that have come to my knowledge that you are more than rejoiced at the result, which I know you have worked hard for, & on which I ask to be allowed to congratulate you.

Yours sincerely [H. S. Foxwell]

[1] Foxwell Papers. From an unsigned copy preserved by Foxwell. Original not traced. Clearly a response to [908].

[2] Bracketed letters omitted in the original.

[3] Foxwell, who had been re-elected a Fellow of St John's in 1905 (after losing his initial Fellowship upon marriage), was also the College's Director of Studies in Economics. He was to continue in these capacities, and in his London posts, for many years, but avoided for several years any association with the Board of Economics. John Neville Keynes recorded:

> Foxwell has expressed his intention of no longer lecturing in Cambridge. At the request of Dickinson & Pigou I went in to see him & to try to persuade him to reconsider the question. But I knew of course that he would not. It was one of the most painful interviews I have ever had. He had felt so confident of being elected that he had even begun to write his introductory lecture. He was quite cordial to me personally, but he was very excited, & at one time I thought he wd break down. I felt and still feel exceedingly grieved on his account. He is very bitter against Marshall, and at this I do not wonder' (*Diaries*, entry for 1 June 1908).

[4] This dictum appears to have gone unrecorded.

[5] The misspellings of preference and Cannan are Foxwell's.

[6] The Foxwell Papers contain a copy of a dignified letter of June 1 from Foxwell to Pigou. Foxwell wrote:

> I cannot pretend to disguise from you that your election to the Chair of P.E. has on its negative side been a heavy blow to me, in as much as it has deprived me of the opportunity for which I have been waiting & planning for many years past, in fact the dream of my life. . . . But I wish to lose no more time in assuring you very heartily that personally you have my very best wishes for your success in your new & responsible post. Our relations have always been, & I hope will always be most pleasant, & I can honestly say that this contest & its result have done nothing in the slightest degree to mar them. What I wish for you now is a free hand & the disposition to use it; for it is my opinion, & I think it will be yours, that there is a great deal that requires to be done before the Cambridge School will get a real hold on the University.

910. To John Maynard Keynes, 10 June 1908[1]

10. 6. 08

Dear Keynes,

I am delighted indeed that you are to join our economic staff. I think it is a brilliant, compact group of earnest men, full of the highest promise for the future. But you are wrong in supposing that I had anything to do with your coming back, any more than the postman had. It did not enter my head that you might do so till Pigou spoke to me of it. As your father is an 'Elector', he could not approach you:[2] so I put his message on paper & the postman delivered it: the postman & I are factors of the second order of smalls & may be neglected.

Yours very gladly | Alfred Marshall

[1] King's College, Cambridge, J. M. Keynes Papers. From Balliol Croft. Reproduced in *Collected Writings*, vol. 15, p. 14. See [902]. The communication from Keynes to which this responds had not been traced.

[2] Neville Keynes being one of the electors and Pigou one of the candidates for Marshall's vacated professorship, it would have been unseemly for Pigou to approach Maynard.

911. To Pierre Émile Levasseur, 17 June 1908[1]

17. 6. 08

Dear Professor Levasseur

I write French so badly, & you read English so well, that I will answer your letter[2] in English; though, in passing from the one language to the other, I am struck by the absence of those stately phrases which give a special distinction to French correspondence.

My work is in a pecular position. In January 1904 I sent to the press the first part of a book on *National Industry and Trade*. By the end of 1905, I had about 400 pages of it in type. I then saw that I could not hope to finish it for several years, & ceased to send my M.S.S. to the press. Since then, and especially in 1907, 8, my progress has been very slow: And I have just resigned my Professorship in order to continue my writing. I have already sent a hundred Kilograms of books and manuscripts to South Tyrol; and I have taken berths for my wife and myself in the steamer which leaves Harwich tomorrow. I hope to write in the high mountain air (1500–1600 metres) during the summer; & then to return to write here. You will see therefore that it is impossible for me to turn my thoughts in another direction, or to be present at the next meeting of the *Institut de Statistique* in Paris.[3]

For this I am very sorry. My weak digestion and my temperament prevent me from attending Congresses generally. But I have the very highest regard for the excellent work that is being done by the Institut: and I think that no question could be more important for their discussion than that of 'Salaires'. I therefore regard it as a high & tempting honour to have been asked to bear a hand in that great work: but I must regretfully decline.

With renewed thanks from the heart, though with British bluntness as to form, I remain

Yours sincerely | Alfred Marshall

[1] Levasseur Papers. In the possession of Arnold Heertje. From Balliol Croft. See [906].

[2] Not traced. A letter from Levasseur of 3 June (Marshall Papers) had acknowledged receipt of [906] and indicated in detail the procedures for nomination and election as Correspondent of the Academy. Marshall had written to Levasseur in French on 15 June to confirm that official notification of his election had arrived and to thank Levasseur for his efforts (letter in the possession of Arnold Heertje).

[3] Details not ascertained. The International Statistical Institute held its twelfth meeting in Paris, 4–10 July 1909. Levasseur took a prominent part and Bowley addressed a session devoted to international wage comparisons. See *Journal de la Société de Statistique de Paris*, 50 (August 1909), pp. 285–314. There does not appear to have been a Parisian conference in the summer of 1908.

912. From Sydney Armitage Armitage-Smith, 20 June 1908[1]

Treasury Chambers, | Whitehall. S.W.
20th June 1908.

My dear Sir,

A short time ago the Chancellor of the Exchequer read a Memorandum, which is in the Treasury, written by you, and printed for the information of the Cabinet in August 1903 on 'The Fiscal Policy of International Trade'.

Mr. Lloyd George was very much impressed by the Memorandum and in particular with those portions of it which deal with the effect of a protective tariff upon the condition of the working classes in Germany, and in his speech in the House of Commons upon the Second Reading of the Finance Bill he made several statements which were based upon your Memorandum.

Mr. Lloyd George has been asked for his authority for the statements made by him, and he is very anxious to have the whole Memorandum printed and presented to Parliament.[2]

But before taking any steps in that direction he desires me to write to you and ask whether you would have any objection to that course, and whether you have any observations to make upon his suggestion.

He is not aware, for instance, whether the substance of the memorandum has been printed in any other form than that of a Cabinet Memorandum, or whether it has ever been published.

Perhaps it may be convenient to you if I refer you, for the debate in the House which I have mentioned, to 'Hansard' for Monday 1st and Tuesday 2nd June Vol. CLXXXIX Nos. 10 & 11.

Believe me, | My dear Sir, | Yours very faithfully, | S. Armitage-Smith

[1] Marshall Papers. Typewritten with corrections added by hand. Armitage-Smith (1876–1932), son of George Armitage-Smith, was at this time Private Secretary to David Lloyd George, Chancellor of the Exchequer. For details on the composition of Marshall's Memorandum see [754–5, 765, 769, 772–3, 776].

[2] Marshall's 'Memorandum on Fiscal Policy of International Trade (1903)' was to be published as a House of Commons Paper (No. 321) on 11 November 1908. It is reproduced as *Official Papers*, pp. 365–420.

913. To Sydney Armitage Armitage-Smith, 27 June 1908 (incomplete)[1]

South Tyrol
27. 6. 08

Dear Sir,

I have just received your letter of June 20th., in which you tell me that the Chancellor of the Exchequer does me the honour of desiring to print & present to Parliament the Memorandum written by me & printed for the information of the Cabinet in August 1903; & that he is good enough to invite me to make any observations on the subject that I may wish.

You call my attention to the references made to the Memorandum in Parliament on the 1st. and 2nd. of June last: but unfortunately I have no access now either to them or to the Memorandum. I recollect only that in an incomplete record of the debates I read that the Chancellor had mentioned my statement as to the change in the relative purchasing power of money in Germany & England, in regard to the ordinary necessaries of life. But I think I am bound to accede to the Chancellor's request, although in so doing, I am departing from the line of procedure which I had marked out for myself, & am indeed acting somewhat inconsistently.

I have always acted on the principle that a professional economist should as a rule abstain from controversy of all kinds. In exceptional cases he may be fitted, as Professor Fawcett was, for an active part in political conflict. But more generally he should, I think, give his attention almost exclusively to those difficulties for which time can seldom be found in the hurry & pressure of political life: he should avoid rather than seek those particular issues of the day as to which it is not easy even for a private citizen to preserve a wholly unbiassed judgement. For this reason instead of publishing my Memorandum, as I was invited to do in the Autumn of 1903, I am writing a large volume on *National Industries & International Trade*, in wh. I am endeavouring to treat solidly those large questions, on which the Memorandum expressed my opinions with a brevity, that necessitated a certain amount of dogmatism. The task is long; & though I have just resigned my Professorship in order to make more rapid progress with it, it will not be ready for another year or two. In the Memorandum I deal only with a few economic causes, & some of their effects: in my book I am engaged more closely with the causes of those causes which are changing the methods & the courses of industry & trade.

The first Part of the Memorandum was written in the Tyrol very hastily . . .[2]

[1] Marshall Papers. From a copy in Mrs Marshall's hand. Armitage-Smith [912.1] is not mentioned by name, but the letter was obviously a response to [912]: see also [915].

[2] The copy breaks off here with one or more pages missing. It seems likely that the missing material was drawn upon in the postscript to the Prefatory Note of the published Memorandum (*Official Papers*, pp. 367–8), dated August 1908 from Ampezzotal. It begins:

Some large corrections of, and additions to this Memorandum were lost in the post abroad in August 1903; and when I read the uncorrected proofs of it in the autumn, I was so dissatisfied with it, that I did not avail myself of the permission kindly given to me to publish it independently. The haste with which it was written and its brevity are partly responsible for its lack of arrangement, and for its frequent expression almost dogmatically of private opinion, where careful argument would be more in place. It offends against my rule to avoid controversial matters; and, instead of endeavouring to probe to the causes of causes, as a student's work should, it is concerned mainly with proximate causes and their effects.

914. To David Lloyd George, 27 June 1908 (incomplete)[1]

27. 6. 08

I endeavoured to make clear that I do not hold the influence, which customs duties may exert on the purchasing power of money in a country, to be important, so long as the duties are confined to a small part of the imports. Disturbances due to strategic trading, including what is commonly called 'dumping' being left aside, it seems clear that such duties raise the prices of the commodities affected (reckoned of course at the frontier & not inland) by the full amount of those duties; & that this rise in price represents an addition almost exactly in the same proportion to their real cost to the consumer (near the frontier).

The argument in the Memorandum that high import duties may raise considerably the general level of prices in a country is designed to apply only to cases in which the tariff affects a large part of her imports. In this case also the prices (near the frontier) of the taxed commodities will generally be raised by the full amount of the taxes. But the causes indicated in the Memorandum are likely to have induced a flow into the country of untaxed things (including gold) in partial displacement of other imports: & consequently to have caused some rise of incomes in general in terms of money. And, in so far as this has happened, the rise in the prices of taxed imports will not have caused a fully proportionate increase in their cost to the consumer (near the frontier).

I have wished to argue that this class of considerations prevents any simple application of statistics of prices to determine whether a tariff can be so arranged as to throw on foreigners a part of the burden of raising her revenue. Other things being equal incomes measured in money are likely to be raised by a high customs tariff: if it were not so the burden imposed on the country by such a tariff w^{d}. perhaps be greater than any modern economist supposes it to be. And in order to prove that the burden of such taxation can be shifted to any considerable extent on to the foreigner, it is necessary to show first that the revenue derived from the taxes is large, & secondly that the tariff has caused nearly as large a rise in money incomes as in prices.

Simple statistics can throw very little light on this matter, for many reasons. For instance [improvements in][2] production & transport are constantly raising money incomes relatively to prices; & if the influence of such improvements is being felt in the same decade in w^{h}. a tariff is raised, the rise in money incomes relatively to prices may be considerable: & yet it may be much less than it w^{d}. have been, if the tariff had not been raised. No doubt the influence of this disturbing cause can be partly illuminated by comparing the movements of income relatively to prices in countries in the same industrial phase, whose tariffs have not moved in the same direction. But, not to mention the difficulties of obtaining such statistics, they cannot be interpreted without taking account of the different influences w^{h}. are being exerted by education & by the development of latent natural resources through the spread of railways & otherwise.

The question cannot be handled effectively except by a study of those causes of causes on w^{h}. the Memorandum touches but slightly. All that could be done there was to indicate that a country could not expect to throw any considerable part of the burden of her tariff on other countries unless she were in a position to dispense with a great part of the goods which she imported from them, while yet she was in possession of such large & firmly established partial monopolies that they could not easily dispense with any considerable part of their imports from her. So far as the latter condition is concerned, England was in a very strong position early in the last century: but not even America is in a very strong position now; while England & Germany are in weak positions, as it seems to me.

Reverting to the old saying[3] that a thaler (three marks) is equal to five francs, which is equal to five shillings in regard to ordinary household expenses, I sh^{d}. like to say that that was impressed on me in Berlin in 1869 and 1870. I then spent about three months in all as a paying guest in a professional family of moderate means where some able journalists were habitués, & the talk often ran on such matters. Since then I have adopted the practice, at first alone & afterwards in company with my wife, of making systematic studies of the character & prices of the food & other goods displayed in working mens quarters in England Germany & other countries. Saturday nights, especially in England, have been the most profitable for this purpose. Frequent conversations with German householders & their wives, together with our own observations confirm the evidence afforded by statistics that the prices of nearly everything w^{h}. the working man needs, except alcohol & amusements are as high now in the industrial districts of Germany as in England, or higher. Houseroom is cheap in some parts of Germany; though it is dearer in Berlin than in London: & the cheap fourth class w^{h}. is provided on most German railways is a great boon to the poorer class of working people.

I have the honour to remain | Sir | Your obedient servant | Alfred Marshall

[1] Marshall Papers. From a copy in Mrs. Marshall's hand bearing the note 'Copy of part of letter to Chancellor of Exchequer'. The original (not traced) appears to have been sent with [913] to Armitage-Smith: see [915]. The opening portion of the letter was not copied and can only be

conjectured. The first six words of the copy were subsequently struck out and Marshall added at some later date 'IT taxes: Influences of frontier duties on prices'. The letter appears to have addressed the specific allusions made by Lloyd George in Parliament: see [912]. For the pertinent sections of the Memorandum (ss. 6–20) see *Official Papers*, pp. 370–80. Revisions based upon the present letter appear to have been incorporated on pp. 371–2.

[2] Words apparently omitted.

[3] Subsequently altered to 'I should like to revert to the old saying (see § 20)'. Section 20 of the Memorandum (*Official Papers*, pp. 378–80) had argued that when Germany had followed a free-trade policy before about 1878, one thaler for a German worker had been the equivalent of five shillings for an English worker, but that in consequence of Germany's twenty-five years of protection the equivalent had become two thalers by 1903.

915. From Sydney Armitage Armitage-Smith, 4 July 1908[1]

Treasury Chambers, | Whitehall. S.W.
4 July, 1908.

My dear Sir,

I beg to acknowledge the receipt of telegram from Cortina and of your letter to me of the 27th ultimo enclosing a letter to the Chancellor of the Exchequer.[2]

Mr. Lloyd-George desires me to convey to you his thanks for your readiness in consenting to the presentation to Parliament of your Memorandum and for the trouble which you have taken in writing the further Note. He is very glad to think that a Paper of such importance will by this means receive the publicity which is deserved by the value of its contents.

If I understand you aright, your desire is that the letter of the 27th addressed to the Chancellor of the Exchequer should form a Preface to the Paper, and that it should be published as such.[3]

I am taking steps at once to have it printed with the Memorandum, and I will forward a proof to you as soon as it is ready.

Believe me, | My dear Sir, | Yours very faithfully, | Sydney Armitage-Smith

[1] Marshall Papers. Typewritten. For Armitage-Smith see [912.1].

[2] The letters referred to were presumably [913–4]. The telegram has not been traced.

[3] [914] was not published with the Memorandum. Instead a short postscript was appended to the original 'Prefatory Note'. This postscript indicates that certain revisions to the original Memorandum were made, perhaps in the light of [914]: see [913.2].

916. To Miss M. Pate, 27 July 1908[1]

Hotel Cimabanche | Ampezzo | South Tyrol
27. 7. 08

Dear Madam

You have probably heard that I have resigned my Professorship in order to make better progress with my writing. But my last half year, partly because it was my last, was very busy: & I have written very little for my book lately. At last I am beginning to write; & I trust I may be able to finish the first draft of my book during the coming twelve months, if not before. I propose to stay here till about August 24th..; then to make a three weeks tour in German industrial districts & return home about Sep 12th.. During those weeks I shall not write of course.

Consequently if the end of August & the beginning of September would be a convenient time for you to type what I may get ready here, that wd suit me well: & I would send you a parcel of M.SS. just before leaving here.

But I am not sure at what time you yourself take holiday; whether it is about that time or later in September. So I write to ask you kindly to let me know what times during the coming four months would be specially convenient for you to have my M.S.S.; & what times wd be specially inconvenient. I think I shall be able, by being warned before-hand, to concentrate almost entirely on the first set. And anyhow I can certainly and easily altogether avoid the second set.

Yours very truly | Alfred Marshall

[1] Marshall Papers. The reading of the hotel name is not confident. The *Cambridge Review* for 13 June 1900 had noted: 'Mrs. Marshall is retiring from the University Type-Writing Office. Under her superintendance the Office has flourished since its establishment in 1892. The office will be in future under the sole direction of Miss Pate, who was Mrs. Marshall's second in command'. Located at 34 Trumpington Street, the office appears to have been a commercial enterprise. Nothing further has been discovered as to the two superintendents. The Marshall Papers contain two further notes from Marshall to Miss Pate of 25 April and May 1908, but they are of little interest beyond showing that typing of Marshall's book was then under way.

917. To Charles Ryle Fay, 3 September 1908[1]

3. 9. 08

My dear Fay,

I have just come home, & taken your book[2] in my hands. It is most fascinating. It develops just the points about wh I most wanted to know: and if I were a free man, I should read it straight through with delight for my own edification. But I hold myself bound to the public—to say nothing of MacMillan—to read nothing & think of nothing that I can help till the book advertised early in 1904 as 'in the Press' has crawled out of the Press. So I will look forward to it with anticipation, getting a double pleasure in this way, as you well suggest that the more ardent devotees of 'Divi'[3] do. Meanwhile I will only say that your book makes me very happy.

Yours sincerely | Alfred Marshall

Just one suggestion. In Edn II consider the plan of putting the title of the *Part*, not of the Volume on your left hand page. E.g. 'Stores, Belgium', describes pp 302, 3 better than the present heading & so does 'Agricultural Societies, Belgium' that of pp 180–1.

And to take a stronger case 'Stores. Industrial significance' makes a good heading for pp 336, 7.[4]

[1] Marshall Papers. From Balliol Croft.

[2] C. R. Fay, *Co-operation at Home and Abroad: A Description and Analysis* (King, London, 1908).

[3] The periodic dividend paid to members of a consumers' cooperative society, typically in proportion to purchases.

[4] That is, the versos should read 'Stores' or 'Agricultural Societies' rather than 'Cooperation at Home and Abroad'. The second edition of Fay's work (King, London, 1920) did indeed follow Marshall's general recommendation.

918. To John Neville Keynes, 27 September 1908[1]

27. 9. 08

My dear Keynes,

I find I get more literature than I can read. I am trying to read a good deal of German: I have always a great stock on hand that I cant get through. And I find the Statist not altogether helpful. It does not seem to me trustworthy; & I should not like to quote anything other than a specific figure from it without verification. And I find that the economic articles in the Manchester Guardian are more useful to me than those in the Statist. (The Times is less useful to me than it was: its ordinary articles are becoming too popular & *tendenziös*, & its Engineering & Commercial are becoming too narrow & technical.) On the other hand the Economist gives me a great deal of reading, more sometimes than I can get through: it seems to me more interesting, but less cautious & responsible than under its last two editors.[2] So I think that on the whole I will not ask you to send me the Statist any more. I am very much obliged for it in the past.[3]

I shall be most delighted to continue to send the Economist to you on the understanding that it goes to Maynard on its way back: if he found that a particular number was worth making cuttings from, that could be bought. And you could, as this year take in the Economist yourself when I am abroad. But it is quite likely that we shall not go abroad much more *to work*. Being less tied, we shall perhaps take more frequent *recreative* holidays in England: but the ever more realistic tendencies of my work make it increasingly wasteful of time & effort, to be compelled to put off looking up authentic statements of fact wh I am using for *illustrative* purposes—I don't much believe in the posssibility of direct induction—till I have come home & got out of the stratum of thought for wh I wanted the reference.

I thought Maynards note in the Ec Journal[4] was a good thing well done.

Yours very sincerely | Alfred Marshall

[1] Marshall Library, J. N. Keynes Papers. From Balliol Croft.

[2] *The Economist* was edited by Francis Wrigley Hirst (1873–1953) from 1907 to 1916. He was well-known as an author on economic, political, and literary topics—a latter-day Bagehot, but lacking Bagehot's genius. Between Bagehot and Hirst, the editorship had been undertaken by Inglis Palgrave and Daniel Connor Lathbury (joint editors 1877–83) and then by Edward Johnstone (editor 1883–1907). See *The Economist 1843–1943: A Centenary Volume* (Oxford University Press, London, 1943), p. 19.

[3] Marshall and Keynes had been exchanging *The Economist* and the *Statist* since the 1880s.

[4] J. M. Keynes, Untitled Note [on Rent, Prices and Wages], *Economic Journal*, 18 (September 1908), pp. 472–3; his first publication in this journal.

919. To Charles Ryle Fay, 17 October 1908[1]

17. 10. 08

Dear Fay

An excellent review in todays *Economist* attributes your book to 'nearly 3 years work at the London School'.[2] I feared that in your case, as in others, Cambridge might be exploited by London. I do not venture to urge you to write to the *Economist* to correct the error: but I think the matter is worth considering.[3]

Yours | A M

[1] Marshall Papers. From Balliol Croft. See [854, 855].

[2] See the favourable review of Fay's *Cooperation* [917.2] in *The Economist*, 67 (17 October 1908), p. 732, which referred to the book as 'the result of nearly three years' work as "Research Student" at the London School of Economics'.

[3] No correction was published.

920. To William Bateson, 24 October 1908[1]

24. 10. 08

Dear Bateson

I listened yesterday with great interest, profound admiration, & some understanding to what you said about 'factors'.[2] But I could not make out how large a part of human nature is of the same order with factors: & especially I could not tell whether there is evidence that variations of *quality* follow the same arithmetical rule as variations of quantity. Also I have long wanted to ask you why twins, *when* similar, are often incapable of being distinguished except by their nearest relations; while no two brothers of unequal age that I have ever known have been so like that a photograph of one at the age of (say) 8 could be mistaken for that of the other at the same age. But I don't want you to waste your time on answering by letter.

I write to ask you whether you know 'The Jukes'.[3] If not, I should like to lend it to you: it will go easily by post. I believe it holds as unique a position among family trees in regard to character, as that wh you showed us yesterday does in regard to night-blindness. The two have rather close outward re-semblance. I don't know in the least whether it will tell for or against your position: & I am sure you will welcome it equally either way. It has been quoted a good deal by advocates of 'sterilization of the unfit'.

Yours sincerely | Alfred Bateson

My wife has read this letter & says the signature must go as it is. It shows how I am dominated by a master mind.

[1] Marshall Papers. From Balliol Croft.

[2] Bateson had given on the preceding day his inaugural lecture as Professor of Biology on 'The Methods and Scope of Genetics'. It was published as a pamphlet by the Cambridge University Press (Cambridge, 1908).

[3] Richard Louis Dugdale, *The Jukes: A Study in Crime, Pauperism, Disease and Heredity* (Putnam, New York, 1877: many further editions). This study of seven generations of a family replete with deviance and degeneracy was much invoked by eugenicists.

921. To William Bateson, 26 October 1908[1]

26. 10. 08

Dear Bateson,

Thanks many.[2] I had not contemplated the divisibility of the ovum: that solves much. But the multiple twins are still to be dealt with.

I should do no good with technical Sheets: work at them must be professional. I have been some months wading through the detestable mud of international trade statistics. They have little interest for me: because I know that everything in them that is of much importance can be got by 'massive' observation & conjecture; & that the apparent definiteness of those aggregates of hundreds of thousands of guesses at value, which are spoken of as 'facts' by the newspapers, offers little real guidance. But that which offers the best guidance to me, is too subjective for external use: So I have to waste time on analysing statistics for other peoples benefit. If such work has done[3] me no other good, it has taught me not to try to interpret statistics, unless in a matter as to wh I know what the statistics will be like before I read them. Partly for that reason I have never worked at the tables of the Jukes.[4]

But of course I am not willing to see what I regard as more or less my own domain invaded by Statistics unless I am sure they are *relevant*: On that, I feel bold to have an opinion; though on the detailed interpretation of statistics I can have none.

I cannot—to be frank—see that your facts are inconsistent with the belief that the *quality* of the life of the parents affects every juice and every fibre & every cell inside the genital organs as well as outside. Every rowing man knows that character is as important as physique: the Johnian freshman of my year who, judged by physique, was easily first, turned out to be *absolutely* useless. After a little while the captain of the sixth boat w^{d}.. not look at him; & mere 'weeds' full of pluck made their way into the first boat. I have just been re-reading *The*

Last of the Barons:[5] the *historical* little Arab horse that carried the huge Warwick past all others was of course well put together, but his real strength lay in his character: & I understand that similar things are told of those queer freaks of wildness & culture intermingled which are found among western prairie horses.

Again, if it is true that good wheat sown year after year on barren soil degenerates, why should it not be true that the social life of many generations of parents—quite independent of any selection—affects the nerves, ie the quality & character of the later generations. That is all that we 'social people' want.

Yours sincerely | Alfred Marshall

P.S. On reading this over, I see that I have not put explicitly my question:—Does the similarity of (some) multiple twins indicate that the quality of the life (physical & mental &c) of the parents at the time of conception, & that of the mother during gestation & perhaps during suckling may possibly affect the qualities of the offspring?

I dont mean that your 'facts' are at all like the newspaper 'facts' about foreign trade. I am sure they are not, because you are you. But I prefer to rest on that massive fact, & not to try to interpret details for myself.

[1] Marshall Papers. From Balliol Croft.

[2] Bateson's response to [920] has not been traced.

[3] This originally read 'If it has done'. The word 'has' rather than 'it' was then inappropriately cancelled when the change was made.

[4] See [920.3].

[5] Edward Bulwer-Lytton, subsequently Lord Lytton, *The Last of the Barons* (Saunders and Otley, London, 1843), one of that voluminous novelist's historical epics.

922. To William Rothenstein from Mary Paley Marshall, with postscript by Alfred Marshall, 10 November 1908[1]

10 Nov 08

Dear Mr. Rothenstein

The portrait arrived safely this morning. It is perfectly delightful. I hardly know whether it is more admirable as a likeness or as a work of art. I can hardly bear to leave it to itself in the dining room where it has just been hung, & the longer I look at it the more it seems to express. Sarah[2] says 'it is all right' & this is the highest praise she ever allows herself to give. Only one friend & 'Harold'[3] have as yet seen it, & they like it immensely, but 'Mrs. Alfred Marshall and the portrait' are going to have two 'At Home' days to the Cambridge subscribers.[4]

I am rather confused about the Spring exhibitions. I had not in mind the society of portrait painters. The one wh. I was thinking of was the exhibition in the New Gallery wh. opens early in May & at wh. I believe I saw your portrait of Mr. Frank Darwin.[5] But whichever exhibition is most agreeable to you & the Committee will also please me best.[6]

The frame seems to me very beautiful in itself & appropriate to the subject. It is indeed a noble achievement & will be my most treasured possession. It will also be associated with those pleasant days during which it was being called into being.

Yours most sincerely & gratefully | Mary P. Marshall

All I have to say is that, considering the abominable material on which you had to work, I think you have made a most surprisingly good job of it in every way. I am *most thankful* that I have never had so difficult a task to tackle; & that you had it.

Yours devotedly | Alfred Marshall

[1] Harvard University, Houghton Library, Rothenstein Papers. From Balliol Croft. See [903–4]. The Rothenstein portrait of Marshall now hangs in St. John's College: see [953].
[2] Sarah Payne, the Marshall's servant.
[3] Not identified. Possibly Harold Guillebaud, Marshall's nephew, now a Cambridge undergraduate: see Vol. 1 Appendix I and [805].
[4] John Neville Keynes called to see the portrait on 14 December: 'It makes him look worn and old, but is otherwise very good' (*Diaries*, 14 December 1908). The portrait committee [867.2] had included some 25 Cambridge residents.
[5] Francis Darwin (1848–1925) botanist, third son of Charles Darwin and a Cambridge resident, who had been Reader in Botany, 1888–1904.
[6] The portrait was displayed at the New Gallery in January: see [931].

923. From James Laurence Laughlin, 12 November 1908[1]

University of Chicago | Department of Political | Economy
Nov. 12, 1908

Dear Professor Marshall:

The account of the volumes you are engaged upon, as described in the last one you sent me,[2] has tempted me to try again to draw you to this country. Seeing Professor Beazley, of Oxford, here sets me to thinking of you.[3]

We have over one thousand graduate students here in the Summer quarter, beginning next June 12. Would you possibly consider coming here next Summer and conducting a seminar course for six weeks—holding a conference of perhaps two hours for discussion once a week, or oftener as you might prefer—open only to advanced students in economics? We could make you personally comfortable; and your coming would enable you to see this big young country. The economists everywhere would give you a welcome which would warm the cockles of your heart.

We would be glad to offer you a compensation which would be satisfactory to you. If a $1000 for the six weeks would be sufficient, with perhaps $200 for your journey in addition, I think it could be arranged.[4]

I hope your health and your writing plans will not interfere. Do come, if you possibly can.

I am leaving next week for Santiago, Chilé, as a delegate to the Pan-American Scientific Congress, to be gone about three months. Therefore kindly send a Cablegram: 'Vincent, University Chicago, yes', (or no, as the case may be) at our expense.

Faithfully yours, | J. Laurence Laughlin

[1] Marshall Papers.

[2] Presumably a copy of *Principles* (*5*): see [876, 877.3].

[3] Charles Raymond Beazley (1868–1955), Fellow of Merton College and University Lecturer in the History of Geography at Oxford. Beazley was Lowell Lecturer at Harvard in 1908, when he also visited several universities in the USA, including Chicago. He became Professor of History at the University of Birmingham in 1909. A prior approach from Laughlin to Marshall is not recorded.

[4] Marshall noted on the letter: 'This seems to work out at £20 an hour for general talk. But I dare not delay my book, though I want immensely to see Chicago business with which one or two chapters of it are closely connected.'

924. To Frederick Macmillan, 17 November 1908[1]

17. 11. 08

Dear Mr MacMillan,

I inclose a copy of the Memorandum, whose strange fate in the Austrian post office I told you in January 1903.[2] Perhaps you may have noticed that Mr Lloyd George discovered the original first proof at the Treasury & quoted from it in the House early in last July;[3] whereon Mr Bonar Law challenged its production, & Mr Asquith undertook to produce it.[4] Really only half of it had been discovered: & this & other causes led to delays. At first I was annoyed at having to prepare it for press: but now I am rather glad. For it makes me more free to keep the controversial element in *National Industry & Trade* very low.

In the passage marked in the enclosed page from the Preface to the new edition of my *Principles*, I give a more exact description of the aim & drift of the book than I have submitted to you before.[5] The contrast in method & aim between it & this Memorandum is indicated in the P.S. to the Prefatory Note to the latter.[6] 'Protection & Free Trade' are in view during a part of its course; but they do not dominate it. It is in the main a study of industry in relation to trade.[7]

My work has been very much interrupted till recently. I am now making relatively fast progress: but that is not saying much. I am however taking my duty to the book seriously; & I propose to live as a recluse till it is out. But I fear that will not be till some time in 1910.

I have again to thank you for your patience with my delays, & consequent change of plan & consequent yet further delays; & I am

Yours sincerely | Alfred Marshall

Frederick MacMillan Esq

The copies of my Memorandum wh had been promised to me have not arrived: but as the Times has a leader on the matter,[8] I will post this letter, & let the document follow. Of course the drift attributed to it by the Times is their own domestic produce.

[1] British Library, Macmillan Archive. From Balliol Croft. See [912–15].
[2] This date is obviously incorrect: see [776, 787]. Perhaps January 1904 was intended.
[3] Actually on 2 June: see [912] where the reference to *Hansard* is given.
[4] See [925]. For details of the publication see [912.2].
[5] Enclosed with the letter was p. vi of *Principles* (*5*) which largely corresponds to *Guillebaud*, p. 46. The marked passage explains of the promised book: 'About one half of it is occupied with the evolution of the present forms and conditions of national leadership in industry, with special reference to the recent changes in the character and functions of giant businesses and of combinations: the second half applies the conclusions of the first half to the modern problems of international trade.'
[6] See [913.2] for the pertinent passage.
[7] This describes *National Industry and Trade*, not the Memorandum.
[8] See [925.7].

925. To the Editor, *The Times*, 21 November 1908[1]

Sir,—Mr. Bonar Law is reported by you as having said at Cardiff on Thursday last that my recently published Memorandum[2] is 'frankly partisan'.[3] The only statement of my purpose is in the first paragraph of the Prefatory Note, which is:—

> This Memorandum is written from the point of view of a student of economics rather than an advocate of any particular policy. I have not held back my own conclusions on the questions to which my attention was directed. But I have endeavoured to select for prominence those considerations which seem at once important and in some danger of being overlooked, whether they tell for or against my conclusions.[4]

No one can be sure that he has acted up to his intentions and Mr. Bonar Law would have been within his rights if he had said that I had failed to act up to my purpose of preserving a non-partisan attitude. But he was not justified in the explicit statement that I had frankly adopted a partisan attitude.

Mr. Bonar Law, at the same time, found fault with the publication of the paper by the Government. He has a bad memory. He, and he alone, is responsible for its publication. For I should certainly have refused to consent to its publication, if he had not extracted a pledge from the Government on June 2 of this year that it should be produced (see 'Hansard', Vol. CLXXXIX, p. 1,743).[5] The quotation which evoked Mr. Bonar Law's remark was stated to be from a paper by 'an economist', no name being mentioned; and this, no doubt, accounts for Mr. Bonar Law not remembering his action on June 2 when speaking on November 19: but, as your Parliamentary report in yesterday's paper indicated, the Prime Minister recollected it.[6]

Your leading article of Tuesday last concluded that, though 'called in to bless' free trade, my 'blessing is a feeble and dubious one'.[7] As to that I am no judge, but your conclusion seems to prove that my paper is not distinctly partisan. The statement that I was called on to bless free trade needs qualification; and there is no ground for the statement made by some of your contemporaries that this paper is the second edition of one which was 'published' in 1903. May I give the facts?

In July, 1903, I received a request from a leading member of the Cabinet for my answer to certain questions, falling into two groups indicated by the headings to Parts I. and II. of my paper.[8] In August, 1903, my answers were printed at the Foreign Office for private circulation. For reasons which are partly set out in the 1908 postscript to its Prefatory Note,[9] it lay dormant till this year. On June 3 I was more annoyed with Mr. Bonar Law than I am now; for your Parliamentary report showed me that I should have to consent to the publication of my Memorandum if requested to do so; and I had meanwhile fully resolved to be silent on the present fiscal controversy, until I could treat it as a side issue to questions of more enduring interest. But after some thought I accepted the invitation to prepare it for publication gladly; because I reflected that, having once done it, I should be free to work quietly at my book on 'National Industry and Trade', with even less reference than I had previously proposed to current politics.

I am, Sir, your obedient servant, | Alfred Marshall.

November 21.

[1] Printed in *The Times*, 23 November 1908.

[2] See [912.2].

[3] Bonar Law had spoken of 'the most remarkable kind of political propaganda which had ever happened in this country. There had just been published an essay in favour of the free-import system written by Professor Marshall. It was five years old and frankly partisan, but it had been published by the Government as a State paper. ([Cries of] "Shame".)' See *The Times*, 20 November 1908 (12c), a report of the conference in Cardiff of the National Union of Conservative Associations.

[4] *Official Papers*, p. 367.

[5] See also [912].

[6] See *The Times*, 20 November 1908 (8b). Asquith, who was the Prime Minister at this time, had refused to arrange a debate on the Memorandum since it had been 'presented to Parliament in compliance with a pledge given by the Chancellor of the Exchequer a long time ago'.

[7] *The Times*, 17 November 1908 (11e–f). This leading article on 'International Trade' had observed of Marshall: 'Called in to bless, he has not indeed cursed the system in which he was trained, but the blessing is a feeble and dubious one.'

[8] See [754].

[9] See [913.2].

926. To Frederick Macmillan, 22 November 1908[1]

Private 22. 11. 08

Dear Mr MacMillan,

Mr Lloyd George's private secretary,[2] who is spending the week end with his father in Cambridge, has just told me that the Copyright of everything printed at the expense of the Treasury, passes to the Stationery Office: And that a publisher has applied for permission to publish my Memorandum.[3] He asked me on behalf of Mr Lloyd George what I thought of the proposal. Of course I told him the history of *National Industry & Trade*: how it was to be a solid structure encompassing the ground covered by the Memorandum; how generously you had acquiesced in the locking up for several years of a vast amount of type; & that it was impossible for me to contemplate without horror the notion of the Memorandum's appearing with the name of any publisher but yourself. He cordially agreed; & promised that no request for its publication by anyone but you should be considered.

Things are moving. Several questions have been asked in the House about it, wh have not appeared in the Times; and several more are pending.[4] There will probably be some attacks on it with siege guns; only light artillery has yet had time to appear. And I may ask you to consider whether it should be published, with perhaps a Supplementary Chapter. But at present, I am inclined to keep on my way steadily, *though slowly*; unless indeed you have a strong opinion in favour of bringing out the Memorandum without waiting for the book.

Yours sincerely | Alfred Marshall

[1] British Library, Macmillan Archive. From Balliol Croft.
[2] William Henry Clark: see [927.1].
[3] [912.2]. The request was apparently from Fisher Unwin: see [958].
[4] *The Times* reported additional questions on 24 November (7e) and 25 November (10a).

927. To William Henry Clark, 22 November 1908[1]

22. 11. 08

Dear Mr Clark,

I have put together all the 1903 correspondence of a semi official character which I have.[2] If you are able to glance through it before coming here—I don't include the print!—you may see your way more clearly than you could otherwise.

Llewellyn Davies & I were, you know on rather intimate terms: & I think it is clear that his letter of 25 Aug 1903, with its reference to Hewins,[3] was private & personal, & must not be shown.

But all those papers which are fastened together with a tag seem to me harmless; & I have no objection to their being shown to Mr Balfour, or in fact treated in any way that may be thought consistent with our duty to Mr Ritchie.

The red marks on p 2 of the first letter show that I have followed my instructions closely.[4] In questions the purpose of the inquiry comes naturally first; but the order must be reversed in answers.

Yours very truly | Alfred Marshall

[1] Marshall Papers. From Balliol Croft. Clark had recently replaced Sydney Armitage-Smith [912.1] as Private Secretary to Lloyd George. Clark, subsequently Sir William Clark (1876–1952), a senior civil servant mainly connected with the Board of Trade, was the son of John Willis Clark (1833–1910) of Scroope House, Cambridge, currently the University Registrary, or chief administrative officer (to be succeeded in 1910 by John Neville Keynes).

[2] Presumably correspondence relating to the Memorandum [912.2]: see [754–5, 765, 769, 772–3]. All are punched so as to be held by a tag. The purpose for which these letters were needed remains obscure, the Memorandum already having been published.

[3] See [769].

[4] See [754.3] for details.

928. To Edwin Cannan, 23 November 1908[1]

23. 11. 08

My dear Cannan,

I am much obliged for your letter:[2] constructive suggestions such as yours are always most welcome. But it happens that the question of international mobility has occupied a large share of my attention almost without interruption for nearly forty years. It took a large place in the text of that MSS on International Trade on wh I worked from 1871 to 1877: (the diagrams wh were printed by Pantaleoni, & circulated privately in other forms, came from the Appendix to that volume).[3] A considerable part of my new book, already in type is given to the evolution & limitations of the notion of 'economic nationality': and so far I may ask for your approval. But I can go no further. For having opened & reopened the question in my own mind many times, I have always come down on the other side of the fence (a mixed metaphor!); & about ten years ago I came down so plump that I fear I shall never climb the fence again: though, if I were still of doubtful mind the cogent force of your great authority might set me on climbing the fence once again.

As to Ireland. I sometimes think I have a policy of my own. But I have never been tempted to utter it in any form: for Ireland, more than almost any other country needs to be studied on the spot: & I have never been there. My point of view is rather that of Plunketts *Ireland in the new century*.[4]

Yours sincerely | Alfred Marshall

[1] BLPES, Cannan Papers. From Balliol Croft.

[2] Not traced. Perhaps a comment on Marshall's Memorandum [912.2]. Cannan recalled that he had suggested 'the real economic "community" is not the "nation" but something much wider' ('Alfred Marshall, 1842–1924', *Economica*, 4 (November 1924), pp. 257–61 at p. 260).

[3] For the surviving portions of this manuscript see *Early Economic Writings*, vol. 2, pp. 3–236. Four of the appendix chapters had comprised the pamphlet 'Pure Theory of Foreign Trade and Domestic Values', printed at Sidgwick's instigation in 1879 for private circulation. For Pantaleoni's diagrams see [850.3].

[4] Sir Horace Plunkett, *Ireland in the New Century* (Murray, London, 1904). Plunkett was an enthusiastic proponent of self-help and character development through agricultural cooperation and technical education.

929. From Frederick Macmillan, 23 November 1908[1]

Macmillan & Co. Ltd. | St. Martin's Street.
London. W.C. Nov: 23 1908

Dear Professor Marshall,

I ought to have written to you before to acknowledge the receipt of your letter of the 17th. & to thank you for the copy of your *Memorandum* which you were kind enough to send me.[2] I have been reading the latter very carefully but I confess that as a layman I find it very hard to understand, but that is due to my lack of training in Political Economy. When one finds oneself unable to form an opinion on a matter of this kind one is struck with the unpractical nature of a system of government under which the settlement of a complicated fiscal question like Free Trade or Protection is left to an Electorate the majority of which is even less capable of understanding it in all its bearings than one is oneself!

When I read arguments about the effect of import duties on consumers, I often think of a story told me by an old gentleman in America about an Irish woman in New York who complained bitterly of having to pay a dollar for a chicken which she could have bought for 25 cents in Ireland. The shop keeper said 'very well ma'm, but if you feel like that why did you not stay in Ireland?' 'Sure' said the old woman 'if I had been in Ireland I should not have had the twenty five cents'!

I believe that the Stationery Office does claim a copyright in Parliamentary Papers, but I never heard that they considered themselves competent to transfer the copyright to anyone else; if the Publisher who asked for permission to publish your Memorandum had been allowed to do so I should indeed have thought that the promised attack on the hen-roosts had begun.

I should think that it would be a good plan to republish your Memorandum in pamphlet form and we shall be very glad to undertake the cost of doing so giving you half of any profits there may be. If you approve will you kindly send the copy to the Pitt Press at your convenience. I think it should be printed in 8vo.. and bound in cloth limp, like Professor Pigous Inaugural Lecture[3] which will appear in a day or two.

Believe me | Yours sincerely | Frederick Macmillan.

[1] Marshall Papers.
[2] See [924, 912.2].
[3] A. C. Pigou, *Economic Science in Relation to Practice* (Macmillan, London, 1908: delivered 30 October 1908). Macmillan's suggestion that Marshall publish the Memorandum as a pamphlet was not adopted.

930. To Frederick Macmillan, 24 November 1908[1]

24. 11. 08

Dear Mr MacMillan,

I gather that you agree with me that my Memorandum should not be published as a book for general reading, unless some change in the situation takes place.[2]

The first two Divisions A & B relating to the incidence of taxation were written when I supposed that only a short paper was needed & that it would be shown only to the Cabinet.[3] Under the circumstances of the moment that really meant Mr Balfour who was supposed to be in doubt. I therefore half-deliberately addressed myself to him: & used as few words as I could.

The substance of those two divisions will be spread thin over several chapters of my Book;[4] & by using footnotes for exceptional cases I hope to make the main discussions easy reading enough. As they stand I admit that they are stodgy: & if driven to publish for the general reader I had proposed either to recommend that those who were not specialists should begin with Division E; or to put into an Appendix B & part of A, C & D.

From E onwards I think there is little difficulty; partly because I was then looking rather at the general reader. For I had learnt that a project—afterwards abandoned—had been formed of issuing a Bluebook containing a sort of Symposium on the Fiscal Problem, similar to that which had been published some years before on the Incidence of Local Taxation.[5]

Of course 'real' wages are high in America: the wonder is that they are not much higher than they are. And the wonder to me in regard to Germany is that real wages are as much below English, except in a few trades, as they are. So far as I can make out employment is *less* steady there than in England. But masters & men there are generally willing that all should work short time rather than some only full time: & therefore an industry may reduce its output by 20% without showing any unemployed: whereas English industries generally wd in like case show 20% unemployed. Of course in the English Coal industry masters & men concur in short time where suitable.

Yours sincerely | Alfred Marshall

[1] British Library, Macmillan Archive. From Balliol Croft.
[2] Marshall appears to be responding to [929] so it is puzzling that he does not react to the offer to republish the Memorandum.
[3] The published Memorandum [912.2] was divided into sections A–O, Part I comprising A–E. See *Official Papers*, p. 369 for details.

[4] The long-promised *National Industry and International Trade.*
[5] Presumably C 9528 of 1899 which had included Marshall's 'Memorandum on the Classification and Incidence of Local Taxes' (*Official Papers*, pp. 327–64).

931. To John Neville Keynes, 5 December 1908[1]

5. 12. 08

My dear Keynes

Only the first few pages of this terribly long letter[2] concern your advice. Please kindly make sure that I have presented it rightly.[3]

If you can find time to read to the end, I shall be glad: & most grateful for any hints. It is on half sheets, so that I can easily cut out any passage which you query [with] '?'

Of course I cannot ask you to endorse the main body of the letter, partly because you are not as free to eulogize the young men as I am.[4]

The difficulty about the Cambridge Associations appeal[5] struck me in the night. It gave me the worst night I have had for years. If Higgs & Co clutch the money, or any considerable part of it, wh we might have got, & divert it from low pay for high energy to high pay for low energy, we may be wrecked. If we can keep our present team together, I believe that we shall have ere long the finest school in the world.

It is more important that this answer should be fitting than that it should arrive speedily. But if you have nothing to suggest please post it direct.

Just after I left you I recollected that the saying 'if x is not elected, it must be a party job' was not spoken to my wife; but to a very responsible lady not specially interested in the issue, who met my wife shortly afterwards, & told it to her with scorn. My wife confirms this.

Also she asks me to say that Rothenstein has been asked to send something to the 'International' Exhibition in January at the New Gallery: & that in consequence a certain picture will be packed up on the morning of Wednesday the 17th..[6]

[1] Marshall Library, J. N. Keynes Papers. From Balliol Croft. There is no signature and the letter may be incomplete.
[2] Presumably an enclosed draft letter, not traced, to Henry Higgs. Higgs was attempting to assemble support for a personal chair in Cambridge for Foxwell. It appears that Marshall had already written to him once on the matter (see [932]).
[3] Keynes's advice was particularly sought on the permissibility, according to University regulations, of an arrangement in which financial support was to be contingent upon a specific individual being the beneficiary.
[4] One of the young economics teachers being Keynes's son.
[5] See [895.3].
[6] See [922]. For details of the exhibition, and of plans for a reproduction of the portrait to be made available to interested persons, see *Economic Journal*, 18 (December 1908), p. 669, which reports that there were 193 subscribers.

932. To John Neville Keynes, (6?) December 1908[1]

My dear Keynes

I am infinitely obliged to you for your kind trouble & most helpful advice. In my first letter to Higgs I had gone on the assumption that he was a devoted friend of Foxwell's, that he would appreciate fully all Foxwell's merits, & not be in a position to note his deficiencies in regard to Cambridge work. I assumed also that he was of exceptionally delicate, fine, & quick perception: & therefore I said nothing deprecatory of Foxwell's nomination in words. I spoke entirely by silence, which I took pains to make prominent. Probably when he rose from his sickbed he had large correspondence, public & private, which needed attention: and I expect that when he got to Statute B, VI, 3, he was content; & did not read the rest of the long letter with care.[2] Otherwise I should think that he had deliberately refused to hear the voice of silence: & in doubt—long & weary doubt—I decided on a P.S. which would leave him no excuse for not recognizing that my estimate of Foxwell's suitability for the higher Cambridge work differs widely from his: especially in regard to the new features of the Economics Tripos.

Also I thought that the appeal, which he made in his second letter,[3] on account of Foxwell's poverty, was setting a dangerous precedent under the circumstances. But, on hearing how the P.S. strikes you, I have no hesitation in suppressing it.

I inclose a copy of the new pp 2, 3, which take the place of the old pp 2, 3, 4: where the reference to Biffen[4] was.

I think myself that when a University has allowed an external body to prepare one of its lecture sheets, nothing short of a palpably incompetent nomination would justify it in refusing assent to such a request as was made to it in Biffen's case. And I gather that in his case all the arguments on the matter were on one side.

Yours very sincerely | Alfred Marshall

I should have agreed more closely with you as to the services wh H.S.F. would render, had not recent events, including the two which I mentioned to you, introduced a new element into the situation.

[Enclosures.][5]

[Page 2] He[6] holds that the section of the Statutes (B vi, 3) which I quoted covers your suggestion: & that since the same Section gives power to the Senate to decide on the method of election in such cases—a point w^{h}. I had overlooked—there w^{d}. be no great difficulty in securing the appointment of the nominee of the subscribers, if that appointment were generally approved.

He called my attention to a precedent recently afforded in the election of Professor Biffen as Professor of Agricultural Botany. I am not myself quite sure that the precedent is perfect: but I gather that he thought it is at all events close enough; & he is an incomparably better authority than I. [Page 3] I have no means of knowing what attitude will be taken generally towards this proposal on its merits. But your first letter implied a wish to know my own opinion: so I will speak more definitely than before.

I think that if a fund is raised on purely personal grounds; & those who raise it desire that a particular individual should benefit by it, then, it being assumed that he is indisputably adequate for it, the University may gratefully accept.

[1] Marshall Library, J. N. Keynes Papers. From Balliol Croft. The letter is undated but probably responds to Keynes's comments (not traced) on the draft missive to Higgs that Marshall had sent on 5 December for Keynes's scrutiny (see [931.2]).

[2] Statute B, vi, 3 for Cambridge University granted the power of creating new professorships for a definite term or for the tenure of the first incumbent only.

[3] Not traced.

[4] Rowland Harry Biffen (1874–1949) had recently been appointed to the newly founded Professorship of Agricultural Botany, funded for the lesser of 20 years or the tenure of the first incumbent by the Agricultural Education Fund. The chair's establishment promoted a new area of study.

[5] These copies of the replacement pages 2 and 3 for the letter to be sent to Higgs are in Mrs Marshall's hand.

[6] That is, J. N. Keynes.

933. To John Neville Keynes, 13 December 1908[1]

13. 12. 08

Dear Keynes,

There has been much more correspondence with Higgs.[2] Its chief items on my side are—

(1) A letter on the 9th resuming that part of my earlier letters which is entirely free from personal references, with an intimation that he may show it to any one.

(2) A letter in continuation of that; written two days later to the effect that after consideration I have decided to urge him to enter into direct communication with you, on the grounds that:—'Keynes has perhaps a higher opinion of the importance of Foxwell's specialty to Cambridge than I have: he has not committed himself, as I have for the last forty years, to the opinion that Professors ought as a rule to resign at the age of sixty: partly for that reason, he does not rate as highly as I do the evils which might arise from the precedent that w^{d} be set by founding a temporary Professorship on the understanding that Foxwell should be elected to it'. I add other reasons connected with your personal qualities & your access to the Council by means informal as well as formal.[3]

(3) Some letters marked 'private' in wh I have explained—in answer to his continued urgency as to the importance of Foxwells experience & judgement—that in my view the specialty of Cambridge teaching is to develop faculty, & to leave judgement to be formed later: & that a lecturer, who imposes his own judgement on youth, is not acting up to the best Cambridge tradition.

(I did *not* add that as Foxwells judgements, while always confident, are apt to be in opposite directions at six months notice, I have a fear of his judgements. On Finance in particular, one of the subjects proposed for him, I think his judgement is extraordinarily bad. He seems never to see more than one side of any complex question.)

In Higgs' last letter but one he half asked my opinion as to the danger of there being 'two Kings in Brentford'. I replied that—though I had not mentioned the matter to Pigou &c—I felt sure there w^{d} be no trouble on that side: but that recent events had made me a little anxious on the other side. And I lifted the veil which covers those events so far as to say 'Foxwell wrote to me in June declaiming against electors, who had set aside the claims of friendship.[4] I shuddered. I did not answer: but that was the forerunner of trouble'.

Holding the opinions which you do, I think you would be right to promote Higgs scheme, provided it is so worked as not to undercut the expected appeal by the Cambridge Association on behalf of the Economic school.[5] But at most I can be 'benevolently' neutral. And if, as is possible, the question is raised whether a second Professorship—should there be one—should go to Clapham or Foxwell, I *must* speak for Clapham.[6] I know you have not come much in his way, & do not share my eager admiration for him. But you must have heard rumours of his success as a lecturer. And I, who have seen a good deal of him, would always go to him as counsellor of the first weight in any difficult matter of judgement. I think his achieved work is of a very high order, full of individuality and strength. Even if Foxwell were still in his prime, I should hesitate to put him on the same intellectual level with Clapham.

I now leave the matter in your hands. For the sake of auld lang syne, I will stretch my academic conscience as far as it will go. But it has a stiff neck. It may be well that you should have learnt at an early stage how far my benevolent neutrality towards Higgs' proposal is likely to reach. I am clear that I cannot *actively* support it in its present form.

Yours very sincerely | Alfred Marshall

[1] Marshall Library, J. N. Keynes Papers. From Balliol Croft. Reproduced in R. H. Coase, 'The Appointment' [908.1], pp. 481–2.

[2] None traced. See [931.2].

[3] A letter from Higgs to Keynes of 14 December inquired 'whether a guarantee would be sufficient or whether the University would require cash down?' and proposed that Keynes come to London to meet with 'half a dozen friends' on 10 or 12 January 1909. Keynes, replying on 16 December, doubted that a guarantee would suffice and disclaimed detailed knowledge of the proposal, foreseeing 'many pitfalls' and a need for 'great circumspection', though 'as a friend of Foxwell's I should like to be able to support the scheme'. Preferring not to be involved with the proposed meeting, he met instead with Higgs individually on 5 January at the Treasury. (Letters in the J. N. Keynes Papers. See also *Diaries* entry for January 5 1909.) Higgs's initiative seems to have come to nothing.

[4] See [909].

[5] See [895.3].

[6] Clapham had recently resigned his Professorship at Leeds to return to Cambridge as Assistant Tutor at King's, replacing Oscar Browning.

934. To Walter Thomas Layton, 14 December 1908[1]

14. 12. 08

Dear Layton

I am vastly glad that you are going to stay here; & that the cause is not in ill health.

As to whether you have decided rightly, I cannot tell. But I always regard India as a mighty Goddess, who gives a high spirit to those who worship her with a pure heart, fervently, but who brings to naught the life of any who treat her lightly.

Yours very sincerely | Alfred Marshall

[1] Trinity College, Cambridge, Layton Papers. From Balliol Croft. Pigou had recently arranged for Layton to lecture for the Tripos at a salary of £100 a year paid from Pigou's pocket. The Indian prospect declined by Layton appears to have been in the Indian Civil Service. See David Hubback, *No Ordinary Press Baron: A Life of Walter Layton* (Weidenfeld and Nicholson, London, 1985), p. 22.

935. To Manohar Làl, 28 January 1909 (incomplete)[1]

28. i. 09

... Thanks for the cutting you sent me.[2] But the writer has not caught my drift. It is true that I think that the reasons, which make Protection specially unsuitable to Britain now, do not apply to India. But neither do I think that simple Protection to Indian industries would work well: and the particular proposals made by the Tariff Reform League, in regard to India, seem to me fraught with the maximum of evil and the minimum of benefit to both India and Britain. I was disgusted at the neglect of India's interests by the Colonials at the recent Conference[3] and I do not like the way in which the Tariff Reformers are arguing now that their scheme is necessary for India's safety. I hold, on the contrary, that any *serious* Preferential Scheme for the Empire would be likely to call into being a formal or informal Middle-Europe-Customs-Union directed against the Empire. Tariff Reformers say that the Continent 'must' have Indian products.

That seems to me true only as to jute. A Tariff war would, I think, exclude Indian tea, silk, cotton, hides, etc. in a great measurement from the Continent. (I expect the United States would not join in the war unless specially attacked: but would remain neutral.) The Tariff Reformers say that roundabout trade is always bad, and that India would do better to sell direct to Britain than to sell to the Continent and pay Britain with the proceeds. But I hold that roundabout trade never exists without good cause. The Continent spins chiefly low count yarns, and therefore is glad to buy short stapled Indian cotton. Who would gain by forcing us to buy short staple yarns at relatively lower prices than the Germans can pay, and causing rather more of the American cotton to go to Germany?

I do not see my way clear as to India's policy. I have never advocated the excise duty on Indian cotton manufactures. But yet I do not like to preach a crusade against it without knowing more of the facts than I do. I hold that, before any such action is taken, the plan should be considered of devoting the excise duties on cotton to subsidizing pioneer works in industries which are still in an infant stage; an industry that employs a quarter of a million people cannot be described as 'an infant'.

But I do not believe that any device will make India a prosperous nation, until educated Indians are willing to take part in handling *things*, as educated people in the West do. The notion that it is more dignified to hold a *pen* and keep accounts than to work in a high grade engineering shop seems to me the root of India's difficulties.... A high authority in an Indian Railway is now in my house.[4] He says—'a native who has discretion is above working in our engine shops'. That is my point. Until the judgment necessary for high grade industry can be developed in native workers, no expenditure on the importation of white foremen will make India a progressive country....

[1] Printed in *Memorials*, pp. 456–7. Original not traced. From Balliol Croft.

[2] Not identified. Presumably concerning Marshall's Memorandum [912.2].

[3] The Imperial Conference of April–May 1907. *The Times* carried extensive reports of the proceedings.

[4] Not identified.

936. To Joseph Robson Tanner, 3 February 1909[1]

3. 2. 09

Dear Tanner

My nephew Walter sent yesterday a new plan for a Manchester career. I did not take to it; & sent full reasons to him & his mother. On getting my letter this morning she wired to him that she had decided it was best that he should come to Cambridge; & wired to me to say so. Of course this decision might be changed, on sufficiently strong reasons shown by him: and therefore I had not intended to tell you anything about it.[2]

I had not clearly understood that Open as well as close exhibitions were offered in June. I incline to think that Walter should enter for one (his brother is of course not eligible[3]): but on the whole I think it will be best to wait for a post or two before writing about it.

My sister will be most heartily grateful to you for your great kindness; as certainly I am.

Yours sincerely | Alfred Marshall

[1] St John's College, Cambridge, Tanner Papers. From Balliol Croft. The Guillebaud twins had lost their father in 1907, a loss which presumably enhanced Marshall's avuncular concern. See Vol. 1, App. I, for family details.

[2] None of the communications mentioned here has been traced. By 9 February (having already reported 'Two satisfactory letters from Bathford and Manchester') Marshall was able to report that 'W. H. Guillebaud will offer himself for an exhibition in June, with the intention of coming up to St John's in any case' (Tanner Papers).

[3] The reason for this is unclear.

937. From Allyn Abbott Young, 3 February 1909[1]

Leland Stanford Junior University
Department of Economics and Social | Science
Stanford University, Cal.,
3 Feb. '09.

Professor Alfred Marshall,
Balliol Croft,
Cambridge, England.

Dear Sir:—

I imagine that the publishers have sent you a copy of the revised edition of Ely's Outlines of Economics.[2] If you have time to examine it you will note that the chapters on Economic Theory, especially those on Value and Price, Distribution, Rent, Wages, and Interest, show more clearly than any other American textbook the influence of your work in Economics. I am writing this letter because I wrote the chapters in question, and because I wish to make this opportunity of saying that to my mind the general view of the economic process embodied in your writings is one which is bound to have an increasing influence in American writing. It is true that the most important recent American publications in the field of Economic Theory have been the developments of Austrian theories. This, I think is due to the fact that the authors in question (with the exception of Professor Clark) got their theoretical impulse at a time when Professor Smart's translations had brought Austrian theory into prominence, and when the dominance of German trained economists in American universities had led to a mistaken revolt against the older English political economy. I am thoroughly convinced that the pendulum is swinging back again; that especially among the younger men there is a strong feeling that an excessive use and development of the marginal utility analysis will not get us very far away from an argument in a circle, and that we have got to apply ourselves to that careful analysis of the forces of demand and supply, which has its best presentation in your writings. It is because I feel that you ought to know that there is in America a growing appreciation of the fact that the Principles of Economics represents the highest achievment in economic analysis up to the present, and that it points the way to the most valuable lines for future work, that I have thought it worth while to write this letter.

Respectfully yours, | Allyn A. Young

[1] Marshall Papers. Typewritten.

[2] Richard T. Ely, *Outlines of Economics* (revised and enlarged by the author with the assistance of Allyn A. Young and others: Macmillan, New York, 1908). The initial publication of *Outlines* had been in 1893.

938. To Allyn Abbott Young, 24 February 1909[1]

24. 2. 09

Dear Sir,

Knowing by experience that the author has often finished with his book long before the publisher gets out all his presentation copies, I will not wait any longer; but send this line to express my deep gratitude for your extremely kind letter.

The paper wh I am sending under a separate cover may perhaps interest you.[2]

Yours very truly | Alfred Marshall

[1] Harvard University Archives, Allyn Young Papers. From Balliol Croft. A response to [937].

[2] Not identified.

939. To John Maynard Keynes, 26 February 1909[1]

26. 2. 09

Dear Keynes,

I don't think it is worth while to have a separate label for those books wh I have put in L.L.R.5.[2] I never thought of such a thing being done: & I cannot countenance it. But that is the only objection wh I have to the enclosed label;[3] wh seems to me excellent of its kind.

Yours sincerely | Alfred Marshall

[1] King's College, Cambridge. J. M. Keynes Papers. From Balliol Croft.

[2] Marshall had written to G. L. Dickinson, Secretary of the Economics Board, on 2 June 1908, handing over to the Board 'all my interest in the books in the L.L.R.5: together with the bookcase'. Literary Lecture Room 5, the lecture room in which Marshall had taught for many years, held a collection of books provided mostly by Marshall for the use of students. He may have augmented the collection from his private library upon retirement. It was not until 27 June 1909 that Keynes was officially appointed custodian of the collection by the Board (Minutes of the Special Board for Economics and Politics, 1903–11: Cambridge University Archives).

[3] A printed copy of the proposed bookplate is preserved with the letter and reads: 'Presented by/Alfred Marshall/Professor of Political Economy 1885–1908'. (This involved a slight inaccuracy since Marshall had actually been appointed in 1884.)

940. To Francis Ysidro Edgeworth, 21 April 1909[1]

21. iv. 09

My dear Edgeworth,

I have just noticed your review of Rea in the *Ec. J.*[2] I don't want to argue. But the hint that a rather rash and random guess has been made by those who suggest that a (moderate) rise in the price of wheat might increase its consumption in England (not generally) provokes me to say that the matter has not been taken quite at random.

When wheat was dear and men were cheap, the estimate of consumption of wheat per head in England was one quarter:[3] now it is, I believe, between 5 and 6 bushels. And thrifty Frenchmen with all their cabbages are said to consume more than a quarter now. Ever since I saw Giffen's hint on the subject,[4] I have set myself to compare the amounts of bread (and cake, wheaten biscuits and puddings) eaten at first class dinners in private houses and expensive hotels, with the consumption in middle class houses and second-rate hotels; and again with the consumption in cheap inns, including a low grade London hotel: and I have watched the baker's supplies to cottagers. And I am convinced that the very rich eat less than half as much bread as the poorer classes; the middle class coming midway. This proves nothing conclusively: but it is a fair basis, I think, for a surmise as to a probability.

In America the waste of cereals is said to be prodigious: I think a rise in price would check that; also all cereals, including even wheat, are sometimes fed to stock. In Germany it is known that dear wheat and rye increase the always enormous consumption of potatoes. I have never seen evidence that dear wheat has a considerable effect in that direction here.

With bad world harvests for two or three years in succession, I suggest that part of English wheat consumption would come from American and Australian waste. If not, then bread might become so dear that our consumption of wheat would diminish.[5] I don't say I am right: but I am not random.

Yours ever, | Alfred Marshall

I forgot to speak of adulteration by bakers. When I was a boy that was done largely by potatoes. Now I think it is seldom done on a great scale: and that maize is used more than potatoes when wheat is dear. I think a great rise in the price of wheat would greatly increase the amount of maize in bread: and this of course tells on your side.

[1] Printed in *Memorials*, pp. 438–9. Original not traced. From Balliol Croft.

[2] 'Rea' was printed as 'Rae' in the *Memorials* version. Edgeworth had reviewed Russell Rea, *Free Trade in Being* (Macmillan, London, 1908) in the *Economic Journal*, 19 (March 1909), pp. 102–5: reproduced in F. Y. Edgeworth, *Papers Relating to Political Economy* [793.6], vol. 3, pp. 164–8. Commenting upon Rea's assertion that an increase in the price of wheat would cause the poor to consume more of it, Edgworth observed that 'Even the milder statement that the elasticity of demand for wheat *may* be positive, though I know it is countenanced by high authority, appears to me so contrary to *a priori* probability as to require very strong evidence'. Marshall had reinvoked the 'Giffen effect' in the context of the English demand for wheat in his Memorandum [912.2] (*Official Papers*, p. 382), largely repeating a suggestion originally introduced in *Principles* (*3*), p. 208 (see *Principles* (*8*), p. 132).

[3] Eight bushels.

[4] Marshall's crediting of the 'Giffen effect' to a hint from Giffen remains a debatable issue.

[5] The sense of the letter suggests that 'increase' rather than 'diminish' was intended here.

941. To Francis Ysidro Edgeworth, 22 April 1909 (incomplete)[1]

22. iv. 09

My dear Edgeworth,

About ten years ago I nearly completed a draft Book (No. X, I think) of my second volume 'On Markets'. It had an introductory general chapter, followed by others in detail.[2] After working some time, I found the task too long to be made complete. So I decided to select two or three typical instances, and work them out carefully. Wheat was—for many reasons—my chief instance. My draft copy on it is about 40 pp. long. I read several thousand semi-technical pages, chiefly American, on the subject: and came to the conclusions which I condensed in 1903 into §§ 23–27 and 29 of my Memorandum.[3] The substance being that, after a special analysis, it appears to be not 'extremely improbable', but *à priori* to be expected, that the elasticity of supply of wheat in those parts of America from which most wheat has been raised in the past would obey wholly different laws from those which did prevail there a generation ago, and which now prevail in the Dakotas and Manitoba etc.: and that the evidence which could be got tended to prove *à posteriori* that this was the case.

Having had means of knowing that the information put before the British public from about 1902, as to the conditions of Northern Manitoba, Assiniboia,[4] etc., was largely fraudulent, and prompted by unscrupulous 'Americans', who had taken options (and in some cases bought outright) a great deal of Canadian land, I began to read again on the same subject, and worked through 'several thousand?' pages more. Whenever I met a high class American I asked him in effect this question, 'Is not the export of wheat from the North American Continent in years of normal harvest highly elastic for a fall and very inelastic for a rise?' and I understood everybody, who expressed an opinion at all, to agree. You may perhaps recollect that there was a dinner party here during the British Association meeting in 1904:[5] and that after dinner, though there were several people to whom I wanted particularly to talk, I spent the whole time—as it was my only chance—in getting from Mavor, who knew much more about it than anyone else in the world, a detailed (illustrated) account of the wheat resources of the Canadian Northwest.

Of course I looked at the matter from the analytical point of view also. And it seemed to me that the common opinion—which I understand you to endorse[6]—is based on a fundamental misconception of the nature of wheat production in a new country. Under some circumstances it is a complete industry; and then it responds but slowly to changes in price. Under others it is a mere department of general agricultural industry; and then it responds almost instantaneously.

There is no paradox in this. Take an analogous case. If a certain pattern of cycle, not patented, were to come into favour, so that it could be sold for £1 more than others into which the same amount of work was put, then its production might jump up from five thousand to half a million instantly: because making a particular kind of cycle merely requires minor detailed readjustments of plant already in existence. That case resembles the case of wheat where highly capitalised *mixed* farming predominates. For the farmer can in 1910 say 'I will have four times as much wheat a year as now', or 'I will not have any wheat at all next year'. As a matter of fact however—and on this all Americans with whom I talked seemed to agree—the Middle West mixed farming might diminish rapidly its supply of wheat, but is not likely to increase it rapidly; because it is not highly capitalised, such an increase would require to be preceded by a large and rather slow increase of live stock (artificial manure being impracticable unless the price of wheat rose very much).

On the other hand, when cement works are fairly busy no increase of price will bring about any considerable increase of supply for a long while; it must wait for the erection of new cement works. This corresponds to the 'sole-crop' supply of wheat in the Far West; where there is very little room for mixed farming as yet. Land already in cultivation is nearly sure to be used for wheat: and in order to break up more land for wheat it is necessary to build new farmers' cabins, attract workers, perhaps get new branch railways and so on. That is to say wheat production under these conditions is a complete industry, like cement production. It is not a department of agriculture, as cycle making is of mechanical engineering. In my view true science and observation completely endorse Rea's conclusions[7] and mine.

I am even more perplexed by what you say about elasticity of demand.... I object to the phrase negative elasticity,[8] because I think it tempts people to carry anaytical mathematics beyond their proper scope. In this case, for instance, it suggests a paradox. And I submit that there is no paradox at all. Take a parallel case. I believe that people in Holland travel by canal boat instead of railway sometimes on account of its cheapness. Suppose a man was in a hurry to make a journey of 150 kilos. He had two florins for it, and no more. The fare by boat was one cent a kilo, by third class train two cents. So he decided to go 100 kilos by boat, and fifty by train: total cost two florins. On arriving at the boat he found the charge had been raised to 1 1/4 cents per kilo. 'Oh: then I will travel 133 1/3 kilos (or as near as may be) by boat, I can't afford more than 16 2/3 kilos by train'. Why not? Where is the paradox? What but needless perplexity can result from calling this negative elasticity, on the abstract ground that that name is in harmony with mathematical symbols, which are being pushed beyond their proper scope?[9] ... I have written this prodigious scrawl because I cannot bear to think that you suppose me to have spoken of elasticity as high for a fall and yet low for a rise, without careful thought; without having in a responsible way convinced myself that the sources of supply from which a great increase would come were not quickly responsive to stimulus, and that the sources of supply which would chiefly shrink against a fall of price would respond in that direction quickly.

Yours affectionately, | Alfred Marshall

[1] Printed in *Memorials*, pp. 439–42. Original not traced. From Balliol Croft.

[2] Almost nothing has survived from the draft manuscript for the proposed second volume of *Principles*. Much of it must have been cannibalized for use in the long-drawn-out composition of *Industry and Trade*.

[3] [912.2]: see *Official Papers*, pp. 381–4.

[4] Printed as 'Assimaboia' in *Memorials*. Assiniboia Territory, created in 1882, became part of Saskatchewan in 1905.

[5] For details of the flurry surrounding the British Association meeting see [792.4, 794, 798].

[6] In his review [940.2], Edgeworth had noted that Rea 'will not accept the assumption that the extensibility, as Mill would say, of the colonial supply may be equated to the contractibility', an assumption Edgeworth imputed to Pigou and justified on grounds of '*a priori* unverified probability'. He suggested that Rea might have confounded short-period reactions in the one direction with long-period in the other.

[7] 'Rea' was printed as 'Rae' in the *Memorials* version.

[8] Marshalls seems to be viewing the Giffen case as one of negative price elasticity whereas Edgeworth had taken it as involving positive elasticity: see [940.2].

[9] Marshall appears to be treating specific commodities as valued not for their own sakes but for the distinct mixes of valued attributes they provide. As shown generally in Richard G. Lipsey and Gideon Rosenbluth, 'A Contribution to the New Theory of Demand: A Rehabilitation of the Giffen Good', *Canadian Journal of Economics*, 4 (May 1971), pp. 131–63, this kind of formulation creates considerable scope for Giffen effects. For a more critical commentary on Marshall's hectoring of Edgeworth on these matters see Peter Newman, 'Reviews by Edgeworth', pp. 109–41 of John D. Hey and Donald Winch (eds.), *A Century of Economics: 100 Years of the Royal Economic Society and the Economic Journal* (Blackwell, Oxford, 1990), at pp. 119–21.

942. To Francis Ysidro Edgeworth, 27 April 1909 (incomplete)[1]

27. iv. 09

My dear Edgeworth,

Many thanks for your all too kind letter.[2] If I made any reply to your gentle criticisms I should be on the inclined plane which leads down to controversy: so my silence under rude blows might be more awkward than it is, if I once broke through my rule to leave controversy to the strong. I am trying to write out my thoughts, including of course those relating to wheat supply, without raising dust. I can't see my way through the huge difficulties of the great issue, even when there is no dust: I work ever slowly. But yet I have a notion that I really have something to say; partly on subtle points, for which my mind is now of little use, only I have a good many notes made before I became a dotard; but more on the One in the Many and the Many in the One, i.e. the relations of details to fundamentals, a matter on which the experience of age is some atonement for its stupidity....

But I wish that some one who has the strength would hit such fallacies.... It wants steady persistent hammering; and it can't well be done except by a trained thinker. Even the generally excellent *Westminster Gazette* gave itself away by saying that the true reason why a German sending goods to the English market need not be charged with the equivalent of English domestic taxes was that the German paid heavy domestic German taxes[3]—an answer fit to make Ricardo's bones rattle in their grave....

Yours most ever, | Alfred Marshall

[1] Printed in *Memorials*, p. 442. Original not traced. From Balliol Croft.
[2] Not traced.
[3] The particular statement Marshall had in mind has not been identified.

943. From William Rothenstein to Mary Paley Marshall, 14 May 1909[1]

11, Oak Hill Park, Frognal. | P.O. Hampstead.
May 14—09

My dear Mrs Marshall—personally I always prefer silver prints, as they give a more vital representation of what a painting is meant to evoke. I quite agree that they are harder, but they are really as it were more honest, & charm is often the result of a *conscious* desire to please, in photographic prints as in other things. So I should myself plump for the silver prints, & if they are done by sound people, & I think Walker's people are, they last for very many years.[2]

It is pleasant to think that a print of the portrait is to hang in the lecture room where so much of your husband's inspiration was given to the world;[3] I have a very vivid recollection of seeing him standing up there, when he gave that wonderful last lecture of his, & I am proud to think that it has been allowed me to suggest something of the man who has for so many years given life to that room. It is just a year since I was with you, & I shall always remember that spring at Cambridge. The affection and kindness you both of you show to me is one of the real things of my life. I am sending you a photograph of an old portrait of myself which has just been bought for presentation to the Metropolitan Museum of New York.[4] You see me there as a kind of brigand, but at least it may amuse you, & it will carry my greetings to you quasi-personally.

It is odd to think of my absurd self in the country of trusts & millionaires & freak[5] dinners, solemnly hanging on a wall in such proper attire. We shall be here until the end of July—is there any chance of your coming up to Town & of our seeing you—your remember we had a promise of a visit from the Doctor. Please give him my warmest regards & remember me too please to Sarah.[6]

Yours always W. Rothenstein

[1] Marshall Papers. A response to an enquiry, not traced, about photographic reproduction of Rothenstein's portrait of Marshall. See [931.6].

[2] The reference given in [931.6] indicates that Mr Emery Walker was to prepare the proposed reproduction. A note in the *Economic Journal*, 19 (December 1909), pp. 647–8, conveyed the message from Mrs Marshall that in addition to the photogravure of the portrait a separate 10″ × 9″ platinotype of the portrait's bust, thought remarkably successful by Rothenstein, would be sent to subscribers upon request.

[3] A reproduction of the Rothenstein portrait, perhaps the one being discussed here, was in 1986 still hanging in Marshall's old lecture room, L.L.R.5 (now part of the Selwyn Divinity School).

[4] Probably the self portrait by Rothenstein bought by a Mrs Chadbourne and presented to the Museum. See Sir William Rothenstein, *Men and Memories* (Faber and Faber, London, 1931–40: vol. 2 covering 1900–22), p. 173. Rothenstein's scornful description of Marshall as sitter on p. 130 of the same volume was in stark contrast with the rather sycophantic tone of this and his previous letter [903] and distressed Mrs Marshall.

[5] 'Steak' may be suspected but is not a plausible reading.

[6] Sarah Payne, the Marshall's servant.

944. To John Maynard Keynes, 30 May 1909[1]

30. 5. 09

Dear Keynes,

I think the L.L.R.5 economic catalogue is excellent, & will be of great service.

I have a good many books, chiefly historical wh are good of their kind, & which I yet seldom use. If you had more space, I sh^{d}.. suggest that some of them should come to you without waiting for my demise. Don't trouble to answer.

Yours sincerely | Alfred Marshall

[1] King's College, Cambridge, J. M. Keynes Papers. From Balliol Croft. See [939.2].

945. To the Clerk, the Girdlers' Company, 2 June 1909[1]

2. 6. 09

Dear Sir

I have recently heard from the Secretary of our Financial Board that the Court of your Company would soon meet to discuss the renewal of their most generous grant to our Economic School: & on consulting with Mr A.H. Adie,[2] I found that he thought it w^{d}. be well that I s^{hd}. write to you some account of its most recent progress.

The chief thing to be said relates to the splendid results of the work of this years staff: & in regard to that Professor Pigou, the first Girdlers lecturer, & now my successor, is not as free to speak as I am: so I am acting on M^{r}. Adie's suggestion.

The scheme of lectures for the present year is on a higher plane than heretofore; partly because several young men of great promise have either begun their work, or settled down to it more thoroughly than before; & partly because King's College has attracted back to Cambridge M^{r}. Clapham;[3] one of the very few living men who can treat in a masterly way the economic history of recent years; a subject which is vital for us but has not yet been worked into shape. Nearly everyone who is teaching now for the school is working on a broad basis of knowledge but is also specialising so far as to be likely to lead the world in his own line are long. They all in their various degrees, are of high ability & zeal; I hear constantly of the attractive force w^{h}. their vigorous personality exerts on the students; &, if the University can retain their services, they will I believe make the Cambridge school of Economics second to none in the world. But the ever growing claims of the studies, which are already firmly set in the saddle, press heavily on the finances of the University: & in spite of the £200 a year which Professor Pigou places at the disposal of the Economic Board, some of them are inadequately paid. The generous aid therefore of the Girdlers Company is of vital importance to the school, & is regarded with deep gratitude.

Until the twentieth century, the time was hardly ripe for a separate school devoted to Economics: & if the numbers of those who sought it had been less than in the case of most other new Schools in the University, there w^{d}. have been no ground for surprise. But it has made a better start than others w^{h}. had less difficulties to overcome; & the most recent figures show that the present staff has a very firm hold on the students.

Part I of the Tripos was held for the first time in 1905, & Part II in 1906. The following figures are of men & women who took honours in the several years.

	Part I	Part II	Total
1905	10		
1906	4	3	7
1907	8	5	13
1908	8	9	17

The entries for 1909 are

	Part I	Part II	Total
	11	13	24

of whom 4 are women.

The number of those who are preparing for Part I in 1910 is 20; of whom 6 are women.[4] Besides these, who obtained the whole of their instruction during the current year from the Economics Staff, about fifty students, of whom a quarter are women, have attended some of the lectures given by that staff. Among these are ten Candidates for the Civil Service examination.

The number of those who will come into residence next October & who are known to intend to read for the Economics Tripos is greater than at the same time in any previous year.

I am asking M^{r}. Meredith who is Chairman of the Examiners for the present Tripos to send you a copy of the papers as soon as he can. I inclose also some more copies of an *Introduction* to the Tripos;[5] & s^{hd}. be very glad to send any number more that you may wish.

I have the honour to remain
Yours faithfully | Alfred Marshall

The Clerk | The Worshipful Company | of Girdlers.

[1] Marshall Papers. From a copy in Mrs Marshall's hand. The Girdlers' Company was to continue its support of the Girdlers' Lectureship during Marshall's lifetime. The Marshall Library lists the recipient as W. Dumville Smythe.

[2] Possibly (reflecting an error in transcription) Marshall's colleague at St John's, Richard Haliburton Adie (1864–1932), or perhaps some relative of the latter—his brother, Walter Sibbald Adie was to become Master of the Girdlers' Company in 1932 after a career in India.

[3] See [933.6].

[4] The numbers of those actually obtaining honours in 1909 and 1910 were Part I 1909, 13 (11 men, 2 women); Part I 1910, 18 (11 men, 7 women); Part II 1909, 10 (8 men, 2 women); Part II 1910, 11 (8 men, 3 women). For the years 1905–8 the numbers of women obtaining honours in Part I were, respectively 5, 1, 2, 1: for Part II the corresponding figures were 1, 1, 4, 2. One man who received an aegrotat for Part I in 1906 was excluded from Marshall's figures.

[5] See [831.4].

946. To Léon Clément Colson, (June?) 1909[1]

Dear Sir,

I write in English, because I start tomorrow for South Tyrol, and must finish some writing before I start: and I write slowly in French.

Briefly—I read Mill's *Political Economy*[2] in 1866 or '7, while I was teaching advanced mathematics: and, as I thought much more easily in mathematics at that time than in English, I tried to translate him into mathematics before forming an opinion as to the validity of his work. I found much amiss in his analysis, and especially in two matters. He did not seem to have assimilated the notion of gradual growth by imperceptible increments; and he did not seem to have a sufficient responsibility—I know I am speaking to a mathematician—for keeping the number of his equations equal to the number of his variables, neither more nor less. Since then I have found similar matters not quite to my taste in the economic work of nearly all those who have had no definite scientific training.

At that time and for long after I knew very little of the realities of economic life. But I worked at what I regard as the central problem of distribution and exchange. Before 1871 when Jevons' very important *Theory of Political Economy*[3] appeared, I had worked out the whole skeleton of my present system in mathematics though not in English. My mathematical Note XXI concentrated my notions: but the greater part of the earlier notes and especially Notes XIV–XX were evolved in substance about the same time.[4] These contained the substance of my doctrine of Substitution; though I did not make use of that term till long after.

As I have said in my original Preface, I owed much to the mental discipline afforded by Cournot; but the one book which really guided me was written by a landowner, who had very slight knowledge of mathematics, and indeed occasionally talked great nonsense in them. It was von Thünen, as you already know.

In 1877[5] I married; found myself committed to writing a cheap popular book, which was necessarily superficial, and which I loathed. After a few years I became very ill, and expected not to be able to write anything considerable. So I took out the diagrammatic appendices which I had written for my book on International Trade;[6] and decided to edit them, showing their uses, and above all their *limitations*: after that was done I expected to depart this life. But I slowly recovered. And so the purely analytical work in Book V of my Principles, with a part of Book III, were the kernel from which my volume expanded backwards and forwards to its present shape. The Austrian School is on lines somewhat similar to a part of mine. But I knew nothing of Carl Menger till my own ideas were nearly in full shape: and Böhm Bawerk and Wieser were at that time at school, or students at the University.

Unfortunately, the French translation of my *Principles* Vol. I was partly published before I received an unexpected call for a new edition which appeared in 1907.[7]

The Preface to that indicates the nature of the changes made in it, and in my plans generally.[8] Age is beginning to tell on me; and I resigned my Professorship a year ago, in order that I might make more progress with *National Industries and International Trade*, which I am writing slowly.

The Austrians, and especially Böhm Bawerk, annoy me (though there is much in their work which I admire) by pretending to have revolutionized the bases of economics; whereas nearly all their doctrines appear to me to have been latent in the writings of the 'classical' economists. Also they offend against my mathematical instincts: though I have now ceased to use the mathematical language easily.

Yours very truly | Alfred Marshall

I know well your *Transports*; and have often recommended it. But I do not know, alas!, your *Cours*; and now I have no more any pupils.[9] I send a Memorandum[10] that may interest you.

[1] Printed in 'Alfred Marshall, the Mathematician, as seen by Himself', *Econometrica*, 1 (April 1933), pp. 221–2. Original not traced. From Balliol Croft. Marshall's mention of resigning his Professorship 'a year ago' and of shortly travelling to the Tyrol, where he was already installed on 2 July (see [947]), makes a June 1909 date almost certain.
[2] That is, Mill's *Principles*.
[3] See [899.4].
[4] The notes in the Mathematical Appendix to *Principles* (*5*) are substantially the same as those in *Principles* (*8*), pp. 838–58.
[5] Printed as 1871 in the *Econometrica* version.
[6] See *Early Economic Writings*, vol. 2, pp. 3–236 for details and surviving text.
[7] See [757.4] for details of the French translation of *Principles* (*4*) with some additions from *Principles* (*5*).
[8] See [877.3].
[9] L. C. Colson, *Transports et Tarifs* (Paris, 1890; third edition Laveur, Paris, 1908)—translated as *Railway Rates and Traffic* (Bell, London, 1914); *Cours d'Économie Politique* (Gauthier-Villars, Paris, 1901–7: 3 vols.).
[10] See [912.2].

947. To Louis Dumur, 2 July 1909[1]

Stern im Abtei, Süd Tirol
2. vii. 09

Dear Sir,

The questions, which the Alliance for promoting the increase of population in France[2] is discussing, are of deep interest. I do not know France well enough to answer them; but I will venture to make a few remarks bearing on them.

From the military point of view a check to the growth of numbers may of course be a source of danger, mitigated by the automatic tendency, which the predominance of any great military nation has, to stimulate alliances or understandings for cooperative self-defence among its neighbours. But such matters do not lie within my scope.

I do not regard a moderate retardation of the growth of population as a great social and industrial evil in itself. And, though I think it often does go together with national decadence, I doubt its being the cause of that decadence. But I think it may often be a consequence of the same causes which bring about that decadence. These are, I think, often associated with the growth of wealth and the cessation of the need for incessant energy and self-devotion in the overcoming of difficulties. In so far as the retardation of the growth of population may be caused by a consequent weakening of individual, and therefore of national character, the remedy seems to me to lie chiefly in combating its evil causes. In so far as it has no such evil origin, I should regard it without grave anxiety.

The rather violent checks to population, which have recently appeared in some strata of some Anglo-Saxon peoples, seem to be partly caused by a selfish devotion to 'sports' and other amusements on the part of men: and partly to a selfish desire among women to resemble men; with the effect that, without rendering any high service to the State in masculine work, they destroy that balance and mutual supplementary adaptation of masculine and feminine character, which enabled a man to secure rest and repose by marriage; though he might probably have been worried beyond endurance by the lifelong incessant companionship of another man. This cause does not seem to diminish the number of marriages much; but it tends to make men delay marriage till their best strength has gone. I believe that these two evil tendencies exist in France, though less than elsewhere.

The evils of town life are being combated by the drift of population from the central districts to suburbs where most families can have separate houses, many can have gardens, and nearly all children can play freely in the open air. The movement of France in this direction has perhaps been rather slow. More energy seems urgently needed to check the drift towards living in small apartments in crowded cities, where children are not easily accommodated; and where placid recreations, which build up strength of body and character, are supplanted by nervous excitements, which consume strength, and consume also a large part of the family income unprofitably. It is of course true that but a small part of the population of France suffers much from this evil.

But there remains one from which I fear that France may suffer much. It is very likely that I am mistaken; and I speak with the utmost diffidence. But is it not true that a preference for a secure income, free from anxiety, and unlikely to be forfeited without grievous fault is specially strong in France? Is not this preference associated, partly as cause and partly as effect, with the law of equal inheritance, and with the large part which dowries play in marriages? Does not a small income derived from land, or from Government employment where promotion goes mainly by seniority, tend to concentrate attention on small cares, and petty savings? No doubt this has its good side; and the masterly, unrivalled economy of many French households is admired and envied throughout the world. But does it not also disincline people for bold creative enterprises? Does it not make the expense of rearing and providing a dowry for an additional child too serious a burden? Does it not make the dowry too important; and thus diminish the chance of marriage for those who come from fertile stocks, and give a fatal premium to infertile stocks?

No doubt it is well to insure people against calamities which are beyond their own control. But is it not a condition of vigorous individual and national life that men should seek, rather than avoid, those risks which are inherent in bold action, and which can be overcome by their own courage and energy? Does not this matter need the careful attention of France, and other old countries? Would not some gain be derived from a little infusion of American audacity, to supplement the splendid industrial qualities of the French people? I am perhaps rash in making this suggestion: but I am encouraged to do it by noticing that some of the suggestions under the consideration of the Alliance point in the same direction.

Taxes on childless people, combined with special privileges to parents of many children, would, I think, have but little direct influence in England: I cannot speak as to France. But in such matters legislation is an expression of the public conscience; and a national protest against the restriction of births from selfish motives might perhaps exert a good deal of influence indirectly.

Yours very faithfully, | Alfred Marshall.

[1] Printed in *Memorials*, pp. 459–61. Original not traced. The recipient was probably Louis Dumur (1860–1933), a Genevan who had lived in Russia as tutor to Grand Duke Michael, returning to France in 1889. His literary output was extensive, although not concerned with population. But fears were rife about France's failure to match Germany's growing numbers and economic and military power.

[2] The Alliance Nationale pour l'accroissement de la Population Française, subsequently the Alliance Nationale pour la Vitalité Française, has left only a skimpy and intermittent published record and appears to have had little impact.

948. To Walter Thomas Layton, 28 September 1909[1]

28. 9. 09

My dear Layton,

What little I have the pleasure of knowing of Miss Osmaston[2] inclines me to believe what you say about her: & under the circumstances that is a very large admission. Mary knows her well: & is sure it is all true. But indeed your letter itself carries conviction. You seem to have been made to fit one another in thought and in hope; & to help one another on the journey towards the Grail. Most heartily do I congratulate you.

Your words to me are all too kind: I wish they could be true; & anyhow they are sweet. When a man gets old, the most precious thing to him, almost the only thing that is really precious to him, outside of his kith & kin, is the affection of younger men; especially when it is accompanied as it is in this case by the trust that they will achieve what he had hoped he might do, but has not done. Again thanks & congratulations!

Yours very sincerely | Alfred Marshall

[1] Trinity College, Cambridge, Layton Papers. From Balliol Croft.

[2] Eleanor Dorothy Osmaston (1887–1959), a student at Newnham 1906–9, obtained a second in Part I of the History Tripos 1908 and a second class, first division in Part II of the Economics Tripos 1909. She and Layton were to marry on 2 April 1910. See D. Hubback, *No Ordinary Press Baron* [934.1], ch. 2.

949. To Lord Reay, 12 November 1909[1]

12. xi. 09

Dear Lord Reay,

I wish it were in my power to give an adequate answer to the questions you have put to me.[2] But my only confident dogma in economics is that every short statement on a broad issue is inherently false. It was in 1903 that the Chancellor of the Exchequer set me two questions.[3] I have done nothing else that I could help except write out my answers to those questions, with their kith and kin. It is now 1909: and the answers are not yet nearly ready. Partly for that reason I have paid very little attention to Budget controversies; and I have remained silent even when my published opinions were misquoted or misinterpreted.

You will therefore kindly understand that the few remarks which I make in answer to your questions do not claim to be true: the most I can hope for is that they are on the whole on the side of truth.

I do not know what 'socialistic' means. The *Times* has just said that it means taking away *property* from individuals and giving it to the State.[4] But the Budget proposes to take *money*: and if, say, £M150 have to be levied by taxation, the Budget, *whatever its form*, must be accordingly Socialistic to the extent of £M150, neither more nor less.

My own notion of Socialism is that it is a movement for taking the responsibility for a man's life and work, as far as possible, off his shoulders and putting it on to the State. In my opinion Germany is beneficially 'socialistic' in its regimentation of those who are incapable of caring for themselves: and we ought to copy Germany's methods in regard to our Residuum.

But in relation to other classes, I regard the Socialistic movement as not merely a danger, but by far the greatest present danger to human well-being. It seems to me to have two sides, the administrative and the financial. Its chief sting seems to lie on the administrative side.

I do not deny that semi-socialistic or Governmental methods are almost inevitable in ordinary railways etc.: though a vigorous despot in America breaks through them occasionally. But the sting of socialism seems to lie in its desire to extend these rather than to check their expansion. I believe that they weaken character by limiting initiative and dulling aspiration; and that they lower character by diverting energy from creation to wirepulling. I therefore regard Protection as socialistic, in that, especially in a democratic country, it gives a first place to those business men who are 'expert' in hoodwinking officials, the legislature and the public as to the ability of their branch of industry to take care of itself.

On the financial side, Socialism may be rapacious, predatory, blind to the importance of security in business and contemptuous of public good faith. But these tendencies lie on the surface: they provoke powerful opposition and reaction; and personally I fear them less than those which are more insidious. In moderation they are even beneficial in my opinion. For poverty crushes character: and though the earning of great wealth generally strengthens character, the spending of it by those who have not earned it, whether men or women, is not nearly an unmixed good. A cautious movement towards enriching the poor at the expense of the rich seems to me not to cease to be beneficial, merely because Socialists say it is a step in their direction.

But it may be urged that, though much of the *expenditure* of the very rich tends to lower rather than to raise human character, yet their *capital* is needed for the expensive methods of modern industry. Britain's capital however grows fast relatively to her area, and a small check to its growth would but postpone a little the day when most of her new accumulations are exported. I admit however that the interest on her foreign investments is a mighty bulwark against the blows of foreign tariffs.

For about fifteen years I taught somewhat eagerly that 'Death Duties' were a grievous evil because they checked the growth of capital.[5] For the next few years I hesitated. Now I think they are on the whole a good method of raising a rather large part of the national revenue; because they do not check accumulation as much as had been expected, and a small check does not seem to me now as great an evil as it did then.

As regards the influence of taxation on employment, I hold it to be indirect only. All income is spent on the purchase of services including that of postponing consumption, or 'saving': excepting in so far as it goes to the owner of land and other forms of wealth that have not been created by individual effort. I have repeatedly stated my opinion that the owners of such land have not truly paid income tax.[6] It is true that they have not 'evaded' it. But the law has hitherto been a sustained social injustice in this respect: what they have been required to return as income is only a part of it. This injustice I regard as 'predatory'; its redress I regard as anti-socialistic.

The case of stock exchange securities which have appreciated is similar in some repects. But (1) to require individuals to make return of all increments got in 1907, and of the decrements in 1908, would be impracticable. (2) Few forms of intellectual effort are more important socially than forecasting the future and contriving so that the future may turn out well. The shareholder who directly or indirectly takes part in the management of a company is generally doing good service; and his rewards, like those of the able and courageous fisherman, come largely in the form of big hauls or 'windfalls'. I do not see how to tax the passive stockholder, without taxing the active one. And I do not want to tax 'increments' except in cases in which *either* it is possible to compensate for 'decrements', *or* the decrements are relatively rare and small.

Lastly. The term land*owner* does not exist in English law: and English public opinion has never admitted that the land*holder* has the same rights of usance, without reference to the public interest, in regard to his land, as he has in regard to his carriage or his yacht. Morally everyone is a trustee to the public—to the All—for his use of all that he has: but the trusteeship under which he 'holds' land is of a specially binding nature.

At the same time I have always scouted the notion that there is a monopoly of land: or that the State can quietly resume the full ownership of land: I am as great a heretic in the eyes of Mr Wedgwood or Mr Fillebrown, as in the eyes of Mr Chaplin.[7]

To return to the relation of taxation to employment. The State by taxes takes part of the national income and spends it almost exclusively on services; just as the individual would have done, if it had been left to him. The small share that goes to those who have rendered no services, in the form of pure rent, may be neglected in either case. Hence I conclude that, if taxes are so levied as to impair enterprise, they *pro tanto* lessen employment at good wages: but if they are so spent as to increase vitality, they increase employment at good wages; because they increase earning power. I am certain that Tariff Reform would, and that the present Budget would not, lessen employment at good wages.

The notion that the investment of funds in the education of the workers, in sanitation, in providing open air play for all children etc. tends to diminish 'capital' is abhorrent to me. Dead capital exists for man: and live capital that adds to his efficiency is every way as good as dead capital. It is not more important to have cheap maize than cheap wheat, merely because maize is the raw material of pigs, and wheat of men.

Foolish ostentatious expenditure by the State, like the similar expenditure of private persons, is, no doubt, an enemy to good employment: because the funds used up in it do not create, as they pass away, fresh sources of future production, and therefore future income; as they would if they were spent on building up improved iron works or human beings.

I think it would be difficult to frame a budget which got so much revenue, with so little burden to the working classes, as the present one does: though I do not entirely approve of all the details of it that I know, and I do not know all.

But if the budget is not to be used as a means of diminishing the existing inequalities of income, then I think it is quite possible to get a total of £M200 a year by the addition of taxes on articles of general consumption, independently of their source; and therefore without taking, as Tariff Reform taxes would do, much more from the people, directly or indirectly, than would be received by the State.

This is I fear a very poor answer, very slovenly and meagre. But my power of work is waning: and it has taken all that I can do in a morning.

Yours sincerely, | Alfred Marshall

[1] Printed in *Memorials*, pp. 461–5. Original not traced. From Balliol Croft.

[2] Not traced. The questions doubtless pertained to the controversy, then at its height, over Lloyd George's 1909 budget. Faced by a need to raise revenue to meet substantially increased expenditures upon Dreadnoughts, old age pensions, and other items, Lloyd George had introduced during the summer a budget proposing substantial tax increases, including a 20 per cent duty on the 'unearned increment' of land value, payable upon transfer of land, and a tax of one half penny per £ on the capital value of undeveloped land. These increases, especially the latter ones, were particularly galling to large landowners. The budget was passed by the Commons on 4 November and rejected by the Lords on 30 November, precipitating a constitutional crisis.

[3] See [754].

[4] See the leader on 'The Word Socialism', *The Times*, 11 November 1909 (9f).

[5] Marshall's only published discussion of death duties before this time was a brief mention in 1897, taking a 'hesitant' position. See *Official Papers*, p. 357.

[6] The 'statements' referred to are not evident in Marshall's publications up to this time, but for his views on taxing the 'public' value of land see the references given in [950.4].

[7] Josiah Clement Wedgwood (1872–1943) and the American Charles Bowdoin Fillebrown (1842–1927) were enthusiastic proponents of site-value taxation. Henry Chaplin (1861–1923), landowner and politician, was opposed.

950. To the Editor, *The Times*, 13 November 1909[1]

Sir,—My attention has only just[2] been called to a statement on page 11 of the 'Budget, the Land, and the People', published in August last by the Budget League.[3] Referring to my answer to questions set by the Royal Commission on Local Taxation[4] ([C. 9,528] 1899, pp. 124–5), it is said that I 'recommended that there should be an annual levy of 1d in the pound on the capital value of land which was worth up to, say, £300 an acre, and that land with higher site value should be made to contribute at a higher rate.... The Budget proposals are not so drastic'. The 1d in the pound, or rather more for urban land, which I suggested was not an additional tax; it was merely a readjustment of the existing burden of taxes, without any increase in their total amount. It therefore was not *in pari materia* with a new tax to be devoted to Imperial purposes.

In my view it was reasonable to levy heavy poor rates, &c., on the 'public value' of land; that is, on 'its value as it stands after deducting for any buildings on it and any distinct improvements made in it during, say, the last twenty years';[5] but I thought that the incidence of such heavy rates on new capital applications was a differential tax against the use of capital in agriculture, a use which deserved special encouragement; and upon the erection of new buildings in towns, a use which deserved no special discouragement. I proposed therefore to place a charge amounting perhaps to about a third of the whole burden of rates, on the public value of the land; leaving the remaining two-thirds as a burden in[6] which alone new capital applied to the land in agriculture or building would pay its proportionate share. I desired to assess this special charge on capital value, because the part of the real annual value of land which does not appear in a money form varies greatly even within the same rating area; and therefore any local rate or general tax levied exclusively on annual value must be to some extent inequitable. So far, therefore, I suggested no new burden; a few minor local inequalities would have been redressed, and farming and building enterprise would have been encouraged. That is all, so far as my main proposal went.

But it is true that I did propose a small new net burden on the owners of urban land. I hold that the most important capital of a nation is that which is invested in the physical, mental, and moral nurture of its people. That is being recklessly wasted by the exclusion of, say, some ten millions of the population from reasonable access to green spaces, where the young may play and the old may rest. To remedy this evil is, in my opinion, even[7] more urgent than the provision of old-age pensions; and I wished the first charge upon the rapidly-growing value of urban land to be a 'Fresh Air' rate (or general tax), to be spent on breaking out small green spots in the midst of dense industrial districts, and on the preservation of large green areas between different towns and between different suburbs which are tending to coalesce. I thought that the gross amount of the Fresh Air rate or tax should be about ten millions a year, till we have cleared off the worst evils caused by many generations of cruel apathy and neglect. But I urged that it 'would not be really a heavy [net] burden on owners, since most of it would be returned to them in the form of higher values for those building sites which remained'.[8]

The proposal made in the present Budget to isolate future accretions of 'public value' and to tax them only[9] was not open to me. I regard it as in many ways a great improvement. Those Socialistic aims, which tend towards the supersession of the responsibility of the individual for his own career, seem to me the gravest of all the dangers that loom on the social horizon. But in so far as the Budget proposes to check the appropriation of what is really public property by private persons, and in so far as it proposes to bring under taxation some real income, which has escaped taxation merely because it does not appear above the surface in a money form, I regard it as sound finance. In so far as its proceeds are to be applied to social problems where a little money may do much towards raising the level of life of the people and increasing their happiness, it seems to me a Social Welfare Budget. I do not profess to have mastered all its details; but on the whole I incline to think it merits that name.

Alfred Marshall.

Cambridge, Nov. 13.

[1] Printed in *The Times*, 16 November 1909. Original not traced. Practically the same letter, dated 17 November, was printed in *The Economist*, 20 November 1909. The two versions differ only in minor rewordings (noted below) and in some trivial discrepancies in the use of commas and capitals. Interpolations in square brackets are Marshall's.

[2] The words 'only just' were replaced by 'recently' in the *Economist* version.

[3] *The Budget, the Land and the People: The New Land Value Taxes Explained and Illustrated: A Complete Guide to the Great Question of the Day*; with a preface by David Lloyd George (Methuen, for the Budget League, London, 1909).

[4] See *Official Papers*, pp. 327–64 at pp. 360–1. Marshall had drawn heavily upon these answers (written in 1897) in adding appendix G to *Principles* (*5*) in 1907. See *Principles* (*8*), pp. 794–804.

[5] *Official Papers*, p. 361, where the additional words 'at private expense' follow 'made in it'.

[6] The word 'in' was replaced by 'to' in the *Economist* version.

[7] In the *Economist* version 'even' was printed as 'ever'.

[8] *Official Papers*, p. 361, where the words 'since' and 'net' are absent.

[9] See [949.2].

951. From Lord Reay, 14 November 1909[1]

Carolside, Earlston, Berwickshire, N.B.[2]
14. xi. 1909

Dear Professor Marshall,

I am indeed greatly obliged for your illuminating letter and the trouble you have taken to answer all my questions.

On the whole I was very glad to see that your opinion of the budget is favorable as regards increment and death duties.

Do I understand that you hold that the interest of capital invested abroad pays for imports to England and *pro tanto* neutralises the evil effects of high tariffs in penalising our exports which otherwise would have to pay for the imports?

I suppose that you regret the excessive outlay in armaments as representing unproductive expenditure, but that you do not object to old age pensions, which may be considered as deferred or supplementary wages.

I take it that your opinion that the landholder has not paid his proper share of income tax only applies to building land, not to agricultural land, and that you approve the concession made to the latter with regard to deductions for repairs and management. I also suppose that you admit that the effect of reducing the spending power of individuals and increasing the spending power of the State is to create a disturbance in the labor market.

I hope I am right in thinking that you do not advocate an addition of taxes on articles of general consumption *independently of their source* except as an alternative of tariff reform.

Again apologising for my inquisitiveness and with very sincere thanks.

Your obliged, | Reay

[1] Printed in *Memorials*, pp. 465–6. Original not traced. See [949].

[2] 'North Britain' i.e. Scotland.

952. To Lord Reay, 15 November 1909[1]

15. xi. 1909

Dear Lord Reay,

You have interpreted my short answers as I meant them. But perhaps I should add a few words on two points.

My view is that foreign import duties on British imports[2] must be paid almost entirely by the consumer (setting aside a few small exceptional cases), unless British exports are thereby reduced to so low an aggregate that Britain is compelled to give up some imports which she urgently needs. If she were, her need would force her to export even at the cost of paying a part or the whole of the duties herself. Such conditions would be unlikely in the present state of world commerce anyhow: and they are rendered impossible in my opinion by the fact that the very few cases in which a foreign country has any approach to a monopoly of an import which we need very urgently are more than covered by our power of drawing about £100,000,000 worth of those things which we most need even if all our exports were barricaded out. This is a complex, but I think important fact; and I am giving a considerable space to it in the book on *National Industries and International Trade* at which I am slowly toiling.

Next as to armaments. I am not a good judge of the question how far we might safely reduce our armaments or even abstain from increasing them now. But I think that, if half a dozen of the noisiest speakers and writers who exulted over the insult inflicted on Germany, when one of her mail ships was taken into a South African harbour, though her captain had given his word of honour that he had no contraband of war, could have been suppressed, and similar conditions stopped, we should have had no call to build ships very fast.[3]

Yours sincerely, | Alfred Marshall

[1] Printed in *Memorials*, pp. 466–7. Original not traced. From Balliol Croft. See [949, 951].
[2] That is, duties imposed by other countries on imports from Britain.
[3] In January 1900 the *Bundesrat*, suspected of running arms to the Boers, had been forced into Durban harbour to be searched. The incident had helped fan the flames of Anglo-German naval competition.

953. From Robert Forsyth Scott to Mary Paley Marshall, 11 December 1909[1]

St John's Lodge, | Cambridge
11 December 1909

Dear Mrs Marshall

I communicated to the College Council yesterday the substance of your letter offering to present to the College Mr Rothenstein's portrait of Dr Marshall.

I was desired to convey to you the thanks of the College for the gift and to assure you that we very highly appreciate the self-denying generosity of your offer.

You will no doubt let us know when we may send for the picture.

Yours sincerely | R. F. Scott

[1] Marshall Papers. See [922]. Scott (1849–1933), Senior Bursar of St John's 1883–1908, had succeeded Charles Taylor [882.4] as Master of the College in 1908. According to Foxwell's much later testimony, Marshall's manœuvrings over the appointment of his successor had set the College against him and the picture was accepted without ceremony. See [1120.3].

954. To Nicolaas Gerard Pierson, 21 December 1909[1]

21. xii. 09

Dear D^{r}.. Pierson

My wife & I were filled with renewed grief this morning on hearing from Mrs Pierson that your illness seems rather to increase than to decrease.[2] There can be very few people in the world whose illness could cause so deep sorrow to so many people in so many lands: and I scarcely know any one else who has touched deeply so many of the hearts with whom he has come into contact among my acquaintances, whether for a short time or a long. After your stay here for a few days at the meeting of the British Association,[3] all the ladies who had met you here, spoke frequently of 'that *dear* D^{r}.. Pierson'; & all the men vied with one another in praises of your bright mind, your perfect quiet oratory and your fascinating bonhommie. You are one of those few to whom it has been given to make the whole world better than it would have been if you had not been born into it. Holland will become still prouder of you as the lapse of years causes sterling work, that masters the future, to stand out from amidst the rococo work of the ready writer & the mere politician, that crumbles under the touch of time: and the world will class you with Adam Smith, the thinker, the patriot, & the cosmopolitan; & with Turgot the Statesman-economist. And it will always be one of my chief joys that I have felt justified in signing myself

Yours affectionately | Alfred Marshall

[1] University of Amsterdam, Pierson Papers. From Balliol Croft. Reproduced as letter 1385 in J. G. S. G. van Maarseveen, *Briefwisseling* [734.1].

[2] Pierson died on 24 December 1909, so that it is doubtful whether he learned the contents of the letter. Mrs Pierson's previous letter not traced.

[3] Presumably the 1904 meeting in Cambridge: see [794, 798].

955. To Macmillan and Company, 30 December 1909[1]

30. xii. 09

Dear Sirs

Your account received in October made me fear that a new Edition[2] might be called for soon; but I have received no other intimation from you. I knew that my book had been adopted officially for general use at Tokio; but I supposed that the copies needed to start the class had already been bought. However I propose to make no fundamental changes in the new Edition; & I am going to make a great effort to keep the pagination unaltered. For my slow progress at National Industries & Trade, my waning strength, & my chagrin at the recrudescence of stupid fallacies even in the speeches of an alert man like Lord Milner[3] make me care about little else than that book. You can, if you like let the University Press know that I will send them copy for two or three sheets of the *Principles* by Monday morning next: & will take care that they are steadily supplied with copy to work on hereafter.

Yours very truly | Alfred Marshall

Messrs MacMillan & Co L^{d}..

Perhaps it w^{d}.. be well to decide rather soon how many copies are to be printed off. I think not less than 5000: I dont want a seventh edition in a hurry.

[1] British Library, Macmillan Archive. From Balliol Croft.

[2] Of *Principles*: *Principles* (*6*) was to appear in 1910. Very recently *Elements* had also been reprinted. The latest (and final) revision of this work in October 1907 had deleted the former appendix C on 'Rent in Relation to Value' but had not consistently altered references to previous appendices D and E, now C and D. These references and other minor errors were corrected in a 1909 reprinting. (Marshall to Macmillan and Company, 14 and 23 October 1909: Macmillan Archive.)

[3] Marshall had known Alfred Milner (1854–1925) at Balliol in the 1880s, before his conspicuous public service, particularly that in South Africa, 1897–1905. Milner, who had become a Viscount in 1902, was strongly opposed to the Lloyd George Budget of 1909 [949.2], but the remarks in question have not been identified.

956. To Sir Frederick Macmillan, 5 March 1910[1]

5. 3. 10

Dear Sir Frederick MacMillan,

I write to report progress & to consult you as to the inclosed proofs of Title page & Preface.[2] The chief point is the suggested suppression of 'Volume I', & the introduction on the Title page of 'An introductory Volume'. For the cover, I suggest 'Principles of Economics' simply. I should be grateful for any advice as to type, and as to method, as well as substance.

In the second page of the Preface I speak with even less confidence about the future than in the corresponding passage of the last edition.[3] I have a great deal of material which seems nearly ready. But the realistic part needs to be largely rewritten once in a decade; & the analytical part is as difficult to my mental muscles as is a steep mountain slope to my feet, though as a young man I could climb it without conscious effort.

This is indeed a chief cause of my inability to make good progress with National Industry & Trade. Another is my endeavour to make my book fairly complete from the scientific point of view, & yet not repellent to able men of affairs. I have been studying their minds much during the last few years. I think they dislike being told that a thing *can* be proved. They may happen to want to form an independent opinion on the validity of the proof. Therefore I never state a conclusion without offering a proof of it. But on the other hand very few men of affairs want to read *many* intricate proofs. Therefore I have relegated to Appendices every piece of complex analysis or hard reasoning that I can; giving a broad statement of what it all comes to in the text. About a quarter or a third of the whole will consist of appendices of this sort, including some history. This will I think help to get the book read by practical men, without spoiling it from the rigidly scientific point of view. I think no book has yet been written in any language on this plan. But the new combination of realism with high reasoning among economists; and of a desire to be independent of academic authority, together with the ever increasing scarcity of time among able men of affairs—these two combinations together seem to me to indicate that some such plan may become general.

There is one Appendix as to wh I shd like to consult you. I shall of course have a chapter on Currency in relation to International Trade. But, partly because the Bimetallic controversy is practically dead, I had proposed to keep that short. I have however recently learnt that parts of my evidence before the Gold & Silver Commission & the Indian Currency Commission (of 1899) are being used as a text book.[4] Their arrangement is of course utterly unsuited for the purpose; partly because a good many questions were in effect duplicates. But a good deal of scissors & paste supplemented by a little writing would I think give a fairly readable result. Do you think that such patch work in an Appendix would be undignified, or otherwise unadmirable?

I think the book may run to about 1000 pages. Later on I will give you a closer estimate & ask you whether it should appear as one volume or two. I do not like to prophesy. But I hope—in spite of the sluggishness of my weary old brain—to begin to print again before the end of this year & to publish before the end of the next. I have tried your patience sorely.

Yours very truly | Alfred Marshall

[1] British Library, Macmillan Archive. From Balliol Croft. Frederick Macmillan had received a knighthood in 1909.

[2] For *Principles* (*6*). The published Preface is simply dated 'March 1910' (*Guillebaud*, p. 61).

[3] See [877.3] for the pertinent passage from *Principles* (*5*).

[4] For the evidence see *Official Papers*, pp. 17–195, 263–326.

957. From William Henry Clark, 23 March 1910[1]

Treasury Chambers, | Whitehall. S.W.
23rd March, 1910.

Dear Professor Marshall,

The Chancellor of the Exchequer has received a request from the Secretary of the Cobden Club asking for leave for the Club to reprint among its pamphlets your paper on the fiscal policy of international trade which was presented to the House of Commons and published as a Parliamentary paper in the autumn of 1908.[2] I have an impression, though I cannot be sure on the point, that when I saw you at Cambridge previous to the publication of the paper, you said something about having agreed to the paper being issued only on condition that it was not reprinted in any form other than as a Government paper.[3] The Secretary of the Cobden Club proposed, if Mr. Lloyd George gave him permission to publish the paper, to write to you himself on the point, but it seemed to me better that I should at once ascertain what your wishes are about it, as I feel some personal responsibility in the matter. I should explain that there are also some technical Treasury difficulties about the reprinting of Parliamentary papers, which will have to be got over and that I have not yet discussed this side of the question with the Chancellor.

I shall be at Cambridge from Thursday to Tuesday of this week. If you would care to see me about it and it would save you the trouble of writing, I should be very glad to call upon you.

Yours very truly, | W. H. Clark.

P.S. I shall be staying at Scroope House.

[1] Marshall Papers. Typewritten. For Clark, still Private Secretary to David Lloyd George, see [927.1].
[2] See [912.2].
[3] See [926].

958. From William Henry Clark, 26 March 1910[1]

Scroope House, | Cambridge.
Mar. 26. 10

Dear Professor Marshall

I meant to call on you this afternoon but got back later than I expected from a ride & had no time. But your letter[2] makes the matter perfectly clear & I am only sorry you should have been troubled through my bad memory, for now you mention it, of course I remember the occasion when Fisher Unwin wished to republish your paper.[3] I will explain matters to the Cobden Club people—or rather to the Chancellor, & let them know that they can't have it.

Wish you could see yr. way to publish the paper with Macmillans as a pamphlet before the next Election. People cant be persuaded to read papers published by the Government—I suppose because we have no system of advertising.

Yours very truly | W. H. Clark.

[1] Marshall Papers. See [957.1].
[2] Not traced.
[3] See [926].

959. From Sir Frederick Macmillan, 6 April 1910[1]

Macmillan & Co. Ltd. | St. Martin's Street.
London. W.C. April 6 1910.

Dear Professor Marshall,

I enclose a letter[2] which we received this morning from the Secretary of the Cobden Club. The question of republishing your Memorandum as a pamphlet was fully discussed at the end of last year & you decided against it. I do not see why you should be persuaded against your own judgement to publish merely to please the Cobden Club & if you approve I will tell M^r. Murray

Macdonald[3] that the republication will not take place as the substance of it will appear in your forthcoming book on National Trade & Industry.

I am | Yours very truly | Frederick Macmillan

[1] Marshall Papers.
[2] Not traced.
[3] John Archibald Murray Macdonald (1854–1939), Secretary of the Cobden Club. A Liberal Member of Parliament 1892–5 and 1906–22.

960. To Sir Frederick Macmillan, 7 April 1910[1]

7. 4. 10

Dear Sir Frederick

The Treasury wrote that the Cobden Club wished to publish my Memorandum.[2] I replied that I did not consider myself at liberty to consent to its publication by anyone but you (I said nothing about any 'promise'): & that I shd specially object to its being published by a Propagandist body. My immediate correspondent was a Cambridge man; & he wrote from Cambridge a second letter[3] in his private capacity suggesting that I shd ask you to publish it. So I took out the half-forgotten Memorandum, & considered it again. I then wrote[4] that I thought it unsuited for popular consumption, because parts of it are difficult, & parts so compressed that they do not contain full answers to all reasonable objections. I added that, if I had known how many general elections were likely to come off before my book appeared, I should have asked you to publish it some time ago. For indeed my book deals with 'causes of causes' too much to be useful for political work. And my conviction that 'Tariff Reform' would lessen employment at good wages under our present conditions grows steadily in strength.

I think it right to let you know the whole position: but I quite approve the answer to Mr Murray Macdonald[5] wh you suggest.[6] But only it must be 'National Industry & Trade' please (not 'Trade & Industry'): for a chief note of the book is that Industry masters Trade.

Yours very truly | Alfred Marshall

Sir Frederick MacMillan

[1] British Library, Macmillan Archive. From Balliol Croft.
[2] See [957].
[3] See [958].
[4] This letter not traced.
[5] See [959.3].
[6] See [959].

961. From John Archibald Murray Macdonald, 22 April 1910[1]

Cobden Club | Caxton House, | Westminster, | London, S.W.
22nd April, 1910.

Dear Professor Marshall,

I wrote rather more than a month ago to the Chancellor of the Exchequer asking whether we might reprint your paper on the 'Fiscal Policy of International Trade'.[2] He referred the request to you, and ultimately replied to me to the effect that you were under an obligation to give the pamphlet to Macmillans for publication, and that, in addition, you thought that, on principle, an economist should not be mixed up in any way with propaganda. He told me at the same time that you had pointed out to him that the Cobden Club was, of course, at liberty to quote from the paper as from any other official document, and that if we were preparing a pamphlet and would adopt that course it might meet our requirements.[3] We have most gladly acted on this suggestion, because we believe it to be of real importance that some at least of the principal points in your paper should be circulated in a form within the reach of the ordinary readers of pamphlets dealing with the fiscal controversy. Mr J.M. Robertson, M.P., undertook at our request to summarise your paper and to include in his summary extracts from it.[4] Before publishing the summary, however, I think it fair to you to inform you of our intention, and in order that you may understand the scope of the publication I enclose a copy of Mr Robertson's prefatory note.

Yours sincerely, | J. A. Murray Macdonald

[1] Marshall Papers. Typewritten. For Murray Macdonald see [959.3].
[2] See [957].
[3] It is not clear when or how this suggestion was made by Marshall.
[4] John MacKinnon Robertson (1856–1933), Liberal Member of Parliament 1906–18: Parliamentary Secretary of the Board of Trade 1911–15. Robertson was a copious author on a wide range of subjects. His books include *Trade and Tariffs* (Black, London, 1908), and *The Political Economy of Free Trade* (King, London, 1928).

962. To John Archibald Murray Macdonald, 23 April 1910[1]

23. 4. 10

Dear M^r^. Murray Macdonald

I am at once flattered & a little troubled by your letter. My suggestion that you could quote freely from my Memorandum was intended to be a mere statement of fact: everyone is at liberty to quote from any Blue & White Paper.[2] But to publish an Abstract of it is rather akin to publishing the whole: & therefore it must be known to be done with my consent. That made me hesitate: for, as I think you recognise, the functions of an academic economist differ from those of a propagandist Association. If the Cobden Club were to act on the two rules which I have marked A & B on the inclosed copy of my Prefatory Note,[3] it w^d^.

repel those readers whom it most needs to influence; & it w^{d}. fail to achieve its high & patriotic aims.

I was however comforted by the statement in M^{r}. Robertsons Prefatory Note, that there would be some 'critical comments': the more there are the better. I will only ask that none of my arguments s^{hd}. be abridged in such a way as to suggest that I have failed more than I have done to act up to my rule A; or that I have made a statement unconditionally, when really I have qualified it. It may be necessary to omit the qualifications, for fear of confusing the ordinary reader. I ask only that some reference may be made to their existence.

I thank you for sending me the Prefatory Note, which is proposed for the Summary. The only part of it in which I am specially concerned is the first paragraph: for that implies that the Memorandum as printed in 1908[4] differs materially from the draft w^{h}. was printed in 1903. But in fact the two drafts are practically identical except insofar as '(0) Possibilities of close relations between England & her Dependencies'[5] is concerned: & the small changes, chiefly verbal, which I have made in the body of the paper, did not materially lessen my original objection to its publication.[6] But M^{r}. Lloyd George had quoted from it in the House; & his statement having been challenged by M^{r}. Bonar Law, M^{r}. Asquith said he was prepared to produce the paper (see Parliamentary Debates Vol CLXXXIX, pp 1670 and 1747).[7] I considered therefore that I had no option in the matter. I did not refer to this in the P.S. to my Prefatory Note,[8] because the Parliamentary episode was then in mens minds. I have ventured therefore to suggest a small alteration on the copy which I return.[9] You may see reason to object to the reference to the House. If so, the words 'a question having been asked about it in the House of Commons' might be deleted, & the sentence would still run. Otherwise the Note seems excellent, barring of course its eulogies.

In conclusion then, I thank you heartily for your kind interest in my poor work; & consent to your proposal. I will tell Sir Frederick Macmillan what I am doing.[10]

Yours sincerely | Alfred Marshall

[1] Marshall Papers. From a copy in Mrs. Marshall's hand. A reply to [961].

[2] See [961.3]. Blue and White Papers are Government publications.

[3] See *Official Papers*, p. 367. The marked rules were probably:

A: 'to select for prominence those considerations which seem at once important and in some danger of being overlooked, whether they tell for or against my conclusions'.

B: 'to distinguish, though not to separate, those suggestions which fall mainly within the province of the economist from those which do not'.

[4] See [912.2].

[5] *Official Papers*, pp. 415–20, the last section of the Memorandum.

[6] A purported copy of the initial 1903 printing of Marshall's Memorandum, found by John C. Wood in the archives of the Treasury, seems to belie Marshall's claim that his alterations were minor. But the anonymous pamphlet identified by Wood is so un-Marshallian in vocabulary and syntax that Marshall's authorship seems highly dubious. See J. C. Wood, 'Alfred Marshall and the Tariff Campaign' [754.1], p. 481 n. 3.

[7] See [912, 925].
[8] *Official Papers*, pp. 367–8.
[9] The following note in Mrs. Marshall's hand was preserved with the letter copy and indicates the amendments Marshall proposed for Robertson's draft. The note is headed 'Change suggested in "Prefatory Note" of Memorandum'.

> *But as is explained in its Prefatory Note*, some large emendations & additions to the original draft were lost in course of post; & *for this & other reasons he preferred that it should not be published. In 1908 however, a question having been asked about it in the House of Commons*, he consented to revise it *slightly*, & *he* re-wrote one portion; where upon it was officially published with his consent' ([Italicised] parts are new matter).

[10] See [963]. Mrs Marshall transcribed Macmillan in its usual form.

963. To Sir Frederick Macmillan, 23 April 1910[1]

23. 4. 10

Dear Sir Frederick,

The Cobden Club want to publish a summary of the argument of my Memorandum, prepared at their request by Mr J M Robertson MP, with 'many extracts' & some 'critical comments'.[2] I am not sure that I should have liked the proposal, if there had been no 'critical comments': as it is, I think I cannot be held responsible for anything they may say. Of course anyone may quote from any Blue or White paper: and so, unless you write to the contrary, I shall take it that you see no objection to their proposal.[3]

Yours sincerely | Alfred Marshall

Sir Frederick MacMillan

[1] British Library, Macmillan Archive. From Balliol Croft.
[2] See [961].
[3] Sir Frederick replied on 25 April that Macmillan's had 'no objection whatever' (Marshall Papers).

964. From John Archibald Murray Macdonald, 25 April 1910[1]

Cobden Club | Caxton House, | Westminster, | London, S.W.
25th April, 1910.

Dear Professor Marshall,

Very many thanks for your letter, and for the permission it conveys to us to publish an abstract of your Memorandum.[2] Your suggested alterations in Mr Robertson's Introduction will be made, and I will ask him to read through his paper again so as to make sure that none of your arguments are so abridged as to omit your qualifications of them.

If you would like it I will gladly send you a copy of the proof before we pass it for the press.[3]

Yours sincerely | J. A. Murray Macdonald

[1] Marshall Papers. For Murray Macdonald see [959.3].
[2] See [962].
[3] There is no evidence that this was done. The pamphlet appeared as 'The Fiscal Policy of International Trade; Being a Summary of the Memorandum by Professor Alfred Marshall Published as a Parliamentary Paper in 1908. By J. M. Robertson, M.P.' (Cassell, London, 1910; for the Cobden Club).

965. To Sir Horace Plunkett, 17 May 1910 (incomplete)[1]

17. v. 10

Dear Sir Horace,

I have read through your instructive and impressive plea for a Country Life Institute[2] twice. I have learnt much from it and profited much by it. But I am not in a position to form an opinion on nearly the whole of its subject matter: and I ought not to sign it. I am very unwilling to say 'no' to an invitation urged in such kind and pleasant words by you, and this morning in a letter by Mr Butcher.[3] But I must not stray so far from my last.

Of course there are some topics raised in your plea which I have considered. But on those I have formed rather definite opinions, which do not march entirely with yours. . . .

There would be no use in my urging my views on you, for you could not be expected to adopt them. And, indeed, many of them are not in accordance with common opinion, and could hardly be expressed in a paper of this kind, without lengthy explanation.

Some of these relate to the history of the relations between classes—landlords, farmers, agricultural labourers, and industrialists in the first half of last century: some to the increase in the purchasing power of the produce of land during the greater part of the second half of the century: some to the opposition between the movements of rural and agricultural population: some to the influence for good of agencies in England and Scotland that are not to be found to any large extent in Ireland and so on.

Perhaps I should add a little on the last two of these groups. I know a good deal of the habits of life of the rural population within an old man's cycle ride of Cambridge, say an area of about 600 square miles. I doubt if there is any rural population on the Continent of Europe, unless it be in Scandinavia, which is so prosperous, so happy, or so much given to thoughts and emotions larger and higher than those of merely local life. I attribute this chiefly to the influence of non-conformist chapels, with whose theological views I have nothing in common; but which I believe give an individuality and a holy sanction to the inner life of even the 14s. a week labourer that is very rare elsewhere. No doubt the farmer's education is generally very bad in the neighbourhood; and a great many Scots are brought in for that reason. But we take in, for the benefit of our servant, a weekly paper—*The Cambridge Independent Press*. It almost ignores the existence of the University, and pays little attention to Cambridge town affairs:

and I think it is ignored by gentlefolk generally in the town and elsewhere. But I often look at it, as a zoologist might look at a kangaroo: and I am astonished at the width of range, the clearness, and—so far as I can judge—the scientific thoroughness of its long weekly articles on things which the agriculturist ought to know, and did not know a little while ago. (These articles are I presume supplied to it by a Press Agency of some sort.) The continued growth of factories in villages; of the free use of cycles by unskilled labourers; of motor omnibuses running out ten miles into the country; of warehouses where there used to be slums and of cottages with gardens where there used to be solitude etc. make me cheerful. An optimistic tone, in nearly all matters except the relations of family life under the influence of aggressive womanhood, fills my voice more and more as I grow old. And though I feel it is a good thing that the weak spots in our social system should be pourtrayed so as to strike into the attention of the negligent, I don't feel that I ought to sign a paper which implies that the conditions of rural life in England are going backwards. I expect what you say as to Ireland is true: there is perhaps no one who knows as well as you do what Ireland needs and how to help her. And no doubt what you say of America is based on knowledge much better than mine: but I could not speak on America from this point of view, without probing some doubts and dreads in my mind as to the dangers of American industrial life (rather than rural) which arise from the aversion of the new strains of immigrants for agriculture.

I have two or three times in my life signed documents with many propositions drafted by others: and every time I have deeply regretted it. My notion is that a document should be the work of an individual, or at most of two or three people working intimately together. If pruned down to please many it really satisfies none, and generally loses all vitality. Then others may express a general approval of its aims, without committing themselves to its details or to the arguments by which it is supported.

I agree with you that even in England and Scotland, a strong Institute might do good work by coordinating all the large movements for the amelioration of rural life, and the dissemination of agricultural knowledge now at work. And I am always glad when anyone takes a hopeful view of any new departure.

I was even enthusiastic when the Institute of Social Service[4] was founded: it seemed to have a definite work to do, and the will to do it. But it has lacked a strong hand at the helm; and its recent history has rather saddened me.

It may prepare the way indeed for a larger semi-official Institute or Bureau. And when one considers the vast number of specialists and business men and others who are working for the increase and dissemination of knowledge in regard to agricultural economy in the country—when one thinks of the literary Department of the Board of Agriculture, the numerous Agricultural Societies, the Agricultural Departments at many of our Universities and so on, may not one incline to urge the Government to summon a meeting of representatives from them to consider how a central Institute might best focus their work? The matter lies beyond my knowledge I can get no further than asking a question.

The work of the Country Life Institute which you suggest for Ireland seems to me a large undertaking; but if your strong hand were in it, I feel sure it would do a glorious work. Little as I am justified in speaking specially of Irish affairs, I would gladly express this confidence in such work in such hands, if you should wish it.

I grieve much not to be able to say more. But I am not in a position to do it.

Yours sincerely, | Alfred Marshall

[1] Printed in *Memorials*, pp. 467–70. Original not traced. From Balliol Croft.

[2] Sir Horace Plunkett, 'A Country Life Institute. A Suggested Irish-American Contribution to Rural Progress' (Dublin, 1909: Plunkett House Series, 2).

[3] Not traced. Samuel Henry Butcher (1850–1910), classicist and Member of Parliament for Cambridge University since 1906, had Irish roots and was an old friend and supporter of Plunkett. See Margaret Digby, *Horace Plunkett: An Anglo-American Irishman* (Blackwell, Oxford, 1949), p. 134.

[4] The British Institute of Social Service published the journal *Progress. Civic, Social, Industrial* (London, 1906–32) but seems to have been inactive generally. The announcement of its formation in the *Economic Journal*, 15 (March 1905), p. 304, indicates that the promotional material quoted a letter of commendation from Marshall (not traced).

966. To George Findlay Shirras, 6 July 1910 (incomplete)[1]

Weybourne, Norfolk
6. vii. 10

. . . I will say briefly one or two things which may possibly be of interest to you.

(1) I made, in preparation for a conversation with Mr Morison and Mr Abrahams,[2] some little study of prices in India in recent years, and compared them with other histories of prices, especially American. I laid stress on America because the lowering of the direct and indirect costs of transport, which has been a chief cause of recent changes in prices, has of course tended to bring up prices of agricultural produce in Indian and American ports relatively to the prices of the same things in western Europe; and to bring up their prices in Upland districts of India and America relatively to their prices at the ports of the same countries. And I concluded that there was a strong *prima facie* case in favour of the opinion that similar causes had produced similar results in the two countries. Cheaper transport and more abundant gold had lowered the value of gold relatively to agricultural produce in about the same degree in the two.

(2) I do not doubt that the facilities for getting currency, in all its forms, back from inland districts where it has done special work in moving harvests or relieving famine, are sadly deficient in India: but it is better that I should not attempt to write about conceivable remedies. I have on the other hand some

conviction that *adaerations*[3] are setting in nearly all over India in various directions and in different degrees: and that consequently a great deal of currency stops up-country, not because it cannot easily get down, but because it is needed where it is. I trust that the important set of local inquiries, which you are organising, will throw light on this subject. American literature, official and unofficial, affords the best means that I know of for studying (1) the influences of cheap transport on prices of imports versus exports; and on upland prices versus prices at the ports; and (2) the varying powers of absorbing a large amount of currency per head under the influences of varying degrees of (a) self-contained life of individual 'farmers' and groups of farmers, (b) payment of wages and in some cases rent in kind, rather than in money, and (c) the use of farm carts etc. rather than railways, carriers' carts, etc., all of which I include under the general term *adaerations*. . . . There is a rather old report, published I think as a 'bookseller' book, on The Purchasing Power of Gold[4] . . . which shows how the price of wheat was rising in some American uplands at the very time when the rapidity of its fall in Liverpool was greatest. . . .

[1] Printed in *Memorials*, pp. 470–1, where it is described as 'In answer to questions arising out of a Government of India enquiry into the causes of the rising prices'. Original not traced. Weybourne is on the Norfolk coast, a few miles East of Sheringham. Shirras was seconded to the Finance Department of the Government of India, 1910–13.

[2] Lionel Abrahams (1869–1919), knighted 1915, was Financial Secretary to the India Office 1911–17. He had brought in October 1909 an 'embassy from the India Office' to discuss Indian currency and prices with Marshall (*Collected Works*, vol. 15, pp. 38–9). Mr Morison was probably William Thomson Morison (1860–1931), knighted 1912, a distinguished member of the Indian Civil Service possessing considerable financial experience in India. (Theodore Morison (1863–1936), knighted 1910, educational administrator, author, and member of the Council of India, 1906–16, seems a less likely candidate.)

[3] Monetization? From the Latin 'adaeratio': valuing or appraising. Not listed in the *Oxford English Dictionary*.

[4] Not identified.

967. To the Editor, *The Times*, 7 July 1910[1]

Sir,—The study of the influence of parental alcoholism recently published by the Galton Research Laboratory[2] has justly attracted great attention on account of its intrinsic importance and the authority of the revered name with which it is associated; and I had hoped that some one more competent than I would have inquired how far the statistical basis of the study is adequate to support large inductive propositions. A certain apparent ambiguity of language at critical points makes it difficult to decide how far the broad conclusions which have been attributed to it in your columns and elsewhere are endorsed by its authors. But I should like, with your leave, to raise a caution as to the interpretation of that particular conclusion which seems to lie in some measure within my own province. It is on page 4:—

> We find that the wages of a drinking man are on the average 25s., and a non-drinking man 26s. It would be reasonable to suppose that the 6d. or 1s. difference shown in the above results is what the employer is willing to pay for the convenience of sobriety. It can hardly mean that there is a great differentiation in physique and intelligence between the alcoholic and the non-alcoholic.

This comparison applies directly to two particular groups of alcoholics and non-alcoholics. But several writers of weight have supposed that it is in a great measure applicable to alcoholics in general and non-alcoholics in general. I desire, therefore, respectfully to submit that these two groups have been so selected that the conclusion reached is practically embodied in the choice of *data*.

There are probably several occupations and many localities in which the wages of those addicted to drink are on the average higher than those of sober men, at all events when they are in full work. A foreman selecting a casual labourer for low-grade jobs at the docks is likely to take a strong man who bears marks of drunken habits, in preference to a sober weakling. But that fact has very little bearing on the relation between alcoholism and efficiency. For the strong drunkard probably came down to that low grade of work merely because he was a drunkard, while the sober man probably came there because he had not sufficient force of character and physique to earn a comfortable livelihood anywhere. The sober man and the drunkard in that stratum are not comparable in regard to the question at issue, because they probably did not start with equal advantages.

Similarly the children treated in the report diverge from the average in such a way as to make the influence of the drinking habits of their parents on their health appear much less than it may probably have been; and much less than it would probably have been shown to be if the *data* selected had represented people who, having had equal advantages at starting, had made unequal uses of those advantages under the influence of different habits in regard to drink.

The report deals only with some 'special' Manchester schools for the mentally defective, and one Edinburgh school. The wage statistics relate only to the latter; and its children come from 'the poorest parts of the city'. We may assume that, with few exceptions, they are of low grade; for stress is laid on the fact that these parts contain some 'old families', belonging to 'the substantially comfortable and thoroughly respectable working class', who continue to live there 'despite the degeneration of the immediate neighbourhood'. Possibly some of these old families stayed on partly because, though reputable, they were somewhat lacking in vitality. And even those who hold most confidently the new doctrine that the habits of life of the parents cannot possibly have exercised any influence on the condition of their children, must admit that there may be some truth in the old doctrine that a great many well-conducted weaklings were the progeny of grandparents or great-grandparents who had fallen into profligate habits, and had in consequence brought up their families in close slums, with no healthy play, and had fed on tannic tea rather than on milk; but these are side issues.

The argument of the report requires in strictness that the figures given should be the average of those actually earned during the course of a year; but I think that this point was overlooked, and that they were really the wages earned in a week of full work. However that may be, I submit that, having regard to the character of the groups under investigation, it would have been reasonable to expect *a priori* that they would show at least as high a wage for alcoholics as for non-alcoholics. For, given the locality in which a man lives, and the rent which he pays, the more he is known to drink the higher must his annual income be supposed to be; while his weekly wage will be even higher in proportion. For the sober man's yearly income will be derived from a larger number of weeks' work than the alcoholic's, and less of it will be diverted from household expenses to drink.

An inquiry into the influence of parental alcoholism on the offspring must suppose that the alcoholism had set in for some time before the offspring were born, and the children were at school at the date of the inquiry. Therefore, assuming the *data* to be truly appropriate to their purpose, we may infer that the alcoholism observed was on the average, say, of 15 years' standing. If 15 years ago one of two engineers who were of equal efficiency took to drinking habits, while the other lived soberly, then, having in view the fact that the latter may possibly have risen to be a foreman, or even higher, I should expect his average earnings for the year now to be 20 or even 40 per cent. higher than that of the alcoholic. In so far, therefore, as the report is so worded as to suggest to some readers that high statistical authority has decided that the 'differentiation in physique and intelligence between the alcoholic and the non-alcoholic' as measured by their respective values to their employers and the nation is only 4 per cent., I doubt whether it will either commend itself to experienced business men and trade-union officials, or further the improvement of the race.

I am, Sir, yours faithfully, | Alfred Marshall.

Cambridge.

[1] Printed in *The Times*, 7 July 1910, under the heading 'Alcoholism and Efficiency'. Original not traced.

[2] Ethel Mary Elderton with the assistance of Karl Pearson, *A First Study of the Influence of Parental Alcoholism on the Physique and Ability of the Offspring* (Eugenics Laboratory Memoirs, 10; Dulau, London, 1910). The report, issued in May by the Francis Galton Laboratory for National Eugenics, provoked a storm of controversy and much correspondence in the press. Ethel Elderton (1878–1954), biometrician and eugenicist, taught at University College, London, 1906–35.

968. From John Maynard Keynes, 11 July 1910[1]

Kings College, | Cambridge
11 July 1910

Dear Dr Marshall,

I was very glad to see your very damaging letter in Thursday's Times[2] criticising Pearson's memoir; for I wrote them a letter on similar lines two or three weeks ago which they rejected.[3] Since then, however, I have got hold of the original account of the Edinburgh investigation, upon which the memoir is founded; and have written a review, chiefly based on this, for the next number of the Statistical Journal.[4] I enclose a proof of this, in case you may like to see it. The facts fully bear out your suggestion, made on general grounds, that the drunken and sober stock were not initially equal. I found so much to say about these facts that I have left out the general considerations arising out of wages, to which I referred in my draft letter, but which you have dealt with as cogently as possible since.

Is it not shameless of K.P. to suppress some of the facts to which I call attention?—for instance that in this supposed random sample 62% of the families were alcoholic.

I have just read his reply to you.[5] The sample *is* in effect selected with regard to alcoholism, and his treatment of the evidence has not been candid.

With regard to the reckoning of actual wages—it is true that an attempt was made by the Edinburgh investigators to allow for irregularity of employment, but the evidence in the individual cases seems to me to show that no data were forthcoming, on which any accurate allowance could be founded. I have a copy of the report[6] (which I have taken out of the Statistical Library[7]) and will send it, if you would care to refer to it on any point.

Pigou has shown me your letter[8] suggesting for consideration the institution of a Social Work diploma. I have talked about it to several of the economists who are up, and they all seem to think it an admirable idea, which might prove a great success. My father and mother are away from England, but I will talk to them about it as soon as they come back.[9]

Sincerely yours, | J. M. Keynes

[1] Marshall Papers. Although dated 11 July the letter appears to have been completed and posted on the following day when Pearson's response appeared in *The Times* (see note 5).

[2] See [967].

[3] The text of this unpublished letter is reproduced in *Collected Works*, vol. 11, pp. 186–8.

[4] This review, signed 'J.M.K.', of the Elderton-Pearson memoir [967.2] appeared in the *Journal of the Royal Statistical Society*, 73 (July 1910), pp. 769–73. It is reproduced in *Collected Works*, vol. 11, pp. 189–95.

[5] See Pearson's letter to the Editor, *The Times*, 12 July 1910 (11f) under the heading 'Alcoholism and Efficiency'.

[6] City of Edinburgh Charity Organisation Society, *Report on the Physical Condition of Fourteen Hundred School Children in the City, Together with some Account of their Homes and Surroundings* (King, London, 1906).

[7] That is, the library of the Royal Statistical Society in London.

[8] Not traced.

[9] Nothing seems to have come of this proposal.

969. From John Maynard Keynes, 12 July 1910[1]

Kings College, | Cambridge.
12 July 1910

Dear Dr Marshall,

I wrote to you this morning[2] offering to send the report and enclosing a proof of a review which I have written on Pearson's memoir for the Statistical Journal;[3] but as I wasn't sure that I had your address correctly, I sent my letter to Madingley Rd to be forwarded. I will send the report by the first post to-morrow morning. You will have no difficulty in showing how much evidence Pearson has had to overlook, in order to regard his sample as random. The more I read his recent work the more I am filled with *indignation*. The public is so completely in the hands of an expert statistician, that his methods seem to me for a man of his reputation peculiarly base.

Sincerely yours, | J. M. Keynes

[1] Marshall Papers. Presumably sent to Norfolk: see [966, 970].

[2] Obviously [968] although it is dated 11 July: see [968.1].

[3] See [968.4].

970. To John Maynard Keynes, 14 July 1910[1]

Kelling
14. 7. 10

My dear Keynes

Very many thanks. I am writing to the Times again.[2] I dont know whether they will have patience for another lucubration. I am keeping as clear as I can of your ground & urging every one interested in Eugenics to read your paper.[3] It is *splendid*.

Yours very sincerely | Alfred Marshall

There is only a box in the wall here; no post office. I will send you the Edinburgh Report[4] tomorrow.[5]

[1] King's College, Cambridge, J. M. Keynes Papers. Kelling lies on the Norfolk coast a few miles east of Sheringham and neighbouring Weybourne.

[2] See [971].

[3] See [968.4].

[4] See [968.6].

[5] The bulkiness of the Report doubtless necessitated delivery to a Post Office.

971. To the Editor, *The Times*, 2 August 1910[1]

Sir,—Professor Pearson has made no attempt to answer my objections to the methods of the recent memoir of the Francis Galton Laboratory, which was stated by Dr. Donkin in your issue of May 31 to 'show that parental intemperance has no causal relation to filial degeneration'.[2] The matter is of far-reaching importance; but I should not have turned aside from my proper work to discuss it if I had been aware that the July number of the *Statistical Journal* would contain a study by Mr. J. M. Keynes of the relations of the memoir to the original report of the Edinburgh Charity Organization Society, on which it is largely based.[3] He has kindly let me see a proof of his paper; he goes deeper than I am attempting to do, and seems to me to prove conclusively that the use made of the report in the memoir is open to grave objection. I venture to hope that it will be considered carefully by those interested in eugenics.

The Edinburgh report, which I have now seen, is of marvellous excellence, and I should like, with your leave, to say a few words more suggested by it. I will trespass as little as may be on the ground occupied by Mr. Keynes.

I will, first, put in another way the central argument of my last letter. Suppose some one to collect statistics of the marks obtained by boys of 14 and 16 years old respectively in the same form, and, finding them to be about equal, to claim to have proved that boys of 16 are not more intelligent than boys of 14. I should say that his conclusion had no value except in relation to that form, and that it was 'practically embodied in his choice of *data*'. That is the charge which I have brought against the memoir. Alcoholics and non-alcoholics living in the same low class of houses and under similar low social conditions are likely to have about the same income, because the inefficiency of some alcoholics causes them to live in a low neighbourhood, just as the lack of intelligence of some boys of 16 causes them to be kept in a low form.

We are told in the Edinburgh report, though not in the memoir, that of the 781 families investigated 425 were 'drunken', in 63 'drink was suspected', and 488 were known to be in receipt of charitable relief. The average weekly wage of the father is stated in the memoir (but not in the report) to be 25s. for alcoholics and 26s. for sober. Professor Pearson now says[4] that 'where there was a difference between the trade wages and the average wages actually received, the latter were used'; but here he must be referring only to the comparatively few cases in which the report gives specific information on the subject. For the rest, it seems that a guess was made; and that the figure, which is the corner-stone of the main argument of the memoir as regards efficiency, does not represent an ascertained fact, but contains a large element of conjecture.

In many cases large contributions to the total income are made by other members of the family. I have examined rather more than 100 cases taken at random, and find the average to be about 4s.; I will suppose the general average to be 3s. 6d. That brings up the steady family income on Professor Pearson's basis to about 28s. Now Mr. Charles Booth puts the equivalent of a regular weekly 21s. as the upper limit of the family income of the poorest million of the population of London; and so far as I know the general drift of official and unofficial studies of town life is consistent with his result. Bearing in mind, then, the above statistics as to alcoholism and pauperization, I suspect that if proper allowance had been made for the irregularity of the work of the drunkards, the ground would have been cut from under the argument in the memoir that drunkenness does little to lower efficiency.[5]

I am, Sir, yours faithfully, | Alfred Marshall.

[1] Printed in *The Times*, 2 August 2 1910, under the heading 'Alcoholism and Efficiency'. Original not traced.

[2] See [967.2] and the letter to the Editor from Donkin published under the heading 'Alcoholism and Offspring', *The Times*, 31 May 1910 (10b). (Horatio Bryan Donkin (1845–1927), knighted 1911, was a prominent physician concerned with public health, prisons, and mental deficiency.)

[3] See [968.4, 6].

[4] In his 12 July letter [968.5], where Pearson actually referred to 'trade-wages of fathers'.

[5] In other words, since 'sober' families had average incomes of 28s., the bulk of the 488 families receiving charitable relief must have been 'drunken', and near or below Booth's poverty line, based on his monumental studies of poverty in London (see [972.6]).

972. To the Editor, *The Times*, 17 August 1910[1]

Sir,—Professor Pearson in his last letter[2] raises several questions with which I have no concern. I wrote to you only because no one else challenged an inference from the recent memoir of the Galton Laboratory which was generally made in your columns and elsewhere, and which caused a great sensation and drew forth high eulogies from some. I waited to see whether that interpretation would be disavowed; but Professor Pearson has appeared complacent under the praise which was given to him for having 'shown that parental intemperance has no causal relation to filial degeneration'.[3] If he had really shown that to be true, economists must have readjusted some of their views as to the conditions of social progress; but if, as I believe, it is wholly untrue, any one who acquiesces in its being taught to the people incurs a very heavy responsibility. That is the only cause which induced me to break my almost absolute rule against controversial correspondence.

I knew that the report of the Edinburgh Charity Organization Society,[4] which is the main basis of the memoir, relates to one of the poorest parts of the city; and I concluded that a comparison of its records of alcoholics and non-alcoholics could at the most prove drunkenness to be a small evil relatively to other causes which bring people into such a district; I knew that the selection of *data* was heavily biassed. A little later, on getting access to the original report, I found that the bias was even more extreme than I had supposed. After a further study

I now assert that the memoir does no more towards establishing the sensational conclusion attributed to it than would be done by evidence that *delirium tremens* was not more fatal than other grievous diseases which sent people to the sick wards of a hospital towards proving that *delirium tremens* has no causal relation to shortness of life.

This particular district is described by Professor Pearson as offering 'a random sample of the populaion'; and no doubt it does contain many who had a good start in life and would be living in good houses in healthy districts if they were not drunken. As it is, they congregate in an atmosphere that is foul physically and morally, where even the sober residents are as a rule weakly in body and devoid of self-respect, insomuch that, as Mr. J. M. Keynes has pointed out, more than three-fourths of the whole of the families investigated were drunken or in receipt of charitable aid, or both.[5] There are indeed a few well-kept homes; of a very few families it is even said that they 'are very respectable and should be living elsewhere'; probably also the outskirts of the district are better kept than its centre in a manner indicated by the coloured borders representing relative comfort to many districts in Mr. Charles Booth's great map of London poverty, where the prevailing colours represent poor and mixed populations.[6]

If the bureau had really desired to obtain 'a random sample of the population', it might have found, or made, a study of some district in Edinburgh or elsewhere which was inhabited almost exclusively by high-grade, sober, self-respecting artisans and labourers, and averaged the results given by that extreme with those got from the district in which less than a fifth of the people had any considerable self-respect. Or, again, the bureau might, with the aid of trade union officials, have compared the families of, say, all the skilled masons in Edinburgh, account being taken of those who had disappeared through drunkenness or other misfortune. If in this balanced sample the children of those who had long been habitual drunkards had been found to be nearly as vigorous as those of the sober members, while the men themselves were earning nearly as high an annual wage on the average as the sober, then the results attributed to the bureau would have been legitimate and worthy of respect. As it is, I maintain that they are not.

Professor Pearson claims that I must accept his figures for the wages of alcoholics and non-alcoholics in the Edinburgh district, because I have described the original report on it as excellent. But he appears to have misinterpreted its column of wage statistics, which, indeed, play a very subordinate *rôle* relatively to the text, and is not capable of being separated from it.

The studies of 781 families, one by one, in the text approach more nearly than anything else I know in any language, covering so large an area in so few words, to the ideal which Le Play set up for social investigations. They are careful, orderly, sympathetic, unassuming word-pictures which focus the experiences of charitable workers, school teachers, doctors, employers, 'factors', pawnbrokers, police, and others who have been brought, on their several paths, into contact with the courage and the cringings, the happiness and the misery, the truth and the falsehood, the virtues and the crimes of that abnormal district.

The wage statistics are not only as good as could reasonably be expected under the circumstances, but better. Those who compiled them took much pains, especially in applying to employers, where such an application could be of any service; but, of course, there were very many cases in which no help could be got from that source. They must have been troubled with the well-known, but very diverse, causes which make the returns obtained from the employer, from the man himself, and still more from his wife, much too low in some classes of cases and much too high in others. These and other difficulties are not discussed in the report; but their existence is tacitly recognized by the refusal of the framers of the report to do exactly that thing which Professor Pearson insists that they are certain to have done, that is to form an estimate of the average weekly earnings throughout the year of every one, however idle or drunken, or however destitute of a permanent connexion with any one employer.

For this mistake of his the report is not to be blamed. The heading of its wage column is 'weekly wage', not 'average wage', and we are told that 'in the cases of regular employment the amounts represent an average taken over a period of time'; thus indirectly being warned against taking them as average wages for 'irregular' or 'casual' or 'idle' workers, save in those few cases in which a separate numerical estimate of the unsteadiness of employment is given. But Professor Pearson insists on treating 'weekly wage' as 'average wage', even when the figure given is the full trade union standard wage, and the man is described in the text if not in the wage column as 'idle', 'often out of work', and so on.

Economists know that nearly all their 'statistics' are mere aggregates of guesses; even such relatively definite figures as those relating to exports and imports are made up largely of conjectural items. Consequently when a mathematical outsider, like Professor Pearson, incessantly upbraids them for setting mere opinions against the statistical 'facts' which he has culled in a hurry, they are apt to observe that if he knew more he would know that he knew less.

Professor Pearson has lightly reached his confident conclusion that the alcoholics in the district earn on the average only a shilling less than non-alcoholics, for the purposes of an argument in which annual averages alone have any place. But he could never have reached it if he had reflected that no one can possibly get at the annual average in the case of the majority of irregular workers who take an odd job where they can get it. No employer knows their history. They do not keep accounts either on paper or in their heads for the year; at all events, if they are habitually drunk as well as feckless. Their wives may do it, if they are acquainted with everything and are sober, but often they are not either.

I pass to consider the use which is made in the memoir of the erroneous results thus obtained. I began my first letter by quoting as an instance of 'an ambiguity of language', which suggests risky broad conclusions, the following passages:— 'We find that the wages of a drinking man are on the average 25s., and a non-drinking man 26s. It would be reasonable to suppose that the 6d. or 1s. difference shown in the above results is what the employer is willing to pay for the convenience of sobriety. It can hardly mean that there is a great differentiation in physique and intelligence between the alcoholic and the nonalcoholic'; and there is a good deal more on the same page[7] to a similar effect; for instance, 'We think it may be safely affirmed that if the alcoholic were markedly inferior in physique or intelligence his average wages would be markedly less than those of the sober parent'.

I will leave the reader, with these passages before him, to interpret as he sees fit the following warning in Professor Pearson's last letter, 'It is needless to add that the memoir does not state, as Professor Marshall's concluding words would lead the reader to believe, that 'drunkenness does little to lower efficiency''.

My position is that the man who was brought up to a skilled trade, who is in good health, and who could have earned a fairly steady 'tradesman's' wage of nearly £2 a week, but who is in fact drunken and irregular at his work, and who lives in a district where physical and moral squalor are rampant, is an instance of great inefficiency caused by drunkenness. I should measure it by the excess of the £80 a year or more, which he might have earned, over that amount which the Edinburgh report, in harmony with innumerable other inquiries, shows to vary from next to nothing up to nearly the full earnings of a sober man with equal natural advantages. Further, his children are likely not to have as good a start as he has; and we may be certain that a large part, often the larger part, of the evils of drunkenness are seen in the next generation, even if we are forbidden to have any opinion of our own as to the influence exerted on a child before birth by the anterior settled drunkenness of either of its parents.

There is one more of Professor Pearson's remarks to which I must reply before I close this wearisome letter. I had observed that misleading inferences might be drawn from a comparison of alcoholics and non-alcoholics selected from an exceptional industry, similar to that which had been made in the memoir in regard to an exceptional district. Professor Pearson now converts this remark into a 'suggestion that those classed as drinkers in the Edinburgh record followed trades in which those addicted to drink received higher wages than those of sober men', and he supplies tables of his own which he considers appropriate to that suggestion. Those tables have no bearing on any question in which I am interested.

The Labour Commission of 1891–4 was occupied a good deal with the tendency of casual employment at the docks to tempt strong men to spoil their lives by alternations of excessively severe work with long debauches. While their strength was still unimpaired they were often preferred to weaker men of steadier habits, who would have been more serviceable to the employer if he had had to find them steady employment; but as it was, his interest in the men did not extend beyond the particular job for which he hired them. It was, for instance, established in the face of severe cross-examination that a batch of strong men would sometimes be taken on to clear a ship, and encouraged to work almost without a break for 36 hours to finish the job. The 30s. or so which each man took away would be spent mainly on liquor during the next four or five days, after which they would again want some work. In the process their vitality was being undermined, and their families, if any, were being degraded; but meanwhile they served the purpose of the employer, who selected his men for each job with regard to their probable efficiency for that job alone. Such malign conditions are rarer now even at the docks than they used to be. It would never have occurred to an economist that they could possibly abound in Edinburgh, where the dominant industries are well known to be exceptionally light.

As regards these personal matters the reader must now judge between Professor Pearson and myself. I have finished. But, as I have said, Mr. Keynes's review of the memoir in the *Statistical Journal* for July has gone more deeply into the main issue than I have attempted to do, and I am glad to leave the matter in his capable hands. Professor Pearson has undertaken to meet his charges.

I am, Sir, yours faithfully,

August 17. Alfred Marshall.

[1] Printed in *The Times*, 19 August 1910, under the heading 'Alcoholism and Efficiency'. Original not traced. See [967, 971].

[2] See Pearson's letter to the Editor, *The Times*, 10 August 1910 (10 b–c) published under the heading 'Alcoholism and Efficiency'.

[3] This repeats the statement attributed to Donkin in [971]: see [971.2].

[4] See [968.6].

[5] See [968.4].

[6] For details of Booth's 'poverty map', which was at one time displayed in Toynbee Hall, see T. S. and M. B. Simey, *Charles Booth Social Scientist* (Oxford University Press, London, 1960), pp. 94, 113–5; see also pp. 184–9 for details of Booth's 'poverty line', alluded to in [971].

[7] See [967] and p. 4 of the Galton Laboratory's report [967.2].

973. To Ernest Stewart Roberts, 22 August 1910[1]

22 Aug. 1910

Dear Master (of Caius)

I am glad to reply to your question about the Economics Tripos.[2] Its progress during the last two years seems to me splendid: I think it is getting a much firmer hold on the University than the experience of other young Triposes seemed to foreshadow. I attribute this success to the conspicuous energy & ability of its young staff; & to the high degree in which its subject matter meets the requirements of the present time.

I take those requirements to be a raising, rather than a lowering, of the standard of high & hard thinking among candidates for University Honours: & at the same time the establishment of such a connection between the studies of Cambridge & the responsibilities of after years, that the seed sown here may spring into full & generous life later on; instead of being dried & put by, as it were, in a cabinet of memories of early life.

For indeed the studies which are tested in the Tripos help the business man to understand the complexity & interactions of the forces which govern the courses of industry & trade. They give him that broad outlook & those habits of patient thought before coming to a conclusion which are every year more required from those who have the charge of large undertakings in private & in joint stock businesses; or in the conduct of the State or of a Municipality. The large space which is given in them to the resources, difficulties, successes of those countries which are sharing with England the leadership of the world, is helping to make the rising generation understand that they cannot hold their own by merely adhering to the ways of strong men who have gone before them; but that they can hold their own by showing an equal energy to that of their forefathers in the work of the modern age, in which disciplined thought & knowledge count for more, & impulsive ready-wit counts for less than in early times.

On another side it helps men, & also many women, to fit themselves for those forms of social work which bring the various classes of the nation into a mutual understanding; which sustains the weak without sapping their courage & self respect; & w^{h}. enables the intervention of State & Municipal institutions to increase their activity for good without enervating individual self reliance. It is being used for this purpose by a rapidly increasing number of persons who hope to be officers of Charity Organization Societies, Inspectors of homes for Municipal Authorities, & so on.

On every side there is strength in the new movement: but, as you know, it is hampered by lack of funds. It came into being late, when several of the newer studies had made out such urgent pleas for pecuniary help from the University & the Colleges that all available funds had been set under contribution: & the Economics Tripos is almost destitute. The Professor gives nearly a third of his income to provide small salaries for lecturers who have no stipend: the Girdlers Company is making provision for another; & one or two Colleges have been able to help. But speaking generally the staff are very poorly paid: & the University cannot be sure of retaining their services.

Yours sincerely | Alfred Marshall

[1] Marshall Papers. From a copy in Mrs. Marshall's hand. For Roberts see [883.1].

[2] The question and the reason for asking it both remain obscure. Roberts's term as Vice Chancellor had ended in 1908. He did serve on Council of Senate, 1909–11.

974. From Francis Ysidro Edgeworth, 22 August (1910?)[1]

5 Mount Vernon | Hampstead
Aug 22

My dear Marshall

I own to not having quite understood Clark's Static State.[2] In putting other factors alongside rent of land I thought he meant much the same as you mean when you say that 'land is but a particular form of capital from the pt of view of the individual cultivator' etc Bk V Ch ii § 5[3] and context—the similarity of the factors of production from the entrepreneur point of view which was indeed not fully recognised by the classical writers. I quote him to that effect on p 185 of my QJE 1904 article.[4] But really I am not certain whether that doctrine is connected by him with Statics. *N'importe.*

Your general impression about Pigou and increasing returns[5] interests and is useful to me.

I am delighted to hear that you are in good health but sorry to think that you have engaged your work of revision. Path breaking which you will now I hope resume will doubtless prove a more congenial occupation than repairing roads.

Yours ever | F Y Edgeworth.

[1] Marshall Papers. Dating poses difficulties. The reference to revision—presumably of *Principles*—suggests 1907 or 1910 as the likely dates, while the reference to Pigou on increasing returns, and the fact that Clark visited Marshall in the latter half of 1910 (see [979.3]) strongly favour the latter date. The tone of the letter also suggests that Marshall had withdrawn from academic activity into retirement. It is true that the preface to *Principles* (*6*) is dated March 1910, but publication seems to have been delayed until September (see [975]).

[2] See [736].

[3] Edgeworth here repeats a slip made on p. 185 of his 1904 paper. The correct reference is to book vi, ch. 2, s. 5. The reference is appropriate for all editions from *Principles* (*3*) onwards. Reference to book v, ch. 9, s. 3 of *Principles* (*4*) or book v, ch. 10, s. 3 of *Principles* (*5–8*) would also have been pertinent.

[4] F. Y. Edgeworth, 'The Theory of Distribution', *Quarterly Journal of Economics*, 18 (February 1904), pp. 159–219. On the indicated page, Edgeworth simply lists 'J. B. Clark, *Political Science Quarterly*, March 1891' among criticisms of Marshall's use of the 'time-honored phrase' that rent does not enter into price.

[5] Presumably an allusion to A. C. Pigou, 'Producers' and Consumers' Surplus', *Economic Journal*, 20 (September 1910), pp. 358–70. Here Pigou first broached the controversial argument as to discrepancies between marginal private and social cost further developed in his *Wealth and Welfare* (Macmillan, London, 1912). For an account and analysis of Marshall's sceptical annotations on the argument, as it was expressed in the latter work, see Krishna Bharadwaj, 'Marshall on Pigou's *Wealth and Welfare*', *Economica*, 39 (February 1972), pp. 32–46.

975. To Macmillan and Company, 8 September 1910[1]

8. 9. 10

Dear Sirs

I am obliged for a copy of my Principles. I think its general effect is excellent: the thin strong paper makes the volume handy.

But may I enter a plea against being described as 'M.A.' on the wrapper. I have never described myself so in my life; & I never buy a book by an unknown author who so describes himself, unless indeed it is written by a manufacturer or somebody of that sort on a technical subject. If he has had a University education, he may reasonably advertise the fact: but an academic writer who so describes himself makes academic people shrug their shoulders. All official letters here are addressed to me as D.Sc: but I do not wish to be described on my own book by any title.

When you are printing off more copies of the wrapper, would you kindly alter 'Industr*ies*' in the title of my forthcoming book to 'Industry'. The title wh you have printed is that which I had originally proposed. But in my new Preface (p vi) I refer to the forthcoming book as '*National Industry & Trade*': that will probably be the title on the back, with 'National Industry & International Trade' as the full title.

The change from 'Industries' to Industry means that I have been forced to abandon the original notion of treating particular industries in some detail.

I have to renew my apologies for the slowness of my progress. I can only say that I give the whole of my little strength to the book: & that I am sure that even from the publishers point of view, it would be unwise to express any imperfectly considered opinion on the difficult & weighty matters with which the book deals.

Yours very truly | Alfred Marshall

Mess[rs] MacMillan & Co

I generally have occasion for a few additional copies, partly to be sent to those who have given me notes of *Errata* &c in the previous edition. May I ask you kindly to send me six more copies.

[1] British Library, Macmillan Archive. From Balliol Croft. The preface to *Principles* (*6*) is dated March 1910, but publication must have been held back: see [956].

976. To John Maynard Keynes, 10 September 1910[1]

10. 9. 10

Dear Keynes,

In my last letter to the Times, I said I had finished with Pearson.[2] So I should not have replied to his pamphlet[3] even if I had thought it very important. I do not know whether you propose to do so: there is more to be said for your writing than for mine. If you do, you may care to look at the rough jottings on my copy. I have not read it carefully, & have omitted most things wh do not directly refer to me. I can lend you the Edinburgh Report[4] and the Times letters &c, if you wish.

Yours sincerely | Alfred Marshall

[1] King's College, Cambridge, J.M. Keynes Papers. From Balliol Croft.
[2] See [972].
[3] Karl Pearson, *Supplement to the Memoir Entitled 'The Influence of Parental Alcoholism on the Physique and Ability of the Offspring': A Reply to the Cambridge Economists* (Questions of the Day and of the Fray, No. 1: Dulau, London, 1910).
[4] See [968.6].

977. From John Maynard Keynes, 13 September 1910[1]

The Little House | Burford | Oxon
13 Sepr 1910

Dear Professor Marshall,

Many thanks for your copy of K.P.'s pamphlet.[2] Has it been out long? I did not know of its existence. What a lying insolent fellow is he! This I knew before. But I have seen nothing from him so stupid as the main argument running through this pamphlet that, *even* if the Edinburgh district is as bad a slum as we make out, it doesn't matter. A great deal of the pamphlet is concerned with debating points and attempted verbal scores, but this, which is a piece of argument, seems to me to bear the stamp of conviction. The rest is part of the method and manner natural to him; but he is not really an enemy of the truth as such, and it is because of this false opinion, I think, that he perseveres.

About replying to it—I shall write to Yule asking him to let me write again in the Statistical Journal and promising to confine myself *mainly* (though not quite altogether) to the important point of reasoning raised by K.P.'s contention referred to above.[3] If Yule is unwilling, hadn't I better let the matter drop? It would be rather absurd to write a pamphlet on such a point (unless K.P. would let me write no II in his series!), and I don't see where else I could deal with the question.

I thought your last letter to the Times[4] was crushing and dealt with him as he deserved. Even if I have no opportunity of replying in the Statistical Journal, I think enough has been said to enable any intelligent person who has followed the controversy to form a just opinion.

With regard to two points of detail:—in the table of wage statistics which he reprints in the pamphlet from his last letter to the Times,[5] there can be little doubt that he *assumes* that, if a drunkard and a sober man are in the same trade, they earn the same wages. I do not see how else he could reach a result from the data in the report.

With regard to housing in Glasgow, I am not certain that his figures apply, as he pretends, to the *whole* population of Glasgow. But even if his figures are perfectly correct, they do not controvert the assertion that he is dealing with the *lowest* part of Edinburgh—which is all that my argument need establish.

I will keep your copy of the pamphlet, if I may, until my own arrives, and I shall be grateful if you can lend me the Edinburgh Report[6]—of the Times correspondence I have kept copies.

I have come across a summary of an investigation into this same question which was carried out on a very large scale by the New York Academy of Medicine in 1901,[7] and am trying to get full details. They investigated 55,000 children. In 20,147 cases the parental habits were recorded. Of the children of drinking parents 53% were dullards; of the children of abstaining parents only 10%. In the case of 3,711 children the family history was traced back through three generations, and the habits as to alcohol investigated—and there are many other figures. If on closer investigation it proves sound, it will be worth while to quote it. It was an *ad hoc* enquiry on more than 10 times the scale of the Edinburgh enquiry, and the results absolutely contradict Pearson's.

I have been spending all this long[8] on my Probability Treatise to the exclusion of everything else, and am glad to say that the end seems in sight.[9] It has occupied all my spare time for the last four years, and I shall not be sorry to be free again for other things.

Sincerely yours, | J M Keynes

I enclose a spare copy of my review.[10]

[1] Marshall Papers.
[2] See [976.3].
[3] Keynes did publish such a rejoinder: see [979.2]. Yule was one of the three Honorary Secretaries of the Society.
[4] See [972].
[5] See [972.2].
[6] See [968.6].
[7] See *Medical Record*, 59 (27 April 1901), pp. 673–4, for an account of the Academy's meeting of 18 April 1901 devoted to the topic of 'Dull and Deficient Children'. T. Alexander MacNicholl, MD, reported on his investigations into hereditary aspects of mental deficiency, which included a study of the effects of parental and grandparental intemperance. He reported further in 'Alcohol and Disabilities of School Children', *Journal of the American Medical Association*, 48 (2 February 1907), pp. 396–8. MacNicholl's study appears to be the one to which Keynes alludes, but there is no indication that he pursued the matter further.
[8] That is, the long vacation.
[9] Keynes's long-projected *Treatise on Probability*, based on his successful 1909 Fellowship thesis for King's, was in the event published only in 1921 (Macmillan, London). Republished as *Collected Works*, vol. 8.
[10] See [968.4].

978. To John Maynard Keynes, 14 September 1910[1]

14. 9. 10

Dear Keynes,

Pearsons paper[2] arrived on Saturday morning in a plain envelope without any indication of the name of the sender. I am in no hurry to see it again.

I think a review of the Paper would be in place in the Statistical Journal: & I think your plan is excellent in every way.

I am very much interested in what you say about the investigation by the N.Y. Academy of Medicine.[3]

The Cost of Living of the Working Classes Blue Book of 1908 says that in 1901 'there were in Edinburgh & Leith 71,907 houses (81 per cent of the total) of less than five rooms, & of these 20 per cent had only one room, 42 per cent two rooms, and 24 per cent three rooms'. . . 'In a Scottish flat both the kitchen & the room measure about 12 or 13 feet by 13 to 15 feet, and there is frequently a "bed recess" in addition to this space' . . . 'In some cases there are two such recesses in the kitchen'.[4]

I think on the whole that I at least had supposed the house accommodation in the Edinburgh district under study to be worse than it really is.

I knew nothing of Pearson before.[5] But I had formed just the same opinion as you express: As you knew it before, it is to be hoped that others know it; & that even those who read only his side of the controversy will discount what he says a little.

I am very glad that your Probability Treatise[6] makes good progress. I have always felt that it is a subject which ought to be handled by some one who constantly reflects that, if people who are firing at a target are in shelter & are not aware that there is a strong jerky North wind blowing between them & the target, the fundamental axiom of the method of least squares will not hold.

When Todhunter's paper in the *Cambridge Philosophical Transactions* on that method[7] appeared—about 1866, I think—I went to him, & asked him whether he thought that there [were][8] many statistics wh could be handled by 'Least Squares', without a careful inquiry into 'the wind': & so far as I recollect he thought not. Even Edgeworth seems to me to think rather too little of 'the wind' in some of his work: & the original advertisement of *Biometrika* seemed to take so little account of it that I doubted whether *Biometrika* would do much good on the balance.

Yours sincerely | Alfred Marshall

If *Biometrika* is in existence, & the *Statistical Journal* won't take your review, perhaps you might write for that.[9] But the *Statistical Journal* is *far* the best. A pamphlet has the advantage of abundant elbow-room: but no one ever buys it, I think. And even if you distributed it gratis, I dont see how you w[d].. know where to send it. But very likely you do. I agree that Pearson seems to overshoot his mark; & therefore not to be very effective with careful readers. But the organs of the liquor traffic who want to prove that the diminution in the yield of the alcohol taxes, subsequent to the increased taxation, is a national calamity, are not careful, nor frank.

[1] King's College, Cambridge. J. M. Keynes Papers. From Balliol Croft.
[2] See [976.3].
[3] See [977.7].

[4] See *Report of an Enquiry by the Board of Trade into the Working Class Rents, Housing and Retail Prices, together with the Standard Rates of Wages Prevailing in Certain Occupations in the Principal Industrial Towns of the United Kingdom* (Cd 3864, 1908), pp. 510, 507, 509, respectively.
[5] Perhaps Marshall had forgotten his approach to Pearson in 1886: see Vol. 1 [190].
[6] See [977.9].
[7] I. Todhunter, 'On the Method of Least Squares', *Proceedings of the Cambridge Philosophical Society*, 1 (1843–65), p. 234. Read 29 May 1865.
[8] Word apparently omitted.
[9] Did Marshall appreciate that Pearson was the founding editor of *Biometrika*?

979. To John Maynard Keynes from Mary Paley Marshall, 21 September 1910[1]

3 Westcliff Terrace | Seaton Devon
21 Sep 10

Dear M^r. Keynes

I wonder whether I am right but I am venturing to send back your paper without letting my husband see it or the letter.[2] This is the only real holiday he is having this summer, & I dont want it to be broken into unless there s^hd. be *real* need.[3] If you think there is, will you kindly send the paper back here. We shall be home in a fortnight, but I did not like to keep your paper till then, as probably you will be wanting it. I will confess my guilt to him then & give him your letter.

Hoping meanwhile for your forgiveness.

Yours very sincerely | Mary P. Marshall

There is no need to answer this, please.

[1] King's College, Cambridge, J.M. Keynes Papers.
[2] The letter has not been traced. The returned paper was probably a draft for Keynes's projected contribution to the December number of the *Journal of the Royal Statistical Society*. This was to appear in the guise of a lengthy letter to the editors (vol. 74, pp. 114–21). It is reproduced in *Collected Works*, vol. 11, pp. 196–205.
[3] John Bates Clark, who appears to have visited Marshall around this time, provided an encouraging description of the latter's condition.

> Professor Marshall is in much better health than I expected to find him in and is working vigorously on a book, which he hopes will appear in two years. It will not be the entire Part II of his work [*Principles*], but will deal with International Values, Protection, and I know not what other subjects.

See Clark's letter of 26 October 1910 to E. R. A. Seligman quoted in J. Dorfman, 'The Seligman Correspondence', *Political Science Quarterly*, 56 (March–December 1941), pp. 107–24, 270–86, 392–419, 573–99, at p. 411 n.

980. To (B. B. Mukerji?), 22 October 1910[1]

22. x. 10

Dear Sir,

My excuse for not answering your question as to my opinions about India is suggested by yourself. If I were to answer all the questions which are sent me, my book would never appear. As it is I shall not live to serve up to table one half of the dishes which I have partly cooked.

I had an hour's talk a little while ago with an Indian on such questions as you ask. By question and answer we got on quickly, each guiding the other. To reach similar results in writing would be a long week's work.

I will however indicate the general trend of my opinion.

I have no objections on principle to the 'Protection' of Nascent Indian Industries. But a customs tariff is an expensive method to this end: and under existing circumstances it would—as you partly hint—enrich European capitalists rather than Indian.

Therefore I think it should not be applied until other methods have been tried, nor until those industries which already receive a *very high* protection from cost of carriage (in some cases double cost of carriage) have succeeded in evoking Indian enterprise: strong cases in point I understand to be the leather, paper and oil seed industries.

If India had a score or two of men like Mr Tata,[2] and some thousands of men with Japanese interest in realities, with virile contempt of mere speech-making in politics and law courts; and with no scorn for work on *things* while the mind was full of *thought*, India would soon be a great nation. Nothing could stop her: no tariff system could hinder her: she would enter into her heritage.

But so long as an Indian who has received a high education generally spends his time in cultured ease; or seeks money in Indian law suits—which are as barren of good to the country as is the sand of the sea shore—nothing can do her much good. So long as, with the exception of Bombay cotton—which after all is of Parsee origin—and a few works, of which Mr Tata's are at the head, all enterprise seems to be in European hands: in spite of the fact that the unhealthiness of India for the young children of Europeans is in effect a Protective duty of perhaps 50–100 per cent. in favour of Indian enterprise in India as against European.

For twenty years I have been urging on Indians in Cambridge to say to others: 'How few of us, when we go to the West, think of any other aim, save that of our *individual culture*? Does not the Japanese nearly always ask himself in what way he can strengthen himself to do *good service to his country* on his return? Does he not seek real studies? Does not he watch the sources of Western power? Is not that the chief reason for Japan's quick progress? Can not we imitate her? Do we need any other change than, like the Japanese, to think of our country in the first place and ourselves a long-way behind?'

You will complain that I have not indicated what I would do if I were responsible for India. My silence is due to two causes. I have not been able to learn enough about India to speak confidently: and I do not venture, in writing to a stranger, to indicate the vague, crude, tentative suggestions which I shall perhaps ultimately publish. I have occasionally discussed them in confidence with Indian friends.

I have said nothing about Preference. The more closely schemes for Preference are examined, whether in relation to India or to Self-Governing Colonies, the more futile and dangerous do they seem to me. Their advocates do not win my confidence.

Yours very truly, | Alfred Marshall

P.S. Perhaps you have already seen the 'White Paper' which I am sending you. I thought a good deal about India when writing it, but my only reference to her is in its last lines.[3]

You will of course understand that I know that some of the Indians who come to the West do really care to make themselves strong in action: I am very fortunate in counting several such men among my friends. But many more are needed.

[1] Printed in *Memorials*, pp. 471–3. Original not traced. From Balliol Croft. The letter is attributed in *Memorials* to 'B. Mukherjee, Lueknow University'. It seems probable that it was sent to Pigou in 1924, together with [1000]. Marshall's correspondent cannot be identified with confidence. The faculty of Lucknow University included in the early 1920s B. B. Mukerji (or Mukerjee) MA, BL (Calcutta), Reader in Economics, who appears to have died in 1947 or 8. The Professor of Economics was the better known Radhakamal Mukerjee (1889–1968). Conceivably the letters had been written to some relative of either of these individuals.

[2] Jamsetjee Nasarwanji Tata (1839–1904), enterprising and far-seeing Indian industrialist, merchant, and philanthropist.

[3] Marshall's 'Memorandum on Fiscal Policy' [912.2] ends with the reminder 'that India is the ward of England; that India is poor, while the Colonies are rich; and that India's commercial policy has been generous' (*Official Papers*, p. 420).

981. To Ludwig Darmstädter, 27 October 1910[1]

27. 10. 10

Dear Sir:

I believe that economics, like the science of navigation has two sides: one the analytical, which is based in eternal laws of nature; the other realistic, which constantly changes, as mans needs and resources develop. My attitude towards the science was set about 1867, when I was engaged in teaching Mathematics in Cambridge, and thought more easily in the Mathematical language than any other. Under the guidance of Cournot and von Thünen, I was led to see that Ricardo's analysis consisted in effect of a series of mathematical equations, in which rates of change in utility or production or any other economic quantity were expressed by differential coefficients relatively to one or several variables:—*time, labor supply, capital supply, productive energy and skill* and so on. It seemed to me that Ricardo scarcely ever went wrong; though of course he never went more than a little way. The present generation has gone further, especially under the influence of books which appeared about 1870: but I hold that the new work has been of real value in direct proportion to its modesty, and inverse proportion to its claims to have substituted new fundamentals in place of Ricardo's.

Realistic work on the other hand is transitional. The knowledge of realities possessed by Adam Smith and even Ricardo and Malthus was extensive and thorough. But few of their practical conclusions are applicable to the modern age of steam, electricity and education of the masses of the people. Perhaps aviation, the further progress of education and other causes not yet in sight may make our own realistic economics utterly obsolete a hundred years hence.

Yours faithfully | Alfred Marshall

Professor Darmstädter

[1] Staatsbibliothek, Berlin. Darmstädter Collection. From Balliol Croft. Ludwig Darmstädter (1846–1927), was a German chemist, industrialist, historian of science, and collector of autographs, author of *Ludwig Darmstädter's Handbuch zur Geschichte der Naturwissenschaft und der Technik* (Springer, Berlin, 1908). Why he sought Marshall's views on the nature of economics (or perhaps just his autograph?) remains unclear: probably a projected work failed to be completed. Marshall accompanied his letter with a note in German offering to make a second try at outlining his views on the nature of economic science, should the one sent prove inadequate. I am indebted to William B. Gaynor Jr. for drawing the letters to my attention and providing further information and assistance.

982. To John Maynard Keynes, 2 November 1910[1]

2. 11. 10

Dear Keynes

You have doubtless seen Galtons letter in todays Times.[2] You can probably read between the lines better than I can. I do not know whether it was of set purpose that he speaks of 'Alcoholism & parentage' & not of 'Alcoholism & Efficiency'. Nor do I know how much justification for his charge there may be in tee-totalist utterance.[3] At present I do not think I shall be drawn, however rude & misleading Pearsons second edition[4] may be. But perhaps it might be well for you to combine some remarks on it with those wh I am so very glad you are making on 'The Day & the Fray'.[5]

Yours ever A M

[1] King's College, Cambridge, J. M. Keynes Papers. From Balliol Croft.
[2] See his letter to the Editor, *The Times*, 2 November 1910 (9b), published under the heading 'The Eugenics Laboratory and the Eugenics Education Society'.

[3] Galton charged that much of the criticism of the work of the Eugenics Laboratory came from those 'who write under a strong bias'.
[4] Karl Pearson and Ethel Mary Elderton, *A Second Study of the Influence of Parental Alcoholism on the Physique and Ability of the Offspring: Being a Reply to Certain Medical Critics of the First Memoir and an Examination of Rebutting Evidence Cited by Them* (Dulau, London, 1910).
[5] See [979.2, 976.3].

983. From John Maynard Keynes, 2 November 1910[1]

Kings College, | Cambridge.
2 November 1910

Dear Professor Marshall,

Galton's letter[2] seems to be a certificate of confidence in Pearson, à propos of nothing in particular—or at any rate of nothing novel. The criticisms which I have seen in temperance magazines seem to me quite fair, and are chiefly concerned with quoting other investigations (of which there seem to have been a surprising number) which have brought out an answer very different from Pearson's. To have put faith in these other investigations is, I expect, the same thing in K.P.'s opinion as to show strong bias. And Galton has probably not looked into the thing himself with any care.

I feel almost sure that K.P.'s second edition will do no more than incorporate parts of 'Questions of the Day and of the Fray No. I'.[3] I am expecting a proof shortly of my reply to this. It is to appear in the Statistical Journal next month.[4] Would you like to see a proof of this, when it comes?

Ever yours, | J M Keynes

I have been able to show that he has not caught me out over the housing question.[5]

[1] Marshall Papers.
[2] See [982.2].
[3] See [982.4, 976.3].
[4] See [979.2].
[5] See *Collected Works*, vol. 15, pp. 197–8 n.

984. To John Maynard Keynes, 4 November 1910[1]

4. 11. 10

Dear Keynes,

Perhaps you may have seen Whittakers letter to wh this cutting refers.[2] I wonder whether he did imply that I had said that the population of the Edinburgh district was 'a mixture of sober degenerates & virile alcoholists'.[3] Of course you would not take cognizance of the correspondence in the Chronicle. But it might be well to make it clear that our contention is only that those who live in worst houses of a bad district (for no district is quite homogeneous) are sure to be, & are shown by the original Report[4] to have been in this case a mixture of artisans & of low-paid labourers: that a labourer might probably get there, though neither drunken nor degenerate: but that an artisan was not likely to get there unless he was either the one or the other; & that Pearson has not shown the contrary, though it is necessary for his argument that he should have.

I am glad the case is good about housing: only don't run the risk of any overstatement.

If you think it distinctly advisable that I should see your proofs,[5] I will do so: but my judgement & my inclination both tend slightly the other way.

Yours sincerely | Alfred Marshall

[1] King's College, Cambridge, J. M. Keynes Papers. From Balliol Croft.

[2] The cutting appears to have been of a letter from Pearson dated 29 October, published under the heading 'Drink and Degeneracy: Prof. Karl Pearson's Rejoinder to Sir T. Whittaker', *Daily Chronicle*, 1 November 1910 (5d). This responded to a two-part article 'Drink and Degeneracy: A Reply to Professor Karl Pearson' by Sir Thomas Whittaker, in the *Daily Chronicle*, 28 October (4d), 29 October (4d). (Thomas Palmer Whittaker (1850–1919), knighted 1906, businessman, Member of Parliament 1892–1919, temperance advocate, and writer on social and economic subjects.)

[3] The coinage of this phrase was entirely Pearson's, Whittaker being charged gratuitously with having 'further reiterated the opinion of Professor Marshall that the Edinburgh population was a mixture of sober degenerates and virile alcoholists'. Whittaker had not referred to Marshall or Keynes.

[4] See [968.6].

[5] As offered in [983].

985. From John Maynard Keynes, 9 November 1910[1]

Kings College, | Cambridge.
9 Nov[r] 1910

Dear Professor Marshall,

I have not seen Whittaker's letter,[2] but I think I have made plain in my contribution to the Stat. Journ[3] the points you refer to. I have just got a proof of it,—but I don't think there is any reason why I need trouble you with it. (Yule has passed it and Pigou is going to look through it for me.) Many thanks for the enclosed quotation[4]—it helps to make more certain that Pearson's argument is of the kind I say it is.

I have just become Sec[y] of the Economics Bd., and in rooting through the archives I read the fly sheets issued by the opponents of the new Tripos,[5]—it is wonderful how thoroughly all their predictions have been falsified.

I have just noted with interest that of the Committee and chief speakers at the Union *more than half* are doing Economics (*six* members of the Com[ee] and three candidates). I should not be surprised if a year hence the President, Vice-President, and Secretary of the Union are all doing the Economics Tripos.[6]

Sincerely yours, | J M Keynes

[1] Marshall Papers.
[2] The 'letter' mentioned by Marshall in [984] was actually a pair of short articles: see [984.2].
[3] See [979.2].
[4] See [984.2].
[5] See [748.1].
[6] Leadership in the Cambridge Union, a debating and social club, was probably the most prestigious non-academic honour that an undergraduate could attain. The *Cambridge Review*, 32, reports the following as speaking at Union debates in the Michaelmas Term of 1910: Robertson, 25 October (p. 54); Shove and Henderson, 1 November (p. 74); Keynes and Dalton, 10 November (p. 95); Robertson, 17 November (p. 116); Robertson, Henderson, and Shove, 24 November (p. 135). On 6 December Robertson was elected Secretary and Henderson was elected to the Committee (p. 182). (Hugh Dalton (1887–1962) was to teach economics at the London School of Economics and rise to eminence as a Labour politician.)

986. To John Maynard Keynes, (10?) November 1910[1]

Dear Keynes,

Thanks for your interesting letter.[2] I am *very* glad that you are secretary of the Economics Board.

The enclosed budget[3] has just come in. I think you will be interested at all events in the last letter, wh is an answer to Pearsons letter in the Chronicle.[4] Whittaker seems to me strong. I am thanking him & telling him to look out for the December number of the Statistical Journal.[5]

Yours | A M

[1] King's College, Cambridge, J. M. Keynes Papers. From Balliol Croft.
[2] [985], whose date suggests that of the present letter.
[3] Presumably a collection of press-clippings and letters.
[4] Probably the letter or short article published under the heading 'Drink and Degeneracy: Sir T. Whittaker Replies to Professor Pearson—Defects in his Family Comparisons', *Daily Chronicle*, 5 November 1910 (3e), a rejoinder to Pearson's letter of 29 October [984.2]. Pearson's further reply appeared on 9 November (5e).
[5] See [979.2]. No letter traced.

987. From John Maynard Keynes, (10? November) 1910[1]

Kings College, | Cambridge.
11. 10. 10

Dear Professor Marshall,

Many thanks for the enclosed.[2] Whittaker's articles[3] seem to me to be quite admirable. I think it will be unnecessary, whatever more Pearson may say, to pursue him further.

Sincerely yours, | J M Keynes

[1] Marshall Papers. Although clearly dated 11. 10. 10, a date of 10 November seems much more plausible.
[2] Possibly returning the 'budget' sent with [986].
[3] See [984.2, 986.4].

988. To Walter Thomas Layton, 2 December 1910[1]

2. 12. 10

Dear Layton,

I have been thinking during the night about your work for the *Economist*.[2] My own opinion is that there is a growing interest among business men in a treatment of business questions from a point of view intermediate between that of the newspaper & the academic lecture-room: & that you might do good service to the *Economist* by writing on that intermediate line in articles, which were in effect somewhat continuous: though each should be apparently self contained, & there should be no continuity of title.

If you could make the same thoughts answer for (1) part of your duty to the *Economist*; (2) part of your lecture work; & (3) a few short books, or rather a collection of Essays, I think your work w^{d}.. have a high quality & the chance of your breaking down through over-strain w^{d}.. be diminished. If you try to ride 3 horses at once, I fear for your health: strong men, who over-tax their strength, often come on the ground with a bigger thump than others.

Of course there may be objections & difficulties in the way of my plan: & I will not ask you to give it over-much attention. But I think Bagehot worked somewhat on those lines. And I am inclined—being a mere old fogy—to suggest as a motto

Live up to Bagehot[3]

Yours very sincerely | Alfred Marshall

[1] Trinity College, Cambridge, Layton Papers. From Balliol Croft.
[2] Layton had contributed regularly to *The Economist* since 1908, serving as a part-time assistant editor. See D. Hubback, *No Ordinary Press Baron* [934.1], pp. 21–2.
[3] Written in extremely large letters.

989. To John Maynard Keynes, 4 December 1910[1]

4. 12. 10

Dear Keynes,

I have found Rau's curves at the end of the inclosed wh I see is the *5th* Ed^{n}..[2] If Prof Liefmann is with you still, he may be interested in them. I thought his talk most instructive.[3] You may be interested in this bit of gossip. I had of course seen Fleeming Jenkin's first paper in *Recess Studies* 1870;[4] but that had no bearing on the short address wh I gave at the Cambridge Philosophical Society, (see *Proceedings* for Oct 1873) to explain the uses of H. H. Cunynghame's glorious machine for drawing rectangular hyperbolas in relation to monopoly values.[5] In that paper however I explained consumers surplus (I then called it 'Rent'), wh I thought was my own property; for I knew nothing of Dupuit. I wanted it of course for the curve, wh I afterwards called 'Compromise Benefit Curve'. Maxwell[6] got up & said, part of the paper reminded him of Fleeming Jenkins work, referring of course to the paper in *R.S.E.* proceedings for 71–2:[7] & that puzzled me, for I had not seen the paper.

At last when my *Principles* came out Jenkin wrote me a courteous letter,[8] somewhat like that wh Walras had written about multiple points of intersection, establishing priority of publication:[9] & I then saw that Jenkin had gone a great deal deeper than I had gathered from *Recess Studies*. I shd have said so yesterday.

Yours sincerely | Alfred Marshall

I have just remembered an incidental reference to Whewell in relation to Gossen in Mathematical Note XIII of my Principles.[10] (It was Note XXIV in my first edition.)[11]

There is no hurry about the return of Rau.

[1] King's College, Cambridge, J. M. Keynes Papers. From Balliol Croft.

[2] Presumably the letter was accompanied by a copy of Karl Heinrich Rau, *Grundsätze der Volkswirtschaftslehre*: see Vol. 1 [59.2] for details.

[3] Further information as to Robert Liefmann's talk, probably to a group of economics students, has not been ascertained.

[4] Fleeming Jenkin, 'The Graphic Representation of the Laws of Supply and Demand, and their Application to Labour', in Sir Alexander Grant (ed.), *Recess Studies* (Edmonston and Douglas, Edinburgh, 1870). See note 7 for reprint.

[5] For the text of Marshall's abstract see *Early Economic Writings*, vol. 2, pp. 283–5. See also the footnote to the preface of *Principles* (*1*) reproduced in *Guillebaud*, pp. 37–8.

[6] James Clerk Maxwell (1831–79), physicist, Cavendish Professor of Experimental Physics at Cambridge, 1871–9. A record of the discussion was not published.

[7] Fleeming Jenkin, 'On the Principles which Regulate the Incidence of Taxes', *Proceedings of the Royal Society of Edinburgh*, Session 1871–2. Reprinted in Fleeming Jenkin, *The Graphic Representation of the Laws of Supply and Demand and Other Essays in Political Economy* (Reprints of Scarce Tracts in Political Economy, 9; London School of Economics, London, 1931).

[8] Not traced.

[9] Marshall had claimed in a letter to Walras of 1 November 1883 (Vol. 1 [133]) to have 'anticipated' the latter's doctrine of unstable equilibrium. It would have been uncharacteristic for Walras not to rise to this challenge, but no reply was recorded by him, although one was perhaps sent. But see Vol. 2 [597] for another indication of Marshall's apparently faulty recollection of his early correspondence with Walras. A claim in *Principles* (*1*), p. 425 n., that 'this theory of unstable equilibrium was published independently by M. Walras and the present writer' was deleted from subsequent editions (see *Guillebaud*, p. 804).

[10] Jevons 'when describing Gossen's work, pointed out the objections to the plan followed by him (and Whewell) of substituting straight lines for the multiform curves that represent the true characters of the variations of economic quantities' (*Principles* (*8*), p. 846: so in all editions).

[11] Closing parenthesis omitted in the original.

990. To John Maynard Keynes, 12 December 1910[1]

The Mauri,[2] | Brixham.
12. 12. 10

My dear Keynes,

The account which I gave at the Cambridge Philosophical Society in 1873 had no other purpose than to explain the high realistic value of Cunynghame's machine. He was an undergraduate, & of course needed introduction. I may say that the ordinary properties of the rectangular hyperbola, though they seemed well adapted for graphic use turned out to be technically difficult. So Cunynghame invented a property that w^{d} work well; & Charles Taylor (late Master of St Johns)[3] the highest authority on the subject, took some trouble to establish its *absolute* novelty. He described his own machine: so I assumed that the Secretary of the Society, who wrote asking me to furnish an abstract of my discourse was asking him also for an abstract, but it turned out otherwise.

My abstract[4] (of which I have a single copy bound up) was less than two pages long; & by itself it explains little. But taken together with the chapter on Monopolies in my Book V,[5] it indicates that I then showed all the diagrams in that chapter, which indeed I had used for some time in the lecture room. Incidentally it suggests the Consumers Surplus curve, wh I had to show separately; & wh elicited Clerk Maxwell's remarks. He spoke rather long & very interestingly. But I cannot recollect what he said.

Yours sincerely | Alfred Marshall

[1] King's College, Cambridge, J. M. Keynes Papers. See [989].
[2] Correctly Wauri: see [1002.1] which reveals that Marshall had misapprehended this name.
[3] See [882.4].
[4] See [989.5].
[5] Ch. 14 from *Principles* (*5*) onwards, but essentially the same in all editions.

991. To John Maynard Keynes, 14 December 1910[1]

I am very glad you, who have girded up your loins so well, are now well Girdled.[2]

This is the shed in wh I have seen prime soles sold to the wholesale dealer at 2/6 a pound. A M

[1] King's College, Cambridge, J. M. Keynes Papers. A picture postcard of Brixham fish market, postmarked 'Brixam DE 14 10'. Reproduced in *Collected Works*, vol. 15, p. 65.
[2] Keynes had been appointed to the Girdlers' Lectureship in Economics, held since 1908 by Meredith, who had recently been appointed Professor of Economics at Queen's University, Belfast.

992. From John Maynard Keynes, 31 December 1910[1]

The Greyhound | Corfe Castle | Dorset
31. 12. 10

Dear Professor Marshall,

I have just got the enclosed letter from Sir Victor Horsley (which I should like back).[2] I am asking him to send the paper here, and I shall call on him as soon as I return to London in the course of the week. Would you care to see his paper before publication or would you rather not? In writing to him I have left the matter open.

Many thanks for your postcards—one on the Pearson letter, and the other on the Girdlers Lectureship.[3]

Sincerely yours, | J M Keynes

[1] Marshall Papers.

[2] Horsley's letter of 28 December 1910 is preserved in the J. M. Keynes Papers at King's College. Marshall wrote the following summary of it on the present letter:

> Abstract of Horsley's letter:—Dr Sturge & I are preparing paper for British Medical Journal on Elderton & Co on Alcoholism. 'Making free use of your crushing letter' in Stat J. Wd like to call on you to discuss it. Quoting also Prof M. Wd he like to look at it? 'Following your lead, the acceptance of the *verified* wage table, we find gives Prof Marshalls percentage loss of wage in the drinkers quite definitely'.
>
> Am declining, because my book goes almost as slowly as Penelopes Webb.

Victor Alexander Haden Horsley (1857–1916), knighted 1902, was a leading medical scientist and surgeon. Mary Darby Sturge collaborated in his work. Their joint paper appeared as 'On Some of the Biological and Statistical Errors in the Work on Parental Alcoholism by Miss Elderton and Professor Karl Pearson, F.R.S.' in the *British Medical Journal* for 14 January 1911, pp. 72–82.

[3] The first apparently not preserved. For the second see [991].

993. To Francis Ysidro Edgeworth (1911?: incomplete)[1]

The Japanese tariff, as handled by the Tarif Reform Commission,[2] has exercised me much. Soyeda[3] sent a director of his 'Industrial Bank of Japan' to me: & I supposed it was to talk about the tariff. But, to my disgust, he knew nothing about it. I have had enough controversy this year to make me shudder at the hateful thing for many years: & I do not want to be let in for it in any way. But if you elect that thorny path, I wd suggest to you to inquire whether these three propositions are not true:—

1. (This point has been made in several journals.) The tariff is supposed to be raised greatly, because what is now published is not the actual tariff but that which will be charged on countries who behave in an unfriendly way to Japan. The others will get remissions. We shall get the benefit of all these.

The present maximum tariff is not *much* higher than the old; & there is no good reason to suppose that the new conventional one will be *in general* much higher than the old.

2. But Japan wants more revenue; & she now thinks she is ready to make for herself many things, which she did not much care to 'protect' before. So she is screwing up a little all round, & especially in regard to simple textiles &c. We are the chief exporters of such things to her; & must necessarily suffer more than other countries: though I think the total effect will be small.
3. As regards iron & steel products Britain & Germany are large exporters to Japan. The duty on pig iron was unreasonably low, in comparison to others: that has been raised greatly, & will hit us more than Germany. But so far as the more important products go, it is *not* true that our specialities are more heavily taxed than Germanys. For instance we are the chief exporters of sheets to Japan (as to other countries) while Germany (& Belgium) rule in bars &c. But the tariff is not specially high on sheets: in fact I think it has been raised less than on bars. I can't verify because the aforesaid Jap took away with him my Tariff Reform paper[4] on the subject & has not yet returned it.

We have often talked of going to Happisburgh,[5] partly because Fawcett used to sing its praises. But we have never been there: the trains from here to it do not fit well. We have been in Norfolk: perhaps we shall go away again for a few days ere long.

Yours very sincerely | Alfred Marshall

I talked to the Jap on these lines & said: Of course if it were true that Japan hits us because we don't hit her, there is nothing to prevent us from hitting back; and we could hit hard, because our doors are generally open. It is just as easy for a free trade country to levy a tax of 10% on all her imports from, say, Japan; as it is for a protectionist country to levy an *extra* 10% on such goods. Free-trade in peace: but a peaceful man wd be free to hit back if peace were regarded as a sign of weakness. A combative or war tariff, pure & simple, is easier to work & more effective as a weapon than one wh is entangled with 'protective' aims.

[1] King's College, Cambridge, J. M. Keynes Papers. The first of three double pages is missing. Keynes wrote on the second one 'To F. Y. E 1911'. The references to recent controversy and having been in Norfolk recently suggest a late 1910 or early 1911 date.

[2] Presumably the Tariff Commission, founded by Chamberlain, of which Hewins was Secretary, rather than the more propagandist Tariff Reform League. Both were centred in London.

[3] Juichi Soyeda (1864–1929), Japanese economist and financier, president of the Industrial Bank of Japan, 1902–13. Soyeda had come under Marshall's influence as a non-collegiate student at Cambridge in 1885.

[4] Probably the Tariff Commission's pamphlet, *The Proposed Japanese Tariff and Its Effect on British Trade* (London, 1910).

[5] On the Norfolk coast between Great Yarmouth and Cromer.

994. To John Maynard Keynes, 2 January 1911[1]

2. 1. 11

Dear Keynes

I am very glad to see this letter:[2] & glad also that you are to revise Horsleys Statistical Methods. For I think he might make some technical slip, the importance of wh Pearson w^d.. magnify.

Alas! my book proceeds about as fast as Penelope's webb: & I must do nothing that I can help.

My fingers itched to be at Alington (Master of Shrewsbury) for his plaint at the cruelty of being compelled to 'learn Euclid by heart'.[3] I wanted to say that such a man ought not to be responsible for the education of people who might have been good scientific men if they had not come under his obfuscating influence. But I thought of the web, & cut my letter to the Times short half way.[4] I think some one ought to go for him.

Yours ever | A M

[1] King's College, Cambridge, J. M. Keynes Papers. From Balliol Croft.

[2] Presumably returning the letter from Horsley [992.2].

[3] See the letter to the Editor, *The Times*, 29 December 1910 (4e), from C. A. Alington, headmaster of Shrewsbury School, published under the heading 'Greek and Algebra', decrying the insistence that non-scientific students be required to pass in algebra. This is the 'science-blind' headmaster, one of the 'ablest and most enterprising' in England, who is referred to in *Industry and Trade*, pp. 820–1 n. Cyril Argentine Alington (1872–1955) was head of Shrewsbury School 1908–16 and of Eton College 1916–33.

[4] That is, did not complete it.

995. To the Editor, *The Labour Leader*, 11 January 1911[1]

Sir,—My attention has been called to an able and interesting article by Mr. Robert Jones in your issue of January 6, in which he describes me as 'stating that capital might well continue to be increased, not only if there were no interest, but even where interest would be negative all along the line'.[2] But if he will look again at the passage to which he refers ('Principles,' p. 582), he will see that I make this statement not in regard to our own world, but to another which may be conceived to exist, with conditions not greatly differing from our own.[3] But in the passages to which this footnote refers, I explain at length my opinion that in our world human nature as it is, and physical resources as they are, make a moderate rate of interest necessary for that continuous increase of railways, ships, buildings, machinery, etc., which enables this little country to maintain a large population in comfort.

It is well known that water increases in density till its temperature approaches the freezing point, and then its volume swells instead of contracting, its density diminishes, and ice floats on the surface. But only 'a small modification of the conditions of (the main fluid of) our own world would be required to bring us to another in which' the increase in density of the main fluid continued as its temperature fell down to freezing point. In that world ice would, in my opinion, go to the bottom of the seas; and in those zones in which even occasional frosts occurred, the bottoms of deep oceans would be solid masses of ice, possibly a mile thick or more. But in expressing this opinion, I do not commit myself to the statement that in this world all the ice may soon have gone down below, so that skaters will have to seek their exercise in rinks alone.

The footnote to which Mr. Robert Jones refers is indeed only a summary of an argument in the chapter on 'The Growth of Wealth,' p. 232, in which the partial symmetry between the supply of labour and that of capital is indicated. After stating that 'we can imagine a state of things in which stored-up wealth could be put to but little use,' and 'the rate of interest could be negative,' the passage continues:—

> Such a state of things is conceivable. But it is also conceivable, and almost equally probable, that people may be so anxious to work that they will undergo some penalty as a condition of obtaining leave to work. For, as deferring the consumption of some of his means is a thing which a prudent person would desire on its own account, so doing some work is a desirable object on its own account to a healthy person. Political prisoners, for instance, generally regard it as a favour to be allowed to do a little work. And human nature being what it is, we are justified in speaking of the interest on capital as the reward of the sacrifice involved in the waiting for the enjoyment of material resources, because few people would save much without reward; just as we speak of wages as the reward of labour, because few people would work hard without reward.

The symmetry is of course only partial. For wages are in the main consumed in supplying the high-class 'fuel' which is 'necessary for efficiency' in regard to various grades of labour; their function as a stimulus to the increase of the energy thus supported is only secondary, though essential; while the position of interest in regard to saving is mainly that of a stimulus. And therefore that gradual rise in the rate of wages, continued[4] with a gradual fall in the rate of interest, which is characteristic of the present age, is a sign of healthy economic conditions; as well as a result most to be desired from higher points of view.—Yours, etc.,

Alfred Marshall.

Cambridge,
Jan. 11, 1911.

[1] Printed in *The Labour Leader: A Weekly Journal of Socialism, Trade Unionism and Politics*, 8/3, 20 January 1911. Original not traced. This journal was an organ of the Independent Labour Party.

[2] The article, one of a series of 'Chats on Economics' written by Jones, discussed issues raised by letters he had received, including one written from Ruskin Hall, Oxford, accusing him of believing interest unnecessary. Jones explained:

The standard text-book at Ruskin Hall used to be our old friend Marshall. If my correspondent will turn to page 582, 5th edition (book vi, ch. 6 § 1) he will find the cautious Professor boldly stating that capital might quite well continue to be increased, not only if there were no interest, but even where 'interest would be negative all along the line'...

[3] The passage in question comprises p. 582, n. 1, in each of *Principles* (*5*)–(*8*).
[4] A misprint for 'combined' may be suspected.

996. To John Maynard Keynes, 31 January 1911[1]

31. 1. 11

My dear Keynes

I was very busy when the *Statistical Journal* came in, & put it on one side. I have just read those parts in wh he refers specially to me; & 'parts of parts' referring to you.[2] I think it is likely you will prefer to ignore it. But if there shd seem to you to be cause for a reply & w[d].. like to see my copy, in wh I have scribbled a *few* pencil notes, I will send it to you.

Yours sincerely | Alfred Marshall

[1] King's College, Cambridge, J. M. Keynes Papers. From Balliol Croft.
[2] See Pearson's letter to the Editors, *Journal of the Royal Statistical Society*, 74 (January 1911), pp. 221–9, a rejoinder to Keynes's review and letter [968.4, 979.2].

997. From John Maynard Keynes, 5 February 1911[1]

Kings College, | Cambridge.
5. 2. 11

Dear Professor Marshall,

I am writing again to the *Stat. Journ.*, partly to make explicit K.P.'s admission, chiefly to sum up the controversy as it now appears from our point of view.[2] I hope to be able to find time to write it in a day or two, and should be very glad indeed to have the benefit of your notes.[3]

I enclose an offprint of Sir V.H.'s article,[4] in case you care to put it with the other documents. Did you see Pigou's admirable article on the general question in the *Westminster* of Feb 2?[5]

Sincerely yours, | J M Keynes

[1] Marshall Papers.
[2] Keynes's final salvo in the battle with Pearson appeared as a letter to the Editors, *Journal of the Royal Statistical Society*, 74 (February 1911), pp. 339–45: reproduced in *Collected Works*, vol. 11, pp. 207–16.
[3] As offered in [996].
[4] See [992.2].
[5] A. C. Pigou, 'Alcoholism and Heredity', *Westminster Gazette*, 2 February 1911.

998. To Macmillan and Company, 9 February 1911[1]

Confidential 9. 2. 11

Mess[rs] MacMillan & Co Ltd

Dear Sirs,

I am glad to answer your inquiry about M[r] Coyagee.[2] A good deal of his work at Cambridge was done after I had resigned my Professorship. But I saw enough of him to be sure that he is a very able, solid, persistent student: & I shall be glad if a textbook on economics for Indian students is written by him in conjunction with Professor Muller.[3] I know rather more of Muller than of Coyagee; & it is perhaps well that I should volunteer some observations about him. He is a Dane by birth (his real name is Müller), educated in England; of a frank charming temperament, but rather fitful & unsteady of purpose. Our relations have always been quite pleasant: but his history, as told me by himself, shows him to be a man rather inclined both to give offence & to take offence, while yet meaning well throughout: for he is generous even to a touch of romance & high minded. I would suggest therefore that you should be rather careful in wording any communications to him, & to allow him a little free play in his. He has a wider experience of the world than Coyagee has; but has perhaps rather less solid strength. I shall look forward to their book with great interest.

Yours very faithfully | Alfred Marshall

[1] British Library, Macmillan Archive. From Balliol Croft.

[2] Jehangir Cooverjee Coyagee (1875–1943), knighted 1928, had studied at Cambridge as an Advanced Student, where he was a member of Caius and took Part II Economics in 1910. He became a leading Indian economist, Professor of Political Economy, then Principal, at Presidency College, Calcutta. See the obituary note, *Economic Journal*, 53 (December 1943), pp. 453–6, which reports that 'Professor Marshall made the prophetic statement that "Coyagee will add one more to the now not inconsiderable number of natives of India who may claim to rank with the ablest and most thorough students of economics in any country"' (p. 454).

[3] See [826.3]. The proposal seems to have come to nothing.

999. To Manohar Làl, 22 February 1911[1]

22. ii. 11

Dear Manohar Làl,

I am very glad to receive your kind and interesting letter.[2] But I must adhere to my resolve not to publish anything about India, till I can incorporate my opinion about Protection to her industries in a more general discussion. I think I have already indicated my reasons: they are too long to be written out; but I think they are strong, and for me at least they are decisive. I never speak of a 'Free Trade Principle.' But I go rather near to one when I say that in my judgment no tax should be levied in such a way as to raise the price of things which are consumed by the people, but yet do not contribute to the revenue, unless it is what the Germans call an 'educative' tax: and I think that a Protective tax on cottons would not now be educative. I think Government should incur economic loss for the sake of industrial education: but I am not in a position to say *confidently* in what ways; I can only speak tentatively.

I do not think that manufactures are more conducive to prosperity than agriculture is, unless they evoke initiative. A score of Tatas[3] might do more for India than any Government, British or Indigenous, can accomplish. The dark spots of western Europe are not agricultural. They are the homes of those manufactures which are divorced from initiative. To try for manufactures as in themselves a remedy for India's ills seems to me a fatal error.

I have understood that the handloom, adapted to the use of the automatic shuttle, is breaking the factory weaving sheds in India. That seems to me a strong reason against laying exceptional stress on the cotton industry.

I am very glad to know of the excellent work you are doing.

Yours very sincerely, | Alfred Marshall

[1] Printed in *Memorials*, p. 458. Original not traced. From Balliol Croft.
[2] Not traced.
[3] See [980.2].

1000. To (B.B. Mukerji?), 12 April 1911[1]

12. iv. 11

Dear Sir,

I am very much obliged for the papers you have sent me:[2] they are most interesting.

I cannot say 'yes' or 'no' to the question whether I am in favour of Protection to Indian industries. Either answer would be as misleading as it would be if given to the celebrated question 'Have you stopped beating your wife?' I have not authorised anyone to say anything on my behalf: but I have suggested to several persons, Indian and English, that the Excise duties should be earmarked for purposes such as were indicated by Sir Sassoon David at the end of his speech.[3]

I do not think the Indian cotton industry has a right to Protection on the exceptional ground that it is 'nascent.' And I am not hopeful that Government can do much for India so long as the best Indian minds seek self-culture, or the barren work of pleading in the Courts, rather than those creative enterprises which might make their country strong. But I hold it bound to do its utmost, in spite of difficulties, to aid new enterprises which are educative, and especially when they are being worked by brave Indians, who care little for either comfort or dignity, provided only they can help India to be great. Would that there were more such men! I am not prepared to say that a Protective duty on imports can *never* be justified when a nascent industry needs help, and no other help is possible. But I think it is a clumsy, wasteful, demoralizing method; and that India can help her young industries much better by other means. I think, for instance, that the Sugar industry needs help; and that a Protective duty would be poison to it. It wants to be waked: and a Protective duty would be a mere sleeping draught.

Yours very truly, | Alfred Marshall

[1] Printed in *Memorials*, pp. 473–4. Original not traced. For the difficulty of identifying the recipient see [980.1].
[2] Not located.
[3] Sir Sassoon David (1849–1926), knighted 1905, was a prominent Indian businessman, a life-long resident of Bombay. A report of a speech by him had probably been among the papers sent by Mukerji.

1001. To John Neville Keynes, 28 April 1911[1]

28. 4. 11

My dear Keynes,

I am great[ly][2] pleased at hearing that Pembroke has honoured itself in honouring you.

Don't trouble to answer.

Yours very truly | Alfred Marshall

Among your many honours there is perhaps none greater than that of being the father of J. M. Keynes: & from what I learn, mainly at second hand, Miss Keynes[3] is as glorious in her way as he in his.

[1] Marshall Library, J. N. Keynes Papers. From Balliol Croft. Keynes had been elected an Honorary Fellow of Pembroke College, where he had previously been a Fellow, 1876–82.
[2] Ending omitted in original.
[3] Margaret Neville Keynes (1885–1970), subsequently Mrs A. V. Hill, the second of Neville Keynes's three children.

1002. To John Maynard Keynes, 18 May 1911[1]

The Wauri | Brixham
18. 5. 11

My dear Keynes,

As you may have heard we have decided to study the evolution of Spring in Devonshire this year: Mary has the most delightful fleet of fishing boats to paint; & we have a long verandah with a tiny garden in front, beyond[2] which are mere rocks & sea. So I shall not be able to attend the meeting of the C.U. Eugenics Society on Monday.[3] But I am hugely delighted that it has been formed & inclose a life composition fee.

Yours very sincerely | Alfred Marshall

[1] King's College, Cambridge, J. M. Keynes Papers. The word 'Wauri' in the address corrected the word 'Mauri' written originally.

[2] The comma was inadvertently placed after rather than before the word 'beyond'.

[3] 'In 1911, the Oxford University Union moved approval of the principles of eugenics by a vote of almost two to one, and meetings of a eugenics society at Cambridge University before the war drew hundreds of people, including high college officials, Nobel Laureate scientists, powerful senior professors, and the young John Maynard Keynes'. Daniel J. Kelves, *In the Name of Eugenics* (University of California Press, Berkeley and Los Angeles, 1985), p. 60. This work is a valuable account of the eugenics movement and provides copious references. For an account of the inaugural meeting of the Cambridge University Eugenics Society on Monday 22 May see *Cambridge Review*, 32 (25 May 1911), p. 459. William Ralph Inge (1860–1954), Lady Margaret Professor of Divinity, gave an address on 'Some Social and Religious Aspects of Eugenics'. This, according to the report, sounded some basic themes of the movement: 'One of the most crying necessities is the segregation of feeble-minded women, whose uncontrolled and abnormal fertility is a source of terrible misery and degradation. Another menace is the tendency to shirk parentage on the part of men and women possessing finely developed physical, mental and moral organisms.... Since in our humanity we inhibit natural selection, it is essential that rational selection should take its place if we are to stem the growing tide of race degeneracy'.

1003. From Francis Ysidro Edgeworth, 25 July 1911[1]

Edgeworthstown, | Ireland.
Jul 25

My dear Marshall

I am glad to think that J. M. Keynes may be willing to become a candidate for the editorship.

I should be happy to give any information in my power. I shall be in town from about the 15th August to beginning of September, and as I think he is often in town it would be easy to arrange an interview. Or before then I could answer any questions that he might ask by letter. I suppose the leading questions are (a) What is the amount of pay? and (b) What is the amount of work? There is a certain indefiniteness—a certain margin of 'probable error' about the answers to both questions.

(a) I have been receiving £50 a year the last two or three years; but previously £60. I gave up £10 the better to endow a colleague[2] (who gets I think the magnificent sum of £25—more or less, between £20 and £30). The Council would be well advised in returning to the figure of £60 for the Editor—without cutting down his Assistant.

(b) As a very rough estimate I should say that the work might occupy an hour or an hour and a half if spread over the year excluding Sundays and say a month in the dead of the Long Vacation. Or again if the whole of the working hours of Sundays (if that is not a contradiction in terms) were devoted to the Journal that would almost suffice. But I am not [to][3] be understood as meaning that the business could be left alone during all the weekdays. Per contra the effort and sacrifice is not to be measured by the time required. A good deal of the correspondence can be done at odd times, when one is in the humour. A good deal of the work too is of the nature of Joint Production: it results in a knowledge of persons and things which is useful to one who is engaged in writing on or teaching the subject.I shall be happy to give any further information.

Yours ever | F Y Edgeworth

P.S. I see no harm in your approaching J.M.K. by letter. You can let him see the preceding if you think fit—explaining that it is communicated confidentially. We have no authority to make any offer on the part of the Council.

The enclosed cutting[4] may interest you.

F.Y.E.

[1] King's College, Cambridge, J. M. Keynes Papers. Keynes was elected to take over the editorship of the *Economic Journal* from Edgeworth at a Council meeting on 17 October 1911, chaired by Marshall. See Donald E. Moggridge, 'Keynes as Editor' in John D. Hey and Donald Winch (eds.), *A Century of Economics: 100 Years of the Royal Economic Society and the Economic Journal* (Blackwell, Oxford, 1990), pp. 143–57 at p. 143. See also Moggridge, *Maynard Keynes* [846.1], p. 208; *Economic Journal*,. 21 (December 1911), pp. 665–6.

[2] H. B. Lees-Smith who had assisted Edgeworth since 1908.

[3] Word apparently accidentally omitted.

[4] The cutting from the *Freeman's Journal* (Dublin), 22 July 1910 (10a) is preserved in the Keynes Papers. It covers an announcement of the Annual All-Ireland Convention of the Town Tenants' League and a report of a meeting of the Edgeworthstown branch, at which it was reported that Edgeworth had agreed to a 20% rent reduction for his tenants, a reduction for which the League took credit and deemed no less than was due.

1004. To John Maynard Keynes, 27 July 1911[1]

27. 7. 11

Dear Keynes

The inclosed letter from Edgeworth[2] puts the case clearly. I am very glad that there is hope that you will allow yourself to be nominated. I ought not to press you. But I may note that the time occupied will not be waste, even from your own point of view. You will read very little for the Journal wh it wd not be worth while to know something about on its own merits. The main point is the writing, with aid, the leaderettes, &c. The task is one of great power combined with exceptional freedom, modified only by the necessity of expressing only in reserved form individual opinions on contentious subjects in a non-contentious Journal.

I expect to be at home any how for the next two months; & I shall be glad to have a talk in case you wish it. For the great thing is that you have a talk with Edgeworth.

I dont think he intended me to send on the cutting: but I send it. I am amused—all to the man who makes money by the agitation, & none to the man who gives.[3]

Yours sincerely | Alfred Marshall

[1] King's College, Cambridge, J. M. Keynes Papers. From Balliol Croft. See [1003.1].
[2] See [1003].
[3] See [1003.4].

1005. To Walter Thomas Layton, 4 September 1911[1]

4. 9. 11

My dear Layton

My wife has brought back the last number but one of the Economist; & I have read the article on the Index number, & re-read your letter.[2] I think you understand that I scarcely ever read anything wh relates to matters that I take seriously, till I get to those matters. I put a note in the appropriate drawer that will guide me to the article when I want it: I read at the time only those things wh I dont take seriously.

I think the article & your letter are very able, suggestive & useful; & are just of the kind to be helpful to the Economist, raising its pitch & strengthening its hold on thoughtful people; while at the same time they further your own growth upwards to economic leadership (not leader-writingship!)

Of course I cannot express any opinion in detail. But speaking generally I think I agree both with your method & your results. The only definite criticism I have to make is that you quote (p 423) as 'retail prices in London' what are really only the prices of Diminishing Return products.[3] If you had thrown in manufactures e.g. cycles!, cost of transport per mile, cost of illuminant per candle-power & so on, you would have got different results to some extent.

As to the causes of the present unrest I agree with all you say: but I should myself lay stress on social & educational changes also.[4]

Yours proudly | Alfred Marshall

P.S. I think Schedule D income statistics need to be weighted by a coefficient representing evasion. I dont believe incomes have increased as fast as the figures suggest.

[1] Trinity College, Cambridge, Layton Papers. From Balliol Croft.
[2] *The Economist*, 26 August 1911, contained an unsigned article 'History of the "Economist" Index Number,' pp. 421–5, presumably written by Layton, and a signed letter from him on 'Some Statistical Aspects of the Labour Unrest,' pp. 440–2.
[3] Layton had written on p. 423 that 'Since 1896 the Board of Trade has calculated [a retail price index] on the basis of prices in London.'
[4] Layton's letter had contrasted large gains in profits and the incomes of the income-tax paying classes with small increases in real wages, and argued that the demonstration effect of middle-class luxury had exacerbated worker discontent.

1006. To Irving Fisher, 16 September 1911[1]

16. ix. 11

Dear Professor Fisher,

I desire to associate myself heartily with your appeal for national, and if possible international, inquiries into changes in the purchasing power of money, with special reference to the costs of living of various sections of the community in various countries.[2] I go with the spirit of your aspirations heartily: but I am inclined to doubt whether a thorough scientific treatment of the whole problem can be achieved quickly; and to suggest that for the present attention should be concentrated on those parts of it which can be treated broadly and quickly.

In particular I doubt whether a study of wages and budgets should be pressed very far at this stage. I do not think we have yet reached satisfactory methods for dealing with those problems. The work that has been done at them is worthy of all honour: but those who have made the chief advances are those who are the least satisfied with what has already been achieved.

Standardisation is as yet in so early a stage that we can get no trustworthy price lists, which range over a fairly long period, and which are applicable to many things which are not either raw or in the first stage of manufacture. No doubt technical progress has been conspicuous in the arts of transport: and in this one direction the commodities that are entered in the artisan's budget do represent fairly well the forces of economic progress. They bring out the fact that his food is still earned at a low cost of effort, although the soil around him may yield small supplies of it. But they seldom represent the economies of modern manufacture which are embodied even in simple clothing: for such things are not yet reduced to any common standard. And scarcely any lists take account of the vast amounts of light, water, reading matter, personal transport and other amenities of life which he does buy cheaply but which would have cost much more than all his wages not long ago. I submit that our main purpose—that of mitigating the evils caused by broad changes in the real cost of production of gold—ought not to wait for further calculations by methods as crude as the best which are within our reach to-day.

Thus for the present I would limit international inquiries to a selection of the best representative commodities for the whole consumption of the world. It must be rather a short list; and each commodity must have a large consumption and a fairly standardised marketing. It cannot therefore be other than crude: it must probably be cruder than our best national index numbers. But it will be simple and definite: and its purpose will be intelligible to the working classes in advanced countries and to the ruling classes in others.

I think the time is not ripe for an official international inquiry into the causes of these variations. The excellent work that has been done recently, for instance, in estimates of the rapidity of circulation of money would perplex the ordinary man, even if it were really complete: and in my opinion it has not yet made a very great advance towards that end.

Only on such a simple definite basis does it seem to me that it could be hoped—if the hope can be entertained at all—to reach an international convention for the establishment of an artificial inconvertible paper currency in which each nation should have its due share; and of which it could truly be said that, though very far from ideal perfection, it was only about half as bad as a gold currency. But I am myself not very hopeful: partly because I do not see how it would work out in a war as intense as that in which Pitt was charged with issuing forged French paper money.

You inquire as to my early scheme for remedying the chief evils that arise out of the ever-changing relations of the supply of gold to the work to be done by it. My proposed 'Remedies for fluctuations of general prices' are set out in the *Contemporary Review* for March 1887.[3] They were on familiar lines already suggested by Lowe, Scrope, Jevons, Walras and others: but they had some little peculiarities. I thought then that any plan for regulating the supply of currency, so that its value shall be stable, must be national and not international. But I thought that each nation might possibly have a paper currency the value of which was in effect tied to that of certain fixed quantities of gold, silver and other commodities which 'have great value in small bulk, and are in universal demand, and which are thus suitable for paying the balances of foreign trade'. I no longer think that such a currency is on the whole at all likely to answer.

But a quarter of a century has made me ever more desirous that every country should have an official 'unit' of general purchasing power, made up from tables of price percentages like those of Sauerbeck and others: and that it should authorise long period obligations for the payment of rent and interest on loans of all kinds to be made at the option of the contracting parties, in terms either of this general unit, or of a selection of price percentages appropriate to the special purpose in hand. Public authority should make out such lists as appeared suitable to particular classes of transactions: but the parties concerned should have perfect freedom to make special selections. Any wages contract, such as a sliding scale in the iron trade, might 'take account not only of the price of the finished iron, but also on the one hand, of the prices of iron ore, coal, and other expenses of the employer; and on the other, of the prices of the things chiefly consumed by the workmen.'[4]

I think that could be done at once. If it succeeded, the world would I think be prepared in say twenty years for an international 'fixed standard' paper currency: provided it can be helped on the way by a vigorous movement such as that in which you are active.

Yours very truly, | Alfred Marshall

[1] Printed in *Memorials*, pp. 474–7. Original not traced. From Balliol Croft.

[2] Marshall had probably received a duplicated typescript of Fisher's 'Memorandum as to an International Commission on the Cost of Living' (1911). (There is a copy in the Library of Congress.) A later version appeared as 'An International Commission on the Cost of Living,' *American Economic Review*, 2, Supplement (March 1912), pp. 92–101. For Fisher's monetary views more generally see his *Purchasing Power of Money* (Macmillan, New York, 1911).

[3] See *Memorials*, pp. 188–211 for the text.

[4] *Memorials*, p. 198 n.

1007. To Sir Frederick Macmillan, 31 October 1911[1]

31. 10. 11

Dear Sir Frederick

I have no objection to the quotations proposed by Mess[rs] Richardson & Walbank.[2] So far as I have followed them, they express my opinions on the subjects to which they refer fairly well without the aid of the context. Their total amount seems to be about six pages.

In saying this I am giving no testimonial to their book. The notice of it which you forwarded to me excites my interest & my sympathy: I wish that the wages of coal miners should rise at the expense of what I believe to be in many cases the excessive profits of coal owners. But the Statistical methods indicated are not convincing to me: they seem to be consistent with a great underrating of average wages & a great overrating of average profits. In particular they seem to make no allowance for the collapse of the value of a mine when a seam runs out: a difficulty to which attention is called indirectly on p 302 of my *Elements* (& at greater length on pp. 620–1 of my *Principles*).[3]

Yours very truly | Alfred Marshall

[1] British Library, Macmillan Archive. From Balliol Croft.

[2] The quotations from *Elements* were to be incorporated into Thomas Richardson and John Arthur Walbank, *Profits and Wages in the British Coal Trade: 1898 to 1910* (NACC, Newcastle-upon-Tyne, 1911). Part II of this work on 'The Economic Aspect of the Minimum Wage' quoted Marshall's book extensively, with only a general acknowledgement and a warning that Marshall should not be assumed to agree with the views expressed. Richardson (1868–1928), miner, trade union official, and local politician in Durham, served as Labour Member of Parliament 1910–18. Walbank, an accountant, was the author of a work on *Builder's Accounts* which remained in print for over 40 years.

[3] The passages in question stress the necessity of balancing losses against gains in judging an industry's average profit rate. There is no particular reference to mining.

1008. To Francis Ysidro Edgeworth, (January?) 1912 (incomplete)[1]

Moore is a night mare to me.[2] I know I must write to him & I am afraid. I do not doubt that he is of great ability; nor that work like his will in the long run be of great service to economics.

But his whole book is one prolonged dancing on what has been the most tender of my beloved corns ever since 1875.

As I think you know, the use of the economic statistical table in pairs by the extreme free traders & the extreme protectionists in the U.S.A. set the corn growing.[3] I think I have spent more time on studying this particular source of fallacies than anyone that ever lived: And I am a red hot fanatic about it.

I scarcely ever used a statistical diagram in lectures by itself, even though I generally got from three to ten allied curves on each sheet. I used to stick up a number of sheets at a time & to preach about the wickedness of deducing conclusions from any one of them alone, save under special conditions.

In general I should say—if I spoke without reserve—I think each of your arguments should run somewhat in this fashion. 'Here are two elements which probably have some causal connection either as father & son, or brothers or cousins. Now if we assume that neither of them has causal relations with any other changing element, they may be safely put into a Statistico-Mathematical machine, & the result worked out to *n* places of decimals. But of course this is mere play. In fact they have many other causal relations: & therefore my results in reference to the real world may have errors not of .5 or .7 per cent, but of 50 or 70 per cent.'

He seems to me to have only proved that there is *some sort of* causal connection in cases in wh no one w^{d} doubt that there was one: & to have reached results not nearly as helpful *practically* as those which he could have got by looking at the world with wide open eyes for a few minutes. Take for instance his figures on pp 11, 12.[4] They are pretty as a beginning. But he should have gone on.

'It is of course well known what are the broad causes which make *money* wages higher generally in almost every occupation (male or female) in one district than another. It is also known what special conditions make a rise in the earnings of men bring about a more than proportionate rise in the earnings of some classes of women especially charwomen.'

'And it is also known what special conditions make the run of mens low where the run of womens wages is high, and *because* womens wages are high: this is of course a common place in regard to many textile districts & especially woollen & worsted.'[5]

'So you will bear in mind that all these pictures & decimals & learned terms are intended to prepare the way for a future generation of workers, who can put all the facts, I have just mentioned, into a group of mathematical machines & turn the handles. But neither our Statistics nor our mathematics are ready for this work. We are like the first assailants of a fortified position: our corpses will fill the trenches so that others can get on.'

All honour to such work, providing it claims only to be mathematical exercises of high value to *future* economists!

[1] Columbia University Library, H. L. Moore Papers. For the circumstances bringing this fragment into Henry Ludwell Moore's possession see [1013]. Marshall had written, on the first of the two double sheets preserved, the following note to Edgeworth: 'I would be much obliged if you wd

at your leisure return these two sheets with comments, say in red ink as frank & outspoken as they [the sheets] are.' Edgeworth's notes were returned separately: see [1013]. Marshall also added, possibly for Moore's benefit, 'Date about 16,1,12.' The double sheets were subsequently separated into four single ones, each written on both sides, comprising pp. 5–12, although only 5, 7, 8, 11, are numbered.

[2] Moore had presumably sent Marshall a copy of his *Laws of Wages: An Exercise in Statistical Economics* (Macmillan, New York, 1911).

[3] See *Early Economic Writings*, vol. 2, pp. 39–42, for example.

[4] Reference to pp. 12–13, where the relationship between men's and women's wages in different States is displayed, would have been more accurate.

[5] For explication see *Principles* (*8*), pp. 556, 715–6 n, where the family is regarded as an economic unit with a given supply price.

1009. To John Neville Keynes, 30 January 1912[1]

30. 1. 12

My dear Keynes,

I am very much rejoiced at learning from the Reporter that Foxwell will join the Economics Board again.[2]

I was much grieved when he left it, his return will be a great source of strength. I do not venture to write to tell him this: but, if you shd think it expedient at any time to let him know how glad I am about it, I shall be much obliged by your doing so.[3]

Yours very sincerely | Alfred Marshall

[1] Marshall Library, J. N. Keynes Papers. From Balliol Croft.

[2] *Reporter*, 6 February 1912. Foxwell had resigned in 1908 when his bid to succeed Marshall as Professor failed. See [909]. He was appointed until 31 December 1912, and was to remain on the Board until 1920.

[3] This note must have been enclosed with a letter Keynes wrote to Foxwell on 31 January. In his reply to this letter on 6 February (Marshall Library, J. N. Keynes Papers) Foxwell wrote:

> I return Marshall's note. It has an unpleasantly false ring about it, & he was right not to address it to me. I have no doubt he is glad now, as he always has been, that others should help in work which he himself despises & neglects, I mean in providing for the poll man, for examinations, & in correspondence with the outside world. But for the people who thus oblige I believe he has in his inner feeling a very honest contempt; & at any rate he has left me in no sort of doubt as to the value he sets on any service it is in my power to render.
>
> However his opinion doesnt affect me one way or the other. I do not think judgement his strong point.

1010. To the Editor, *Daily Chronicle*, 25 March 1912[1]

In answer to your question, I reply that I can readily believe that the Government have not sufficient data in their possession to decide how a 5s. minimum would work; and I am sure I have not nearly enough data. I have not followed the discussions fully, for, indeed, I am not quite well, and am about to go for a few weeks to the South of Europe.

But I have not noticed that attention has been called to one of the chief objections to the proposal in question. It is that a uniform national minimum would very greatly increase the evils without materially increasing the benefits of collective bargaining as to wages. It is well known that a minimum wage works almost entirely for good when it causes those who are a little slack in temperament to rouse themselves and make themselves worth having to the employer at that wage; and of course when it checks the real 'sweater,' that is the employer who is 'good at a bargain.' But it does harm when it is so high that, except in times of booming trade, a considerable number of those who seek employment either cannot make themselves worth it at all at that wage, or can do so only by working harder than is good for them. So long as a man can enjoy both his work, and his rest after it, the harder he works the better it is generally for him and the State; but work that is so hard as to destroy the joy of rest is almost wholly evil.

[*The Strong and the Weak*]

Collective bargaining for a standard time wage is responsible for much unemployment, and for much work that is so hard as to be injurious to all but very strong workers. I have often been told by men not yet in full middle-age that night was almost as dreary as the day, because they were too tired to sleep; and yet a man of 25 would take a 20-mile walk or a 60-mile cycle ride on a Sunday or other holiday, in the intervals of such work; what was food for him was poison to them. This evil is great, but it is much less than would be caused if national standard or minima wages were substituted generally for local.

As things are, the stronger and abler men in low-waged districts frequently migrate to the larger opportunities of high-waged districts, and prosper. Weaklings, or [those who][2] overrate their own abilities, migrate also; but, unable to get continuous employment at the higher standard, they go home, and they are not very unhappy after all. When a unionist cannot get steady employment at a high-waged district, his union pays his travelling expenses to one in which the standard of ability is not beyond his reach, and tell him he must go there.

Such geographical sorting is, of course, not made with perfect ease and accuracy; there is a considerable ragged edge of failure. But on the whole local minima and standards evoke healthy energy, raise average wages, and do not do incidental harm comparable to that which would be done by a national minimum high enough to be suitable to the more prosperous districts.

[*Local Minima.*]

I agree that local minima are needed in the public interest in coal mining more than in other trades, because supervision underground is difficult, and disagreements as to facts are inevitable. None but fairly energetic men should go there; and 5s. is not too high a wage for such men, especially where there is much danger. But a national wage makes no allowance for local variations of danger.

I have not referred to the broad and grave danger that would arise if the State were to make a beginning of fixing wages. I hold that such a course might probably bring national disaster. I must not develop this theme. I will only say that I desire that the State should be active, resolute, cautiously venturesome in destroying the present grievous inequalities of wealth by measures that give as nearly as possible equal starts in life to rich and poor; but I do not desire that Government should be responsible for the nation's business.

P.S.—To simplify negotiations the minimum wage for an ordinary labourer might be fixed at, say, half the minimum agreed locally for hewers, with 2s. added.

[1] Printed in the *Daily Chronicle*, 25 March 1912, in conjunction with an article headed 'To End the Deadlock.' With the country in the grip of a coal strike, the Government had recently rejected demands for a national minimum wage for miners of 5s. per day, proposing instead local regulation, a decision endorsed by Marshall. The subheadings were presumably inserted by the newspaper.
[2] Words apparently omitted.

1011. To John Harold Clapham, 17 May 1912[1]

17. 5. 12

My dear Clapham

Our talk on Wednesday about University Reform[2] drifted away on to German Doctorates. May I say a little more about it.

I hold that the University s^{hd}. be represented to the world as German Universities are mainly by their chief students, being also their chief teachers: & that all such persons should receive the title of Professor from the University, as they do in London. I would wish that those professors who have no official duties except to the University sh^{d}. be increased in numbers but that, in order to avoid any attack on the College system, their ranks s^{hd}. be further enlarged so as to include all College lecturers, whose work in study & in teaching is of so high a quality that they would be 'generally recognised' as worthy candidates for full University Professorships, when suitable vacancies occurred in them.[3] 'General recognition' s^{hd}. I think be expressed by a vote of the Senate on a Report made by a General Professorial Electorate. That s^{hd}. I think be made up of men of the same class as those who are now electors for particular Professorships: & number about twenty in all. The Electorate w^{d}. of course appoint a Committee, partly consisting of their own members, to report to them, & they w^{d}., if they thought fit, report to the Senate. (I dont bother you with details: but I s^{hd}. wish, while conforming to the general idea of the present reports on candidates for Doctors degrees, to avoid certain evils, w^h. experience has shown to be likely under the present system.)

Probably the initiative s^{hd}. be taken by the College, w^h. desired that one of its lecturers s^{hd}. receive the rank of Professor: it s^{hd}. conform to certain general rules as to the extent to w^h. his terms w^d. be occupied with College work, & the salary (fellowship included) w^h. he would draw from the College.

I think that there are perhaps 150 men at Cambridge at present whose work is in the main Professorial; that is, advanced study combined with high grade teaching.

I have some more fads: but I wont bother you with them.

Yours very sincerely | Alfred Marshall

[1] Marshall Papers. From a copy in Mrs Marshall's hand.

[2] For details of the University Reforms Committee, formed in February 1911, of which both Clapham and Maynard Keynes were active members, see D. E. Moggridge, *Maynard Keynes* [846.1], p. 193.

[3] At this time, many teachers in Cambridge held only college posts, although those holding University posts were frequently associated with a college, as Marshall had been.

1012. To Sir Joseph Larmor, 18 May 1912[1]

18. 5. 12

Dear Larmor,

My wife & I will not be at home in August: but we should be glad if our house could be of service as night quarters to Mathematical Congress visitors,[2] in case there should be any difficulty about [putting][3] up them (& their wives).

When the British Association last met in Cambridge,[4] Tanner was away; and we got leave to put up some of our § F guests in his house. They were offered their breakfasts there: but, as it happened, they preferred to have all their meals here. At the last S.J.C. great Commemoration, the rôles were inverted; & some of Tanner's guests slept here. The plan worked well on both occasions.

The plan might be specially convenient for you; if people, who had an attraction for you, brought wives or daughters with them. If you think you would not care to adopt it, but that Hobson[5] perhaps might, my wife will call on Mrs Hobson & talk it over. There is no hurry whatever about an answer. We are to go away about July 15, as at present arranged. But our redoubtable housekeeper could make all the necessary arrangements on a few hours notice, if she had reason to think she was likely to be called on. In that case a P.C. to 'Miss Payne',[6] sent by you on the day before the visitors arrived would be sufficient.

Yours sincerely | Alfred Marshall

[1] St John's College, Cambridge, Miscellaneous Letters. From Balliol Croft. Joseph Larmor (1857–1942), knighted 1909, had been a Fellow of St John's since 1880. He was Lucasian Professor of Mathematics, 1903–32.

[2] The fifth International Congress of Mathematics was to be held in Cambridge, August 22–8 1912. Edgeworth and Bowley were active in the section on 'Statistical, Economic, and Actuarial Mathematics': *Economic Journal*, 22 (June 1912), p. 349.

[3] Word apparently accidentally omitted, as was the parenthesis concluding the sentence.

[4] In August 1904: see [792.4, 794, 798].

[5] Ernest William Hobson (1856–1933) of Christ's, Sadleiran Professor of Pure Mathematics, 1910–31.

[6] Sarah Payne.

1013. To Henry Ludwell Moore, 5 June 1912[1]

5. 6. 12

Dear Professor Moore,

When your letter[2] arrived, I had been sent to a London nursing home for a trifling dental operation: this explains delay.

I will be frank. I have had your book on Laws of Wages[3] in a prominent place near my writing chair ever since it arrived, intending to read it when opportunity came. It has not come: & I fear it never will come. For what dips I have made into the book, make me believe that it proceeds on lines which I deliberately decided not to follow many years ago; even before mathematics had ceased to be a familiar language to me. My reasons for it are mainly two. (1) No important economic chain of events seems[4] likely to be associated with any one cause so predominantly that a study of the concomitant variations of the two can be made as well by Mathematics, as by a comparison of a curve representing those two elements with a large number of other curves representing other operative causes: the '*coeteris paribus*' clause—though formally adequate seems to me impracticable.

(2) Nearly a half of the whole operative economic causes have refused as yet to be tabulated statistically.

I have worked at the comparative diagrammatic method, (indicated in a paper read at the Statistical Society 'Jubilee Volume' 1885 pp 252 &c)[5] persistently: and each of the last 40 years has confirmed me in the belief that your method is not likely to have practical fruit for a long while.

I am extremely glad you (& I hope others)[6] are working at it: it may do good practical work in your life time; but I feel sure it will not in mine.

My power of work is *very* small. I have half done many things wh I cannot hope to publish. Talking fatigues me in a very unusual manner. And, finally, it would be wrong for me to encourage you to come to Cambridge for a serious conversation.

But if you are coming to Cambridge to see others, & would like to take lunch (1.30) or afternoon tea (4.15) with my wife & myself; & discuss general topics, we shall be honoured by the opportunity of making your acquaintance.

Next Friday would not suit us: but we have *at present* no engagement for any other day. If you write nominating a time, I will write (or if necessary wire) should that particular time be already mortgaged.

Yours very truly | Alfred Marshall

P.S. I have plucked up my courage to perhaps a point where it should be called rash, or even impudent, audacity. I have decided to send you two sheets of a letter I wrote early in the year to Edgeworth in answer to one of his[7] in which he spoke of your book among other things. I wrote, just before posting it, the lines underscored at the top of p 5 (the first which related to you).[8] His answer was on a separate letter:[9] but he has told you his position in the *Economic Journal*[10] & perhaps elsewhere. I am afraid that my remarks will seem to you very wild prattle in comparison with his. But they are the sort of things wh I should be glad to read, even with a wry face, if written by others about my own work. So I send them; & trust that you will (1) forgive me & (2) kindly abstain from asking me to defend them.

[1] Columbia University Library, H .L. Moore Papers. From Balliol Croft.
[2] Not traced.
[3] See [1008.2].
[4] Followed by 'to' in the original.
[5] See *Memorials*, pp. 175–87, for the text of Marshall's 'The Graphic Method of Statistics.'
[6] In the original this parenthesis is placed after the 'it' that follows.
[7] Not traced.
[8] Pages 5–12 of Marshall's letter to Edgeworth, forwarded to Moore with the present letter, are reproduced as [1008]. The underscored lines comprise the note given in [1008.1].
[9] Not traced.
[10] See Edgeworth's review of Moore's *Law of Wages*, *Economic Journal*, 22 (March 1912), pp. 66–71. This elicited a reply from Moore (June), pp. 314–17, followed (pp. 317–23) by an uncharacteristically acerbic rejoinder from Edgeworth.

1014. From Henry Ludwell Moore, 6 June 1912[1]

Moscow Mansions,[2]
June 6, 1912.

Dear Professor Marshall:

I have just this moment read your letter[3] and I am aglow with pleasure over its sincerity and frankness. Do not think that I am using words carelessly when I say that, in consequence of what you have written me, I now associate with my admiration for your work, an affectionate regard for you. I hope I do not say too much; but I am anxious that you should know how wisely you have acted in speaking out your whole mind as to what I have done.

What you say in the way of general criticism I shall take as caution in my future work: I do not feel that it applies to what I have already done, and consequently I am not dispirited. If you should ever read the work and should find that your first impression was not just, you will I am sure tell me so in a word. I am very far indeed from wishing to ask you to read even so much as a chapter.

You will not misunderstand my not accepting your invitation to lunch with you and Mrs. Marshall. My reason for asking you to let me call on you was not that we might have a serious conversation on economic questions, for I was quite sincere in limiting the visit to half an hour. I simply wished to know you in person.[4] But you should not be subjected to the excitement of meeting me, and this is my sole reason for not accepting your invitation.

I shall treasure your letter and the outspoken criticism you sent to Professor Edgeworth.[5] I doubt whether I shall ever again receive so frank and so generous treatment from a fellow-worker.

Yours very sincerely [Henry L. Moore]

[1] Columbia University Library, H. L. Moore Papers. From an unsigned transcript retained by Moore, together with his rough draft.
[2] 224 Cromwell Road, London.
[3] See [1013].
[4] The rough draft had added here 'I have spent profitable years in the study of your work'.
[5] See [1013, 1008].

1015. To James Bonar, 18 June 1912 (incomplete)[1]

18. vi. 1912

Dear Bonar,

... Speaking generally I may say that the chief interest in Symmetallism departed with the collapse of Fixed-ratio-mintage: and that the changes in the arts of extracting gold from the earth, etc., in which it is embedded have been so great, and the discoveries of gold fields so extensive, that the facts of a quarter of a century ago—with which my evidence[2] was largely concerned—are mostly obsolete. As to the analytical part of the evidence I have not consciously changed my position. It is set out in some directions more fully in my evidence before the Committee on Indian Currency of 1899[3] ...

Yours ever, | A.M.

[1] Printed in *Memorials*, p. 375. Original not traced. From Balliol Croft.
[2] To the Gold and Silver Commission 1888–9: see *Official Papers*, pp. 17–195.
[3] See *Official Papers*, pp. 263–326.

1016. To Ludwig Joseph Brentano, 18 June 1912[1]

18. 6. 12

Dear Professor Brentano,

The bearer of this, C. W. Guillebaud (a 'Huguenot' name) is a nephew of mine. He was in the first class of our Economics 'Tripos' Part I last summer. He is to take Part II of the Tripos next summer. He wants to know Germany more intimately than he does yet; & so he is a member of the German-Tour party of English students. That brings him to Munich now. But his main cause for venturing to break in on your busy & important occupations is that he hopes to sit at your feet during the Autumn of this year. Possibly you may kindly find time to give him some hints as to University work: he need not occupy it as to his private affairs—lodgings &c—: for, as to those he is already cared for.[2]

Yours very sincerely | Alfred Marshall

[1] Bundesarchiv, Koblenz, Brentano Papers. From Balliol Croft.

[2] In a note to Brentano of 9 October 1912, Marshall told him 'My nephew took a great fancy to Munich; and he was especially delighted with your very kind reception & helpful conversation'. On 21 March 1913, following his nephew's longer visit, he wrote (in German) further thanks for Brentano's kindness (Brentano Papers).

It must have been in this or the preceding year that Claude received from his uncle a letter criticizing the buying of inessential books and advising him to live hard, work hard, and spend little, until established in a career (undated fragment, Marshall Papers).

1017. From John Harold Clapham, 12 October 1912[1]

55, Bateman Street, | Cambridge,
Octr 12

Dear Dr. Marshall

Will you accept this? It is not Economic History—tho it contains a few economic fragments. If it is anything it is my little monument to the second of the two men from whom I drew my chief inspiration in earlier days.[2] And as I cannot give him a copy I give one to the first, with the fear that he may think that all my strength should have been put out elsewhere. He will be glad to know that this was off my hands in the spring, since when all my leisure has been economically employed.

Yours very truly | J H Clapham

I believe you will like the motto on the title page.[3]

[1] Glued to the cover of a copy of J. H. Clapham, *The Abbé Sieyès* (King, London, 1912) inscribed 'To Alfred Marshall from his sometimes errant pupil JHC'. The volume is now in the Marshall Library. Emmanuel Joseph Comte Sieyès (1748–1836), French prelate and Revolutionary leader.

[2] Lord Acton.

[3] 'On parlait à Sieyès du mépris qu' affectent éternellement ses détracteurs pour ce qu' ils appellent les grandes théories. Les théories, dit-il, sont la pratique des siècles; et leurs pratiques sont la théorie du moment qui s'écoule—Roederer, Works IV, 204'.

1018. To Irving Fisher, 14 October 1912 (incomplete)[1]

14. x. 12

Dear Professor Fisher,

... The scheme for a national stable-value currency which you send me has very great attractions.[2] But as you know I now, though not in 1887, think that international trade would be too much troubled by a set of national currencies; and that a national value-unit (or groups of such units) should be kept for long period domestic contracts and customary rates (wages etc.) only. I admit heartily that, if national currencies on your plan were generally set up, the limits of fluctuation of the Foreign Exchanges would be less than on any other plan for artificial national currencies which I know. But I can get no further than that.

And I would ask you to consider whether your regulations would supply a sufficiently powerful force to keep the volume of the U.S. currency at the level required for your purpose, unless the other chief countries had nearly the same regulations. When $100 purchased *more* than a hundred dollar units of general commodities, gold might indeed be brought to the mint in spite of the seignorage which was still being charged (though charged at a lower rate of course than when prices were higher). But even in this case the adjustment might not be very rapid: the speculative strain involved in deciding whether the seignorage was likely to go lower or not would be considerable: and the new dollars might for a long while be insufficient for their work; might they not?

And on the other hand if, when the gold dollar, i.e. the unit of value, was much above its gold value, a development of banking or other cause reduced the total purchasing power needed to be held in coin, might not there be a great rise in prices in U.S. while prices elsewhere were at rest? Would not the gold dollars need to stay until their value had been caught up by that of gold bullion?

These are only hasty half-thoughts. But even so they throw me out of my feeble stride. I *must* adhere to my rule of not going into any complex matter that does not arise out of the particular writing which I have in hand at the time. May I therefore ask you to be so very good as to let these few weak words be my last on the subject?

I am yours very sincerely, | Alfred Marshall

[1] Printed in *Memorials*, pp. 477–8. Original not traced. From Balliol Croft. See [1006].

[2] Fisher had probably sent a duplicated transcript of his 'Memorandum on a More Stable Gold Standard: A Proposal for a "Compensated Dollar" as a Partial Remedy for the Rising Cost of Living' (1912). (There is a copy in the Library of Congress.) The idea of varying the gold content of the dollar so as to stabilize the price level was to become something of an obsession to Fisher. See his 'A More Stable Gold Standard', *Economic Journal*, 22 (December 1912), pp. 570–6; 'A Compensated Dollar', *Quarterly Journal of Economics*, 27 (February 1913), pp. 213–35, 385–97; and his retrospect (with Hans R. L. Cohrsson), *Stable Money: A History of the Movement* (Adelphi, New York, 1934).

1019. To Irving Fisher, 15 October 1912[1]

15. x. 12

Dear Professor Fisher,

On further consideration it occurred to me that I could not have advocated an artificial national currency in 1887. I have just looked up my article in the

Contemporary Review,[2] and I find that my goal was an artificial *unit* for long standing contracts and arrangements, and the restriction of currency to passing bargains. When Giffen uttered his vehement trumpet blast against 'Fancy Monetary Standards' (No. XIX of his collected *Inquiries and Studies*),[3] I chaffed him about his energy; and I recollect that he said that his argument was not opposed to my scheme. Recollecting that just now, I further remembered that my doubt about the practicability of my original scheme was connected with International Stock Exchange securities bearing a fixed rate of interest (among other things).

Yours very sincerely, | Alfred Marshall

[1] Printed in *Memorials*, p. 478. Original not traced. From Balliol Croft, an addendum to [1018].
[2] 'Remedies for Fluctuations in General Prices': see *Memorials*, pp. 188–211 for the text.
[3] R. Giffen, 'Fancy Monetary Standards', *Economic Journal*, 2 (September 1892), pp. 463–71; reprinted in his *Economic Inquiries and Studies* (Bell, London, 1904).

1020. To John Harold Clapham, 4 November 1912[1]

4. 11. 12

My dear Clapham

I s^{hd}. like much to attend the meeting about University Reform on Thursday: but I fear I must not do so.

As I made to you a part of my Confession of Faith about it, I will add one more item.

I think that working men at Oxford or Cambridge will seldom profit as much as they would at a non-residential University, where they w^{d}. be on equal terms with other students without inordinate expense. And I think that the revenues of Oxford & Cambridge are inadequate for their own needs as leaders of study & as teachers of the teachers at other Universities.

But I think our foundations are held in trust for the nation, & are not the property of the well-to-do: & that therefore they ought to be devoted mainly to the necessary expenses of teaching & study in those branches of knowledge w^{h}. contribute most directly to national well-being. I interpret this to mean that our revenues s^{hd}. be so distributed as to promote preferentially work that will directly affect the future of the world, while studies of the past, w^{h}. affect the future only indirectly, s^{hd}. be supported mainly by the private purses of the well-to-do.

I am aware that money will not effect all that is needed in this direction. So long as Headmasters are out of sympathy with scientific study, they inevitably draw towards classical studies nearly all those boys who are resolute in character & keen in mind, & therefore capable of good scientific work.

I say this the more freely, because I do not think that Economics can advantageously be taught at school: & I do not think it w^{d}. be well that Economics s^{hd}. be studied by very many men even at Cambridge.

I write this to you as an individual & not as a member of the Reform Comt[ee] but it is not private.
Yours very sincerely | Alfred Marshall

[1] Marshall Papers. From a copy in Mrs Marshall's hand. See [1011].

1021. To John Maynard Keynes, 12 April 1913[1]

12. 4. 13

My dear Keynes,
I am delighted to know the youngest member of the youngest Commission; & I think almost the youngest of any. You are the right man for the place. But you will need to husband your strength.
Yours happily | Alfred Marshall

[1] King's College, Cambridge, J. M. Keynes Papers. From Balliol Croft. Reproduced in *Collected Works*, vol. 15, p. 98. Written on the occasion of Keynes's appointment at age 29 to be a member of the Royal Commission on Indian Finance and Currency.

1022. From Sir Frederick Macmillan, 14 May 1913[1]

Macmillan & Co. Ltd. | St. Martin's Street
London W.C. May 14 1913

Dear Professor Marshall,
I am very glad to learn from your letter received this morning[2] that you are now restored to health. I hope that you will be careful to obey the doctors orders & that you will not allow your natural anxiety to get the new book off your hands, to lead you into over-working.

I understand that your present scheme is to go to press with volumes I and II of 'National Industry and Trade' in the Autumn of this year leaving volume III to follow as soon as may be. This strikes me as a very good plan, & I hope you will not allow the necessity to have a good deal of the book in type at once to worry you. We can easily arrange with the printers to meet your convenience on this point.

I quite agree with you that the double leading is not necessary: indeed I think that the page with the thin lead is better to look at and quite as easy to read as the more open one. I return the specimen pages with the Preface & Introduction[3] which I am glad to have had the opportunity of reading.

We will certainly not fix the price of the book without first consulting you & shall be glad to make it as low as is reasonable.

With kind regards I am | Yours very truly | Frederick Macmillan

Professor Marshall
Cambridge

[1] Marshall Papers.
[2] Not traced.
[3] Presumably for *National Industry and Trade* as it then stood and subsequently revised or abandoned.

1023. To the Vice Chancellor, Cambridge University, October 1913[1]

Oct. 1913

Dear Vice Chancellor

In view of the cessation of the triennial Essay Prize provided by the Cobden Club,[2] I desire to offer to the University funds for a prize to take its place.

No doubt the earlier work of a student in economics can be best tested by examinations: but his mature & higher work seems to need a stimulus similar to that elsewhere offered to men of the age of our junior Graduates by writing Doctor's Degree Dissertations on subjects of their own choice: and under existing conditions our best means to that end seems to be an Essay Prize with a similar free choice of subjects.

I should therefore like the new prize to be of the same value & title, and to be awarded under the same conditions as the Adam Smith Prize, at present given by Professor Pigou:[3] but I propose that the University shall be free to modify the arrangements for the Prize in case occasion should arise.

The new prize would naturally be awarded at the same times as the Cobden Prize has been; so that equal intervals, of eighteen months each, shall intervene between two successive prizes.

Professor Pigou has suggested that, since some students find it difficult to hit upon suitable subjects for their essays, the Examiners should set out a few specimen subjects as aids to the choice; but not so as in any way to limit the freedom of that choice. It seems that this can be done under the existing Regulations; provided the additional examiner is appointed early, as is usual in the case of Prizes for which subjects are set.[4]

I remain | Dear Vice Chancellor | Yours very truly | Alfred Marshall

[1] Cambridge University Archives, Records for the Marshall and Adam Smith Prizes. From Balliol Croft. The Vice Chancellor at this time was Montague Rhodes James (1862–1936), Provost of King's.
[2] The Cobden Club had recently withdrawn the triennial essay prize it had offered since established in 1876.
[3] The triennial Adam Smith Prize of £60, established in 1891 (Vol. 2 [337]), had been continued from Pigou's pocket after Marshall's retirement in 1908.

[4] There was some change in the proposal by the time it was brought to the attention of Senate in a report of 17 November by Council of Senate (*Reporter*, 18 November 1913). This report printed a revised letter of 7 November from Marshall. This deleted the third and fourth paragraphs of the present letter and inserted between its first and second paragraphs the following additional paragraphs

> My first notion was that a second prize should be awarded at the same time as the Cobden Prize has been; but that it should be of the same value and title and under the same conditions as the Adam Smith Prize, at present given by Professor Pigou.
>
> But it has been suggested that the income, proposed for this purpose, would be better applied in awarding an annual prize of about £20 under like conditions, to be supplemented for the present by the money which Professor Pigou would have otherwise devoted to the present triennial Adam Smith Prize. He is, I believe, writing to you independently approving the suggestion, in which I heartily concur.
>
> I propose, subject to the approval of the Financial Board, to transfer to the University £600 Great Western Railway Four per cent. Debentures for this purpose.

There was also some minor rephrasing. Pigou's letter, also reproduced in the Report, proposed to contribute whatever was necessary to bring up the prize to £40 (with an extra £5 for an examiner additional to the Professor of Political Economy). Since the annual income from Marshall's endowment was £24 less income tax, Pigou was thus paying about half the cost and over three years, more or less the same amount as before (£60 + £10 for an examiner). The recommended regulations specified 'an Essay on some unsettled question in Economic Science, or in some branch of Economic History or Statistics subsequent to the year 1800 A.D.' The examiners might suggest—but not prescribe—topics, and in awarding the prize should have regard to 'the constructive ability and the grasp of scientific principles rather than to the erudition displayed', thus continuing the principles established in 1891.The report was discussed on 27 November (*Reporter*, 2 December) the only recorded remarks being by J. N. Keynes who, on behalf of those 'specially interested in the study of Economics in the University', warmly welcomed the gift and expressed deep gratitude for it. The Vice Chancellor wrote to Marshall on 19 December to inform him that the Grace accepting his gift had passed Senate, adding 'I do not think that the Vice-Chancellor is often called upon to acknowledge a more generous & public-spirited offer than yours' (Marshall Papers).

1024. From Charles Booth, 10 November 1913[1]

28 Campden House Court, | Kensington, W.
10 November 1913

My dear Marshall,

Your letter[2] was delightful to get; but you are far too kind, too good, & too generous; and I should be sorry indeed to think that your kindness had led you away even for an hour from the path of your own work.

My pamphlet[3] is crude, and the practical application of its proposals very difficult. All I can hope for is to widen the ideas of the Trade Unionists. But if my proposals should come to be realised & put in practice, I think there would be sufficient natural check on misuse; since if a long-sighted broad minded[4] policy were not pursued failure would quickly result.

I look forward much to the coming volume.

My wife is in Scotland but would wish to join in love to Mrs Marshall & yourself.

Ever yours sincerely | Charles Booth

[1] University of London Library, Booth Papers.

[2] Not traced.

[3] C. Booth, *Industrial Unrest and Trade Union Policy* (Macmillan, London, 1913).

[4] 'broad minded' reiterated in the original.

1025. To Edwin Cannan, 16 January 1914[1]

16. 1. 14

Dear Cannan,

Many thanks for *Wealth.*[2] I envy the brevity of your title, & hope to get much profit from the book, when I can get at it.

Yours very truly | Alfred Marshall

[1] BLPES, Cannan Papers. From Balliol Croft.

[2] E. Cannan, *Wealth: A Brief Explanation of the Causes of Economic Welfare* (King, London, 1914), based on first-year lectures given at the London School of Economics.

1026. To John Maynard Keynes, 9 March 1914[1]

9. 3. 14

Dear Keynes,

The I.C. Report[2] came in at lunch time. I am behind hand with copy for the Press; so I thought I would not do more than get to know its general drift just at present.

But I dipped in here & there, & then read the conclusions: & finally turned negligently to the Annexe. But that held me. I had had no idea you had written it. Much of it, as of the Report itself, deals with matters beyond my knowledge and judgment. But there is quite enough of it within my understanding for me to have been entranced by it as a prodigy of constructive work. Verily we old men will have to hang ourselves, if young people can cut their way so straight & with such apparent ease through such great difficulties.

I thought of several objections as I read: but on going further, I found all of them met except one. Probably there is an answer to that also: but I did not see it. The objection is that in being generous to the shareholders in the Presidency Banks, you may possibly have been a little less than just to other credit institutions (I purposely use a broad vague term), English & Native; and also perhaps to the Indian State. I have always felt a little jealous of those Presidency Banks: they seem to me to have none of the obligations of a State Bank, & yet some of its sources of profit: & the new Bank wd be able to override competitors who might have held their own against the Presidency Banks.

Again I have always thought the Bank of England Parlour as it was described by Bagehot contained elements, wh a State Bank should consider; & try to get something of them if possible. I admit that the fortunate accidents, which made it so strong say 40 years ago, are not as prominent now as then: and that state banks are for many reasons in a stronger position than then. But yet, I think, I should like to inquire—if I ever went into the matter, which of course I shall not do—whether some Assessors might not be nominated (subject perhaps to conditions, including a veto in exceptional cases) by other financial authorities. Also *some* of them might perhaps have the right to subscribe for a few shares of The Bank at par.

I found in talking to the Indian experts in 1898 that the work of the native financiers (Banyans I fancy they were called) was not fully understood: and I doubted even whether Englishmen in India understand it. Several natives of India have talked to me confidentially about the relations of Indians & English: & they were unanimous in the opinion that Anglo-Indians, even the best informed, have no conception how much there is to be known about India which is beyond the knowledge of Englishmen. The extent of native hoarding was one of the subjects to wh these conversations referred.

But I have made a sufficient display of matters on which I certainly know much less than you: so I will end

Yours enthusiastically | Alfred Marshall

[1] King's College, Cambridge, J. M. Keynes Papers. From Balliol Croft. Reproduced in *Collected Works*, vol. 15, p. 268, where the surrounding material provides background. Also reproduced in *Memorials*, pp. 479–50.

[2] The Report of the Royal Commission on Indian Finance and Currency: see [1021.1].

1027. To the Editor, *The Times*, 22 August 1914[1]

Sir,—I think that all will welcome Dr. Prothero's suggestion[2] that means should be taken to explain to the nation that the war on which we have entered is one of self-defence, as well as a debt due to France and Belgium in return for aid which we have expected in time of our need. It is certain that Germany has long resolved to obtain so firm a hold on Antwerp, or Rotterdam, or both, that she will be able to control the narrow sea. I have never come across a German who avowed a preference for force as the means of obtaining control of those ports, but I have repeatedly been told that Germany's trade is becoming so vital to Belgium and Holland that a threat to divert a large part of it by hostile tariffs, railway rates, &c., will ere long be sufficient to force them into a close commercial alliance with the Zollverein, which would include full access to their ports at all times. And Napoleon's saying that Antwerp is a pistol pointed at the heart of England is not forgotten.

But Dr. Prothero refers to the danger that popular lectures might be made attractive by bitter denunciation of the Germans. Experience shows that acrimony and the repetition of lurid tales come ready to the mouth of an excited lecturer bent on holding the attention of a general audience. I think, therefore, that those who know and love Germany, even while revolted at the hectoring militarism which is more common there than here, should insist that we have no cause to scorn them, though we have good cause to fight them. For instance, tales of their shooting civilians in cold blood should never be repeated without inquiring whether the laws of war had been broken by hostile action on the part of non-combatants. I was in Berlin in the winter of the Franco-German war, and my friends complained bitterly of the willingness of Englishmen to believe that civilians, who had not so offended, had been ill-treated by them. As a people I believe them to be exceptionally conscientious and upright, sensitive to the calls of duty, tender in their family affections, true and trusty in friendship. Therefore they are strong and to be feared, but not to be vilified.

Their jingoes boast that they can 'waste' a million men and yet have a strong army. If every means of annoying them, even if it do not affect the main course of the war, is sought out, as some of your correspondents urge, then they will waste two millions rather than give in. If after all they conquer they will hold Antwerp and be provided by a war indemnity with the means of building innumerable Dreadnoughts. It is therefore our interest as well as our duty to respect them and make clear that we desire their friendship, but yet to fight them with all our might.

Alfred Marshall.

Cambridge, Aug. 22.

[1] Printed in *The Times*, 22 August 1914, under the heading 'A Fight to a Finish'. Original not traced. Britain had declared war on Germany on 4 August 1914. That the letter should have been written on the day it was published seems improbable, and a composition date of 21 August seems more likely.

[2] See the letter 'A Fight to a Finish' by George Walter Prothero printed in *The Times*, 20 August 1914 (3b). Prothero (1848–1927), editor of the *Quarterly Review* from 1899 to 1922, had been a Fellow of King's and was University Lecturer in History, 1883–94, before migrating to Edinburgh where he was Professor of History, 1894–9. Knighted 1920.

1028. To the Editor, *The Times*, 25 August 1914[1]

Sir,—The letters in your issue of to-day by Mr. Page and 'Union Jack'[2] show that my letter, published by you last Saturday,[3] lends itself to misinterpretation. Before Germany had answered by deeds the question whether she intended to respect the neutrality of Belgium, I was asked to sign a statement that we ought not to go to war because we had no interest in the coming struggle. I replied:—'I think the question of peace or war must turn on national duty as much as on our interest. I hold that we ought to mobilize instantly, and announce that we shall declare war if the Germans invade Belgium; and everybody knows they will.' Then came Dr. Prothero's letter published by you last Friday.[4] It emphasized the dangers with which Germany's recently developed ambitions threaten us, and suggested that these dangers should be explained in popular lectures.

My 'professorial' duties have made me endeavour to ascertain at first hand the conditions and points of view of other nations. In 1900 I came across the *Alldeutscher Atlas*, a clear manifesto of the Pan-Germanic League.[5] I have shown it to several people, who were surprised at finding their own countries painted 'Germanic' in its maps; and I have talked to German and Austrian military men about the matter. In consequence I regard these dangers very seriously; and I adopted Dr. Prothero's uncompromising heading 'A fight to a finish.' But I go with him, and perhaps even a little beyond him, in anxiety lest popular lectures on the subject should inflame passions which will do little or nothing towards securing victory; but may very greatly increase the slaughter on both sides, which must be paid as the price of resisting Germany's aggressive tendencies. It is to be remembered that a great many Germans, especially among the working classes, are averse to wars of exploitation, but, like similar classes at home, are exasperated by insults to the Fatherland.

Among the people at home to whom it is most important to explain the necessity of a fight to a finish are those described by Mr. Maddison in your columns yesterday:[6]—

> The invasion of Belgium added to the enormity of the crime committed by the Prussian military caste and not by the great German people. Now, nothing would be more likely to convert the present sober determination of the people to break the power of this dominant militarism into a feeling of doubt, if not of disgust, than to let loose on them, especially in the north, the suggested perambulating bands of speakers, who would be regarded as little more than Jingo spell-binders.

Great responsibility, in which I personally am unable to share, must attach to those who undertake to select lecturers not liable to such reproach. It is to be remembered that those who conquered at Vicksburg were Lincoln's own men, careful of speech; those who ran away at Bull's Run had shouted insults against the Southerners.[7] The true 'craven' is he who vents his courage in the reckless use of offensive adjectives.[8]

Yours faithfully,

August 25. Alfred Marshall.

[1] Printed in *The Times*, 26 August 1914, under the heading 'A Fight to a Finish'. Original not traced.

[2] These letters were published under the heading 'A Fight to a Finish', *The Times*, 25 August 1914 (d–e). Page had written: "No rhetoric or denunciation can exaggerate the grim realities we may have to face, and talk about 'knowing and loving Germany" or about "a people exceptionally conscientious and upright", is not only idle and fatuous but at the present time misleading, hazardous and disloyal. It is by listening to such fantastical and academic stuff that we have been lured to apathy in the past.'

[3] That is [1027].

[4] See [1027.2]. Prothero's letter was actually published on *Thursday*, 20 August.

[5] Probably published by the Alldeutscher Verband, a German patriotic and expansionist association, based in Berlin and active 1891–1910.

[6] See the letter from F. Maddison of the International Arbitration League, *The Times*, 24 August 1914 (4d).

[7] At Vicksburg in 1863 the Union forces in the American Civil War, under Ulysses S. Grant, had won a decisive victory. The First Battle of Bull Run in 1861 had turned into a rout of the Union side due to overconfidence.

[8] The letter from 'Union Jack' had characterized Marshall's recommendations as 'craven'.

1029. To John Maynard Keynes, 8 October 1914[1]

8. 10. 14

Dear Keynes, I have just read with great admiration & profit your splendid article on war finance.[2] I think I agree with you on all points on wh I can form an independent opinion. But there is a good deal of ground beyond my ken. I have never seen my way to form an opinion on the controverted questions as to the relative advantages of the English & Continental methods of dealing with (1) specialized bills, or (2) the financing of businesses. My general notion is that system counts for less than men; & that the British system suited British conditions in Bagehot's time. But the consolidation of banks since his time opens out new problems, which I cannot grasp.

As to the ill conduct of particular banks in recent times, I know nothing: I am not inclined to suppose them all to be raised above sin. But on the other hand, my little experience inclines me to think that those whose stories of the wickedness of banks are the most incisive, are often those of whom the banks (if free to speak) could tell wicked stories.

Yours very sincerely, | Alfred Marshall

[1] King's College, Cambridge, J. M. Keynes Papers. From Balliol Croft. Reproduced in *Memorials*, p. 480.

[2] J. M. Keynes, 'War and the Financial System, August, 1914', *Economic Journal*, 24 (September 1914), pp. 460–86: reproduced in *Collected Works*, vol. 11, pp. 238–71.

1030. From John Maynard Keynes, 10 October 1914[1]

Kings College, | Cambridge.
10 October 1914

Dear D^{r}.. Marshall,

Thanks very much for your letter.[2] It was impossible to do justice to the question of the behaviour of the banks in the early days of the war without going into personalities, which was not possible in the Journal. Schuster and Holden[3] were the spokesmen of the bankers and the men whom the Treasury looked to as their leaders. The one was cowardly and the other selfish. They unquestionably behaved badly, and it is not disputed that they pressed strongly for suspension of cash payments by the Bank of England. By no means all of the other bankers either trusted S. and H. or agreed with their immediate proposals; but they were timid, voiceless and leaderless and in the hurry of the times did not make themselves heard. I think, however, that, taking a long view, the banks themselves are to blame for this. They are too largely staffed, apart from the directors, on what in the Civil Service is called a second division basis. Half of their directors, on the other hand, are appointed on hereditary grounds and two fifths, not on grounds of banking capacity, but because they are able, through their business connections, to bring to the bank a certain class of business. Naturally when the time comes they find themselves without a leader of the right kind. And no one but themselves is to blame. Parker,[4] here, tells me that the meetings at the Treasury took place before the Board of Barclays had an opportunity to meet. Of course they did. In crises you must have a few men at the top capable of taking wise decisions immediately. Fortunately we had a few such—but not amongst the Joint Stock Bankers.

At least that is my view of what happened.

Yours sincerely, | J M Keynes

[1] Marshall Papers. Reproduced in R. F. Harrod, *The Life of John Maynard Keynes* (Macmillan, London, 1951), pp. 197–8, with the names or initials of Schuster and Holden replaced by dashes. The version reproduced in *Collected Works*, vol. 16, pp. 30–1, replicated the Harrod version as 'the only version ... available'. The individuals involved were eventually identified from the Marshall Papers original by R. Skidelsky, *John Maynard Keynes* [846.1], p. 292.

[2] See [1029].

[3] Sir Felix Otto Schuster (1854–1936), Governor of the Union Bank of London, 1895–1918; Sir Edward Hopkinson Holden (1848–1919), Chairman of the London City and Midland Bank, 1908–19.

[4] Probably Edmund H. Parker [761.14], Borough Treasurer of Cambridge and a Director of Barclay's Bank, 1896–1925.

1031. To John Maynard Keynes, 12 October 1914[1]

12. 10. 14

Dear Keynes,

Many thanks for your letter,[2] which interested & informed me greatly.

Your experience goes on similar lines to that wh I had on the Labour Commission: the preponderance of heavy minds in the management of businesses that can be reduced to routine is a great evil. The minds of leading working men seemed often more elastic & strong.

I had this danger partly in mind when I thought of the need of some financial agencies outside of the banks, whose chief concern is with routine: much of which could, theoretically at least, be discharged by automatic machinery. I had mistaken the nature of the fault wh you found with the bankers.[3]

But I must stop. | Yours very sincerely, | Alfred Marshall

[1] King's College, Cambridge, J. M. Keynes Papers. From Balliol Croft. Reproduced in *Memorials*, p. 481.

[2] See [1030].

[3] This perhaps refers to conversation as no correspondence has survived on the points mentioned.

1032. To John Tressider Sheppard, 12 October 1914[1]

12 10 14

Dear Mr Sheppard,

I cannot talk for more than a short time without suffering from 'blood pressure': & therefore my wife & I are cut off from the power of offering hospitality to Belgians.[2] But my wife has just gone to the Claphams[3] to inquire as to your work for them, & find out whether we might be allowed to help them through you. She has just returned with the recommendation:—'offer to pay the expenses of half-a-Belgian'. We should like to do that, if we may. Will you tell me what & how I should remit.

I wonder whether you are related to the Sheppard who was Senior Wrangler in 1884; & who, unless my badly confused memory serves me amiss, was one of the first & most agreeable attendants at my lectures on my return to Cambridge.[4]

Yours very truly | Alfred Marshall

[1] King's College, Cambridge, Sheppard Papers. From Balliol Croft.

[2] Sheppard was active in the settlement of Belgian war refugees in the Cambridge area. Reports of German atrocities in Belgium had produced outrage and an outpouring of sympathy.

[3] Presumably the home of J. H. and Mrs Clapham (née Mary Margaret Green).

[4] William Fleetwood Sheppard (1863–1936), born in Australia, who found a career in the civil service. Apparently no relation.

1033. From Nina Cust, 16 October 1914[1]

Chancellor's House | 17, Hyde Park Gate, S.W.
Oct. 16 1914

Dear M^r^. Marshall

May I use the name of Lord Rayleigh or M^r^. Balfour as an introduction and add a personal note to my husband's more formal letter. We feel that your name will carry great weight abroad and we shall be exceedingly grateful if your are able to help us by permission to use it as suggested. I may add that any attempt

at instruction or pressure will be carefully avoided. If you are so kind as to send us an answer, would you perhaps address it to me (M[rs]. Henry Cust) here.
Yours very truly | Nina Cust

[1] Marshall Papers. Emmeline Mary Elizabeth (Nina) Cust (?–1955), née Welby-Gregory, novelist and daughter of a former maid-in-waiting to Queen Victoria, was the wife of Henry Cust (1861–1917), editor of the *Pall Mall Gazette*, 1892–6, and Member of Parliament, 1890–5 and 1900–6. He was Chairman of the Central Committee for National Patriotic Associations, formed in 1914, in which G. W. Prothero [1027.2] also played a leading rôle. The accompanying letter from Henry Cust has not been traced.

1034. To Nina Cust, 17 October 1914[1]

17. 10. 14

Dear Mrs Cust

I am highly honoured by the letters just received from M[r] Cust & yourself. But early last month, when sending to D[r] Prothero a small contribution towards the expense of disseminating accurate information as to the origins of the war, & the call it makes on Englishmen, I added that my lack of strength & other causes w[d] prevent me from taking any responsibility for the way in which this work was done. To that decision I must regretfully adhere.

I have read with great pleasure D[r] Prothero's excellent—*Our duty & our interest in the war*, & the short manifesto of your Committee.[2] But even these moderate & guarded pronouncements are not such as I could adopt without reserve. I am old: my mind has become fixed in grooves on some subjects, & in particular on the ethico-political-economic relations of England to other countries; & I cannot be sponsor for any opinions but my own. To write a single controversial, or even argumentative letter sets up 'blood pressure' & almost loses the day for me.

Thus I rejoice that the Manifesto warns people to be prepared for the possible, not probable, arrival of great national misfortune. And yet, I think that past history & recent events alike show that the people, even if left to themselves, w[d] rise to difficulty & danger; & I could have wished that to be put in the foreground. Again I entirely agree with D[r] Prothero that (p 13) a 'half & half victory is of no use to us': but I am not sure that the German people wish us to (p 9) 'drink the cup of degradation to the dregs': & I am sure that we ought to use our expected victory over them in such ways as may secure our own ends, while imposing the least possible degradation on them.

I believe it to be quite as true of a nation as of an individual that 'no one is ever written down by anyone but himself'. Bernhardi[3] has written down the Germans, I think, a great deal more effectively than any Englishman can do. Germanys assertions that we have been disloyal to Belgium seem to me innocuous: for Belgians know better.

On the other hand, when I read the *Board of Trade Journal* about taking the opportunity of the war for dishing German merchants in neutral countries, to say nothing of the less restrained arguments on the same subject in some newspapers, I am hurt by Germany's assertion that England alone among her foes regards the war as a means to sordid ends. If, as I fear, we have pushed this aspect of the war with disproportionate eagerness, we have perhaps written ourselves down more than the German Foreign Office have.

This letter is in a way the ending of some correspondence with Dr Prothero.[4] Perhaps you may be able to let him see it.

Yours very truly | Alfred Marshall

[1] Marshall Papers. From a copy in Mrs Marshall's hand. See [1033, 1033.1].

[2] G. W. Prothero, *Our Duty and Our Interest in the War* (Murray, London, 1914); The Manifesto has not been traced, but see *The Times*, 9 October 1914 (3c), for an account of the Committee's inaugural meeting. A letter from Prothero and Henry Cust announcing the formation of the Committee had appeared in *The Times*, 5 September 1914 (9d).

[3] Friedrich von Bernhardi (1849–1930), soldier and author of *Germany and the Next War* (1912), proposing Germany's world dominion.

[4] Not traced.

1035. To the Editor, *The Times*, 27 October 1914[1]

Sir,—I desire respectfully to endorse your plea for the dissemination of accurate information as to the conditions under which the civil population of a country may oppose the violence of an invading army. It should, I think, be in two forms: one statement should be technically exact, and somewhat full; while the other should be short, and expressed broadly in plain language. The Belgian Government had no time to arrange this; and a few errors by Belgian civilians seem to have been to some extent the real occasion, and to a greater extent the pretended occasion, of violence that has horrified the world. Invasion of our land is no doubt improbable; but that is no reason for omitting so easy a precaution against some of its worst evils.

There are scoundrels in every nation and in every army. The criminal population has been known to promote disorder and conflagration in order to cloak plunder; and soldiers of the same class may incline to goad peasants into fury in order that the 'punishment' of a village may remove obstacles to looting. But it seems that many troubles have been caused by soldiers who were not scoundrels, but had lost full control of themselves through drink. Sometimes firing at random, sometimes provoking an outburst of anger, like that which kindled into Wat Tyler's rebellion,[2] they have inaugurated carnage, for which they had no desire, but for which they were determined not be held responsible. Confused in their memories, they made up easily stories which exonerated themselves and were accepted by their officers in preference to the perhaps not wholly consistent explanations of terrified peasants speaking in a strange tongue.

When we have been at war, other nations have sometimes accused our soldiers of cruelties of which we have been certain they were incapable. The reasoned but unbridled ferocity which the Germany military caste has avowed has undoubtedly been palliated in the minds of the German people by the care with which official news has concentrated their attention on what have appeared to the rest of the world as mere wanton outrages, but could be plausibly represented as not without provocation. The dissemination of simple, sound knowledge among our people as to the rights and obligations of civilians in war time would diminish each one of these sources of disaster.

Yours faithfully, | Alfred Marshall.

Cambridge. Oct. 27.

[1] Printed in *The Times*, 28 October 1914. Original not traced.
[2] The peasants' revolt of 1381.

1036. To Lewis Fry, 7 November 1914[1]

7. xi. 14

Dear Mr Fry,

My favourite *dictum* is:—Every statement in regard to economic affairs which is short is a misleading fragment, a fallacy or a truism. I think this dictum of mine is an exception to the general rule: but I am not bold enough to say that it *certainly* is.

Also I am able to work only for a very short time without a break: and my long promised book goes very slowly. I am quite well: but feeble. So I generally avoid letters and conversation. But I do not like to leave your letter without some poor attempt at an answer.

My patron Saint is Abbe,[2] who, in control of the 'Zeiss' works, has done more than anyone else, I believe, to revolutionise the higher glass industry, and attain results which a little while ago were thought impossible. His maxim was—keep financial control, but allow yourself for personal expenditure only as much as will enable you to keep your (and your family's) physical and mental energies at their highest. That is, my attitude towards 'luxuries,' in the distinctive sense of the term, does not get beyond toleration. Nevertheless I was not altogether sorry when, at the outbreak of the war, some cold-blooded and perhaps not altogether disinterested people cried out:—'Don't alter your mode of expenditure more than you can help. By refusing to buy accustomed luxuries you throw out of employment highly specialised workers, who cannot turn to anything else. Presently they will be wanting charitable relief. Pay for work would have been better for them, and would have avoided disorganisation of labour, with its attendant financial nervousness: and that is a thing specially to be dreaded from the point of military efficiency at the present time.'

But I also think that everyone ought to begin to turn his expenditure into channels, which tend to the general good. A panic movement, which caused a wholesale discharge of elderly butlers would have been an evil: but a steadfast diminution in the demand for unnecessary domestic servants would turn people, who were not too old to change their vocation, into work that would make for the public good. Just at present of course the best of that work is at the front in the North of France and in Belgium.

Meanwhile chauffeurs, who are not able or willing to render direct public service, should, I think, be employed, as many of those belonging to my neighbours' establishments are, in taking convalescent soldiers for drives in the country. Other neighbours are retrenching in small ways, and either taking refugee Belgians into their own houses, or subscribing for their relief otherwise: and so on.

So now I think the time has come for the general principle:—Make towards a more steadfast suppression of personal luxuries and a larger devotion of resources to public ends. When the war is over, let the new seriousness, which it has brought into life, endure. Let more of the resources of the nation go to keeping children longer at school, and at better schools; to clearing out all unwholesome dwellings; and to levelling up the incomes of the poorer classes by an extension of the general principle that all may use freely roads, bridges etc. which are made at public expense.

By this means the employments that are subservient to luxury will be depleted gradually, without shock, and with no considerable hurt to any one: and the nation as a whole will grow in physical, moral and mental strength and joyousness.

On the question whether, when such a thing as sugar threatens to become scarce, well-to-do people should stint their consumption of it, I should be inclined to advocate moderate stinting: but I do not think the matter is practically important. If grain supplies ran short, I think educated people should eat oats etc. to which those with less elastic minds cannot accommodate themselves easily. Horses might put up with other food. The conversion of barley etc. into beer and spirits should be almost stopped. And, if milk runs short, healthy adults should leave it for children and invalids as much as possible.

As to the expenditure by Public Bodies on undertakings, other than relief works, I hesitate: because I cannot forecast the needs of the country after the war. Of course any unnecessary borrowing is a grave injury to the general business of this country. We ought to be financing our weaker allies, perhaps more than we are. It is said that we have lent fifteen millions to Australia. Our power in this direction is less than our will: and any one who still further lessens it without cause, is not acting rightly.

I have maintained from the first that, so long as the sea was open, there was no reason to expect much unemployment in the country *during* the war. Some persons would of course have to shift their occupations a little: but the whole trend of modern industry is towards the removal of impassable barriers to migration from one occupation to another of *the same kind*. The number of subdivisions is increasing: and when work becomes slack in any one, those in it say truly that they cannot get work in any other. But that only means that they cannot get it easily. If pressure lasts in their special work, they can, with a good-will, gradually get fairly good employment in other work. This was nearly certain *à priori*: and the experiences of the last three months have shown it to be true. See e.g. Board of Trade Labour Statistics for October; and Prof. Ashley's recent investigation into the conditions of work in Birmingham.[3]

The building trades are, I admit, likely to become slack when the work arranged before the war is done: and though I think it would be most unwise and even wrong for any Public Body to commit themselves to large expenditure without most urgent need, there may be cause for getting plans ready for building and navvy work *after the war is over*. The unemployment, which is to be expected in many trades then, will be specially heavy in building trades: partly because they are so large, and those in them have no wide alternative openings; and partly also, I think, because ordinary people will then first realise how much the resources of the country have been depleted by the war and how much incomes generally must shrink; and will be on the look out for cheaper houses rather than larger. Of course, if we are invaded, the building trades will be busy after the war in some places: and have no employment at all in those which have not been devastated. But our present concern is not to keep at home young strong men—such as affect the building trades—but to help them to the front.

Such alone are the poor and fragmentary remarks which I can offer you as an expression of my particular views on large questions.

Yours very sincerely, | Alfred Marshall

P.S. On reading this over, I see that it ought to be re-written: but I trust you will kindly pardon its slovenliness.

In forecasting, as best I may, conditions after the war, I have made no allowance for an indemnity from Germany. Though I think she should be forced to pay for the havoc she has wrought in Belgium and France, I think also that the world does partially endorse Germany's charge that we alone among her enemies are influenced by sordid commercial considerations; and partly for this reason I hope that all *our* demands will be concentrated on lasting security against her military pretensions.

[1] Reproduced in *Memorials*, pp. 484–7, where it is attributed to 'the Right Hon. Louis Fry'. Original not traced. From Balliol Croft. Lewis Fry (1832–1921), was an old acquaintance from Bristol days when he had been a prominent member of the Council of University College, Bristol. See Vol. 2 [700]. His letter, not traced, had presumably sought advice on how a civilian might assist the war effort.

[2] Ernst Abbe (1840–1905), German physicist, Professor at Jena and partner in the optical works of Carl Zeiss (1816–88). These passed after the latter's death into Abbe's control. See also *Industry and Trade*, pp. 353–4.

[3] Immediately following the outbreak of war Ashley provided regular reports (some printed) on the local labour situation to the Birmingham Citizens' Executive Committee and the Intelligence Department of the Local Government Board. See Anne Ashley, *William James Ashley: A Life* (King, London, 1932), p. 150.

1037. To Sir William Ramsay, 9 December 1914 (incomplete)[1]

9. xii. 14

Dear Sir William Ramsay,

In my chapter on Germany's contribution to 'Industrial Leadership' I talk about Lorraine and Luxemburg ores and Gilchrist in few words: but I did not know that the Germans were held up for a time by patents. That is an important fact. I will put it on to the proofs.[2]

§§ 78, 79 of the inclosed[3] indicate that I have no objection on principle to 'combative' taxes on dumped goods. But though I have read carefully everything that throws light on the practical working of such taxes, I have found nothing to show that they can be worked efficiently.

What is said about ether leaves me cold.[4] If the Excise people are pigheaded, the scientific world is able to bring pressure on them. Possibly however the Excise may have a stronger case than appears at first sight. During the last thirty years I have come across scores of instances in which there is more to be said for the regulation than is admitted by those to whom it is objectionable.

But generally I agree that the Government in general and most especially the legal members of the House of Lords need to be bullied into common sense and some knowledge of business. Of course Moulton[5] does not belong to the old gang.... But Halsbury[6] went out of his way to preach an economic sermon in favour of unlimited freedom to grant rebates: and had no idea that American economists—who are the highest authority on this particular subject—are convinced that those rebates strengthen the destructive and antisocial effects of unscrupulous trade combinations more than almost anything else: and, as far as I know, English economists agree....

Yours very sincerely, | Alfred Marshall

[1] Reproduced in *Memorials*, pp. 487–8. Original not traced. From Balliol Croft. Apparently Marshall had sought Ramsay's advice on points of industrial chemistry touched upon in the long-promised *National Industry and Trade.*

[2] The passage in question does not seem to have survived into *Industry and Trade* when published, but see pp. 94–5: also, pp. 125–6, 135 n., 557. Marshall there refers to the Thomas process. Sidney Gilchrist Thomas (1850–85), aided by his cousin Percy Gilchrist, invented in 1875 the Bessemer process for removing phosphorous from iron in steel making. This benefited the German steel industry by allowing it to use abundant local phosphoric ores.

[3] Marshall's 'Memorandum on the Fiscal Policy of International Trade' [912.2]: see *Official Papers*, pp. 414–5, for the passage in question.

[4] The point at issue here remains obscure.

[5] John Fletcher Moulton (1844–1921), an early acquaintance of Marshall—he had been Senior Wrangler in 1868—had become Baron Moulton and was Lord of Appeal in Ordinary 1912–21.

[6] Hardinge Stanley Giffard (1823–1921), first Earl of Halsbury, had been Lord Chancellor for 17 years under Conservative administrations. He, like Moulton, was a 'Law Lord'.

1038. To Sir William Ramsay, (1914?)[1]

Dear Sir William Ramsay,

I was told by a youth, who had been taught chemistry for two years at a leading University, that his teacher dictated a sort of text-book of his own; and that the lesson was chiefly one in writing from dictation facts useful to be remembered. Allowing for some exaggeration I thought this a bad sign; and there were others of the same kind on a smaller scale elsewhere.

Impressed by the personality of Sir David Dale (whom I met at the Labour Commission) I invested some of my small means in the Dundesland Iron Ore Co.[2] I was *disgusted* when I found that they had recourse to Edison[3] for a method of dealing with the ore, and spent enormous sums on setting up plant on his method; when a small experimental station at home might have indicated that the plan was not suitable for the ore. I was *terrified* when the directors, with millions of money at their back, went (as it seemed to me on their knees) to Krupp; and asked him to let one of his chemists make some experiments for them. Dale had died meanwhile. Krupp's chemist made them successfully: but I was chagrined by his success.[4]

In consequence I have scarcely ventured to touch on industrial chemistry in revising my old proofs;[5] though I have felt able to speak with confidence on a good many matters connected with industrial mechanics.

Your letter heartens me very much; but I am not yet in good spirits. Ought not you, and the few men who, like you, are raising the reputation of British chemistry throughout the world, to set yourselves to see whether the rank and file of British teachers of chemistry work up at all near to your own high ideals?—This is the question which occurs to me: it may probably show nothing but impertinent ignorance. And in any case do not trouble to answer. We ought both of us to be at our own hard work.

Yours very sincerely, | Alfred Marshall

I would rather have your testimonial as to a pupil than that of any body of examiners: but I would not give a halfpenny for one by the man who dictated a text-book.

[1] Reproduced in *Memorials*, pp. 488–9, where it is dated as '1914'. Original not traced. From Balliol Croft. The letter bears no indication of war-time concerns, suggesting that an earlier date (say 1908–14) may be possible.

[2] David Dale (1829–1906), ironmaster, railway director, and pioneer of industrial arbitration in the North East, knighted 1895, had become Chairman of the *Dunderland* Iron Ore Company on its establishment in 1902.

[3] Among the many researches and inventions of Thomas Alva Edison (1847–1931) had been the magnetic concentration of iron ore.

[4] The Krupp steel and armaments empire, founded by Alfred Krupp (1812–87), was headed from 1902 to 1943 by Gustav Krupp (1870–1950), husband of Alfred's granddaughter, Bertha.

[5] Proofs for the long-promised *National Industry and Trade* had been accumulating since 1904.

1039. To John Maynard Keynes, 14 December 1914[1]

14. 12. 14

Dear Keynes,

I have to thank you for what seems a most important article once more.[2] I am too far away from all monetary questions, & too imbecile, to be able to read it through properly. But I seem to find myself agreeing with all I read. I think your concluding paragraph clears up your position well.

I don't think you have said anything about invasion in regard to the B. of E.'s stock of gold.[3] I have always regarded the two as intimately connected. We have been warned that the Germans did intend, though *perhaps* they do not now, to risk the loss of many ships & lives in the endeavour to put 150,000 or 200,000 men at least on our shores: weather, *new model* submarines (capable of firing torpedoes without turning), &c. may conceivably favour them. If so many people will go mad with terror; & demand gold to bury in their gardens, &c. Until the danger of such mad, senseless terror is over past (perhaps it nearly is now) I do not want the Old Lady's stocking to be thinned out.

My reasons are partly political: partly a fear that such a panic wd put a premium on gold, if the Old Lady did not oblige. And in this matter also I look at the sentimental side more than the material: but our national credit seems to have a larger sentimental element in it than that of any other country: & to have a very large gold value.

Yours very sincerely, | Alfred Marshall

Don't trouble to answer.

[1] King's College, Cambridge, J. M. Keynes Papers. Reproduced in *Memorials*, pp. 481–2. From Balliol Croft.

[2] J. M. Keynes, 'The Prospects of Money, November, 1914', *Economic Journal*, 24 (December 1914), pp. 610–34: reproduced in *Collected Works*, vol. 11, pp. 299–328.

[3] The B. of E. is the Bank of England, the so-called 'Old Lady of Threadneedle Street'.

1040. To John Maynard Keynes, 2 February 1915[1]

2. 2. 15

My dear Keynes,

So far as I can judge the Governments declaration as to Germany's trade[2] is required & wise. I am glad that no precedent is to be made for declaring food unconditional contraband.

Take care of yourself in this heavy strain.
Yours ever | Alfred Marshall

[1] King's College, Cambridge, J. M. Keynes Papers. From Balliol Croft. Reproduced in *Memorials*, p. 483, where it is dated '22 ii 15', a clear transcription error.

[2] The British fleet was exercising increasing control at this time over Germany's overseas trade, creating friction with neutrals, including the United States.

1041. To John Maynard Keynes, 21 February 1915[1]

21. 2. 15

Dear Keynes,

I know so little about either war or politics that I am afraid of speaking publicly lest I do mischief. But some time you—with your full access to knowledge—will perhaps tell me whether I am right in fearing that our attitude to food supplies may cost us dearly in the future; though of course France and Russia can see no danger in the new precedent.

I shall not live to see our next war with Germany; but you will, I expect. For I am convinced that Germany is resolute in saying her quarrels with Russia & France are capable of adjustment: but that she will not accept our superiority at sea, unless we allow her unhampered expansion—which of course includes unlimited fortified coaling stations: so I think of the next war almost as much as of the present; & the two together oppress me.

The more severely we use our power of starving Germany, the more eagerly do I think that she will set herself to prepare during a generation for a war with England, turning nominally on questions in which France & Russia have little concern: that she will at last spring it suddenly, & have several score of fast cruisers already out to sea.

The Alabama, always evading battle, did immense mischief to North American trade:[2] & though aerial telegraphs have helped our cruisers more than the Emden,[3] a great number of Emdens might stop most of our food supplies, except such as were convoyed by powerful fleets.

Further, submarines, some swift, but most broad & able to fire torpedo's in all directions would be ready by the hundred; with light engines & large displacement, so as to be independent of fresh air for a day & of fresh supplies for a month.

Such a war would cost her but little; for we could not hurt her; while we should need to keep incessant guard during perhaps several years against invasion & hunger; unless Russia vetoed German ambitions.

So I say to myself anxiously is the present gain to be got by bringing hunger to the people of Germany, against the judgment of many neutrals, worth what it may cost to England a generation hence? You must be busy, so don't answer till we can meet.

Yours ever | A. M.

Of course I do not think that peace ought to be concluded on terms which fail to make Germany regret that she engineered the War.

Don't bother about this if you are busy. It is merely an old man's nervousness.[4]

[1] King's College, Cambridge, J. M. Keynes Papers. From Balliol Croft. Reproduced in *Memorials*, pp. 482–3.

[2] The *Alabama*, a Confederate cruiser, active 1862–4 in the American Civil War, inflicted damages on US shipping valued at more than $6 million in the settlement of the Alabama claims.

[3] This German light cruiser sank 15 ships in the Indian Ocean before she herself was sunk on 9 November 1914.

[4] This sentence was added to the *Memorials* version but is not in the original. Possibly it was written on the envelope, now lost.

1042. To Charles Ryle Fay, 23 February 1915[1]

23. ii. 15

BRAVO!

M. le Professeur

Capitaine Fay!

I am glad every way. I shall be delighted with analogies between economics and militarics. I don't guess what they are, except that the relations between long- and short-period policies and causations are—I suppose—rather similar in the two cases.

Life and Labour, 1800–1850 is a fascinating study.[2] But a thousand years hence 1920–1970 will, I expect, be *the* time for historians.

It drives me wild to think of it. I believe it will make my poor *Principles*, with a lot of poor comrades, into waste paper. The more I think of it, the less I can guess what the world will be like fifty years hence.

Yours affectionately, | Alfred Marshall

[1] Reproduced in *Memorials*, pp. 489–90, original not traced. From Balliol Croft. The occasion for the letter was probably Fay's commissioning. He was to serve as a Lieutenant and acting Captain in the Buffs and the Machine Gun Corps, 1915–18. See *Memorials*, pp. 76–7, for his slightly improbable recounting of military tutelage received from Marshall in 1918, a story amplified in Fay's 'Reminiscences' [897.4], pp. 89–90.

[2] Fay was to publish his book *Life and Labour in the Nineteenth Century* only in 1920 (Cambridge University Press, Cambridge), basing it on lectures he had given in 1919. Marshall's allusion thus remains puzzling. Possibly Fay had broached the general scheme at this time.

1043. To Frank William Taussig, 27 March 1915[1]

27. 3. 15

Dear Professor Taussig,

If I had a single free copy of the chapters for wh you ask,[2] it should seek its resting place in the Harvard Library—a noble Mausoleum. But it is many years since I have had more than one (in addition to that which is bound up in a copy of my *Miscellanea*[3]): & about 4 years ago that was cut up to make an Appendix to my book on 'National Industry & Trade'.

I send you a waste copy of an introductory section to that Appendix. On consideration I thought it too full for publication; & rewrote it briefly: but your kind eyes may not complain of its minute detail.[4] I may add that the discussion of International Trade will not come into Vol I of '*Industry & Trade*' (the new title); but into Vol II. It is—especially on the abstract side—so far finished that it could be published, even if I should not finish Vol II, to say nothing of Vol III. I am in excellent health: wholly free from illness of any sort. But the smallest excitement sets up blood-pressure & cripples me for the rest of the half day. And I may not even write quietly for much more than an hour on end; and, still less, talk. I tell you this, because one of its chief hardships is that it prevents me from seeing visitors; among whom no place has been higher in my esteem than that of Americans, & especially American economists. And next to them came German economists. Alack the day! But I love them still.

I think with you that the outlook is evil. I think more about the next war, in some moods, than even about the present. For if Germany were to declare war on England alone, we could do nothing against her, except to push her commerce into indirect channels, and harry her Colonies: & that would strengthen Germany's opinion that our attitude to her is one of mere commercial jealousy. That may be true of the Germanesque tendencies of the 'Tariff Reformers': but it is not true in the least of the people at large. Our dread, which latterly has become envenomed, is that in such a war, we should need to spend perhaps two hundred millions a year on defences by sea & land against invasions, which might reduce a part at least of the land to the condition of Belgium. They would then have ready beforehand perhaps two hundred submarines, some swift, others with immense power of life without return to a base; and we might be brought to misery during many years, even if we escaped perdition. That is why many of us, who w^{d}.. be glad to see private property at sea immune, if it might be, feel that the right of capture at sea is our only bulwark, other than our alliances, against the monster-army of Germany.

And yet, I love the Germans through it all. They are not what they were in the 60's; because they have all passed under the schooling of German officers; and these are, it seems to me, far more selfish as well as arrogant, than Germans in general. That is I think shown by the particular form which they have given to Agrarian Protection. The broad lines, wh Wagner advocates for it, may be wise or foolish: but they are not lines of class-selfishness in any narrow sense. But protection, nearly the whole of the pecuniary gains of which come to the class from wh the officers are almost exclusively drawn; while many of the smaller cultivators gain nothing net by them, seems to me to indicate a narrow class-selfishness.

I fear *that*: & I fear the sayings of Bismarckians that the use of German colonies, is not to draw the population away from the Fatherland: i.e. it is not economic. It is to supply bases for naval stations, from which military operations may be worked.

If we thought that Germany would use her colonies merely for commercial purposes, many of us would most heartily welcome the extension of her colonies far & wide; even though we know that her present colonies afford immense opportunities, wh she has no real inclination to develop with her full energy.

Yours in prolixity, but most heartily | Alfred Marshall

[1] Harvard University Archives, Taussig Papers. From Balliol Croft. Partly reproduced in *Memorials*, pp. 490–1.

[2] The chapters on the 'Pure Theory of Foreign Trade' that Sidgwick had caused to be printed in 1879. See *Early Economic Writings*, vol. 2, pp. 111–81.

[3] Marshall had bound a collection of his occasional publications under this title. A copy is preserved in the Marshall Library.

[4] The appendix presumably became eventually appendix J to *Money Credit and Commerce*. The abandoned introductory section has not been traced.

1044. To Jacob Harry Hollander, 22 May 1915[1]

22. 5. 15

Dear Professor Hollander

I am much obliged for Fauquier:[2] what I have read of him is extremely interesting, & he was previously unknown to me. Some time ago I collected a great many early Tracts, partly in original copies: but I have no hope of being able to read such things now. I found their interest cumulative: when I had had half a dozen belonging to a period in my hands, I was greedy for more. But my digestion was not strong enough for such diet in between my regular meals: so I gave it up. All the more do I wish to express my gratitude to those who are like you able fully to read mark & digest them.

Yours vy truly | Alfred Marshall

[1] University of Illinois, Urbana-Champaign, Hollander Collection. From Balliol Croft.

[2] Francis Fauquier, *An Essay on Ways and Means for Raising Money for the Support of the Present War, without increasing the Public Debts* (Cooper, London, 1756): republished in a series of economic tracts edited by Hollander (Lord Baltimore Press, Baltimore, 1915).

1045. To John Maynard Keynes, 14 October 1915[1]

14. 10. 15

My dear Keynes,

I agree heartily with what has been said on behalf of the Treasury as to the need for ever increasing taxation, especially such as will tend to increase[2] consumption: but, as I have nothing to say that is new, I am not writing.[3] If however there is political cause for such writing, even by unimportant people,

I will write to the Times, on the chance of their finding room for it. You are more likely than anyone else, with whom I am [in][4] touch, to know whether there is such need: hence this note.

I do not want to waste your time: so I shall assume no answer to mean that there is no special reason why I should write.

Yours sincerely | Alfred Marshall

[1] King's College, Cambridge, J. M. Keynes Papers. From Balliol Croft.

[2] Presumably 'decrease' was intended.

[3] To the press.

[4] Word apparently accidentally omitted.

1046. To John Maynard Keynes, 25 October 1915[1]

25. 10. 15

My dear Keynes,

Perhaps I did not take your point about America rightly. I don't think I rate as highly as you do either the influence of the German faction in the U.S.; or the danger of a popular outcry[2] against the exportation of munitions & other products, as causes of delay in railroad building &c.

But I think that there are from time to time opportunities for making tremendous profits in America; & that if, in various ways, the Allies make the supply of capital too scarce to go round even among these choice ventures, the consequent demand for capital will put up interest so high that we shall not be able to borrow at anything like five per cent. Also I think that if a furious rise in prices is caused by dumping of gold in America, the people at large will go for anything that can be supposed to be its cause, especially if it enables them to vent ill temper on Government. So I agree with you that the flow of capital from America may be checked rather abruptly.

Babson, in *The future of the world peace*,[3] which seems to me likely to influence opinion, is on the side of the Allies: but points out that, from the military point of view, Germany's fleet even if very strong would be less dangerous than ours: because we could 'take New York' &c 'within 48 hours from our base in the West Indies'. If friction between us & U.S. ever arose, this latent source of U.S. jealousy might perhaps become patent.

Dont answer | Yours very sincerely | Alfred Marshall

[1] King's College, Cambridge, J. M. Keynes Papers. From Balliol Croft. How Keynes had communicated the views to which Marshall reacts remains unclear, as does their precise character.

[2] In the United States.

[3] Roger Ward Babson (1875–1967), *The Future of World Peace* (Babson, Boston, 1915). See pp. 130–1. Marshall paraphrases rather than quotes directly.

1047. To John Maynard Keynes, 15 November 1915[1]

15. 11. 15

My dear Keynes,

I am drifting to the opinion that there is much to be said for commandeering American & other foreign stocks, & putting the proceeds into war loan. Perhaps it would be inexpedient to give notice: for shirkers might evade it: and yet I don't want to be commandeered.

Before this point had occurred to me I had inclined to sell my few American shares: because I think that the country has begun to face its difficulties with clearer sight than when I said—with your agreement, I think—that such sales should be postponed in the public interest. I don't ask you to write about this, unless inclined.

There is however one matter, on wh I have strong views, & in wh the Treasury is concerned. I see great difficulty in commandeering for the war loan the surplus wages of adults, though I wish that could be done. But I see no harm & great advantage in commandeering the wages of boys. I should like (say) a half of all that they earn in excess of a number of shillings weekly equal to the number of years in their several ages, to be compulsorily invested in their names in the hands of a Public Trustee; to be released when they reach manhood, or special occasion arises. The economic waste caused by the excessive wages of some boys is a great evil: but the physical & moral deterioration which is being caused by the stress put on them in twelve hour shifts, & the huge sums of money at their disposal, seems to me to be a national calamity of the first order.

I think twelve hour shifts for any but adult males should be stopped: I hear that the numerous leavings of high class boys from Woolwich Arsenal are due to this feeling on the part of their parents: it seems to me a mistake even from the 'munitions' point of view.

Yours sincerely | Alfred Marshall

My thoughts were turned on boys wages by a message from Lavington sent thro' Pigou.

[1] King's College, Cambridge, J. M. Keynes Papers. From Balliol Croft.

1048. To John Maynard Keynes from Mary Paley Marshall, 15 November 1915[1]

15. 11. 15

Dear M^{r}. Keynes

My husband does so enjoy & value his confidential talks with you (& you managed so well last time that he was not overtired), that I dont like to suggest that you sh^{d}. come when other people are here. But, next Sunday, for the first time in two years, we are having people (not members of the family) to lunch (at 1.15). They are Prof Pigou & M^r. Lavington: & no doubt the talk will turn on boys wages.[2] If you sh^d. care to come we sh^d. of course be very pleased.

I hope you will come for a tête a tête talk at tea time, whenever the spirit moves you. Of course the lunch will be enough talk for next Sunday. We shall be here on the 28th., but probably we shall be away on the 5th. Dec.

Yours very sincerely | Mary P. Marshall

[1] King's College, Cambridge, J. M. Keynes Papers. From Balliol Croft.
[2] See [1047].

1049. To the Editor, *The Times*, 28 December 1915[1]

Sir,—My vivid recollection of the horrors of hunger during the siege of Paris, of which I heard much while staying in Berlin in the winter of 1870–1, has made me regret that our Government has thought it necessary to restrict the importation of food into Germany. But Germans decided that it was right to reduce two millions of people of all ages to the brink of absolute starvation, until Paris surrendered not merely herself, but France. Before the pressure of starvation became extreme she was willing to surrender herself; but the Germans held back English and other supplies of food, which were on the way to Paris, until she surrendered in the name of all France, though the Government of France was not within her walls. It seems, therefore, that the Germans should be the last people in the world to protest against some small restriction of their food supply.

But the *Cologne Gazette*, quoted by you today,[2] continues the attempt to engender hatred of England among the children of Germany by dwelling on the scarcity of milk, which has arisen because 'England's sharpest weapon is aimed at the lives of our children and of our weakest and most helpless.' Now German economists have long boasted of the abundance of milk, which their methods of agriculture supply; and for this and other reasons it is certain *a priori* that German children will have sufficient milk, if precedence is given to their needs. I have no knowledge as to the possibility that some milk may have been intercepted by manufacturers of glycerine for high explosives. But I know that England has not intercepted Germany's external supplies of milk. For a list of her chief sources of imported milk and milk products in 1913 is before me, on pp. 192–3 of the *Staatisches Jahrbuch*, 1914.[3] They were Denmark, Russia, Switzerland, and France. The single milk product that entered Germany from the sea and was of sufficient importance to be shown on the list was a third of a million tons of butter from Sweden; and some part of the 18 million tons which she got from Holland may possibly have come from far. On the other hand, she imported from America a hundred million tons of lard and 20 million tons of oleomargarine.[4]

Yours faithfully, | Alfred Marshall.

Cambridge, Dec. 28.

[1] Printed in *The Times*, 29 December 1915, under the heading 'The Overseas Supply of Fats'. Original not traced.

[2] See *The Times*, 28 December 1915 (7c).

[3] The *Statistisches Jahrbuch für das Deutsche Reich* was an annual publication of Germany's Statistisches Reichsamt, 1880–1919.

[4] A short letter of correction by Marshall appeared in *The Times*, 31 December 1915 (9e) under the heading 'German Imports of Fats'. It read:

> Sir,—By a strange mistake I wrote 'million' instead of 'thousand' in the figures of German imports of fats. Germany imports from America, in normal times, a hundred thousand tons of lard: and so on./With apologies, I am yours faithfully,/Alfred Marshall.

1050. To John Maynard Keynes, 29 December 1915[1]

29. 12. 15

My dear Keynes,

In continuation of our conversation about conscription, I should like to tell you my latest notions.[2] There are a few people who—from temperamental & other causes—are so averse to serving in the army that they would almost rather die at once, than serve: they are often brave, but they w^{d}.. be depressing influences in the ranks. But many, perhaps most of them are patriotic & unselfish. They serve as a screen to shirkers, & selfish neer-do-wells of all sorts.

The well-to-do used to protect themselves by allowing a man to escape conscription by paying the expenses of a substitute. But this plan favours the rich & is an insult to the poor.

Like objections do not seem to lie against the proposal that any unmarried man of military age, who is not needed by the country at home, & is unwilling to go to the front, may be exempted from conscription if he contributes (say) *one third* of his total income (in addition to general taxation) to the services of the war.

Some mitigations might be needed for special cases: e.g. that of a man earning less than £1 week, & supporting invalid near relations.

It seems to me that such an arrangement would fulfill Asquith's pledge;[3] & would bring into the army nearly all those who ought to be in it.

If you think it advisable, I will write to the Times in this direction. You know what is happening in the higher strata of the political atmosphere & I do not. But as it is a matter on which I have *no* special knowledge, I am disinclined to write.

Yours ever | Alfred Marshall

[1] King's College, Cambridge, J. M. Keynes Papers. From Balliol Croft.

[2] Conscription was a delicate issue for Keynes, partly because of his own convictions, but also because many of his friends and Cambridge colleagues were conscientious objectors. For a detailed account and assessment see D. E. Moggridge, *Maynard Keynes* [846.1], pp. 253–61. It is doubtful whether Marshall was fully aware of these complexities.

[3] A registration scheme for military service, directed by Lord Derby (1865–1948), had faltered as it relied on voluntary compliance. Asquith, the Prime Minister, had pledged on 2 November 1915 that the Government would introduce conscription rather than call up married volunteers while unmarried men with inessential jobs held back. The threat had not produced the hoped-for unmarried volunteers. For contemporary details see *The Times*, 28 December 1915 (e–f); 29 December 1915 (e–f), where the pledge and related statements are reproduced in a short history.

1051. To John Maynard Keynes, 4 January 1916[1]

4. 1. 16

Dear Keynes

I agree: & that is one reason why I want a great increase of taxation. I was only searching for a way out, in case the pledge, which Derby led Asquith into giving, be thought absolutely binding.

Yours ever | A M

[1] King's College, Cambridge, J. M. Keynes Papers. From Balliol Croft. The nature of Keynes's reply to [1050] can only be surmised. See [1050.2,3].

1052. To Eli Filip Heckscher, 28 January 1916[1]

28. 1. 16

Dear Sir

I have to thank you much for the two pamphlets which you have kindly sent me.[2] I am specially interested in the statement that the Swedish income tax reaches downwards very far. I am a great admirer of direct taxation; & I should be glad to see any increased taxation, which it may be necessary to impose on English working classes, levied directly: but that would involve much additional work on an already over-taxed Government.

Unfortunately I am not able to read Swedish: but my wife has been told by a Swedish friend, Miss Paues of Newnham College,[3] the general purport of that which you have sent me: & it makes me proud.

Yours very truly | Alfred Marshall

[1] Royal Library, Stockholm, Heckscher Papers. From Balliol Croft.

[2] A copy of Heckscher's pamphlet, 'Statsfinanserna—De Offentliga Hushållningarna Tilsammantagano' (Sveriges Land och foch. 1, Stockholm, 1915) is preserved in the Marshall Library. The other pamphlet can hardly be guessed at since Heckscher's writings of the period were copious.

[3] Anna Caroline Paues (1867–1945), Lecturer in English at Newnham, 1906–27, University Lecturer in Swedish, 1927–36; born and educated in Sweden.

1053. To William Harbutt Dawson, 2 February 1916[1]

2. 2. 16

Dear Mr Dawson,

It is with the very greatest unwillingness that I decline the great honour of taking part in your enterprise for the highest wellbeing of our country.[2] I have never received an invitation of the kind, which it has caused me so much regret to refuse. The purpose & the plan of your book seem to me excellent in every way. And this chapter which you propose has special attractions for me; in spite of the fact that the technical detail wh must be considered in drafting a budget lies outside of my province, & would need a good deal of study.

But I am not a free agent. A good part of a book on *National Industry & Trade*, wh MacMillan advertised about seven years ago as 'in the Press', has been standing in type ever since. It had swollen out in design to three volume size: but these volumes will never be completed. For I have for some years not been allowed to work for more than an hour at a time; & the output of an hour diminishes without cease. It does not bear *directly* on the new problems of the present time: but it is directed towards broad principles which are for all time. And when I come to matters of international trade & tariff policy—wh are to find place in the second volume—I shall hope to say something on the situation after the war, then ended.

Yours very sincerely | Alfred Marshall

[1] Marshall Papers. From Balliol Croft.

[2] Dawson was organizing and editing a collection of essays on 'After-War Problems' and had asked Marshall to contribute one on fiscal policy. Dawson's letter has not been traced.

1054. From Sir Frederick Macmillan, 4 April 1916[1]

Macmillan & Co. Ltd | St. Martin's Street, | London, W.C.
April 4th 1916.

Dear Mr. Marshall,

You will remember that the sixth edition or your *Principles of Economics*, which was published in 1910, consisted of 5,000 copies. The sale has gone on very steadily, and we now find ourselves with only between two and three hundred copies in hand: and, I am glad to say, a continuous demand for the book. I write therefore to ask what you propose to do. By far the simplest plan would be to give us permission to reprint the book word for word and let us issue it as an exact reproduction of the sixth edition. If you saw your way to allow this, we could guarantee an exact reprint and it would not be necessary to send you proofs. There is a great deal to be said for this plan, and I cannot help thinking that if you once allow yourself to go through the book and make corrections you will find it a much heavier piece of work than you would care to undertake: and after all a book must at some time or other reach its final form.

I shall be much obliged if you will take this matter into consideration and let me know your decision as soon as may be.

With kind regards, | I am, yours very sincerely, | Frederick Macmillan.

[1] Marshall Papers. Typewritten.

1055. To Sir Frederick Macmillan, 5 April 1916[1]

5. 4. 16

Dear Sir Frederick,

I have anticipated the danger that I might be called on for a seventh edition of my Principles before I had got free from even the first volume of my new book. So I have made changes from time to time, as criticism or other cause led me to think that any passage in my *Principles* needed a different emphasis or wording; or again as statistical & other statements in it had become obsolete. I have just gone over the whole of them; & I am ready to hand the book over bodily to the Press as soon as I hear from you. It could be put in pages at once from the title page to the index without break; & the Press could be told to send me proofs only where any doubtful point arose.

I am preserving the pagination of the fifth & sixth editions: & I am changing the title 'Preface to the Sixth edition' into 'Preface to the Sixth & Seventh editions,'[2] to indicate that there is no substantial change: but I find the number of small changes is more than I had expected.

I make very slow progress with my new book. I have now got nearly the whole of the first volume into slips: but if the thing is ever finished, it will run to three volumes, each about three fourths as long as my Principles.

I am dropping 'National', & calling it 'Industry & Trade'. Vol I consists of:—

Book I Origins of the present problems of industry & trade (a historical introduction)

Book II The organization & administration of business (very realistic)

Book III Tendencies to monopolistic aggregation.

Vol II is to be on International Trade, & some monetary problems. Most of it is typewritten.

Vol III exists only in fragments & old material. It is designed to cover social & Governmental applications of the other two, &c.

About three years ago I found myself unable to do much work. I found that diseased gums had brought on blood pressure. I fell into able hands, & am in relatively good health, though I cannot work much. But I find that what I wrote before I knew I was ill is not satisfactory: & I cannot expect to bring out Vol II without much re-writing.

I had therefore proposed to suggest that Vol I should come out as soon as ready. But in view of the war my own inclination is now distinctly to wait & bring out Vols I & II together.

If I do not finish Vol III (I am now in my 74th year), I propose to arrange that it should be converted in large measure into a collection of essays &c already published, & selected with a view to the main purpose, which I propose for the Volume, if I should be able to complete it.

This is a long letter: but your patience has been tried by my terribly slow progress with 'Industry & Trade' far worse than even by this letter: & you have been very kind.

Yours very sincerely | Alfred Marshall

Sir Frederick MacMillan

[1] British Library, Macmillan Archive. From Balliol Croft. See [1054].
[2] In the event the title was 'Preface to the Seventh Edition': see *Guillebaud*, p. 61.

1056. From Sir Frederick Macmillan, 7 April 1916[1]

Macmillan & Co. Ltd. | St. Martin's Street, | London, W.C.
April 7th 1916.

Dear Mr. Marshall,

I am very glad to learn from your letter of the 5th inst. that you are so well prepared for the news that a seventh edition of your 'Principles' is likely to be needed soon. I was afraid when I wrote to you that I might be asking you to undertake a troublesome piece of work.

As printing is rather a slow business now-a-days I think it would be as well to set to work at once. I shall be obliged therefore if you will send the corrected copy to the Pitt Press.[2] I will give them instructions only to trouble you with proofs when any doubtful points arise.

With regard to 'Industry and Trade' I quite agree that it would be best to bring out Vols. I and II together. As you say that the greater part of Volume II is already typewritten, I expect this only means postponing the publication until the war is over, and the discussion of the matters with which you deal will be very apropos.

I am very glad to hear that your health has improved so much, and hope that you have before you many years of (moderately) active work.

Believe me, yours very sincerely, | Frederick Macmillan

[1] Marshall Papers. Typewritten. See [1055].
[2] The University Printer in Cambridge, where all Marshall's books were set up. The preface to *Principles* (7) is dated 25 June 1916: see *Guillebaud*, pp. 61–2. However, a finished copy seems to have reached Marshall only in November: see [1066].

1057. To Johan Gustav Knut Wicksell, 8 April 1916[1]

8. 4. 16

Dear Professor Wicksell,

I am ashamed of having forgotten what you had said long ago about the currency. But as I forget what I have written even a week ago, I may be pardoned for forgetting others' words.

I am to this extent in agreement with your suggestions, that I think international understandings as to rates of discount may play an important part in the business of the world in the distant future. But I doubt the possibility of exercising any *permanent* influence on interest, whether nationally or internationally, by the action of the banks.

I dont object to Government notes being printed on silver: but I dont like them being printed on gold, as I have indicated in print: I think that if ever international agreements for the regulation of prices are made, they should perhaps take the form of a central committee to arrange for the taxation of gold at the mines, when prices are rising: the proceeds of the tax being so distributed that it does not press hardly on any gold-producing district. Then we could keep the kilo of gold in its present (peace) position, as the unit of international currency. If gold ran short, on the other hand I would call in some kilos of silver to help it, *if necessary*.

When I get to Utopia, I think, I shall lay some project of this sort before the public: but not in this world.

Meanwhile I must keep on my blinkers, & look only at the humdrum.

Yours very sincerely | Alfred Marshall

I must not write any more

14.4.16

I mistook your address: and this has just been returned from the 'Dead letter' office.

16.4.16

This has been returned from your London address. So I send it to Sweden.

[1] Lund University Library, Wicksell Papers. From Balliol Croft. Wicksell had visited England in February 1916 to investigate wartime monetary policy. In Cambridge he had a 'long conversation with Marshall, nota bene that it was he who was talking all the time'. In London he lunched with Maynard Keynes, who impressed him. See T. Gårdlund, *Life of Knut Wicksell* [800.1], pp. 294–5.

1058. To Arthur Cecil Pigou, 12 April 1916 (incomplete)[1]

12. vi. 1916

My dear Pigou,

I am charmed by the brilliancy and 'go' of your book.[2] But I am also a little frightened. I am certain that almost everything you say is true, with the qualifications that are latent in your mind: but some of them seem to me in danger of misleading people who do not know the ropes of economic complex interactions. For instance, what you say on p. 19[3] means something that is true: but I think it may be taken to be inconsistent with the *vitally* important fact that, if our soldiers and their families consume in various ways at Government expense much more than the German soldiers do, and the war last long, then Lloyd George's silver bullets[4] in the last campaign may fail us.

Again, if A buys old lace from B, and B saves the money, the country is not weakened. But in fact B probably sells lace in order to spend—perhaps on maintaining a big establishment, dances, etc. Therefore I should be glad to hear that A had decided not to buy the lace, so long as I know nothing about B. The only thing which I have noted as apparently opposed to my own opinion is on p. 93, about railways.[5] I have been working off and on at railways for several months; and I think I know nearly all of importance that has been said by the best authorities. I believe that they hold that it costs more to earn £100 on first class than on third class traffic; for first class insists on something like solitude, and the dead weight involved is portentous; but that, the excess of receipts over direct costs being high, they would lose net revenue by dropping first class carriages. I believe these opinions are certainly valid. My own estimate, based on no inside knowledge, is that, the direct cost to the country of A's railway journey for which £1 is paid is something like 6d.; though, especially if there is luggage, it *may* rise to a shilling. If the £10[6] is distributed over a dozen journeys, the cost would of course be higher. I make allowance for the time spent by ticket clerks, etc. on A's own needs: but none for the need which increasing traffic may make for increased services, and not merely tight packing of trains. (Of course that is fairly reasonable under war conditions.) If allowance is made for probable lengthening of trains, I would add half as much again: if additional trains are in view, a good deal more; and more again if A travels at times of the day at which the line is heavily worked. But I can't get beyond 4s. in any case. On the other hand I regard unnecessary motor car hiring as exceptionally unpatriotic....

Alfred Marshall

[1] Reproduced in *Memorials*, pp. 433–4. Original not traced. No address given.

[2] A. C. Pigou, *The Economy and Finance of the War* (Dent, London, 1916).

[3] Here Pigou argues that it is a fallacy to think that low pay for soldiers would save resources for then dependents must be supported by the state.

[4] Lloyd George's metaphor for Britain's vast financial reserves. See J. H. Edwards, *David Lloyd George* (Sears, New York, 1929), Vol. 2, pp. 404, 463.

[5] Here Pigou argues for individuals travelling less by rail or car in order to conserve resources, observing that switching from first- to third-class travel would save less resources than the fare differential might suggest.

[6] Presumably £1 was intended.

1059. To Sir Edwin Ray Lankester, 27 April 1916[1]

To Professor Lankester 27. 4. 16

Dear Sir,

I regret much that I cannot attend the meeting, to which you do me the honour of inviting me, in regard to the Neglect of Science. I am quite convinced that England cannot maintain her position in the world, unless she calls science to her aid in a much more thorough way than hitherto. The causes which have enabled an Englishman in almost any industrial occupation to earn more, on the average, than a man of equal ability and industry would in any other 'old' country, are quite definite; but their force has declined rapidly during the last few decades. Meanwhile in Germany, and to a less degree in several other countries, organized scientific work is enabling many industries to do their work with less effort than ours can; and some industries to attain results beyond our power. I am therefore in hearty agreement with the second of the resolutions to be proposed on Wednesday next.[2] It points the way to a great increase in the number of those who have some knowledge of science. But to me it seems even more important to raise the quality of the scientific work of our chief schools: and I do not think that can be done until a fair proportion of the head masters of those schools are themselves scientific students of no mean order.

A young boy probably exercises the highest spontaneity of which he is capable in translating from Latin into English, and *vice versa*. But when he reaches the age of fifteen or sixteen, germs of scientific faculty may begin to show themselves; and a head master who was himself a scientific student would be likely to cherish and develop them. But a classical head master is not likely to recognize them; and under present arrangements the boy may probably be lost to science, unless he happens to be averse to classical studies. I think, therefore, that science will not get its proper share of the best ability of the people until more of the leading schools of the country are under the control of scientific head masters.

Yours truly | Alfred Marshall

[1] Printed in *The Neglect of Science. Report of the Proceedings of a Conference held in the Rooms of the Linnean Society, Burlington House, Piccadily, W. on Wednesday, 3rd May, 1916* (Harrison, London, 1916), at pp. 46–7. The conference was organized by Lankester (1847–1929), eminent zoologist, knighted 1907, and presided over by Lord Rayleigh. The report (p. 1) indicates that a memorandum, signed by several dignitaries, had appeared in *The Times*, 2 February 1916, and was then sent to 'a number of men of science, educational experts, and heads of industrial organizations' who were invited to attend the conference. Marshall was presumably included in the list. His letter was from Balliol Croft and the original has not been traced. As reproduced in the report, the letter is described as from 'Alfred Marshall, Esq., M.A., late Assistant Master of Harrow and Professor of Political Economy in the University of Cambridge'! Marshall's was one of a group of letters from sympathetic non-attenders.

[2] This resolution urged the government to give much greater weight to scientific subjects in the entry examinations for the civil service and Sandhurst. The first resolution had called for more prominence for science in school curricula and university entrance examinations.

1060. To Kumakichi Kawabe, 2 May 1916[1]

2. 5. 16

Dear Sir

Your courteous & high minded letter convinces me that you would not have proposed to translate a book which its authors had deliberately suppressed if you had been aware of that fact.[2] I am so much impressed by your noble sentiments, & by the trouble & expense to which you have gone that, I give my consent to the publication of matter of which I am not proud, with the proviso that you kindly translate the inclosed explanation, which I have just written, either exactly or without any important change.[3] The new *Economics of Industry* was made rapidly chiefly by scissors & paste out of my *Principles*; & it is less attractive to a beginner who wants to talk about economics with the least possible exertion. But the new volume maintains a much larger circulation than the old one; & as I am more anxious to clear away misunderstandings[4] than to provide light literature, I prefer it.

Yours sincerely | Alfred Marshall | Mary P. Marshall[5]

[Enclosure][6]

This volume was begun in the hope that it might be possible to combine simplicity with scientific accuracy. But though a simple book can be written on selected topics the central doctrines of Economics are not simple and cannot be made so. For the first half simplicity was given the preference; but in the second no progress could be made without more accurate foundations. Most of the first half being already in print, some patching was necessary: and the second half was written on lines somewhat similar to those of the *Principles of Economics*. When that was published in 1890 we saw the difficulty of keeping in circulation together opinions as divergent as some of those in this volume and that: so we decided to suppress it. The place was taken by a new Economics of Industry, made chiefly out of the *Principles* and that has been translated into Japanese. There are however some discussions in the third Book of the earlier volume which lie outside the scope of the later. That Book[7] was written with some care, and may be taken as representing well considered opinions: the same cannot be said of the whole of the present volume.

[1] Marshall Papers. From a retained draft copy on Balliol Croft notepaper. Kumakichi Kawabe (1873–1945) studied abroad for several years and lived in America. Returning to Japan, he founded a translation company, publishing in 1916 a translation of the 1889 edition of *Economics of Industry*. This incorporated a translation of Marshall's enclosed disclaimer, which was there dated 2 May 1916. Marshall's letter has previously been dated to 1910, the more likely reading of the handwritten date. But the above details, together with the character of the handwriting and the style of the printed letterhead, strongly suggest 1916. (I am greatly indebted to Professor Shoichi Hashimoto, author of a 1981 Japanese translation of the *Economics of Industry*, for the above information and for his persuasive arguments for a 1916 date.)

The letter is largely reproduced in Rita McWilliams-Tullberg, 'Economics of Industry', *History of Economic Thought Newsletter*, 9 (Autumn 1972), pp. 14–18 (reproduced in J. C. Wood, *Critical Assessments* [897.4], vol. 4, pp. 245–50). The enclosure is reproduced in *Early Economic Writings*, vol. 1, p. 82.

[2] This sentence is preceded by the deleted 'I concur in my wifes letter'.

[3] The remainder of the draft is struck through and the final letter may have ended here.

[4] The following alternative continuation from this point—also struck through—is preserved with the letter:

> [more anxious to clear away misunderstandings] on serious difficulties than to provide light instruction. Those who suggested that an educational work on economics should be written by a young student (who had attained only a very elementary knowledge of it) were not economists, & did not know that the task of combining simplicity with thoroughness is more difficult in this than in almost any other subject. Several scores of books have been written in the hope of doing this: but they have all perished quickly. My wife and I began by trying to make the book simple.

The parenthesized phrase was separately deleted.

[5] The intention was presumably to redraft Marshall's letter to make it a joint statement, as the enclosure was.

[6] This statement was included as an additional authors' preface to Kawabe's translation, with the attribution 'the second day of May 1916 at Cambridge, A. & M. Marshall' (information from Professor Hashimoto—see note 1 above.)

[7] That is, book iii of *Economics of Industry*.

1061. To William Harbutt Dawson, 5 June 1916[1]

5. 6. 16

Dear Mr Dawson

It had struck me that the number of books on the war had already become too great: & I do not feel inclined to read many recent books which I should have welcomed eighteen months ago. Knowing also the high cost of paper, & the scarcity of printers—the University Press here can hardly get along—I have wondered what view publishers might take of the situation. In consequence I had felt inclined to make to you a full statement of my position; which I now do, being emboldened by your recent letter.[2]

Some time ago the Vice Chancellor sent an official circular to resident members of the Senate asking each to specify any sort of national service which he would be willing to contribute. I had to reply that my age—now about 74—, & my inability to work or talk for more than an hour at a time prevented me from doing more than contributing a considerable part of my income to public uses; & taking great pains over any questions addressed to me by responsible persons. I would like to have contributed my quota in kind; but could not see my way.

I now find that you are quietly doing that very thing; I want to go in with you; & have *no* honorarium.

I may say that so much of my half-done work will in any case have to be scrapped when I depart this life, that no honorarium however great wd have led me even to consider a suggestion for any work wh I could not represent to myself at all events as 'doing my bit'. But your project offers me a chance.

I will now tell you how my M.S.S. stands at present in rough first draft. It enticed me beyond my original intentions, though I spent some pains on re-writing in order to attain compression. I left it early in March containing about 8000 words, under the following heads:—

1. Britain's financial position after the war. (I do not think many people realize how grave it will be: & have spoken very frankly about it.)
2. Principles of equity & policy in taxation.
3. Taxes on income, property & general expenditure under normal conditions.
4. Influences of the war on the policy of taxes on capital.
5. Shifting of the burden of taxes: 'a new (indirect) tax is a bad tax'.
6. Taxes on houses as representative of general expenditure.
7. Taxes on particular classes of commodities produced at home.

The plan provided for two more sections: (8. Taxes on imports; 9 General observations): but I have not yet written any part of these. I had intended 8 to be short: but the sudden activity of the Tariff Reformers makes me think it will need to be long, & even to be broken into two or more sections. The MSS of my book on *Industry & Trade* has a great deal on the subject; but most of what is said there would be inappropriate for the present purpose. I should however like to be free, if I may, to add about 3000 words on the subjects proposed for the two last sections.

My wife & I propose to spend July & August, & perhaps a little more time, in a remote farm house. I could undertake to let you have the first seven sections at almost any time in August: but if I do not keep back the Mss of the last sections till rather late in September, I may want to make considerable alterations on the proofs by aid of literature, wh I shall not be able to take to the farm.

I shall be grateful for any suggestions you may make in regard to this scheme; & I will do my utmost to comply with your wishes.

In §2 I had contrasted the positions of rich & poor: but what you say about the middle class shows me the importance of adding a paragraph or two about them. Some time ago the lower middle class, though doing (as I think) lower-grade work than that of the artisans, were paid higher. Their conventional expenditure will no doubt need to be reduced after the war. But it has always been the province of the economist to put the case of the weak as strongly as he can. And though I want the numbers of the lower middle class to be much reduced, I think it would be right to lay stress on the injury which Tarif Reform would inflict on them.

In cordial appreciation of the great services wh you are rendering to the country I remain

Yours very truly | Alfred Marshall

[1] Marshall Papers. From Balliol Croft. See [1053]. It is evident that Marshall had rapidly reversed his February decision not to contribute to Dawson's book, and that composition was now well under way. The volume was to appear as W. H. Dawson (ed.), *After-War Problems* (Allen and Unwin, London, 1917). Marshall's chapter (the eighteenth of nineteen) was entitled 'National Taxation After the War'. It occupies pp. 313–45, and is partly reproduced in *Memorials*, pp. 347–52.

[2] Not traced.

1062. To Macmillan and Company, 20 July 1916[1]

Rollington Farm
Corfe Castle
Dorset
20.7.16

Mess[rs] MacMillan & Co

Dear Sirs,

I accede willingly to M[r].. Nourse's request, inclosed.[2] It may save trouble if I give you a general authority, as I hereby do, to sanction all such quotations, in case you yourselves see no objection thereto.

Some time ago I wrote to Sir Frederick MacMillan about *Industry & Trade*.[3] In the result it was arranged that I should bring out the two volumes together at the end of the war, if possible. Since then progress has been slow. The last few chapters of Vol I are taking much more work than I had expected: & I have been unable to refuse to contribute to a sort of manifesto in support of a resolute, but moderate, policy after the war.[4] Also my power of work rapidly diminishes.

The Cambridge University Press is at work on the Seventh Edition of my *Principles*; which is entirely in their hands. But of course their staff is depleted. So they acceded readily to the suggestion that I should send them no more copy for my new book, till they have worked off the old one.

As things are I do not expect that my new Vol I will be ready much before the end of the war. If any notice of it is published,—as to the advisability of wh I have no opinion—it may perhaps be described as concerned with 'Origins and problems of the present industrial structure, with special reference to its monopolistic tendencies.'

I should have liked to publish the somewhat elaborate discussion of the fiscal policy of international trade, which is to occupy a considerable part of Vol II, before the country settled down to post-bellum conditions: but I now find that that is impossible. The matter however is very old; & it will always be new.

Yours faithfully | Alfred Marshall

[1] British Library, Macmillan Archive.

[2] Not traced. Presumably a request from Edwin Griswold Nourse (1883–1974) for permission to include a selection from Marshall in E. G. Nourse (ed.), *Agricultural Economics: A Selection*

of Materials in which Economic Principles are applied to the Practice of Agriculture (University of Chicago Press, Chicago, 1916). Selection 133 (pp. 421–6) of this work adapts pp. 167–83 of *Principles* (*6*) under the heading 'Utility and the Demand Schedule'.

[3] See [1055].

[4] See [1061.1].

1063. To Lady Margaret Ramsay, 24 July 1916[1]

Rollington Farm | Corfe Castle | Dorset
24. 7. 16

Dear Lady Ramsay,

You will be overwhelmed with letters from far & near, which speak with better knowledge than mine of the terrible loss that has befallen the worlds science: my only claim to speak of him is that he rendered me the greatest of all services. In the autumn of 1880 I was rapidly dwindling: I knew that each month of my stay at Bristol materially lessened my chance of living to do any considerable part of the work on wh I had set my heart. The Council of University College, Bristol, declared that the condition of their finances prohibited their advertising for a new Principal. The new Professor of Chemistry began his work in late September: by the middle of November I knew I was free. For a true strong MAN had come to the College; &, young as he was I knew that the destinies of the College were safe in his hands. They turned out to be much more than safe. In most grateful & affectionate remembrance of him, I remain,

Yours very sincerely & sympathetically | Alfred Marshall

[1] University College, London, Ramsay Papers. Sir William Ramsay had died on the previous day. The Marshalls had been well acquainted in Bristol with Mrs. Ramsay (née Buchanan), as she then was.

1064. To the Editor, *The Times*, 26 August 1916[1]

Sir,—I hear from an officer serving in Mesopotamia that that far-off region seems to be rather out of sight; and that, though the officers are fairly well off, the rank and file have not the same generous supply from private sources of those minor comforts and luxuries which do so much to lighten the tedium and cheer the spirits of their comrades on other fronts. My correspondent whispers of cigarettes, and suggests that the Mesopotamia Branch of the Y.M.C.A. might well receive some special aid. I venture to pass on their pleas to your readers.

Yours faithfully,

August 26. Alfred Marshall.

[1] Printed in *The Times*, 29 August 1916, under the heading 'Comforts for Mesopotamia'. Attributed to 'Professor Alfred Marshall' in *The Times Index* for 1916.

1065. From John Rickards Mozley, 29 September 1916[1]

1 Holly Bank | Headingley | Leeds
29 Sept 1916

My dear Marshall,

I was much touched by, and very grateful for, your letter.[2] The days of one's youth cannot but recur to one; and though in one sense they never return, in another sense they are perpetually with one. I never think of Henry Sidgwick as dead, or otherwise than as truly living, though beyond our ordinary knowledge. I do not think it unreasonable to hope for greater faculties than we have now—It is true what Clough says, that friends separate;[3] and there is apt (as you say) to be something tragic in this; but we are all on voyages of discovery, and may communicate to one another the light we separately obtain, and there is much compensation here. By the bye, my son Kenneth[4] quoted Clough in a sermon the other day: 'Say not the struggle nought availeth &c':[5] I was pleased to hear him do so.

I have always thought you more able than any modern economist whom I know to carry on *both* sides of political economy, which Mill[6] keenly appreciated—the scientific side, in which it deals with unalterable facts, and the emotional and expansive side, in which it aims at improving human affairs, and at changing the face of the world. I have always found the plain facts very difficult to understand. When I was a a boy at Eton, the one rule of arithmetic which I could not understand was 'Stocks'; what the reason was of stocks going up or down was a perfect mystery; and nobody explained it to me. Directly I began to possess shares, I understood it at once. Similarly, a bill of exchange is even now something of a mystery to me; after great efforts, I think I have obtained a theoretical understanding of it; but a living practical knowledge of it as a commonplace fact of the world I have not got. I think economists might do more than they do to make these first elements imaginable to people who are not practically conversant with them. A person who is practically conversant does not understand the ignorance of a person who is not practically conversant.

I wonder if I have gone wrong myself in my book in this way. Prayer, though sacred, and full of mystery and difficulty in some aspects of it, has yet its commonplace side; and it is possible that I may not have been clear enough in explaining this. I wonder if Mrs. Marshall would say I have been intelligible here. However, let me quote two sentences from your letter which I think have some pertinency to the subject.

'I have come to the conclusion that the Unknown probably has concerns in which this world plays a part almost as insignificant as that played by a single small insect in the history of this minute world x x x'

'Every year my reverence to the Unknown becomes deeper; my consciousness of the narrow limitations of all the knowledge in this world becomes more oppressive; and my desire to add to that quantity something that will count, though it is a microscopic fraction of that microscopic whole, becomes stronger'.

Of these two sentences, the first expresses the theory of the Unknown; the second expresses what ought to be our practice in actual life. But I think I should add to what you say, that the Unknown, being spiritual in its essence, helps us in our efforts to add something 'that will count' to human experience and knowledge; and in religious language, 'the Unknown' is God, and our appeal to the Unknown is prayer. Thus though the essence of God is unknown, our communications with God, and the results of those communications, are known, and God enters into our ordinary experience. In this way we perpetually grow towards the Infinite.

If you care to read a short chapter in my book, not very argumentative and rather outside the ordinary lines, read the fifth, on China and Japan. I don't think it would give you much trouble; but of course don't tire yourself.

I have never been to Mürren since we were there in 1867,[7] nearly half a century ago. I should like to see that magnificent mountain wall, with its array of peaks, again; and still more I should like to see the dolomites again—However, to have seen is something.

I forget if Mrs. Marshall knows my sister-in-law, Mrs Nutt,[8] who lives in Millington Road, and who is full of the spirit of curious inquiry, though she doesn't agree with my book; she is worth knowing—I believe however that Mrs. Marshall does know her.

Now I must not trouble you to answer this letter, though I hope, if I come to Cambridge, I may see you for a few minutes; though when that will be I do not know. With kindest regards to Mrs Marshall believe me yours ever

J R Mozley.

P.S. I will ask Kenneth about your nephew,[9] whom I have not myself met.

[1] Marshall Papers. Mozley (1840–1931) had been 12th Wrangler and 5th Classic in 1862, and a Fellow of King's 1861–9. Marshall had made his acquaintance in 1865, while both were teaching at Clifton College. Subsequently, Mozley served as Professor of Pure Mathematics at Owens College, 1865–85, and thereafter lived in retirement in Leeds. Marshall's (untraced) letter to Mozley had probably been written to congratulate him upon the publication of his *The Divine Aspects of History* (Cambridge University Press, Cambridge, 1916: 2 vols.).

[2] Not traced.

[3] Arthur Hugh Clough (1819–1861), English poet, brother of Anne Jemima Clough (1820–92), first Principal of Newnham. Possibly the allusion is to Clough's poem 'That out of sight is out of mind'. See A. L. P. Norrington (ed.), *The Poems of Hugh Arthur Clough* (Oxford University Press, London, 1968), p. 101.

[4] John Kenneth Mozley (1883–1946), churchman and theological author, who had a distinguished student record at Cambridge.

[5] The title of one of Clough's best-known short poems. See Norrington, p. 63.

[6] John Stuart Mill.

[7] Marshall had shared a climbing holiday in 1867 with Mozley. Mürren, the Swiss mountain resort, commands a fine view of the Jungfrau massif.

[8] Probably the wife of Rev. John William Nutt of Harpsden Lodge, Millington Road, sometime Fellow of All Souls, Oxford, whose daughter May Geraldine had married Mozley's son Kenneth in 1910.
[9] Probably Marshall's clergyman nephew, Harold Guillebaud. See Vol. 1, App. I.

1066. To Macmillan and Company, 3 November 1916[1]

3. 11. 16

Mess[rs] MacMillan & Co

Dear Sirs

I have to thank you for a copy of my *Principles.*[2]

The paper wrapping describes my work that is in the Press as on *National industries & international trade.* I think I had written to you or to Sir Frederick MacMillan that the title is to be *Industry & Trade*: but perhaps I omitted to do so; & any how the error is of no consequence. The correct title is given on the first page of the Preface to my *Principles.*[3] The change of title was caused by the slowness of my progress, which convinced me that I cannot hope to bring out any considerable work after this: & therefore I am changing the scope of this, & giving it a more elastic title. My work at it has been interrupted, chiefly by causes connected with the war; but I am now proceeding with it.

Sir Frederick MacMillan, having learnt incidentally that I had bought a copy of my Principles, asked me not to do that again: but to apply to you for any copies that I wanted. I have for some time been without a spare copy, & occasions arise on which I cannot easily avoid presenting one. I shall therefore be much obliged if you will kindly send me six or eight copies of the new edition.

Yours faithfully | Alfred Marshall

[1] British Library, Macmillan Archive. From Balliol Croft.
[2] The newly issued *Principles* (*7*).
[3] See *Guillebaud*, p. 61. Marshall had indeed communicated the change in title—see [1055].

1067. To Sir Frederick Macmillan, 7 November 1916[1]

7. 11. 16

Dear Sir Frederick,

I thank you much for the six copies of my *Principles.*

I am not sure whether I told you that I have found the plan of bringing out my two volumes of *Industry & Trade* together impracticable.[2] Vol I will, I hope, be ready so far as I am concerned about Easter: you must decide when it is to be published. I now work so slowly, & propose to put so much matter into Vol

II, wh had originally been relegated to Vol III, that it is not likely to be ready for two or three years.

Yours very truly | Alfred Marshall

[1] British Library, Macmillan Archive. From Balliol Croft.
[2] He had: see [1055].

1068. To William Harbutt Dawson, 18 November 1916[1]

18. 11. 16

Dear Mr Dawson,

I am much troubled. My old draft of my chapter contains far less than 19,000 words. I can't recollect how—if the publishers have counted right—the draft I sent has been increased from that. The last post of the day is in: & no M.S.S. has arrived.

I cannot help fearing that the publishers have an aim different from that which I supposed to be yours when I consented to do 'as my bit' a thing that no number of hundreds of pounds would have induced me to do for payment. As I warmed to my subject I got to see that this is an occasion on wh it may be possible to do some public service by a bit of work as thorough as I could make it. I have given in all a full quarter of a years work to it: & I have so few quarters before me that in consequence I must let other half finished work go unfinished. Many plans have occurred to me: but none seem likely to answer the publishers purpose & mine. When you wrote to me in June that I should write freely & not bind myself to a limited number of words, I thought you recognized that the subject allotted to me is of exceptional scope relatively to those originally suggested, to say nothing of some recent additions: & I tried by frequent re-writing to comb out superfluous words.

The chapter could be divided into two parts easily: but the two would need to be read together; & I do not see what is to be done.

It never entered into my head that the book was to be [a][2] small one; smaller even than the Labour Year Book,[3] which supplies about 350,000 words for 2s (1s in paper) & has a table of contents rather distressingly like that now adopted, though not so very like the parts of the original draft of it, wh I liked most heartily. So I am very very sad.[4]

Yours very sincerely | Alfred Marshall

[1] Marshall Papers. From Balliol Croft. See [1053, 1061].
[2] Word apparently accidentally omitted.
[3] *The Labour Year Book*, vol. 1. Issued under the auspices of the Parliamentary Committee of the Trades Union Congress, the Executive Committee of the Labour Party, and the Fabian Research Department (Cooperative Printing Society, London, 1916).
[4] *After-War Problems* [1061.1] had 366 pages and 19 contributors. Marshall's 33-page essay was the longest, although Viscount Haldane on 'National Education', at 32 pages, was close. Only six of the essays exceeded 20 pages in length. At approximately 450 words per page, the published version of Marshall's essay contained about 14,500 words, and the entire volume contained about 165,000 words. Its price was 7s. 6d. net.

1069. To Mary Booth, 24 November 1916[1]

24. 11. 16

Dear M^rs^. Booth,

I write a line to express my sympathy with you, & yours; & my grief at the loss which the world has suffered. Mr Booth's name is imperishable: it will live not only in history, but in popular language; as we speak of an Achilles, a Socrates, or a Parsifal. He was strong & gentle, wise & simple, earnest & placid, resolute & tolerant: he was broad in his conceptions, & minutely careful in his unparalleled mastery of details.

To know him was an education: it was also one of the chief honours & pleasures of my life.

Yours very sincerely | Alfred Marshall

[1] University of London Library, Booth Papers, on mourning paper. No address given. Mary Booth (1847–1939: née Macaulay) was the wife of Charles Booth who had died the previous day.

1070. To the Editor, *The Economist*, 30 December 1916[1]

Sir,—May I make a humble contribution to the support which you give to Profesor Pigou's plea for increased taxation to defray the expenses of the war.[2] In the early stages of the war a considerable part of the nation did not realise the extent to which the future of Europe, and to some extent of the whole world, depends on the frustration of Germany's purpose to make Berlin the centre of a military empire, which would dominate Europe and imperil the security of other continents. Also nearly everyone greatly underrated the preparations which she had made for the war, and the expenditure which it would involve. Therefore our Government judged it prudent to avoid checking the eagerness with which the people entered into it, and were slow to increase the burden of taxation. The difficulties of a courageous policy would have been greater than now, and the need for it was less urgent.

Almost every great increase in a nation's wealth and prosperity has been preceded by a period of hard living. And there is therefore some little justification for the boast of the Germans that they are working as hard as we are and consuming much less; that, therefore, their resources are not being diminished as rapidly relatively to ours as might have been anticipated, and that the hardships which they are enduring are a better preparation for energetic work after the war than are the unwonted luxuries which some of us are enjoying at the expense of mortgaging the future for the benefit of the present. There is great exaggeration in every part of this boast, but small kernels of truth will remain in it unless there is a generous, ungrudging response to the appeal to 'men of all ranks and conditions to play the game.'

Those below the income-tax level, and those whose incomes are in such forms that they cannot conveniently be brought under the tax, though in equity they should, must escape lightly. But taxes on alcohol, inelastic as their yield is, should be increased; and some taxes might be levied on ordinary articles of consumption; a tax might be taken, for instance, on every animal that enters a registered slaughter-house, imported meat being, of course, taxed correspondingly.

The main sources of increased revenue would, however, necessarily be taxes on income and on capital. For, as Professor Pigou has well argued,[3] capital cannot easily emigrate during the war in large quantity, and taxes imposed merely for the duration of the war will not do much towards setting capital on the move. But the vast indebtedness which the country is heaping up now will require heavy permanent taxation after the war, and that will greatly retard our command of the capital which will then be grievously needed.

A further increase in the intensity of the income-tax will, of course, aggravate the inequalities of its burdens on people with like incomes but unlike responsibilities, and no thorough remedy for these evils can be worked out during the stress of the war. But while maintaining the unity of joint incomes of husband and wife for the purposes of assessment, allowances of various degrees might be made at once for all the members, adult and young, who depend on the family income.—Yours faithfully,

Alfred Marshall.

[1] Printed in *The Economist*, 30 December 1916, under the heading 'The Need for more Taxation'.

[2] See Pigou's letters of 19 November, 4 and 17 December 1916, all published under the heading 'The Need for More Taxation', *The Economist*, 83: 25 November 1916, pp. 1003–4; 9 December 1916, p. 1087; 23 December 1916, pp. 1180–1. Pigou urged a greatly increased reliance on the income tax for war finance, and was supported by *The Economist* in an unsigned article 'Taxation and Consumption', 2 December 1916, pp. 1031–2, which suggested, however, that saving be spared.

[3] In his letter of 23 December.

1071. To Charles Kay Ogden, 15 March 1917[1]

15. 3. 17

Dear M^{r}. Ogden

I am very sorry to be unable to comply with your request.[2] I really know nothing about the matter. Though I subscribed to the funds of the Fight for the Right movement, when it was first started, I have lost sight of it; & I did not know that it had come into conflict with the Cambridge Magazine.[3]

The fact is that the work on w^{h}. I am at present engaged, while bearing indirectly on economic policy after the war, is largely concerned with facts, that need to be collected from scattered sources: & my eyes, w^{h}. are now easily tired, give out before they have done what I require of them. So I scarcely read anything else: my wife reads aloud to me a good deal, but I have no clear idea of what the Magazine is doing. I ought perhaps to add that what I read of the

Magazine some time ago impressed me with high respect for the character of those who were conducting it; but represented a view so different from my own as to the consequences of the partial success of German aims, that I thought they w^{d}. be injurious to the best interests of the world, if read by people who had not a full knowledge of the other side of the case.

With great respect for your high purpose & courage, I remain

Yours very truly | Alfred Marshall

P.S. In my early days I had a warm regard & even affection for nearly all the Germans whom I got to know: but even then I knew that the Prussian Junker was the embodiment of evil. He has been the schoolmaster of the Prussians, & indirectly even of the Saxons & others since then; & every time I met Germans in later years I seemed further away from them: but even the early horrors of Belgium did not make me dread the expansion of their influence as much as I do now.

[1] Marshall Papers. From a retained copy in Mrs Marshall's hand. Ogden (1889–1957) had obtained a first in Part I of the Classical Tripos of 1910. He founded and edited the *Cambridge Magazine*, 1912–22, and became well known as a linguistic psychologist and the founder of Basic English.

[2] Not traced.

[3] See *The Times*, 13 November 1915 (11b), 29 March 1916 (11b), for information on the activities of the Fight for Right movement. With its motto 'Fight for right till right be won', the organization sought to harness musical and poetic feeling to patriotic ideals.

1072. To John Maynard Keynes, 9 June 1917[1]

9. 6. 17

My dear Keynes,

I am out of the world: but I have just learnt from the Economist that you are a C.B.[2] I am glad. That is the first step upwards on a noble staircase. Macte virtute![3]

Yours ever | Alfred Marshall

[1] King's College, Cambridge, J. M. Keynes Papers. From Balliol Croft. Keynes had recently been made a Companion of the Order of the Bath in recognition of his wartime services, but only after Lloyd George as Prime Minister had made a point of refusing to forward a previous nomination. See *Collected Works*, vol. 16, pp. 222–3.

[2] *The Economist*, 84 (9 June 1917), p. 1060, in a note on Birthday Honours, had observed that 'Mr J. M. Keynes's C.B. recognises arduous and very practical work for his country by a brilliant economist'.

[3] Persevere in virtue, or keep up the good work.

1073. To John Maynard Keynes, 13 June 1917[1]

13. 6. 17

My dear Keynes

I do indeed hope that you will not abandon science for administration. But you have a better chance than any economist has ever had in this country of rendering high services to the State on critical occasions: for you will know more of economics than any professional statesman has ever done; & you will know more of Whitehall's difficulties—whether founded in the nature of things or in bureaucracy—than any professional economist has ever done. So when you are K.C.B.[2] and are yet thinking out your best thoughts to their foundations, and from your foundations, you are to suppose that my shade is hovering over you, & dropping an ethereal wreath from Elysian fields on your head.

Yours till then, & after | Alfred Marshall

[1] King's College, Cambridge, J. M. Keynes Papers. From Balliol Croft. Reproduced in *Collected Works*, vol. 16, p. 223.

[2] Knight Commander of the Order of the Bath, an honour Keynes was not to receive.

1074. To Sir Frederick Macmillan, 25 August 1917[1]

25. 8. 17

Dear Sir Frederick

So far as I am personally concerned, I should prefer no change to be made in the prices of my *Principles* & *Elements*.[2] For they have ceased to give any considerable trouble; & I should have thought that their costs of production— mental & material, to writer & publisher—were not rising on the whole.

I have several times been on the point of writing publicly on the side of those who hold that—save for every exceptional reasons—no one should push prices up. For instance I think that neither wholesale nor retail dealer ought to add his full ordinary *rate* of profit on an increase of his turnover which results from an increase in the prices which he has to pay for his goods. I think he should add only his *actual* extra costs; consisting of (1) extra payments (a) for his goods & (b) for the services of his employees; & (2) normal profits on extra locking up of his capital. I am not sure that this principle would apply to the case now in hand. But I think an economist is bound to be more scrupulous in such matters than other people. So I should prefer no change. But I feel specially bound to speak with humility on the matter.

For indeed I must wrap myself in the white sheet, & hold the candle of the penitent, when I pass to speak of my new work. For I know I have run up a huge printers bill on it, which will eat a considerable way into the publishers share of the earnings on my other books. I had been on the point of writing to you about it, when your recent letter arrived.

I will not narrate the history of my vacillations as to scope and arrangement of the work. They have been caused partly by external events; partly by my tardy recognition of the magnitude of the task proposed: but chiefly by the mental inertia caused by 'blood pressure' before I knew that such a malady existed, & by the extreme slowness of work, which I am told is the only condition under which I can hope to work at all. So long as I obey orders, I am in excellent health.

The upshot is that nearly the whole of Vol I—the winding up alone excepted—is now in slips. I think the Volume will be a little shorter than my Principles, but certainly not much shorter.

As the publication of Vol II is put off for an indefinite time, I am shifting to Appendices nearly all matter relating to the development of the policies of international trade. Many other changes, mostly small, have been gradually made in the slips: but I hope to be able to get through with only a single revise, & that of course in pages, with but few exceptions.

I have however practically rewritten the first chapter. I had hoped that new slips of that would have come in this evening; when they do come, I will send you a copy. It describes the plan of the work definitely.

It does not however give the title: & that has been modified since I last wrote to you. It now stands:—

INDUSTRY AND TRADE

A study of industrial technique and of business organization, and of their influences on the conditions of various classes & nations.[3]

Yours very truly | Alfred Marshall

More than half of Vol II is typewritten: but it will need a good deal of re-writing. None of it is in print.

[1] British Library, Macmillan Archive. From Balliol Croft.

[2] In a letter of 22 August (Marshall Papers), Macmillan had proposed increasing the price of *Principles* (7) from 12s. 6d. to 16s., and that of *Elements* from 3s. 6d. to 4s., in recognition of increased costs. He did not expect the increases to affect sales seriously since similar increases were being made by other publishers.

[3] This was, indeed, the title given to the published work.

1075. From Sir Frederick Macmillan, 29 August 1917[1]

Macmillan & Co. Ltd. | St. Martin's Street. | London. W.C.
Aug 29 1917.

Dear D[r] Marshall

I have your letter of the 25 and write to say that we are quite willing to fall in with your suggestion that the prices of your two books should remain unaltered. It happens that we have a considerable stock of each consequently the increased cost of production will not affect them except in the matter of binding.

I quite agree with you that prices should not be put up without good reason and that is why we have refrained from taking action for so long. The cost of manufacture has been rising ever since the war began and as we do not as a rule carry more than a year's stock of the books in most demand we have been constantly reprinting books at an increased cost without any corresponding increase in our receipts. You will realise this when I tell you that the cost of paper has gone up 300%, Binding 37%, Printing 20%, in addition to business expenses which have risen enormously owing to a general increase in wages. The price of paper will no doubt go down somewhat after the war but not I think to its former level, and I don't expect to see any decrease in the other items as the rise has been largely due to wages.

I am much obliged to you for the proof of Chapter 1 of 'Industry & Trade' which I shall read with great interest. I quite understand why this book has been so long in the press & hope that you will not attempt to hasten it by trying to work quickly against your doctor's orders. I am delighted to hear that you can keep in good health by obeying him.

As for the Title pages,[2] I prefer A: the type used for the sub-title in B is very ugly in my opinion. I quite agree with you that the line 'The many in the one', Etc should be in the larger italic type as on specimen C.

Believe me | Yours very truly | Frederick Macmillan

[1] Marshall Papers.

[2] When sending the proofs of ch. 1, Marshall had also enclosed three specimen title pages for Sir Frederick's judgement. (Covering note of 27 August 1917: British Library, Macmillan Archive.)

1076. To Walter Thomas Layton, 23 September 1917[1]

23. 9. 17

My dear Layton,

I have just heard you are a C.B.E.[2] I am heartily glad & proud. I think it is a noble position & fits you well. I know you declined another honour: but I think C.B.E. is the more solid.

I am vastly pleased to think of the great services you are rendering to the country: I hope you may yet return to Cambridge, for the sake of Cambridge. But if—after the war—you find more vital work to do in London, I shall regret & rejoice by turns.

Yours affectionately | Alfred Marshall

[1] Trinity College, Cambridge, Layton Papers. From Balliol Croft.

[2] Companion of the Order of the British Empire, an honour awarded for Layton's wartime contributions, for which see Hubback, *No Ordinary Press Baron* [934.1], ch. 3. Details as to the declined alternative award have not been discovered. Layton was to decline a knighthood in 1919, and was then made a Companion of Honour (Hubback, p. 50).

1077. To the Editor, *The Times*, 26 December 1917[1]

Sir,—Sir Conan Doyle in your issue of to-day suggests that the position of Britain and her Allies would have been stronger now if they had made the development of hatred against Germany a chief aim of their policy.[2] By doing always what seemed to us to be right we have enlisted the sympathy of the world on our side, and therefore we are strong: but we should lose much of that sympathy if we cultivated hatred as a weapon of war. Clear, well-authenticated statements of German cruelty ought no doubt to be published without reserve. But to foster hatred as an end would strengthen the position of pacifists, whose noble sentiments seem to me to make for a premature peace which would inflict a disaster almost unparalleled in history on the coming generation.

Yours faithfully,

December 26. Alfred Marshall.

[1] Printed with other letters under the heading 'The Uses of Hatred' in *The Times*, 28 December 1917. Original not traced.

[2] See the letter from Sir Arthur Conan Doyle (1859–1930), the well-known author, *The Times*, 26 December 1917 (9d).

1078. To Arthur Raymond Marshall, 18 January 1918[1]

18. i. 18

My dear brave Arthur,

How good and strong you are under your grievous pains! The latest news if you is always *the* news of the day, rivalled only by the inch high headings—if there are any—over the war news in the 'Times.' Poor dear lad! It is sad that you are thus struck, and in parts of the body that are specially sensitive and self-willed. But all brave soldiers, when hit, have the consolation of being able to say, 'it was for my country': and in this war there is even more to be said. The whole world—other than Germany—is in a sense 'the country' of those who are fighting for a future of peace: you suffer on behalf of the world; and the world will be grateful to you in coming times. Even should the worst befall and the world seem to darken before you, you can say '*Dulce et decorum est pro patria mori*': and then you can say it over again, and put *pro orbe* instead of *pro patria*. But that is only for moods when you are cast down. In other moods you will be looking forward to a noble life in quiet hero garb. First you will be looking after recruits, and then you will be settling down to engineering work, in which your mind will be all the keener, and have all the qualities of true leadership, because you have seen so much, and done so much, and felt so much. And this is the mood that you should foster. Among the happiest of men, are those who have gone through great tribulation, and have worked through it all to a noble life, ever nearer their Ideal, ever nearer to God.

Your loving, anxious, hopeful | Alfred Marshall

[1] Reproduced in *Memorials*, pp. 495–6. Original not traced. From Balliol Croft. Arthur Marshall, son of Alfred's older brother Charles, and a Captain in the Royal Garrison Artillery, had been wounded in action on 8 December 1917 and was to die in hospital at Rouen on 2 February 1918 (see *Memorials*, p. 495). Little detail has been discovered as to this branch of the family, but see Vol. 1, App. I, for general family background.

1079. To Lady Catherine Courtney, 13 May 1918[1]

13. 5. 18

Dear Lady Courtney

I desire to offer my tribute of respect and regret to him whom you have lost; & whom his country will not soon forget. Strong brave & wise, but open-minded & sympathetic, he has been a model representative of British character and statesmanship. He ever went on his own path, without turning to the right or the left: but his utterances were so well-informed and so well considered, so intensely patriotic and sincere, that he was respected by his opponents as fully as by his allies.

He has long been a chief glory of Cambridge University, & of St John's College in particular. He was specially reverenced by economists; & the Economic Society was proud that he consented to be one of its Vice-presidents. Every one of these fine qualities has a special claim on my homage and affection; & he was particularly kind & helpful to me at a time when I was most in need of guidance from that sound and penetrating judgement, of which he was an eminent master.[2] You know this far more fully & intimately than I can. But it is a relief to me to say it; while tendering you my heartiest sympathy for your great loss.

Yours very sincerely | Alfred Marshall

[1] BLPES, Courtney Papers. From Balliol Croft. Catherine Courtney (née Potter) had married in 1883 Leonard H. Courtney (Baron Courtney of Penwith since 1906). He had died on 11 May.

[2] The occasion for this advice and assistance is unclear: perhaps Marshall's campaign of 1902–3 for a new Economics Tripos.

1080. To Sir Frederick Macmillan, 8 June 1918[1]

8. 6. 18

Dear Sir Frederick

The University Press, though of course undermanned, is likely to have some energies to spare during the Long Vacation; & my *Industry & Trade* Vol I is now so far advanced that I think I may get it out in the early Autumn. I have postponed as long as possible the suggestion that it should go to Press; because the far-reaching changes in public opinion & in the activities of Whitehall, which were notable before 1914, are now moving at an unprecedented pace. This is one reason of the great changes which I have made since the first proofs of the book were set up long ago: though the chief reason is to be found in my failure to anticipate the extent to which my task would grow on my hands. Also things changed in perspective, as time went on; very much as the apparent contour of the Alps does when one travels past. Some of the things that I have still retained are less appropriate to actual conditions than when I wrote them: but a good deal of the book happens to bear directly on large issues, which have risen above the horizon only recently.

Mr Peace is writing to you about paper.

With renewed thanks for your tolerance of my delays, & consequent extravagances, I am,

Yours sincerely | Alfred Marshall

Sir Frederick MacMillan

[1] British Library, Macmillan Archive. From Balliol Croft.

1081. To Sir Frederick Macmillan, 11 June 1918[1]

11. 6. 18

Dear Sir Frederick

Thanks for your kind letter.[2] I think the number of copies you propose—2000—is appropriate.

But there are two, or perhaps three, sheets more to come.[3] The last chapter—which may become two—deals with monopolistic tendencies in Britain, in relation to 'Industrial Reconstruction'. The Whitley Report[4] seems to mean different things to different men: to some it is an improvement in organization; but to others it is to confer vast benefits on particular classes. If the latter interpretation is right, some must lose at least a part of what others gain. I want the clouds, that obscure this matter, to lift as far as they will, before I send anything to press about it. That is why I began my revise before getting quite to the end of the book. My revise is almost ended & I am now turning towards 'the clouds'.

Yours very sincerely | Alfred Marshall

[1] British Library, Macmillan Archive. From Balliol Croft.

[2] Dated 10 June 1918 (Marshall Papers). Macmillan had projected a book of about 700 pages, assuming it to be 'now all in type'. He looked forward to adding the title to 'our very attenuated Autumn List'. Supply of paper was a concern given wartime scarcities.

[3] A sheet contained 16 pages (8 leaves). The published version had xxiv + 875 pages.

[4] See P. and G. Ford, *A Breviate of Parliamentary Papers, 1917–39* (Blackwell, Oxford, 1951), pp. 319–21, for details of the various reports issued by the Committee of the Ministry of Reconstruction on Joint Industrial Councils, chaired by John Henry Whitley (1866–1935). The Final Report (Cd 9153, 1918) recommended industrial and works councils, bringing together representatives of workers and management, as a means of improving industrial relations. These councils were commonly referred to as 'Whitley Councils'. See also *Industry and Trade*, pp. 393–4, 643–5.

1082. To Sir Frederick Macmillan, 28 June 1918[1]

28. 6. 18

Dear Sir Frederick

Sir H Llewellyn Smith wrote to me a day or two ago,[2] to say that he had heard I was writing something about railways: that the Board of Trade are now giving great attention to their future; & that he would be glad if I could let them see confidentially what I had written.

So I have asked the Press to pull off some copies of my three chapters on the subject & print them on its own paper: all charges of course being given to me.

I feel sure you will approve so do not trouble to answer.

Yours very truly | Alfred Marshall

Llewellyn Smith knows that it would not be possible for me to give oral evidence.

[1] British Library, Macmillan Archive. From Balliol Croft.
[2] Letter not traced. Llewellyn Smith was Permanent Secretary of the Board of Trade, 1907–19.

1083. To Sir Hubert Llewellyn Smith, (1918?)[1]

Dear Sir H Llewellyn Smith

Thank you for your letter of the 12th.[2] I think we are in full agreement so far as those matters reach, of which I have knowledge. And, if I knew all the reasons which oppose the temporary return of the railways to their pre-war status, while a thorough study was being made of one of the largest & most difficult economic problems that have ever been faced by British Statesmanship, & on the solution of which her future greatly depends. Being already at least half-way inclined towards railway nationalization, in association with other transport developments, I should not be specially anxious on that particular matter, if I were not afraid that it might be the source of troubles in other directions. I am one of those who think that soon—though probably not in my time—the working classes will enter into their long deferred heritage; & that, as commonly happens in such cases, the lessons of experience will be learnt too suddenly to be well learnt. Therefore I have been made anxious by the somewhat excessive courage which has appeared to me to have inspired some suggestions for immediate action in regard to railways.

The terms of reference to a Select Committee of the House of Commons, which you kindly inclose,[3] seem to me admirable. And, if they take evidence from all concerned & publish it in the ordinary way, I should expect nothing but good from it. But I will venture to unburden my soul about the group of Departmental Committees on the position of particular trades after the war.[4]

In time of war it was of course impossible to keep open house; to invite representatives of every important interest & trend of opinion concerned to give witness; to accept rebutting evidence from suitable witnesses who took exception to some of the arguments or statements made by other witnesses; & thus to act the part of judges rather than advocates. But I submit that any conclusions on large matters reached without these advantages—which belong to all public Commissions—lack something of authority. I have myself learnt more from Blue-books than from all others: but that is because any statement or conclusion in a Report which interests me sends me to the index. I then find the evidence on which it is based; get to know the personalities of the witnesses concerned; watch them & their interrogators, & finally know on what basis the statement or conclusion rests. But when as sometimes happens—as for instance in regard to the actual working of cartel-like organizations—I find a difficulty in accepting the conclusions of a Committee sitting with closed doors, I cannot avoid the impression that such a method of study is full of dangers; especially to a country which is becoming increasingly democratic.

Take for instance the opinion, that has been voiced in perhaps unduly strong terms in the *Economist* & elsewhere that the Committees underrate the difficulties of organizing marketing.[5] I am not an authority on that matter, but I cannot avoid the conclusion that the Committees have sometimes supposed that they were only suggesting that British associations should do what German cartels habitually do: and, if that is so, think it should be ignored: & yet the method of inquiry which alone is practicable during the war, almost necessarily excludes all-round treatment. That is what I mean, when I urge that nothing should be done, without urgent cause, in the hurried time of war which would reach far forward into the leisured time of peace.

I have not overlooked the 'Reservations' &c of individual members of the Committees; some of which are very helpful to me.

The length of this letter is inexcusable: I can only trust that your kindness will pass a lenient judgment on it.

Yours sincerely | Alfred Marshall

[1] Marshall Papers. From Balliol Croft, undated. The preceding letter suggests that the letter was written in the summer of 1918.

[2] Not traced.

[3] Probably the Select Committee on transport questions appointed August 1918. See P. and G. Ford, *A Breviate* [1081.4], pp. 255–6, for details of its terms of reference and reports.

[4] For details see Ford, pp. 151–60.

[5] See, for example, the leading articles 'Trade and the Board of Trade', 'After War Perhapses', and 'Industrial Leading Strings', *The Economist*, 86: respectively, 26 January 1918, p. 111; 4 May 1918, pp. 699–700; 22 June 1918, pp. 1039–40.

1084. To the Editor, *The Economist*, 21 September 1918[1]

Sir,—One of the most instructive episodes in the history of cartels is found in the relations of the *Prussian* Government to the potash industry, of which it is a chief member. The deposits are mainly in Stassfurt, but that is not, as you say in your issue of to-day,[2] in Saxony; it is in 'Province Saxony,' which is part of Prussia.

Yours faithfully, Alfred Marshall.

September 21st, 1918.

[1] Printed in *The Economist*, 28 September 1918, under the heading 'The Supply of Potash'. Original not traced.

[2] *The Economist*, 87 (21 September 1918), p. 363. An unsigned note entitled 'Home Supplies of Potash', had observed: 'Of course we have no natural potash deposits such as those which exist at Strassfurt in Saxony, and are sufficient to supply the needs of the whole world . . .'.

1085. To John Hilton, 3 October 1918 (incomplete)[1]

3. x. 1918

Dear Mr Hilton,

I am delighted to find that you are Secretary to the Committee on Trusts:[2] it is a most important post; and, I think, admirably filled. . . .

I began the study about twenty years ago; and have given most of my time to it during recent years. I began with a bias against American developments, and in favour of German. But the American situation has greatly improved; and—except for the good mingled with the ill in the Stahlwerks-Verband[3]—I do not think the German situation gets better. The Americans are absolutely frank, I think; and the pictures of German cartels which seem to have been supplied to some of the Board of Trade's Committees on particular trades after the war[4] differ widely from those which I have formed as years went on. It is very unfortunate that they have not published the evidence on which they have based opinions, which are not, I think, in accordance with the evidence on the subject furnished by the Kartell-Enquête[5] and the discussions at the Social Verein[6] on the subject.

As to the relation of law to monopoly I have learnt very little from English sources: it seems never to have been thoroughly studied here. But American analysis and experience seem to show that in almost every difficult case there comes a stage at which the right of appeal to a 'Supreme Court,' or its equivalent, becomes necessary. But I do not think that a Court of Law is at all likely to find out what are the really significant points in such a problem, unless guided by highly trained specialists: and I think that some of the *obiter dicta*, even of many able judges, as to matters of economic policy might have very disastrous results if any authority came to be attached to them.

In short, I think the Federal Trade Act[7] (somewhat modifying the duties of the old Bureau of Corporations and preserving in the main its personnel, though changing its name to Federal Trade Commission) is a master stroke of genius. It has been repeatedly argued, both here and in America, that the Common Law in regard to monopolies etc. has done admirable service, because its traditions are so vague as to be incapable of exact interpretation: it merely suggests a general tendency; and each generation has interpreted its vagueness with more or less success, in accordance with the needs and the administrative resources of the time. If that great heritage is to be swept away in the troubled waters of war time, I trust that nothing will be done of a far-reaching character without a careful study of the toilsome steps by which American expedients have been developed. I presume you have full access to the official literature relating to the work of the Federal Trade Commission. I have learnt from it, and that of the Bureau of Corporations, more perhaps than from any other source relating to the functions of a democratic government in regard to complex economic issues. On the other hand I have learnt nothing from *official* German pronouncements on such matters, unless it be in the art of saying what one does not mean. I am still a great admirer of Germany, in some connections, but those sides of her character, which the war has made prominent, seem to have misguided the policy of her cartels, and of her Government in relation to them.

I concur in the suggestion made by the Engineering Committee (Cd. 9078), p. 26,[8] that secrecy is at the root of many of the evils of cartel policy: but not in their proposal that the constitution of a cartel should be registered *privately* with the Board of Trade. Bureaucratic rule has been necessary during the war: but if it became permanent, grave evils might arise from it, I fear, in this country, which is rapidly becoming a true democracy.

At such a time as this I think everyone who has studied a matter that is becoming urgent should submit his conclusions without reserve to those who are responsible, and, though I do not suppose that mine will be found very helpful, I have ventured to burden you with a long letter.

Yours faithfully, | Alfred Marshall

[1] Reproduced in *Memorials*, pp. 491–3. Original not traced. From Balliol Croft.

[2] Of the Ministry of Reconstruction. See P. and G. Ford, *A Breviate* [1081.4], pp. 195–6, for details. The Committee grew from an earlier report on post-war problems by the Garton Foundation of which Hilton was secretary.

[3] The pre-war German steel cartel.

[4] Ford, pp. 151–60 gives details.

[5] The official German inquiry into cartels of 1905–6.

6 The Verein für Socialpolitik, the association of German economists with historical-school learnings led by Schmoller, was founded in 1872. It held periodic meetings and sponsored an extensive series of monographs. Industrial matters were a frequent topic.

7 Of September 1914.

8 See Report of the Departmental Committee on the Engineering Trades after the War (Cd 9073—not 9078—1918). Ford, pp. 156–7, gives details.

1086. To Sir Frederick Macmillan, 12 October 1918[1]

12. 10. 18

Dear Sir Frederick MacMillan,

I omitted the words 'Volume I' from the title page of my Book, wh I sent to you: & I see that it has been followed in the notice which you were good enough to insert in the current *Economic Journal*.[2]

Perhaps it may cause disappointment to purchasers. For Vol I does not get very far into the study of 'the conditions of various classes', & does not touch directly on those of various nations. I do not think any great harm has been done: but perhaps some notice—you will best judge how—should be given that the range of Vol I is narrower than that of the full title, when again the volume is described. Perhaps inserting 'Volume I' will suffice.

I have been working fairly well. But my progress is slow, partly because the subject of my two last chapters is very complex; but partly also because the Board of Trade has published, & the Ministry of Reconstruction (with a special 'Committee on Trusts')[3] is preparing a vast quantity of new matter on the subjects of those chapters. It is however fortunate on the whole that I know what is going on.

Yours very truly | Alfred Marshall

1 British Library, Macmillan Archives. From Balliol Croft. A copy, dated 12 October 1918 and in Mrs Marshall's hand, of what appears to be an earlier draft for this letter is sufficiently different to merit reproduction (Marshall Papers):

> Dear Sir Frederick Macmillan,
>
> I have only just noticed that the title page of my new book, w^{h}. I submitted to you for approval did not contain the words 'Volume I.' You have naturally followed the lines of the title page in your notice of the current Economic Journal; & I fear it may disappoint some readers. For Vol I is little more than 'a study of business technique & business organization': 'their influence on the conditions of various classes & nations' will be the main concern of Vol II.
>
> I have just sent to press the last chapter but one of my book, after in effect re-writing it about four times. This is partly because the Board of Trade & the Ministry of Reconstruction are at work on the same lines as those of that & the last chapter. Blue books, one after another are coming out w^{h}.. give new information & alter relative proportions of the matters I am thinking about: there never has been in the whole history of the past so much official & important new work on a particular class of problems. This *embarras des richesses* causes delays: but it is lucky that my book was not printed off a little while before the flood came. It tends to make some parts of the book rather opportune.
>
> Yours very truly | Alfred Marshall

2 Vol. 28 (September 1918). The notice was printed on the back cover.

3 See [1085.2].

1087. To Sir Frederick Macmillan, (23?) October 1918[1]

Dear Sir Frederick MacMillan,

I think you are right about dropping the words 'Volume I.'[2] There is enough matter in semi-final form for my second volume to be printed, even if I should be unable to do anything more at it. I propose to speak of it in my Preface to this volume as a companion volume: and perhaps to indicate, more or less precisely, that its title will probably be 'Industry and Trade, a study of the organization of employment, of international trade, and of other influences on the conditions of various classes and nations'.

I cannot think of any other fitting titles on the backs than 'Industry and Trade' in both cases. The companion volume might have * * on its back: & perhaps this might have a single asterisk. I think there is some precedent for this: but you will know better than I do.

Your announcement of the book in the Economic Journal[3] (for which many thanks) has set up a little comedy; in which you, as a Cambridge man[4] may take some interest. I had no idea that such a title as 'Emeritus Professor' of Cambridge existed: and, when I inquired about it my disengagement from all such mundane affairs stood out rather ludicrously. My attention was called to a passage in the Calendar (p 308 of the 1914 edition), which stated that according to Grace passed in 1897,[5] a Professor on retirement after the age of 65 became 'Emeritus' automatically: & I had retired at the age of 66. A little later, it was discovered that that statement, though official, was incorrect! The Regulation creating the word 'Emeritus' was really passed in 1912; and was intended to be retrospective. But the only other Professor affected by it, beside myself, objected *vehemently* to the Regulation—on some side-issue—I do not know what. The Council was given to understand that, though I had not expressed a similar objection, I really shared it—though in fact I knew nothing of the matter. I avoid the use of all titles—even honorary membership of foreign Acadamies: but, as the matter had once been raised, I acquiesced in its being brought before the Council. The result is the inclosed Grace.[6]

Yours sincerely | Alfred Marshall

I am in close touch with the 'Committee on Trusts', set up by the Ministry of Reconstruction;[7] and I give and receive confidential papers on the subject.

[1] British Library, Macmillan Archive. From Balliol Croft. Macmillan's response [1088] suggests the date.

[2] Macmillan's response of 14 October to [1086] had thought it 'best to allow the title-page of *Industry and Trade* to remain as it stands and to insert a few words in the Preface explaining that a second volume is contemplated' (Marshall Papers).

[3] See [1086.2].

[4] The Macmillan firm had been launched in Cambridge, but Sir Frederick had never studied at the University. His brother Maurice Crawford Macmillan (1853–1936) had, however, been a member of Christ's, obtaining a first in the Classical Tripos of 1875. He had joined the family firm in 1880.

[5] The Grace of 11 February 1897 establishing a Professor's and Reader's Pension Fund.
[6] *Reporter*, 25 October 1918. The Grace conferred on Marshall the title of Professor Emeritus.
[7] See [1085].

1088. From Sir Frederick Macmillan, 24 October 1918[1]

Macmillan & Co. Ltd. | St. Martin's Street, | London, W.C.2
October 24th 1918.

Dear Dr. Marshall,

I am very glad that you agree about dropping the words 'Volume I' from the title-page of *Industry and Trade*. We will certainly adopt your suggestion that a * should be put on the back of the cover of Volume I, so that if and when a second volume ever appears * * can be put on the back to indicate that it is a second volume.[2]

I am very much amused to find that the mistake we made in our Announcement List has led the University of Cambridge to put itself into line with our advertisement and that we shall be justified to go on calling you 'Emeritus Professor of Political Economy'.[3]

I am, | Yours very truly, | Frederick Macmillan.

[1] Marshall Papers. Typewritten.
[2] *Industry and Trade* was published without the asterisk on the spine.
[3] See [1086.2, 1087.6].

1089. To Walter Thomas Layton, 9 December 1918[1]

9. 12. 18

Dear Layton,

I don't know whether I have ever received a letter, at once so delightful & so difficult, as that w^{h}. you have just sent me.

It is most delightful, because the honour conferred on you is almost unique, reminiscent a little of Turgot. As President of the Steel Whitley Council, the most important member of the most important class to w^{h}. it belongs, you w^{d}. have singular powers of doing good.[2] You w^{d}. be the right man in the right place you w^{d}. learn much that all economists have wanted to know, & have difficulty in learning. Your time wd. be very much at your own disposal, & you w^{d}. be able to write & think out general problems relating to employment & industrial organization, with unexampled knowledge. No doubt you w^{d}. seldom be at liberty to quote specific facts of just the kind most important for your purpose: but, there is much force in the maxim 'seldom quote specific facts, but embody the essence of multitudes of facts in the words w^{h}. you utter & in your abstinences from expressing opinions that seem plausible at first sight.'

Those who talk to you & those who talk before you w^{d}. be always saying important things, not easy of access, & full of significance for the larger economic problems both technical & 'human.'

If all went well, you w^{d}. have a splended career, more fortunate in many ways & more capable of being turned to good account in the public interest than any other economist has had. All this is most delightful.

But there are difficulties, w^{h}.. I may not ignore, though I am not in a good position to know how far they are real & how far merely apparent. Moreover I am conscious of a certain bias in the matter. I may say confidentially that I wrote (confidentially again) to Llewellyn Smith, contrasting the report of the Board of Trade Com^{tee} on the Iron & Steel Trades[3] with some others in the same group; on the ground that, except for some of the reservations, & especially those of Sir Hugh Bell,[4] it seemed written rather by men with blinkers on. I don't know whether the Federation of the Steel Trade w^{d}. include its 'higher' branches w^{h}. were dealt with mainly by the 'engineering' report to the Board of Trade;[5] that (the Engineering Report) seemed on a much higher level. Again I am prejudiced a little by my study of German Cartels; on w^{h}.. I have probably spent more time than any other Englishman. I recognize indeed that the Stahlwerkes Verband[6] has greatly increased the benefits & considerably diminished the evils w^{h}.. Cartels in the various strata of the Iron & Steel Trade brought to the German nation; but as a general result, I think worse of German cartels than I did ten or twenty years ago. I have had also some correspondence with the leaders of the Federation of British Industries,[7] of w^{h}.. your Federation w^{d}. be a chief, if not the chief member. I learnt much & found much to like: but my anxieties are not wholly stilled.

If, as time went on, you found yourself in opposition to the policy of your Federation, as regards Protection, & especially as regards using Protective tarifs as a shield for selling *much* more cheaply abroad than at home {of course selling rather more cheaply abroad than at home is often inevitable} I think you might find yourself in an uncomfortable position.

If I were in such a position I s^{hd}. be killed, unless I got out of it very quickly. I think you are tougher than I am, but yet not as tough as the average student, & much less tough than the average business man. So you might be worried a good deal: but I dont lay stress on this point. Nor do I lay stress on the risk that after a time the Federation might like to make the tenure of the Presidentship circulate among the heads of the chief businesses in it. But I do lay stress on the absence in your account of any reference to an understanding that you w^{d} be free to express your own opinions on such questions as Protection the remuneration of employees & other matters.

This is my great difficulty. If it could be left out of account I s^{hd}. have no hesitation in wanting you to accept. But I think you must face the difficulty straight; & if possible manage to get in writing a statement as to whatever liberty can be allowed to you, in expressing opinions as to matters in which the interests of members of the Federation may point to policies that are not the best in the interests of the Nation.[8]

This difficulty might be evaded in your unofficial utterances, though not without some loss, by your avoiding thorny questions. But if the Federation decided, say, to issue a manifesto or to interview a Minister, in regard to Protective Duties, or to a tax on Germany for even such milder forms of dumping as British manufacturers commonly practice, you might be in a tight place.

If you dont feel this difficulty or if you see your way to get round it, then I think you should accept. If you can't accept I shall be very sorry but I think you *must* look before you leap.

Yours in proud anxiety | Alfred Marshall

[1] Trinity College, Cambridge, Layton Papers. No address given. In Mrs. Marshall's hand, but signed by Marshall.

[2] Layton, now freed from wartime duties, had been offered the lucrative position of Director of the Iron and Steel Federation. He had served in the last months of the war as chairman of the Reconstruction Committee on post-war iron and steel requirements and had been heavily involved in the wartime management of steel and munitions. See Hubback, *No Ordinary Press Baron* [934.1], pp. 34–51, especially pp. 49–50. For Whitley Councils see [1081.4].

[3] See *Report of the Departmental Committee on the Iron and Steel Trades after the War* (Cd 9071, 1918). P. and G. Ford, *A Breviate* [1081.4], pp. 155–6, gives details. Correspondence with Llewellyn Smith not traced, but see [1083].

[4] Sir Hugh Bell (1844–1931), industrialist, active in iron and steel, coal, and railway businesses in the North-East.

[5] See [1085.8].

[6] See [1085.3].

[7] Founded 1916. Correspondence not traced.

[8] Layton was to accept a five-year appointment as Director at the end of January 1919, but only after 'making it clear that he was a firm believer in free trade, that he was convinced that labour should have a greater say in industry, and that any important industry should not follow sectional interests which might conflict with wider national economic policy' (Hubback, p. 51).

1090. To Walter Thomas Layton, 13 January 1919[1]

13. 1. 19

My dear Layton,

Mary is writing for me. I thought yesterday evening & again during the night, a great deal about your plans; & I found my opinion swinging round steadily against your taking a position in w^{h}. your vote w^{d}. be demanded *ex officio*, on the side of the Masters, through thick & thin. During our conversation I had not paid sufficient attention to the fact that the votes on the two sides are exactly balanced, with the obvious purpose of opening out questions by free discussion, & arranging that no conclusion sh^{d}. be reached save by general agreement.

If an individual employer upset the apple cart by voting against his kind, he might get some rough language: but yet he w^{d}. clearly be within his rights. But if that were done by the salaried officer of the employers there w^{d}. arise irration, w^{h}. might make his position unhappy until he left it, accompanied by some unjustly severe criticisms. In that case you might rather have lost prestige than have gained it, & after all you w^{d}. not have learnt much, *w^{h}. you w^{d}. be at liberty to reproduce*, & could not have been got from other sources.

I repeat that your position of Chairman w^{d}. make you, to a certain extent, *ex officio* mediator & intepreter; & that w^{d}. be all to the good for you & for the country. But I think you w^{d}. be in an impossible position, if you found yourself unable to vote with the employers, with the consequence that an employees motion was carried by a majority of one.

So, on the whole, my voice goes, for whatever it is worth, against your joining the Federation. And, now that I think decidedly that by joining it you w^{d}. make a mistake from your own point of view, I feel at liberty to urge other considerations, w^{h}. constantly got half way to the end of my tongue yesterday, but w^{h}. I felt bound to swallow. They concern the nation & the world but they concern your Cambridge friends, including myself, in a special degree.

When I resigned my Professorship I s^{hd}. have felt very anxious as to the provision of lectures on 'Structure & Problems of Modern Industry',[2] if you had not been at hand. Under your care the subject flourished; because your heart was in the matter; & now your head holds more of it, probably than does that of any other economist. And, if you teach the coming generation, how to bring heart & mind together in working at it in conjunction with Section B. 'Wages & Conditions of Employment', you may do more towards fashioning the life of Britain in the second & third quarters of this century than anybody else. In this matter Cambridge seems to be the main hope of the country. Some fatal influence seems to prevent Oxford men from uniting hard thought & persistent study with energetic social policies. Either half alone is well represented there but not the two together. No other University seems to have a Curriculum comparable in scope with that of our Tripos.

But Manchester is strong & growing in strength, & not long ago the head, I think he is the Vice Chancellor, of the University, wrote to ask me if I could suggest a successor to Chapman.[3] I said I could not: because Economists were scarce, & those whom I knew best were, so far as I knew, well settled. But if the post is not yet filled & if you have a feeling that you w^{d}. rather steer your own ship, Manchester may have great claims. You w^{d}. there be constantly called on to act as Mediator & Interpreter between Employer & Employed, in the finest center of the finest industries of the world. All your knowledge & all your faculties w^{d}. be turned to account. You w^{d}. have a large & noble life, & if you lived long the country w^{d}. be left a much happier & more harmonious country than if you had not gone there. Your direct influence w^{d}. be much greater there than at Cambridge: though you w^{d}. not have as great a power of influencing many academic generations of young men who were to become leaders in social thought & social work for the country.

I am quite certain that, leaving Cambridge out of the question, (because I may be prejudiced) it is much better for you & the country & the world, that you s^{hd}. go to Manchester, than that you s^{hd}. want to give an employees vote, when you were a paid official of the Steel employers.

Chapman had wanted to be a candidate for the Professorship here.[4] I did not give him to understand that I s^{hd}. support him against Pigou, but I urged him to stand, & he decided to do so. But shortly afterwards he wrote to say that the Manchester Authorities, when raising his salary to £700, had understood that he undertook in return to stand by the Manchester School; so he was not free to run for the Cambridge post.

Yours in affectionate prolixity | Alfred Marshall

[1] Trinity College, Cambridge, Layton Papers. In Mrs Marshall's hand, but signed by Marshall. See [1089.8].
[2] For Part II of the Economics Tripos.
[3] This proved eventually to be Henry Clay.
[4] In 1908.

1091. To John Hilton, 14 April 1919[1]

14. 4. 19

Dear Mr Hilton

I think I s^{hd}.. like you—if you can spare the time—to glance at my plea for chivalrous competition:[2] I think it is a chief factor of progress, & am therefore a little troubled by any suggestion that competition must be greedy.[3]

My notion that it is an essential stimulus for many forms of activity was developed long ago in a racquet court. I found that if my friend—& opponent—came late, I could knock about the balls by myself for some ten minutes without discontent. But then I got tired; & became lively again when he arrived to compete. I did not care whether he won or I did: I enjoyed the competition; & I think it did me good. Some forty years later I put the same notion but other words in the paper w^h. I enclose. Do not trouble to answer. You have more important things to do.

Yours sincerely | Alfred Marshall

[1] Marshall Papers. From a retained copy in Mrs Marshall's hand. No address recorded. See [1085].
[2] Presumably Marshall enclosed an offprint of his 1907 paper, 'Social Possibilities of Economic Chivalry' [863.2].
[3] Remarks to this effect by Hilton have not been identified but may have been in one of the several reports with which he was associated.

1092. To Sir Frederick Macmillan, 31 May 1919[1]

31. 5. 19

Dear Sir Frederick MacMillan

The whole of *Industry & Trade*, except the Preface, is now in its final form: & M.SS for the Preface are with the Press.

Partly as a consequence of rapidly changing economic conditions; but chiefly as a result of my slowness of work, & changefulness of purpose, the expense of setting the book up must have been extraordinarily heavy. Also paper & other costs of production are, I know, almost at war level. Therefore the price of the book cannot be low.

But I have £100 with nothing in particular to do. I therefore send it to Mess[rs] MacMillan & Co, with the request that it be turned to account in pulling down the price of the book as far as it will reach towards a normal level.

I have put so much more work into it than I put into my *Principles*, that I think it may run to a second edition—though, being more largely concerned with details that change from decade to decade, it may become super-annuated ere long more completely than is likely to be the case with discussions of general 'principles'. But I think that a very high price might militate against its getting such a hold, as would make its life tolerably long.

Yours very faithfully | Alfred Marshall

[1] British Library, Macmillan Archive. From Balliol Croft.

1093. To Sir Frederick Macmillan, 26 June 1919[1]

5 Devonshire Buildings | Weymouth
26. 6. 19

Dear Sir Frederick MacMillan,

I sent off from here a few days ago the last sheets of *Industry & Trade*, including the Preface & Index, marked 'for Press': so I trust you will soon be able to set the binding in hand.

It so happens that almost every days newspaper gives me some additional reason for regretting that the book is not already out: but I know that the blame for the delay rests wholly on me.

Yours sincerely | Alfred Marshall

[1] British Library, Macmillan Archive.

1094. From Sir Frederick Macmillan, 1 July 1919[1]

Macmillan & Co. Ltd. | St. Martin's Street, | London, W.C.2
July 1st 1919.

Dear Professor Marshall,

I have your letter of the 26th June telling me that you have sent off the last sheets of *Industry and Trade* for press, and write to assure you that we shall lose no time in getting the book bound and issued.

The question now arises as to the price at which it is to be sold. I have looked into the cost of production and have had an estimate, of which I enclose a copy, made up to show you how it will work out.[2] I do not see how we can possibly make the price less than one guinea, which, especially in these days, is not at all dear for a volume of 900 pages. Even at this price the estimated profit on the whole edition is not what it should be, but I know that you want to have the book as cheap as possible. I shall be glad to have your views on the matter.

I am, | Yours very truly, | Frederick Macmillan.

[1] Marshall Papers. Sent to the Weymouth address given in [1093]. Typewritten.

[2] Rounded to the nearest £, the estimate showed costs totalling £1,128, made up of composition and printing £605, materials and binding £423, and advertising £100. For a selling price of 21s. (15s. 9d. net to the publisher), with 250 copies sold to the New York branch at 10s. 6d. per copy and with 100 complimentary copies, sales receipts on a run of 2,000 copies would be £1,431. With Marshall's contribution of £100 (see [1092]) this left a surplus of £403 (incorrectly calculated as £353) to share between publisher and author.

1095. To Sir Frederick Macmillan, 2 July 1919[1]

Weymouth → Cambridge
2. 7. 19

Dear Sir Frederick MacMillan,

I confess that I should myself prefer the price of 18s or even 16s to 21s: partly because I think that if the first edition of a book, which aims at a fairly long life, pays its way, it has done its share. The little '*Economics of Industry*' was priced at the record price—for smallness—of 2/6, after a conversation in 1877 (I think) with Mr Alexander MacMillan; in which we considered that books on economics are largely read by people of limited means, to whom they are not essential, as means of preparation for a technical examination.[2]

So far as I am concerned, the money to be got from *Industry & Trade* is of little moment. It is the main product of many years hard work, for which I would not have accepted £1000 a year, if I had not cared for the substance of the work. And both MacMillan & Co & myself have derived considerable gains from later editions of my *Principles*, which have not cost much trouble of any sort. Therefore I should myself much prefer the price of 18s, even if it were necessary to forego all profit *to myself* from the first edition. If paper were not still rather dear—I notice that the Times has returned already, tho' not before the paper for my book must have been bought, to 24 or 26 pp—I should have liked an even lower price. But as things are, I feel I am asking much of your kindness by pressing for 18s.

Yours very truly | Alfred Marshall

Many thanks for your instructive 'estimate.'[3]

[1] British Library, Macmillan Archive.
[2] See Vol. 1 [40, 41], for pertinent correspondence.
[3] See [1094.2].

1096. From Sir Frederick Macmillan, 3 July 1919[1]

July 3rd 1919.

Dear Professor Marshall,

I have your letter of yesterday's date, and write to say that we will agree to make the price of *Industry and Trade* 18/–. I fear that this will do away with the chance of any profit, but in the circumstances we are quite prepared for that.

I am afraid that the prospects of a second edition being producable at a lower rate are not very hopeful. It is true that paper is going down slightly but not to anything like pre-war prices; and printing and binding, owing to the demands of the wage receivers, are if anything likely to go up.

I am unable as yet to fix a date for publication, but we will see that no time is lost.[2]

I am, | Yours very truly, | Frederick Macmillan.

[1] Marshall Papers. To Balliol Croft from the same address as [1094]. Typewritten.
[2] A subsequent letter from Macmillan promised publication on 26 August. (Marshall Papers, letter dated 19 August 1919.)

1097. To Sir Frederick Macmillan, 4 July 1919[1]

Cambridge
4 July 1919

Dear Sir Frederick MacMillan

I am very grateful to you for consenting to reduce the price of my book to 18s. I did not intend to suggest that the price for any eventual edition should be lowered: for on general grounds I dislike such changes. And as to special reasons that might justify a reduction, when war conditions have passed away, I agree with you that any great fall in costs in the *near* future seems improbable.

Yours very truly | Alfred Marshall

[1] British Library, Macmillan Archive.

1098. To James Bonar, 8 August 1919[1]

8. viii. 1919

My dear Bonar,

I have just returned home, and found your letter of August 2nd.[2] I agree that no very large indemnity can be got from Germany by any *one* of the routes you mention: but I think they might be used simultaneously. I am however opposed on principle to every sort of attempt to exact a sum approaching to ten thousand million pounds, even though the greater part of it might in fact be paid in *territory*. If—as appears to be the case—Germany must be forced to cede much territory in Africa as well as in Europe, I think that such territory should be accepted at the very high money value which she would naturally set on it: and the remainder of our demands on her might be covered mainly by the transference of securities representing command over property in various parts of the world.

In any case, I think, no transfer should be enforced which cannot be put through quickly. For the military occupation of Germany, which would be required to enforce large payments spread over many years, would involve so much expenditure and so greatly retard that quenching of the military spirit, which is needed to restore British industry to its sober, earnest habits of work, that its net effect might probably be an economic loss. The hatred which it would cause, even among those numerous though not specially vocal Germans, who try to see our side of the conflict, would, I think, be an enduring calamity.

I have not read Giffen's article on the payment of the French 1873 indemnity[3] in recent years, but I recollect that I thought it exaggerated the harm which the purely economic side of the inflation did to Germany. The main source of the mischief appeared to me to be the enormous increase of influence which the results of the war (geographical, political and economic) gave to the German jingoes. In 1869, they were, I believe, a relatively small minority of the population of Germany, except in the North East provinces; but the war set school teachers, among others, to wallow in jingoism; and the average German as he entered manhood was very much more jingoistic than he would have been if born a little earlier. And, though the milliards were an important contributory cause to this deterioration of quality, I think that a similar, if milder, madness would have spread over the people without it.

In fact the milliards did this good; that they made German business men so over-confident as to intensify the subsequent depression of trade. That depression was a wholesome medicine and mitigated much of the evil influences which the indemnity exerted on German business; though it did not check the domination of the military caste over society, over the universities, and—partly through them—over the schools.

I therefore oppose the demand for a *huge* indemnity in the interests of the British nation, even more than on ethical grounds: but I think that, if liberal allowance be made for Germany's property in land and its fixings in Africa and elsewhere, even £M10,000 might be got out of her.

I don't go into detail: but I do not regard a compulsory gift of German goods to us as necessarily a danger. Any violent disturbance of a *particular* British industry is of course an evil: but most of the goods which Germany could send us would be such as she might have exported to other countries in Europe or outside of it. It would probably not be well to export those goods: but we might export similar goods of our own to the markets to which they would have gone if Germany had been free in the matter. Again our agriculturists could do with any amount of German potash. German sugar is also in elastic demand; but of course no vast quantity could be handled in the next few years: and so on.

I have recently been much tempted to publish some of my opinions on current financial and social problems: and also on the strange compound of good and evil in the character of the German population—most people who write on the subject seem never to have associated, as comrades, with Germans, and to recognize only the evil. But my strength fails fast; and I have much half-ready material, belonging to my special province, which will need to be cremated on my funeral pyre. So I dare not write controversy on matters as to which I have no direct responsibility: and indeed I have to cut down even my reading of current events rather severely.

I live so much out of the world that I did not know you were in England: that good Mother must rejoice in your return even as does one of her humbler sons.[4]

Yours very sincerely, | Alfred Marshall

[1] Reproduced in *Memorials*, pp. 375–7. Original not traced. From Balliol Croft.

[2] Not traced.

[3] Robert Giffen, 'The Cost of the Franco-German War', privately printed 1872. Reprinted in Giffen's *Essays in Finance* (Bell, London, 1880) and in his *Economic Inquiries and Studies* (Bell, London, 1904).

[4] Bonar had served as Deputy Master of the Canadian branch of the Royal Mint, 1907–19.

1099. To Macmillan and Company, 26 August 1919[1]

26. 8. 19

Mess[rs] MacMillan & Co

Dear Sirs,

I desire to thank you for all the patience which you have shown with my endless changes of plan & delays; & for the energy with which, in spite of the great difficulties of the time, you have brought out *Industry & Trade* in a volume which is not disagreeably bulky; & yet contains nine hundred pages printed on solid, substantial paper. I am grateful also for the concession you have made to me in regard to price: for I know that a higher price might probably have yielded larger net profits; while the benefit, which an author derives from bringing his notions to the attention of an enlarged circle of readers, is not shared equally with his publishers.

In the absence of Sir Frederick MacMillan, with whom I have chiefly corresponded about it, & who has given prompt and wise counsel and aid on every occasion, I send, without delay, these my most hearty thanks to the Firm.

Yours very gratefully | Alfred Marshall

[1] British Library, Macmillan Archive. From Balliol Croft.

1100. To Walter Thomas Layton from Mary Paley Marshall, 10 September 1919[1]

10. 9. 19

Dear M[r] Layton

Alfred thanks you heartily for your letter.[2] The last year has been a great strain for him, for he went on & on without any regular holiday for many months & the result was that though he finished with the proofs in June, he has only just recovered strength to begin writing again. He is now engaged on Money & Foreign Trade for w[h]. he has a great deal of material in quite an advanced stage. I think you will agree that it is best all round that he s[hd]. bring out as much of this as he can for it contains a great part of many years work. You will find that in the latter part of Industry & Trade he deals somewhat with current topics; but with his very small power of work it seems best that he s[hd]. work up his old material rather than enter into immediate problems, much as he is tempted to do so.

I wonder how you like your new work.[3] Perhaps you have hardly got into it yet. We shall miss you greatly here though, as you may have heard, there are some brilliant additions to the Economic Staff.

This needs no answer. My love to all your troop

Yours very sincerely | Mary P. Marshall

I believe I ought to put all sorts of letters after your name.[4] Perhaps your wife will let me know sometime about this delicate matter!

[1] Trinity College, Cambridge, Layton Papers. From Balliol Croft.
[2] Not traced.
[3] See [1089.2, 8].
[4] See [1076.2].

1101. From Sir Frederick Macmillan, 11 September 1919[1]

Sep 11 1919

Dear Professor Marshall,

Your book has made such a successful start that we find ourselves today with a stock of not much over *600* copies & a demand for about 20 copies per diem. If this keeps up we shall have disposed of the Edition within a month, and even if as is probable, the rate of sale goes down the Edition will not last very long.

In the circumstances I should like to have your permission to print another 2000 copies without alteration (except correction of any misprints that you may have noted) and without sending you proofs. I suggest this for two reasons firstly because only in this way can we hope to have the reprint on the market within a reasonable time and secondly because it would seem hardly fair to the buyers of the first edition to put on sale a new and revised one within such a short time. If I can have your assent to my proposal I shall set the Pitt Press people to work at once & do my best to persuade them to get on with it at a good deal more than their usual pace.

I am | Yours sincerely | Frederick Macmillan

[1] Marshall Papers. From the same address as [1094].

1102. To Sir Frederick Macmillan, 19 September 1919[1]

19. 9. 19

Dear Sir Frederick MacMillan,

I am very much obliged for the corrections which you have forwarded to me from Mr Maurice MacMillan:[2] they are all important.

Craik's History of British Commerce[3] has dropped out of sight: but I think it has some points of superiority over any similar book that is accessible.

Yours very truly | Alfred Marshall

Craiks book is a reprint from *The Political History of England* (Knight).[4]

[1] British Library, Macmillan Archive. From Balliol Croft.

[2] Sir Frederick had enclosed with a letter of 18 September 1919 (Marshall Papers) four misprints noted by his brother Maurice [1087.4] who had 'been reading *Industry and Trade* with some care'. Sir Frederick also intimated that the printers promised to complete the reprint before Christmas.

[3] George Lille Craik (1798–1866), *The History of British Commerce from the Earliest Times. Reprinted from the Pictorial History of England with Corrections, Additions, and a Continuation to the Present Day* (Knight, London, 1844: 3 vols. in 1). This work is referred to three times in *Industry and Trade*.

[4] G. L. Craik, Charles MacFarlane, and others, *Pictorial History of England, Being a History of the People, as well as a History of the Kingdom* (Knight, London, 1837–44: 8 vols.).

1103. To Karl Gustav Cassel, 22 September 1919[1]

22. 9. 19

Dear Professor Cassel

I wish I had sufficient time & strength to respond to the suggestion, with wh you honour me, that I should give you my views on your *Sozialoekonomie*.[2]

But I am in my 78th year. My strength fails very fast. I have already type-written material in first draft for a third thick volume; which I can hardly hope to complete: and rough manuscripts, most of which I have at one time or other designed to publish, amounting to twice as much more.

So I must plod on my slow way looking neither to the right nor the left; whatever the pleasurable incitement.

From what someone else said, I rather think that you may suppose my 'Principles' to have some claim to be exhaustive, which it has not. It is almost confined to a preliminary study of the 'causes of the causes' which govern value *under normal conditions*.

One or two passages in your book on wh my eye has fallen, but which I only skimmed, suggested to me that you were occupied with a different class of studies from those which seemed to me appropriate to a Volume which is described on its title page as 'Introductory'.

However that may be, I must plod on my chosen path—not to its end, for I shall not get near that, but—to the end of my little remaining life & strength.

Meanwhile I remain with great respect | Yours very sincerely | Alfred Marshall

P.S. It has just occurred to me that possibly you may not have noticed my hobby—for which I have been assailed more often & continuously than for any other; & of which I am, perhaps in consequence more fond than any other—is the insistence that in nearly all profits & earnings, even under normal conditions there is an element of value, due to scarcity. To this element I have given the suggestive name 'quasi-rent', but it is often more, as e.g. when the demand for a certain skill has increased fast. The poor thing was remorselessly kicked for many years; but now at last it seems to be partially tolerated even in highly respectable economic society. If your insistence on Knappheit,[3] is akin to this idiosyncracy of mine—as to which—to my great regret—I lack the time to form an opinion, we ought to be allies.

[1] Royal Library, Stockholm, Cassel Papers. From Balliol Croft.

[2] G. Cassel, *Theoretische Sozialoekonomie* (Winter, Leipzig, 1918: second enlarged edition 1921). Translated by Joseph McCabe as *The Theory of Social Economy* (Unwin, London, 1923). Cassel's communication to Marshall has not been traced.

[3] That is scarcity or deficiency. See the pages listed in the index to the translation under 'Scarcity, the principle of'.

1104. From John Maynard Keynes, 29 September 1919[1]

Charleston | Firle Sussex
29 Sept[r]. 1919

Dear D[r]. Marshall,

Very many thanks for the copy of your new book.[2] Its appearance is a great event, and is one more great step forward into converting Cambridge Economic Doctrine from an oral tradition into a corpus of written teaching available to all the world.

As you may have heard, I have at last escaped from Gov[t]. service and shall be back again lecturing at Cambridge next term. My six months at Paris was a terrible experience. I was the British financial member on the Supreme Economic Council and principal Treasury representative at the Peace Conference. And I saw enough of horror, wickedness and folly to satisfy a life time.

For the last two months I have lived on the Sussex Downs and have nearly finished a book entitled *Character and Consequences of the Peace*[3] which is a vehement criticism of the Peace and, in part, an explanation of my resignation from the British Delegation shortly before the final presentation of our terms to Germany. This resignation was attributed to ill-health at the time (not by me), but was handed in, as a matter of fact, entirely on grounds of policy.

Yours ever, | J M Keynes

[1] Marshall Papers.
[2] *Industry and Trade.*
[3] Keynes's magnificent polemic against the drift of the peace negotiations was to appear in December 1919 as *The Economic Consequences of the Peace* (Macmillan, London). Reproduced as *Collected Works*, vol. 2.

1105. To Sir Frederick Macmillan, 20 October 1919[1]

20. 10. 19

Dear Sir Frederick MacMillan,

It occurred to me yesterday that the miscalculation which caused me to send to an Appendix some of the most important things which I wanted to say in *Industry & Trade* could be remedied with comparative ease by cutting out sixteen pages from Appendix P & adding them to the text. I had, as you know, started the Appendices with a sheet,[2] so that most of them could be printed off while I was still at work. Consequently I devised the plan, which is indicated in inclosed first draft of an addition proposed for the Preface.[3]

I find it best to avoid conversation: my wife does that for me. She has just returned from a long conversation with Mr Peace, to which the head compositor was called in as Assessor. Mr Peace heartily approved the plan; & said that I might tell you that the change would not delay at all the date at which the new issue could appear: & that it would cost but little.

I have observed that some important reviewers have not read the Preface & therefore not Appendix P:[4] small blame to them!

Necessary changes in the index have been discussed: they will be numerous, but not difficult; & my wife will take them in hand at once.

I hope you will approve of this proposal: & shall be grateful for any amendment suggested by you.

I have already made a little progress with the semi-final draft of the companion Volume.

Yours very truly | Alfred Marshall

[1] British Library, Macmillan Archive. From Balliol Croft.
[2] That is had them printed starting with a new 16-page sheet.
[3] This was doubtless similar to the PS of 14 November 1919 added to the preface of the 'second edition' of December 1919. The change involved is fully explained there.

[4] The preface to the first edition had warned: 'Some matters considered in the final chapter of the volume have been affected by events and discussions, so recent that adequate place for their study could not be carved out of the text: and consequently much of Appendix P, and especially its last two sections, may be regarded as properly belonging to that chapter' (p. viii). This passage was left unchanged in the second edition, also in the 'third edition' of 1920 and the final 'fourth edition' of 1923, qualified in each case by the PS of 14 November 1919.

1106. To the Editor, *The Times*, 17 November 1919[1]

Sir,—Though I am unwilling to enter on the discussion of current politics, I am impelled to take some share in the protests which are being raised against the proposal that the State should in effect become the holder of a gaming table. Surely this would be a grave error.

The spirit of adventure is a chief factor of progress: it strengthens the character, while advancing our knowledge of difficulties and of the routes by which they are to be approached. But mere gambling is at best a barren amusement, and, when it has once obtained entry into the practice of men and women who are excitable and lack strong purpose, it mars their lives. Many thoughtful Germans and Austrians have spoken to me with envy of the comparative freedom of the great body of the English people from a morbid craving for excitement, and have attributed to it much of that solid strength of purpose which they regard as the chief source of England's strength. In consequence I have visited several Continental gaming resorts, and have been much impressed by the unwholesome nervous expressions of the faces to be seen there.

Our statesmen in past times seem to have shared this opinion. They have not attempted to suppress private gambling, but they have curbed the growth of gambling resorts, and they have, as a rule, condemned without reserve suggestions that the State should itself seek the paltry gains that are to be got by lotteries of any kind. We have inherited a great birthright; shall we sell it for a very small mess of pottage!

Yours obediently, | Alfred Marshall.

[1] Printed in *The Times*, 17 November 1919, under the title 'Premium Bonds. A Form of State Lottery'. Original not traced. Premium bonds appealed to lenders' gambling instincts by converting part of the yield into periodic lotteries yielding substantial prizes, bond holdings serving as lottery tickets. They had long been popular on the Continent. For details of the extensive debate and correspondence during November and December 1919, ensuing from their proposed introduction in Britain, see *The Times Index* (October–December 1919) under 'Finance-Premium Bonds'.

1107. To John Maynard Keynes, with postscript by Mary Paley Marshall (January 1920?)[1]

My dear Keynes,

I am much interested in the faint rumours I hear of your lectures.[2] About three years ago I spent many hours in turning over the pages of a German Atlas & in giving what room for 'Expansion' could be conceded to Germany without enabling her cruisers to cut chief communications of the British Empire. If I had succeeded I shd have written to the Times. But I could find no place except South America, & as we have no rights there & the United States have strong interests there I did not think the proposal could appropriately come from an Englishman. These remarks cant be of use to you but they may interest you.

I wonder whether you wd. like to borrow Jahrbuch der Welt Wirtschaft by von R. Calwer. 1911., over 1000 pages.[3] It gives much the fullest description of Deutsches Reich that I have come across: 301 large crowded pages. It was almost certainly suspended during the war. You are welcome to borrow it if you like, but I daresay you have all the information you want.

I have often shown my little German 6 mark Atlas to people who seemed not to recognize the points in w^{h}. the Germans are superior to us. I say that I have £20 of English atlases in the house & that I use the little German atlas a great deal more than all the rest put together.

I thought I had thanked you for 'Economics of Peace Treaty'[4] but Mary tells me she thinks I have not. I am not able to use either my eyes or my mind very much but I have derived an exceptional pleasure & profit from it.

Yours ever | A Marshall

I have put the book in the hall, in case you sh^{d}. call when I am not in, but Alfred w^{d}. be glad to see you if there were any cause. MPM

[1] King's College, Cambridge, J. M. Keynes Papers. From Balliol Croft. Signed by Marshall, but otherwise in Mrs Marshall's hand. The reference to Keynes's book, published in December 1919, suggests the dating.

[2] Keynes was lecturing in the Michaelmas Term of 1919 on 'Economic Aspects of the Peace Treaty'. See Harrod, *The Life* [1030.1], p. 286.

[3] Richard Calwer [858.3], *Jahrbuch der Weltwirtschaft* (Jena, 1911), pp. xxxiv + 1070.

[4] See [1104.2].

1108. To Sir Frederick Macmillan, 2 March 1920[1]

2. 3. 20

Dear Sir Frederick MacMillan,

I have just returned home & looked up the correspondence of 1899 relating to the French translation of my *Principles*. I then, being kindly left a free hand by you, stipulated only that the translation should be carefully made & brought out by a good firm: I asked for no payment. (As matters turned out, the translator became ill & the French edition was long delayed).[2] I am now even more indifferent than I was then to pecuniary conditions: for my income exceeds the amount which my semi-socialistic principles permit me to spend on private uses: & therefore I think I shall do best by leaving the matter of a translation of *Industry & Trade* entirely in your able & judicious hands. I should like the quality of the work to be as high as may be; & the price to be as low as may be: and with that I shall be content.[3]

I cannot find the French translation of my *Principles*: I think I must have given it to one of the Belgians who sought refuge in Cambridge during the recent war. So I do not know who published it. There would perhaps be some advantage in putting *Industry & Trade* into the same hands, if practicable. But you are the best judge of that.

Yours very truly | Alfred Marshall

[1] British Library, Macmillan Archive. From Balliol Croft.
[2] See [757.4] for details of the French translation of *Principles*, published by Giard and Brière.
[3] A French translation was to appear only in 1934: *L'Industrie et le Commerce* (Giard, Paris, 1934; translated by Gaston Leduc).

1109. To Herbert Somerton Foxwell, 13 March 1920[1]

Don't trouble | to answer

13. 3. 20

Dear Foxwell,

I am engaged on a chapter dealing with index-numbers &c.[2] By accident I have referred to the first edition of Jevons *Investigations*—a most wonderful book w^h.. is not known as it should be.[3] On its p 130 (p 122 of Ed II) I find a pencil comment:—'The foot-note seems out of place: it seems to belong to an earlier page'. Also on p 129 the reference to an extraordinary rise of prices between 1833 & 1843 is difficult. I think perhaps 1843 is a misprint for 1840. I trouble you with this, because I think I may claim to be, after you, the most ardent worshipper of Jevons still living 'Nihil tetigit quod non ornavit':[4] & yet once Cairnes was more in repute than Jevons!

I don't suppose I shall finish the book on wh I am engaged; though I have huge masses of crude material for it, together with some that are in a more advanced state.

Yours sincerely | Alfred Marshall

[1] Foxwell Papers. From Balliol Croft.
[2] Index numbers are discussed in book i, chs. 2, 3, and in appendix B of *Money Credit and Commerce.*

[3] Foxwell had edited W. S. Jevons, *Investigations in Currency and Finance*; first edition 1884 [840.3]; revised and abridged edition with preface by H. S. Jevons (Macmillan, London, 1909). The passages referred to are from Jevons's 1865 paper 'The Variation of Prices and the Value of the Currency since 1782'. *Money Credit and Commerce* makes only general references to *Investigations*: see pp. 29n, 279–80n.

[4] 'He touched nothing that he did not adorn'.

1110. To Macmillan and Company, 7 April 1920[1]

7. 4. 20

Dear Sirs

My wife has just taken a copy of *Industry & Trade* to Mr Peace, with some corrections on a small scale. He seemed (but see P.S.)[2] to question the expediency of printing a small edition now, unless the book was stereotyped. In the past I have been averse to stereotyping. But the little strength, which is left to me, must be given to a forlorn attempt to get its companion volume ready: so I now concur in the suggestion, if you think it right.[3]

Mr Peace told my wife that the rather rapid sales—for so stodgy a book—indicated that it was being read by business men: & that, if so, the sale might be maintained. I should be interested in any information you can kindly give me as to the direction of its sales: e.g. whether it has gone in considerable quantities to places, where there is little or no academic activity.[4]

Mr Peace understands that there is no hurry about the second edition.[5] Indeed your letter to me was shown to him.

Yours truly | Alfred Marshall

Messrs MacMillan & Co

P.S. My wife says I misunderstood her as to Mr Peace's having expressed any opinion as to the proposed third edition. But the rest of my letter holds.

[1] British Library, Macmillan Archive. From Balliol Croft. Macmillan and Company had written to suggest a second reprinting of *Industry and Trade*, the stock of the first reprinting (the 'second edition' of December 1919) being down to 980 and likely to be exhausted within six months. A reprinting of *Principles* was also proposed, the stock only covering a year's sales. (Letter of 1 April 1920, Marshall Papers.)

[2] This phrase was inserted as an afterthought.

[3] Macmillan and Company proposed in reply that plates be made after a further reprint of 2,000 had been run (letter of 9 April 1920, Marshall Papers).

[4] The 9 April letter from Macmillan conjectured: 'It is probably true that the book has been read a good deal by businessmen as we circularised the book in such quarters, but the large provincial towns such as Manchester, Leeds, Birmingham, &c., are not only centres of business but also of Universities.'

[5] The second reprinting of *Industry and Trade* of August 1920 was to be termed the 'third edition', as the letter's postscript suggests.

1111. To Jogis Chadra Sinha, 14 May 1920[1]

14. 5. 20

Dear Sir,

I have to thank you for your friendly letter of 8 April last.[2] If I do not reply to it at length, my excuse must be that I have but little strength left, & a great amount of unfinished work on hand.

The third quarter of p 460 of my Principles[3] seems to me to tend in the same direction as the passage, you quote from the Economic Journal.

I prefer my own definition of 'Representative firm': but 'average firm' may serve for rough uses.

My own attitude to the difficulties, noted by you, is indicated by the suggestion on pp 809, 10 that a *curve* does not represent adequately Increasing-Return-Supply; & that a *surface* would get nearer to the requirements of the problem.

Yours very truly, | Alfred Marshall

There can be *many* Representative firms. They are *not* such as produce at the greatest cost.

[1] King's College, Cambridge, J. M. Keynes Papers. From a 'True copy of a letter written by Prof. Marshall to J. C. Sinha' sent by Sinha to Keynes with a covering letter of 18 February 1929, addressed from Hampstead. Sinha (1893–?) was an Indian economist, author of *Economic Annals of Bengal* (Macmillan, London, 1927) and other works.

[2] Not traced. However Sinha recollected the queries he had addressed to Marshall [Herbert Joseph Davenport (1861–1931) was an American critic of Marshall's economics]:

Q.1 Do you agree with Davenport's view that the representative firm 'in the long time adjustment with all its ups and downs will pass for a marginal firm'?

Q.2 Is it an average firm or a marginal firm ie a firm producing at the greatest cost?

Q.3 Can there be more than one representative firm for an industry at any particular time?

Q.4 Does the average cost of the representative firm or its marginal cost, determine the long period supply price? Evidently you do not abandon the marginal analysis in the case of increasing returns industries.

Q.5 How is the marginal cost of the representative firm to be calculated? Are we to calculate it, as you suggest in your article on Distribution and Exchange in the Economic Journal Vol 8 p 51 ...

Q.6 Is it possible to draw the long period supply curve of a commodity obeying the law of increasing returns, on the basis of the marginal cost ... of the representative firm, varying with the changes in the aggregate scale of production in the industry, in different periods of time?

[3] References are to *Principles* (*7*) but also serve for *Principles* (*8*).

1112. To Sir Frederick Macmillan, 2 June 1920[1]

2. 6. 20

Dear Sir Frederick Macmillan[2]

You have been good enough to let me make my own terms as regards translations in the past, & I have thought it best to press for a careful translation

& not ask for any payment. I do not care about any payment now, but I think I ought to consult you in the matter, so I enclose Prof Salz's letter.[3]

It might be reasonable to ask him the name of his publishers, but I am rather run down & am to start for the Italian Alps at the beginning of next week, so perhaps it might be assumed that only a strong publisher w^d^. undertake the task. My wife often acts as my secretary, as now, & I am amused by a tendency on the part of strangers to write to me through her.

I am cleaning up work with the University Press before starting. The only important change I am making in the Principles concerns the Preface. I think that to the first edition indicated the drift of the book better than the others so I am printing that in full & following up with a Preface to the eighth edition, w^h^. is practically a reproduction of that to the seventh edition.[4]

Yours very truly | Alfred Marshall

[1] British Library, Macmillan Archive. Signed by Marshall, but in Mrs. Marshall's hand. From Balliol Croft.

[2] Mrs Marshall wrote the name in its normal form.

[3] Not traced: possibly addressed to Mrs Marshall. Arthur Salz [827.2] had been one of the translators of the German edition of *Principles* (*4*), and was requesting permission to publish a German translation of *Industry and Trade*. No such translation was to appear, although Marshall did grant permission (postcard from Italy to Sir Frederick Macmillan, postmarked 'Piccolein 21 VII 20'. British Library, Macmillan Archive).

[4] See [1110.1]. The preface to *Principles* (*8*) is dated October 1920. Writing to Macmillan and Company on 26 August 1920 from 'St Martin/n^r^ Bruneck/North Italy', Marshall confessed that he had forgotten to send his corrections to the press and that Mr Peace had been forced to hunt them up at Balliol Croft in the Marshalls' absence (British Library, Macmillan Archive). As the new academic year opened, with burgeoning student numbers, both *Principles* and *Elements* were out of stock for a while, much to Marshall's chagrin. *Principles* (*8*) appeared early in December at the elevated price of 16s. (Letters of 26 and 30 November 1920 to Sir Frederick Macmillan, Macmillan Archive: the latter's mollifying responses of 29 November and 1 December are in the Marshall Papers.)

1113. To Sir Frederick Macmillan, 29 June 1921[1]

Address for at least two more weeks
↓
Sea Vale House | East Lulworth | Wareham
29. 6. 21

Dear Sir Frederick MacMillan

I am quite indifferent as to any payment for an Italian Edition of *Industry & Trade*: but I cannot give my assent to an *abridged* edition, until I know what abridgements are proposed. I do not anticipate any difficulty in the matter: but a translator might chance to regard some discussion as unimportant, which seems to me to be essential for my main purpose.[2]

Yours very truly | Alfred Marshall

[1] British Library, Macmillan Archive. Someone other than Marshall has written 'Fratelli Bocca' on the letter.

[2] An Italian translation was not to be published.

1114. To Dennis Holme Robertson, 20 September 1921[1]

20. 9. 21

My dear Robertson,

I am approaching the subject of credit fluctuations (& incidentally of 'industrial fluctuations'): & I observe on your p 5 a statement that my account of consumption excludes the services of a piano.[2] I have not explicitly mentioned a piano in this connection: but pictures are even more inert than a piano: and I find that their 'consumption' is mentioned on p 64 of my *Principles*.[3] This is a *very* small point, but it gives me an excuse for saying that, in the Chapter of 'Commerce & Finance' which treats with 'Fluctuations of Credit', I often refer to your study.[4]

Don't trouble to answer

Yours sincerely | Alfred Marshall

[1] Robertson Papers. From Balliol Croft.

[2] D. H. Robertson, *A Study of Industrial Fluctuation: An Enquiry into the Character and Causes of the so-called Cyclical Movements of Trade* (King, London, 1915). Based upon Robertson's successful Cobden Prize Essay of 1913. Robertson here proposes to 'include in our estimate of consumption of the year the utility of the capital goods created during the year'. A footnote adds: 'This Marshall's plan would *not* do—so far at any rate as the instruments render their services directly, e.g. a piano: it is not clear whether it would when they render them indirectly, e.g. a factory'.

[3] 'The "consumer" of pictures, of curtains, and even of a house or yacht does little to wear them out himself; but he uses them while time wastes them', *Principles* (*8*), p. 64.

[4] 'Commerce & Finance' was published as *Money Credit and Commerce* which does not cite Robertson and deals only sketchily with economic fluctuations.

1115. To Henry Ludwell Moore, 15 December 1921[1]

15. 12. 21

Dear Sir,

I am much interested in the papers you have kindly sent me.[2] Even twenty years ago I should have given much time to an endeavour to coordinate them with my own conjectures: but I am eighty years old; & I have half-finished work on hand that wants about twenty years. So I must restrain my appetite.

I will however burden you with a note as to my own work. About fifty years ago, when still rather more a mathematician than an economist, I was appalled by the complexity of economic interactions. I thought that *a priori* reasoning had great scope in deciding what events *might* be, in part at least, causes of any given result: but that the statistical method of concomitant variations was the only one that could give much help in deciding how far the influence of any one set of causes had prevailed generally.

So I caused half a ream of large paper to be ruled with 100 horizontal lines, so that each page would represent a century. (To be exact, my stationers told me that they could not guarantee the correct marking *in red* of every fifth line: So I caused every fifth line to be left blank.) Then for each recent century, & especially of course the nineteenth, I drew on each of several pages all the consecutive statistics which I could get in inks of various colours. Then I spent hour after hour, during several years, in trying to get *a posteriori* results by the method of concomitant variations. I always had a group of allied sets of such curves hanging in my study: &, after a time, ventured to set up a group of them in my lecture room; to illustrate my reasonings on a particular class of causal relations. The result was that I found the depths of my ignorance as to the relations between the development of different economic phenomena to be even greater than I had supposed: & that is saying much. I learnt a good deal about realities: but even more about my own ignorance.

Now, in my old age, I am returning to what may be called 'Ricardian' methods of analysis: using statistics, whenever available, to check my thoughts. But I am convinced that as time goes on[3] much may be achieved by the method of concomitant variations applied to groups of curves in each of which the same distance from a given vertical (or it may be horizontal) line indicates the same year; & transverse distances indicate quantities.

It is all very well to have a planetary theory which starts on the basis of an ellipse, with the sun in one focus; & express the influences of one planet on another by a waving line in the neighbourhood of that ellipse. And during peace time in the seventeenth & eighteenth centuries much might be done in regard to prices, & some other things, on the basis of the prices of wheat or-other dominant human-food grain. BUT I am 80 years old.

Yours very truly | Alfred Marshall

[1] Columbia University Library, Moore Papers. From Balliol Croft.

[2] Presumably a selection of Moore's recent journal articles eventually republished in his *Generating Economic Cycles* (Macmillan, New York, 1923). See especially his three 1921 papers published in the *Quarterly Journal of Economics*: 'Generating Cycles of Products and Prices' (vol. 35, February, pp. 215–39); 'Generating Cycles Reflected in a Century of Prices' (vol. 35, August, pp. 503–26); 'The Origin of the Eight-year Generating Cycle' (vol. 36, November, pp. 1–29).

[3] Followed by a repeated 'on' in the original.

1116. To Sir Frederick Macmillan, 28 December 1921[1]

28. 12. 21

Dear Sir Frederick MacMillan,

I am now in my eightieth year; & I have a huge mass of M.S.S. in various stages of preparation for printing. They fall in the main under two heads:—

A Currency, The Money Market, and International Trade:—

B Functions of Government and Possibilities of Social advance

A is practically ready to go to press, & will consist mainly of matter that has not yet appeared in print

B will consist mainly of reprints: &, while A is passing through the press, I propose to make arrangements for B's being printed—after my departure if necessary.

Shall I begin to send A to the University Press early in January?

Yours sincerely | Alfred Marshall

[1] British Library, Macmillan Archive. From Balliol Croft.

1117. To Hubert Douglas Henderson, 10 January 1922[1]

10. 1. 22

Dear Mr Henderson,

I am extremely glad to see 'Supply & Demand'.[2] The great difficulty of Cambridge men when lecturing on Economics in this country has been, I think, that treatments of parts of economics were generally pitched low. On the other hand the class seldom had time for extensive study: & books that met their wants in other respects, were generally elaborately elementary. Your book seems to me to succeed in keeping on a high level, & yet being a fairly compact whole, wh even busy men can read.

At Bristol University College (now University)[3] my evening classes were of exceptional interest to me: but I could seldom recommend a book which was thorough and short. The series edited by Keynes & you has made an excellent beginning. I am happy thereat.

Yours sincerely | Alfred Marshall

[1] Nuffield College, Oxford, Henderson Papers. From Balliol Croft.

[2] H. D. Henderson, *Supply and Demand* (Nisbet, London, 1922: Cambridge Economic Handbooks, 1, with an introduction by J. M. Keynes).

[3] Since 1909.

1118. To Dennis Holme Robertson, 14 January 1922[1]

14. 1. 22

My dear Robertson,

Many thanks for *Money*.[2] It happens that I am just now writing a chapter on it:[3] & I find your strong book of exceptional interest & value. I think The

Cambridge Economic Handbooks promise to add much to the glory of Alma Mater.

Yours very sincerely | Alfred Marshall

[1] Robertson Papers. No address given.
[2] D. H. Robertson, *Money* (Nisbet, London, 1922: Cambridge Economic Handbooks, 2).
[3] Book i and appendices A, C of *Money Credit and Commerce* are devoted to the topic of money.

1119. To John Maynard Keynes, 14 January 1922[1]

14. 1. 22

My dear Keynes:

I am no politician: but I have long wished that some economist would become recognized as an authority on the economic foundations of the larger politics. The work requires a combination of rapidity with thoroughness, which is rare: I know no one who has it in nearly as full a degree as you have.

If I have any opinion on the present issue, it is—to speak in Irish—not on it, but on generalities, which bear an ancestral relation to it. I incline to think that the mixture of good & evil, which is universal in human nature, is exceptionally deep-coloured and turbid in German human nature.

Bismarck, I think, mastered German nature; & his success made his influence last long and strong. It is I think for the good of Germany, as well as of the rest of the world, that she should have tribulation. I am not sure that she has yet had enough of it. But I doubt whether she can get as much of it as is good for her, without France's getting more glory & more cash out of military success than is good for her.

Yours ever | A. M.

[1] King's College, Cambridge, J. M. Keynes Papers. From Balliol Croft.

1120. From John Maynard Keynes to Mary Paley Marshall, 7 June 1922[1]

King's College | Cambridge
7th June, 1922.

Dear Mrs. Marshall,

A little time ago the Council of the Royal Economic Society decided to do themselves the pleasure of arranging an Address to Dr. Marshall on the occasion of his forthcoming eightieth birthday.[2] The Address is of quite a simple character, which will be transmitted through the post, and the signatories will be confined, for the most part, to members of the Royal Economic Society who are old friends, pupils, or academic economists in England.

The terms of the Address have now been drawn up by a Committee consisting of Edgeworth, Pigou, Flux, Chapman and myself, and we are about to circulate it for signatures.[3]

I do not, however, like to do this without letting you know in advance, and to make quite sure that what we are doing would be in no way disagreeable or upsetting to our venerable master.

Yours sincerely, | J M Keynes

[1] Marshall Papers. Typewritten.

[2] 26 July 1922.

[3] The address, with an extensive list of signatories, together with Marshall's reply [1123], was printed in the *Economic Journal*, 32 (September 1922), pp. 287–9. This material is also reproduced in *Memorials*, pp. 497–9. The *Economic Journal* printing was preceded by the photograph of Marshall that faces p. 64 of *Memorials*. Foxwell was a conspicuous non-signer. An undated 'Private' note from Foxwell in the J. M. Keynes Papers (King's College, Cambridge) explains:

> I did not sign the Marshall Letter, partly on the merits, as I thought it exaggerated & fulsome: but mainly because he played me such an ingeniously dirty trick just before the election to the Professorship here [in 1908] that as soon as I learnt of it from Ashley, I broke off all communication with him [Marshall]. Long before, & for somewhat similar reasons, the Master of St. John's not only refused three times to subscribe to Marshall's portrait, but refused to accept it, after we had got it done, on behalf of the College. Somehow or other it got into the College ... but there was no ceremony of acceptance.

On the portrait's acceptance by St John's see [953].

1121. From John Maynard Keynes, 25 July 1922[1]

46, Gordon Square, | Bloomsbury
25 July 1922

Dear D^r^. Marshall

It falls to me as Secretary of the Royal Economic Society to forward to you the enclosed. We all wish you many happy returns of the day with deep affection and respect for all you have done.

Signatures to the enclosed have only been invited from Members and Correspondents of the Royal Economic Society.

Yours ever | J M Keynes

[1] Marshall Papers. See [1120].

1122. From John Maynard Keynes to Mary Paley Marshall, 25 July 1922[1]

46, Gordon Square, | Bloomsbury.
25 July 1922

Dear M^rs^. Marshall,

I hope this crumpled copy will be excused! The printers are on strike and we cannot obtain what was to have been our fair copy.

It is impossible at this moment when we are thinking of our master and his life not to think of you too, so much a partner in everything he has done. We owe you too a great debt, and I wish I could convey to you on behalf of all his old pupils and friends what emotion they feel in thinking of your great love and devotion.

Yours ever | J M Keynes

[1] Marshall Papers. See [1120].

1123. To John Maynard Keynes, 27 July 1922[1]

Sea Vale | East Lulworth | Dorset
27 July 1922

My dear Keynes,

The address, which you have sent to me on my eightieth birthday, fills me with gratitude and joy. It is all too kind: but I am so avaricious that I would not give up a jot of it.

It is true of almost every science that, the longer one studies it, the larger its scope seems to be: though in fact its scope may have remained almost unchanged. But the subject matter of economics grows apace; so that the coming generation will have a much larger field to study, as well as more exacting notions as to the way in which it needs to be studied, than fell to the lot of their predecessors. The Chinese worship their ancestors: an old student of economics may look with reverential awe on the work, which he sees young students preparing themselves to do.

If I have helped in putting some young students on the way to grapple with the economic problems of the coming age, that is far more important than anything which I have been able to do myself: and, resting on the hope that I have done a little in this direction, I can depart in peace.

Yours happily | Alfred Marshall

[1] King's College, Cambridge, J. M. Keynes Papers. See [1120]; also [1120.3] for details of previous reproduction.

1124. To John Maynard Keynes from Mary Paley Marshall, 27 July 1922[1]

Sea Vale | East Lulworth | Wareham
27. 7. 22

Dear M^{r}. Keynes

I don't know how to thank you for your letter. It warms & cheers me, & I shall treasure & often look at it.

To have been for so many years his companion, & to have helped, however little, such a life as his is an enviable & delightful lot.

Yours ever | Mary P Marshall

[1] King's College, Cambridge, J. M. Keynes Papers. See [1122].

1125. To John Maynard Keynes from Mary Paley Marshall, 31 July 1922[1]

Sea Vale | East Lulworth | Wareham
31. 7. 22

Dear M^{r}. Keynes

Thank you very much for the two extra copies of the Address. We are very glad to have them.

I wish you could have seen how delighted Alfred was when it came on his birthday.

He is now working away at Money Credit & Commerce much of w^{h}. is about 50 years old!

This place suits us exactly it is right on the Downs & close by the sea: & the weather has not served us so very badly here

Yours ever | Mary P. Marshall

[1] King's College, Cambridge, J. M. Keynes Papers. See [1120].

1126. To Herbert Somerton Foxwell, 20 October 1922[1]

Dear Foxwell

I cannot conveniently go to S.J.C. chapel tomorrow: but I wish to tell you that your brothers gentle face always attracted me: & that his death has caused me sorrow.

Yours sincerely | Alfred Marshall

[1] Foxwell Papers. From Balliol Croft. Foxwell's brother Ernest had died on 18 October in the rooms he occupied in St John's College during his latter days. *The Times*, 20 October 1923 (1a), noticed the demise and funeral in its death announcements.

1127. To Sir Frederick Macmillan, 1 December 1922[1]

1. 12. 22

Dear Sir Frederick MacMillan,

I write to you individually in accordance with auld lang syne. *Money Credit & Commerce* is now out of my hands: it has rather less than 400 pages. As you know, I am a strong partisan of low prices for books that are not specially technical: & I hope you will kindly keep the price as low as you can. Low priced books increase the sales of their comrades: and that illustration of 'group interests' among books has some special attraction for me.[2]

I have no intention of writing anything new: but I am lazily collecting various selected essays &c for publication after my death, if not before.

Yours very truly | Alfred Marshall

[1] British Library, Macmillan Archive. From Balliol Croft.

[2] *Money Credit and Commerce* was published in January 1923 (the preface is dated August 1922) at a price of 10s. Marshall told Sir Frederick 'I should have liked the price to be 7/6: but I must admit that 10s is a very reasonable price' (letter of 7 December 1922, Macmillan Archive).

1128. To James Phinney Munroe, (1922? incomplete)[1]

I have a rather vivid memory of the day on which I called on him in Boston in 1875, I think. I believe I had brought a note of introduction to him from President Eliot, so he knew what I was interested in.[2] He sat still for a minute, saying 'I wonder what I had better talk about.' He must have known that he might talk for a week without getting to the end of what I wanted to know. But he was wont to be fond of parables, and he seemed to decide that the best thing he could do was to make me see how different fundamentally were American economic problems from British: either country might learn from the other, but the learning had to be re-distilled before it was fit for use on the other side of the herring-pond. At last he said, 'I know what I'll do,' and he fetched a book of photographs of Indians, gave it to me, talked about some of them, and his personal relations with them and filled my mind with them. I do not recollect the details of the conversation which followed, but in some way it led up to this: 'British economics has a chief corner stone in Ricardo's theory of rent; in a sense that is universal, but the particular developments of it which are of most importance in an old country don't count for much in a land where the nominal owners of a hundred million acres or more are the people whose photographs you have just seen. . . .'

[1] Reproduced in J. P. Munroe, *A Life of Francis Amasa Walker* (Holt, New York, 1923), pp. 308–9, where it is said to have been written recently, presumably in response to a request for recollections of Walker. Munroe (1862–1929) was a Boston businessman, active in local affairs and in the life of the Massachusetts Institute of Technology, where he had served as Secretary of the Faculty, 1882–9, under Walker's presidency. Munroe edited Walker's *Discussions in Education* (Holt, New York, 1899) as well as writing several books.

[2] The meeting was in New Haven, not Boston. See Vol. 1 [26]. Marshall's mistake as to place led Munroe to think that the 1875 date was too early.

1129. From Edwin Cannan, 25 January 1923[1]

11 Chadlington Rd., Oxford
Jan 25 1923

Dear Professor Marshall

I was extremely pleased this morning to receive your new book, and have already devoured a great part of it. I am sure it will be a great help towards the revolution against the impostures which the war foisted on the tired intellect of mankind. P. 47 will, I hope, give me a leg up in my effort to insist on the importance of variations in people's willingness to hold currency.[2]

Yours ever | Edwin Cannan

[1] Marshall Papers. Typewritten. One of a batch of 21 notes of thanks for complimentary copies of *Money Credit and Commerce* that is preserved in the Marshall Papers. Besides the 12 reproduced here, there are largely formal notes from the following: G. U. Yule (25 January), Leonard Alston (27 January), E. A. Benians (29 January), H. Llewellyn Smith (30 January), Gustav Cassel (31 January), W. Jenkyn-Jones (Vol. 2 [531.6]; 1 February), Charles Gide (1 February), A. T. Hadley (15 February), and T. N. Carver (17 February).

[2] Marshall there writes, for example, 'an increased issue of inconvertible paper currency may lower its credit, and therefore lessen the amount of ready purchasing which the people care to hold'.

1130. From Gerald Frank Shove, 25 January 1923[1]

12[a] Sidney Street | Cambridge.
25th January 1923.

Dear D[r] Marshall,

I must write at once to thank you for the honour you have done me in sending me a copy of your book.

I need not say that I shall treasure it all my life and how much it will mean to younger students like myself to have the privilege of travelling over yet one more wide & difficult tract of country under your guidance.

Yours sincerely | G. F. Shove.

[1] Marshall Papers. See [1129.1].

1131. From Arthur Cecil Pigou, 25 January 1923[1]

Kings
Jan 25

Dear Marshall

Thank you very much indeed for sending me the book. It is what we have all been wanting for a long time. And I'm very glad too to see in the preface that you hint at another volume to come. I am looking forward to reading both this and that one very much.

Sincerely | A C Pigou

[1] Marshall Papers. See [1129.1].

1132. From Alfred William Flux, 25 January 1923[1]

Board of Trade, | Great George Street, | S.W.1.
25 January 1923

Dear Marshall,

I have not waited to try to glance through your new volume, much less to study it, before sending you my most hearty and joyful congratulations on the accomplishment of this further stage in your self-imposed task, and my grateful thanks to you for sending me a copy of the book.

I trust I may find that, on making more detailed acquaintance with your new written views in the field covered, my training of nearly 35 years ago, over which you so generously presided, will prove to have been sufficiently sound, and soundly worked out, to insure that I do not now find reason to revise most of what I have written or said on the topics with which the new volume more particularly deals. I am certain to find it an invaluable resource.

With every good wish for your progress with the remaining volume

Yours very sincerely | A.W. Flux.

P.S. My wife will not be back from Sierre[2] for a fortnight, but I know her well enough to be sure that, if she were here, she would wish me to send you a very cordial greeting from herself, both to you & to M[rs] Marshall

AWF

[1] Marshall Papers. See [1129.1].

[2] In Switzerland—however, the reading is doubtful. Flux had married Emilie Hansen, a Dane, in 1895.

1133. From Frederick Lavington, (25?) January 1923[1]

Emmanuel College
Thursday

Dear D[r] Marshall,

It is most kind of you again to send us copies of your new book. I am already nearly half way through on my first reading. While sending you my thanks for my copy may I add the wish that it will be well within your strength to complete the final volume for which you allow us to hope.

Yours very truly | F. Lavington.

[1] Marshall Papers. See [1129.1]. 25 January was a Thursday.

1134. From Herbert Somerton Foxwell, 27 January 1923[1]

1 Harvey Road Cambridge
Jan. 27. 1923.

Dear Professor Marshall

On my return from London yesterday I found a copy of your new volume on Money Credit & Commerce sent me by Macmillans at your instance.

I have not had time to do more than glance through the book: but it is safe to say that by such a publication at your age you have made a record in economic literature.

I am much obliged to you for sending me the volume.

Yours sincerely | H. S. Foxwell.

[1] Marshall Papers. See [1129.1].

1135. From Stephan Bauer, 29 January 1923[1]

International Association for | Labour Legislation
Basle, January 29 1923
Leimenstrasse 58.

Dear Prof. Marshall,

An old disciple wishes to thank you for the splendid gift of Money, Credit and Commerce.

I have just had the time to glance at the preface and I am most enthusiastic to see that the fourth volume on the possibilities of social advance is in perspective. Having most modestly been labouring in this field, your announcement gives me some courage to submit you my last publication on labour legislation, which although written in German will prove you (page 403 i.f.) the importance attached to British initiative.[2]

I hope to be in England about at Whitsuntide and hope then to be able to express you orally my gratitude.

With best wishes for your and Mrs Marshall's health as well as for her brother's,[3]

believe me, | most gratefully yours | Stephan Bauer

[1] Marshall Papers. Typewritten. See [1129.1].
[2] Presumably S. Bauer, 'Arbeiterschutzgesetzgebung', in L. Elster and others (eds.), *Handwörterbuch der Staatswissenschaften, Fourth Edition* (Fischer, Jena, 1923), Vol. 1, pp. 401–71.
[3] Probably George Knowles Paley—see Vol. 1, App. I, for family details.

1136. To Macmillan and Company, 6 February 1923[1]

6. 2. 23

Messrs MacMillan & Co

Dear Sirs

I am not at present very well acquainted with *Industry & Trade*: So I am inclined to let it go its own way. But some reference to the new volume of the series may be advisable; as suggested in the inclosed.[2] I am making progress with a group of selected (& abridged) 'Essays'.

Yours very faithfully | Alfred Marshall

[1] British Library, Macmillan Archive. From Balliol Croft.
[2] Probably a draft for the PPS of March 1923 added to the Preface of the 1923 'fourth edition' of *Industry and Trade*. This drew attention to the appearance of *Money Credit and Commerce*.

1137. From Francis Ysidro Edgeworth, 7 February 1923[1]

5 Mount Vernon | Hampstead | London NW
Feb 7 1923

My dear Marshall

Having been absent since the beginning of the Term from Hampstead to which Macmillan directed your new book I only last night received this remarkable present. I value it highly for many reasons. Firstly it shows that I am remembered by you, in your thoughts as you are in mine. Secondly it proves that you are 'going strong' as the golfers say. Thirdly there is the intrinsic value of the contents. I distinguish topics to which I have paid special attention such as Index-Numbers and International Trade and others which I only have known well enough to lecture about them, without really getting inside the subject.

Under the first head it is pleasant to find that your earlier constructions on which I had built remain firm. I have learnt much from your new lessons on the second class of subjects, your treatment of which seems to me admirably clear and chaste.

Yours ever | F Y Edgeworth

[1] Marshall Papers. See [1129.1].

1138. From H. Oshima, 7 February 1923[1]

21, Cricklade Ave., | Streatham Hill, London S.W.2
Feb. 7th 1923

Alfred Marshall Esq.
Dear Sir,

Please allow me to inform you that I am a Japanese student in Economics and have been here more than two years and a half devoting in the study. I have been deeply inspired by your recent work 'Money Credit & Commerce' and cannot help presenting you short notes of my deep congratulation and admiration for your courage you have shown to the world in your old age.

My memory goes eight years right back, when I, a boy of eighteen, entered a Japanese College and the first economic book I acquainted with there was your 'Elements of Economics of Industry' which I read line after line with great difficulty. But it was through this book that I learned the principles of that difficult study and you have been, if I may be allowed to say so, the first guide to me who has lead to the world of Economics.

Now the world is suffering from chaotic[2] state of economic disorder and restoration of peace is most important and urgent and the only means by which our common aim can be realized is correct application of economic theories to the world with cooperation of the nations at large. To this end, your recent contribution is invaluable and youngman like me will do his best to achieve this great task.

In conclusion, kindly allow me to present once again my hearty congratulation and pray God to bless you forever.

Yours very faithfully, | H. Oshima

[1] Marshall Papers. Oshima has not been further identified.
[2] Written 'caotic' in the original.

1139. From Herbert Stanley Jevons, 15 February 1923[1]

Allahabad
15th Feb. 1923

My dear Dr Marshall,

Very many thanks indeed for sending me a copy of your new book 'Money, Credit & Commerce'. I shall read it with great interest, and particularly so Books III & IV.[2] As a result of the Indian Fiscal Commission[3] we are plunged into the controversy of Protection v. Free Trade. If this becomes the issue at a general election the Protectionists will undoubtedly win; but we are expecting some definite statement & perhaps a step towards protection in the Budget Statement on March 1st.[4] For myself, since coming out here I have become a supporter of 'discriminating protection' which is much the same thing as 'modified free trade', & not much different from our old friend the protection of infant industries.

There will be 320 millions of people within the ring of protection & people must make some present sacrifice in regard to luxuries for the future benefit of the country. India cannot afford to be for ever dependent on a culture developed in great seaport cities. There is a want of balance.

I am glad you have at last published the graphical presentation of the problems of internat. trade. I have been the lucky possessor of the copy of your private print[5] which you gave my father, & have used it with some senior students.

Yrs sincerely | H. S. Jevons

[1] Marshall Papers. Written on notepaper bearing the printed seal of the University of Allahabad. See [1129.1].

[2] Respectively entitled 'International Trade' and 'Fluctuations of Industry, Trade and Credit'.

[3] See *Report of the Indian Fiscal Commission, 1921–2* (Cmd 1764, 1922).

[4] See *The Times*, 2 March 1923 (11f, 12d) for details of the 1 March budget statement of the Government of India. Jevons's expectation was hardly met.

[5] The 1879 chapters on the *Pure Theory of Foreign Trade*: see Vol. 1 [59, 59.3].

1140. From Frank William Taussig, 20 February 1923[1]

Cambridge, Mass.
February 20, 1923

My dear Marshall:

Thank you very much for sending me the copy of the book on Money, Credit and Commerce, which has reached me here, forwarded from the Washington address, which evidently still lingers on your publishers' records. As of course you know, I left Washington nearly three years ago, and have been in service at the University[2] ever since. I have quite ceased to be in any sense a public character, and am trying to give myself entirely to the sort of work which most interests those of our profession.

I have done no more than glance at the book, but have read enough to see once again the unmistakeable evidences of your wide range of learning, your catholic judgment, your extraordinary ingenuity in dealing with illustrative figures and formulae. Your place in the intellectual world is so firmly established that it would be superfluous for me to add a word of praise.

I send my cordial personal regards to yourself and Mrs. Marshall, and am as always,

Faithfully yours, | F. W. Taussig

[1] Marshall Papers. Typewritten. See [1129.1].

[2] Harvard University.

1141. From James Mavor, 21 February 1923[1]

The York Club | Toronto
21st.. Feb 1923.

My dear Profr Marshall.

Yesterday I had the great pleasure of receiving your newly issued '*Money and Credit*'. I was looking forward to it; but I did not expect to see it so soon. Let me congratulate you upon achieving another milestone. I have only had time to glance at it but it is evident that it is a worthy continuation of '*Industry and Trade*'. I was talking to Fay this afternoon. He remarked that in teaching he found '*Industry and Trade*' by far the best guide; in this I thoroughly concur. We have set our faces here against the use of a single text book and indeed against the use of text books in any numbers. Our object is to stimulate the student to master the literature of the Subject and as well to enable him to select from the voluminous field what ought to be read. For this purpose we counsel our students to read all of your books. Although we have many copies in our libraries, they are well worn, for our students are not invariably well enough off to acquire what they ought.

I can assure you that we all value immensely, the 'painful labour' by which you have made clear for us the economical processes. You know that we have on our staff in economics three men who have come directly under your influence, Fay (Christ's), and Jackson and Dobbs (John's)[2] while all of the rest of us have come under it through reading. This year all told we have about 1200 students in economics besides numerous extra mural classes. I hope that now you have seen the book issue from the press, you will take a rest for a bit before attacking another installment.

I am writing also to Mrs Marshall.

With kindest and most respectful regards,

Yours very sincerely | James Mavor

P.S. I am just bringing out another edition of my book on '*Russia*';[3] but I am sorry that owing to the impossibility of procuring the necessary material from Russia, I am unable to write a third volume which I had always projected—upon inner and outer trade and upon transportation. I tried to get some material out of Russia but it was stopped by the Soviet people. I did get some but not sufficient. JM

[1] Marshall Papers. See [1129.1].

[2] Gilbert Edward Jackson (1890–?), associate professor and author of *An Economist's Confession of Faith* (Macmillan, Toronto, 1935) and other works, had obtained a first in Part I of the History Tripos, 1910. Sealey Patrick Dobbs, lecturer, author of *The Clothing Workers of Great Britain* (Routledge, London, 1928), soon returned to Britain, lecturing at Sheffield University.

[3] J. Mavor, *An Economic History of Russia, Second Edition Revised and Enlarged* (Dent, London and Toronto, 1925: 3 vols.). The volumes dealt respectively with Economic Conditions, Social Conditions, and Politics and Government.

1142. From Sir Sydney John Chapman, 6 March 1923[1]

3 Oak Hill Park | Hampstead | London N. W. 3
6. 3. 23

My dear Marshall,

Thank you so much for your new volume. It was very kind of you to send me a copy—but that is a kindness for which I have always to thank you as your fresh works come out, and the stream since your relief from teaching has been wonderful. I did not write at once, as I wanted first to get the reading started, & unfortunately the pressure on my time is such that I do not get on very fast with what lies outside the daily task.[2] But I know you will forgive the delay; & I can now in all sincerity express my admiration as well as my gratitude. I do not know how you manage to keep on doing it. I shall look forward, too, to the new volume which you forecast—& will I trust have the strength to complete. I hope that you & M[rs] Marshall are in the best of health.

I enjoy my work as an official but my hands are always pretty full.

With kindest regards | Yours very sincerely | S. J. Chapman

[1] Marshall Papers. See [1129.1].
[2] At the Board of Trade, where Chapman served as Permanent Secretary, 1919–27. He had been knighted in 1920.

1143. From Guisseppe Ugo Papi, 26 (?) 1923[1]

Ministero dei Lavori Pubblici
Ufficio Speciale delle Ferrovie
Rome 26th 1923

Pr. Alfred Marshall
Balliol Croft | Cambridge
Sir,

I am indebted to your magisterial work 'Industry and Trade' for my volume[2] written during violent dissensions[3] of the whole country after a considerably long period of meditation.

No word can tell you how I have learned from your classical principles of economic science. Before the universal admiration for the Master my little name is confused, my young audacity is hesitating.

But I am trusting that your indulgency may appreciate my pure devotion and may welcome to my great admiration.

With kind regards I remain | Yours very truly | Guiseppe Ugo Papi

Corso Umberto Uffizi 6 Roma

[1] Marshall Papers. Why Papi unambiguously wrote Rome 26th 1923 in lieu of a full date remains a puzzle.

[2] Papi published two works in 1923: *Prestiti Esteri e Commercio Internazionale in Regime di Carta Moneta* (Signoreli, Rome, 1923); *Il Lavoratore alla Gestione dell'Impresa* (Vallardi, Milan, 1923). It is probably the latter to which Papi alludes.
[3] Written 'disenssions' in the original.

1144. To John Maynard Keynes, 19 December 1923[1]

My dear Keynes,

Many thanks for your fascinating *Monetary Reform.*[2] I have several times as much 'half baked' work on hand, as I can hope to bring out of the oven; but I have been unable to keep my eyes off it.[3] As years go on it seems to become ever clearer that there ought to be an international currency; & that the—in itself foolish—superstition that gold is the 'natural' representative of value has done excellent service. I have appointed myself amateur currency-mediciner: but I cannot give myself even a tolerably good testimonial in that capacity. And I am soon to go away: but, if I have opportunity, I shall ask new-comers to the celestial regions whether you have succeeded in finding a remedy for currency-maladies.

Yours ever | A. M.

[1] King's College, Cambridge, J. M. Keynes Papers. From Balliol Croft. Reproduced in *Collected Works*, vol. 19(1), pp. 162–3.
[2] J. M. Keynes, *A Tract on Monetary Reform* (Macmillan, London, 1923), reprinted as *Collected Works*, vol. 4.
[3] That is, Keynes's new book.

1145. To Hubert Douglas Henderson, with a postscript by Mary Paley Marshall, (January 1924?)[1]

Dear Henderson,

I happen to have taken today a Sabbath days journey over a bundle of old papers relating to the scope of economics; & my wife has just come in, saying that you are a hearty friend of it. In 1906 I circulated (in & out of Cambridge) seven thousand copies—I think—of the 'Introduction' to our Tripos;[2] because I found that its existence was not generally known in the Country. I send you a copy of it & of one or two others. Eighteen years is a short time in the history of a nation, but probably only a small number of those to whom it was sent are now alive and at work here.

Yours sincerely | Alfred Marshall

P.S. Unfortunately there is not a single copy of the 'Plea' to be found w^{h}. is the first document. It was sent round to all members of the Senate in 1902 & first set the ball rolling but it is very much like the 'Social education' address w[h]. is enclosed.[3]

[1] Nuffield College, Oxford, Henderson Papers. From Balliol Croft. The postscript is in Mrs Marshall's hand. The mention of 'eighteen years' since 1906 suggests a 1924 date, but the letter's relative vigour suggests a date early in the year, if not before.
[2] See [831.4].
[3] For Marshall's *Plea* see [734.7]. The 'Social education address' is Marshall's pamphlet *Economic Teaching at the Universities in Relation to Public Well-being* (Spottiswoode, London, 1903), a paper read at a conference of the Committee on Social Education. Besides this address, the Henderson Papers contain copies of Marshall's 'New Cambridge Curriculum' [751.4], and the printed letter extracts [747] circulated to the Senate in May 1903.

1146. To Macmillan and Company, 21 January 1924[1]

21. 1. 24

The Macmillan Co[2]
Dear Sirs

There are a few changes to be made in Money Credit & finance.[3] with one exception, they are small; & can be easily set right. But pp 286,7 each contain the same paragraph of thirteen lines![4] I will send you a corrected copy by tomorrows post probably, yours faithfully

Alfred Marshall

[1] British Library, Macmillan Archive. From Balliol Croft.
[2] Remarkably, in this his last recorded letter, Marshall abandons the form 'MacMillan' to which he had adhered so tenaciously and quixotically.
[3] That is, *Money Credit and Commerce.*
[4] Details as to reprintings of *Money Credit and Commerce* are unclear, but it appears that this slip went uncorrected. It survives in the standard reprint (Kelley, New York, 1960).

1147. To John Maynard Keynes from Mary Paley Marshall, 27 June 1924[1]

27. 6. 24

Dear M[r]. Keynes

D[r]. Bowen[2] (in whom I have great confidence) has been for another consultation. The last was 6 weeks ago. He says that Alfred is much weaker than he was then. He (Bowen) thinks that Alfred cannot last longer than a month, & that if the disease of the kidney were to increase suddenly he might become comatose at any time. Bowen says we must keep up the illusion that Alfred will be free of nurse & doctors & start work to-morrow! He is very cheerful and free from pain.

Yours ever | Mary P. Marshall

[1] King's College, Cambridge, J. M. Keynes Papers. From Balliol Croft.
[2] William Bowen, physician and surgeon, of 24 Lensfield Road, Cambridge.

1148. To John Maynard Keynes from Mary Paley Marshall, 14 July 1924[1]

14. 7. 24

My dear M^{r}. Keynes

I do not know how to thank you for your very kind letter.[2] I only wish that the words you say about Alfred could have got into the inadequate article w^{h}. is in todays Times.[3]

I shall anyhow be staying in Cambridge till the end of July, so 30 July w^{d}. suit me very well & I will put together any material I have w^{h}. might be useful for your Memoir.[4]

He was unconscious during the night of Saturday & at 10.15 on Sunday he passed so peacefully away that I could not believe that he had gone.

I shall always be glad to think that you had that little talk with him,[5] & he spoke of it afterwards.

Ever, dear Mr. Keynes | Yours affectionately | & gratefully | Mary P. Marshall

He looks so beautiful now.

[1] King's College, Cambridge, J. M. Keynes Papers. From Balliol Croft. Marshall had died on the previous day.

[2] Not traced.

[3] *The Times*, Monday 14 July 1924 (16 c–d) published an obituary under the heading 'Professor Alfred Marshall. Doyen of English Economists'. Marshall's death was also briefly noted in the same issue (15b) under 'Court and Personal'. As the first published assessment of Marshall's career and influence, the obituary is of some interest. It was evidently written by a former pupil in an affectionate, laudatory, but hardly sycophantic manner. There are some minor inaccuracies, and the treatment of Marshall's economics verges on the superficial, nevertheless it hardly merits dismissal as 'inadequate'.

[4] Keynes's remarkable memorial essay on Marshall was to appear as 'Alfred Marshall, 1842–1924', *Economic Journal*, 34 (September 1924), pp. 311–72; reprinted with minor changes in *Memorials*, pp. 1–65 and in *Collected Works*, vol. 10. It drew heavily on notes provided by Mrs. Marshall.

[5] Probably the pathetic 'last visit' Keynes recorded in a letter of 16 May 1924 to his future wife, Lydia Lopokova (1892–1981). See Polly Hill and Richard Keynes (eds.), *Lydia and Maynard* (Deutsch, London, 1989), p. 195.

APPENDIX I

Reports of Marshall's Speeches to the Cambridge University Senate, 1903–8

Discussion of Report of the Economics Syndicate, 7 May 1903[1]

Prof. Marshall said that he would like to add one suggestion to the admirable remarks which Mr Dickinson had made.[2] It was that the Historical Tripos as at present constituted was an almost exclusively *English* Historical Tripos, especially on its economic side. That was because it had been found that in three years a student could not trace the detailed history over eight centuries of more than one country: any glances he might take at other countries must be hasty: and his studies were cut short for want of access to secret documents just about the time when the electric telegraph and other modern means of communication were leading up to the economic conditions of our own time. Economically the western world was now a single organism: so that no nation could understand its own economic problems without constant reference to the recent and contemporary international history of other countries. Recent international history was absolutely essential to the economist, and that was not represented at all in the Historical Tripos.

It was almost impossible to overrate the value of Historical Studies as an end in themselves. He hoped and believed that they would attract, as time went on, a largely increasing part of the best intellect of the world. But history to the economist was a means towards his ends, and they must consider what his ends were.

The purely material aspects of wealth could not be neglected even by the philosopher. The British Empire contained only one white family to each of its eleven million square miles; and part of this territory was coveted by other nations whose population was growing faster than ours, and who were not wearing out their natural sources of wealth as rapidly as we were. Some of us might be expansionists and wish to add a few million miles more to the Empire; some of us might think that we had enough. But we all hoped that, if we were forced to fight for what we already had, we should win; and for that we should want very large sinews of war. Thirty years ago he had thought it was right to urge people to turn to a life more like that of the Greeks, who, blessed by their favourable climate, and helped by slaves, as we were by machines, could afford to work little and indulge in mental luxuries a great deal. It was right to press in the same direction now; but, in view of the growing expenses of war and the preparations for war, it was not safe to press so strongly as it was then.

The material aspects of wealth were those with which the man in the street supposed the economists to be chiefly concerned; but the man in the street was wrong. The motto at the beginning of the treatise on Political Economy by him whom they all most regretted was: 'Things are in the saddle and ride mankind'.[3] What had made men become Economists, in three cases out of four, was the belief that in spite of our growing command over nature it is still things that are in the saddle, still the great mass of mankind that is oppressed—oppressed by things. The desire to put mankind into the saddle is the mainspring of most economic study.

Mere pain and poverty might be endured without much loss of the higher life: though to acquiesce in their continuance was deadly. But the absence of fresh air, of repose, and of healthy play for children lowered the tone of life; and all the more when work was long and food scarce. Wealth which was now almost wasted might be used so as to secure the benefits of *rus in urbe, urbs in rure*;[4] with full opportunity for wholesome energetic life, physical, mental and moral. It was easy to devise remedies for such symptoms of social disease. But if the remedies did not reach the causes of the disease they were likely to increase instead of curing it. The diagnosis of social maladies was very difficult, and no study of them could be worth much that was not as thorough as that which was given to Physics or Mathematics.

It had just been said that the older economists were *doctrinaires*.[5] It was a remarkable fact that those who had passed into history as *doctrinaire* economists were scarcely ever people who had been able to give a large part of their lives to the study of Economics; they were men of much knowledge of affairs, of first-rate practical experience, but who had to settle economic questions in a very short space of time. What they said was generally true with reference to the special conditions they had in view: but they said nothing about the conditions: they spoke in general terms; and careless followers converted their conclusions into dogmas. Where there had been long-continued professional study, there had often been a certain vagueness about results, but this extreme *doctrinaire* method was not to be found.

To treat Economics as on the same lines as Physics and Mathematics was a task which seemed to be pointed out for the University, which had developed all its studies with sedulous thoroughness. The unwillingness to arrive at a conclusion without adequate data had spread from Mathematics to other studies, and had marked off Cambridge studies from parallel studies in other Universities. To be thorough at all costs was the Cambridge peculiarity, which now found vent in a desire to have done with the exclusively superficial study of Economics, for which alone there had been scope here.

It had been said that one year's study would suffice.[6] That was very easily said dogmatically. But experience was on the other side. When he returned to Cambridge in 1885 he had hoped that one year's reading for the second part of the Moral Sciences Tripos might set mathematical and other trained students fairly on their way to become economists. A considerable number of such men had started to try, and they had obtained a better grasp of general economic principles than many able undergraduates obtain in two years. But they had no time for the study of the subject-matter: they did not become realistic. Only some five or six of them had been able, through great self-denial, to continue their studies after they had left Cambridge, and thus to become real economists with a true sense of proportion. This partial failure had been a deep disappointment to him. The instinct of proportion seemed to be developed by the students for this[7] Historical Tripos; but very few of them got beyond the merest elements of economic science: they could not afford the time.

He had often endeavoured to give an advanced course of Economics. He had never succeeded. He had always found it necessary that he should go back to first principles, and spend two-thirds of the time upon work which ought to have been done before the advanced course began. There had been in the whole of the eighteen years since he returned to Cambridge only two men who had had in their third year a knowledge of the realities and a grasp of the machinery of their science, such as a tolerably able student of Physics had in his third year. For the full development of Economic studies here they had got to create an adequate staff. There would be needed half a generation to get the staff in perfect order; but, as Prof. Sorley had shown, the Historical Tripos had developed well from beginnings very much smaller than those with which they now proposed to start.[8] He trusted that they would ere long have a Tripos which should not be much inferior in regard to the number of its students, or the intellectual strain it required from them, to any other Tripos; and which would be superior to any in the extent to which it developed the intellect in relation to the sympathies and imagination, and the sympathies and imagination in relation to the intellect.

The great reason why the two older Universities held their eminent place in the affections of the nation was that they trained the individual character and sympathetic faculty in relation to the intellect, as only a residential University could; and it was for that reason more than for any other that business men would send their sons here, in spite of the risk that they would be less inclined for the rougher side of their work at the end of their University course than at the beginning.

But there was need for another kind of sympathy,—that which united not one individual with another, but one class with another. They had to prepare for the coming time when the masses would be endowed with colossal strength; when anything could be put through that the masses desired, and nothing could be put through which the masses did not desire: and then, even more than now, the work of interpreting between class and class would be most urgent. The employer was apt to live in the employers' class, and look at things from the employers' point of view: and thus he could not without effort throw himself into the point of view of others. But undergraduate sympathy here has naturally a bias towards the weak; and the undergraduate, who had learned to look at social problems here, had been found to help the older and more experienced employer by enabling him to enter into the employees' point of view.

He thought some attention should be paid to the exceptional consensus of expert opinion in support of enlarged opportunities for the study of modern realistic economic problems in Cambridge. The Memorial presented to the Council on the subject a year ago bore an almost unprecedented number of weighty signatures. Almost every non-resident member of the Senate who was specially interested in economic studies had signed: the list contained the names of Courtney, Leslie Stephen, Roby, J.B. Mayor, Cunynghame, Nicholson, Flux, Bowley, Chapman, Aves, Wynnard Hooper, Moulton, Sanger, Clapham, T. Llewellyn Davies; all of whom had exercised or were beginning to exercise an important influence on the economic thought of their age.[9] In fact the two dissentient members of the Syndicate[10] were almost the only Cambridge experts resident or not resident who had not signed. Cambridge moralists who had not specialised on economics such as Lyttelton (late Bishop of Southampton), Caldecott, and Mackenzie had written very heartily in approval. Dr Lyttelton wrote, 'I hope that some real good to the country and the University may come of your movement'. Dr Caldecott, Professor of Logic and Mental Philosophy at King's College, London, writes that most Moral Science students have taken up Economics only as a part of their discipline; and he adds: 'I trust that Economics will always be retained as a part of the Moral Sciences discipline, and of the History Tripos too: but for training for constructive work, a separate Tripos is indispensable'.[11]

One of the speakers had complained of the smallness of the number of the letters from eminent men of affairs which had been submitted to the Syndicate in support of the opinion that the proposed curriculum would meet a great public want, and attract to Cambridge students who might otherwise not have come here.[12] The number of letters was not large: but they gave the opinions of a large percentage of those to whom he had sent a copy of his *Plea*: for he had not ventured to send it to any save those few with whom he had been brought into some personal contact; together with one or two others who had recently published their views as to the best education of business men.

He ventured to protest against the suggestion that such men were going beyond their proper province in expressing an opinion as to what kinds of high class education for their sons were most likely to bear fruit in later years. Many of these men were of very high culture. They belonged to a class which contained within it probably much more than half of the finest and strongest ability in the country: and for observing how the after-effects of different kinds of education developed in later life they had opportunities which were not generally accessible to resident members of a University.

The providing a good education for business men was indeed not the main object of the movement: the main object was to render possible a thorough scientific and therefore realistic study of economics. But as a secondary aim it was important, for its own sake; and possibly also in relation to that poverty of the University, on which the opponents of the movement had dilated so eagerly. For if this University should refuse to do what business men required: if in return they should, as it was said they were already doing, tend more and more to send their sons to new Universities (even though thereby the glorious training of Oxford or Cambridge corporate life were lost); and if, in consequence, the rising generation of wealthy business men became the loyal sons of the newer and not the older Universities, then he thought this University might regret too late that it had seemed somewhat indifferent to the opinion of business men.

Discussion of Report of the Moral Sciences Board, February 1904[13]

Professor Marshall said that it would be seen that three out of the four members of the Board whose special study was Economics had not signed the Report. They held that it was desirable that an opportunity should still be afforded for combining the study of Economics with that of Philosophy. Full provision was now made for those who were to be professional Economists, or who were preparing for a business career. It was true that the Economics Tripos did not find place for Economic History, except in quite recent times; but facilities for combining one Part of the Historical Tripos with one of the Economics Tripos, afforded by the recent alterations in the Historical Tripos,[14] gave everything that Economists could reasonably desire in that direction. But though he did not agree with the view that all students should be made to study Moral Science as a preliminary to becoming Economists, he thought that there were many for whom a combination of Economic and Moral Science was the best possible training. He referred specially to those who proposed to be clergymen, or other ministers of religion, and to those who were looking forward to social and philanthropic work. Now that Part I was to be lightened by the dropping of Economics it would have been an opportunity for saying that Part I should not by itself entitle to a degree and thus encouraging this combination of Moral Science and Economics. This plan would be simpler than retaining Economics in the Moral Sciences Tripos: and he wished to urge it.

Many members of the Senate held that the efficiency of the University as a place of general education would be much increased if the first Part of every Tripos were kept light enough to be taken at the end of the second year; so that, except for professional students it might be a common practice to take a Part of each of two Triposes, and thus avoid extreme specialization: but were yet unwilling to adopt this course for the Tripos in which they were specially interested, so long as the general practice of the University seemed to imply that every Tripos should catch all the men possible and keep them for the whole of their undergraduate career. The Historical Tripos had adopted the principle that the first Part must be taken at the end of the second year and should not by itself qualify for a Degree. This experiment appeared to have been quite successful and to have improved the quality of the work done by the students. These facts seemed to indicate that the question of the combination of Triposes was perhaps rather for the Senate or for the recently appointed Studies Syndicate than for a Special Board; it was one of the faults of our Constitution that there were few opportunities of discussing broad questions of University policy. Discussions in the Senate House were mainly on Departmental issues. But of course there were many who, in private conversation, expressed doubts as to the excellence of the Cambridge Tripos System. He was a partisan of that system for young students, but only for them. It was most beneficial for a student to work for a Tripos till the end of his second year. In the third year he thought that perhaps an option should be given between working for a Second Part and engaging in original work, and after the third year all working for an examination was generally mischievous.

He agreed that Metaphysics was an ideal subject of study for adults, but no subject was so bad for examination purposes. But an excellent mental training could be got by combining a Part of the Moral Science Tripos with a Part of the Mathematical or the Classical or the Natural Sciences or the Economics Tripos. His attention had been called to the fact that a student of Philosophy had to take two Triposes in order to include Ancient and Modern Philosophy: but he did not wish to express an opinion on that point himself.

He regretted the Report had been brought forward without waiting for the Report of the Studies Syndicate, and he hoped the Council would consider whether it should not be held back until the Syndicate reported; or at all events referred to the Syndicate for its consideration.[15]

Discussion of Report of the General Board of Studies on the Girdlers' Lectureship in Economics, 17 May 1906[16]

Professor Marshall said that he hoped the University would express its indebtedness to the Girdlers' Company, and he was sure those who were interested in Economic studies would like to express their gratitude. He did not think it was generally understood that, although the Economics Tripos had now been in existence two years, and although the entries during the present year were understood to be twenty—he said understood, because there was no formal roll on the subject—yet nothing was paid towards the teaching specially adapted to the needs of students for that Tripos by the University or by any College, except by St John's, to Mr Foxwell; and he held no lectureship in the subject, although he held a fellowship. Every other person, except himself, who was lecturing to the students for the Economics Tripos was giving the instruction specially needed by them without any payment from the university or the Colleges.[17] ... Economics had been removed from the control of the Moral Sciences Board. Some of the teachers on the list of the Economics Board did receive salaries, but not one of them received anything from the University or any College in recognition of the work done by them specially for that Board. Mr Dickinson received a salary, Mr Green received a salary, and Mr Head received a salary, but all of these were in connexion with other departments. The work they did specially for the Economics Tripos was entirely voluntary; and their incomes would not be diminished if they ceased to take any part in teaching specially for that Tripos. Those who were concerned with the other studies enjoyed the main body of the resources of the University; and they suffered comparatively little from any action that might divert benefactions from this to other Universities. But *Delirant Reges, plectuntur Achivi*;[18] those endowed with the royal wealth of existing foundations flouted the opinions and the wishes of business men; and the consequent blows fell chiefly upon the newer studies. The commercial element which was associated with some of the newer studies was often contemned. But even a classic was sometimes forced to earn his living; and then the commercial instincts asserted themselves vigorously. Thus, in favour of Regulations which tend to repel those interested in the newer studies, it had been recently urged in the Senate House: 'The commercial value of the Classical Tripos was that it gave a kind of opening to the schoolmaster, and if the Greek ceased to be taught in the schools classical men would not be wanted as masters, and would often go in for some other Tripos'. So an appeal was made to the Senate 'to reject any proposal that would tend to make Greek merely an extra'.[19] The way in which business people were affected by the action of the University, although it might be a matter of indifference to those who were already endowed, was likely to prove the destruction of studies which had no endowment at all. He had gone rather beyond the strict limits of the discussion, and had all along been in fear that the Vice-Chancellor would call him to order: and he had to thank him for allowing him to say that much, which had been an appeal to those who were strong and those who were rich to have compassion on the sufferings of those who were weak and poor.[20]

[1] *Reporter*, 14 May 1903, pp. 772–4 (the report of the entire debate covers pp. 763–74).

[2] Dickinson, the previous speaker, had countered complaints about the limitation of the new Tripos to nineteenth-century history: 'It was, of course, to be regretted that everybody could not know everything. . . . But surely it was not necessary to cover long periods of time in order to understand the historical method . . . . There was, however, an equally important method, namely, the analytical method, which consisted not so much in tracing consecutive causes and effects in time as concurrent causes and effects among coexistent phenomena. For this method . . . there would in his opinion be better opportunity in the proposed Economic Tripos than in any existing Tripos' (p. 772).

[3] Henry Sidgwick, *Principles of Political Economy* (Macmillan, London, 1883).

[4] 'Country in town, town in country'.

[5] Cunningham in his speech had charged: 'Economics was a science which had suffered from over-specialisation, from the *doctrinaire* character of those who had been its experts—exponents of the science who had allowed themselves to get out of touch with ordinary life' (p. 766). Foxwell, the next speaker, agreed that 'to furnish men with a system of abstract principles, the application of which to actual affairs was supposed to be safely left to commonsense' was likely to produce *doctrinaires*. But instead of Cunningham's remedy of less economics, Foxwell sought more emphasis

on applied economics: 'the power of applying principles to actual affairs was extremely rare, and could only be developed in economists by making their study more realistic' (p. 767).

[6] In Cunningham's speech (p. 766).

[7] A misprint for 'the' is to be suspected. (By usual practice Marshall would have had the opportunity to correct and emend the proof of the report of his speech before publication.)

[8] Sorley's speech is reported on pp. 769–70. See also [746.4].

[9] See *Reporter*, 29 April 1902, pp. 762–3, for the Memorial and the complete list of signatories: Chapman was, in fact, not one. Marshall can hardly have helped his case by representing all the individuals he names as significant economic thinkers. (Henry John Roby (1830–1915), Senior Classic 1853 and sometime Fellow of St John's, Professor of Jurisprudence at University College, London, 1866–8, and subsequently a cotton manufacturer and Member of Parliament. Wynnard Hooper (1854–1935), City editor of *The Times*, 1885–1914. Joseph Bickersteth Mayor (1828–1916), Fellow of St John's 1852–64 and moral science teacher. For Aves see [870.4].)

[10] Cunningham and MacTaggart.

[11] These letters have not been traced. All three individuals mentioned had signed the Memorial: Arthur Templeton Lyttelton (1852–1903) first Master of Selwyn Hostel 1882–93, Suffragan Bishop of Southampton 1898–1903; Alfred Caldecott (1850–1936), sometime Fellow of St John's and Professor of Logic and Mental Philosophy, King's College, London, 1891–1917.

[12] The complaint came from MacTaggart, who claimed to have met 'a very successful business man in the cotton business who said that the best training for the cotton business up here would be Latin verses' (p. 769).

[13] *Reporter*, 23 February 1904, pp. 540–1. In its Report of 3 February 1904 (*Reporter*, 9 February 1904, pp. 454–5) the Board had recommended that Political Economy be eliminated entirely from the Moral Sciences Tripos. The proposed elimination of the Economics and Politics specialization in Part II was hardly controversial in the light of the new Economics Tripos, but expulsion from Part I, in which Political Economy had hitherto been a required subject, was something of a rebuff to Marshall and his supporters, Foxwell and Neville Keynes.

[14] See [779.2].

[15] The Report was approved and the changes made without such a delay.

[16] *Reporter*, 22 May 1906, pp. 960–1. For the Report see *Reporter*, 14 May 1906, p. 859. The Girdlers' Company had in 1904 provided £100 a year for three years to fund a University Lectureship in Economics, known as the Girdlers' Lectureship. The Company now offered to continue this arrangement for a further three years, the Board recommending grateful acceptance. The Lectureship was held by Pigou from 1904–8.

[17] An interjector enquired at this point about stipends received by Economics-Board lectures for unrelated duties.

[18] The people pay for the blunders of kings (Horace).

[19] In the 1905 debate on the retention of Greek in the 'Little Go'. See [816.2].

[20] Questioning of Marshall ensued as to the proper classification of Cunningham, whose lecturers were currently listed by the Economics Board but who was not to continue after July.

APPENDIX II

Comprehensive Listing of Archival Sources for Volumes 1, 2 and 3

This appendix classifies by source every item from archival collections that is either reproduced or cited in the present work, providing fuller archival detail (collection or item number) when that seems desirable. Citation is to be understood as encompassing all references or quotations (partial or whole) occuring in editorial footnotes. Permissions to draw upon the listed archival sources are indicated in the Acknowledgements prefacing Volume 1 and are not repeated here.

For each archival collection a list of 'items reproduced' is followed by a list of 'items cited'. Items reproduced are identified by their letter numbers (for example [640]), while items cited are identified by their footnote numbers (for example [641.3]). A full description of the item or items involved may be obtained by referring to the indicated letter or footnote. It is helpful to bear in mind that letters 1–332, 333–732, and 733–1148 are in Volumes 1, 2, and 3, respectively.

When the archival label for a specific item is reproduced it is normally placed immediately after the listing of that item. Thus, '[442] 43/116–7' indicates that the document reproduced as letter [442] is identified by label 43/116–7 in its archival source. The few exceptions to this procedure are clearly indicated. Archival labels for items cited in a footnote are given in the same fashion, but when a footnote cites more than one item *from the same collection* the listing is in the order of citation. Thus, '[936.2] 11.72 and 11.59' indicates that the first of the two items from the collection cited in the footnote has archival label 11.72 and the second 11.59. Of course, the same footnote may cite items from different archival collections and thus appear in more than one list of citations. The notation 'n.c.' (not classified) for an item indicates that it does not have an archival label.

MATERIALS IN THE MARSHALL LIBRARY, CAMBRIDGE

Introduction: The pertinent manuscript holdings of the Marshall Library consist of the Marshall Papers, a substantial collection of the correspondence of John Neville Keynes, some papers of James Bonar, and a small collection of the correspondence of Charles Ryle Fay. For the purpose of this work, the last has been treated as part of the Marshall Papers.

A useful conspectus of the Marshall Papers as a whole is provided in Rita McWilliams [Tullberg], 'The Papers of Alfred Marshall Deposited in the Marshall Library, Sidgwick Avenue, Cambridge', *History of Economic Thought Newsletter*, 3 (November 1969), pp. 9–19, reproduced in John C. Wood (ed.), *Alfred Marshall: Critical Assessments* (Croom Helm, London, 1982), vol. 4, pp. 193–203. The correspondence contained in the Marshall Papers was for many years collected in four boxes, labelled Marshall 1 to 4, Box 1 being letters received, Box 2 correspondence with Macmillan and Company, Box 3 letters written, and Box 4 xerox copies of *most* of the correspondence from the records of Macmillan and Company now preserved in the British Library's Macmillan Archive. Within each box the items were numbered consecutively so that, for example, Marshall 1(33) or M1(33) would refer to item 33 in Box 1. In addition to the items collected in these boxes, a few unclassified letters were scattered through the Marshall Papers generally. The Fay correspondence was included in the first of two boxes of miscellaneous correspondence, with items referred to as Misc 1(44), and so on.

The Marshall correspondence has now been reclassified into a main Marshall collection with items numbered 1/151, 1/152, and so on, while Marshall's letters to Foxwell and Fay have been incorporated in new Foxwell and Fay collections. A largely complete listing of the new main Marshall collection, giving both the new and the old collection number for each item, is provided in Frances Willmoth, 'A List of the Marshall Correspondence in the Marshall Library of Economics, Cambridge', appendix A (pp. 199–208) of Rita McWilliams Tullberg (ed.), *Alfred Marshall in Retrospect* (Edward Elgar, Aldershot, 1990). Since the old collection numbers have been widely used, the Library intends to maintain convertability between old and new. Both are given here where possible, the new number appearing first. The main Marshall correspondence and Marshall's correspondences with Foxwell and with Fay are listed in that order and then followed by listings relating to the Neville Keynes correspondence and the Bonar Papers which have always been maintained as distinct collections. A listing of miscellaneous materials drawn from the Marshall Papers is given last.

The Neville Keynes correspondence was for many years kept in five boxes, Keynes 1 to 5, with Keynes 1 (120) or K1(120) denoting item 120 in Box 1, and so on, while the Bonar material was kept in three Boxes, with items labelled Bonar 2(7), and so on. These collections are being reorganized and new as well as old collection numbers are given where available.

The Main Collection of Marshall Correspondence (The first-listed new collection numbers are all prefixed 'Marshall'.)

Reproduced: [14] 1/34, M3(101); [21–3] 1/289–91, M3(66–8); [25–32] 1/292–9, M3(69–76); [33] 1/75, M1(9); [34] 1/182, M2(49); [35–6] 1/175–6, M2(36–7);

[40–2] 1/179–81, M2(40–2); [50] 1/182, M2(49); [59] 1/35, M3(103); [64] 1/37, M1(14a); [65] 1/38, M1(15); [83] 1/183, M2(43); [102–3] 1/40–1, M1(16–17); [104] 1/109, M1(146); [119] 1/42, M1(18); [146] 1/43, M1(124); [148] 1/44, M1(19); [150] 1/68, M1(107); [156] 1/45, M1(125); [167] 1/46, M1(20); [177–8] 1/284–5, M3(86); [191] 1/47, M1(126); [195] 1/6, M1(120); [204] 1/48, M1(127); [206] 1/193, M2(7); [213] 1/49, M1(128); [237] 1/97, M1(39); [249] 1/15 M1(10); [254] 1/50, M1(129); [276] 1/306, M3(77); [289] 1/95, M2(9); [298] 1/87, M1(35); [304] 1/196, M2(8); [313] 1/53, M1(21); [318] 1/100, M1(41); [320] 1/54, M1(132); [324] 1/55, M1(22); [325] 1/7, M1(6); [332] 1/56, M1(135); [333] 1/198, M2(2); [334] 1/88, M1(36); [335] 1/91, M1(37); [339] 1/278/1 and 2, M3(57); [343] 1/104, M1(43); [346] 1/85, M1(33); [349] 1/105, M1(44); [350] 1/2, M1(2); [354] 1/277, M3(58); [355] 1/279, M3(59); [362] 1/69, M1(108); [363] 1/106, M1(45); [376] 1/305, M3(81); [378] 1/58, M1(135); [401] 1/93, M1(143); [402] 1/205, M2(3); [406] 1/280, M3(60); [408] 1/281, M3(61); [411–2] 1/8–9, M1(7–8); [413] 1/86, M1(34); [414] 1/10, M1(8); [422–3] 1/60–1, M1(137–8); [433] 1/62, M1(139); [437] 1/19, M1(11); [438] 1/101, M1(42); [476] 1/1, M1(1); [479] 1/108, M1(47); [575] 1/70, M1(109); [593] 1/11, M1(121); [651] 1/82, M1(29); [652] 1/283/1 and 2, M3(83); [653] 1/83, M1(30); [674] 1/71, M1(110); [678] 1/125, M1(59); [688] 1/116, M1(64); [692] 1/128, M1(61); [693] 1/3, M1(3); [694] 1/114, M1(50); [695] 1/127, M1(62); [696] 1/126, M1(60); [697] 1/115, M1(51); [698] 1/118, M1(53); [699] 1/120, M1(111); [700] 1/122, M1(56); [701] 1/130, M1(63); [702] 1/124, M1(58); [703] 1/113, M1(49); [704] 1/94/1 and 2, M3(82); [705] 1/119, M1(54); [706] 1/117, M1(52); [707] 1/121, M1(55); [711] 1/123, M1(57); [754–5] 1/252–3, LBB(24); [765] 1/254, LBB(24); [766] 1/327/1 and 2, M3(64); [769] 1/255, LBB(24); [772–3] 1/256–7, LBB(24); [786] 1/20, M1(12); [804] 1/366, n.c.; [847–8] 1/24–5, M1(13); [850–2] 1/78–80, M1(27–8); [866–7] 1/22–3, M1(163); [874] 1/145, M1(83); [877] 1/144, M1(77); [878] 1/143, M1(82); [879] 1/139, M1(78); [880] 1/141, M1(80); [881] 1/137, M1(74); [882] 1/136, M1(73); [885] 1/215, M2(11); [887] 1/142, M1(81); [888] 1/134, M1(71); [891] 1/146, M1(84); [892] 1/147, M1(76); [893] 1/133, M1(70); [894] 1/138, M1(75); [903] 1/98, M1(40); [905] 1/95, M1(38); [912] 1/258, LBB(24); [913] 1/260, LBB(24); [914] 1/259, LBB(24); [915] 1/261, LBB(24); [916] 1/304, M3(79); [920–1] 1/272–3, M3(1–2); [923] 1/74, M1(24); [927] 1/262, LBB(24); [929] 1/216, M2(12); [937] 1/111, M1(48); [943] 1/99, M1(144); [945] 1/29, M3(91); [953] 1/102, M1(145); [957] 1/263, LBB(24); [958] 1/266, LBB(24); [959] 1/217, M2(13); [961] 1/264, LBB(24); [962] 1/265, LBB(24); [964] 1/267, LBB(24); [968–9] 1/269–70, K5(28–9); [973] 1/96, M3(92); [974] 1/135, M1(72); [977] 1/271, K5(30); [983, 985, 987, 992, 997] 1/271/2–6, Red Box 1(2); [1011] 1/13, M3(90); [1020] 1/14, M3(90); [1022] 1/218, M2(14); [1030] 1/64, M1(67); [1033–4] 1/16–17, M1(164–5); [1053] 1/274, M3(3); [1054] 1/219, M2(15); [1056] 1/220, M2(16); [1060] 1/63, M3(85); [1061] 1/275, M3(4); [1065] 1/89, M1(31); [1068] 1/276, M3(5); [1071] 1/90, M3(99); [1075] 1/223, M2(18);

[1083] 1/103, M3(84); [1088] 1/230, M2(22); [1091] 1/30, M3(62); [1094] 1/232/1 and 2, M2(24); [1096] 1/234, M2(25); [1101] 1/239, M2(30); [1104] 1/65, M1(68); [1120] 1/66, M1(150); [1122] 1/67, M1(149); [1129] 1/153, M1(88); [1130] 1/169, M1(102); [1131] 1/168, M1(101); [1132] 1/158, M1(92); [1133] 1/164, M1(97); [1134] 1/159, M1(93); [1135] 1/151, M1(86); [1137] 1/157, M1(106); [1138] 1/166, M1(99); [1139] 1/162, M1(95); [1140] 1/171, M1(104); [1141] 1/165, M1(98); [1142] 1/156, M1(91); [1143] 1/167, M1(100).

Cited: [185.2] 1/188 and 1/191, M2(46) and M2(45); [205.1] 1/192, M2(1); [348.3] 1/28, M1(23); [355.4] 1/282, Misc 1(99); [384.2] 1/51, M1(130); [399.2] 1/202, M2(52); [400.2] 1/203, M2(51); [468.4] 1/208, M2(4); [747.6] 1/131, Misc 2(31); [767.4] 1/214, LBB; [848.1] 1/26, M1(14); [858.3] 1/12, M3(100); [906.2] 1/76, M1(25); [907.2] 1/107, M1(46); [911.2] 1/77, M1(26); [916.1] 1/302 and 1/303, M3(78 and 80); [963.3] 1/268, LBB(24); [1016.2] 1/367, n.c.; [1023.4] 1/33, M1(66); [1074.2] 1/221, M2(17); [1081.2] 1/225, M2(19); [1086.1] 1/228, M2(21); [1087.2] 1/229, M2(21); [1094.2] 1/232, M2(24); [1096.2] 1/235, M2(26); [1102.2] 1/240, M2(31); [1110.1] 1/241, M2(32); [1110.3, 4] 1/242, M2(33); [1112.4] 1/243 and 1/244, M2(34) and M2(35); [1129.1] respectively 1/172, 150, 152, 170, 155, 163, 160, 161, 154 (previously M1(105, 85, 87, 103, 90, 96, n.c., 94, 89)).

Correspondence with Foxwell (The first-listed new collection numbers are all prefixed 'Foxwell'.) Note that [882, 1134] are listed in the main collection.

Reproduced: [110–15] 1/29–34, M3(7–12); [120–1] 1/35–6, M3(13–14); [122] 1/37, M3(6); [123] 1/39, M3(16); [125–6] 1/40–1, M3(17–18); [128] 1/42, M3(19); [130] 1/43, M3(20); [134] 1/46, M3(23); [514] 1/49/2, M3(26); [515] 1/49/1, M3(26); [517] 1/50, M3(27); [521] 1/56, M3(32); [522] 1/51, M3(33); [523–6] 1/57–60, M3(34–7); [533] 1/61, M3(38); [536] 1/62, M3(39); [580] 1/63, M3(40); [643–4] 1/64–5, M3(41–2); [673] 1/66, M3(43); [681] 1/67, M3(44); [682] 1/69/1, M3(45); [684] 1/70/1, M3(46); [836–7] 1/72–3, M3(48–9); [839] 1/74, M3(50); [875] 1/78, M3(52); [895] 1/79, M3(55); [908] 1/80, M3(56).

Cited: [121.1] 1/36, M3(14); [126.1] 1/44, M3(21); [513.4] 1/48, M3(25); [515.2] 1/53, M3(29); [517.4] 1/53/1, M3(29); [520.6] 1/55, M3(31); [681.13] 1/68, M3(44); [682.4] 1/69/2, M3(45); [684.5] 1/70/2, M3(46).

Correspondence with Fay (The first-listed new collection numbers are all prefixed 'Fay'.)

Reproduced: [853–5] 1/23–5, Misc 1(44–6); [897] 1/27, Misc 1(48); [917] 1/29, Misc 1(50); [929] 1/31, Misc 1(52).

Neville Keynes Correspondence (The first-listed new collection numbers are all prefixed 'J. N. Keynes'.)

Reproduced: [90] 1/77, K1(75); [91] JNK Testimonial file, M3(65); [124] 1/76, K1(74); [136] 1/296, K3(40); [149] 1/73, K1(71); [155] 1/66, K1(64); [196] 1/60, K1(58); [198] 1/61, K1(59); [221] 1/62, K1(60); [222] K3(68); [225] 1/78, K1(76); [226] 1/56, K1(57); [227] 1/79, K1(77); [228] 1/58, K1(56); [229] 1/57, K1(55b); [231] 1/67, K1(65); [232–3] 1/80–1, K1(78–9); [234] 1/63, K1(61); [235] 1/59, K1(55a); [236] 1/82, K1(80); [238] 1/55, K1(54); [239] 1/54, K1(53); [240] 1/69, K1(67); [241] 1/52, K1(51); [243] 1/71, K1(69); [245] 1/72, K1(70); [246] 1/83, K1(81); [248] 1/84, K1(82); [250] 1/53, K1(52); [251–3] 1/85–7, K1(83–5); [255] 1/88, K1(86); [257] 1/90, K1(88); [260] 1/91, K1(89); [262] 1/68, K1(66); [263] 1/92, K1(90); [266] 1/93, K1(91); [267] 1/143, K1(143); [268–9] K3(69–70); [270] K3(72); [271] K3(67); [272] K3(66); [275] 1/94, K1(92); [278] K3(73); [279] 1/74, K1(72); [280] n.c.; [281] 1/95, K1(93); [282] 1/65, K1(63); [283] 1/96, K1(94); [284] 1/97, K1(95); [291] 1/99, K1(97); [299] 1/98, K1(96); [300] 1/51, K1(50); [309] K3(71); [321–2] K3(74–5); [336] K3(93); [345] 1/246, K2(103); [347] 1/103, K1(101); [358] 1/245/1, K2(102); [370] 1/101, K1(99); [371] 1/100, K1(98); [397] 1/106, K1(104); [398] 1/49, K1(48); [421] 1/108, K1(106); [451] 1/109, K1(107); [453] 1/107, K1(105); [471] 1/110, K1(108); [481] 1/111, K1(109); [502] 1/112, K1(110); [531] 1/113, K1(111); [532] 1/104, K1(102); [537] 1/114, K1(112); [539] 1/115, K1(113); [541] 1/116, K1(114); [543] K3(111); [582] 1/117, K1(115); [605] 1/118, K1(116); [607] 1/119, K1(117); [618–9] 1/120–1, K1(118–9); [622–3] 1/122–3, K1(120–1); [625] 1/124, K1(122); [647–8] 1/125–6, K1(123–4); [675–6] 1/127–8, K1(125–6); [680] 1/129, K1(127); [690] 1/130, K1(128); [750] 1/133, K1(131); [778] 1/134, K1(132); [801] 1/136, K1(134); [918] 1/137, K1(135); [931] 1/138, K1(136); [932] 1/140, K1(140); [933] 1/139, K1(137); [1001] 1/141, K1(138); [1009] 1/142, K1(139).

Cited: [114.6] 1/24, K1(23); [162.3] 1/47 and 1/48, previously K1(46) and K1(47); [240.5] 1/69, K1(67); [257.2] 1/50,K1(49); [272.1] K3(64); [283.1] 1/89, K1(87); [359.1] 1/245/2, K2(102); [362.1] 1/105, K1(103); [622.3] 1/64, K1(62); [623.7] 1/41, K1(40); [693.4] 1/230, K2(87); [722.1] 1/132, K1(130); [768.5] 1/250, K2(107); [778.2] 1/135, K1(133); [933.3] 1/231 (previously K2(88)) and K3(131); [1009.3] 1/145, K1(44).

Bonar Materials

Reproduced: [359] Bonar 2(7).

Cited: [680.4] Bonar 3(20) and Bonar 3(19); [704.2] Bonar 3(3).

Miscellaneous Materials in the Marshall Papers (Consult the listing by Rita McWilliams mentioned above.)

Reproduced: [490] from Scrapbook; [545], [722], [747], [748], [1121] all from Large Brown Box; [737], [1017] from inserts in books. The 'enclosures' to [21–3] and [25–32] come from Box 6(1).

Cited: [155.2], [326.1] refer to items from the Marshall Scrapbook; [448.3], [744.3], [747.3], [748.1], [776.8], [782.3] all refer to items from the 'Large Brown Box'; [277.6], [637.4] refer to the 'Red Book' of statistics; [123.7] refers to Box 8(6); [205.4] refers to Box 9(6); [705.3] refers to a book insert; [421.5] refers to an unclassified annotated pamphlet.

MATERIALS IN OTHER ARCHIVES

Balliol College, Oxford

E. Caird Papers: reproduced [542].

B. Jowett Papers: reproduced [382–7], [389–92].

Bishopsgate Institute, London

G. Howell Papers: reproduced [828].

Bodleian Library, Oxford

Bryce Papers: reproduced [567].

Harcourt Papers: reproduced [687] dep. 243 fols. 5–6, [689] dep. 734 fols. 202–4, [691] dep. 243 fols. 87–92.

Bristol University Library

Archives of University College, Minute Books: cited [99.1].

British Library, Macmillan Archive

Letters from Marshall are arranged chronologically in Add Ms. 55174. Copies of replies by Macmillan and Company are in the voluminous letter books, Add Ms. 55376–55834, which are arranged chronologically.

Reproduced: [101], [185], [205], [219], [290], [295], [305–6], [311], [315–17], [375], [380], [399–400], [403–5], [468], [500], [548], [550], [562–3], [569–71], [573–4], [576], [579], [731], [733], [751], [757], [787], [797], [810], [814], [831], [849], [864–5], [868–9], [876], [884], [886], [890], [896], [924], [926], [930], [955–6], [960], [963], [975], [998], [1007], [1055], [1062], [1066–7], [1074], [1080–2], [1086–7], [1092–3], [1095], [1097], [1099], [1102], [1105], [1108], [1110], [1112–3], [1116], [1127], [1136], [1146].

Cited: [468.4], [579.2], [751.3], [864.3], [876.4], [955.2], [1075.2], [1112.3–4], [1127.2].

British Library of Political and Economic Science, London

Beveridge Papers: reproduced [898] IIb; cited [898.1] IIa 54.

A. L. Bowley Papers (Coll Misc 773/1): reproduced [632], [634], [637], [670].

E. Cannan Papers: reproduced [431] 1020(18–19), [474] 1020(46–52), [475] 1020(53), [505] 1020(100–1), [507] 1020(116–7), [596] 1020(187–8), [716] 1021(36–7), [774] 1021(52–3), [838] 1021(113–4), [841] 1021(85–93), [842] 1021(122–6), [843] 1021(127–8), [844] 1021(129), [845] 1021(130–1), [928] 1021(156–7), [1025] 967(36); cited [841.2] 1021(121).

Courtney Papers: reproduced [630] VIII f41, [631] XIX f49, [1079] XIII f51; cited [630.2] VIII f15.

F. Y. Edgeworth Papers (Coll Misc 470): reproduced [80–1], [94], [96–7], [105], [109], [176], [192], [202–3], [217], [307–8], [340], [424–5], [427–8], [504]; cited [217.2], [242.1].

Giffen Papers: reproduced [464] I.84(f128), [677] II.25(f39).

Miscellaneous Letter Collection: reproduced [873] III.68M203.

Passfield Papers: reproduced [261] II.2.28, [265] II 1(ii)204, [377] II 1(ii)114, [395] II 1(ii)116, [396] II 1(ii)205, [555] II 4 9(4)67.

Royal Economic Society/British Economic Association Minute Books: cited [406.9].

H. Solly Papers (Coll Misc 154): reproduced [153], [157]; cited [157.3] (all from Sec 4(b) Item 1).

L. Stephen Papers (Coll Misc 476): reproduced [341–2], cited [343.2].

Bundesarchiv, Koblenz

L. J. Brentano Papers: reproduced [274], [310], [621], [661], [714], [715], [720–1], [724], [740–2], [744], [758–60], [763–4], [767–8], [770], [776], [794], [796], [827], [1016]; cited [502.4], [1016.2].

Cambridge University Library

Acton Papers (Add 6443, 8119): reproduced [544] 6443(205), [546] 6443(206).

Add 4251: cited [497.5] 4251(B)940.

Archives of Board of Extra Mural Studies: reproduced [595] BEMS 55/9.

J. N. Keynes Correspondence (Add 7562): cited [619.3].

J. N. Keynes Diaries (Add 7831–58, covering 1874–1908): reproduced [162], [220], [230]; cited [51.8], [90.1,4], [123.2,3], [124.1], [145.3], [149.2], [158.2], [162.1,3,7], [164.2], [172.3], [180.8], [198.2], [203.1], [215.2], [220.1], [224.2], [225.3,4,6], [226.1], [227.2], [228.1], [229.1,2], [230.3], [236.5], [239.1], [240.1, 5], [243.5], [250.2], [251.4], [252.9], [255.2], [257.2], [260.4], [262.1], [267.1], [268.1], [272.1], [284.3], [302.3], [309.3,4], [321.2], [322.6], [336.5], [345.2], [358.2], [408.4], [446.3], [462.6], [532.6], [533.4], [539.2], [575.3], [619.3], [648.2], [674.3], [846.1], [909.3], [922.4], [933.3].

B. Kidd Papers (Add 8069): reproduced [450] M251, [461] M252, [559] M253, [560] M254, [561] K41, [679] M255, [709] M256, [710] K80.

Librarian's Correspondence (Add 6463): reproduced [372] 1666; cited [502.5] 2748.

F. W. Maitland Correspondence (Add 4251): reproduced [808] 887–8.

Rare Book Room: reproduced from rare pamphlets in the collection: [12], [790].

University Archives
Collection of Fly Sheets (UP60): reproduced [611]; cited [611.1].
Guard Book on Local Examinations and Lectures (CUR57.2): reproduced [209]; cited [209.2,4].
Guard Book on Prizes and Awards (including records of the Marshall and Adam Smith Prizes), CUR38 (Lea-Muir): reproduced [1023].
Guard Book on Professor of Political Economy (CUR39.26): reproduced [883].
Minutes of Cambridge University Association (Min IX.4,9): reproduced [587]; cited [778.4], [790.1].
Minutes of the Economics Syndicate (Min VI.68): reproduced [723], [726]; cited [722.1], [726.1].
Minutes of Special Board for Economics and Politics (Min V.114 for 1903–11, Min V115 for 1911–23): reproduced [907]; cited [778.4], [836.7], [854.7], [895.3], [907.2], [939.2].
Minutes of Special Board for Moral Science (Min V10 covering 1860–88, Min V 140–4 covering 1889–1963): cited [238.4], [345.4], [471.2], [514.2], [582.3], [605.6], [778.1].
Records of the Whewell Benefaction (Char.1.14,14i): reproduced [871]; cited [871.2].
Records of the Women's Degree Syndicate (Synd II.3): reproduced [508].

Columbia University Library

J. B. Clark Papers: reproduced [184], [296], [357], [365–6], [373], [617], [727], [730], [732], [736].

H. L. Moore Papers: reproduced [1008], [1013–4], [1115].

E. R. A. Seligman Papers: reproduced [319], [369], [443], [452], [465], [478], [485], [491], [498–9], [501], [590], [610], [612], [615], [728], [826], [900]; cited [369.3].

Foxwell Papers (in the possession of R.D. Freeman)

Reproduced: [13] 9/89, [15–16] 11–12/229, [18–20] 13–15/229, [43] 19/71, [44] 45/155, [45–6] 41–2/155, [47] 44/155, [48] 49/155, [49] 46/155, [51] 36/155, [52] 38/155, [53] 48/155, [54] 42/155, [55] 37/155, [56] 35/155, [57] 7/9, [58] 20/9, [60] 4/9, [61] 1/9, [63] 14/9, [66] 17/9, [67] 16/9, [68] 18/9, [69–70] 12–13/9, [71] 15/9, [72] 9/9, [74] 8/9, [75] 6/9, [77] 19/9, [78] 4/252, [79] 5/252(2), [82] 9/252, [84] 1/252, [86] 6/252, [87–8] 7/252 (1 and 2), [89] 8/252, [92] 28/245, [98] 17/150, [99–100] 3/252, [107] 16/150, [137] 12/73, [138] 49/23, [139] 13/73, [141] 19/73, [142] 7/73, [144] 5/73, [145] 11/73, [147] 10/73, [154] 77/6, [159] 76/6, [161] 11/84, [164–5] 70/6, [172] 25/95, [173] 49/98, [175] 47/98, [179] 51/98, [180] 42/98, [186] 50/98, [200] 33/69, [207] 28/69, [208] 19/128, [214] 22/168, [215] 24/168, [216] 23/168, [218] 26/69, [224] 30/69, [264] 20/124, [285] 6/124, [286] 2/124, [287] 9/124, [288] 3/124, [293] 14/124, [297] 12/124, [302] 4/124, [303] 1/124, [330] 8/124, [367] 16/56, [368] 40/56, [374] 43/56, [388] 17/56, [393–4] 41–2/56, [426] 3/224, [444] 9/127, [445] 8/127, [446] 5/127, [447] 7/127, [454–6] 1–3/127, [458] 23/104, [472] n.c., [480] 13/228, [534–5] 59–60/17, [626] n.c., [645] n.c., [649] n.c., [650] 19/217, [655–6] n.c., [658] n.c., [685] 61/186, [752–3] 9–10/244, [761] 13/244, [762] 12/244, [777] 8/244, [909] 11/252, [1109] 19/42, [1126] 87/4.

Cited: [18.2] 13/229, [60.3] 5/9, [61.1] 1/9, [93.1] 27/245, [138.1–3] 48/123, [147.3] 6/73, [159.2] 74/6, [173.3] 67/6, [207.1] 35/69 and 31/66, [213.2] n.c., [299.4] 13/124, [339.3] 12/56, [374.1] 14/56, [454.2] 6/127, [456.3] 11/127, [456.4] 4/127, [462.6] n.c., [657.3] n.c., [761.17] 6, 4 and 5/244, [909.6] 11/252.

Girton College, Cambridge

College Archives: reproduced [85] ED X11/1(14).

Greater London Record Office

Papers of the Toynbee Memorial Fund: cited [218.2] A Toy 1/1–2.

Harvard University Archives

C. W. Eliot Papers (UAI 5.150): reproduced [466] Letter Press Volume for 8 February 1889 to 3 November 1898 p. 102a, [467] and [470] Box 138 Folder 1270, [819] Box 228.

F. W. Taussig Papers: reproduced [352], [364], [409], [434–5], [439–41], [459],

[469], [482], [492], [506], [509], [511–12], [551], [554], [558], [1043] (HUG 4823.4.5 for 1891–7, HUG 4823.5 for later material); cited [511.5].

A. A. Young Papers: reproduced [938] (HUG 1891.5, Box 2 File A–W 1906–10).

Harvard University, Baker Library

Foxwell Papers: reproduced [581], [583], [585–6], [588–9], [591–2]; cited [93.1], [137.2, 3], [591.2].

Harvard University, Houghton Library

W. Rothenstein Papers: reproduced [904], [922] (both bMS Eng 1148(981)).

Jevons Family Papers (in the estate of the late Rosamond Konekamp); reproduced [140].

John Rylands-University Library, Manchester

W. S. Jevons Papers: reproduced [17], cited [126.3].

King's College, Cambridge

O. Browning Papers: reproduced [183], [473], [477], [487–9], [493], [518], [529–30], [624], [640–1], [725], [743], [745], [782–4], [822]; cited [186.1].

College Archives: reproduced [668]; cited [668.2] (from Col 42/1902/Pigou).

J. M. Keynes Papers:
File L/M: reproduced [846], [857], [860], [902], [910], [939], [944], [989–91], [993–4], [1002–4], [1021], [1026], [1029], [1031], [1039–41], [1045–7], [1050–1], [1072–3], [1107], [1111], [1144]; cited [1003.4], [1111.1,2].
File A24(1): reproduced [76], [1123], [1125]; cited [311.2].
File CO13 Pearson: reproduced [970], [976], [978–9], [982], [984], [986], [996]; cited [992.2].
File L/MM/Mrs Marshall: reproduced [1048], [1124], [1147–8].
File A26(2): reproduced [460].
File RP/1(2)/Corresp: reproduced [1119].
Undated Letter File: cited [1120.3].

J. T. Sheppard Papers: reproduced [1032].

King's College, London

College Archives: reproduced [242] KA/1C/E63, [360] KA/1C/M141.

Levasseur Papers (in the possession of Arnold Heertje)
Reproduced [906], [911]; cited [911.2].

Library of Congress, Washington, D.C.

S. Newcomb Papers (79 34629): reproduced [415–7], [419].

D. A. Wells Papers (80 45062): reproduced [24] 1781–2.

Lund University Library

J. G. K. Wicksell Papers: reproduced [800], [802–3], [813], [815], [817], [835], [1057].

Manchester Central Library

T. C. Horsfall Papers: reproduced [606] 244, [635] 247, [638] 248, [795] 251; cited [635.2] 245 and 246, [638.5] 249 and 250.

Newnham College, Cambridge

College Archives: reproduced [211], [495].

Nuffield College, Oxford

F. Y. Edgeworth Papers: reproduced [95], [106]; cited [242.1].

H. D. Henderson Papers: reproduced [1117], [1145]; cited [1145.3] (all in Box 21).

Oriel College, Oxford

L. R. Phelps Papers: reproduced [327–8], [361], [432], [520], [604].

Palgrave Family Papers (enquiries to National Register of Archives, London) Reproduced [244]; cited [442.3].

Public Record Office of Northern Ireland, Belfast

J. K. Ingram Papers: reproduced [292], [312], [331] (D2808/60/5,11,17 respectively); cited [292.2] D2808/60/9.

W. R. Scott Papers: reproduced [672] D 1884/4/4.

D. H. Robertson Papers (previously in the possession of the late S. R. Dennison, now transferred to Trinity College, Cambridge)
Reproduced [1114], [1118].

Royal Economic Society Archive, Cambridge

Reproduced [329], [381], [420], [429–30], [486], [510], [513], [565]; cited [303.1], [326.1].

Royal Library, Stockholm

K. G. Cassel Papers: reproduced [659], [1103]; cited [659.2].

E. F. Heckscher Papers: reproduced [1052].

Saint John's College, Cambridge, College Archives

SB21 file 57: reproduced [152]; cited [152.1,6].

D 93 file 19: reproduced [806], [829], [859].

J. R. Tanner Papers: reproduced [683] 4.27, [686] 4.29, [729] 4.112, [746] 5.123, [779] 5.270, [780] 5.274, [812] 6.145, [816] 7.12, [936] 11.54; cited [487.2] 1.3, [936.2] 11.72 and 11.59.

D. 104. 109 and 110 reproduced in Volume 1, Appendix III.

Saint John's College, Cambridge, College Library

E. A. Benians Letters: reproduced [830], [889].

Miscellaneous Letters: reproduced [497], [1012].

Rare Pamphlets: reproduced [8] 10.17.28, [11], [12] 12.12.11(11), [657] Foxwell Box (6); cited [867.2] 10.17.16(204).

Seeley Library, Cambridge

Minute Books of the Special Board for History and Archeology: cited [447.3], [589.6], [624.2], [640.2], [641.2,3], [643.2], [686.3], [779.2], [780.2], [782.1], [784.2].

Sheffield University Library

W. A. S. Hewins Papers: reproduced [436] 43/112, [442] 43/116–7, [462] 44/12–15, [463] 43/187–8, [597] 44/226–35, [598] 44/236–7, [602] 45/1–2, [613] 45/12–13, [633] 45/5–6, [654] 45/77–80, [708] 45/129, [756] 46/35–8, [872] 50/227.

Staatsbibliothek, Berlin

L. Darmstädter Collection: reproduced [981]; cited [981.1].

State Historical Society of Wisconsin, Madison

R. T. Ely Papers: reproduced [212], [662–4], [666–7] (all from 2212).

Trinity College, Cambridge

W. T. Layton Papers: reproduced [820–1], [823–5], [934], [948], [988], [1005], [1076], [1089–90], [1100] (respectively 2(26–38)).

H. Sidgwick Papers: reproduced [7] c 100(96), [9] c 104(41), [10] c 104(38), [614] c 94(114), [616] c 94(115), [861] c 106(4/1).

Trinity College, Dublin

C. F. Bastable Papers: reproduced [108] 5879/1.

University College, London

College Archives: reproduced [93], cited [95.1] (both from Coll. Corr. Applications).

K. Pearson Papers: reproduced [190] 759/7.

W. Ramsay Papers: reproduced [1063] Vol 16(ii)206.

University of Amsterdam

N. G. Pierson Papers: reproduced [348], [356], [566], [609], [743], [954].

University of Illinois, Champaign–Urbana

J. H. Hollander Collection: reproduced [1044] 4053.

University of Lausanne

Fonds Walras: reproduced [117], [127], [129], [131–3], [143], [158], [166], [187–8], [273].

University of London Library

C. Booth Papers (Ms. 797I) reproduced: [181–2] 1310–11, [210] 1312, [407] 1324, [410] 1325, [449] 1352, [636] 5769, [739] 5770, [870] 1715, [1024] 2037, [1069] 5771.

University of Newcastle-upon-Tyne

H. Bosanquet Papers: reproduced [717], [719], [771], [775], [781].

University of Toronto, Thomas Fisher Rare Book Library

J. Mavor Papers: reproduced [527], [788].

Yale University, Sterling Library

A. T. Hadley Papers: reproduced [791]; cited [791.2] (both from YR G 2A–13, Box 105).

W. G. Summer Papers: cited [26.5] 291 Box 29 folder 815.

ADDENDUM

In addition to the items listed above, [901] is reproduced from an original in the possession of Peter Groenewegen and [704.6] cites an original in the possession of Arnold Heertje.

Further letters of Marshall, mostly of limited interest and neither reproduced nor cited in the present work, are preserved in some of the archives listed above. The Marshall Library collections, the Macmillan Archive of the British Library, and the Foxwell Papers each contain a substantial number of such letters, while the following collections contain one or more:

Balliol College (Strachan–Davidson Papers)
BLPES (Cannan Papers, Edgeworth Papers, Giffen Papers)
Cambridge University Library (Acton Papers, Add Ms 4251(B), Librarian's Correspondence, Archives of Board of Extra Mural Studies; University Archives: Guard Book CUR 116.1 on Advanced Students, Minutes of the Moral–Science and Economics Boards)
Columbia University Library (Clark Papers)
Greater London Record Office (Records of the Toynbee Memorial Fund)
King's College Cambridge (Browning Papers, Col/42/1902 Pigou)
Oriel College, Oxford (Phelps Papers)
Royal Economic Society Archive
St John's College, Cambridge (Benians Letters, Tanner Papers, File SB21 Building Estates)
Sheffield University Library (Hewins Papers).

Additional letters of Mary Paley Marshall are to be found in the Marshall Library collections, the Macmillan Archive, the Foxwell, Acton, Clark and Hewins Papers, and also in the following collections (and doubtless elsewhere):

BLPES (Courtney Papers)
Bundesarchiv Koblenz (Brentano Papers)
Harvard University Archives (Taussig Papers)
Harvard University, Baker Library (Foxwell Papers)
King's College, Cambridge (J. M. Keynes Papers)
Public Record Office of Northern Ireland (Scott Papers)
Royal Library, Stockholm (Cassel Papers)
Trinity College, Cambridge (Sidgwick Papers).

Several items of Marshall's correspondence published in other places have not been reproduced in the present work. The following might be noted.

The letter to di Martiis cited in [757.3].
The letter from Maitland cited in [809.2]: the source cited there also reproduces letters from Maitland of 13 March 1885 and 17 April 1897.
The letters of 1887 from Walker cited in [189.7].

The memoranda and transmittal letters reproduced in *Official Papers.*

Three letters reproduced in Giacomo Beccatini and Nicolò Bellanca, 'Marshall and the Italian Academies', *Marshall Studies Bulletin*, 2 (1992), pp. 14–26.

A letter to Achille Loria partly reproduced in Italian translation in the latter's review of *Money Credit and Commerce*: 'Marshall sulla Circolazione', *Riforma Sociale* (1923), pp. 234–40 at p. 240. The letter responds to Loria's criticism of the calculation of the net benefit of international trade on pp. 162–3 of *Money Credit and Commerce.* Enquiries have failed to locate the original. It seems likely that Loria had sent an earlier draft of his review.

A testimonial of 1910 for Eva Hubback (née Spielman) partly reproduced in D. Hopkinson, *Family Inheritence: Life of Eva Hubback* (Staples, London, 1954), at p. 47.

A description of the Grote Club printed in A. and E. M. Sidgwick (ed.), *Henry Sidgwick: A Memoir* (Macmillan, London, 1906), at pp. 137–8. The original, dated 7 October 1900—just after Sidgwick's death—is in the Sidgwick Papers, Trinity College, Cambridge (c104:65). It was accompanied by extracts (also preserved) from a commonplace book Marshall had kept in 1866 and 1867. Marshall's note was substantially pruned and reworded when printed. The full version together with the extracts will, it is hoped, be reproduced elsewhere.

INDEX OF LETTERS BY CORRESPONDENT

Each of the 1148 letters reproduced in Vols 1–3 is a communication between Alfred or Mary Paley Marshall and some correspondent, either an individual or an organization. The present index groups all letters with the same correspondent under the name of that correspondent, listing separately the letters to or from that correspondent. Letters reproduced or quoted only in notes or appendices are *not* covered. The entries are grouped by volume, the symbols I, II, and III indicating Vols 1, 2, and 3 respectively, and take the form of the *letter number* followed in parentheses by the *page* number on which that letter begins. Superscripts attached to letter numbers are to be interpreted as follows:

a—the letter is from or to Mary Paley Marshall
b—the letter includes a postscript by another individual
c—the letter is jointly authored

For the user's convenience an entry for Mary Paley Marshall is included in the listing of correspondents. This simply collects together all letter numbers having an 'a' superscript in the other entries.

INDEX OF PERSONS

This index cites each appearance of every person referred to in the letters, notes, and appendices of all three volumes, with only the following limitations:

(i) A correspondent is cited only for appearances in the letters for which that person is *not* one of the correspondents. *Thus, for a correspondent, the entry in this index must be supplemented by the entry in the preceding index.*
(ii) Appearances of a person in any notes consequent upon a cited appearance of that person in the text of a letter or appendix are *not* also cited.
(iii) Authors and editors are usually *not* cited if their works are mentioned only as either (a) a convenient alternative edition or translation of a cited primary work, or (b) the source of another printing of a document reproduced in the present work. Translators are usually *not* cited.
(iv) Names of persons incorporated in the titles of publications, professorships, prizes, archives, businesses, etc., are *not* cited.
(v) This index does not include Alfred or Mary Marshall (on whom see the Subject Index), nor does it cover the Appendix on archival sources (Appendix II, above).

There are a few persons for whom the number of citations remains large, even when thus narrowed. Specific searches may remain manageable in such cases as the citations are chronologically ordered (or relate to specialized appendices). Moreover, the analytical entries for key individuals included in the Subject Index provide a more selective and informative treatment for most persons heavily cited in the present index.

Citations in this index are by *volume, page, and note* number. Vols 1, 2, and 3 are denoted by the symbols I, II, and III, respectively. Citation of a page relates to the text of that page only. Citation of a note refers to a note commencing on the indicated page. Occasionally a page and a note on that page are both cited.

The names of certain persons listed in this index are followed by symbols in parentheses. These symbols have the following interpretations:

C—The person is a correspondent.
S—The person also has an analytical entry in the subject index.
1, 2, 3—The person is described in the Biographical Register for Vol. 1, 2, 3, respectively (only the fullest entry being indicated).

Persons not listed in a Biographical Register will normally be identified, or have a cross-reference to an identification, at every cited appearance (authors and editors being deemed identified by the bibliographic description of their work).

For individuals who appear under two names, the alternative name is added in parentheses or a cross-reference is provided. Cases where a name has been conjectured are indexed under the conjectured name, and cases where a person is clearly referred to but not named are treated as if the person was named. All persons who are correspondents or who have an entry in a Biographical Register are listed in the present index even if they have no citations. Citations of *Memorials*, *WSJ* or *LW* (see Abbreviations for Vol. 1) are indexed under A. C. Pigou, R. D. C. Black and W. Jaffé, respectively.

SUBJECT INDEX

This index is divided for convenience into the following sections:

1. Alfred Marshall—Personal and General
2. Alfred Marshall—Writings, Speeches, and Official Evidence
3. Mary Paley Marshall—Personal and General
4. Other Individuals—Personal and General
5. Cambridge University and Colleges
6. Other Institutions and Organisations
7. Economics—Method, Theory, and Applications
8. Other Topics

Section 2 is further divided into subsections. The first three, covering Marshall's publications, are organised chronologically using abbreviated titles. (See Abbreviations and Chronologies in Vols 1–3 for details.) Elsewhere arrangement is alphabetic. The 25 individuals included in Section 4 are also covered in the Index of Persons, where comprehensive lists of references to them are to be found.

Citations in the present index are by volume, page, and footnote number. Volumes 1, 2, and 3 are denoted by I, II, and III, respectively. Citation of a page *covers the associated footnotes*. Citation of a footnote refers to a footnote with the indicated number starting on the indicated page. Volume preliminaries and Appendix II of the present volume are not indexed.

1. ALFRED MARSHALL—PERSONAL AND GENERAL

2. ALFRED MARSHALL—WRITINGS, SPEECHES, AND OFFICIAL EVIDENCE

a. Books

b. Articles and Pamphlets

5. CAMBRIDGE UNIVERSITY AND COLLEGES

6. OTHER INSTITUTIONS AND ORGANISATIONS

7. ECONOMICS—METHOD, THEORY, AND APPLICATIONS

8. OTHER TOPICS